March 1988

Mom—

I dedicate this book to you with special thoughts on how Yeet and how your love, prayers, and support pulled me through. (p. 333)

I love you, mom!

Andie Mac

The Poetry of Life:
A Treasury of Moments

Edited, with introduction, index
and biographical sketches

By

JOHN FROST

And the staff of the American Poetry Association

THE AMERICAN POETRY ASSOCIATION
Santa Cruz, California

INTRODUCTION

Listening to his radio, a man feels chills run down his spine when he hears a crescendo in a Mozart symphony. A woman pauses on the street on her way to work; she lifts her face to momentarily savor the snowfall gliding silently earthward. A child strokes his dog's head, comforting his old, sick friend.

These are the people whose experiences fill the pages of **The Poetry of Life: A Treasury of Moments**. They are people who've felt the thrilling effect of powerful emotional experience. Because they feel passionately, they are moved to read and write poetry. As poets, they are particularly conscious of those significant moments that have shaped their lives.

To capture a moment in history, that fleeting emotion, and then to distill it in words: this is the art that we celebrate in **The Poetry of Life.** Moreover, we celebrate the artists themselves, the poets, for through their example, they encourage all of us to appreciate the *moments* in our lives.

John Frost

John Frost
Chief Editor
Santa Cruz, California
December 8, 1987

RETROSPECTION

From 'The Princess'

Tears, idle tears, I know not what they mean.
Tears from the depth of some divine despair
Rise in the heart, and gather to the eyes,
In looking on the happy autumn fields,
And thinking of the days that are no more.

Fresh as the first beam glittering on a sail,
That brings our friends up from the under world;
Sad as the last which reddens over one
That sinks with all we love below the verge, —
So sad, so fresh, the days that are no more.

Ah, sad and strange as in dark summer dawns
The earliest pipe of half-awakened birds
To dying ears, when unto dying eyes
The casement slowly grows a glimmering square;
So sad, so strange, the days that are no more.

Dear as remembered kisses after death,
And sweet as those by hopeless fancy feigned
On lips that are for others; deep as love,
Deep as first love, and wild with all regret, —
O Death in Life, the days that are no more.

Alfred Tennyson

THE CHANCE O GOD LIES IN LOVE'S SIMPLICITY

The grasses came, though not to necessarily seed the grave
of man. Verily creation doth gather around us in fair measure
burdening her blessings to stay, while anon our watch the greater
bubble of awareness doth burst forth into another season begun.

Midst all quiet (and its sequel) lies a dialectical gem, or our
moral escape into eternity. Here in the material presence of a plume
is a salute to the literal possession of all tense . . . ascribed as
a godlike embrace anon the masterful strain of wisdom. Hence the
necessary form of all set, while fro the habits of a quill merge
gracefully with our sense of discovery. And man is endowed by a
dovelike wake of letters, and logic with their many victories in the
triumph of faith. In sooth the flower of our abstraction simply
transposes in the beauty of access gently manifesting into the enatic
mark of our greater understanding sainted by the labors of a soul.

Thus altruity hath being in prayer at eternal crossings, and the
fruits of language are matched by the alternate in the balance of
recorded time. Singular to all Sacraments of God, if our motif fosters
not a metaphysical principle of access, then truly render unto
humanity the feather of the eternal vane whose finger merely points
to the stir, and not else too the prayer of creation.

Daniel R. Malloy

A SHIP IN A BOTTLE

He lived his life like a ship in a bottle.
Then all of a sudden the ship started to throttle.
The bottle went pop.
The ship floated out.
Now the little man is no longer on the bottom.
Now the little man is on top.
He now sees things from a different angle.
He was tired of being trapped in that rectangle.

Andrea Fruman

SAD MEMORIES

The sweet and sad memories
Of my early years
Still fills my eyes with tears
When I think of all my poems
Un-wit-tingly, burned as thrash paper
My brothers never knew I wrote
They thought, I just played jump the rope
I was only ten,
And I never talked about my work
Not even then
However, mother understood
And fixed a barrel for me in the shed
Where I would go to read
Before going to my bed
After mother passed away,
I went to live with my older brother and his wife
Starting to work and going to school, changed my life
Though it was difficult to forget
The happier years of writing in the shed
And filling the barrel, before going to my bed

Rose Mary Gerlach

THIS LAND

This land will forever stand
In memory of God's loving hand
The daffodils on the hill
The love-songs of the whip-poor-will
How sweet the memories
Of the path where the roses grew
And of feeling the coolness under the willow trees
Best of all,
In late summer and fall
I knew
It was time to sample
One of each
Pear, peach and apple
And to thank God
For *His* birds, flowers, and fruit
Which was so ample

Rose Mary Gerlach

OUR LIFE CANDLE

Our Life is like a candle burning bright,
  And we have only one to burn.
We have just one bright day, then comes the night;
  Just once to live, we have our turn.
A bright flame burns, then death puts out the light.
  When we are gone we can't return.

Shall we turn our flame low or to its height,
  Live Life full or forever yearn
For the things in Life that bring us delight?
  From Life what lessons will we learn?
Love, joy, and pleasure, and things that excite,
  And great happiness will we earn?

Life is so fleeting! Let's do what is right,
  Find joy in a world that is stern!
Against the things that would hurt us we must fight,
  The Devil and temptation spurn.
Then e'er steady will burn our candlelight,
  Nor cast flick'ring shadows astern.

Carol Boyer Mitchell

THE NYMPH'S REPLY TO THE SHEPHERD

If all the world and love were young,
And truth in every shepherd's tongue,
These pretty pleasures might me move
To live with thee and be thy love.

Time drives the flocks from field to fold
When rivers rage and rocks grow cold,
And Philomel becometh dumb;
The rest complains of cares to come.

The flowers do fade, and wanton fields
To wayward winter reckoning yields;
A honey tongue, a heart of gall,
Is fancy's spring, but sorrow's fall.

Thy gowns, thy shoes, thy beds of roses,
Thy cap, thy kirtle, and thy posies
Soon break, soon wither, soon forgotten —
In folly ripe, in reason rotten.

Thy belt of straw and ivy buds,
Thy coral clasps and amber studs,
All these in me no means can move
To come to thee and be thy love.

But could youth last and love still breed,
Had joys no date nor age no need,
Then these delights my mind might move
To live with thee and be thy love.

Sir Walter Ralegh

IN WILDNESS IS LIFE

The river doesn't wait
For someone to watch it flow;
The sun doesn't shine
Only when it's noticed;
The wind doesn't look
For someone to caress,
Yet caresses.
We need to learn the ways
Of wildness.

Mary C. Mc Dyer

IF, BUT AN EAGLE

Peering over the cliff's edge
Moving twigs to the side
It's a long way down
Steep and ominous
Truly risky, I knew
But, few would ever dare
What I thought I could do
A death leap
Or, life's first step
Instinctively knowing why
I must
Span my wings and plunge
Feel the wind below my belly
And fly

J. V. Presogna

LIFE GOES ON

A War is fought,
Kingdoms are bought;
  Bridges are crossed,
  Battles are lost;
    But Life goes on!

Skies are clouded,
Foxholes crowded;
  People are killed
  And graves are filled;
    But Life goes on!

Lies are spoken,
Hearts are broken;
  Feelings are hurt,
  Heart's in the dirt;
    But Life goes on!

I try to keep
From falling deep
  Into despair.
  Why should I care?
    But Life goes on!

Carol Boyer Mitchell

WRITTEN ON THE WIND

A love like ours, can never be again,
Only once in a lifetime —
For it's written on the wind.

It's deeper than the ocean,
Beyond the rainbow's end,
It extends to heights of heaven,
For it's written on the wind.

The poets write about it,
Due to love, the bluebird sings,
The joy we share together,
Transcends all other things.

Just as long as there's tomorrow,
We will live until the end,
Yes, in laughter and in sorrow,
For it's written on the wind.

Toni Figueroa

STILLED HANDS BESIDE LYRE

The song that floods the soul
And rises with a glory and a prayer
To burst full-throated on the morning air

Shall cease before nightfall.
Memory will be all.

The heavy beat of your persistent sorrow
Outlasts my every song;
And retrospection on a laden morrow
Shall banish caroling
Which from the heart would spring.

Mary Whitenack

BEWARE!

I find that Cupid is a god to know,
He shoots his arrows anywhere he wills,
For he's the god of Love, and can bring woe,
And all the plans he makes, these he fulfills,
Then choose your steps, watch where you go,
    Beware his quills!

For love is blind, and it may be a blow
To find that it may bring the tear that spills,
Yes, it can break your heart, and bring you low,
For it is often said that false love kills,
Take heed, I say, for love's a show
    With bitter pills.

Before you give your heart, let wisdom grow,
And ask, ''Is this pure love, or is it thrills?''
True love's a precious gift, and this is so,
Unselfish love imparts a peace that stills
The mind and soul; with radiance glows,
    All being fills!

Georgiana Lieder Lahr

TO GOD

God, take my Mother
If you must —
Don't let her suffer anymore
Her sight is gone and her heart is heavy.
Her dreams have dribbled away.
Her life is empty —
Now that Daddy died.
And so, God, if you must take her . . .
Let her fly with you . . .
Through the sky —
Let her taste the heavens above . . .
And meet the angels . . .
Flying with the doves.
Let her see the dawn . . .
As it wakes up . . . and let the night . . .
Fill her with love —
Of days gone by on earth . . .
When she had her will and . . .
Spirit to live —
Before she died and gave up.

Marilyn Gold Conley

LET FREEDOM RING

Giant footsteps etched on foreign shore
Painfully separated from heart and home
Call to duty in the corps
The sky serving as a battle dome
A rugged marine symbolic answers the call
For duty demands entry into the fray
Protecting rights so preciously cherished
Forsaking loved ones to be dutybound
Alas, some shall not return again
To childhood abode's familiar sights
Lads and lassies — adults too soon
Struck down in distant trenches
Guadalcanal, Korea and Viet Nam
Names seared in memory's shifting sands
Battle fatigues, fabric torn
Silently display the violent aftermath
Thousands sacrificed to let freedom ring
For all who would hear its toll

Stanley S. Reyburn

TREE OF LIFE

My Tree of Life, as it has grown through the years,
  Has borne sharp thorns, as well as flowers sweet.
I have known sweet hopes, and I have known dread fears;
  I've known winter's cold, I've known summer's heat;
I have known lots of laughter, and lots of tears;
  I have known vict'ry, I have known defeat!

My Tree of Life each bright spring herself adorns
  With such beautiful leaves of fairest green,
With outward smile covers up the hurts, the thorns,
  With bleeding heart within appears serene;
Even though with inner pangs lost joys it mourns,
  My Tree in a forest remains a queen!

Some of these leaves from my Tree of Life are here
  Within this handsome book pressed and displayed,
Leaves that have sprouted from a heart that's sincere,
  Leaves that have grown through both sunshine and shade.
I hope a few might bring you joy and good cheer,
  Lend color to your Life that will not fade.

Carol Boyer Mitchell

CAROL BOYER MITCHELL. Born: In our beautiful Montana winter wilderness, I have memories of moonlight on snowclad pines, snow on those majestic Rocky Mountains, the howl of coyotes in the moonlit canyons, snow on the roof of our cabin, frost on our windows, and the crunch of snow beneath our snowshoes. Oh, it was like a beautiful fairyland, truly a winter wonderland! Poetry: 'Carol's Tune,' 'Good Night, Dear,' 'I'll Go With You,' 'Patchwork Memories,' 'When I Hear a Whistle'; Comments: *Poetry is the art of painting word-pictures.*

SEPTEMBER PLEASE CHANGE

September for me is a month of sorrow
Like there may never be a Beautiful Tomorrow
I do remember when it was oh so good to me
A Delightful Blessing for the world to see
Why does life go so wrong — And always rearrange
Why can't it pause and choose — Let just the bad be changed
And let the good and beautiful like forever be
Now I hate September — It is such a pain to me
I can see just nine days left that I will have to mourn
Then fantastic October is once again newborn
My burdens then will go — And I will feel so light
No more heavy heartache for me — In deep of night
September is my month of my birth — This is true
I used to find it Great Delight — It never made me blue
Exciting — Warm — and Loving — Always such a treat
It moved my heart — and rested my tired and aching feet
Nineteen-hundred-and-eighty-three changed all of this for me, you know
Nineteen-hundred-and-eighty-four, a repeat of a year ago
September please, *I Love You — Be Like You Used To Be*
Bright — and Light — and Loving — When You were Good to me.

Hetty M. Schroeder

MY BRIGHT STAR

When I was a very young girl — This did happen to me
The man I was to marry — Went away you see
I was very sad and lonely — Each and every day
Why did he go away — And leave — Me here to stay?

I did not understand the reason — He was gone
I only knew the days and nights — Seemed so very long
Then early one A.M. I was searching — Way up in the sky
I was saying to *God* — You must need him — Much much more than I

I then spied a bright Star — Shining down at me
I knew right then — My Love was watching over me
I found a Star in the evening — It shown brighter than the others
As if to say don't pine for me — I will protect you like a brother

I will shine down on you — And I will guide you from above
No need for you to fret, worry, nor fear — You still have My Love
So when I goof — And I need proof — He twinkles so gently
And to this day — I have to say — My Star — Sparkles just for me

Yes, this all happened to me — Some thirty-seven years ago
Yes, someday — I will be a Bright Guiding Star — This I truly know
Thank You — For the Star Light in the night
  — As well as the Bright of Day
But most of all — *I thank you, Lord* — For Your *life long stay.*

Hetty M. Schroeder

SILENTLY

As a young boy — Born into a life of tragedy
He fought so hard — And long — Alone so gallantly
Just to win a cause — That he would never see
Because fate fled with his mind so silently
This Someone with such very high ideals
A Someone — Who would never from you steal
A Great Someone with honor and glory
A Someone with great need for victory
His world was — Reaching out for first class
His needs were met — But not for long to last
For when they finally did for him come true
The man that succeeded — Never even knew
He had worked so long and hard — Just to be
A Knight In Armor — To serve you and me
But then fate stepped in — And did destroy all
His Mastered Plan — Crumbled — And he did fall.

Hetty M. Schroeder

What has this child in the grasp of its hand?
Something unreal, I don't believe I understand.
Watching images expand, different worlds at its command.
Merely the creative frolicking of a mind unmolested.

Experience, little one, and to your emotions be always true.
And when you've had enough or too few,
There's always something new in an escape nowhere to.
Lose yourself beyond your tensions and anxieties.

Merely the creative frolicking of a mind let free.
There's a place in my mind you'll never see,
There I flee from your judgement and cruelty.
And there I search for an end with no pain.

M. W. Maccree

LIFE

Life that is full of hope
Has many of God's folk.
Life that is full of troubles,
May be fraught with transient bubbles.

It needs God's support,
To sustain and cavort,
In a world where materialism is rampant,
And the Golden Rule is seldom used;
And where man is much abused.

Man is put on this earth
With a purpose in his divine birth;
To help his fellowman;
To share his burden as best he can.

Elbert R. Moses, Jr.

BASKET OF FLOWERS

Near his casket
Lies a basket
Of flowers red, blue, and white,
Ne'er to brighten death's night,
Heretofore his breath was warm,
His eyes twinkled with a charm,
But nevermore he'll tread this earth,
And he will derive no mirth
From a basket of flowers.

Betty J. Silconas

MADMAN

Too mad you were
For me to gain to ought but the periphery.
You threw at me in circles, squares,
Formations geometric superposed,
All that you had.
And then you wept
That I should fail to build
A structure wrought with form and sense.

Mary Whitenack

THE LOVE SPRITES

Dreams, like smoke, fill the air
After daily toil and care,
Dreams are gossamer fairies
Float on blossoms of cherries
In the spring,
When peepers sing
Of Eros dreams,
These Love Sprites
Fly by night,
Touching the tired
With passion's fire,
Enchanting the air
With love dreams fair.

Betty J. Silconas

DEMISE OF A HILL

Murdering by evisceration,
The gargantuan bulldozer
Severs the hill's bowels,
Columbines and infant maples
Are robbed of their sustenance,
Hapless meadow mice and killdeer
Shriek!
And the little meadow stream
Is choked with silt,
Inevitably, a parking lot
Replaces Nature's Hill,
The figment of memory,
Mourned only by the esoteric.

Betty J. Silconas

BETTY J. SILCONAS. Born: Franklin, New Jersey, 8-3-48; Education: County College of Morris, Upsala College; Occupations: Vegetable farmer and amateur planetary scientist; Poetry: 'A Mother's Day Blessing,' *Ideals Magazine;* Comments: *Writing gives me a sense of identity. I enjoy manipulating the English language. My main interest in life is the English language, and my best friend has always been a dictionary!*

THE CARDINAL

Today I saw a Cardinal,
Perched on a limb of a tree.
'Twas near my bedroom window,
And he was beautiful to see.

It was in the early morning
That I heard his joyful song.
I quickly opened the window,
For I knew his stay wouldn't be long.

As he perched atop that leafless tree,
A brilliant spot of red was he,
He stayed for only a moment or two,
Then flew away into the blue.

Yes, a Cardinal I saw today,
And it made my heart rejoice
For it means spring is on its way,
And winter's cold will soon be away.

Mary Louise Brooks

MY FRIEND,
THE REDWOOD FOREST

Whenever I am lonely,
And feel depressed or sad,
I go to see the Redwood trees
They lift my spirits and make me glad.

When I want peace and quietness
And a need to be alone,
I seek the cool Redwood forest,
For there tranquility roams.

When I need to worship God
I visit those forests of trees,
I can feel His presence there,
And all my cares and worries cease.

I love those forests of Redwood trees,
And no matter where I be,
I know God watches over them,
As well as over me.

Mary Louise Brooks

FAME OR FOOLED

Oh! Brilliant mystic and elusive fame, how
you do blink, at hopeful hearts and minds that
think — to bestride you hand in hand.

But was it not you, and kin kind pride, that
beckoned old Lucifer to the side — prior to
rebellious and feebled stand.

Curious to know, from whence thee came,
always and forever remaining the same — with
never a sign of tired old age.

The gifts you give, are falsely fleet,
leaving a nothingness incomplete — yet
followers do stoop, by every stage.

The world sets defense, at need of you,
for many lost hopes, may haps this true — but
the righteous do warn and often tell.

To seek and find, the revealed word,
once spoken to man, then forever heard — can
hold paths straight in fame's old spell.

Lonnie Louis

STONE AMONG STONES

How strange, to wander alone,
As alone is each pebble and stone.
No tree knows the other
Though they are growing together.
Filled with friends was the world around me,
While the bright life I could see;
Now, that most of them are gone,
I am in deep darkness thrown.
Only those, who are plunged into darkness
Can really feel separation's grief and stress,
And to them, too, it is then known
That *everyone* in life is *alone*.

Hartwig Heymann

FICKLE APRIL

"O, the uncertain glory
of an April day!" (Shakespeare)

Today blue April mourns.
At first she wails as violent gusts of giant flakes
    whirled madly in the way of icy winds.
But now, emotion spent, she softly weeps,
    quite blinded as her tears drop silent
    into overflowing pools.
A pair of crows flap idly by in black-winged mourning;
They but add notes to an already drear lament:
"Today King Winter's dead! O weep for him!"

Tomorrow . . . grief forgot, her somber garb replaced
    with virgin white, bright April, with her sparkling smile
    and laughter sweet, will pay allegiance to
    the new-crowned Queen . . .

As in her path, on dancing feet, she gaily scatters
    springtime flowers . . .

    Ruby A. Jones

HE RIDES THE WIND

I've sought His hand in moments rich and rare
When head was bowed in whisper of a prayer;
I've dreamed I heard the rustle of His robe at night
When pain and fear clutched heart in icy fright;
I've heard the murmur of His voice in rippling,
    soothing music of a brook;
I've caught the admonition of His word when buried deep within
    the pages of a book.
I have held Heaven in the hollow of my hand when He, in Indian Summer
    strode tall across the land.
I've glimpsed His touching flash of bird-wing white,
    and in the passage of a flock in flight;
Felt His compassion in dark hours of grief,
Knelt humbly at the glory in a leaf.
I've harkened to the laughter of a child, found joy in lads whose
    small hands cling,
Discovered treasure in the magic of a smile, as I recalled His love
    for little things.
I've felt deep reverence gazing at His skies, found faith reflected
    in another's eyes . . .
. . . Fear you the night? The turmoil of the storm?
He calms the raging seas, the tempests of alarm.
All ye who seek, yet cry in anguish loud,
    He is not here! have thus unknowing sinned.
Thrust back your shoulders! Staunchly lift your heads!
    Behold! He rides upon the Wind!

    Ruby A. Jones

THE BATTLE SONG

It is dawn and I am ready.
The battlefield lies gloomily before me.
Yet I fear not for the armor of God.
Though I am one, I am not alone.
I cannot see but yet I know,
The holy one is in me — the Father, Son go with me.
I have prepared no thought, I am humble before the Lord.
My faith is my breastplate, His word is my sword.
I shall not lose this battle, Lord.
Nevertheless the outcome, you've already won the war.

    Rick Redmill

WEAVER OF WORDS

His slender hands were gnarled and wrinkled
The same as the spindly body he wore;
But, his mind was sharp like a razor
As through the well-worn pages he bore.

He spent days chasing one special thought,
When at last, within his grasp, he had it tied;
He spent weeks foraging another thought,
Then, placed them side by side.

He weaved his thoughts like finest tapestry
And with skillful art he formed the frame;
Mixed musical thoughts with words and called it poetry
And gave those treasured thoughts a name.

He stacked the thoughts, line on line,
And so it grew, like a budding flower.
His thoughts became words and words became love
And in the weaving, became precious power.

Some say even a thousand years from now,
When the book is opened, from the weaver's hand;
The woven thought of the sealed-in mystery
Will be revealed, to those who understand.

    I. J. Evans

PREFACE

The world isn't all darkness, sadness, cold war, atomic
bombs, nuclear fallout, famine — just look around — open
your eyes and see and feel the beauty of the trees in
spring, open your ears and hear the song of the birds,
children laughing at play, beautiful inspirational music,
and feel God through the wonderful power of prayer.
The words on the following pages should lift your heart,
and make the world a brighter, better place, especially
within yourself.

    Olive Hickerson

GAME OF LIFE

I have wandered long this lonely spot
Where emotional hurts are hung to dry;
Haunting memories cling like evening fog
And shroud the course that sea gulls fly.

Heartaches ride on the tossing tide
And roll with the waves, until they sleep.
The salty air heals the pain they bear
And there is nothing to do but weep.

The filtered ashes from a cremated love
Ride the hissing water and slashing foam.
They have knocked these rocks a thousand times,
No door was opened, they have found no home.

The fathomed depth of solitude hangs heavy
On winds where screeching night birds fly;
To seek the sound of other anguished souls,
Who find this spot and nightly come to cry.

Thoughts are cooled by the crawling waves
And air scrubbed clean for the new-born day.
This solitary place doesn't bring forth answers,
It's just a game of life we play.

    I. J. Evans

NEVER TOO LATE

Apocalyptic riders, of the grizzle
gray, and escalated unpeaceful bay — more
swing their scythes from sudden still.

Evil sets a youth, to herbal madness,
with unchained lust and morbid sadness — so
much famine seeds cannot fill.

Pharohs of today, still think to be true,
'tis only they who are able to do — what
pleases their minds with never a shame.

Must wayward minds be taught through
show, once again how little they know — with
tribulations and eternal flame?

It's not too late, if but we pray, for change
of hearts and repent of way — the sins
mortals do commit.

So great is his find, forgiveness to our
kind — for with wisdom he sits, in praise of
acts, found to be fit.

Lonnie Louis

FRIENDS

What on earth would
   one do without a
     friend?
What field could one tend?
The world would surely end.

Suppose alone, a castaway
   on a desert isle.
Without a trace of
   bath or tile.

Sans mechanics, fellow
   workers.
No storekeepers or
   even a relative,
To whom could one give?
How could one live?

And like the beachcomber
   Lost on a little
   Spit of land
   In the ocean blue
Only the combers would
   remain,
The hope of rain.

And so as we plod
   Through life,
Let's be thankful we
   Receive the friend
   Not the knife.

James T. Mackey

POET'S BEAUTY UNSEEN

With eyes to heavens
and all in between.
The poet gives form,
to that we know, yet
never have seen.

As winged fowls fly,
and siblings do cry.
Hustle — rush the people,
to nothing to go.
Oblivious to sight,
earth's gifts to show.

All too soon, does the
miracle of being, fall
suddenly away.
With few and true poet,
to walk with beauty, in a
graceful and humble way.

Lonnie Louis

ROBINSON, LONNIE. Pen Name: Lonnie Louis Born Fordyce, Arkansas, 11-30-34; Education: Lassen College, California, A.A., 1955; U.C. Berkeley, California, SDS Credentials, 1975; University of San Francisco, B.S., 1984; Occupations: Computer specialist, Employment development specialist; Memberships: The Planetary Society, University of California Alumni Association, NAACP, Society of Technology and Culture, Biblical Archeology Society; Comments: *I write due to forceful urges, to personally show worldly inhumanities, and what seems to be man's unsuccessful and relentless search for true origin and peaceful co-existence.*

LOVE DESTROYED

For many years your cruel words
Have fallen like drops of acid
On my tender loving heart;
And oh, the pain, the seething pain,
The seething, burning pain
That turned to icy ashes
Any love I ever had for you.
Now only dreadful scars remain.

Joy Bischof

THE RIVER OF MERCY

The green river wound through meadows
less green, shaded by Cotton Wood
and Willow.

It splashed in crystal bangles
against the rocks, piled across
its breast, that supported the
wooden span joining two meadows.

It swirled into a quiet, deep pool
that mirrored sky, clouds, mountain
and bird.

It housed darting fish and youngsters
diving to its cool, clear bottom,
looking eye to eye curious of
each other.

The green river wound its way to the
sea, home to many a creature,
touching the earth in green.

Helene A. Donohoe

THE SPELLWEAVERS

Who hears them,
They who weave a spell:
Is it you, who
Could not sense a dream:
Can you ask,
Was it shiny?
Was it glossy?

Ellen Malis

WE BECOME ONE WITH LIFE

All we know for sure is movement
But from whence does it come?
Time and space overtake form
That knows only change and is
   ever becoming.

We pursue our outflowing world
And express a creative will that
   forever comes and ceases
   to be
In our shuffling, we learn to play
We deal the cards, a full hand
   is laid
And we become one with Life.

Wilson Reid Ogg

VIRGIN THOUGHTS

I believe some thoughts are mine alone
Too sacred for other minds to share;
The memories of my lonely talks with God,
Of how we meet and where.

Quiet, faltering footsteps I lightly make
In fields of freshly falling snow;
Too dim for other eyes to see
And paths that only I should know.

I hang the stars to give me light
To see the place where I am free;
Seek deep within my soul each night
And find the self that is truly me.

I offer love upon my chosen altar,
A sacrifice with sacred wine.
A million lights I use for candles
To seek a voice that says it's mine.

My nimble fingers play the muted violin
And music jumps the clouds to unknown height.
Wind songs harmonize upon the strings of time
And I dream my dreams at night.

I. J. Evans

COLEMAN STREET

A voice in my mind coaxes me back
to the little white house on Coleman Street
in the drowsy, picturesque town of my birth —
where shade trees canopied roof and yard,
where flowers sprang from clean brown earth.

A nudge in my heart backtracks me
to a time of summer dreams: wiener roasts;
Saturday night dancing in the park to a brassy band;
whispered secrets between two best friends;
the lake where sweethearts walked hand in hand.

Whispers deep inside remind me of a first love,
a gentle love — so innocent and so unhurt —
a love gone by, like clear water flowing over
smooth sun-kissed pebbles in a stream;
like honeybees tiptoeing fields of clover.

A smile in my mind mirrors the way back
to my sanctuary, to my garden of memories,
to the placid town and tree-lined Coleman Street —
I picture the years from child through teen;
I count the tracks left there by younger feet.

Rosa Nelle Anderson

If it weren't for "you,"
I never would have had the joy of living.
If it weren't for "you,"
I never would have had the courage to accept the sorrows.
Without Life, you cannot have Love
And without Love, you cannot live.

Olive Hickerson

A MEDITATION

This ever changing, growing life
Has wonders sealed within
Which, step by step, revealed to each
Bring mysteries within our reach.

Awaken reverence for its grandeur:
It makes us fold our hands and kneel.
Is this our souls reaching up to God?
Is this love of life we feel?

Is this awareness our belief in Him?
Is this faith and hope and love?
This life, this light we experience within
Where there is no illness, exists no sin.

Is this the sacrifice of God, the Creator of worlds wide?
Is this the Comforter the Great Teacher sent forth?
Whatever it is, whatever it may be,
I thank God, from the depth of my heart.

Maaike van Thiel

THE WORLD IS WIDE OPEN

Yellow tulips sing to the greens of
elephant ears.
Roses of red charms beam which reflects
piercing comet sharps.

Diamonds are loyal to glimmering lightning
flashes.
Little drops of rain are buttons of spindles
stop machineries that sew.

Orange and red threads mingle gorgeous
gowns to decorate African Violets.
To Summer Marriages:
May they last forever.

Bracelets line halos and cloud pink cotton
candies of angel's frills.
Complete beautiful dresses, and lace
every vivid smoothness to purple petaled plums.

Thomas R. Shoemake

THOMAS ROARK SHOEMAKE. Born: Commerce, Texas 8-23-49; Education: East Texas State University, B.A., Dramatic Arts, 5-74; Occupation: Freelance Writer; Membership: First Christian Church, Commerce, Texas; Poetry: 'Shadow Posing'; Other Writings: ''The Talk Show,'' Comedy Screenplay, privately sold, 5-74; ''Fate of the World,'' Dramatic Screenplay, privately sold, 8-84; ''The Children We Love,'' Dramatic Screenplay, privately sold, 9-74; ''Twilight Zone,'' Dramatic Screenplay, just completed and up for submission; Comments: *I like to write poems that are realistic in their overtones. I try to express romantic virtues and the picture of the true self.*

WHEN WE ROMP
AND DANCE

We are not destined for toil but for frolic
Those who labor miss their clues
And act meagerly their roles
We who play need no utterance but
    the breath of life itself.

In our rollicking, we capture nature
That plays hide and seek with us
    shunning and yet yielding to us
In our taking, we find beauty
    skipped by those who submit to
    life's grind
From castaways of others are gems of
    artists and gist of thinkers.

And when we romp and dance
Love wells up within us
Waxing our compass one to the other
In granting us a parcel of eternality.

Wilson Reid Ogg

JUST A MINUTE OR TWO

When is there time to
be alone?
The kids are always
on the phone.

A minute here. A
minute there.
So little time to say
I care.

Pick up your socks. Don't
trip over the block.
Is there any time left
on the clock?

Just give me a minute or
maybe two.
Then I will be able to
get over my blues.

Karen Buak

LET US PLAY

How much freedom can we catch in one night?
For we only have our lives to live,
Before we die, let us play.

Time is unlimited distance.
Playmates of the night
Come to make up the distance.

Alone, we have found our precious toy.
Passion games without a rule —
Spirit of the moment, a double joy.

Soon, the distance is growing,
Playmates slip away — off to find another game.
Wondering if anyone is winning.

Karen E. A. Carlough

To paint my world in swirling grays
to storm and slash through endless days
    and so I strive
    to be alive
yet no man here will lend me praise

To clothe my night in desperate dreams
of blackest silk I weave my schemes
    and thus repair
    the gaping tear —
my heart has bled a thousand streams

To sheathe my soul in walls of mail
to burn beneath an armoured veil
    and use the shell
    to thus repel
the stones and spears of fiery hail

To wield the ancient, mythic sword
to see them kneel and call me lord
    and turn to sand
    I understand
into my hands their lives are poured

Debra Gasthalter

the chain
    goldly gleaming

    solid
        indurate

        into my flesh
        closely pressed

for this I yearned
while freedom burned
    and smoldered
    and sparked

    to fire I turned
        all fear consumed

        heart flung to his feet
my blood his wine

    the chain I crave
    to be his slave
    from fern to coal
    from green to the grave

Debra Gasthalter

My daddy has a great big chair
In his office near the door
It's hard for me to sit in it
'Cause my feet don't touch the floor.

Winifred J. Johnston

THOUGHTS ON SPRING

Cool morning following
    peaceful night
Birds, flowers, early
    sunrise
First day of spring
Taking a long look
At a weary world
Willing to give it
Another try.

Mary C. Mc Dyer

FOREVER

Regardless of
What you feel,
I have you
In my heart.

In your heart,
You may feel,
There is no
Room for me.

You forget;
The Entirety;
Of your own
Heart and Soul.

Karen E. A. Carlough

BEYOND LOVE

Is there a reason
For forgetting to write
When I think of you
My heart swells
And I cannot be with you

You asked me to trust you
So I did, blindly
You stepped on me
Now, my head turns for
Other stimulation

Half of the time
We would like to marry
And with you I feel
That despair would tarry

Beyond love is where
I would like to be

Beyond pleasure and pain
Feeling no bane . . .

Kirk Harris Wolfe

ON THE SONNET

If by dull rhymes our English must be chained,
  And, like Andromeda, the Sonnet sweet
Fettered, in spite of pained loveliness;
Let us find out, if we must be constrained,
  Sandals more interwoven and complete
To fit the naked foot of poesy;
Let us inspect the lyre, and weigh the stress
Of every chord, and see what may be gained
  By ear industrious, and attention meet;
Misers of sound and syllable, no less
Than Midas of his coinage, let us be
  Jealous of dead leaves in the bay-wreath crown,
So, if we may not let the Muse be free,
  She will be bound with garlands of her own.

John Keats

DRUNK CITY

After some five marriages gone berserk,
I was beginning to tire of the work;
I reflected and turned to the bottle,
I drank and went after it full throttle;
'Twas a girl I met at a bar called Buck's,
I was so sure she would bring me some luck;
Almost like a fool, I reached for her bod,
She pushed my hand away, and called me a clod;
Within her eyes I could see the pity,
Lord, I've been ten years into drunk city;
A few more days of this and I will sob,
I wish I could stop and hold a fast job;
Two weeks back, I turned short and wrecked my car,
Since then, I've been walking from bar to bar;
Many days I am absolutely down,
Oh Lord, how I wish I could leave this town.

Don Bedwell

A NEW BABY

A wee little baby's a precious mite,
And a miracle is its birth.
And no matter whether 'tis a girl or boy,
Its parents will love it, when it arrives on earth.

'Twill be tiny and very very sweet.
While its eyes will be blue as Heaven above.
And its rose-bud mouth, when it smiles,
Will tell of God's infinite Love.

Its soft baby skin will be like peaches and cream,
And its tiny hands will seem fragile indeed,
Yet its fingers take hold of a finger very tight,
And won't let go to that person's delight.

God has devised a wonderful plan.
For those seemingly fragile-like hands,
And He alone knows what someday they'll do,
So I think a wee babe, is God's Masterpiece, don't you?

Mary Louise Brooks

TWINS

That magic moment, magnificent in life,
When one becomes a mother, as well as being wife.
I lay there wondering, waiting to know
Was it daughter or son, please, yes, or no!
Then the nurse came in, stood very near.
A smile for me, ''How are you, dear?
And did you want a girl, a boy?
Which would give you the greatest joy?''

I told her then it mattered not,
But please to let me know then *what!*

''Surprise,'' she said. ''You have one of each,
To feed, to clothe, to love, to teach!''

A nurse at the door then came over to me,
A babe in each arm, so I could see
Those two tiny faces, so perfect and small —
If I'd been standing, would have taken a fall!
''Hope you have names for them,'' she said,
Laying them down upon the bed.
I called them by name then, Judy and Pete,
Took each little hand, inspected the feet.

Without a doubt, some forty years past,
'Twas a miracle moment, 'twould always last!

Mary Whitenack

Witness of two miracles,
  You shall witness no more

  Remaining lives are committed to the ground

    Encircling the altar,
    we cast flowers at your feet —

      The reign has ended

        All magic be stilled

Angel of my awakening:
  mother to my secrets
    protectress of my dreams

  Your voice has always
    followed me

  Your smile — my comfort

  Would that I may revive
  the roses given by one so loved

Debra Gasthalter

SEXUAL PAIN

Why I hurt I know, I know
  I was tossed into the sea
Once upon a time long, long ago
  You pushed me into the lea
Love, Love me
Love, Love me

Please do not put me into your sepulchre
  Your sexual sea
Cover not my tomb
  With liquid not from me
I would have died for thee
  Could we not have said we

Your amorous behavior is chilling
  Your darkness is killing
Your lies were seemingly from above
  I took your feelings for love

I wanted you for my bride
You stabbed me in the side . . .

Kirk Harris Wolfe

INTUITION

Dearly beloved, you whisper,
''What happiness will come to us
  at dawn.''

And I, seeming to believe,
Pray God that I can bear it
  when you're gone.

Neva Dawkins

How admirable,
He who thinks not, ''Life is fleeting,''
  When he sees the lightning!

Basho

PERSISTENCE

I lift my hands in weariness,
And think, ''I must look old,
With no existent happiness,
A broken heart and soul.''

Then, looking at my mirrored face,
I marvel when I see
The lonely hours have not erased
The beauty love gave to me.

Neva Dawkins

NOCTURNAL QUIET

Tonight my heart is still,
Empty and still.

The twinkling stars,
Points of steel,
Stir no memory.

The south wind
Brushing my lips,
Caressing, passes.

Love dreams
Breaking my heart
Broke so carefully.

Broken hearts are still,
So deeply still!

Neva Dawkins

EVEN TO ME

God
is so much more
gentle to each
human being
than each human being
is to every other human being.

God is so good
to each human being
because God is good
and cannot
be otherwise.

God is kind
to each human being
so His kindness
can shine
on all
through all.

Mary Frances

EVERLASTING LOVE

Almighty God,
without You
I am nothing.

You give to me
all that I have,
all that I am.

And I give to You
all that I have
and all that I am.

Yet, I do not
cease to have
nor cease to be.

You give to me,
I give to You —

a constant
exchange
of
love.

Mary Frances

DUE PRAISE

Holy God,
make me
as holy
as I can be.

Holy God,
make each
person on this earth
as holy as
each can be.

Then we will
all sing
with one voice,

''Holy, holy, holy
God,
Fountain
of all
holiness!''

Mary Frances

CHALLENGE OF LIFE

Things are seldom what they seem,
Before the end there's an in between.
There are ups and there are downs,
There are laughs and there are frowns.
Whene'er there is a silver lining
A big black cloud appears before,
As the waves roll o'er the ocean
The sand gets wet upon the shore.

So life can deal you a winner's hand,
And on your feet you will land,
When suddenly life becomes a storm
And no longer are you safe and warm.
Even when you dream at night,
It can be a sheer delight
And suddenly the scene will change
And your goal is out of range.
Life will keep you on the hop,
Because what you see is what is not.

Joan M. Lacey

SUNSET RADIANCE

Embryonic oaken, maple buds,
  their pinkish-red hues,
capture the crimson of the setting sun,
  mutate into a new prism,
magical, magnified into undefinable mirrors,
  of breeze-blown sparkle-splashes,
illuminated a few fleeting ephemeral moments,
  during three early April sunsets,
to those knowing inner-eyes.

Mark E. Durand

HAVE YOU BEEN THERE?

Pouring yourself into a drink —
Storing it with everything, backward.
Far away into tomorrow.

Beginning with your mind softly,
Slipping through every round,
The ''hardluck'' now goes nowhere.

Possessing no living heart
Or maybe, it is being flooded
Washing out to the returning sea.

For smooth sinking into oblivia,
Until, everything is neatly stored
Inside your hardening shell.

After awhile, the semi-safe shell has only,
The aftertaste of the returning sea —
And the sense of being on the verge of drowning.

Karen E. A. Carlough

PASSING THROUGH

There's something there that will never leave. Something
deep in my soul.
A feeling, a moment and memories gone by to cause what
I'm about to say:
   I loved you, my darling, I truly did.
   But it's time to leave and close the door.
   What we had were dreams before.
   Dreams we tried so hard to fulfill but never
     understanding how.
   I need a man who I can turn to and lean on in
     time and need.
   A man who will talk and comfort me, not afraid
     to take the lead.
   Not some person who waits around never uttering
     a single sound of what he wants, feels or likes
     or what he hates and/or despites.
   We had good times, but they're over now.
   I need my dreams to become realities.

Lynn Walsh

MY MOTHER

She, is a Patron Saint.
A lady with a touch of tenderness as warm as the sun's rays
Her smile gives way to a silent reverence in passing days
She . . . is my Mother.

She, is a Mother Confessor.
One who never fails to listen with a sympathetic ear
One who smooths the path of trouble and wipes a away a tear
She, is my Mother.

She, is a Guardian Angel.
Her quiet vigil during the awesome times of fear and sorrow
A steady hand to hold for comfort I can borrow
She . . . is my Mother.

She, is a Lady.
Gracious and inspiring, she fulfills the love of life
Her soul so blessed from fear and strife
She . . . is my Mother.

Neola M. Eichmeier

THE HIGHER FORMS OF MIDNIGHT

They came lightly last night
   All were among us
From the other time
   Space was entered and moved
As I reclined in repose
   After intuiting for days and nights on end
We were lain to rest
   And darkness shrouded
As the apparitions moved space
   I thought of you
While the visitations were stimulating
   And the forms were higher
Since they were the higher forms
   of midnight . . .

Kirk Harris Wolfe

KIRK HARRIS WOLFE. Born: Chicago, 4-2-50; Education: University of Georgia; Georgia State University; St. Leo Indian River Community College, Stetson; Occupation: Poet; Award: Rhodes Scholar Nominee; Poetry: 'Wings of Spring,' *American Poetry Anthology*, 1987; 'One Demon Dreaming,' 'The Curse of the Dove,' 'Vulcan,' 'The Last Man,' all *Just Before Dawn*, 1987; Comments: *My collected work is entitled* The Empire of the Sun. *In addition to miscellaneous topics, sex, death, and love are exploited and explored as themes.*

MEMORIES

I was born in England, it seems so long ago.
I was educated there and mind seeds did I sow.
I dream of my childhood and the excitement of my life.
And then I remember the day I became a wife.
A fine American Soldier came and stole away my heart,
And we promised true love to each other 'till death us did part.
Then I came to America, the Land of the Free,
Bought a home, started a life and we were as happy as can be.
He was quite wonderful, a real part of my heart
That I never really thought that we would ever part.
Death came and took him, he went ahead of me.
It was lonely without him, but it had to be.
But I had such a happy life, my memories so complete,
That I won't accept sorrow or ever bow to defeat.

Joan M. Lacey

MY LITTLE GIRL

I do not own a mansion,
Nor a diamond ring;
But I have something of value,
That makes my heart sing.

Her cheeks are a rosy red,
Her eyes a bonnie blue;
Shiny curls atop her head,
That's of a golden hue.

She skips along beside me,
Of me she is a part;
She's my darling daughter,
My little girl, my heart.

Fredrica Williamson

FUTILITY

I wonder if life will ever be,
Half as sweet again to me?
I used to watch for every dawn,
But now my vitality is gone.
For darling since you went away,
I care not for night or day,
For you held within your hand
My cup of joy you understand,
But I hear your voice and feel you near
As time goes relentlessly on, my dear.

Fredrica Williamson

MOTHER'S HANDS

The touch of my mother's hand
Was like the touch of down;
Like peach blossoms on the tree,
Or a crinkled leaf of brown.

Soft as the dusk at night,
The touch of her hand like dew;
Rough and work-worn as they were,
But kinder than anyone knew.

Stilled now are her weary hands,
Gentle as the breaking dawn;
Sleep has closed her lovely eyes,
And my tears have come and gone.

Fredrica Williamson

A PRAYER FOR THIS DAY

Lord, in my going out, and in my coming in,
  this day, direct me.
In my downsitting, and in my uprising,
  this day, protect me.
If there's unkindness in the words I say,
  this day, correct me.
Before each daily task, let me first ask
  for Your direction,
Then at the close of day, I can truly say,
"I lived 'this day' in Your Reflection!"

Nancy Fowler

SERENITY

When all of my six kids
were little, and really
"raising cane," I remember
the day I lost all control,
and thought they'd drive me insane!
I rushed upstairs to be alone,
and I prayed to the Mother of God,
"Your only Child was perfect,
please help me to discipline my mob."
Serenity descended as
soon as I did, and I
knew She had answered my plea.
From then on, I always
called on Her, when my
job got too trying for me.

Grace Frigo

THE WEDDING PORTRAIT

Boutonniere,
    spats,
And golden watches.
Crystal moments,
Jeweled flamboyance,
Flowers and dreams,
Sunshine peeking in.
Grandmama, haunted by memories,
Churning, like the sea
That does not want to be.
Oh, all of you,
Like deserted attics:
All those darling
        yesterdays.

Ellen Malis

THE NAME WAS MARYJANE

Her dreams were dressed
In silky gauze.
The hue of the time
Was pink and gold,
And all the flowers
Were in bloom.
Maryjane had a pretty, print frock:
No one played with Maryjane,
So she went home.
She once heard birds,
Chirping, a certain way,
Before she dressed her dreams all up.
She was still listening to songs,
When she got killed.
Maryjane
And all her dreams.
Her dreams,
Ode to her dreams:
They bled all over
        these streets.

Ellen Malis

NEVER

In all my life I could not find
Another person to be mine

Green grass now has turned to rust
And fallen leaves have turned to dust

The trees stand bare
And wait to die

As burial snow
Downs from the sky

Others romp around and play
For them the snow is fun and gay

But trees stand stiff
Like crosses on a grave

And mark the time
I could not save

Carolyn Apel

DON'T CRY

Don't cry for me;
I did my best.
My life's been full
As I go to my rest.

Though time's cut short
I did my part;
Performed each task
With all my heart.

Don't cry — just pray
For my poor soul.
I leave with hope
To make it whole.

Don't cry — remember
Now and then;
And I'll be given
Life again.

Barbara Oaks

WAITING

Days move swiftly along
Months march quickly by
Still lonely she waits
No letter has come
Since last July . . .

Time passes her by
The years are sped
Still quietly she waits
She seems afraid to ask
Her heart fills with dread . . .

Seasons come in their turn
Holidays pass swiftly on
The mother still waits
No word is heard
Where is her soldier son?

Lolita Parkhurst

EYES OF LOVE

I've sung a Song of Sixpence a pocketful of Rye,
I've watched his little hands reaching for the sky,
I've seen his baby face when it holds an expression of delight,
And I've listened for his cry far into the night.
I see how proud he is when upright he stands,
And how clever he feels when he claps his little hands.
I see him growing up each and every day,
And how sweet is the sound when a name he tries to say.
I look into his wide blue eyes, and see such wisdom there.
I love picking out clothes for this little man to wear.
I've watched and I've worried when he is sick in bed,
And I've laughed at his antics when he is being fed.
All in all I love him, this is plain to see,
For his very presence here on earth brings so much joy to me.

Joan M. Lacey

C'EST LA VIE

After much heart, feeling, revealed, penned, spent,
   personal, private letter was not sent.
Tucked, still stamped, sealed, in worn secret folder,
   wise words, with time, grew dim, foreign, colder.
Re-read, years past, I wonder what they meant.

Mark E. Durand

OCEAN FRONT PROPERTY

Abalones kiss, broken battered stone,
   Flat crusty city, silent spiral shells.
    Terra firma bound, granite citadels.
Suction cups suck, grasp, cracking crumbling throne.
Their rock fortresses minutely shift, groan.
    Flashing, flaunting, mother-of-pearl lapels,
Abalones kiss, broken battered stone,
   Flat crusty city, silent spiral shells.

By brackish salt threads, crude ice needles sewn.
   When sea waves end all, only Father Time tells.
    The mollusks care not, and need no farewells,
They have no real feelings, for the home they own.
Abalones kiss, broken battered stone.

Mark E. Durand

IVY

There have been many tributes paid to thee,
Ivy, that growest fair about our walls;
Symbol of love which ever more shall be
Binding us closely to these well-loved halls.
Thou dost recall our growth, as thee we view;
Stronger and greater with each sun and rain,
Rising yet higher, as each day anew
Calls thee, and us, to meet its joy and pain.
These thou hast been, yet more than these thou art;
Thy fragile leaves pointing aloft so bright,
Gleam like the myriad flames which form a part
Of all the incandescent glow of light:
Light that is life, and glows in pure flame;
Light that shall live and change, yet ever be the same.

Frances R. Brown

OBERAMERGAU

Do you suppose it has changed greatly now,
That tiny village where the Passion Play
Was lived full richly, where each player vowed
To consecrate his life anew each day?
Those many hundred years the new-old tale
Had been fulfilled at Oberamergau
Seemed to have made Christ's spirit there prevail.
Is that still true? Is His town Christ-like now?
Do people come in wondering awe and see
Sharp lightning split the Crucifixion scene?
And sleep 'neath feather bolsters, glad to be
At Jesus' house? Or do I only dream
The tree on which the Christ was crucified
Is putting forth new buds this Passiontide?

Frances R. Brown

A CHALICE SPILLED

So many poets through all the ages past
Have poured their wine of pain upon the world,
Seeking surcease through sorrow thus unfurled,
Some pouring from pure crystal, some from glass.
Dare I presume to add to this? To cast
My drop of beauty like a plummet hurled
Against the sweeping flood, till it lies curled
Within the aching vortex of the vast?
It will not bring you back, that well I know.
Not all of Isolt's poignant lines could sing
Tristram from death, nor prove the magic ring
Of love as strong as cold death's stronger blow.
Yet I must try, as all who've gone before,
To spill my chalice at this bleak closed door.

Frances R. Brown

ARACHNID

Weave, weave and weave the thread so frailly spun
In a round circle glimmering and fine.
Sit at its center, watch its every line
And find anew the pattern once begun
Under the rays of a soft-fading sun.
You have your web a delicacy divine
Made from yourself, a growing febrile sign
Laid up in air as light and lively spun.

Your web? Ah yes, the web Arachne wove
On a slim loom, and bragged its purity
Was better than Athena could put forth.
She learned Athena's power and could prove
Her own slight web had no security
Against a strong wind blowing from the north.

Charlotte Louise Groom

PORTRAIT OF STEPHANIE

How can I paint you so young and so fair
With big brown eyes and red-gold hair?
When I need you to pose, you're sure to be
Occupied elsewhere, a mere fantasy.

A will-o-the-wisp, a bright butterfly,
Elusive as mist or clouds in the sky.
You would much rather run, laugh, and shout,
Or wickedly tease me, dancing about.

I have faithfully sketched you so many times;
So far I have gotten only your lines.
To perpetuate you in your tender youth
So far I have failed; that's the sad truth.

This time I'll paint you quick as a wink
Forever to hold in my heart, naughty minx.
There you are! You are captured at last!
Never again shall I paint one so fast.

Laugh, Grandma, laugh! Be joyous and free.
Whenever you are lonely I'll be company.
I'll try hard to please you, your gloom to dispel.
Thank you for painting me as a belle.

Carol S. Meyer

IN THE SLEEPY MEADOW

The grass is soft and green
where the soldier hugs the earth,
his arms curled about his head,
the summer breeze in his hair.

Is it home of which he dreams,
the girl he left behind,
the joys of life he knew,
now lost in the distant past?

What if he should open up his heart
and describe the myriad pictures of his mind,
his ten thousand dreams in shadows,
would the song of life then be revealed?

What if his lips should never speak again,
and his words be lost forever,
would we still dare to be nonchalant
and not fear his awesome silence?

Matthew Weiner

A JOURNEY

As I wept in the fields
of memory, a girl's voice
aroused me, calling me
to the edge of the river;
I went, empty-handed,
on the river's path, and saw
by the water a woman, whose eyes
held my harvest tears.

George N. Braman

THE FUNERAL

Bells tolling,
Workers toiling,
An open grave.

Hearse driving,
Mourners weeping,
To open grave.

Hearse stops,
Remains lowered,
In open grave.

Minister praying,
Birds twittering,
At open grave.

Flowers strewn,
All depart,
From open grave.

Winds blowing,
Workers toiling,
To close grave.

Monument placed,
Rest in Peace.

LaVerne H. Jackson

NEVER SAY FAIL

Keep pushing — it's wiser
  Than sitting aside
And dreaming and sighing
  And waiting the tide;
In life's earnest battle
  They only prevail
Who daily march onward
  And never say fail.

With an eye ever open
  A tongue that's not dumb
And a heart that will never
  To sorrow succumb,
You'll battle and conquer
  Though thousands assail;
How strong and how mighty
  Who never say fail!

LaVerne H. Jackson

TRUE COLOURS

The break of dawn,
a new beginning,
in the hands of God.

Without a palette,
or a brush,
colours of truth to drink of.

Debra A. Knapik

A SUNBEAM

A merry sunbeam in a glen,
Far from the busy haunts of men,
Lay thinking what it best could do
To render others happy, too!

It wandered to the forest grey,
And found the wild winds in their play
Had stripped the noble woodland trees
Of half their pretty, brilliant leaves.

The wildflower lifted up its head
To see the sunbeam pass its bed.
And thought within its tiny self —
Who was that laughing, dancing elf?

It next tripped by a cottage door
And shone across the polished floor.
Until the children stopped their play
To watch the little golden ray.

May we all like this sunbeam be
From every selfish motive free —
Willing all in our power to do
To render others happy, too!

LaVerne H. Jackson

LaVERNE H. JACKSON. Pen Names: Jackie;
Born: Chicago, Illinois, August 9; Married: Bryne
Ambro Jackson, 9-14-63 (deceased 3-23-84);
Education: Northwestern University, 1950-52;
University of Chicago, Journalism, Business Ad-
ministration, 1954-56; Occupations: Editor of
Garden Glories, official publication of the Gar-
den Clubs of Illinois; Finance/accounting coor-
dinator, Cantigny, the home of the late Col.
Robert R. McCormick, editor and publisher of
The Chicago *Tribune;* Memberships: Professional
Writer's Guild; Awards: Golden Poet Award,
1987; Poetry: 'Enigma,' *American Poetry Anthol-
ogy, Vol. VI, No. 1*, Spring, 1985; 'Enigma,'
Great American Poetry Anthology, Fall, 1987;
'The Squirrel's Arithmetic,' *Masterpieces of
Modern Verse*, 1985; 'But For Me,' *The Art of
Poetry: A Treasury of Contemporary Verse*,
1985; 'The Peaceful Bay,' *Best New Poets of
1986;* Comments: *I started writing poetry after
the death of my husband, in 1984. The writing
seemed to be an out for my feelings of tremendous
loss. I seemed to phase into a metamorphosis and
be oblivious to the world around me — a beauti-
ful sense of euphoria. My themes tend toward the
Spiritual and Nature. Creativity through writing
is a great consolation.*

PEOPLE

There is a place to be,
  with friends who love thee.

In a mirror of master reflections,
  Christ is shown to me.

With loving kindness in their lives,
  for all to see.

For how much brighter they appear,
  before me.

So soft and cuddly, they are his chosen angels,
  to me, and to other people that may see.

AnnaMarie Kilbreth

LIFE

The happy things in life are not of me.

There're a lot of things that disturb me.

There are strange noises and vibrations that
  do affect me and, I'm not happy.

So sad in heart am I to be.

I am so thankful that Jesus died for me.

Because I know if I believe in him,
  he shall set me free.

Free from the bondage that I feel from thee.

Free to do what's inside of me,
  to be all that I can possibly be.

I'm so happy, so very happy, that
  Jesus has set me free.

AnnaMarie Kilbreth

FOR A FRIEND

I'm walking on the sidewalk
I don't talk much anymore
I've said all there is to say
My ship has reached the shore
They say everyone has their problems
And I'm no different I know
But somehow I've learned to live with them
And with my friends I have learned to grow

Pain comes in so many ways
And love sometimes slips away
But you realize that it's all worthwhile
When there's the comfort of a smiling face
We all have a story to follow
But someday the story must end
And wherever we are tomorrow
I thank God today for a friend

Above the city I sit alone
And pretend to be a king on his throne
Though the things I see are not for me
My friends are forever, wherever they may be.

Richard Clark

WHATEVER RETAINED

A whining still voice I hear
  Longing for whom I have known
But they are so far removed
  And meant for me alone.

Such details come to my mind
  Where memories now abide
As time and space may recede
  But lying dormant inside.

What was no more is here
  At least it makes me seeing
Before a dividing gulf
  Sounds left I am hearing.

May unexpected appear
  Stirred by whatever reason
By power of my will
  Or vestige of one vision.

Whatever is retained
  Keeps surfacing anew
Dormant feelings rising
  Deep from inside you.

I hear this inner whimper
  Long for whom I have known
Echoic of past life
  And are for me alone . . .

Howard Deutsch

DARK KNIGHT

Soldier of death mounts the green monster,
Nearer doth he ride.

Black the sky, lightning strikes;
Reality dissolves before my eyes.

Steam of hell 'round me boils,
Insanity rises high.

Wildly searching as I'm felled,
No aide steps to my side.

All earthly talismans fail me now,
Alone must I face the Dark Knight.

Inner strength my only shield,
Stout enough to hold?

If faith be all we have to guide us,
Then naked is our soul;

Alone, each one will surely fight
To death, our ultimate goal.

Rose Marie Brandon

AGING

I reach for my "specs" each morning
The moment I get up.
Then off to the bathroom for the teeth
I left soaking in a cup.

Each month there's a B-12 shot
To supply red cells I make no more.
Plus a daily dose of insulin
I buy at the corner store.

My hair has long since faded
My step is getting slow.
My doctor bills and taxes
Are the only things that grow.

Some parts are not working well
And others are not even there.
Yet somewhere in the heart of me
Still lies the capacity to care.

But there is one thing left intact
It's the joy within my soul.
And that will live forever
Jesus cleansed and made me whole.

Clara G. Stinson

CLARA G. STINSON. Born: Chester County, Pennsylvania, 12-17-10; Widow; Education: High school, 2 years; Occupations: Retired housewife; Memberships: Windsor Baptist Church; Awards: 2 Golden Poet Awards; 13 Awards of Merit for: 'Wintertime,' 'Strawberry Time,' 'Added Years,' 'Little Things,' 1987; 'I Hear His Voice,' 'We'll Never Walk Alone,' 'Our Anniversary,' 1986; 'An Angel,' 'That Little Thing Called Love,' 'Safety,' 'Confidence,' 'Love,' 1985; Writings: 'Confidence,' *American Poetry Anthology;* 'The Babe in the Manger,' 'Only a Leaf,' 'Wintertime,' 'Paintings'; various recorded poems; Themes: *Religion, family, nature, patriotism and verses written for special occasions (weddings, birthdays, anniversaries, etc.).* Comments: *My purpose is to be uplifting, to bring happiness to my readers.*

TIME LIKE SNOW

Time must fall like snow and drift and drift
Over me — empty as a discarded pod —
Before my heart breaks open as sea-thrift
Driven by frost into stone; before the load
Of love's great woe, swollen with heavy tears,
Will burst the seed and tender as young moss
Uncurled by coaxing sun new love appears,
Born from buried planting of past loss.
Your love, so deeply rooted in my soil
Was not the source but only aril coat
around my heart; not yours the lovely toil
Of this unfolding love. But I will hope the note
    Sung by a wind-swayed leaf may filter through
    My running sap and find response in you.

Charlotte Louise Groom

WHEN NIGHT HAS DRAWN

When night has drawn its treadbare moleskin cape
Across the sky, at every fraying rent
And pinhole prick some brilliance will escape
The cover, tautly stretched where day is pent.
Likewise my love — long hours past its noon —
Underlays my sorrow with relief,
Memory's zodiacal stars and moon,
To mark a north and south on spacious grief.

As long as life is beating in the veins,
Or living earth is molten at the core,
Or planets loop their constant airy lanes,
And comets trace on night a glowing scar,
So love again will strike through the heart's lens,
Reaching the point of orbital recur.

Charlotte Louise Groom

CHARLOTTE LOUISE GROOM. Born: Cincinnati, Ohio, 1908; Education: College Preparatory School, University of Cincinnati; Occupations: Poet and Painter; Memberships: Pen & Brush, New York; National League of American Pen Women; Ohio Poetry Day Awards: 'Ocean Impulse,' 1st prize; 'A Silver Whistle;' 'Pythagoras' Curve,' 1st prize; Poetry: 'Street of Women,' Dorrance & Co., 1936; 'Writing on the Wall,' Dorrance & Co., 1939; 'Sun Up Sun Down,' Dorrance & Co., 1947; 'A Reed's Slight Span,' Exposition Press, 1953; 'Esau,' Dorrance & Co., 1964; Themes and Comments: *Cities of the world, war poems, love poems, nature poems, people poems. I am interested in ancient Egypt. I have written on it both in prose and poetry; it holds my fascination. I have painted in oil, in watercolor and lino-cut.*

LIFE IN PARTICULAR

Up a mountain, down a valley —
Meet the multitude, seek the solitude.
Win a victory — feel a great defeat!
Make a new friend, make a new enemy.
Show a kindness, know a slight —
Find great peace, experience a great conflict.
Give a good testimony — learn a new temptation!
Understand a new concept, fail an old principle.
Gentle winds of joy, violent storms of sorrow —
Think all is secure, figure later nothing is.
Say, ''I've never had more'' — wonder where it went.
One day goes well — then three like hell!

Nelson Wilhelm

A GIFT WORTH MORE THAN GOLD

Friendship is a treasure
More valuable than purest gold,
It's as priceless as an authentic pearl,
Radiant and bold!
Friends are there to listen
And offer wisdom too,
Friends understand, lend an outstretched hand
When azure skies turn blue.
Possessions are so meaningless
Without someone to share —
After all, what worth is tea served in an
  antique cup
If nobody visits or cares?
Yes, true friendship is a love-filled gift
Homemade by God and wrapped up with a bow,
Untie it quickly and you'll see
A touch of heaven's glow!

Linda C. Grazulis

  may the seasons' changings be as moments of
life awakening within you each day like the birth
of a newly born child.
  live anew each hour of understanding as the
spring brings forth life to the trees and
tranquilizing freshness to the crisp flowing mountain
brook, making easy your heart of compassion
which will bloom into fullness in the heat of
summer love as do the gardens of the earth
expressing life's love in creation.
  accepting all, remember the fall is the stripping
away of the beautiful of what has been, leaving
clear your achievements lost of their color as do
the leaves falling from the bark of the new
growth blending it with the old.
  fear not the winter's cold for it is in preparation
for the coming of the blessing of purity to be
bestowed upon thee. such is why the heart of the
earth does freeze as land turns hard stopping life
in expression to feel the touch of the freshly fallen
snows to begin life again with anewed purity.

Richard J. Ingrao

TRACES

Soon, our picnic lunch was ready!
Like my dreams, I held it high —
As we raced to catch the trolley,
Heard the river rolling by.

Gleaming white, our boat was waiting —
Long ago in brilliant spring;
How the mood was captivating,
Buoyed by feelings love can bring.

Then we sailed with lyric motion,
'Neath a cloudless, azure sky —
Through the islands, to the ocean,
With the gulls in joyful cry.

True our love that first was spoken
On the beach's silver strand;
Recollection now the token
Of the future that we planned.

Gone the years, as fleeting footprints;
Gone the shifting, silent dunes.
Still aglow in retrospection
Are those lovely afternoons.

Eugenia McWilliam Short

ASCE

One little boy played on the floor
Another lay sleeping on the couch
by the door

She came out of the bedroom
Tears streaming down her face
Her voice shook as she spoke
The child on the couch
Stretched and awoke

"I'm so glad you're here
How did you know,
This was the day
I needed you so"

"I'm so glad to see you
Once again share my hurt
and make it go away"

"Mamma, Daddy it's so hard to say
Our old faithful dog, Asce,
Was killed on the highway today"

Fran Pinson Bergman

LANA'S LEAVING EARLY

For sure I'm glad
We had some time
To spend together
Am I wrong
For wanting more
My heart, my soul
Lies herein
The rest of life
Is but the fringe —

Max Sheffield

COMING HOME

I have come home. So many years have gone by

I have walked the streets of an alien reality
As false dreams flogged my tired steps

I have touched unknown faces
Blinking with toothless smiles

I have drunk from rusty tin cups
Half-empty of my burning desires

I have encountered leaching ghosts
Who dragged my screams to a land of arid sand

I have learned the lesson of oblivion
Dancing at the beat of a shattering rock sound

I have reached for distant suns
But icy rains have scorched my bones

I have come home with wounded wings

The roaring fire of my creativity is no more
Thousands of tempests have sapped its vitality

Take me into your loving arms
Soothe my cry with your sweet tears

Take me back into your womb
I am home at last

Floria N. Parmiani

REBIRTH

O Nature! You gave birth to
Geniuses, monsters, angels

Geniuses to build power
Over your divinity

Monsters to ravage
And pillage you

Angels to cry out
For they can't save you

At the end of Life
You await with revenge

In a bang, furiously
You wipe blank the lurid canvas

Winter comes, and a a terrifying night
Sizes the deafening silence

The Glacial Ages purify the Creation

Then, in a warm and snuggling breath
You give life to the rainbow
The rivers, the forests and the beasts

Minus the human race

Floria N. Parmiani

LOVEBIRDS

Upon a spring day bright and fair
I heard the bird songs fill the air.
I saw two lovebirds hand in hand
Approach a tree and by it stand.
Because I knew them both quite well
I joined them while on her lapel
He pinned peach blossoms from the tree.
He winked at her and then at me.

A twinkle came into his eye.
She meekly blushed and gave a sigh.
He squeezed her hand and kissed her cheek,
Then jovial words to me did speak,
"For fifty years she's been my bride
To walk through life near by my side.
If she is good for thirty more
I'll try her for another score."

Elzie D. Gayle

I'VE TOUCHED THE HEM OF YOUR GARMENT!

May I touch the hem of your garment?
That your "Spirit" may flow within?
May I touch the hem of your garment?
That your touch would heal my sin!

May I touch the hem of your garment
That my faith would make me whole?
May I touch the hem of your garment
To cleanse my heart and soul?

May I touch the hem of your garment
That your love would flow in my heart
May I touch the hem of your garment
That your grace to me would impart!

May I touch just the hem of your garment?
That your peace may dwell in me?
May I touch just the hem of your garment
That from sin my soul will be free?

Oh! I have touched the hem of your garment!
What a blessing! No sin and no strife!
Oh! The wonderful grace of Jesus!
Oh! What joy that has filled my life!

Mrs. La Forrest Lucas

I'D RATHER CHEAT MYSELF THIS WAY

Although I'm badly missing you,
I'd rather not see or hear you.
I can't behold the time's trail
Across the face I used to hail;
I can't endure the life's bruise
Amidst the voice I fear to lose.

I'd rather see you in my frame,
A budding rose that lasts the same;
I'd rather hear you by my mind,
A jingling bell in Santa's hand.
I'd rather cheat myself this way:
Assume time stopped in our teens' day.

Z. Lite Cai

OH GREECE!

How I long for your mystical shores
Homer and the Odyssey
A Grecian Ode and Knight from afar
Your mystic sea-oceans (mythical)
Pillars of fire
Ancient statues of love and glory
And your lamentations of sadness
Nights of wonder and splendor
Small villages and fishing boats
Quite a catacosmic sight
Sunshine, shining gaily in my face
The warmth of my body and my feet
Moving briskly toward the shore
Oh! Athenian delight, will you be my
Eyes and ears to this beautiful land,
As I continue on my wondrous mystical journey.
Oh! Greece you lay somewhere deep
into my heart, like a mystical paradise.

B. Devi

WHEN I CONSIDER

When I consider the moon and the stars,
The work that God's fingers have perfectly made,
When I consider the depths of the ocean,
The earth's foundation that He wonderfully laid,
When I consider the heights of the mountains,
The valleys, the deserts, the day and the night,
How mindful I am that all His creation
 is perfect to Him, in His all-seeing sight!
When I consider how much He desires
That we enjoy all His wonders, so glorious to see,
Dominion He's given us, o'er all His creation,
I consider how much He must love you and me!

Nancy Fowler

IT WAS A VERY SPECIAL TREE

It was a very special tree that cast its shade about.
It lived for almost thirty years, since my husband set it out.
A little house swayed back and forth, where sparrows raised
 their brood.
Their mothers hovering over them, providing them with food.
When each bird was ready, and the nurturing was through,
They ventured out and left their nest, as they were meant to do.
The tree that had weathered many storms, weakened day by day.
They brought their axes and their saws and took the tree away.
My heart was overwhelmed with loss, of that very special tree,
Until a tiny twig grew up near where it used to be!
Now it is growing strong and tall, and I know it won't be long
Until the birds make it their home to cheer me with their song!

Nancy Fowler

THE DREAM PLACE

Shadows, dreams, fantasies unreal,
lust, depression, and loneliness is most of what I feel.
Reality is a pain that never goes away.
I wonder where a sentimental romantic slob can go to get away?
Away from rejection and the death of hope . . .
Away from this new society and it's wholesale sex, death, & dope.
I dream of a bright tomorrow,
full of joy and happiness, instead of sorrow.
I pray for love and peace of mind,
so each night, I consult the great *Divine*.
Questions plague me constantly.
My mind wanders off into endless fantasies.
I look for places to go to dream silently.
I look for a true love to share my life with me.
There is only one place I have found that's always safe & true.
Dear *God,* that is the one I keep deep inside myself for only *You!*

Karen Denise Bynum Jones

MADE FOR EACH OTHER

On March 28, of '33, a baby boy was born you see, may I present my
pal Anthony? On March 28, of '34, another boy, this date was born,
his name became Wayne! On March 28, of '35, God knew they'd one day
need a wife, so to me, He then gave life! As the years rolled on with
the march of time, God arranged for our lives to intertwine.
I met Anthony first as you recall, the feelings we shared with one
another were like those shared by a sister and a brother! . . .
The years flew by so very fast, and the Korean War came to pass.
Into the Air Force the two of you went, and in San Antonio the two of
you met! 'Twas after Tech School you all parted ways, and you arrived
in Tampa Bay! Anthony being the man he was, said ''Look up my
brothers, they will show you around'' . . . So, Papa, Mama, brothers
and sister too, introduced me then to you! . . . In a few short
months, you asked if I'd share your life, and I became your Air Force
wife! . . . Three lovely children God sent to us, a boy, a girl,
and a big surprise!
A lovely girl our son did meet. Her date of birth? March 28th —
was there ever a doubt? Now my friends, if you think this is the end,
please bear with me once again . . . March 28, of '82, we waited and
cheered, but all in vain — our grandson applied his brakes, and
he stopped our daughter's labor pains! A day of his own, is what
he sought, a few hours late, to us he was brought! March 29th is his
claim to fame! But we all love him just the same. So, to all of us on
this our day, Good Luck, God Bless, and many more years of good
health and happiness!

Dolores Rey Partie

BACCALAUREATE

When I graduated from Hughes with my class
Our church's old paster gave the address.
The poem he read, ''The Fittest Shall Live''
Was of value to me; I'm sure he'd forgive
My mentioning it now.

He read his good poem, gave his address
With feeling, much fervor, yet with finesse.
In silence we sat in cap and long gown.
The old hall was filled with friends from the town,
There to help us rejoice.

That faithful old pastor had much more to give
Concealed in his work, ''The Fittest Shall Live.''
I listened intently, his message to hear,
In one magic moment, His meaning was clear;
He was saying, ''Be Fit to Live.''

Carol S. Meyer

LOVE SURVIVES

Burning on my eyes
Outlines of a distant face
Words that pierced through my heart
And your love survived

How could you love me
After all this time
All the memories that press against my mind
Still love me after all this time

You look at me and deep in your eyes
I see cool blue waters
How many rivers have poured from those eyes
All because of my deceitful lies

Sweetly I want to touch your face
Brushing my fingers softly against your skin
And I hope slowly I can try to erase
All the hurt you still embrace

Diane M. Bryan

UNFORGIVEN

A lonely lover's silent breath!
Wanting the night's so he could rest.
Thinks about the times he cried,
Asking himself the reason why.

A lonely heart's silent beat!
A sound which echoes to his feet.
Pulling apart his inner soul,
Knowing one day he'll grow old.

A lonely hand's silent grasp!
Trying to get a hold of the past.
Reach out with all his might,
If only he would have one more night.

A lonely mouth's silent lips!
If only he could say the words he missed,
To speak them then they weren't clear,
To speak them now would seem so real.

Lonely eyes silently stare!
Oh, how I wish that you were here.
You would give me a breath to share,
A beat to hear, a hand to hold,
Words of love while I grow old!

Diane M. Bryan

JOLLIES

Roley-poley bumpkin-Fats
Scurrying hither-thither, graceless
Pandemonium's rising tides
Arch into unsequenced chuckles
And guffaws galore,
Belting-out wallops of belched acoustics:
Ring-a-ding plunk-plunk,
A riot's roar;
And then the jump and the cuddle
By the Fats cat's muddle.

Roy D. Benson

IN THE SANDBOX

She sprinkles the sand with perfume,
down from the nursery to shape battlements
around a courtyard, encircling, imprisoned,
her yellow hair ribbon tied to a stake,
from the tower room a pale tongue
to mock at armies advancing
out of the nursery,
launching walnut shells
to cross the moat with red oak sails.

A breath of triumph tips and routs them;
toothpicks bob away from
armless knights that float limp
'til she buries them deep
under hurried splats of scented mud.

She marches away but returns at dusk,
out of the nursery,
a secret undoing
to rinse the tall wet sails,
to bind and press some damp brown leaves
in the folds of an unwritten diary.

Anne Wallace

FIFTEEN

A spherical puzzle unsolved,
fragments of warring identities
struggle for ascendency, wanting union,
rattling raw angled in a bone bowl;
untested selves,
perilously contained in
a walled circle of repudiation,
polarize, yet strive to merge
in a womb of awakening flesh, beautiful,
alien, searching the need to know, but
remote with the fear
of the bowl tipped,
the wall breached,
the womb pried open too soon, and
the self, premature, spilled
and scattered all over the floor.

Anne Wallace

MAGIC BULLET

The tines of forked revolvers
Recoiling into oblivion
Rage against the motions of a conscious ploy;
Blood-beats and fluid-flows
Upon my unransomed neck
Beguiled by the untimely snap
Of the trigger's swinging bomber
On a fabled day, in a screeching moment
The wrath was unleashed
To soothe the bloated mangy beast.

Roy D. Benson

TO MY CHILDREN

Many times I've tried
To write a poem to each of you.
Some feelings run so deep
That words just will not do.

Each of you controls the essence
Of the fibers of my life.
You're the masterpieces of accomplishment
That I have done with teetered strife.

So, my dearest children,
You will never know
The pride I have for each of you,
To each, I love you so.

So, forgive me, my darlings.
I cannot find a single word
To write a poem to each of you;
I've tried, but it's absurd.

Just know and try to understand
What I'm trying to say to you,
A mother's love and pride's fulfilled,
In what you are and what you do.

Frances P. Brown

WEARY TRAVELER

I am a weary traveler,
Going down a lonely road;
Seeking rest for a weary body,
And peace for a tired old soul.

I've met a lot of strangers.
Some good, and some were bad.
Many were just happy people.
But a few were very sad.

I've slept in lots of places.
Much food I haven't had.
But for each human kindness,
My heart is very glad.

I will continue on my journey —
Wherever it may lead.
I was born to be a weary traveler,
Until I reach the end, indeed.

Frances P. Brown

UNTITLED

It's the same old thing
and the same old face
the same old time
and the same old place
It's the same old line
and the same old dress
the same old bed
and the same old sex.

Elizabeth A. Brown

PIPE DREAM

The gold harp is still in the sunroom
Of this house which once was our pride.
It has been there since I was twenty
And brought Helen home as my bride.

Most of our things are tattered or time-worn.
Their heyday has long passed away,
But the harp is majestic as always;
It stands tall, unscathed to this day.

Relaxed in my armchair at nightfall
I see Helen come into the room,
Dressed in a gown of soft white chiffon
Plainly visible there in the gloom.

Her skin is like ivory, her hands gentle doves,
Sweeping the strings like birds in their flight;
Enhancing my dream with the harp's tinkling music.
Dark is her hair — dark is the night.

At last I retire; the hour has grown late,
But when I arise she is gone from my sight,
Vanished completely into the shadows,
Alas, she was only the smoke from my pipe.

Carol S. Meyer

THE PLEDGE

When I was young I had a pledge
For life to come to all my friends
Now that I'm older so much has changed
Young dies the soldier, but the pledge remains

As a teenager I had a prayer
May grief and danger hold no one there
Now I seem to be a stranger to so many people
But when I heed my savior I am not deceitful

When I became a man I had a call
That rang across the land, freedom for all
But I see so many held by the chains of war
What I feel seems plenty, but not enough to soar

Now that I'm old I have a new pledge
May the stories told about life and death
Have a happy ending to those I reach
May the pledge I'm sending bring hope and peace.

Richard Clark

HIS SONG

As I speak of the Almighty's love song ''Let it be,''

It is the love of he, that the love may flow from within,
    to a special kind of friend like thee.

I took thee's hand, and sat silently holding it ever so
    gently, as I was saying how much I love thee.

It's only from within, my heart it did sing
    ''Let the love of Christ flow within.''

I saw with his heart of gold which did give him golden glow
    and I love even more so.

Sharon, thee quietly said to me.
I turned toward thee and said, ''So it shall be.''

AnnaMarie Kilbreth

ONLY BECAUSE OF A POEM

There we were, in high school,
A time when we thought we were cool.
That's when I first met you,
And finding out, that you wrote poems too.

It was from then on,
We felt like we could do no wrong.
We had our own song to sing,
And the dreams of what that song would bring.

Dreaming of the very biggest of times,
Knowing Nashville was where we would take our rhymes.
We knew our time had come, to call,
We wanted everything, we sure wanted it all.

We knew it was something we had to do,
Even when our selfish ways made others so blue.
It all ended up, costing our families' love, and the warmth of our home,
Only because of a poem.

But we believed in all we could do,
That's what you've done for me, what I've done for you.
We put our lives in each other's hands,
But only to find out, time washed us away, like water does the sand.

Tina Marie Ivers

YEARNING HEARTS

The snow that melts when the season ends.
The yearning for better times.
Worries of the world yet the happiness of spring.

Millie R. Curtis

SWEET YOUTH

Ah, sweet youth! 'Twas ever thus
Why do old folks make such a fuss?
Must Dad be such a mean sort of cuss?
Can't they leave our lifestyle up to us?

Mary can do this or Johnny can do that
While 'my folks' say ''no'' at the drop of a hat.
They're forever saying ''you're not allowed''
What's wrong with being one of the crowd?

Although youth never agreed with Mom and Dad
They've given you more than they ever had.
So all you young folks better look twice
Before you rebel and refuse their advice.

One day they were young and carefree too
And probably felt the way you do.
Think, before you go on today's kind of trips
For you have the world at your fingertips.

Once they were young and rebellious like you
They thought their parents were 'old-fashioned' too.
Many years passed before they finally knew
Because of their love, parents act like they do.

Clara G. Stinson

CHILDHOOD MEMORIES

When I was just a child,
On the farm I liked to be.
Around the corner behind the barn
Stood a huge apple tree.

I climbed its branches many a time
To fetch an apple to eat;
Big, red, and just right
Its juices ever so sweet.

Sitting on a limb of that old apple tree
Gazing out across the field,
I dreamed sweet dreams of faraway places —
Childhood fantasies — instilled.

Did they come true, those dreams?
I can't remember now —
Whether they did or not
Is not important, somehow.

Such sweet dreams I dreamed
In that old apple tree.
Cherished they will always be . . .
These memories remain a part of me.

Frances P. Brown

YOU'RE ON MY MIND

You make me see
How good life can be
You're on my mind
Not only now but
All of the time
When I close my eyes
I see you, I hear you
I touch you and love you
It's so real when
You're on my mind
Sometimes I see you
Like a reflection on the water
But the image slowly fades away
Yes you're on my mind girl
With every heartbeat
You touch my very soul
So believe me honey
You'll find it's true
You're on my mind
All of the time

Gene Roberts

GIVING, OR TAKING?

Do we get our strength each day
From peace which God has given?
To keep us in the right path
Today — where we are living!

Do we *give* help to others,
Or *take* time from them each day?
Do we trust God's loving care,
Or make others go our way?

God has *given* — let us give
Freely — without selfish thought —
By taking God's greatest gift,
Our freedom here has been bought!

Edna M. Parker

DEBTS OF LOVE

Our parents worked and struggled
To teach us right ways from wrong
We owe them a debt of love
As we find where we belong —

To family, friends, and neighbors
We can pay our debt each day
By little acts of kindness
All along life's busy way —

When life's evening comes to us
And our mission is fulfilled
Our debts of love will be paid
If we have lived as God willed!

Edna M. Parker

A CHILD'S PRAYER ANSWERED!

Flowers were hurting — dry again
A small boy asked: "Can God help pain?"
Let's pray to Him *now* for some *rain* —
A gentle rain answered his prayer
He called me on the phone to share:
"He did it! God does really care!"

The look on his face when he came
Was a moment of childhood fame
True faith — no longer a game!

Edna M. Parker

THE LAST BABY

You were born in a time of strife
Heartsick to be pregnant & give you life
Caught in a web of babies and work
I could not cope, yet could not shirk.

I've loved you always, but with a guilt
I was ashamed and did not make a quilt
To cover your little body and hold you close
The last in line and breakdown close.

Loving family and friends not there
To guide and counsel and say a prayer
I held 'til the explosion came
Then the sick-depression, shame.

I grieve that I was not wise
That I feel the pathos and anger still alive
Please forgive — We can't forget
But life has love for us yet

To hold you close and feel your love
I need and you need, while we live
There is not world enough or time
To make amends — *I love you — baby mine*.

Fatima Mosey

NOTHING AT ALL

Do you ever sit and people watch?
It's remarkable and fun
None of us came from the same batch
We're not alike — not one.

Did you know you were unique?
There is no one just like you
It's not the frame that does the trick
It's how you think, what makes you tick.

Catch a glance, exchange a grin
Who was that? Just her or him
They're enjoying life and living too
That is the bonus, and the roux.

It's life teeming all around us
Busy scurrying to and fro
From where to whence?
I don't know, must I though?

Fatima Mosey

YOU CAME BY

Did I say I'm glad you came today?
Did you know the glow you made?
I sit and wait to end the play
Silent, tearful, lonely, unafraid.

Did you say I'm glad you came today?
I got to listen to someone's voice
Speaking to me — about the way
I feel and look and "My food of choice?"

Did I say I'm glad you came today?
You filled my mind, made me smile
A laugh, a story along the way
Your visit will be recalled and beguile

Did I say I'm glad you came today?
Oh yes! you made me feel a closeness
A human touch, one hour, one day
And I can think and fret a little less.

Fatima Mosey

FATIMA 'TINA' HAYES. Pen Name: Fatima Mosey; Born: Sioux Falls, South Dakota, 3-31-22; Married: William M. Hayes, 3-1-86; Education: High school; Occupation: Accounting clerk in hospital; Awards: Golden Poet Awards, 1985-87; Poetry: 'Valley of the Shadow,' 'Brown Eyes,' 1985; 'My Bequests,' *American Poetry Anthology;* 'Freedom,' 'Our Son,' 'I Thank Thee,' 1986; Comments: *After 65 years I have things to say! I enjoy words and their flow and flow and flow.*

STRAWBERRY TIME

Early each summer when the skies were blue,
The fields were green and covered with dew.
We each took a bucket and a straw hat, too,
And headed for the patches where wild strawberries grew.

If we were lucky to find one larger than a pea,
We called for the others to come and see.
It took the morning to pick a pail of them,
And all afternoon just to sit and stem.

Precious little time we had to ourself,
Till fifty quarts of preserves were on the shelf.
Although there were times we thought we'd roast,
They tasted mighty good in the winter on toast.

Sometimes we made ice cream for a special treat,
And licking the paddles was kinda neat.
But it always was strawberry way back then,
And I vowed I'd never eat that kind again.

Those days hold memories of long ago,
No longer are there fields where berries grow.
But when I look back on the childhood of mine,
I can see Mom in her apron at strawberry time.

Clara G. Stinson

THE FIRST TIME

I remember the first time I said,
''I Love You.''
It was hard to say but I did it.
I knew what I was getting into;
I hoped you did too.
Now we say it in ways that we never thought of before.
I'll take this moment to take us back to the beginning,
''I Love You.''

David Allen Mills

THINK IT OVER

  Life is a game of give and take
Are you willing to give whatever it takes
          Think it over
  Sometimes justice digs a well of joy with a
ske
  Are you willing to give whatever it takes
          Think it over
  Sometimes justice digs a well of joy with a
spade of sorrow
  Try and do a good deed today, don't wait
until tomorrow
          Think it over
  If your load is heavy, just stop and rest a bit
  Believe you are a winner, a winner never quits
          Think it over
  Time and life is your paycheck, to use or
throw away
  If you don't use it wisely, you'll regret
it some day
  Just keep thinking, remember thoughts are things
  You'll be happy with what positive thought will bring
  Every problem you have can be solved
  If you let God become involved
          Think it over

Jerry Belton

THE APPLE TREE AND THE SEED

How many seeds are in one apple
You can count them and you will know
But how many apples are in one seed
And what's the power that makes them grow

Why do some apples turn red
And others hardly change at all
But they all must do what nature says
Eat, grow, get ripe and fall

We should appreciate the apples that grow on the trees
The tree loves and appreciates its apples and leaves
If we loved each other as the tree loves its leaves
We would understand, and not be so hard to please

Jerry Belton

A TORN AND FADED TAPESTRY

A torn and faded tapestry, life gathers dust.
A byway of loneliness, age winds blindly into a sunset.
Leaping and dancing, today's children understand so much more.
I cannot talk to them.
I was never one of them.
They will never be like me.
Angry and frustrated, the still green grass defies winter.
Snow beats endlessly against life.
Tomorrow is new and I am old — far too tired to fight again.
I have no more defenses: mind and heart open.
I have given up, yielding to time with all its dust and wear.
The wind, cold as death, has worn me down.
I am a gingerbread man standing alone in the ice cold rain . . .
Melting and shifting, I am traveling far away.
A freed soul, drifting alone, knocks at the children's doors.
No one is at home.
There is no one who believes in the gingerbread man.

Daniel Jay Marker

THE FABRIC OF THE UNIVERSE

I wonder about the fabric of the universe
of its content being woven by what hand
an intricate array of patterns
so delicate and beautiful to behold
colors mesh together
forming tree and sky and land
a nighttime blanket of brilliant stars
to every grain of sand
I wonder about the fabric of the universe
silky smooth
vibrant textures
deep rich softness
I am often amazed at the interwoven complexity
on the surface clear as an ocean
but made up of layer within layer of life
variation upon variation
It's a joy to know and see
we are all participants in the art

Christine Miletta

MEMORIES OF THE SEA

My mother brought me
To the ocean when
I was young.
She taught me to love
The tides, the waves, the blue
Of the calm sea, the gray
Of the stormy sea, the white
Of the salty tide line,
The shells, the agates, the driftwood.
The memories of that time
Return when I walk
The beach with my daughter.
The joy returns when she
Claims from the tides
Her first agate.

Linda Yaple

A CLOWN

Sometimes I'd like to be a clown
And dress in real bright colors
My snow white gloves
My painted face
My bright orange hair
Almost a disgrace.
My baggie pants
My roomy pockets
My great big feet
As big as rockets.
So when I have a real sad face
Nobody really knows
Am I playing a ''happy game''
Or sad down to my toes?
But most of all I like to see
The funny faces I can be
To bring a smile and a sparkling eye
To a little child
This clown and I.

Winifred J. Johnston

THE CLOTHES CHUTE

There's a great big hole
In our bathroom wall
It even has a door
It's used for feeding dirty clothes
Then they fall on the basement floor
It's good for dumping dirty sneaks
My sister's comb and more
I put her brand new sweater in there
We nearly had a war.
My sister says it's a *clothes chute*
And I may *live* in there real soon
But it's dark and I'd have to stand all the time
I'd rather be sent to my room.
I'll try being good to her
Instead of a tangle with Dad
She's not too mean, but it sure will be tough
'Cause I like to make her mad.

Winifred J. Johnston

LANGUAGE OF THE SOUL

The wisdom of words
The center of emotions
The winds of the spirit
The throbs of the soul

I seek for expression
Of the Creator's magnificence
That I might speak
Of the Wafting of the Eternal
As His Stirring sweeps over me

I want to go into unentered realms
That I might see
Mysteries and truths untold
And then attempt to convey
The unending beauties they hold

Though as I strive for attainment
I am humbled by the vastness
That God Holds in His Hand
Yet daily I breath His Breath
That He bestowed upon me

Richard D. Cagg

BITTERNESS FROM THE WAR IN VIETNAM

How bitter to arise
To an American demise
To wake up and see
Allies no longer free

How bitter to give yourself to a cause
Only to see retreat and pause
To see your efforts in vain
To see your adversaries gain

So the VC and NVA prevailed
While we simply failed
But not surprising when you compare their will
With the ground that we would till

But if we were so wrong
Why do boat people long
For an alternative
In which to live

Steven Koven

MAN OF THE SEA

Horizons hold your eyes
As now you do hold me,
A tallied time from sea —
Before goodbyes,
Before goodbyes.

Ah time is timeless now,
These minutes out of years —
Until a tide of tears
Anoints the love I vow,
Anoints the love I vow.

Donna Ohl Allen

OF JOY

Oh give my heart
An autumn day —
An autumn day
Of brilliant blue
And sun still warm;
A spicy wind
Whose laughter shakes
The golden leaves
From golden trees
And grabs the ground
In bright brocade.
Oh give my heart
An autumn day
And it will have
More joy than my
Whole heart can hold!

Donna Ohl Allen

MORNING SPLENDOR

There are lush grassy meadows;
There are glad songs in the night;
There's a land of milk and honey;
And there's Pisgah's lofty height.
There are streams in the deserts;
There are springs in the valley;
There's the Bread of Life awaiting,
And a rest for all the weary.

Though scenes like these amaze us —
They truly cannot compare,
To the joy that will surmount us
When we meet Christ in the air.
And there dawns that special morning
Which I so longingly await,
When I meet my God and Savior
Just inside the Eastern Gate.

JoAnn Wollam

DUSTY ROOM

The dust drifts across the room
appearing in the sunbeam.
It crosses against the window
across the picture of the stable earth.
It disappears into the invisible air
hiding behind the layers of light
appearing again in another beam.
Outside the window
leaves whip up
in the torrents of the wind
spinning in a vortex
and rising up.
A gusty fog of sand bursts up
and beats against the window
while the dust still drifts steadily
against the violent scene.
The sand attacks the window,
but the dust merely drifts along
feeling only the warmth of the sun
that shines unaffected.

Kenneth Idler

ALICE

I have loved you, Alice, from the very start.
I love you, dear, from the bottom of my heart.
I loved you then and I love you still,
I love you truly and I always will.

If love could be weighed, I want to say,
There is no train big enough to haul my love for you away.
If love could be measured it would be very tall.
The way some people act, they don't have any love at all.

My love for you will never grow old.
The pleasures we've shared are more precious than gold.
I'm so thankful I love you the way I do
For I know that you love me too.

We've loved each other through hardships and pleasures too.
I would tell the world that's what love can do.
We loved our children and watched as they grew.
Sweetheart, my three famous words are
    I LOVE YOU!

Forrest M. Moore

MY OLD PORCH SWING

If I could change some things around, here is what I would do,
I would be the master of many arts, and be a friend to you.
But I can't play a musical instrument, neither can I sing.
The only thing that I can do well is swing in my old porch swing.

When my day's work is over and I need a place to rest,
Of all the places I can think of, the porch seems the best.
There I forget all my troubles and never worry about a thing,
With all my thoughts and pleasures in my old porch swing.

When winter is over and warm weather is here to stay,
We can enjoy our front porch every single day.
Some people think I'm crazy, others say I'm a ding-a-ling,
But I just keep on swinging in my old porch swing.

Forrest M. Moore

LOLLYGAGGING

I took a ride on the Iron Mountain train.
It was fun and excitement until it started to rain.
The rain came in and we all got wet.
Everyone began to fuss and to fret.

The chug, chug of the engine and cinders in your eyes,
With smoke coming from the stack like clouds in the skies,
I always enjoyed a trip on the old steam-engine train,
Up and over the mountains or down through the plains.

A funny thing happened and it must be told,
When I took my last ride on the Iron Mountain Railroad.
The conductor cried out loud and clear, "This is a train, not
    a hay-ride wagon,
And I want everyone to know, there will be no lollygagging!"

Forrest M. Moore

THE CHILD'S FIRST FUNERAL

To market to market to be a fat pig . . . but
across the street, out of the market
is carried a thin tall lady with a three-foot
grasshopper hunched on her back . . .
The Funeral Director looks away
as he hands me out of the limousine.
We take care of all that, he says.

On stage the pianist preys over the keys,
and Piglet in the wings peers at Pooh,
from behind a gorse bush . . . It's small,
he says, and runs round and round
the body looking, but all I can see
is the thin tall lady getting smaller
and smaller . . . the priest prays over her . . .
Mother . . . mother . . . it's dark . . . and the organ
swells as we set off piggyback out of the church.

Anne Wallace

ANNE MILLS WALLACE. Born: Englewood, New Jersey; Married: Kenneth Dean Wallace; Education: Harvard University, B. A., Magna Cum Laude, 1968 (under name Anne Mills Connors); Occupation: Radio producer; Poetry: 'Ghetto,' 'Return to Sender,' 'Treasuries of the Snow,' *American Poetry Anthology, Vol. VII, No. 2,* 1987; Comments: *Most of my poems are a means of intensely personal catharsis and healing; they are also a reaching out to touch one other probably unknown person in one tender, secret place, yet in images that also touch those places where all of us have wordlessly hidden the same kinds of experience. For this publication I have chosen poems that uncover the often unconscious memories of childhood moments — regal anticipation, personal loss with its self-generated guilt, and the pregnant fear of growing. The original images are spontaneous, but if some nameless "other" can read the finished poem and say "yes," with surprise, "it was like that!" then for me the poem has succeeded.*

OH PLEASE GOD?!

That feisty swain doth cometh once
Again to trounce my bursting chasms,
As Death, that grand shatterer of worlds,
Enters my humble bumbling dwelling
As if, God had not said: "My child,
Ye shall dwell in the house of the Lord, forever!"
So I raged within
A thousand chanting rituals:
Begone trouble!
I bellowed
And I wallowed
And I followed
A callow youth, with sunken chest, and island eyes;
I think not, therefore I am also.

Roy D. Benson

IT IS TIME TO LEAVE

Take my hand, my Love,
if for just a while.
Walk close to me, my Love,
if for just another mile.

Hold me tightly, darling,
I am afraid to die.
Be near until the time has come,
for then I shall not cry.

Do not worry for me,
pity, please feel none.
Shed no tears, my dearest,
for what is done, is done.

I shall live forever,
if you wish it so.
I will live in memory,
it is just the shell that goes.

The time is near, my dearest,
and now I have to leave.
Remember I am with you.
If only you believe.

LeAnne M. Emery

UNFULFILLED

Unfulfilled this heart of mine
and wanders so through life.
Some Voice, some Face,
some heartfelt glance.
For just a moment, warms,
then dies.
Yearn on you foolish, dreaming mass.
To find and cherish what you seek.
Would last but just a heartthrob long,
and wither into not.
The dreams are worth a dozen haves.
The yearns a thousands keeps.
For time has spoiled every dream.
The tarnished silver threads
of home,
are not, when they are possessed.
So keep the voice, the face, the glance.
Hold it dear and rare.
To keep, possess and conquer these
are dreams yet Unfulfilled.

LeAnne M. Emery

UP ON TOP

Have you been on a narrow, winding, road
Way up high,
Between the earth and sky?
All around are mountains
Beyond wide open space . . .
You get a feeling that is hard to describe.
As if the world below is far away
And nothing down there is important.

Marie Wills

GREAT AMBITION

I was born in Newport News in 1947,
and I was playing the piano by eleven.
I had played this instrument in Carnegie Hall,
and I had my winner's certificate on my wall.
I did pretty good work in high school
just to let people know that I was no fool.
I had made the Honor Roll by fourteen,
and this would make the ignorant grow mean.
Great Ambition!

I was born on November 23rd,
and I hope that this poem will be heard.
I often dreamt as a child,
and my temperament was described as mild.
I often did what I was told,
with the hope that I would grow old.
In college I made the Dean's List,
just by often using my wrist.
Great Ambition!

Michael Leroy Porter

MY CHILD

Tiny, and crying,
and taking my time;
oh, for some solitude
I would whine.

Older, and learning things
you had to know;
I tried to be patient
though it didn't show.

Finally, you're ready
to go off to school;
you get on the bus —
please, obey the rules.

Sitting alone now
surprised to say;
I can't wait to see you,
and hear about your day.

Judy Tomkiel

TAKE AWAY ALL THE THINGS THAT MAKE ME GLAD

Take away, all the things, that make me glad,
  take away, all the things, that make me sad.
Take from my memory,
  all the things that meant so much,
  to you and me.
Give me, just one more, sunny day,
  when you leave, my sky, will be forever gray.
Don't kiss me goodbye,
  unless you want to see me cry.
The new love you'll find,
  you think, will be greater than mine.
Someday you'll see,
  there was no greater love,
  than the love that was between, you and me.

Robert L. Willyard

MOTHERHOOD

Yes, dear one, he is sweet and small,
Still a part of your very heart
As he will always be.

But do not make your love a burden
And all your hopes for him too high.
Let him become what he must.

Keep only memory of his early years,
Of his early love and need of you.
A man must transfer these.

Prepare yourself now for that distant day
When family union will be broken
And a barrier is born.

When no more he shows affection
His eye is critical, his comments sharp.
Remember, his life's untried.

May you find the ways to learn
To let the day suffice — then keep
Your past in a quiet heart,
Your future, leave to faith.

Eleanor F. Miller

LONGING

Oh, daughter that I do not have,
Where are your arms about me
Your loving eyes that say, "I love you"?

How empty my heart
Tonight, without you.

This longing that the years have held,
Unanswered, makes the crying deep.
I miss the closeness others have
The exchange of glance, the message warm.

I cannot ease the cause of my distress
Left comfortless and still alone
No mother, sister, daughter dear,
My love to give, it to receive.

The years are long, ahead of me.
My sons now grown, though dear and good,
Are, in the course of life, bestowed
Their gift of birth no longer mine.

Mothers of daughters, you hold, still, the cord,
The heart's dear lease your full reward.

Eleanora F. Miller

Simple trust:
Do not the petals flutter down,
  Just like that?

Issa

OCTOBER MORN

Oh, October morn, the sky is blue,
October blue.
Sunlight breaks the dawn,
The world is new, and so is love.

Grass is wet with dew,
And time stands still,
When you are near, close to me, dear, ever so clear,
October morn.

Birds sing us their song,
They sing farewell
Until it's spring.
Leaves are red and gold,
They frame our love,
October morn.

Bernice Prill Grebner

JEALOUSY:
THE DEATH OF LOVE

You see Her walking with another male,
Smiling, laughing, talking, carefree and gay.
Something inside flares up, sunshine turns grey,
A shock runs down your spine, your face turns pale,
Wild passion blows the fuse of Reason's frail
Logic. Love and Law's strictures die today,
No fear of any consequence can stay
The madness, after this all life is stale.
She's walking and She's laughing down the street,
She holds his arm and looks up in his face;
A million years of female wiles displayed,
From flying hair right down to dancing feet.
Built-in emotions of the whole male race,
Flare out, a Super-Nova on parade.

Joseph E. Barrett

FLOWERS FOR DONALD

Donny Boy we miss you by the Seashore,
We miss you when the tide comes in at dawn.
The wind blows soft and lonely down the lawn,
Now we hear children's laughter as once more
It echoes on the sands just like before,
The giggles of sweet Marylou and John
As Alice Mary's stories led us on
To bright delights for memories' deep core.
Those days will never die, those sunny days,
Though flowers hide the stone that bears your name;
The others are long gone into the blue
And Donald you have gone a long long ways,
But that's not you, that old man you became,
You still play on the beach with Marylou.
You live some way in each of us who shared
Light days and bright days and days we all cared.

Joseph E. Barrett

THAT SOMEONE WAS ME

Someone called you today,
    She wanted to tell you,
        She was moving away.

Someone thought,
    You really cared,
        Love is something,
            That must be shared.

Go ahead,
    And have your fun,
        She thought I was,
            The only one.

Someone you kissed,
    After a long walk,
        Along the shore,
            Said they would love you,
                Forevermore.

Now there are only memories,
    of the joy,
        She thought would always be.

She wants you to love her,
    as you did before,
        Return to her,
            Like the ship that comes back,
                To the shore.

Someone still loves you,
    Can't you see,
        that someone who called,
            That someone was me.

Robert L. Willyard

GRANDMOTHER

She sits upon her rocking chair,
 sadly reminiscing long ago,
wishing she was still there,
 and didn't have to go.

On her aging brows,
 sunbeams meet,
and her silver hair, they also greet.

She gazes upon the ocean,
 at the same old blues and greens.
Her aging soul wants to escape
 into her youthful dreams.

She's had good health, a loving heart, a strong mind,
 and pleasure she has endured as well,
The feeling of friendship, kind and warm,
 Oh, she certainly knows love's spell.

Her hopes and dreams have gone now,
 so she rocks away the remaining days,
and clings to her memories,
 with weary, solemn, faded eyes,
she recalls her youthful paradise.

Cindee Rubin

MY DEAR

Never again to see you
Never again to hear you
Never again to touch you —
Death is final.

Remembering the friendship we shared
Remembering the children we bore
Remembering the long years together —
Love is constant.

There is the beautiful smile
There is the loving reply
There is the protective hand —
These are with me.

Eleanora F. Miller

REMINISCENCE

Reminiscence costs me little
But the energy it takes
To bring forth the memories
That looking back awakes.

Remember when we worked so hard
From dawn 'til setting sun.
It seemed that life was full of work,
With little time for fun.

Yet when the time to rest
Would finally arrive,
That rest was quite relaxing.
It was good to be alive.

I try to be real positive,
As I think back through the years.
I dwell upon the happy times
And forget about the fears.

Ivan L. Coe

THE GOLDEN YEARS

Even though we look to the future,
Our thoughts are oft backward turning.
We would not care to live in the past.
Nostalgia should not be a yearning.

We are apt to dream of the future.
We can boast of past sweat on the brow,
But contentment comes to us only,
When we cherish the here and the now.

Old age brings great satisfaction —
Enjoyment in so many ways.
It makes the present and the future look better
Than the so-called good old days.

Ivan L. Coe

THE HARVESTER

Before the days of the combine,
The reaper was the magic machine.
To us it was known as a binder,
As it bound the bundles so clean.

The sickle shuttled back and forth.
It severed the stalks skillfully.
The reel tumbled them backward.
At last they were entirely free.

Onward and upward the grain moved along —
On canvasses stretched very taut.
Finally it started downward —
By the beaters so firmly caught.

The needle encircled the straw
And the knotter caught the twine.
The bundles were kicked onto the carrier,
And they were dropped in a line.

The sheaves were settled into the stubble,
And lay there in shining glory.
Later they were put into shocks,
But that is another story.

Ivan L. Coe

I DON'T KNOW WHY

I love you Hope;
I don't know Why,
but your smile
warms me up inside;
your soft voice
keeps me going
when I feel the need to hide.

I love you Hope;
I don't know why;
to others you're not the most beautiful;
you're not the most shapely,
but you're all I need;
you're beautiful to me.

There is something about you;
there is something inside me
that just won't die.
I love you, Hope Marie,
and I don't know why.

Robb Allan

SO SOON

The time we've spent together
Is but days, and just a few
But I feel deep in my heart
I've something special, you

I can't explain, it makes no sense
To feel like this so soon
But I know when I'm with you
I'm walking on the moon

I know not what the future holds
Or where this road will end
I do know that you'll always be
More than just a friend

James D. Denam

NEVER ALONE

The time we're forced to spend apart
Each and every day
Reminds me that you're in my heart
And there I know you'll stay

When I feel that I'm alone
And long to be with you
I need only close my eyes
And your sweet face I view

All the things you've said and done
Since our first day together
Dwell within my memories
And will be there forever

For when the days seem darkest
And I think I can't go on
Your loving touch, your shining smile
Fill my heart with song

You show your love, while being you
You let me know you care
I know I love you truly
With you my life I'll share

James D. Denam

HEARTACHE

A sweet dream,
Turning into nightmare.
Finding out he doesn't care.
All the love you have given,
Never to be returned.
Everything cherished,
Becomes perished into pain,
A pain hard to overcome.
Leaving the memory,
Never to be forgotten.
Leaving a scar,
Never to heal.
Finding it hard to believe real.
Not wanting to try again,
You lock and chain,
   the doors to your heart.
Trying to keep it from falling apart.
If another comes along,
You'd look back and have to run.
Thinking of he who hurt you.
Fearing your heart would shatter,
   and your life could end.

Deborah D. Herington

FOLLOWING MY HEART
TO SCOTLAND

I am following my heart to Scotland,
 over the ocean today.
I don't know if I will return,
 or if I shall stay.

He has written me with love,
 from the land of bagpipes and kilts,
and living alone without him,
 makes my poor heart wilt.

I love him in a way no other woman can,
 that is why I am following my heart to Scotland!

We carved our names together on a tree
 made of Scot's Fir wood,
and he held me in his arms,
 the way a man should.

Now I must be leaving for my restless heart is grieving
 to be in Scotland with him again.
I bought a ticket for one way,
 hopefully I will stay
in the land across the sea
 with my lover in my sight when day turns into night.

Cindee Rubin

ODE TO OLDSTERS

Especially those poetically inclined

What do we do when we can do no more?
What do we do when we can't reach the door?
What do we do when our legs won't work?
What do we do when we cannot *hear* a thing?
What do we do when our vision grows double?
What do we do when our *hearts* palpitate . . . (*omen* of trouble!)
What do we do when our *tears* overflow the cup? Stop crying?
What do we do when we grow faint and dizzy . . . *give up?*
What do we do when *memory* fails or so it seems . . .
Try again and *try* prayer . . . and with a *resolute* . . . grin
I'll keep right on 'spouting *poetry'* until the . . . *end!*
If it is the end . . . be of good cheer! A new adventure is near!

For the *one who* endowed us with Poetic Lore
He'll stand by us as *He always did . . . before!*
What we experience is . . . *complete loss of fear!*
Not only our 'Guardian Angel' but our loving *Father* is here!
If *He* grants us one wish for *Eternity* . . .
What would it be? As for me . . .?
Ah! To be *young* again 'Spouting Poetry' . . . forever . . . *Free!*

Mabel Lagerlof

BELIEFS ECHOING TESTIMONY

Wings lapsing in the liberating wind
Declarations of honor extending over the mountains

Talons of abandon
Eclipse the savage heart

A gentle promise emerges
Victorious over the forest

In the eagle's eye
Dawn dances

Richard Dana

THE THIEF

Fear's a thief, but what does it steal
It steals the courage, it steals the strength, it steals the will
to win
It makes us feel we cannot go on
We're defeated and that's a sin

Fear's a thief, but who does it rob
It robs the child, it robs the tired, it robs the faint of heart
It takes from those with the least to give
We're beaten before we start

Fear's a thief, but when does it plunder
It plunders when weary, when we're in doubt, or when we've been
beaten down
When life has thrown us too many curves
In our sorrows we're sure to drown

Fear's a thief, but can be brought to task
By facing it straight, measure it true, bring it out in the light
By putting our faith in a power far greater
With His help we'll put fear to flight

James D. Denam

DAD

This poem is dedicated to my father,
James V. Howell.

You have been a father beyond compare,
Whenever I need you, you are always there.
You pick me up when I fall down,
And kiss my hurts without a frown.
I have made some blunders in my life,
And you always listen, but never criticize.
You have given me love, and lots of laughter,
And you're proud when I meet the goals I go after.
Now time has passed, and along the way,
I've stopped to notice your hair turning gray.
Your shoulders are stooped, but your eyes are bright,
And — *Dad* — you're still my guiding light.

Delva L. Wolfe

REMEMBERING

The last time I saw my mother, I was in a hospital
suffering from severe kidney failure, and was attached
to a kidney dialysis machine. Since then, I have been
the recipient of a successful kidney transplant, but
my mother didn't live to see me get better.

My mother left this world behind,
And memories of her haunt my mind.
The things she did, the things she said,
Keep going around inside my head.
Years have passed since she's been gone,
But in my heart she still lives on.
Could she come back for just one day
I'd have so many things to say.
I would take the worry from her face,
And put a smile there in its place.
If she could know how much I wish
For, one more time, her face to kiss.

Delva L. Wolfe

GOSSIP AND TWITTER.

EMOTIONS

Emotions play tricks on the eye.
Emotions encourage stability to fly.
Emotions determine a child from a man —
And discourage a life with the wave of a hand!
Beliefs are blind, immortal, untrue;
Beliefs destroy all that you do.
Beliefs possess a man's soul,
Often obtaining complete control.
The heart rules the ears, the eyes and the mind,
The ears often deaf, the eyes often blind!
A mind so untouched, unbiased and true —
Is merely a dream that encourages you.
You need not encouragement, not in the least;
For the bravest of animals, is certainly a beast!
My heart and my mind are open once more,
Until some stranger closes the door;
The door to my dreams, my hopes and my loves —
The dreams I embrace, I have and I love.

Linda Copp

BOXES

My soul finally joined with the masses last night
    (I awoke with a terrible fright)
My soul, in a bundle of flat, empty shells,
Was formed by machine that was deaf to my yells
And blind to all life which this cold system quells
    (I woke at the thought of the sight)

My soul scuttled down the conveyor of doom
    (The nightmare continued to bloom)
My soul, in a square dry and empty as death
And suddenly, painfully, stuffed out of breath
Was sent to be stifled by glue down its breadth
    (The vision: my soul as its tomb)

My soul, in its destiny, journeyed to fate
    (I sorrowed in the plight of my state)
My soul, as a box in an endless routine
Of boring precision attuned by machine
Entrapped in this dark diabolical scene . . .
    (A witness of this that I hate)

Steve Orwoll

TRUE FRIENDSHIP

Let me tell you what your friendship means to me,
For it was through God alone that this friendship came to be.
The golden rays of sunshine cannot begin to warm a heart,
Like the glittering rays of friendship from my friend when we're apart.
No mountain top or autumn tree,
Can compare with the smile my friend gives me.
There is not a thing that can stir my soul,
As much as this friendship that I know.
No mortal tongue can ever tell,
Nor pen would ever spell,
The feeling I get within my heart,
As my friend and I talk before we part.
They say that gold and diamonds are precious jewels to find,
But none of them compare to my friend, for he is one of a kind.
As I think of how my love continues to grow for you each day,
I thank my God above who cares for us in the very same way.
Yet His love goes deeper far surpassing what I could say,
This is why over the years our friendship will always stay.
God truly blest me with a wondrous gift,
When He gave to me such a friend as this.

Chuck Clemons

SLOPPY LETTERS

I sit on the porch staring at the mailbox across the street.
I'm waiting for a letter to come to get me back on my feet.
And when the mailman comes driving right on by,
A glassy stare will take form in my eye.
He shoves the mail in the mailbox and shuts the door so tight.
I jump up and run across the street hoping with all my might.
There it is, a letter — from one of my little friends.
One glance at the envelope and again my heart mends.
I rip it open in expectation and pull out the letter inside.
I see where a small hand wrote and made the words collide.
Tears begin to stream down my face touching my very heart,
The words leap into my inner being as though he had thrown a dart.
The misspelled words and wrinkled paper send off a message of its own.
Just to know that someone thinks of me touches the marrow of my bone.
I read where he says he thinks a lot of me and hopes that I am fine.
Oh, there is no other friend around quite like the friend of mine.
So you see it's not the big fancy letters that mean the most to me,
But its the sloppy, misspelled ones of a child's earnest plea.
So as I go through life I'll always sit near the mailbox
    where I can see,
And hope that in the future there will be another letter
    in there for me.

Chuck Clemons

A JOYFUL DAY

I had a visit today from two I love dear.
This rarely happens; maybe once in the year.
They took me to dinner, it was like Italy.
The food was authentic and tasty as can be.

Too numerous to mention and I would if I could.
Rare delicacies, which is quite understood.
Baked clams, rice balls and Panella eaten with ease.
Fried squid, potato croquettes and wine if you please.

To my home we proceeded, without empty hand.
With Scotch, Panella and cookies, which I thought was grand.
Good conversation and music to play.
This was how we spent the rest of the day.

The time swiftly flew, I knew that it would.
This always happens when you share what is good.
When they departed, I could honestly say;
''Thank you for coming, I had a wonderful day.''

I'm sure you are wondering, these two I acclaim.
Marion and Andy, who share the same last name.
They are my kin folk and I'm proud as can be.
That I am a part of their family.

Marie Gennaro

LAMENT

Why is it that no one sees me quite the way I am
    Do I somehow gilt or distort reflections of myself
        . . . perhaps wear a cover opaque to the light of other's empathy
Or are they blind to what it is that stirs within me

O, surely I am not as others say
    There must be something else they fail to see
That in the brilliance of the light of truth
    They will at last perceive the real me

Ronald G. Ribble

EACH ONE

We all have a place on this earth.
There's a reason for each one's birth.
Each one special. Each one unique.
Keep a smile upon your face.
Mile after mile. Each road you take
learn from each mistake.
Don't turn the other cheek.
And one day you will find it.
So proudly there you'll arrive.
All your answers will come alive.
You'll find your place in the sun.
Victory is yours. You've won.
Keep believing in yourself, and you'll succeed,
in whatever you do.
Your heart will open. Don't give up.
You'll find whatever you need.
A whole new world is just waiting for you.

Rita M. Sutherby

FOREVER FRIENDS

He came to me with extended arms.
A smile beyond compare.
So clearly could I see, that
I'd find a true friend there.
Eyes so beautiful! And sincere,
sparkle like the stars above.
More I have still to learn about love.
What can I give in return?
So sweet, kind, a friend, so true.
Pensive, caring, very handsome, too.
He will sail every sea, touch every star,
and travel so far.
And he will be free.
A friend to cherish forever.
Though distance may keep us apart,
a special place will be held always,
just for him, deep within my heart.
Thank you, Michael, for being a friend!

Rita M. Sutherby

TRUE KNOWLEDGE

The spell is broken
    the die is cast
There's no more future
    it's all the past!
My mind spins circles
    it twists and turns
My heart sheds tears
    from eyes that burn.
So much has happened
    but, finally I see —
Those things that once
    had eluded me.
Before the morning
    the day must dawn
Before the echo
    you must sing the song.
Before you're loved
    you first must love
Before you fly
    you must first be a dove.
Don't mourn your past
    or fix on a star —
Just give all you can
    and be what you are!

Linda Copp

YOU CAN HAVE THE MOON

You can have the moon
    but you can't have the sky
You can have the answers
    if you don't question why?
You can live forever
    in silent mockery
If you live your life
    never wanting to be free!
You can have tomorrow
    at the price of yesterday
You can walk alone
    through life's turning, twisting maze.
You can live forever
    bored by man's distress
But, then you'll never know
    what you could possess!

Linda Copp

FIRST LOVE

Love, at first brought me so much joy
The kind I never knew could be felt with a boy

I was altogether different
All the times with him I spent

Not feelings of sorrow, but of happiness
Embraces by his gentle caress

I was on top of everything in my world
I was on earth the luckiest girl

For I had love in my heart
The love I never wanted to depart

But, to my shocking surprise
I had to acknowledge the lies

Of that first love, I gave all of me
Nothing left but sadness inside of thee

I could never give love like that anymore
Because the pain is still there from before

Often I sit and wonder, what did I do
Then I realize I had only loved you

My first love seems to be my last
Can't forget him and leave him in my past

Brenda L. Johnson

COMPANY

Angels walked the earth today
I saw them in the clouds
Their radiance shone through
the morning mist
They danced in the dewy flowers
Soft wings glistened in the sun
as they soared on high
Their voices mingled sweetly
with the songbirds' thrilling cry

Rose Marie Brandon

THE SEARCH

Mirrors on a placid sea,
thoughts, reflecting all the past;
solitude, the cure for me,
freedom soul, free at last.

Reasons now, becoming clear,
among the misty web-spun mind;
friends and lovers, held so dear,
friends, not lovers, so hard to find.

So many people among the friends,
sharing much, but none so real;
so many beginnings, so many ends,
to share so much, but never feel.

Looking for love, prepared to hail,
the faulty promises of wedding chimes;
the dismal ache, of search and fail,
the lonely reality, of endless times.

Searching and searching, fore and hind,
longing for love, among the Blue;
endless searches, never to find,
never to found . . . 'til there was You.

Glenn T. Fugitt

CHILDHOOD MEMORIES
UNDER THE LILACS

Under the lilacs we spent many a day,
Drinking our tea and talking at play.

Listening to the birds sing,
To welcome the morn air,
And the bright white daises,
Dressed especially for a fair.

Flowers were our wonder of nature,
And of God's special way
Oh he'd make them grow in abundance,
Day after day after day.

In spring how we loved to pick them,
Wind blew lavender scents as they grew,
And we'd bring them home to Mother
Who was made happy, as we knew.

Lovely were the days,
That have long ago been past,
And the truthful saying is,
The present is all thou hast . . .

This, and the very precious memories,
Of our childhood, under the lilacs.

Marcella Ann McDonell

THE POET

The Poet
    Paints A Picture
        With Words . . .

Marie Wills

THE TWILIGHT OF SENSIBILITES

I sensed its presence long before
I dared to look and see what it was
in that inky-black darkness which is
sire to so many terrifying images
I anxiously lifted, then turned
my head and there it was
at once darting in and out of a well circumscribed and
irradiant mist

I could not move, my body seemingly frozen in place and
screams of help lodged inextricably in
my throat
when all at once my senses were bathed in a sea
of blinding light out of which a hand
extended and a voice urged softly, "It's time . . .
it's time for you to come to bed."

The creature was eradicated with a flick of
the televison switch and I arose and
retreated with a sigh of relief to
another chance at dreams that no longer seemed
such forbidding things.

Ronald G. Ribble

FOR GORDON

When the lights were going out
one by one you'd come into the bedroom
with your ball and say Dad, want to play catch?
If Guidry were pitching you'd climb up
on the bed and I'd run my fingers through your
beautiful blonde hair.
I'd stagger down the steps behind you
blinking in the light and we'd walk over
to the patch of drive next to the house.
We'd catch a hundred in a row
then go back inside to the devils.

Tonight I have laid out my clothes, made my plans
for the bus ride to New Hampshire for your
high school graduation. I am lying here
watching the ballgame & Guidry is pitching.
I reach out and stroke the pillow with one hand,
remembering your beautiful blonde hair.

Gordon Murphy

OTHERS

God did not make His people to live on isles apart.
He carries every one of us within His loving heart.
He is our caring Father and we all are sisters and brothers
So our slogan should always be the little group word "others."

A day we don't help somebody is a day that we have lost.
We can help other people with no, or little, cost.
When homeless and hungry walk our streets
And swords begin to rattle,
Don't waste our money on human greed —
"Help others" is our battle.
Affordable housing, decent food, health care for all, we need.
Don't feed the corporate vultures with their everlasting greed.

To help my brothers and sisters is why God put me here,
To lighten folk's heavy burdens, to speak a word of cheer.
We never need be bored to death, my sisters and my brothers,
If we live by the little six letter word "others."

Ashley J. Kroterfield

FELINE FANCIER

Two beautiful cats have I
These are the "apple of my eye."
"Princess" is a Persian so very blue.
She is affectionate and lovingly true.

"Boots" is black with four white feet.
This Tom's disposition is ever so sweet.
To my loneliness they are an antidote;
To them much loving care I devote.

In return they afford me much pleasure.
Their companionship is something I treasure.
I am a cat lover of much repute;
Their playful antics and coyness I can't refute.

Kathlene Hicks

CHRISTMAS

C — is for the Christ Child born that holy night.
H — is for the heavens so gloriously bright.
R — is for the rejoicing at the *Good News*.
I — is the innkeeper; room for Christ he did refuse.
S — is for the star shining brightly in the sky.
T — is for the thrill at the sound of that newborn cry.
M — is for Mary, God's chosen mother of the King.
A — is for heaven's angels, and praises they did sing!
S — is for the Son of God, the supreme gift of love,
    Sent down to the earth from Heavens above!
    Christmas (God with us) this acrostic spells out,
    And tells what it is *really* all about!

Luke 2:1-20

Kathlene Hicks

THE OLD PLACE

Beyond the great lawn — far back in the trees
Sits an old ancient house, gruesome everyone agrees
But, great in its time with fame, sublime
And Oh! If I could only go in and see
I would glory in its *Majesty!*

The grass has grown tall beyond the wall
And the old gate protests loudly
As I venture forth, and lay my hand on the old wrought iron
The old house seems to beckon me.

I feel — I belong, and the past is mine
The old trees out of shape and grotesque seem to know my mind
And seem to urge me on.

And I know it is just what I want it to be
The *Old Mansion* is sitting there just waiting for me.

Arettia Coomer

THE CONQUISTADOR

It is done
   . . . finished
      . . . over with
The hard work, the joys,
   the exasperations
But — finally — the triumph

I do not feel
exultant as others
say I ought,
only pleased that
once again I have
climbed to the
top and, surveying the horizon,
see yet another challenge to
test my mettle

It is my lot to
relish the battle
but . . . regard the victory
with benign indifference

Ronald G. Ribble

OH MOTHER, MINE

Oh Mother, mine.
Beside your grave I reminisce and pine
For happy days that I once knew
Until the day you passed away . . .

Full of patience and so good.
You were the example of motherhood;
Endowed with God's gift of love,
You imparted it to all of us.

Also the sweetest, dearest Mother
To my sisters and my brother,
You brought laughter to our hearts
And sunshine into our home.

Oh Mother, mine,
Upon my knees
I join my hands and pray
That you may rest in peace.

Irene T. Xavier

MORNINGS BRING TOMORROWS

Silently, I stroll
Where emerald waters meet coral sands.
Rainbow-hued near sleeping skies,
Merge majestically across life's endless horizon
As if suspended at the water's edge.

As lingering rays of the parting sun
Bid me farewell,
I feel awash like tiny pebbles
Mirrored before me,
Resting in the coolness of soft shifting sand.

I become part of God's masterpiece,
Joyous in the knowledge
That mornings bring tomorrows
On coral sands or perhaps suspended
Where emerald waters meet sleeping skies.

Sherry Bryant

DEEP JOYS

How sweet the sight of bright moonlight
   On virgin snow,
Of sunshine sifting through a pine
   Where bird nests show,
The gentle beat of waving wheat,
   The sound of rain,
The bright sunrise, the butterflies!
   I'll not complain
As years go by, nor shall I sigh
   While growing old,
For life goes on. When this is done
   We may behold,
And hear new things. Our Father brings
   Deep joys unknown,
On Earth unshared, delights prepared
   For His alone.

Alta McLain

MID-STREAM

Change calls, I can no longer stay.
Along the shore, I've walked too long.
I miss you, but I must go away
And leave the busy throng.
Today, I walked within the deep,
Where others have gone before.
Way, way out from the distant shore;
I felt the waves around me creep.
My anchor held!
I turned, for I cannot walk
Upon the deep.
The tide swelled.
I knew, I must go through
Alone, and without you.
Why be a *hesitator?*
It will be music to me later.

Mina Huffman

REFLECTION

Empty chairs around the table
   at the annual family gathering
A reminder of years gone by when
   all our relatives eagerly attended
'Twas a delightful celebration
The years have been good to us, having
   had our dear ones for a very long time
But now many are gone
Memories are the dominant bond to
   remind us of joy and laughter
   that was always prevalent
Loving embraces kept the family units
     together
   Presently —tranquility
How wonderful then, now so sad
   And sadder when we view
   Additional vacant chairs
   As the family dwindles —
   — All in a lifetime

Dorothea Schoener

KIND WORD

A bouquet of flowers
   A gift to make it right

A note expressing gratitude
   While *my heart burst with pain*

Hurt, sadness, unhappiness
   I longed a warm embrace
An understanding of my life
   A caress to assure me
But most of all
   I desired
A kind word.

Alice Viola

WHAT IS LIFE?

What is life?
And what does it mean to us?
Do we plan our future or destiny,
or does it just happen along the way
like the starting of a brand new day?
Do we instantly know what the future brings,
or does each of us have secret dreams, or
secretly planned our goals in life?
Should we get depressed when life's secret
desires not go as we wish?
Should we cry when we feel sad or hurt
over things we cannot control?
And dare we be completely different from
each other, to find that we are the
same as our parents or grandparents before us?
Not as sure of ourselves, nor of them,
as we would like to be.
Our lives would be so much better if we
took the time to look around us.

Michele Roy

LIGHT UP WITH WOE

My soul is slave to a smoke —
   A puff.
Anyone knows it's the devil's
   Stuff.
Righteousness and God, it turns
   Out the door.
I know I'll never reach
   Heaven's shore.
Just one more smoke I surely
   Need.
U can see I'm hooked on the
   Devil's weed.
Albeit comes as a staff-o-light,
   But turns to a demon's rod.
Never shall I be free until I'm
   Under the sod.
And then — oh my soul — too late
   To reach God.

Margie Edwards

LOVED ONE

As I sit here by your bedside, weeping
And as I see you lying there, suffering
Knowing that soon you must go.
I feel so very helpless, trying my love to you show

There's so much to be said — So much to ask, I need to know
Thinking of our past life, I need you so —
And as the Angels linger to carry you safely home
I will wander back home alone
And as I ramble aimlessly through the empty rooms

Touching this and that, remembering — keeps taking me back
There are always good days and bad, joyful times
And also sad.
But, knowing you, and having you for awhile
A blessing beyond compare

And it helps to ease my heart, knowing you are with ''Him''
on ''High'' up ''There.''

Arettia Coomer

WINTER'S MORN

The snow has fallen through the night
The fence posts marching down the lane
With their white caps on again
Red birds perching, so bright
To sing their song of delight

And quails skipping along the fence row
Tidbits to find, as they leave little footprints
In the snow

A rabbit hops by twitching his nose
Then off into the bush he goes

Then the ''bluebirds'' come and stay awhile
Lending array to the view
There we have ''our'' Red, White, and Blue
Then an icicle comes dripping down from the eaves

Then the wind gives a little howl
Arresting my attention from the scene
As I turn I hear the coyotes yell down by the stream
I can picture them now, on this lovely ''winter's morn.''

Arettia Coomer

TO CLAROLA RUTH

Born in April, on the eighth day
I watched you grow — so happy and gay
Playing and swinging, by the cherry trees
Back and forth with the summer breeze.

Then summer turned to winter and snow
You played and loved to feel soft winds blow
Another day the trees were coated with ice
The sun came out making a picture nice.

In my mind I see the picture yet
Our childhood days give *memories* without regret
Thankful for thoughts such as these
Carefree play, snow and ice, summer breeze.

Rowena Bragdon Holt

MY FRIEND

When my house is silent because only I am home,
There's a little friend I turn to so I won't be alone.

Sometimes he comes so softly that I hardly know he's there,
But other times he rants and raves or puts music in the air.

His presence picks me up when my heart is filled with gloom,
But sometimes when I am happy, he brings me words of doom.

He's a teacher and a preacher; a sinner and a saint.
He's many things I want to be; he's many things I hate.

I know he'll never leave me because I take him wherever I go.
For you see this steadfast friend of mine is my little radio.

Judy A. Deeter

HOMEWARDS

The last leg of one hundred mile
of car vacations, towards home,
seem to have a unique atmosphere;
It's usually dark
and reality cannot always be recognized;
A distant possible rabbit concretizes into a real stone,
an apparent mile-post begins to sprout
two glittering eyes and turns out to be a fox.
Inside the car a conversation with the beloved,
and sometimes we are silent,
but think about the same;
Tomorrow starts the working routine, the grind,
for yet another year;
Should one make a drastic change?
Towards some freer, simpler life?
How could we make at least minor improvements?
Have our breakfast in the porch?
Could one improve some personal relations?

　　''It was a nice vacation,
　　　　next year we may go to'' —

George Mueller

VELVET

A smooth and gentle velvet mist
begins to cover, to hide
the rough scars and crags of the landscape of life;
The mists of oncoming age, of ageing,
soothe, soothing,
like a half-forgotten coral sand
of a beach in the Bahamas
— like a balm —
on the vicissitudes of my fate —

Or shall I try to force again
the course of my destiny —
— if I can —
The roughness of living provokes self assertion —
then the will weakens once more.
Then agitation, then calm, assertion, peace,
　　rebellion, acquiescence, turbulence, peace —
Life appears as a flickering light house
— receding — receding
　　　I am growing old.

George Mueller

CALL ME

When the quiet closes in,
and there is no other near
   so you have no one to talk with,
then it's time to call me dear.

I have no elixir for your sorrow
as you struggle to attain,
   the life you now must build
and what comfort you can gain.

I know it helps to share your loss
with ones that understand,
   so please feel free to call me
should you need a helping hand.

Talk and tears can soothe you
as the days go slowly by,
   I am here to listen
and your tears, we then can dry.

If you need a shoulder to lean on
mine are pretty sturdy yet
   as I offer you my friendship
that's been yours since first we met.

Rita Dingman

LIVING

Fifty years ago we met
and the first spark of love did glow,
what the future held for us
we surely did not know.

Times were hard. Depression days!
But still we two did wed,
our love would sustain us
though we knew not what lay ahead.

We weathered the loss of a child
that we both loved so well,
it brought us closer together
for on our loss we dared not dwell.

In forty years my loved one
joined our child up above.
I was so lost and lonely
but I was sustained by their love.

I am much older now
and still I feel their love
as I wait until the day comes
that I'll join them up above.

Rita Dingman

UP ON TOP

Have you been on a narrow, winding, road
Way up high,
Between the earth and sky?
All around are mountains
Beyond wide open space . . .
You get a feeling that is hard to describe.
As if the world below is far away
And nothing down there is important.

Marie Wills

A SECRET PLACE

There is a place I know of,
I've seen it in my dreams.
It's deep within the forest,
Where the ferns grow lush and green.

Where all the woodland creatures
Accept me as their own.
Where my days are filled with beauty,
And I never feel alone.

I can gaze in speechless wonder
At the splendor God has wrought;
And feel Him close beside me
On every path I walk.

If there is reincarnation,
I know what I will be;
A creature of the forest,
Forever wild and free.

With no need for power nor riches
That we mortals always seek;
But with a feeling of contentment
As I lay me down to sleep.

Arbie Warren

AUGUST SONG

Let us go down to the sea, beloved.
The waves will swirl around us
  and curl strands of seaweed
    round our feet.
We will clothe ourselves in sunlight,
And I will pluck wildflowers
  and braid them with my hair.
We will watch the sun
  as it falls into the sea.

And as the night claims us,
  we will make love in the rolling surf,
  and our children will play
    with mermaids.

Nancy Lee Taylor

FOOTNOTE

Alone.
It's never far away,
  even when I'm with you.
Some I've loved have loved me —
I sometimes think *you* do
  in your own way.
We share a word, a touch,
  a dream,
But *alone* is always out there —
  waiting.
I touch other hands,
  other bodies, sometimes.
Sometimes, perhaps,
  I touch another heart.
But all the time I know
  alone is out there —
  somewhere
  in the dark —
  waiting.

Nancy Lee Taylor

ONLY A MONTH

You've been away a month today,
  But yet I feel you near,
It's been a while since I've seen your smile,
  But memory keeps you here.
I'd like very much your cheek to touch.
  To hold your hand in mine.
I'd like the choice, to hear your voice,
  And visit one more time.
I cannot fret, I've no regret.
  We were close as could be.
We talked each day, wrote when away,
  And I still have each memory.
Though you had to go, I'm sure you know,
  That whatever else I do,
In each busy day, I'll find a way.
  To still have a talk with you.

Eulaliah T. Hooper

MEMORIES

Sometimes there are memories
   that hurt me.
There are memories
   that make me glad.
Some memories excite me,
And those that make me sad.

Sometimes there are memories
   that haunt me;
Yet, memories
   can be so sweet.
Some memories terrify me;
So many that lay incomplete.

Mark Allen Atterson

SLEDS AND SNOW

In honor of granddaughter — Julie

Sleds without snow
Haven't much use you know
Girls and boys as they play
Hope for a snowy day.

There are sleds oh so nice
Among the sleds without a price
Little hands fashioned a sled to treasure
This kind gives the most pleasure.

A fast run down the hill
All laughing, waving, then — a spill
Up again, brushing off snow
My! what a heavy blow
Come friends, climb the hill
Hot drinks, our stomachs we will fill
In years to come, children *think back*
To times spent on an icy track.

Rowena Bragdon Holt

WE, THE TOURISTS

We appear — and disappear
the viewers of this world
our tourisms are brief.
We are the prisoners of the fleeting instant;
We may only remember the past,
and anticipate the future
but our presence is locked into the ever-shifting ''now.''
So we form our queues
to have our fleeting glance. —
Why is our stay so brief?
Perhaps,
because it is for the best
for the world to have upon it
a greater number of short and fresh impressions,
than a more prolonged bored look.
Are we the pawns of some cosmic justice?
How was this ordained?
How did it come about?

George Mueller

THE PLANETS

The planet Mercury is fleet and small,
For nearness to the Sun it beats them all.
Next is Venus, twin of Earth and evening star,
A lovely sight that none can bar,
Earth is third from the dear old Sun,
And it is here that we have our games and fun,
Mars is the planet with a tinge of red,
Many think it has long been dead,
Jupiter, the mighty, is largest of all,
With gravity so strong you could hardly throw a ball,
Saturn, the planet with fascinating rings,
Is the most beautiful sight among heavenly things,
Uranus, discovered by William Herschel in 1761,
Is third in size and seventh from the Sun,
Neptune, number eight, is very far from us,
It's fourth in size, after Jupiter, Saturn and Uranus,
Pluto, the most distant from the sun,
Is small and cold and no place for us to run.

Brad Lee

LAMENT

I want them to like me when I am old . . .
The people who listen to tales I have told
And patiently listen again and again . . .
    When I am old.

I want them to love me when I am old . . .
The people who feed me and don't ever scold
When I scatter the food my hands cannot hold
    Because I am old.

I hope they'll remember when I've gone away
The care that they gave me day after day,
The heartful of *'thank you'*s my lips could not say . . .
    Because I was old.

Dorothy E. Alger

PIECES OF MYSELF

There was a time when life was sweet.
Dreams were simple and clear as a summer sky on
a sunny day.

I chased the clouds and wondered how far I could go
to find the end of the rainbow after a spring shower.

Dandelions made lovely bouquets.
Trees were made to climb with just a touch of
adventure.

Secrets and promises shared with the deepest sense
of cross my heart and hope to die, not to tell
another soul.

Right was right and wrong was wrong, home was where
the heart belonged.

Cigar boxes filled with treasures hidden away so
no one could find them.

Pieces of myself no one else could touch.

April B. Ramburg

DAYDREAMS

A gentle swan floats slowly by, on a lake of clearest blue.
I am all alone, in this barren park, daydreaming of you.

The carnival lights are blinking, as we're blissfully holding
hands. You take me on the roller coaster, and I scream as
hard as I can.

We throw popcorn at each other, missing by a mile.
You start making funny faces, causing me to smile.

You drag me through the haunted house, though I do not want
to go. Next, we're on a tiny boat, rocking to and fro.

Then the harsh and frozen winds bring me back to reality.
I am all alone, as I sadly realize it was all just a silly daydream.

Dawn Stanton

FUCHSIA FANTASY

Coral, purple bouffant skirts topped by
  pale pink petals gracefully bending,
    open under small white heads pirouetting
      on long, slender legs as the breeze
        gently twirls the white flower pot
          hanging from a branch of the pink dogwood tree.

Like ballerinas performing a dance of beauty,
  charm, enchantment and leaving one with a
    feeling of having witnessed their beckoning
      for a fleeting moment away from adversity
        and unhappiness to come spin and be free.

As I watched them gaily spinning around
  side by side, in small clusters or alone,
    I wanted, for a fleeting moment, to be
      one of them but suddenly one fell lifeless
        to the ground while the other watched
          knowing she would never pirouette again. How sad.

June Alexander

MANY YEARS AGO

A Son Was Born

Altho' many years have come and gone
I still remember that September dawn
Wrestling through the livelong night
You were born just after daylight.

My! such a handsome baby boy
You filled our hearts with joy
When nurse held you for us to see
We were as happy as we could be.

Watching you grow was pure delight
Your dimpled cheeks and eyes so bright
Enhanced your smile each time
And we felt a love so sublime.

Thank God for all your days here,
We'll meet again and have no fear
Of being separated in another land
Praise God for the heavenly band.

Rowena Bragdon Holt

ROWENA FERN HOLT. Pen Names: Rowena Bragdon Holt, Robert Endicott Bragdon; Born: Merom, Indiana, now living in Camden, Arkansas; Married: Louis J. Holt; Occupation: Homemaker; Memberships: Community Concert Association, First Christian Church; Awards: Award of Merit certificate, Golden Poet Award, 1987; Poetry: 'Mon Fils,' 8 others poems,' various subjects, *American Poetry Showcase,* 1985; 'Falling Leaves,' nature, *American Poetry Anthology,* 1984; 'First Winter on Charlotte Road,' nature, *Best New Poets of 1986;* 'Five Loaves and Two Fishes,' religion, *Masterpieces of Modern Verse,* 1985; Comments: *I write mostly about nature, love, religion. Some serious, others about nature, as I enjoy it. My aim is to make ability out of a disability.*

Dawn, Dawn
The beautiful sunrise
It is so revealing
With the wonderful feeling to be alive,
And know there is a God.

Olive Hickerson

GOD AND I

Every morning at the start of day,
I bow my head and begin to pray.

I thank God for bringing me through the night
And praise him for the morning light.

Friends of mine say I'm a fool,
Because prayer is such an out-dated tool.

They laugh and say, "There's no one there,"
And tell me I'm just talking to the air.

And if I told them I'd heard God speak,
I know they'd say I'd become a freak.

But God does listen, God does care,
And God lifts me from deep despair.

So I'll not listen to what they say,
And I'll keep on prayin' every day.

Judy A. Deeter

THANK YOU

Thank you for your loveliness
Thank you for your unconditional love
Thank you for presencing God back in my life
Thank you for peace and serenity
Thank you for your listening and kindness.

The gratitude and love I have for
              you
Is boundless.

The Good Lord tells us:
"Seek and ye shall find"
After you, I need not seek
Anymore.

Rosann Claeys

THE HARROWING

Coming late in April, home,
I found the field
Between the house and cemetery
Turned for harrowing —
Your illness coming
As the seed went in —
A gauzy droning
Past the curtained room.

The earth, regardless,
Churned itself to corn,
The tasseling coming on
As you went down.

By harvest
You were gone.

Today the field waves parchment
In the wind
And stubble glints
Like nails
In the late sun.

Jean Holmes Wilson

AFTERIMAGE: ECLIPSE IN JULY

I smoked the window glass
And held it close to eye
And turned my face up, innocent,
To watch the moon pass by

And witnessed such a syzygy —
Corona pulsing orange —
I couldn't pull my eyes away
From the celestial burn —

And after it had passed
And spheres cooled into place,
A light there was that holds an eye
That can't accomodate.

Jean Holmes Wilson

JEAN HOLMES WILSON. Born: Rochester, New York, 4-28-37; Married: T. Kenneth Wilson, 9-2-61; Education: University of Buffalo, B.A., 1960; M.A., English, 1966; University of Pittsburgh, Ph.D. program; Occupation: University instructor, English; Memberships: Speech Communication Association, Academy of American Poets; Awards: First prize, Grand Prize Category, American Poetry Association, 1987; First prize, *The Lyric,* 1960; Honorable Mention, *The Lyric,* 1959; Poetry: 'A Salvaging,' *American Poetry Anthology,* 1987; 'Wait But A Moment,' *The Lyric,* 1960; ' 'Twixt the Granite,' *Manuscripts,* 1960; 'I Surmise A Remnant,' *The Lyric,* 1959; 'Sonnet,' *Voices of America,* 1959; Comments: *I find metaphors in common things.*

PRAYER TO THE LORD

Every day we do what is wrong
Ask the Lord to forgive us our wrong.
Every day and night
Let us ask Him to show us the right.
In His service we do not know what to do.
Pray He will show us what to do
Today is another day
Still by my side stay.
How wonderful it is when we go to bed at night
To tell the Lord I am in your care good night.
On this earth let Him by our side stay
In heaven we will be forever by His side stay.

Ella H. Hollander

A LAMENT

O World! O Life! O Time!
On whose last steps I climb,
  Trembling at that where I had stood before;
When will return the glory of your prime?
  No more, — O nevermore!

Out of the day and night
A joy has taken flight:
  Fresh spring, and summer, and winter hoar
Move my faint heart with grief, but with delight
  No more, — O nevermore!

Percy Bysshe Shelley

A MESSAGE FROM THE SEA

A shell from the sea, will give a message to me,
If I would but incline my ear, close enough to really hear
The cry of the gulls, flying high,
The sound of foam, floating by,
The feeling of dampness in the air,
As if I were surely there.

The crunch of sand, beneath my feet,
Makes my heart skip a beat.
Seeing great waves riding high,
Until they almost touch the sky,
Clashing like cymbals, as they reach the shore,
Is joy to my soul forevermore.

Dorothy W. Mundy

FLIGHT MEMORY

Your mouth moves, arms wave,
eyes light and fade
like some over-made black-and-white film star:
voiceless to my thoughts
and memories that block the sound
with bitterness and better times:
a cabin, a mountain,
the silence of late autumn
that harbors so many words,
that large black bird
spiraling in the valley,
sailing 'round and 'round us —
tireless — as if testing the patience of human nature,
pressing itself against the soft white clouds, high, higher
and falling fast, faster, wings enfolded,
feigning some aerial deathwish dance.
It made you laugh like you haven't laughed in years;
a sound so real, so colorful, so lovable,
still pitiably audible to me, echoing
as you stand there now: angrily saying nothing.

Susan Carol Hines

OLD DOODLE AT CHRISTMAS

There once was a Christmas when I was a child,
Times were hard, and we had nothing to make us smile,
I sure didn't think that Santa would forget about me,
But I was wrong, for he did you see.

Never did I blame him, for I still loved him well,
There's really a lot to this story to tell,
Old Doodle barked at Santa when he came to the door,
Dragging a large, dirty bag full of toys galore.

My brother grabbed his shotgun and off it went with a bang!
I was screaming and crying, but he didn't give a dang,
He said that old Santa ran away dragging his sack,
And that the old, fat rascal would not be back.

This story is very much true that I'm telling you,
My folks were so poor, they didn't know what to do,
They didn't have any money to give old Saint Nick,
So they chased him away when he came, real quick!

Willard Lee Skelton

SEASON'S FASHIONS

Winter clothed in gray and white for its cold dark
  days and shivering nights.
Spring adorned in dazzling green, sprinkled with colors
  warmly seen.
Summer's green lazily borne midst honeysuckle and a
  rose thorn.
Just when we think we can bear no more, Fall strides
  through another door —
Dressed in brilliant orange, gold and red and when all
  things are said;
Though worldy fashions come and go as their hues,
  God's creations always receive rave reviews.

Mildred Schlagle

ONLY RESTLESS SLEEPERS

  Only restless sleepers
  Pacing in the night,
  Gazing out a window
  Touched with lunar light,
Will ever see a string of wild geese
In flight across the silent moon's wan face,
Or ghostly silhouettes of guardian trees
Loom massively, will note that darkest place
Where one high-perched, soft-plumaged great horned owl
Hoots eerily, observe his yellow eyes
That scan the homes and street lights partially
Enveiled by puffs of rolling mist . . . that rise
Along the road where solitary cars
Go whispering along. That world, apart
From ordinary slumberers, can stir
The questing mind with wonder, touch the heart
  Of every restless sleeper
  Pacing in the night,
  Gazing out a window
  Touched with lunar light . . .

Mauricia Price

AN EPITAPH ON
MASTER PHILIP GRAY

And if I had no more to say,
But here doth lie till the Last Day
All that is left of Philip Gray,
It might thy patience richly pay:
For if such men as he could die,
What surety of life have thou, and I?

Ben Jonson

DISCOVERY

On a deep autumn path
With branches overhead,
Mother Nature speaks.

Margaret E. Danielson

BOUQUET

My life is just a dried bouquet,
Of flowers that bloomed yesterday.

A fragrant memory or two,
Recalls a day when youth was new.

Robert Emmett Clarke

BIG MOUNTAIN, ARIZONA

I am white and angry
that the past has not
opened our eyes . . .
of what brotherhood
does to the
spirit of life.

I am white and angry
about the history
of our forefathers,
who took land
from the red man.

I am white and angry
that history . . . is repeating
itself.

Naedeen McWalters

FROSTY BEES

Over the dry peach ridge
of summer

frosty bees fly through
the raisin thin land
into a breeze

blueberry windmills
blow across
the wild prairie sun.

John Svehla

GRADUATION DAY

Black gray gowns
blow into the wind
red harness bees
hidden inside a purse shell

mockingbirds swing on
chairs of bone
tears flow into
wooden lakes.

John Svehla

broken window panes
    on an old farmhouse —
blurring rain

Charles B. Rodning

LAUREL LIDS

Laurel lids
close the day up

dolphin winds fly over
into lower white ridges

south years land on
a barge at sea.

John Svehla

JOHN J. SVEHLA. Born: North Platte, Nebraska, 1946; Married: Sharon Rubenstein, 11-12-76; Occupation: Senior typist/secretary; Awards: Finalist's award for 'Autumn Buds,' The Eye of Saint Agnes 1985 Poetry Competition, published in *Negative Capability,* 2-86; 2nd Prize for 'Summer,' California Federation of Chaparral Poets, 1977; 2nd Honorable Mention for 'A Jar World,' Pennsylvania Poetry Society's Experimental Poetry Award, 1977; Poetry: 'Ships,' *The Poet,* Winter 86/87; 'Two Broken Horses,' *Poetic Symphony,* 3-87; 'Red Collar Ants,' *Wide Open Magazine,* Summer, 1987; 'A Shuttered Breeze,' *Wind Magazine,* Vol. 16, No. 56, 3-86; Comments: *I am putting forth a new idiom in nature poetry.*

ASTRONOMICAL

Far moon seem some pearl
Pour sands of time.
View how it whirl
Say waves wisdom rhyme.

Slow flow old ages
Never pass freedom.
Fix diamond pages
Meet readers agree from.

So treasure hallows
Dream to be taxless
And love told shallows
Dew sing soul as waxless.

Night ensure pleasure
Sweeter for having
Truth at fond leisure
Peace give wound salving.

Orien Todd

PONDERING

As the sun came up this morning
And the sky turned to azure blue

Portraying in all its glory
The beauty of my mountain view

I sat and sipped my chocolate
Thinking of today and you

And wondered how God would view us
In the light of this brand new day.

It's been given us to do as we will
Let's not waste it with trivial things

Be proud of the things done in our life
The great effect we've had on others

And know that through this beautiful day
You hold God's love in your hand.

Joan Lee Schetter

RAINBOW

A rainbow presented itself to me today
    outside my dining room window
A myriad of delicate colors.
    It stayed as the rain softly fell
Becoming faint in the mist of the morning
    I wondered as I sat there
Remembering all my past
    of all life's simple splendor
Would it fade really soon or last?
    Would the memory linger still
As the sun slowly came forward
    or would it like life and its treasure
Fade to only a memory — but last?

Joan Lee Schetter

THE WRITER'S LAMENT

Inspired to write, and no space left, on my writer's desk —
Twiddle, with paper, and pens — looking around,
Books — here, and there — lying on top, of one another
Pens, and papers — encyclopedias — making a mound.
Keeping them from falling, is the back lip, of the desk.
No space left, for me to write upon.
These beautiful thoughts, must be put down.
 Screaming, in hysteria, I see the right wall —
White, and of a beautiful lustre —
Words going down, in fast appraisal,
A manuscript — for all the world to see
My mind empty, but tired —
I've written all day, and the wall, is replete, with my writing.
 No room, on my desk, to write?
Use the wall — near, and wide — happily satisfied.

Annette N. Ashbough

BRANDI

In my life there have been many joys
The birth of my daughter and my two baby boys
I never thought there would be a way
To outshine or equal what I felt on those days

But one Friday morning on September 13th
The Lord gave me more than I ever had dreamed
He brought to my life a precious new gift
When my daughter gave birth to Brandi Elizabeth

The joy of a child is greater it seems
When the child is born to your offspring
Making you grandma or grandpa is a blessing
Giving your life what it seemed you'd been missing

A new baby girl who is precious and sweet
A new generation to make the family complete
Brandi is life — life that goes on
As it has forever, since time first dawned

Peggy Simmons

ALOHA '87

The trade winds whirled by my window . . .
 as the storm broke over the horizon.
A sleepy sun rose over the clouds . . .
 and a rainbow appeared across the sky.

We finally landed on a sea-green island . . .
 and the gentle trade winds greeted me.
A mystery now lay in front of me . . .
 as the many warm smiles sang Aloha.

I met a man and his beautiful daughter . . .
 and together we shared many stories.
We travelled over mountains and rocks . . .
 through deep caverns above and under water.

We swam among magical sea creatures . . .
 as they guided us through the corals.
I narrowed my eyes as I faced the bright sun . . .
 I saw deep cobalt waves crash along the shore.

I heard stories of yet another island . . .
 that shelters amazing crystal waterfalls.
I can still hear the laughter of children . . .
 all happily playing on the endless beaches.

Kim Hardiman

UNSELFISH LOVE

Matthew was born on March 20, 1987 and adopted on April 1, 1987.

She will always carry in her heart his love, his blessing and the sacrifice all her own.
He was not left abandoned, he was not left alone, for out of her love, in love she had to let go.
I can't feel your pain, I can't feel your sorrow, I can as a friend understand. That today was the day you put your little boy in God's hands.
I know someday he, too, will understand the reason and the why. And know his mother truly loves him; she gave him the gift of life!

Linda Sue Wynn

CAROLYN

On your confirmation today,
Let your heart and soul never betray,
The rights & wrongs, which life may have in store,
Strengthen your beliefs, to your core,
Shield yourself with knowledge and pride,
For you shall need this worldwide,
God's rules have been set for your course,
Live by them & you shall know no remorse,
'Tis easy for me to say,
But life is a turmoil in every way,
How pure you look all dressed in white,
You're cherished and loved and such a delight,
Your peer pressure you shall soon meet,
Strengthen yourself, plant firm feet,
No, I shall not let you sway from your course,
For then heartache shall be your boss,
Fifteen years on earth you've been,
Never to have committed a mortal sin,
Let all ''All Mighty'' hold you close to his breast,
For then, I know, you shall do the rest.

Maxine Loffredo

CHARLENE

This child has sorely touched my heart.
I've worked, I've prayed and sometimes wept.
I've watched her grow year after year.
Her needs are great; her talents few.
I've walked beside her as she grew.
I've helped her through each varied part —
The constant vigil kept —
Of pain, of joy, of fear.

Kaleidoscopic day on day.
Dwarfed, tragic clown with unshed tears;
A world unsuited to her need.
Guileless and lost; a homeless child,
Sometimes meek, sometimes wild;
Unarmed of rules for games we play;
Maturity outstripped by years;
Her case I often plead.

Yet I know not this child of mine,
Though as bodyguard and friend,
Through twenty-seven years of pain.
When she's unveiled, some morning bright,
And stands before me whole and right,
With burnish and refine,
My broken heart will surely mend.
For joy I'll weep again.

Ruth C. Rowley

PRECIOUS MOMENTS

Sometimes when life is very still
And all about you dark
Sit quietly just by yourself
And listen to your heart.

Precious moments of your life you'll find
Sometimes long forgot
They're what made your life worthwhile
And to others what you've taught.

So think of all the lives you've touched
By being a wonderful you
By sharing your love, your life, your caring
Dear one, there's no one like you.

And when at each day's new dawning
If you begin each day with a smile
You'll know as you go ever onward
You've done your best with each mile.

So when life is still about you
And things seem oft so dark
By yourself just sit quietly
And listen to your heart.

Joan Lee Schetter

EMPTY SWINGS

Quiet schoolyard
Empty save a man
Too old to gambol
he can only sit
and remember

M. Johnathan Anderson

LINES

Look not in my eyes
For fear they mirror true
The sight I see, and there
You'll find your fare
Too clear, and love it
And be lost like me.

Margaretbelle Borham

AMBIVALENCE

I see an old man
Walking down a street
He looks at me
He sees arrogance, youth, vitality
And envies me
I see wisdom, knowledge, stubbornness
And envy him
We continue to contemplate one another
Though never a word of greeting spoken
And we remain walking
Passing one another
In awkward silence
And continue on in our ways
Filled with ambivalence

M. Johnathan Anderson

THE RETURN OF RAIN

Did you forget the smell of rain?
The air is cool as once again
The drops come slowly down.

You feel the rain, can touch it and revel
In its delight. The soft winds blow,
The rain swirls about,
And it is cool to know.

The flowers need the natural rain.
God did not forget our sun-parched lands.
It comes so quietly, with no loud claps
Or noise — just steady, life-giving flow
From the clouds above.

Thank you, God, for this welcome Sunday rain!

B. J. Brunson

A WOMAN'S QUEST

I want a voice,
but you say I can't speak.
I want to make changes,
but you say I don't understand.
I want the knowledge,
but you say it's not available.
You don't understand, yourself,
and all I want is Peace.

Ruth Gilbert

old friend —
    falling chrysanthemums
across the gravestone

Charles B. Rodning

POOL GAME

He wasn't my lover;
we were playing a game.
The colored balls of life
sat on the table.
He made the first move,
with the cue stick
he broke.
Colors flew, landed in a pocket.
His options were open,
he could choose.
I chalked my stick,
waited to play.
He shot over and over,
all dropped in.
Then came the eighth,
black as his eyes.
I shot it in, lost.
He wasn't my lover;
we were playing a game.
He found another player.

Ruth Gilbert

LIVING BY THE OCEAN

Living by the ocean
just to see the sea
and to feel the cool sea breeze

Living by the ocean
so I could be free
and let the anger loose of me

Living by the ocean
I measure night and day
as though it's far away
but even though, it's here
to stay!

Melissa Belanger

ODE TO A DRY MARTINI

Our cocktail hours are not the same
The nights we don't have you
A whiskey sour is just too tame
And even scotch won't do

Sometimes on a cold, cold night
With beef stew in the pot
Manhattans do seem almost right
Although we know they're not

On summer days beside the pool
To hold a frosty glass
A gin and tonic may look cool
To someone with no class

A frozen daiquiri to some
Is thrilling to the taste
But though we try to hide our glum
On us they're just a waste.

New cocktail fads may come and go
But you still rise above
Your cool clear beauty makes us glow
You are the drink we love.

Betty Lapham

WAKING

In the early hours
of this dour day
no one can help
but consider the end
before the beginning begins.
In vulgar dreams
the night washed through heads
and limbs and swollen bellies.
In the morning
I exhale
black clots of air
sigh, and rise.

In the garden
I sense
the sound of tennis ball and laughter
lazy leaves touched gold
and the air
delicately butterflied.

Lisa Forestier

A TRUE FRIEND

Through fields of sullen he ran and played.
Stayed with me when I was lonely and afraid.

Listened to me when others could
not, and guided my steps through
the hidden and gloomy night.

He gave to me an inspiration
to motivate my heart and mind,
to be happy rather than to cry.

And showed me loyalty
and love like no
other could.

He had given me so much,
even to sacrifice his life for mine.
I'll miss that companion of mine.

Alvin Moses

EMPTINESS

Moments to remember, too delicate and cherished
    to share,
Cannot re-light ashes remaining there.
Thumping, pounding, gnawing
    torment deep within, I know not where,
Nor why it stays and grows
Until my blood grows colder
No longer warmed by memory
Of every hope and dream fulfilled
For just the barest moment
    Less than one grain of sand
A desert
Upon eternity.

Betty B. Pruett

THE BIRTH OF DESIRE

I laughed in the sunshine that spread a gentle glow
 from the light of your special smile;
 and reflected the sparkle from your eyes,
 that cheered my heart as we talked awhile.

I reveled in the delight of your gestures and jokes
 and shared a little of my tormented past;
 then wondered, deep inside my anxious soul,
 if this new friendship would die . . . or last.

The peacefulness of each new chat, lifted us quietly
 into a constant joyful bliss that stayed all day,
 and filled the empty halls of our waiting minds
 with memories, that were carefully filed away.

Our easy talk spun a web of friendship 'round our hearts
 and very soon, secrets from the past we did share;
 how could we explain our compelling desire to touch;
 how were we to know . . . love was waiting there.

Alice Miller

KINGDOM IN THE SKY

As a child, I read that in days of old
Kings and queens lived in palaces of gold;
Their robes were velvet, their coaches grand —
Everything glistened and gleamed in the land.

Where, oh, where did this splendor go?
Sometimes I think I really know,
When I look above and observe the sky
With fluffy clouds piled mountain-high,
And a great golden light streaming from behind:
I feel that in back of this mountain I'd find
A vanished kingdom, flourishing in glory,
Just as it did in a fairybook story!

Elsie Walush

ODE TO CHRISTMAS 1986

  Dwell eerie upon the edge in time
frail heart that tears at a sad liar.
  Shout moot phrases that sadness mourns
diminutives that carry forth with love.

  Presume not upon the world at large
because indifference dulls your sanctity.
  Rescue trysts with lovers from the past
tumultuous likings dauntless produce disdain.

Michael Varbadian

NO . . . NOT ME

It's not my problem, no not me . . .
  I have a nice warm house you see.
The sidewalk homeless, well . . . let them stay,
  I'll just look the other way.

It's not my problem, no . . . not me,
  I have a job and a family.
It's the cities, no the county . . . or somebody in the state,
  but someone better help before it's too late.

Because out there in the winters cold . . .
  are people who are getting old.
Old waiting . . . look he is almost thirty-four,
  been without work six weeks or more.

Came down here from Tennessee . . .
  but that's not my problem, no . . . not me.
There is another, she is forty-one,
  came from Ohio . . . she has a little son.

That old couple, they are almost fifty,
  came here with hope from Mississippi.
Here is a man from Minnesota, lost his farm,
  there is a Vet . . . he lost an arm.

You with the big backyard and an apple tree,
  it is our problem . . . you and me.
We all better stop and think and care,
  so with them we may all share.

Share where to find a home and a job,
  so they the homeless may not be robbed.
Robbed of the American Spirit . . . the Dignity,
  we all have the right to in our Land of the Free.

D. J. Winkelman

CHANGES

Houses no longer stand on the
busy, bustling two lane street.
Sounds changed considerably
with rolling bulldozers passing
through the construction crews.
Sounds of children playing cease
existing; modern times bring changes,
yet past memories linger forever.

Maria Valeri-Gold

WE WERE THERE

In memory I see the old home place,
and see again each familiar face.
I can hear the laughter, see the tears
of all those carefree childhood years
when we were "best friends" long ago.
We made angels in winter's snow
hunted wild strawberries on summer days
trimmed mud pies with Queen Anne's lace.
We played our games of "let's pretend"
and thought those days would never end.
but Time, like sand in an hourglass,
all too swiftly seemed to pass,
and childhood friends drifted apart
leaving empty places in the heart.
But in my memory we are always three
Carrie and Kathy and Me.

Florence R. Dixon

THE GARDENER

What is this strange need
   To grow a garden of your own?
Your harvest will indeed
   Let you reap what you have sown
Or whatever may have blown
   Into your garden and has grown.

You throw away extraordinary seed
And grow a stray and ordinary weed.

Betty B. Pruett

I REMEMBERED

I suffered it all again today
The pain of the crippling Blow.
Why was I crippled? I don't know.
I was not maimed or dismembered,

How did it happen again, you say?
I remembered.

Betty B. Pruett

MURRAY

The only predictable thing he'll do
Is to be unpredictable through and through.
   There's a Pruett streak for all to see
   And yet he's got a streak of me,
But greater than these there flows a tide
The essence of the man that grows inside.
   He is himself. There is much to bless
   Though he tries to hide his tenderness.

No one knows how hard he strives
   Or the motives he was given.
No one knows whether he drives
   Or whether he is driven.

Betty B. Pruett

DIET

I'll lose my fat this very year
Though it took three to get it here.
What thrilling plans, my heart is beating
At the thought of just not eating.

When I saw shock in people's eyes
I felt I should apologize:
"I roll this way because I'm round,"
(And went on gaining pound on pound).

If my plan works out like I'm hopin'
In the future if their eyes pop open
I'll be glad; I'll feel so clever,
And never again, no never, NEVER!

Will I feel compelled to say
"I roll because I'm built this way,"
I'll say, "There's nothing in a name,
But *everything* stands on a frame."

Betty B. Pruett

BECKY SPRINGS

The spring of clear water
Runs over white sand
Straight into Black Creek
Through miles of land.

How it came by its name
I do not know
A woman named Becky
May have lived here long ago.

There's old broken brick
Lying on the ground,
Some old pieces of wood
Scattered around.

Plum trees still stand
On this beautiful land
Where Becky once walked
With pail in hand.

Did she ever think
That her name would live on
By the spring of cool water
That some other would own?

Vivian Thomas

OLD WOMAN

The cold winds came
The tree branch cracked
The old wood heater burns
The wood pops and cracks.

The old woman rocks
And dreams of her past
And wonders how life
Flew by her so fast.

The old cat lies
Close by her feet
She keeps him covered
With her old pink sheet.

She longs for her children
To come sit by her side
That cold winter night
The old woman died.

Vivian Thomas

FIFTY

I'm just as happy at fifty,
As I was at twenty-two
Now I can blame old age
For the silly things I do.
I may not be as pretty,
But who gives a care,
With the help of Miss Clairol
There's no gray in my hair.

Vivian Thomas

You can turn from the grave site,
the hearse may drive away.
But,
the pain, anguish and memories,
still linger on.
It may have been sudden,
or prolonged and painful.
But,
the end was the same,
Death.
The death of someone you love,
someone you cared for,
possibly never realizing,
how much you really needed.
But now, there seems to be nothing,
nothing that can change things,
nothing that can make you feel better,
nothing,
nothing but, pain and memories.

Teresa M. Brown

I remember dressing up
and
playing Barbie dolls.

I remember trick or treating
and
show and tell.

Beautiful Easter Sundays
and
brand new Easter bonnets.

There was sleigh riding,
Christmas caroling
and jolly old St. Nick.

But, most of all,
I remember when
Love didn't hurt.

Teresa M. Brown

HALLOWEEN

I remember when it was fun to go out
And say the words ''Trick or Treat'' in a shout.

People entered into the fun
And to the door they would run

To see the varied costumes there
And for them their goodies would share.

But now happy times like this we'll miss
Because bad things happen doing this.

Since times change these days
We'll have to change our ways

To save our child harassment
Supervise some special event.

Happy Halloween!

No tricks — just *Treat!*

Doris L. Brown

WHAT OF HONOR

The wars that crushed the socialists;
We fought them and died so with grace,
We defended whatever it took to be free,
Is freedom just too hard to face?

The spine of our nation belongs to us all,
Its backbone is, henceforth, in our hands;
We, the people, the spirit, the union,
Made choices for which we all stand.

What of honor do we dare not do,
To maintain that level of love?
For a country that gave its people their lives,
Do we dare not return the same blood?

This young America belongs to me,
As it belongs to all those who care,
Who'll speak of honor, of love, and of trust,
And who'll give it a damn to dare?

Jane Abbott-Bird

THE WISDOM OF BABES?

When tots depict themselves in groups,
What a wealth of color they use!
Orange caps top purple coats
And pants of greens and blues.

But very often there remain
Several empty spaces:
''They have no color,'' the babes explain,
''Those are only faces!''

Elsie Walush

DISTANCE

I couldn't sleep last night
As I listened to the raindrops fall,
I know the way we're living
Somehow just isn't right,
I tossed and turned,
Thinking solely of you
As my passions burned,
My mind was opened wide.
Thinking of the distance between
Wishing you were by my side.

Sherrie Lynn Mantooth

MY FRIEND

I stumbled
He helped me up

A tear slid down my cheek
He brushed it away

I was alone
He sat by me

I felt despair
He made me joyful

I will forever call Him
My Friend

Teresa Miller

THE CHOSEN ONE

Mama and Daddy looked everywhere
For a very special baby boy,
A sweet and gentle little fellow
Who'd fill their hearts with joy.

Of all the tiny tykes in Texas
I'm proud to be the *chosen* one,
To be called Robert Joseph Myers
And become their loyal, lawful son.

P.S. — Jesus must have loved me a lot
To give so much to such a tiny tot.

Mrs. Joe P. Lyon

FRAGMENTAL MOMENTS

Fragmental moments:

  enticing sunsets
    birds in motion
  lakes aglowing
    ripples twirling

  winds chiming
    ships asailing
  squirrels frolicking
    children laughing

  flowers blooming
    snowcaps melting
  cattle lowing
    leaves crackling

  people smiling
    church bells ringing
  dazzling rainbows
    family unity.

Life is full of special moments;
  it makes each day worth living!

Maria L. Canales

The first snow,
Just enough to bend
  The leaves of the daffodils.

Basho

LITTLE FOSTER ANNIE

When God sent us little Annie,
We realized she couldn't stay;
But time has passed so quickly —
She'll be leaving us just any day.

We learned patience and compassion
While her heavy cast she wore;
Then one day the doctor took it,
And she'll never need it anymore.

We won't forget her dimpled face,
Her rosy cheeks and funny nose;
We'll picture dainty, lacy clothes,
See patent slippers, wiggly toes.

We have loved her like a sister,
And we're so sad to see her go;
But we're happy for her mother,
Because she loves her baby so.

Mrs. Joe P. Lyon

HOW GREAT IS OUR FATHER

Oh how great — how wonderful — it is
To know *Our Father — God — is in control!*
His love enfolds us — His precious arms hold us —
No matter the time — No matter the place —
His precious, beloved, smiling face,
       Is leading the way,
       We cannot stray.
       No harm to us can come;
       Each day sees us nearer home,
       Where love, and peace, is forever ours:
       For ''The Eternal God is our refuge,
       And, underneath are the Everlasting Arms.''

Deuteronomy 33:27

Joy S. Pearce

MATA HARI

As I sit on the grass looking over the horizon,
Another sunset, another day gone by,
I think back through how my life has been,
Leaves me here to wonder why.

A warm night on the Caribbean, I saw a sparkle in your eye,
The moon shown brightly on the calm sea,
And the breeze blew through your hair,
Looking at one another, without hostility and carefree.

Reaching out to sip the nectar, I held onto you,
A feeling went through my body, tingling up and down my spine.
My lips touched yours don't hesitate, the feeling made me blue,
It felt like it was true love to me, or was it just the wine?

The palms are blowing outside in the wind,
The sight of native dancers dancing around a flame,
A feast of native treasure, we're guests of a special kind,
The night with you, Mata Hari, a feeling I cannot tame.

Jeffrey David DeBry

HEARTSONG

Come to me in the night
And extinguish all but one light
The light that burns in my heart for you
The light you can trust will always be true

I may sing a song for you
And you may join me if you care to
But my song will be of love and of fate
Two things I sometimes think you hate

Then other times I feel I could fly
Your love for me sends my heart to the sky
Then I sit back and wonder when the love seems gone
Have you ever really heard my heart's song?

Can you see it in my eyes?
My love for you should be no surprise
But how can I know if you love me?
There's never been a light in your eyes that I could see

Can you love me when it seems there's only hate?
I sometimes doubt that you are my fate
A solitary heart that is full of light
Can't carry us both through even one single night

Denise Lorraine Cogswell Tucker

MEMORIES TRAPPED

I wander along this deserted beach
Searching for memories just out of my reach
Semi-familiar faces, places go by
People, things I should know but I don't know why

This old town has changed so much
But as I walk I can feel the past's touch
Some of the faces, places seem the same
Maybe these are the ones that will never change

There's a man with a camera, talking to himself
Brings back memories I thought were put far back on a shelf
As the slow parade of memories goes by
Good ones, bad ones, they seem to haunt me, don't know why

As the sun sets, I see my dreams fade
Hopes and dreams from long ago, how I wish they'd stayed
But new hopes, dreams, have replaced the old
The new ones seem warm, the old dead and cold

But the old dreams aren't dead as I once thought
They are only trapped in a mind maze, caught
Held there so long, just out of my reach
Slowly coming out as I walk alone along this beach

Denise Lorraine Cogswell Tucker

HIS REWARD

God promised all good men a mansion over there,
Calling Uncle Bud while he slept in his chair;

So tired and worn, his steps were short and slow;
He'll have a new body . . . the Bible tells us so —

No pain, no sickness there, no crying nor care,
The day forever fair . . . there's no night there;

No need for worry here while he is in the care
Of the Maker and Caretaker of everyone there.

Mrs. Joe P. Lyon

TWO RIVERS

Thy summer voice, Musketaquit,
Repeats the music of the rain;
But sweeter rivers pulsing flit
Through thee, as thou through Concord Plain.

Thou in thy narrow banks are pent:
The stream I love unbounded goes
Through flood and sea and firmament;
Through light, through life, it forward flows.

I see the inundation sweet,
I hear the spending of the stream
Through years, through men, through Nature fleet,
Through love and thought, through power and dream.

Musketaquit, a goblin strong,
Of shard and flint makes jewels gay;
They lose their grief who hear his song,
And where he winds is the day of day.

So forth and brighter fares my stream,
Who drink it shall not thirst again;
No darkness stains its equal gleam,
And ages drop in it like rain.

Ralph Waldo Emerson

WRITER'S CRAMP

It simply will not go away
    this thought
    this plot
Until a more convenient day
    it haunts
    and taunts

It sits upon my swollen mind
    I give in
    you win
When I write it down, I find
    a brief
    relief

Lorraine Standish

THE ARTIST

When you see the waves of the sea
Or just feel the warmth of the breeze
When you smell a flower
Or just plant the seed
When you look up in the blue sky
Or see a bird fly by
When you see the tall trees
Or have a feeling to believe
When you see the rain
Or hear it on your window pain
When you see the color of the fall
Or read *Ten* important laws
When you see the mountains
Or water flowing fountains
When you touch the earth
Or remember a special birth
When you, or do, it's more than that
It's the *Artist* of these things that you're
feeling, thinking and looking at:

Sandra Specht

NEVER A FRIEND

When we started high school,
We did so together.
Many of our classes were the same,
Even homeroom.

When they changed my schedule,
Your distress seemed genuine.
I know it upset me.
You were my closest friend in a strange place.

Then something changed.
I know it wasn't me.
Was it you?
That I do believe.

Why the vehemence?

I did nothing so wrong.
A friend is through thick and thin.
Mine you could never have been.

Michael Crouthers

TOO LONG APART

I was in a huge hall,
In some strange building,
Descending stairs unknown to me.
I was looking for you.

The place turned out to be a school.
A college, I'm sure.
A strange one, indeed.
The students were behind glass walls.

Looking amongst them,
I still could not find you.
I was overwhelmed with sadness.
So long ago had been our last parting.

Then I saw a lady.
In her hands was an obituary.
In it I found you.

With a sense of urgency,
I awakened to the morn.

Michael Crouthers

YOU CARED ENOUGH

Because you cared enough, I love you truly
and tonight, I'm high on love.
Yes darling, you cared enough.
Thank you for caring for yourself.
Thank you for sticking your funny
broken nose in my business.
Thank you for your feeling, loving
hands, and toes,
and thank you for caring enough to
make me high on love,
yes darling, you cared enough!

Loretta R. Sullivan

HE IS SILENT

He sees her crying.
He is silent!
What is he thinking?
He loved her once. Does he love her still?
He can still make her laugh.
He cares enough to do so.
Why, why, why is he silent?
There has to come a time when he isn't silent.
There has to come a time when he will talk to
her. Talk *to* her, not *at* her.
Will there be a renewed relationship?
He is silent.
His silence is cruel!
He doesn't say yes, he doesn't say no.
Why, she doesn't know.
She doesn't cry much any more.
She just waits and
he is silent.

Loretta R. Sullivan

HEAVEN AND EARTH

Water, sun, wind and sands
reached out as so many hands
enfolding.
Holding you in my arms
your body an unending delight
so subtle and light
on mine.
Sunshine, brassy and bright
forming aureoles over your hair
so soft, glaring, fair
almost blinding.
Ancient rhythms welled up there
caressing, caressed,
loving and blessed
being one
by the water, sand, wind and sun.

*H. S. H. Sylvia Magdalena
Czartoryska*

PROFESSOR GUINEA PIG

*Dedicated with tongue-in-cheek to
Washington State University*

There was a guinea piglet
who became professor
successor to many famous men.
Standing on his hind legs
he held forth to the perplexed
about quantum mechanix
and international lex.
Oh, yes and grammar,
etiquette cum solar spots,
all that and what nots . . .

*H. S. H. Sylvia Magdalena
Czartoryska*

**H. S. H. SYLVIA MAGDALENA CZAR-
TORYSKA (née POLONY).**

RETIREMENT

The word sounds awesome and grim
  It leaves me empty within.

I realize the day had come
  It's confinement or freedom to some.

But I feel as if the clock stopped its hands.
  Yet I had so many plans.

My partner left many years ahead
  And passed away while asleep in bed.

Now I face this move alone.
  I reap the seeds that I have sown.

Perhaps a vacation on a cruise.
  Now I have time to use or lose.

Or maybe a fast trip to Mars.
  Out of this big world of ours.

No longer do I rise with the sun.
  Nor go to sleep when the day is done.

I'll eat when I feel the need.
  I'll come and go at my own speed.

This is retirement that has to be.
  Because the world no longer has a need for me.

Mignon P. Butler

HE

As Jim holds the swing till Maggie gets on
I sit on the porch and think back in time:
He holds the swing till I get on
He sings me songs and tells me nursery rhymes
He whistles a tune or two
He told me about the man in the moon
He took me fishing and showed me how to skate
He stayed up late to hear about my first date
He walked me down the aisle, with his sad yet happy grin
And gave me away to Jim
He was old and a bit grey
But, I went to see him every day
I wear his overalls when I'm in the garden,
which are a little baggy
But, I was glad that he lived long enough for
the birth of Maggie
These memories are memories I'll always have
Memories of me and my Dad
As Jim holds the swing till Maggie gets on
I sit on the porch and think back in time

Sandra Specht

SANTA CLAUS

A girl getting ready for bed
When in a distance came a sled
Footsteps I did hear
And lots of jingles coming near
When in came Santa a jolly old soul
Happy were the eyes, of this 6-year-old
I watched very carefully as he put the
presents under the tree
And knowing that one of the big ones was for me
I tossed and turned all night
I couldn't wait until daylight
But, when it came up, I went to see
What Santa had given me
It was a dollhouse of pre-painted rooms
And lots of furniture pieces, and bride and groom
My heart was so happy, this year was great
I got a peek at Santa, on this special date
I haven't caught another glimpse of him since then
But, I know he always drops in, on this same date
Because, there's always a piece missing out of
the Christmas cake

Sandra Specht

THE DENIAL OF REALITY

I never imagined this day would come.
Even now I stand incredulous.
It seems impossible, but it is so.
Some things not expected do come to be.

The pain I feel now cannot be described.
The shock is too much to bear.
Now that you're gone the world seems so empty.
Yet something in me continues to say, it can't be true . . .
it can't be true.

I must learn to accept that you won't be around.
I must try my hardest to let you go.
That won't be easy, I can assure you.
For so long now, *dear*, I have held you.

That is why this seems so unreal,
as if it were a dream from which I would awaken.
But the only thing to which I must open my eyes,
is the realization that what we had is now over.

Michael Crouthers

POETS OF THE KEYS

Famed Poets of the keys,
  How you can put one's mind and heart at ease.
Some joyous melody to unfold,
  That reaches the heart of the waiting soul.
Waiting for the rapture of sounds,
  An etude, a sonata, a waltz.
You can go on and mention more,
  The beauty of every written score.
God bless the hands and minds forever,
  Who composed the masterpieces of yesteryears.
Such gems from generation to generations,
  Those priceless treasures left for all nations,
Poets of the keys,
  Truly, gifted by God for mankind.

Josephine Sadowski

THE TOMATOES

It is quiet now in the garden
The silence tells the tale
Of limp rotten forgotten
Decay, frozen in frost

But the tomatoes grew like crazy though
You could hear them pop
They grew so fast
They could not stop
And they gave not to plunder

Yet, they have had their fun
And known the pleasures tomatoes know
And won!
For the weeds
Have hid about a dozen seeds
And in the fresh beginning of the year
The earth will sprout a volunteer.

Herbert V. Short, Jr.

GUIDED BY THE MOON

Let your imagination
flow like the River:
with beauty and calm,
with rapids and rage;
with mystery in each bend
of what lies beyond;
with intrigue and fascination
of all that is in these surroundings.
The hidden caves,
secluded from all but the River,
hold treasures of old,
perhaps a touch of gold.
The River has to end
as the ocean begins.
So spread your horizons.
Let your imagination be
as the neverending waves:
constantly changing
and guided by the Moon.

Jerrie M. Poindexter

TOOTIE'S THRENODY

In memory of a friend

Like a butterfly
you flew,
but never ventured far;
and always shining bright
like a twinkling star.
You thought things through
so carefully
as not to do things wrong;
and never were you nonchalant
but always brave and strong.
Like all living beings,
for you life ended
and no more will we cry;
for the memories we have of you
will never ever die . . .

Jerrie M. Poindexter

AS I SAID TO MYSELF

What shall I do with a new little grandson
asleep and melted on my shoulder?
Lay him gently in his basket
where he allegedly belongs?
    No.

Cherish this communion of flesh and soul.
Pray that through some sort of osmosis
he will absorb, even personify
certain intangibles you hold dear.
    Yes.

Treasure these precious moments of bonding.
Savor the sweetness of his breath.
Ponder the miracle of his birth,
the perpetuity of generations.
    God Bless.

Vera Current Thummel

THE END OF ALL?

The night is falling too soon —
It is too early,
There are many plans
Left undone.
There is sorrow
For all that is unsaid and undone.
There is joy
For all that was said,
Was done —
Left many happy beings
In its wake.
Fight the night —
Keep it at bay,
For the day
Has yet awhile to go.

Billie E. Henthorne

IN MEMORIES

Softly, softly now,
Golden, fluffy down,
Smooth petals
In colors pastel,
Her face.

And movement fluid,
Running, bubbling water,
Gentle chimes
From far away,
Her laughter.

And warm, yellow sunshine,
A favorite, old blanket,
Hot cocoa
By the fireplace,
Her love.

Matthew C. Warner

COMING HOME

Come running home,
If you have one
That you hold
Dear to your heart.
And if not,
Find where your heart lies;
For eventually
All must come home.

Matthew C. Warner

IN THE END . . .

I stood Alone amidst Chaos
Knowing the End and the Beginning;
Realizing that Start and Finish
Are two different Things
With the Same Meaning
That happen at the Same Time.

Matthew C. Warner

GERRY

Baby Gerry on display
For visiting aunt.

Baby cries when hungry.
And mother feeds him.

Exercise time.
Tiny legs kick the big soft ball.

Then mother bathes baby.
Close by are helping father
And admiring aunt.

Mother with washcloth
And soothing chatter,
Warm water on pale smooth skin.

Suddenly Gerry smiles.

Esther Rosenstock

PARTING

Wait.
Don't say anything.
I don't want you to say it.

I know.
You don't love me anymore.
Maybe you never did.

Gone.
But still in my dreams.

Esther Rosenstock

NO FAITH IN ME

Faith can move a mountain even the sea
  Such a shame you never had no faith in me
My love was strong my dreams come true
  I wanted to share my whole world with you
I wanted to be with you the rest of my life
  My dreams came true when you became my wife
A world full of joy for us so soon could be
  Such a shame you never had no faith in me
You cheated on me lied and you ran around
  Took my heart and you dragged it on the ground
My faith for you was so strong and so true
  Shame you never shared in that faith too
Had so much of a dream for you to share
  Never did I realize you just didn't care
Shattered pieces much too soon was all to be
  Broken heart and promises is all you left of me
Never did you know we could have had it all
  Tell me why did you have to let your end fall
Our love and faith could have set us free
  Such a shame you never had no faith in me

Gene A. Ward

GOODBYE LOVE

When we first married it was so happy to be
  Too soon you grew tired and wanted to be free
You promised me a love that forever would last
  But isn't it funny how forever ended so fast
I don't understand why you wanted to be free
  Can't you visualize what you are doing to me
We had it all sweetheart until our dying day
  Can you tell me baby why did you throw it away
Never had any idea of what you could do to me
  Didn't know soon I would have to set you free
Yes it's over now the finale is coming on fast
  You left me broken there's no future in my past
You'll never understand my heart full of fears
  I know I will love you the rest of my years
Inside I know you will never come back to me
  But baby its destroying me to set you free
How could God let our love come to end so fast
  Why didn't God make forever eternal to last
Somehow now is here it is time for me to go
  Darling always remember all ways I love you so

Gene A. Ward

YOUTHFUL PAIN

Oh the sorry times of life and death intermingled with spring air
and robins' song in early evening calm.
What is the torment of the soul which crushes the last of hope
and spring and leaves the shambles of a dismal past run into present.
What is the happiness we seek throughout our short and endless life,
The price we pay for love and comfort
The things which fill our hearts with renumerating thoughts of joy —
Our very definition of the infinite good which each holds up as God.
Time heals or magnifies at will;
Evening is as infinite as the trail of air and space around the
small places we call existence.

Doris Beausoleil

MOTHER ROSE

To my mom

Women are often referred to
as a budding rose.
With thorns, we tend to be
everybody knows.
As a rose with age
we tend to wither away.
Time shows no mercy.
Too soon will come our day.
As for you, Mother Rose,
your thorns I've often seen.
I have picked your petals
and felt your punishing sting.
Never was there a rose so sweet
or shall there ever be.
You have stood in the garden and watched me grow
and mothered me patiently.
I dream of being half the rose
with things I say and do;
but I could never bloom so brilliantly
as the rose inside of you!

Jerrie M. Poindexter

THE SOCIAL WORKER WAITS

You need help
You're not alone!
You need to talk out loud
Where the rules of the game are four walls.
You find that you cheat and cavort and avoid.
The walls have mirrors — and the ceiling and the floor
And you run from the truth the only way you can —
Close your eyes.
But your heart pounds and your head bangs out its many tunes
Some in harmony, some in discord —
All within you.
The message is noted, not yet fully understood
For the room has more than reflections
A mind and a heart with eyes open
Trying to see.

Doris Beausoleil

ETERNAL WARRIOR

He stood alone, on a hill, in the dark.
Timorously, I approached
to see tears from the sky wetting his face,
or did these spring from yesterday's memories?
Acquired through years, virtue burnt within eyes
held taut as the weapon in his fist,
both wearied from battle.
Clearing my throat I spoke to him.
Slate eyes turned in my direction
but, like Lot's wife, he could not move;
could not step down until a champion replacement was found;
could not rest until another willingly took up The Cause.
Strong fingers contracted and uncurled as
the mist-kissed lips I would have liked to.
And still those eyes burned through me.
''If you will not step down — may I come up?''
No answer, but his silver head nodded.
I walked to join him and touched his wet clothing
feeling muscles tense beneath my fingers.
I so seldom, if ever, had touched a hero.

Elizabeth King

GERIATRIC

A young man walks down the corridor.
Carrying one small child, leading another,
He whistles the theme of ''The Twilight Zone.''

Residents crowd into the elevator,
Some in wheelchairs, flaccid or shrunken.

Others use walkers or canes
Or walk carefully without aids.

The less fortunate lie bedridden and helpless,
Or wander the halls in a demented state,
Not knowing where or who they are.

My father, no longer muscular,
Now speaks in a soft voice,
But his personality remains the same.

Esther Rosenstock

REFRAINS OF PORTER STREET

Whenever I hear classical music
I think of you, and you are here:
Wearing your smoking jacket,
sitting in your favorite chair,
listening as Verdi's music
combines with the spiraling
cigarette's smoke.
We are all together again,
present in this nighttime
living room
of red drapes and LaTraviata.
Daddy . . . ?

Elizabeth King

CHELMSFORD HEIGHTS

There is a cold moon rising
which paints the birch branches
in shadow inks across the yard.

It reawakens memories of you
to cross my mind,
to feel your touch,
to smell your scent.

This teasing moon,
this compelling force,
coerces me each night
to search for the promise of you.

Elizabeth King

MYSTERY OF LIFE

My life is still a mystery,
The plot continually unfolding.
I may not solve the puzzle
With the clues I am able to see.
Like a sleuth I try my best and
Expect to do until the day I die.

Dolores G. Schorr

RHYME WITH REASON

A rhyme without reason
Is like weather without season.
Monotony is created on such a base,
So must put on another face.
Some like it hot, some like it cold.
There's room for the casual
And room for the bold.
For rhyme to be sublime,
And endure for all time,
It must have some meaning for you and me;
Or else what's the use of it to be.

Dolores G. Schorr

THE JOY OF WORKING

The joy of earning with a certain yearning
   is a challenge.
When work is done, the yearning may
   be left behind.
New sights set on other aims beyond oneself
   is true altruism,
Bereft of gluttony, vanity, false pride,
   and other qualities that subvert happiness.

Dolores G. Schorr

COMES THE DAWN

At the end of those eight hours
   of resting in our sack
There's one thing we are sure of
   and that is dawn will crack
When it does our daily tasks
   begin once out of bed
Before engaging in activities
   planned for the day ahead
The first thing that confronts us
   as we beeline for the bath
Is that reflection in the mirror
   cause for someone's wrath
But with a bit of grooming
   we clean up pretty good
Before heading for the kitchen
   to take on breakfast food.

Russell T. Gratner

MOTHER'S DAY 1987

My soul is in darkness
   My spirit is quelled;
My son is in prison
   And I am in Hell.
My sweet, affectionate, handsome son
   Never in his life hurt anyone;
Victim of genetic flaw;
   Subject to archaic law
      And macho judge who
Heedless of a mother's tears
   Gave my dear son sixteen years.

Gladys Manning Rogers

We're all here visiting,
Leaving a lot of littering.
No concerns for respect,
A world filled with reject.
We're lost in confusion.
We've misplaced the solution.

Sharon J. Davis.

PIANO KISS

Quixotic notes shimmering
Dulcated melodic ring
Piano strings singing true
Miasma rainbow colored blue
Shades of sound, nuance of audible
Heard through freckled openings translatable
Ivory blacks syncopating white jumping jacks
Cacophony fast friends with non-verbal tracks
Mind aglow with the spread of abstracts
Streaming across a keyboard of tic-tacs
Spoken tongueless ear-drum bliss
Percussion notes never amiss
Through the light particles swim
Igniting that which once was dim
Inspiration engineered translucence
Imagery sparkling on dusk set suns
Capturing the days timelessness runs
Exposed full-meter ecstatic strums
One last warming sips' blend rums.

D. F. Mendleson

UNIVERSITY WITHOUT WALLS

To Pacific Western University

Here the flame of knowledge
burns without quenching
unearthing various kinds
of tools the craftsmen use
to ignite and polish their
various crafts while assessing
and giving them the recognition
they deserve. Here the spring of
knowledge flows to those who
strive to achieve.

Apostle J. P. K. Appiah, Jr.

How brief
a spelling is!
How long is the rhythmatic
austere?
The imperfect of fighting for freedom.
The silence increased love . . .
Years doubt, affirm
my moment and stainless worthy?
Building a human boat
anchors anywhere.

Ling

SOMEONE TO TALK TO

You can talk to Him whenever you please
You don't have to get down on your knees
He listens to whatever you have to say
Whether it is once a week or every day
No one will interrupt you when you talk
It can even be done while you take a walk
You can tell Him whatever is on your mind
You won't have to worry about the time
He will never laugh at what you've said
It can also be done when you go to bed
If you find it difficult to perform a task
You will have the strength, you won't have to ask
You have to believe for what He stands
He is not your ordinary mortal man
You can tell Him secrets, He listens well
You won't have to worry, He will never tell
He will not betray you, He is always there
He will always listen, He really cares
When things get tough and you feel alone
You can talk to Him, you won't need a phone

Mary P. Criniti

OUR LEGACY

To Wole Soyinka with love
(on hearing that Wole Soyinka had won the
1986 Nobel Prize for literature)

Kokrokoo — Kokrokoo — Kokrokoo —
Kon — Kon — Kon — Kon — Kon —
Africa 'Muntie!' Africa 'Listen!' Africa 'Muntie!'
Our legacy is linked with
our ancestral past; the stories
of our grandmothers, recounted
at night gatherings and in the warmth
of our huts. Fables and tales of
different shades, inspiring us to
dig deep into the fountain of knowledge.
Ananse stories, Yoruba mythologies,
and the others, are remnants of the
golden treasures of our past heritage.

And now the richness of our culture
has been laid bare on the African
palanguin for the world to adore.
The scales have turned, and literature's
elegance sits on Mother Africa with
the victory celebration of drums.

Apostle J. P. K. Appiah, Jr.

WINNIE'S FAREWELL

You know in what manner I have loved, ever since we met!
I loved you with all humility through times we will never forget!
I kept back nothing good for you, I swear by God above!
Oh, let us come together, and enjoy once more Our Love!
But, no, they come! You must go! You must go! You know where!
I know pain awaits in that prison, I know what will happen there!
But you fear none of these, tho' assailed by every strife!
God, let us finish Our Course! That is more precious than Life!
And, now my dearest Nelson, I can be with you no longer!
Remember we never stepped back, and pray God make us stronger!
We coveted no one's silver or gold! Our hands provided our needs!
And now if war must leave its spoor, I hope for the poor it bleeds!
But I can say no more! Just let me touch your face!
Nelson, My Love, I must leave you! Oh, how I'll miss your embrace!

Martin J. O'Malley

SUMMER RAIN

My window's unshuttered; my view, unobstructed.
  The mind unclutters as the haze scatters.
Up, the leaves turn and first drops splatter.
      Summer Rain, I observe.

  It's cool and it's wet and refined.
Summer Rain, oh, Summer Rain has arrived.

The steambath cools and clear heads rule.
    The rain collects and pools.
    It gets dark real fast . . .
Then, a lightning flash, and children splash.

The rock & roll thunder. The rainswept plunder.
    The breeze, it turns to gusts.
    The Wonder of it fills my Cup.
And, it's cool and it's wet and refined.
Summer Rain, oh, Summer Rain has arrived.

Miguel Letto

MISSING YOU . . .

Tonight, sitting on this beach,
Ocean breezes caressing softly . . .
I am missing you,
And I know in my heart you are missing me
too.

I wish you were here . . .
So we could savor each tender moment . . .
Loving . . .
Sharing private eternities.

For me . . .
For you . . .
Time must now stop for awhile
Until we can be together again.

Our time spent, yet brief . . .
Brought love's sweet moments
That welcomes home the longing heart.
Oh precious time, fly beyond the realm of today . . .
tomorrow . . .

Let not dust gather, in years spent . . .
Until we reach our eternity, loving, one lifetime!

Glenna Gardner-Wimett

THE GIFT TO THINK
DEEP IN STILLNESS

About Yesterday, Today and Tomorrow,
Foolish mind, is enslaved by the Shadows.
Treacherous thought-forms, Creatures, in the lower world.
Just seems to be real. Mind made in darkness —
Long, long ago, in the beginning of Earth.

The old age beliefs, are melting away, by Truth.
I could see and understand, Pride is lack of understanding.
Impatiences express in mistakes — jerks and groans.
Mental agony and distress is the curse.
From invaders from the past evil, "We made."
I was thinking, are we able to bear so much pain?

All at once, I was the Center of Light, "Myself,"
The Eternal Light, "*Mind*" that knows Truth and Love.
In the natural path, "*Mind is the guiding ray.*"
Mind must be generous and Love.

Dorothy Carter

HELPLESS NIGHTS

I feel the presence within your eyes
  of an emotion catching on fire.
Tell me what is on your mind,
  Let me feel your desire.

You touch the burning shadows,
  Is there living after dying?
You're willing to take the chance
  though your lonely mind is crying.

Don't be afraid to hide your tears
  — the pain will go away.
I'll be your friend through the desperate years
  going slowly day by day.

You can count on me forever
  but there's one thing to be done.
For you to find out who you are,
  you must reach out to the sun.

I know that you are very scared
  and that's the hardest part.
But keep in mind
  you've got the guts
and the strength that's in your heart.

Angie Flauto

FALLING STAR

A star fell from the heavens
and vanished without a trace.
The dark clouds now were crying,
and the moon had a sad face.

An emptiness filled the night
and a stillness filled the air.
As it watched the clouds weeping,
the huge moon could only stare.

Behind clouds, stars stayed hidden,
so the moon left too, to hide . . .
and sadness filled the heavens,
for their friend, the star, had died . . .

Arlene P. Devine

PENS AND ROSES

Say much without trying
They need little effort to convey
And no time to realize
The thoughts in a troubled mind
When one cannot sleep or think or eat
Or know that which comes with time
Known only to the wise
Comes softly with Pens and Roses
Leaves happy tears in kind eyes.

Unsure but feeling you know
They sat it all
Without moving a sound
Fall lightly to the air
Like snow upon the ground
Leave my mind open to the truth
"Love," "Forever," and "Trust" come in time
But if that is not so
Then, in these Pens and Roses
Be True, and ever so Kind.

Virgie M. Tabaco

ENDEARMENT

As the wind whispers across the land,
I see you dancing upon the sand.
Caressed by the gentle breeze,
I kneel before you and take your hand.
Basking under stars so bright,
Shining from celestial heights,
I gaze into your face so fair,
Glowing with the tranquil light.
I look into your wond'ring eyes,
Sparkling like the star-filled skies,
And ask you by the deep blue sea,
To join in harmony our separate lives.
  And as the sea doth sigh and seethe,
  To you I do my love bequeath.

Stephen Kalandros

THE MAKER'S SONNETT

I stood upon a high steep hill,
  And up above me the sky was still.
I saw the herd, the grass, the lakes,
  The beauty no human man can make.
Then far beyond a mountain rose
  A perfect view that God had chose.
Still further tops of forest trees,
  Had caught my eyes amid the breeze,
Specks of colors here and there,
  The flowers' fragrance filled the air.
How very perfect was his plan,
  That he should create this beauty for man.
Yes, fortunate man, that I am,
  That God should be so good to man.

Josephine Sadowski

BILL

The house way up in the hills
belongs to a man named Bill.
They say he's killed many.
And will continue to kill anyone
who'll dare go into his hills.
I believe they're wrong.
I'm strong. I made the climb.
I found a peaceful man
who took my hand, showed me his land.
Here, I'll stay with Bill.
And in the distance I hear
the people say, ''Bill killed her.''

Linda Rosalie Farley

WARMTH TOUCHES

I open my eyes
The sun is sleeping on my bed.
Touching my arm, ''nice''.

Warmth touches, The Great Law.
The morning opens my windows
I open my doors —
I was alive —
Gravity has not let go
Love is in the air
With no questions.

Dorothy Carter

A WALK WITH ALMA TADEMA

Dressed for the Epicenium thou must
  wave farewell; to this end
the wand will hurl its magical
  curse onto that path beyond.
At thy breast tuck an eolith
  that portends the storm to come.
Atop that crown laden with silken
  hair rests a bow braided with lilacs.

Loosen that sheath that flows from
that bladed shoulder perfumed to scent.
  And stroll beyond this universe
unto that lane that reaches
  never never land.

Michael Varbadian

LOVE

Mind yearns for Love
Restless to see repose
Thinking change — Love flows.

Various powers inhabit
Makes nerves against
Memory makes unsteadiness
Dictates to the emotions.

A sense of torment at times
Continues to roam. I *find*
My Love just in time.

Dorothy Carter

GAY PAREE

Life is so grand
  in ol' *Paree*
a wicked city to be sure,
  but the mesdames are so lovely
    toujour, toujour.

Sitting on the sidewalk café
  sipping red wine,
under the striped awning
  watching the ladies swish by,
Oh, how the garçons give them the eye.

Oh, gay *Paree*
  Eiffel tower and Arch of Triumph
The Louvre and the Tuilleries
  Opera grand and the follies bergeriere
Boats gliding down the Seine.

The sun shines down on the golden roofs
  of Chartres and Notre Dame
Palace of Versailles
  Ah, *Paree* is the summer of sighs.

Marilyn Vanistendael

THE SONG OF PHILOMELA

The sky is vast and spacious,
  And if perchance the day is fair,
White clouds drift in countless numbers,
  No descrimination of size,
  Still higher overhead a perfect blue to compromise.

The sky is vast and spacious,
  And only that which has wings,
Can know the thrill of taking flight,
  Higher still higher past the white clouds and into the blue,
The ceiling destination reached.

The sky is vast and spacious,
  And at appointed time comes nightfall,
The line of day meets the dark nightward clouds,
  And from the still quite forest, taking her wings into the night sky,
Comes the nightsong of Philomela.

Gone is the daylight bright, gone is the sunset glow,
  And now night skies are here all birds are not still.
Philomela, Philomela sing your midnight song of love,
  Philomela, Philomela how you thrill the stars above.
Philomela, Philomela how you must cradle the woodlands
  With your song so gay, Philomela, my dear Philomela,
Carry my love song to my true love some day.

Josephine Sadowski

JOSEPHINE SADOWSKI. Born: Chicago, Illinois, 7-16-19; Education: Grace Street Grammer School (now called Canty), 1929-36; Steinmetz High School (College Preparatory 2), 1936-39; Art Institute of Chicago, scholarship, 1938-39 (eye surgery in 1939 required giving up anything that would cause eye strain, unfortunately); Occupation: Retired, previously four years of medical work, 17 years of clerical work office work, 10 years of analyst work/medical papers, 15 years of teaching Sunday school; Memberships: Grace Evangelical Free Church; Directed two Christmas pageants during the 1970s, completely designing costumes, programs, etc.; Always active in church choral groups; During World War II, was given the War Manpower Commission, training people within industry; Awards: Honorable Mention for eight poems appearing in *Important American Poets and Songwriters of 1947,* Valiant House Publishers, and two poems in *Talented Songwriters and Poets of 1947,* Heaven Publishers; Poetry: 'Amber Skies,' 'Ode to the Oceans,' 'Little Fisherman,' *Important American Poets and Songwriters,* 1947; 'When Springtime Comes Again,' 'Play a Symphony to Fall,' *Talented Songwriters and Poets,* 1947; Comments: *I write by inspiration. My themes come easily and vary somewhat. I like to write about Truth, and the four seasons. The desire to write has always been with me. As a child, my first poem,* The Beauty of Spring, *appeared in the school paper. I have done a lot of writing through the years. Since I have retired, I have been trying to finish many of my manuscripts. I have always had a busy and very active life, and I only wish I could do it all over again — however, now, at sixty-eight I can look back and like the life I lived walking close with God; the beauty that's left is in the heart. I was born of Polish parents, the seventh of nine children.*

GOLDEN DAYS

When life seems like a heavy load,
And you begin to wonder when you took the wrong road,
Let's take a trip, on a memory ship,
And recall the carefree years.

Think of the fun you had, and your spirits will raise.
You played with everyone
Those were the Golden Days
Their race or creed made no difference to you,
For you liked them as friends,
And knew they were true.

But time changes the way things used to be,
And life is not so simple for you and me.
But we still can have a good life, if we try to find,
The good in all the races of mankind!

Ruby M. Olson

PEACE OF MIND

When we lose our peace of mind,
We're not happy anymore.
All we seem to see, is trouble coming to our door.
We start each day with worry.
We cannot think or do our chores.

No one seems to understand,
Or wants to stop, as they go by our doors.
Everyone is in a hurry, to do their own thing.
Life for them is fulfilling their own needs,
Just have their own fling.

And make a mark in the world to bring them glory.
But for us, our world is another story.
Our guiding light shines no more.
Each day in our mind.
Things seem worse and so unkind.

What's the answer? I don't know.
But maybe soon the day will come.
When someone will find,
A way to help those, who have lost their Peace of Mind!

Ruby M. Olson

UNDERSTANDING

The world would be a better place,
If we could see the good in each other's race
If we would show kindness and consideration,
And give our friendship to each nation.

Without the problems that spawn hate, war and turmoil,
  to all the world
And distrust where our flags are unfurled.
There's room for all the people to live,
So when we take, we should also give.

And prove that we understood the words,
''Peace on Earth, Good Will to All.''
And remember His Holy Birth, in a lowly stall.
He was born to be our king
And to our world, His love did bring.

To help us live each day with friendship for strangers,
Helping them to avoid the dangers.
And showing them, if we all help as one.
We will all share the glory, when our work is done!

Ruby M. Olson

THE BABY THAT NEVER WAS

I never had a daughter, never a son.
I always needed, wanted one.
   To love me, to be loved by me.

He could be dark, or fair,
With a little head of little hair.
   To love me, to be loved by me.

To see the beginning walk —
To hear the beginning talk —
   To love me, to be loved by me.

I saw a little shirt, a shoe.
A cuddly stuffed bear, a kangaroo;
Dream time, Baby, dream time for you.

I never had a daughter, never a son.
I always needed, wanted one.
   To love me, to be loved by me.

Madelene Middleton

WE

We are long together —
Through stormy, through sunny weather.
The many days never apart
The many nights heart to heart.
The babies came, they grew with loving care,
They grew up and are gone; we are here.

He died in early summer and is away
He died in early summer; I cannot stay
No place other than with him can I be
No place other, is never for me.

How can one live, who so long was two?
The world all dark, no light shining through
Dear God, let him linger at Thy gate
Let him linger, I'll not be late.
No place other than with him can I be
No place other, is never for me.

Madelene Middleton

I REMEMBER

I remember not when I was born —
  or do I remember?
  From shadows of eternities past
I see a face, fleeting memories cast
Shadows, and dream scenes that last
And haunt me night and day
As I reach out for landmarks on my way.

From heaven's realm a fugitive —
My soul in birth, my life to be
Is not tied to earth, I now am free —
Free to hear and feel and give
Free to die — but free to live!

I remember, with misty eyes —
  But, I do remember!

Charles E. Haggerty

TO WHOM I LOVE

When I receive my special call
  To leave you whom I love
And take my journey
   Into another realm
Grieve not, nor shed tears.

Do not let your thoughts be sad
  I'll love you as I always have.
I may live on some distant shore
  Where other loved ones have gone,
They'll take me to their hearts.

Talk of me and laugh
  As if I were by your side.
I'd come and take your hand in mine
  Could I only find the way,
But I cannot see afar.

Behold the morning sunrise,
  Listen to the song of the bird,
Watch the roses burst into bloom,
  Then think of me with joy — not tears,
I loved them all — and you.

Remember how I loved to talk with you
  We bandied ideas to and fro
You stimulated my mind.
  There are many things I longed to do —
Who realizes all his heart's desires.

Know that I do not fear
  But leaving you behind
Is so hard to bear.
  This I know without a doubt —
Some things each must face alone.

I know God loves you — and me.
  He has tasks for me to do
He parts the curtains of eternity
  That I may see through.
Come join me on some fair day.

Charles E. Haggerty

DOG NEEDED GLASSES

The dog needed glasses.
I didn't know.
I was over my neighbors
Shoveling snow.
Dropped the case of glasses
Onto the ground.
Went back over to find them;
They couldn't be found.
On my way up my yard,
Looked back over to his;
The dog was running, glasses in mouth,
Like a toy for a kid.
If I'd known he needed glasses,
I'd set up a fund.
For all dogs that can't afford
Glasses — let it be done.

Mary Frances Hayes

cold water
   overflowing an oaken bucket —
rusty pump

Charles B. Rodning

THE RETURN

You returned to me so suddenly
To brighten up my day.
How I wish it could stay this way,
But I know that's an impossible dream.
My love for you is hidden
Beneath a mask of friendship.
I hope the friendship will swell like a wave
And crash upon us,
Spraying love on the sand where we stand.
But all of this is just a seashore dream,
Dreamt by a lonely girl in white,
Standing on a lonely pier at midnight.
She can't unveil herself because she is afraid,
Afraid of rejection by her
Prince Charming.

Kristi Hurd

O. R.

If you still heard me
  talking my love,
if you still knew me
  I asked your freedom
   wanting
to breathe for you —
For a moment so dear
I held your hand in mine
  blinded by a sky
   offering beauty
among the welts of tears —
Then I could close my eyes
open to the formidable image
of childhood memories —
if I could take back the pain.

Monique Adam

THINGS WE DIDN'T SAY

When we were last together
I didn't say much to you.
I didn't ask you to be mine,
I didn't say I loved you.

But I took you in my arms,
and when your lips touched mine
I felt a tingle in my heart
and I knew we would be fine.

You didn't say you loved me,
you didn't say you cared.
But something bound us closely
in the feeling that we shared.

Apart now, we must call or write,
knowing without fail
that we each wait eagerly
for phone calls and the mail.

I count the seconds and the hours
as I await the day
when I return and we will say
the things we didn't say.

Ken Coomes

MY BELOVED . . .

Beloved, one lifetime to meet . . .
Laugh, dance, love . . . one moment to change
two lives.
A quiet stare, magnetically pulling my heart
Into tide's full stream of love.

I am enraptured with each word
That holds the heart spellbound . . .
Teasing delightfully, my homing beacon you've become,
Loving, we know what few have found.

Tonight I am dreaming, oh sweet love . . .
Lost in the elegance of your caress . . .
Softly drifting, sweetly touching,
Cascading on delicate tendrils of my soul.

Slowly teardrops drench
Upon this sea of loneliness . . .
Remembering parting tides quietly pulling you away
One soft spring night . . .
Leaving me . . . you silently die . . . no good-byes!

Now I grieve in reminiscence of thirty years . . .
My beloved, my lifetime!

Glenna Gardner-Wimett

BEGINNINGS . . .

A quiet stare, brings two sets of eyes in
contact . . .
Feelings stirring within,
With smiles parting sweet lips,
A beginning . . .

Now whispered words
Find two contented hearts . . .
Lost in love's sweet rapture,
A loving wonderment . . .

Moments become eternities
Stopping time . . .
When all else ceases to exist
But the flesh of love . . .

Lost in a sea of romantic illusions . . .
Grasping life's one elusive dream . . .
Feelings locked within the heart, all mine, hard
to define . . .
So special, my collected treasure you've become!

Glenna Gardner-Wimett

THE MOON

The moon is on the rise, can you see the man in the moon?

They say he is there, do you believe it? I do!
I do because I want to believe it, it is a part of the universe.
I wish there were a lady in the moon, then we would have a universal
delight plus more moonlight.

Lorraine F. Lewis

GIVE ME THE ROSES

Please give me the roses while I live,
So I can be happy while living.
Please shower me with the petals from morn till night
The same as I too, am giving.

I give you a rose in the smile that I have,
As you come in at the door
Not just on my lips, but down in my heart.
And more so than ever before.

I give you a rose in my tolerance of faults,
In the kindness and patience I show.
I give you a bouquet in the love I feel,
And the happiness I want *you* to know.

Please give me the roses you want me to have,
Don't wait ere I've gone from your sight.
Just one word of kindness, thoughtfulness shown.
Would make me *so* happy tonight.

Willie Johnson Cummings

HAVE I MEASURED UP?

Have I asked thee humbly, my sins to forgive,
And to guide me as I walk the right road,
To brighten my life and help me to live,
So that it is easier to carry my load?

Have my footsteps been straight on God's pathway,
So my Children can easily follow along,
If not, oh God, help me live each day,
So they will never, no never do wrong.

The golden rule I shall remember for thee
For in loving others, there is no time to weep,
And, I shall let my light shine for all to see,
For "as ye sow, so shall ye reap."

My faith is so much bigger than a mustard seed,
And I shall knock and knock at the door.
For it is always open to those in need,
Even if they have never knocked before.

For knock and God will open the door.
Seek and you will surely find,
Happiness here on earth, life forevermore
And a serene and peaceful mind.

Willie Johnson Cummings

MY WORLD

On this lovely hill I'll make my home.
Where my eyes can see and my thoughts to roam.
I paid — I don't remember the price —
For my little acre in paradise.
A field of yellow daisies at my feet,
The whole wide world is mine to keep.
Spring will bring courage, a promise in the sun.
Knowing life for me has just begun.

Helen Pastushin

SOUL TO SOUL

Thought to thought
we found respect, a common bond,
friendship.

Hand in hand
we found strength in each other,
to make it through rough times.

Heart to heart
we found love, one-ness together,
a more complete sharing.

Body to body
we found pleasure, the joy of touch,
wonder in each other.

Soul to soul
we'll find eternity.

Ken Coomes

FREE FROM TEARS

I will show no tears from troublesome
years.
God swept away all my fears.
For when I placed my hands into His
I could finally say — I'm absolutely free.

Phyllis M. Cumbie

DEATH: A FRIEND

Death is the end of being
Who I am and of who you are to me.
We are but things of a day . . .
The shadow of a dream is man; no more.

The grave is dark and silent,
But the paths that lead
From it, are, to the righteous,
Strewn with flowers.

We mourn for the dead
But in truth it is for ourselves;
For afraid, we cannot see
Beyond the veil between us and God.

Death is a gentle friend who
Comes with quiet release of pain.
Some believe it is a new beginning
Of a life of the spirit.

A brightness of the spirit and God
Gives it; a shining of light of the
Soul; and Death is sweet . . .
A walk with God, throughout Eternity.

E. F. Schmidt

Lifting up a rock,
  I was bitten by reality.
My identity stood naked
    to my eyes.
I tried to hide in a dream
  but the mist quickly lifted.
And I found myself crying
  with a rock in my hand.

Mike Shanta

GOLDEN TREASURE

I found a golden treasure,
  no, not the usual kind,
because it is, you see, in
  the middle of my mind.
I tap into a golden mist
  filled with healing balm,
and share it by the handful
  with all of what I am.
To the ends of my fingers,
  to the tips of my toes,
through all the lanes and
  byways of me that
golden treasure flows.
Endless is the bounty of
  that misty trove I find,
however many times I tap it,
  more is there each time.
I found a golden treasure in
  the middle of my mind,
more precious than any I had
  ever thought to find.

Mary D. Welker

IT IS NOT DONE

It is not done
I have not finished yet
I must give to the world
something they won't forget
I must create, I must do my thing
I must write a poem, I must learn to sing
I must make an impression on the sands of time
I must learn a lesson, I must be sublime
I have a mission that God has given to me
I must write his words down
for all the world to see
So I write a poem and hope that you see
It is the love of God as it shines through me
I will never be famous or rich
but I will always have this wish
Think of me kindly when I take my leave
Pray for me kindly, do not ever grieve
I will be happy in the Lord
for having written his great word

Hazel Carestia

THE GIFT

Every leaf on the tree
is a gift from God, given to me
Every flower in my yard
given with sweet regard
Every blade of grass
I must mow
The finest carpet he can sew
The cool breezes of the night
The moon a lover's delight
Each star a little light
completing the tapestry of night
Spring has come to our town
all the colors of nature's gown
Spring has come to my heart
a new beginning, a lovely start

Hazel Carestia

SOUR GRAPES

My phone, it doesn't ring
I have no dates
I hung my hopes on just one
and found that I really have none
Oh, sour grapes, that's all I get
no true love, no not yet
sour grapes, sour grapes
the bitter taste of love rejected
I sit alone and quite neglected
never hang your hopes on one man
and put the sour grapes in the jam

Hazel Carestia

THE TOUCH OF GOD

Today I felt the Touch of God,
in answer to my prayer.
I knew my prayer was answered *now* —
I felt *Him* everywhere.

My answer came as if *Someone*
had placed His hand on me
and murmured low but very clear:
"It will be well. You'll see."

"My Child — today your prayer's been heard.
Your answer has been made."
I felt His Love surrounding me.
At rest my heart was laid.

Arlone Mills Dreher

WILD ROSES

When the wild roses begin to bloom,
They bring a memory of days of yore,
And a little log homestead shack,
Where wild roses bloomed by the door.
Often the lovely fragrance crept inside
And seemed to fill that little room.
What a very special treat —
When the wild roses were in bloom!

Romie Clouse

SIGNIFICANT OTHER

She clung to his exit coffer
wailing in gasping cries
of a "fire in her heart
that would never die."
I didn't understand.
I was a child,
and her uncontrolled outburst
frightened me.
The entire event was coated
with a much too sobered atmosphere.

Time continued, she was gone,
I was grown.
I met a man;
he became my love, my life.
One day, I stood gaping
as he sauntered through an exit door;
and I thought of Gran,
and I understood.
For I, too, had a "fire in my heart
that would never die."

M. C. Evangelista

LAS VEGAS

Dark shadows of dry desert hills roll by on the road
the clouds quickly pass over the moon and stars,
a cosmic wind from eons blows them over.
The Desert: where few stay long, all must be strong.

The sky brightens in the distant horizon,
wherein lies a shining oasis, a saving grace for the unknowing
only the glitter and glamour showing
of Las Vegas.

Neon dancing on the strip,
giant cowboys flip their hats in greetings,
crowds lured by star-studded marquees,
sights of card sharks, sounds of slot machines.

And the dry wind blows in off the desert,
offering no relief in the stale city air,
only the flickering lights of pleasure
can stimulate a feeling of fleeting despair . . . in Las Vegas.

Janet Castiel

JANET E. CASTIEL. Born: New York, New York; Married: Howard Levy; Education: Vassar College, University of Madrid; Occupations: Writer, Video director; Memberships: International Radio and Television Society, American Film Institute, AMI-New York; Awards: 'Secrets,' *Hearts on Fire, Volume II*, Certificate of Merit; 'Simplicity's Sewing it Up!', International Film and Television Festival; Poetry: 'Land of Ah's,' *Best New Poets of 1986;* 'Nevada,' *American Poetry Anthology, Vol. VI, No. 5,* 1986; 'More Secrets,' *Hearts on Fire, Volume III,* 1986; 'Candle Glow,' *A Treasury of Contemporary Verse,* 1985; 'Secrets,' *Hearts on Fire, Volume II,* 1983.

WEB

You cease attempting to understand
By utilizing self-reasons.
Then begin to act mostly as they want of you
Only in rebellious mannerisms.
To cause them concerting tones of,
'Where have you suddenly gone?'
When all along you are there;
Once donned in natural splendor
Now cloaked in shaded shawls
To conceal intelligible ideas
They firstly disparaged now come to comprehend:
Your original morals were voiced, unheard;
As conflicts shut-off avenues
Due to outside influences' opinions;
For they are lost, too.
So. You begin again to breathe
Attempting to understand
By utilizing self-reasonings
Until such time; you cease attempting to understand . . .

Diane M. Saucier

VICTIM OF CIRCUMSTANCE

An Autobiography

In this life, consider it made
    to take side streets; to lead the parade
Caught from behind, and sidestep the cause
    making it happen; when it never ever was
A feeling within, a feeling without
    a calm resurrection; and it's all about
Seems friends that all know, the secrets beyond
    are friends who'll not tell; for these friends are gone
To hide behind tears, that never can fall
    to reminisce tomorrow, before it can call
To sanctify his God, from a soul deep within
    just to walk from the beach, and not let him in
The word, the wisdom, the power, the cause
    shall be just an echo, as I only was
To friends who are foes, with the blink of an eye
    I really do love you; but it's so hard to try
So, when the breath of my body, the just to my cause
    can no longer exist; remember, I was
Hence, the secret of luck will somehow be born
    as no one single person, can relish; but mourn

Lucky Rimpila

SONATA

Until the end my tears will fall on an errant
Tamarind that tells me it is you. Are not the
Leaves more green than when the sun and rain alone did
Caress them? I stand not in the way of nature's fare
And yet I wonder if the unkind arm of fate
Might once have ripped away the bark, twigs and blossoms
Of my tree. All through the night I heard a call as
From some saddened bird that glimpsed a garden on a
Hill and flew to find no herbage there, naught but a
Lichen cramped within a stony crag. Perhaps
Someday, when wandering is done this bird will drop
Beneath the tamarind, its soul to rest within
The tree. Are you the tree, am I the bird, and will
We two, forever nomads, living, dwell apart?

Karl Gasslander

SOME COWBOYS COME OF AGE

Jesse Montana and Colorado Reed
Ridin' Wyoming; without a care or need
Dusty boots and saddles, and a trail that winds the range
Of the Shenandoah Mountains; of some cowboys come of age

Wild mountain roses; and a dew that glistens green
On a trail with no beginning; that just cowboys have ever seen
Thirsty days and star-filled nights; long riders in a valley wind
No home to linger on to; no messages to send

It's wild Wyoming roses for a sweetheart in the pines
A ride across the Beartooth, and down the mountainside
Together riding sunsets; forever with a friend
Jesse and Colorado; this trail will never end

Sweet Karianne of Cody, is waitin' by the stream
That winds its way to heaven, and heaven is a dream
She's waitin' for her cowboys; it's an end to her lonely nights
'Cause when her cowboys come a ridin'; it makes everything all right

And the time they spend together; the heartaches that they mend
Seem like to last forever; but all forevers have an end
So, ride away Jesse Montana; and Colorado Reed
And Karianne of Cody; mountain souls from a sagebrush seed

Lucky Rimpila

AUTUMN'S SUNRISE
ON THE MALIBU

A quarter moon hangs heavily in the Western sky.
It seems most reluctant to bid us good-bye.
Our souls welcome the symphony of wild bird songs.
Their exuberance will stay with us, all day along.

The Eastern sky blushes, as the light increases.
The beauty of it all breaks our gloom — to pieces!
It's hard to believe you can see the distant mountains,
As the slanting rays become a sparkling yellow fountain.

The miracle of a halo brings us a brand new world,
And sets our Beings in a spinning whirl.
From Santa Monica — to Point Dume.
The world's awake — all will be busy — soon.

I lift my hand and say — Good Morning, Sun,
    I'm glad you're here!
Make it a good day! A good one, you hear!

Helen Pastushin

MY SPECIAL HOUR
BETWEEN SUN AND MOON

The glorious summer kisses the silver sea
On a bit of beach that belongs to me.
A lingering sunset floods the sky.
A gentle gull tips his wing as he flies by,
To bid farewell to another day.
I love this place, more than I can say.

The first stars so dazzling, so bright,
Lift the curtain of a blue velvet night,
To make way for the moonlight's path of gold.
No northern wind, no northern cold!
So — open your eyes, so you can see
This special place — that means so much to me.

Helen Pastushin

FATIMA

Apparitions of Our Lady of Fatima

Our Blessed Lady of Fatima like in Lourdes,
appeared to young folks like Bernadette
Soubiron, namely Lucy, Jacinta & Francisco, there
in the valley & prairie of Spanish-shephards' sheep-herd.
The Blessed Virgin appeared five consecutive times
predicting the conversion of Russia to the Mother Church
in a far expected time. She forwarded the hope
of world peace to those children, the Rosary Prayer
by the Spanish & Portuguese multitudes and a
deeper consecration to her immaculate, miraculous heart.
The Miracle of the Sun happened in Portugal just three
months before the German invasion of Austria,
the great miracle was kept silenced until the Holy Father
revealed this scientific apparition to the clergy
of the Catholic Church in Rome.
Continuously the recent pilgrimages bring along
healthy cures, grand faith & fervent hope in our
Blessed Lady of Fatima at Cova da Iria.

Misericordia Dei ad multiplicanda miracula,
quotidie sunt elargenda per Fatimae Virginem Mariam.

Allan De Fiori

ALLAN DE FIORI. Born: Barre, Vermont, 1-24-15; Married: Catherine Florio, 2-37; Education: High school, graduated cum laude from the Episcopal Seminary of Reggio-Emilia, northern Italy; Graduate from Gymnasium School, 1932, Italy; Occupations: Bookbinder, Nurse, Lyric poet; Membership: Y.M.C.A. of Norwich since 1974; Awards: Second place from Peace World Arts for 'Willow Bitter'; 12 Honorable Mention Certificates and 3 Golden Poet Awards, 1985-87, for poetry; Poetry: 'Cypress,' 'The Resurrection Star,' 'Ode to H.M. Elizabeth II, Queen of England'; 'Mt. Hermon' 'Mt. Horeb,' 'Mt. Taylor,' 'Mount Aetna,' *American Poetry Association,* 1982-86; Comments: *I enjoy writing poetry. Most of my poems are dedicated to my dear fiancee, Catherine Mary Florio, R. N., for her beautiful inspiration & talent.*

FAIRBANKS

It is midnight up in Fairbanks
    all the bars are running full.
Every tenderfoot is lit up
    like the Northlands' midnight sun!
Helen and her dancing girls
    are kicking up the sky,
Frilled dresses high above their knees,
    gold nuggets on their thigh!
Prance away, you merry chicks
    in the Malamute Saloon,
While the wolves howl in the timber,
    at the mountains of the moon!
Red garters flash on shapely legs,
    flushed faces all aglow,
Who cares what bleak tomorrow brings
    tonight we love the show!

Harry C. Helm

A TRAIN WHISTLE CALLS

I hear a train whistle blowin'.
The lonely sound echoes on the wind.
It seems to be callin' me,
To climb aboard and go back home again.
How I'd love to step aboard, settle back
And watch the scenery go by
As I listened to the clickety-clack —
Ah, it brings a tear to my eye!
Whenever I hear that lonely call
Of a train whistle echoin' on the wind —
If I could only answer
And go back home again.

Romie Clouse

AND EASTER COMES

Like a garment — the snowtide
Covers — smothers —
Nothing grows.

But O, the springtide!
Emerald jewels, dawn glistened,
Wave upon wave
Like flecks of sea-foam
Birthing — breathing —

    And Easter comes.

Almost — I understand
Those capricious motions
Expectant in the springtide
For I am transient, too.
I wear a changing robe

    And Easter comes!

Elated — I lift up my hands.

Bethell Whitley Hice

SELF-PORTRAIT

My dress is prim and proper
    and precise as it can be.
The cloth is sturdy, color black.
    Plain and conservative me.
But oh, the riot of colors
    and frills a man could find.
If he'd just forget the way I look
    and peep inside my mind.

Beverly C. Graham

TIME TRAVELS

On the wings of night
And memories
And diffused dreams
There are half-remembered places
Lost in time
And peoples from another place.

The adventures of the night
Await —
Each day in toils
Sinks into the fading Sun.

We watch the night sky
Where troubles fade
On wings —

The traveled heroes
Of our dreams
Recall and re-create
Life and love
And beauty.

Virginia Weber

MUSING AT SAINT PAUL

This river runs before me
On its journey to the sea:
Longest yet of any river
Landlocked by an inland lea.

What of tales this river tells me
On its journey to the sea?
Tales of life and manly measure
As it moves along to be.

Weak and starting at this bending,
Flows it slowly to the sea.
Who would think that at this trending
It is set about to flee?

Lo, behold this Mississippi,
Flowing long and moving free,
Soon to reach the greatest distance
From its source unto the sea!

At its Minnesota starting
Moves the water from its lea;
Moves it deep into the ocean
Far beyond its delta, free!

Harris Hollis

SOMEWHERE

Somewhere there's a place for us,
With a just-right house and a garden fair,
A barn, an orchard, and a cool green lawn.
Oh, I'll be so glad when we get there!

I hope there's a trout stream near,
Where our small sons can fish and swim.
And an ancient oak with wide, strong limbs
To build a treehouse in.

A wide front porch would be so nice,
And a kitten curled up in a rocking chair,
A lilac bush, and a red rose tree
With a pair of bluebirds nesting there.

Contentment will reign in our dream home
While time flits swift as a swallow's wing,
Enriched by boyish scuffles in the big back yard
And girlish laughter in the garden swing.

Vivian Harvey

OOPS!

O sweet sweet inspiration's flight
When I'm in bed at dead of night.
The close deep dark, inside and out
Does make the muse foment and spout
And so I grab my little pad
To scribble brilliant verse like mad —
And in the morning's bright sunlight. . .
I can't read what I wrote last night!

Flo Salo

A CHEERFUL PRAYER

Give me a good digestion, Lord
    And also something to digest
Give me a healthy body, Lord
    And sense to keep it at its best.

Give me a healthy mind, good Lord
    To keep the good and pure in sight
Which seeing sin is not appalled
    But finds a way to set it right.

Give me a mind that is not bored
    That does not whimper, whine or sigh
Don't let me worry over much
    About a fussy thing called I.

Give me a sense of humor, Lord
    Give me the grace to see a joke
To get some happiness from life
    And pass it on to other folk.

Helen deLong Woodward

I'M OLD

I turned 62 — before I knew
I am an old lady. Don't know what to do —
I filed for Social Security — feeling so bad.
3 great-grandchildren, I realized I had.

I listened to people — talking about age,
When anyone asks me how old, I flew into a rage.
Growing old gracefully — was never my cup of tea.
They all could get old — but never me —

I'm a mother to a 47-year-old son —
My baby is 45 — yes, the very last one —
3 grown grandchildren — married and gone —
I'm divorced now — and all alone —

When I look into the mirror, at the wrinkles & grey hair,
I wonder often — how long it's all been there —
I've been weak & tired and wondered why:
Old age creeping up — now I sit and cry.

40 and 50, soon slip away —
Social Security — the government will soon have to pay.
Don't feel guilty — you paid it in —
Remember — you're old too — find an older friend —

Mabel D. Green

TRYST

Come, my latter-day Lindbergh,
Fly with me over the north Atlantic to Norway.
Share a mystic cruise in slate green fjords
We'll wrap ourselves in furs and gaze at the clear
     midnight sky
Laugh at sailors speaking Norwegian who sound like
     they have marbles in their mouths.
If you ignore my plumpness
I'll ignore your hairpiece.
Gawky teen-age sweethearts, remember us —
Arms linked to keep warm. Crunching, stamping
our feet in the snow.
Snowflakes circling.
Window shopping at the festive windows on the Plaza.
Spanish arabesque building outlined in thousands
of colored lights.
A magic romantic evening which never happened.
But could have
Should have.

Gerry Storms Frerichs

IMAGINE

Imagine . . .
     four boys in Liverpool struggling for a gig,
     did they know then, they would make it so big?

Imagine . . .
     thoughts of their first sights in the U.S.A.,
     all the screaming teen-agers held at bay.

Imagine . . .
     the Sixties: Flowers, Peace, Love for all,
     sit-ins in front of City Hall.

Imagine . . .
     what type of music would've changed us all,
     if it weren't for George, John, Ringo and Paul.

Deana M. Lo Galbo

DILEMMA

Have I traveled on this road before?
     Ah, yes I see the same stones
          and remember more.

I look around; I feel the pain
     that this road
          brings once again.

And, I can see beyond.
     There is a fork in the road
          and I have no choice but go on.

Although I walk slowly, what I
     have dreaded is here.
          I stand, look at the fork, and cry.

Standing here looking at the choices
     will not do. I have to go
          left or right and not listen to their voices.

I want to go left. No, I want to go right.
     Oh, I don't know what to do.
          I have to hurry lest I sleep tonight.

Going left would only bring more pain.
     So, I'll go the right way
          and pray I never come this way again.

Gina Marie Moss

DRUGS

Drugs can make you happy,
Drugs can make you sad,
Drugs can make you hurt yourself,
Or just make you mad.

Drugs may make you happy,
Drugs may make you sad,
But for sure it can make you hurt yourself,
And it will make you mad.

Drugs aren't something to get happy over,
But something you should get sad about,
Because when you realized your dreams are gone,
You'll want to quit but you can't.
Then you'll start to wonder where the happiness went,
Or what happened to the money for the rent.
Then you'll realize where it all went.

Drugs won't make you happy anymore,
Because drugs were the only way your messed-up life was spent.

Cindy Blevins

JESUS CHRIST

He came from above, He reached out in love,
Which was shown by the spirit in the form of a dove.
He came to stamp out hate and to boost men's
faith. He's got a gentle touch to show — He's there.
A touch to show He really cares.
A simple nudge to point the way, to keep us all
from going astray. A kind word, a simple story
all point to Him and show His glory.
A sacrifice to take our place, for sin and pain
this Lamb was slain. He rose again to make
it plain, that He alone is fit to reign.
Our priest, our king, our Savior, our Lord —
No one can possibly ask for more.

Lynn Jones

SHARING WITH YOU

In 1957, I was 14 and free
the adult strange ways
I couldn't see.

To be alone was easier than
persecution.
But I didn't choose drugs or
prostitution.

If any hope of my future to
know
was to learn and search for
the truth; will it show.

Your question may be why this
happened to me.
I say we were chosen in
the future to be
and to change the wrong
you so clearly see.

You'll need several things to
complete your task;
God, Love, Knowledge and
be kind to yourself.

You're not alone,
you but need to ask.

Bob Simpson

JACK FROST

When the trees have dropped their leaves,
And the ground is white with snow,
When the woods are still, and the glow
Of the stars is bright upon the meadows,
Then Jack Frost comes softly creeping —
Sneaking on tiptoes in the night.
With a palette and a brush
He paints coconuts on the trees.
My windows become forests of fern —
Magic places of white delight
For me to see.
Then just before the morning hush,
He takes his palette and his brush
And tiptoes back to Fairyland.

Lucille J. Conboy

MY BELOVED

Loving you was easy
Liking you was fun
Losing you was harder
Than anything I've done
Time has helped a little bit
But the pain is always there
Your smile, your glowing wit
The way you wore you hair
Such different looks upon that face
I loved so much so very long
If only there wasn't an empty space
Where only you should be
I'm thankful for the time we had
I've forgotten the days that were bad
I promised you that I'd be brave
But promises are hard to keep
I'll try again tomorrow
Now please Lord let me sleep.

Louise McPhail

GONE IS THE LIGHT

Our relatives and friends are so dear
With their love our lives function
Things seem to be so clear
We can see each junction
But when someone goes the light dies
A part of us falls away
Something within us cries
We want them to stay
But life is a revolving door
Coming and going we are
We constantly want more
As in the drunk at the bar
There are those we know only briefly
Others we hold on for life
We try to hold them tightly
But most are consumed with strife
We enter each other's lives for a while
Then we're gone
Never to rest for another mile
Just moving on.

David Devore

THANKSGIVING

Thanksgiving is just a special chance
For us to refreshingly begin anew
To think about things we've done
and those we plan to do.

A time for us to keep in touch
With old friends we hold dear
And join in Love with family
Thinking in hope of the coming year.

A time to firmly put aside
The distress that we have known
And count all joys and blessings
That are ours and ours alone.

A time to revive our favorite dreams
And start them on their way
To the wondrous fulfillment
That we hoped for . . . yesterday!

Most of all — a perfect time
To praise the Lord above
For thankful joys and blessings
of His Everlasting Love.

Susan K. Kichline

VISITING SNOWFLAKES

They arrived like an early snowfall
There long enough to touch you and melt away
Leaving echoes of laughter only children make
And the happiness it brings

Pauline Schwendinger

GEE, MISTER!

That skateboard flew
Around the corner
And met me, an old man,
Leaning on my stick.
It took my breath away
As well as my feet,
And down I tumbled.
Somehow the youngster
Spun his board
Back to me
With the formal grace
Of a prima ballerina.
Back on my feet —
Saying, ''Gee, Mister!
Here's your cane;
I'm awful sorry!''
''No harm done, son.''
A barrier drops.
I like the idea
Of a caring exchange
Between yesterday
And tomorrow.

Harry E. Beebe

SHE MOVES ME

As the air she moves me
psyche flying high
light of the eyes
life's dance an open gift
tender as a soul's kiss
remembering her eye its gleam
hopeful and shiny clean
rosy amber her colored dreams
reflecting back when new
spring leaves swayed in
a loving breeze shadows
painting your quiet face
the changing patterns of its smile
knowing her gentle strength
gives me reason to think
once she knew the feverish
grab of many a hellish day
gentle and kind-hearted
a fawn among the thorns
keen-eyed and sure-footed

Dawn Pittenger

CHILD OF THE UNIVERSE

I am a child of the universe
unbounded, free,
no labels heavy weighing
me, no backward glance,
nor downward pull
can thwart my upward flight.

Christine Bonner

IF I HAD KNOWN

If I had known you were going away
What would I have done that previous day?
I might have been unusually kind
   Perhaps I was
Then too, I would reaffirm my love
   I hope I did
There was a reason that bleak November day
Why I didn't know you were going away
Such a wonderful life we'd had together
Both good and bad like the changing weather
The piper was paid, the songs were sung,
Our sons grew up — then suddenly gone
With lovely families of their own
Through all the years your courage kept me going
Now there's only one thing that I'm knowing
The earth is warmer where you've lain
To gather the sun
To welcome the rain.

Louise McPhail

BAD KREUZNACH SPA

Take a walk on a tree-lined street beside the Nahe.
Pass great houses, fancy stores and kliniks.
Look at rich people strolling to get some air.
See middle-class people licking ice-cream cones.

There's a young clown —
Face painted red, white and blue.
There's a big legless man in a wheel chair,
Who looks and smiles like FDR.

Look up at the trees by the river.
When sun slant, waves and light
Are aligned just right
You'll see a mystic sight.

On the bottoms of the leaves,
Flickering in the fading yellow light,
Tiny images of boats and people
Are there for your delight.

Royston W. Donnelly

LETTER TO A DEPRESSED FRIEND

My friend, I know your pain,
And have felt it many times before
  In places deep within my soul
    That I never knew existed.

I understand your sadness,
  When tears well up from that hollow place inside your stomach
  And erupt in burning rivulets of anger and grief.

I have felt the heavy hand of hopelessness pressing me down
Until only death promised relief
  And no light shone anywhere
    No matter where I looked.

There were times when my world was so unbearable
I wanted to run away.
But I found solaces only temporary reprieves.

Some days were so long and so hard
I wondered how I got through them.
But I did (even despite myself)
  And you will too —
    I promise you that.

Mary E. Dyson

BEACH-BALL MOON

"Come play with me, bright beach-ball moon;
  Provide the night with gambol-fun,
  With jack-straw games and run-sheep-run;
  Cavort with me; be my balloon.

"Undrape the mantle, picayune,
  That hides the nightwing's garrison
  From light of day and sight of sun;
  Amuse, diffuse, ideas impugn."

"I'll play with you and be your friend,
  But beach-balls often do deflate,
  And then my shine may sublimate
  The merriment that you intend.

"If only I could comprehend,
  I'd send the world to consecrate."

Bud Christian

INTROSPECTIVE TIME

Introspective time is often silent,
  But the message is still clear.
  The mind divides and collides
    With times you've spent
    Separating and renovating
Life as fine and grand as it dictates.

Percussions sound as loud as drummers bang;
  The tympanum beats a different pace.
  The verse collates with chord and beat,
The programmed life sometimes adverse.

Choral swells may tell a tale,
  Evoke a tear, provide a smile.
Mind-silence oft relates its theme as well;
  The song is sung without a tongue.

Introspective time is often silent.
  Sans voice and word, yet sent
  Into mind and soul as though
Symphonic chords were struck and echo
In the chambers of rhapsodic memories.

Bud Christian

CLASSICAL SONNET
THE ETERNAL MUST

There is no doubt that somewhere I shall wake
  Once more, and as I open eager eyes
  I'll sense the azure glint of summer skies
Reflected from some distant mountain lake;
But when I rise again, I shall forsake
  The clutching fingers of those mortal ties
Which bind me now; for that in me which dies,
Is not the part which lives without a break.

That "I" goes on, ignoring death and birth,
  Observing with a gleam of rueful mirth
    The eons as they pass. Yes, I go on
Though constellations fade and turn to dust;
'Til earth and stars, and sun alike, are gone . . .
Yes, "I" go on and on because "I" must.

Barry Green

LOVE FOR THE BAD BOYS

Bad boys don't cry,
  Growing up fast only to have to endure
ultimate emotional pain, yet you'll never
see those bad boys cry, they just turn
their heads and walk away. They're victims
of political persecution, but yet those
bad boys don't cry. They're used for
stepping stones by the local police
for promotional reasons, but yet you'll
never see those bad boys cry, they just
turn their heads and walk away. They're
the everyday topic and victims of
community persecution by the so-called
just citizen, but yet all and all you'll
never see those bad boys cry, they just
turn their heads and walk away. But
all in all I have to confess that those
bad boys really do cry night and day

John J. Rivera, Sr.

EVENING

Evening — and a hush
has fallen;
It's quiet now;
So quiet
the smallest sound seems loud;
We can almost hear
spiders spinning their webs
in the cedar
by the front porch.

John Craig Carpenter

CAROUSEL MUSIC BOX

The music box plays "Carousel,"
The horse dances 'round and 'round,
With every spin of the platform's tin
Its hooves beat out the sound.

The old lady lies in the nursing home bed
Listening to "Carousel;"
The drumbeat of her heart thump-thumps
With the tune she knows so well.

In childhood days the merry-go-round
Was a ride of joys and thrills;
But the music box sounds ominous,
As the tune so slowly stills.

She, too, in her bed, winds down toward death,
As the music mirrors her fate;
And the carousel horse is out of breath,
And the end of the tune won't wait.

She doesn't fear the trailing notes,
Nor the slowing down, but then,
She longs to rewind her music box,
Mount up, and ride again.

Sheila Insley

BUTTERFLIES

I watched a butterfly today
  winging merrily on its way . . .

Fluttering in the summer air
  pausing briefly here and there.

How daintily it goes about its way
  on rainbow wings so bright and gay . . .
Such a pretty sight.

I wonder where butterflies go at night
  or when skies are not so bright?

Only on a summer's day
  do they appear and wend their way . . .

Pretty butterfly so fair and free . . .
  Won't you come and light on me?

Valerie Cummings

HERE COMES SUMMER

Summer's come — time for fun!
Robins singing, church bells ringing.
Berries ripening, flowers brightening.

Children running, jumping, hopping . . .
time for play, without stopping.

"School is out," hear them shout . . .

Skipping rope and bouncing balls
  Riding bikes and climbing walls.

Ice cream cones with
  chocolate sprills . . .
Lemonade and popsicles.

Rakes and hoes and garden tools
Bats and balls and swimming pools.

Summer's come, time for fun!

Valerie Cummings

ALLEY CAT

Skit, skat, old alley cat!
  Go away and don't come back!
Ragged ears and tattered fur . . .
Pussy cats are meant to purr.
All howl and growl you spit and spat
  Go away, you nasty cat!

Stalking by night . . .
Sleeping in my garden by day.

Now leave those birds alone
  Vamos, you stray!

Crouching by my garbage pail
I see you there, you skraggle tail.

Glaring at me with pleading eyes
Spare me of your mournful cries.

Old alley cat, so lean and keen

Oh, all right . . .
  I'll get some cream.

Valerie Cummings

THE QUEST

Once before a crowd I stood,
In this dream which my mind did impress.
I told of God's love, how I'd sought Him.
To find Him was my deepest quest.
As I told of His great wonders,
How He'd called me, and made me His own,
I was filled with the light of His presence,
And the power of Pentecost came down.

"Of physics I am supposed to be speaking,"
I said in my dream long ago,
"Of velocity, speed, weights and measures,
Electricity, light, rain and snow —
Our God made them all by His word.
It is of Him that I want you to know!
He is not to be sought in the ether,
Nor to be found in the far away sky,
But His presence will dwell now within us.
Don't wait for the sweet bye and bye."

Lauretta Williams

BETRAYAL

Her heart ached beyond endurance.
What could she say to him,
Her lover,
Whom she had betrayed?
She prayed that he would call,
And she waited by the phone.
Hours passed,
But the phone never rang.
Where was he?
What was he thinking?
Oh God,
How she wished she could change
  what she had done.

Helen G. Cornish

TRY IT!

One lovely ray of sunshine
— At the close of a stormy day —
Can erase the shock of the thunder,
Experienced along the way.

One moment of joyful laughter,
— Rippling through the air —
Can fill with — remembered — happiness,
A heart, burdened down with care.

One little word of love — in greeting —
— As you pass on a busy street —
Can lift a cloud of depression,
From a soul, in the clutches of defeat.

Joy S. Pearce

THE GREAT-GRANDMOTHER

She was known as a very wise woman —
They say wisdom comes with age, and grace.

Her life was not one of luxury,
It could be seen by the lines etched upon her face.

God gave to her twinkling gray eyes, a warm loving heart,
and open outstretched arms.

I can see the silver hair that she kept neatly tied in a bun,
I can hear her laughter, I can feel the love that she instilled
in each and every one.

Is time a fragment of reality — ?
Or is reality a fragment of time — ?

All the questions remain unanswered as to wrong or right . . .
Are all the dreams of ''could have been,'' out of reach and
out of sight . . . ?

Since she has been gone the world has grown colder, and colder.
With every passing day I become a little older.

I know though she is near to us and not far.
She is in heaven each night, up in the velvet sky,
She now is with God, she is one of His stars . . .

Monica M. DeMarinis

THE ROSE PETAL

Memories of a tropical night take me back,
To reveries of the past . . .
Memories which will forever linger and last . . .

The hot sands of weathered white,
An endless view of twinkling stars to light the balmy nights.
Clean, fresh scents of a thundering surf pound
the gentle, sloping shore.
I long to return to that ethereal paradise once more.

Magical memories of my sweet reveries grows, and grows,
Of the night you picked a petal from my blushing Red Rose,
Placed it in the nectar from which your tender lips
sipped, and tasted.
Not one precious moment we shared was misspent or wasted.

I still hear our laughter.
Voices of the palm trees sway in the warm breeze,
I still recall the graduated blues of the restless foamy sea.
Most of all, I see, the strength and storm in your
piercing dark eyes, a petal from a blushing Red Rose,
And stars in the velvet sky.

Memories of that tropical night, reveries of my past
Precious, treasured memories . . .
Forever to linger . . .
Forever to last . . .

Monica M. DeMarinis

AN ANSWERED PRAYER

A true friend, a treasured friend,
Is an answered prayer.
A gentle and compassionate heart which assures you,
She'll always be there.

A counselor, a confidant untold . . .
As beloved as the most precious of cherished gold.

God's gift to us is our life . . .
Filled with joy and happiness, pain and strife.

Somewhere along the individual path we journey upon,
A true friend we chance to meet . . .
A true friend we rely on . . .

No matter how this world forms and changes,
. . . from new to old,
A treasured friend . . . an answered prayer,
You will forever endear and behold . . .

Monica M. DeMarinis

ACROSS THE WATERWAY

The Golden Gate Bridge built during the depression,
Was the centerpiece of an outing that afternoon.
Going over this span, we had a walk,
Sightseeing much beyond the extension line.
George explained the history and background to us.
I was in awe seeing it hung as a hammock,
Between two towers suspended by cables.
Dazzling me on the stroll,
'Twas magnificent as a whole,
San Francisco, the City by the Bay.
Mary Elizabeth held a deep rose woolen shawl,
Around her head with beauty and grace,
A striking Prarie-like cameo she made,
Against the gentle winds.
We watched the surfers, yachts, that is to say,
Also the sailing boats from the other shores,
Seen from the bridge is a panorama so grand.
Upon returning on the same pedestrian side,
There! At the other way we noticed a pelican,
On a pier resting; truly this lovely web-footed bird.

Rose Mary Gallo

PHILOSOPHICALLY MINE

If only shadows did not appear!
God whispers His spirit is here;
In our earth is the farmer's touch
The lemon citrus tree in a tract growing much.
To suppose I had extensive years,
Or the power to relive this life!
Would I have drawn a different card?
Fate had its own reasons.
This is not to discount the good fortune.
A closely-knit family beloved.
Friends who mean a lot.
The grass is not greener on other parts;
Such circumstances that are dealt,
Can make a deep furrow.
There is time for all seasons,
Moreover the reminder to reap and fruitfully sow.
These oblique hints one must ignore,
And whatever there is in strife,
As I have God-given talents,
His hand has found me that place in the sun.

Rose Mary Gallo

A HELPING HAND

Will there come a time
  when the serious-minded,
  pleasure-loving segment
  of society outlaws TV news?

Oh! We should listen —
  solutions, even aid
  may be far beyond our means
  to secure and administer.

But the fact we know
  and care and are deeply troubled
  may be the ointment
  for the needed healing salve.

Those of us who take for granted
  fresh air and sunshine —
  love and laughter;
  shy away from unseemly comparisons.

Therein may lie our salvation.
  Arriving at a universal truce.
  Extending a helping hand.
  Refusing always to render judgment.

Irene Leach

IRENE LEONA LEACH. Born: Beeler, Kansas, 1-31-16; Married: Ephriam Densmore Leach, 11-15-36; Education: Three hours extension college, Creative writing, Graphoanalysis, 1977; Occupations: Newspaper worker, Volunteer church secretary; Memberships: Rebekahs, church group, EHU, farm social club; Awards: Third place for 'The World We Want After the War,' District Farm Bureau, Garden City, Kansas, 1943; Poetry: 'Jeweled Moments,' *American Poetry Anthology,* 1983; 'Daddy's Home,' *News Chronicle,* 1974; 'Good-Bye My Love,' *News Chronicle,* 1976; 'An Invitation,' church letter, 1978; 'Echoes,' church bulletin, 1979; Comments: *I like to write about about the good things of life: beauty, love, laughter; I think I have shared this enjoyment with the world. I have written a book-length true story of an intriguing plot with counterplots taking place in my life. For about five years I have searched for a publisher for* Haunted By A Good Deed.

ED

Ed is the backbone of our team.
He never wastes any precious steam
but watches for every winning gleam.

Now Ed's not much of a talking man
he just holds on to each choicer plan
and pushes it just as much as he can.

His running is fast and to the base
with tight control of time and space
he nearly always wins the race.

Some of the men just fool around
others are slow upon the mound.
But Ed is to the winning bound.

In everything he tries to do
he thinks of ways both old and new
and plays right loyal to his crew.

Whenever things are getting rough
and we have taken just enough,
then Ed steps up and calls the bluff.

Ruth E. Beckwith

LITTLE "DINO" FINALLY CAME!

Thoughts from Grandma

It was on St. Patrick's Day, that
  "little man" arrived!
Five lbs., 13 oz. in the morning
  at 3:25.

Dark hair like his Dad's, and his
  nose, too — he must confess.
Peach-fuzzed cheeks, but his eyes,
  "they look like my Tess!"

He's a tiny, pretty boy, and so
  precious, I must say!
Day and night, he'd be with me,
  if only I'd have my way!

The way he stretches, grins, and
  yawns so cute,
Just picture him, if you can, in his
  cap and baseball suit!

I prayed all along, he'd be healthy,
  complete, and neat.
God surely answered, because that
  "Little Man" is "Heaven Scented,"
  and, oh, so "sweet."

Juanita Joyce Avila

A PERFECT CHOICE

With a Mother's love — Mom B.

Once in a while a man comes along
Who knows just what to do
To make a woman feel real good.
That's what I see in you.

When a man can let his heart show
And not think it makes him weak
He's the very type of man
Women everywhere seek.

To know my daughter has you
Really lightens my load a lot
I want the very best for her
And that's exactly what she's got —

  In you.

Terry Ann Braaten

GROW OLD WITH ME

As friends
we formed the foundation
each day
we added more of ourselves —
our thoughts
our feelings
and with time
we grew.

Strengthened by hope
protected with trust
we created a solid relationship
from life's strongest emotion,
love.

We have built a special place
to share our commitment of life
together.

Rose Teresa Guyott-Avitia

MY KITCHEN

My kitchen is a homey place
In it we give grace
For the morn we are about to face
Hold tight to another day
As ahead it does lay
We bless the ones around our table and
From us apart
With the love in our heart.

My kitchen is a homey place
In it I give *God's grace*
For I am free
Just to be me
There are times a bird's song
Stays with me all day long
As I see him in a treetop high
Almost touching the sky.
My kitchen is a homey place
For in it I feel *God's* grace
At the close of another day
As I pause in silence to pray.

Jimmie Renee

TENDER MEMORIES RENDERED

Every nature of recalling the past,
That is, dwelling upon the yesterdays,
Are heartbeats anew,
Reflections above value,
Still remaining unshattered.
There are treats to be remembered;
These fascinating sights and everything,
A lovely restaurant with woodsy tables at the Fort,
Reading road maps to another journey's end.
Mother Nature's paint box coloring the scenery,
At the amusement park bells did ring.
The children's carousel,
Vintage railroad cars, planes and a missile,
Were not just for buffs to see.
Kinship wedding was on the list of things,
And as for plane-hopping to and fro,
Had us manipulating trips and reservations.
While glancing back at our pleasure's status quo,
To state, the happiest hours, memorable times.
It was for the three of us, most endearing.

Rose Mary Gallo

THE BRIDGE TO ALZHEIMER'S

There he stood before me, so happy and alive
He must have gotten something in his eye,
Or were those tears forming in his eyes?

Today he headed for his normal stroll, just as
He has for the past three years, strange, for today
He did not take his best friend Bow!

I am excited, it is a hot summer's night,
The kind that invites you to unleash your heart
He must have changed our favorite spot, for I
Found him lying, bundled between the blankets of wool.

There are invaders in this house; they are
Flashing their evidence in this man of mine.
He is the victim and I the observer.

These invaders are seducing him like that of a child
All he speaks of is a mother and of a father.

With the strength of a nation, I remember to
Remind him that it buttons in the front!
But, he does not hear me anyway.
Silently, reluctantly, I surrender, for you have
already taken him away.

Cindy L. Carlson

WITHOUT MOTHER'S LOVE

What kind of person would I be now; without ever having your love.
Without your tender care and understanding words.
Where would I be in this world without your helping hands;
Showing me how to create masterpieces from high fashion to fixing
    apple pie
To perfection.
I might be like Ms. Brown lost and alone.
No family who cares and no place to call her home.
She wanders from place to place, searching for someone to care.
I am forever blessed because of your love.

Phyllis M. Cumbie

LIFE

You are the planter and harvester of the heart.
You sow and reap the soul just as frost melts
When it is brushed by the morning sun.
All that is done is known from the start — and lost.

As I wander the earth beyond the misty world
Of the meadowlark where violet flowers fade,
Among dew-drenched dreams and bright prophecies
Forever eternal, and eternally stranded,
You are my master still.

You lead me down unfrequented paths,
Instilling your magic at every turn,
Borne on the wings of white doves,
Foraging, you express a silent calling.

Hold me gently as a babe in the womb
For you are all that I am,
And will ever be.

Ronald Russell Enders

THE VISION

Fair was the day for she was with me;
Not in the flesh or presence of touching,
But in spirit . . . a companion.
I felt her gentleness in everything.

Her voice was like the lyric poetry
Of the mountain stream —
Her soul soared in the breasts of the birds
In the sky's awning.

The wildflowers blushed at the mere thought
Of her smile,
Ancient trees bowed their heavy branches in reverence;
Her vision brought the sunshine to a bleak
And windswept world.

Love had risen above all that exists
And filled the universe with rapture and beauty —
I could not believe I was not in heaven . . .
Until I awoke and she had vanished.

Ronald Russell Enders

RONALD RUSSELL ENDERS. Born: Hartford, Connecticut, 9-13-52; Married: Nancy Messenger, 4-12-86; Education: University of Hartford, B.A., 1974; Syracuse University, M.A., 1978; Ph.D. candidate; Occupations: Teaching; Historical interpreter (Mark Twain Historical Society); American Automobile Association travel consultant; Memberships: Archeological Society; Other Writings: *Mirror of the Heart*, collection of poems; 26 fiction novels — histories, mysteries, occult, adventure; Comments: *When poetry becomes anything other than an illusion, it is no longer creation. My poetry reflects a release from the world of fiction which dominates my historical and other novels which I hope one day will reach the public for some real gourmet reading.*

IT HAPPENED TO ME

It happened to me
  I can't believe it's true
Could I really fall in love
  With someone like you

It happened to me
  Things are different somehow
And now I'll have someone
Lonely nights are over now

What a surprise to me
  It wasn't even suspected
That I would be the one
  You really and truly respected

It happened to me
  I can't believe it's true
Could I really fall in love
  With someone like you

Eldred L. Douglas

DOESN'T HURT AS MUCH

The time we had together I
will remember. I thought
we'd stay ''in love'' forever.

It was over before it started,
No explanation was given, we'd
just parted.

When you left, I thought I would die,
for many nights I even cried.

You went away as quickly as
you came. I don't even hate,
nor do I blame.

I couldn't go back to you.
It's hard to believe we're through.
Time has gone by and with it,
some strong feelings for you. So
now, it doesn't hurt as much
As it used to.

Dwayne Bailey

LONELINESS

Darkened days
  which pass by so slowly.
Not knowing if anyone cares.
Being tortured by thoughts
  of unhappiness.

No one to lean on.
No one to talk to.
No one there to wipe away my tears.

Facing my true enemy of life.
It is not hate,
  nor war, nor death.
Yet, it is almost
  as frightening.

It is:
  Loneliness.

Ellen Coates

ON MY OWN

Me providing all the needs
Taking care of a little girl
The cleaning and cooking, too
Make life a dizzy whirl.

Me to work and her to school
On the go at morn's first light
No time for playing games
It'll have to wait 'til night.

She and I are always together
Best friends all the way
Thanking God for each other
As we bow our heads to pray.

Juggling money and bills
Finding excitement in all we do
Always learning about ourselves
Seeing everything as brand new.

Hearing my girl's laughter ring,
She's happy as can be
Knowing her life is stable again
And her love grows for me.

Trisha M. Haydon

Evening cherry-blossoms:
Today also now belongs
  To the past.

Issa

ELUSIVE DREAMS

Sometimes I sit and reflect on my life
Going over the path of my being.
Wondering things far out of reach
Visions only for my seeing.

Knowing I'll never be wealthy
Yet, I have richness of the heart.
I can't give millions away
But love won't keep us apart.

My beauty won't win many crowns.
I feel it grows from deep inside.
You can see it in my thoughtfulness,
And my gentleness I do not hide.

My homelife will not be perfect
For hard times, I've dearly paid.
Memories and love I have now
And what I have, I would never trade.

When we are young we have dreams
Never realizing the changes we'll face.
Yet, we reach for all we want
Praying God will watch with grace.

Trisha M. Haydon

TAKEN BY THE NIGHT

Some people say that Death is hard,
And that he only shows disdain
For all the lives he sweeps away,
And that he never feels the pain.

Some people say that Death is cold,
That he enjoys catastrophe,
And when people grow meek and old,
That he only laughs carelessly.

Death is a grim star, that is true;
But when he strolls the evening sky,
He gazes softly at the blue
Wisps of the clouds as they float by,

And at the sun orange-glowing
Upon the end of its long flight,
He gently watches swallows fleeing
Swiftly across the moor, far from his sight.

Perhaps he wishes to be taken by the night,
So that he, too, may rest within eternal light.

Hugo Walter

THE WORLD IS NOTHING
IF NOT PRAYER

The world is nothing if not prayer;
Even as I sit along the sea,
I watch the silences portend
Haunting murmurs of eternity.

I fold my prayers from the sands
And from the softly scented spray,
And raise my hands up to the stars
Beyond the fragile whims of day.

Even as I watch the sea and wait,
I know that you, O Lord, are there;
The roaring waves may shape and shatter fate,
But the world is nothing if not prayer.

Hugo Walter

THE RED GLOW

The red glow lingers furtively
Behind the dark green trees;
The evening stalls against the sky
As the last sunlight flees.

Dark shadows slowly stream across
The pale-pink cloudy haze,
Which swells up from the silence lost
Among transfigured days.

Hugo Walter

THE STRIVE FOR ITS LIFE

Many times I saw an end to its use.
Each time, like a miracle, it got like new.

Then, there came a time when I heard a peculiar sound.
It seemed to struggle, like it was carrying its last bundle.

To the shop it went again.
The repairs seemed to have no end.

Finally, it was like new.
The miles in store were more than a few.

There was no longer any sign of auto trouble.
It got dressed with new tires and a new seat cover.

Everything was OK until the third day, when it got into a traffic jam.
From far and near all could hear when it got hit; it was loud and clear.

A monstrous vehicle in front led the line to suddenly halt.
An ambulance found no one hurt and left the scene to the police.

In evaluation, it was said: ''It is a total loss — the auto is dead.''
''It can't be,'' I said. ''It has new parts in it to live again.''

''Insurance is there, and it will live.''
But, the company said, ''This is all I give.''

The auto's age of a few years meant it got too old for such a debt.
The strive for its life had come to an end.

Frances D. Rosenthal

JEANIE

''Just call me Jeanie,'' she would say
To every guy who came her way
Her bisque-like skin on fragile bone
Did set the stage for amber, saucer eyes
That gleamed like sunlight inside the rays
Of curled lashes, so like the gold-brown hair
Around that angel face

When she pursed her lips to smile
Each one that caught her eye she could beguile
Now, when in reveries, our youth goes by
Though nearly forty years have passed, I still can see
My sister's lovely face and hear that sweet voice say
''Just call me Jeanie''

Pauline Schwendinger

RUBIES & SALT

He had found this ''child of the light''
She, whose value was ''that above rubies''
''Salt of the Earth,'' she said he was
They came to wed here in this bleak place
Where not even a dandelion dared grow.

The Countenance shone upon that place — that day
Kaleidoscopic images of color, much as a garden
Family, friends, laughter, delicious scents
This bleak place transformed
Their Eden.

Here they wed, these shy children, Solomon & Dorothy
Lips quivering as they said their vows
Promising to honor each other
To live by God's laws
Fifty years ago today.

Pauline Schwendinger

SO IT GOES

A man has dreams; however, it seems
The time will never come
When he can follow that star, no matter how far it leads.

Night turns to day and they both slip away
Still he waits for the perfect time,
Knowing what to do but afraid to pursue his needs.

Marching to the drumbeat
Dancing to a tuneless tune
Following advice and meaningless direction
So it goes!

I'll soon see the day when I'll cut away,
He says with a weary smile.
I'll kick up my heels and learn how it feels to live.

First, work must be done, there are miles left to run
And, then, I'll be free at last.
But that's a mistake, the world's born to take, not give.

Waiting for a dream world
Seeing life through someone else's eyes
Living with delusion and self-deception
So it goes!

Jo A. Perlberg

THE QUICK PICK-UP

An allegory

The quick pick-up, might seem a pretty sight;
A new used-car, reflecting neon light.
Yet evening flash, exposed to morning rays
Shows shines as shades; turns rainbow hues to grays.

To those in heat, used-cars look pretty good,
But boys beware — a look below the hood
Might signify, a car that's seen its share
Of dusty roads that seem to go nowhere.

The wise appraiser, checks his credit line
For confidence, before he goes to sign
The documents, which might affect his life;
A faulty car, is like a faithless wife.

Used-car buyers: take heed upon this warning,
Or else you might wake oily in the morning.

James Scileppi

MOTHER

She's faced so many hard times through all her life; yet her eyes never showed fear.
When you look into them you would be surrounded by her love.
She kept me so surprised, by always giving freely from her heart.
Her love will never leave me; no one can take it away.
Let her forever know that I love her.
Let her know no one can ever take her place in my life.
Let me keep making her proud.
For with my love, respect for others and good deeds is how
I keep showing her I love her still.
Our love is unison like the sun and the sky.
The bond of love between my mother and I shall forever last all time.

Phyllis M. Cumbie

TIME FLIES

Let's talk about the future
In veiled and rosy hues.
Let's walk across the meadow
In the lazy morning dew.

Let's talk of former pleasures
Of gentle morning smiles.
Let's walk o'er sandy beaches and
Kiss a little while.

Let's talk on inane subjects,
Don't give too much away.
Let's walk and I'll pretend you'll miss me
When you go away.

I'll don a mask of self-defense,
That I may pass this rigid test.
No pleas of endless love, no tears,
Just tender words to calm my fears.

Let's walk! Let's talk!
Let's tell each other lies.
Time runs, Time races, Time flies . . .
It's time my love to say good-bye.

C. K. Pancoast

THE ART OF BEING

Ours is the ability to find happiness
   through the simple art of being. A
   creature bound by language, I strive
   to name all that my senses experience,
   but, alas, I cannot for fear of
   jeopardizing the simplicity from which
   these emotions are generated lies
   foremost in my mind.
Thus, it must suffice to say that being
   with you constitutes being fully me.

Stephanie A. Kepner

MY QUEST IN LIFE

My quest in life,
Is to reach for the sky,
To rise above the trees so high.

To roam the earth alive and free.
To be the best that I can be.

To follow the light,
Of a radiant star.
To continue to follow,
No matter how far.

To float on a wave,
The way a leaf does.
To share with our world,
Forever, my love.

John Albert Biasetti

AND TIME WILL BUILD

And time will build,
On what we hold dear.
And hope will guide us,
Every day, every year.

And day will extend,
our tranquil night.
And our future will plan,
for things that might.

And love from heart,
will flow to see.
To act on ways,
Our life should be.

John Albert Biasetti

WEDDING SONG —
TO MY DAUGHTER

Now comes the time to stretch the heart,
for love will turn into a stone
when the heart shrinks to itself alone.

Now comes a life that's set apart
from all the world that went before —
a greener field, a wider shore.

On this glad day, reach out and cry:
''This is my love, for whom I'll live and die!''
In this bright hour, lift up your voice,
and tell each other how your souls rejoice!

Then leave the altar, keep the fire,
and burn the message in your minds:
Life's not for Self alone designed!

So, never, in your spirits, stand apart:
Now comes the time to stretch the heart!

Hal Barrett

A LOVE

A love
so bright
yet so compassionate
mixed with emotions
the feeling exploding
like a bomb, bursting
into flames, like
firecrackers falling
from the sky.
A love
so tender.

Loramor

FAMILY ALBUM

Faded pages of our photo album
Stained with tears and deckled with time,
Tell the story of our life together
The story of your life and mine.

We stood close together, acting as one,
And cherished each day as it came;
Committed ourselves to making it good
Then year after year did the same.

In the days we were raising the children
There were triumphs as well as some strife,
But we blamed not a soul for the trouble
Picked up and got on with our life.

Tattered corners of this fine old album
Reminiscent of places and time
Enhance all the pages, yellowed with love,
The love which remains yours and mine.

As we reprise our commitment together
Soar with the eagles as long as we last;
Do you see clear . . . the anticipation . . .
Or the memories made of our past?

Jacqueline Rowe Gonzalez

REACH DEEP, MY FRIEND

Reach deep within your heart, my friend,
And seek the treasure there;
Precious thoughts and memories
You tucked away with care.

Take each treasure, one by one,
And stroke it with your mind;
Each facet is a precious jewel
You must reach deep to find.

Your youthful escapades — remember
How they shaped your life;
The teen-age years; the busy years;
The sweetness and the strife.

Remember friends from long ago;
Recall their loving faces;
Return in fondest memory
To old familiar places.

Then, when you have touched each one,
And held it to your heart;
Let it nestle there in warmth;
No longer kept apart.

Delphine LeDoux

WHEN YOU TOUCHED ME

when you touched me
why did I run
dissolving quickly
into a disappearing sunset
only to reappear
as the thunder
that engulfed you
never ceasing to rain
into your precious soul

Sylvia Ann Murray

SOLITUDE

Allow me a moment that I might embrace —
      The dark soul the silent thought follows,

Alone is not lonely; there's no one to face —
      No one dwells in the mind's lonely hollows.

Alone in a landscape that's softened by rain —
      No sharp lines — no contrasts — no thinking,

No passionate sun to shed light on my pain —
      Just an island that's silently sinking.

There's no time; the cosmos fade back to a cell —
      All motion dissolves into matter,

In truth, Heaven's only the flipside of Hell —
      Whose borders are ready to shatter.

Enclasp me in chains, so at least I might dream —
      Of a freedom that's never existed;

How lucky the slave in whose eyes it must seem —
      Freedom's somewhere but somehow he missed it.

Alas, if I might in my mind lie alone —
      In my dark universe left to brood,

There's really just one person living — just one —

      Alone in his own solitude.

James Scileppi

NINE MILE FOREVER

Written in 1918

I know a place that's not far away
It's very lonesome I've heard some say,
But there is none so dear to my heart
And from Nine Mile I hope that I never depart.

Dances, oh yes! and picnics too, oh, my!
I can hardly wait until the Fourth of July.

It took so long to get the bunch together
But they never stay home because of the weather.
Rain or sunshine, windy or lots of snow,
Don't you ever think that this bunch won't go.

Just to prove that we started the New Year right,
We went to Potomac and danced all night.
Fourteen of us, all in one big sleigh
And we laughed and sang all of the way.

We were slow in getting started this spring,
But at last we'll make these old hills ring
With the joy and gladness that we bring today,
And it shall last forever and a day.

Viola J. Smith

WHAT DOES GOD SUPPOSE

Strife, famine, pestilence, and death,
From our first gasp to our last breath,
What does God suppose makes life worth living,
The fearing, the daring, the taking and the giving?

From first remembrance, there were slights,
Suspicions, accusations, arguments, and fights.
There was confusion, delusion, frustration,
Pointless learning and enigmatic illustration.

The obstacles were many, the gates were few
More storms than lulls, more frost than dew.
Where were the lakes and ponds and meadows,
Where were the elms and palms and willows?

All those hopes, those plans, those dreams,
That seemed always to tear at the seams,
All those ideals, morals, and teachings,
All a waste of time, empty preachings.

The ephemeral success, the fleeting friend,
The departing lover, the unfulfilled end,
The lonely sigh, and even lonelier cry,
Till the day I die, I'll be asking God why.

J. D. Edgar

JOHN DELBERT EDGAR. Born: Salineville, Ohio, 4-6-44; Single; Education: Merlington High School, Alliance, Ohio; Malone College, Canton, Ohio; Occupation: Writer; Themes: *Religion and philosophy; politics and economy; often combining drama and comedy.*

TO DWELL IN THE MARIGOLD'S SPELL

Oh strain melancholy fears — strain to rip asunder ropes
That entwine, shackles and pinchers that hurt and confine,
Forever shall a deceitful breast and ruby-sculpted lips
  fall short of tranquility's doorstep — or an evening blessed —
For the mistress of love has set my heart on a lofty peak
  beyond your cruel and unladylike jests.
No more can warmth elude this once cold, cold chest
  for there was a stormy night, a time
When pleasure was bereaved of sight and sorrow,
The true reaper, scythed my past joys
  and stacked them in bundles three
Until (to my everlasting delight!) Love's errant messenger
  found the labyrinth leading to this sinner's heart
And planted a kiss on sleeping care,
Sweet care that had dined on a corpse's shell —
To arouse the spirit of docile passions —
  that flit hither and thither
In yonder garden of midsummer gold;
And now a million joyous deeds on diaphanous wings
Suck ambrosia that can be found only in our dreams.

Lonnie Bailey

THE CIRCUS AM COMIN'

The circus am comin' to town, yeah, man!
The circus am comin' to town!
With lions and tigers and ellyphants,
And acrobats in their skin-tight pants!
The calliope, and the bears that dance!
The circus am comin' to town!

Gonna buy me a ticket and see the show!
Yeah, man! Off to the circus I go!
With hotdogs and peanuts I'm goin' to stuff!
And cotton candy — I can't get enough!
If I gets sick, well, that's jes' tough!
'Cause the circus am comin' to town!

Delphine LeDoux

AN ODE TO THE SAFETY-PIN

Don't know the original intent
For the use of the oddly bent
Safety-pin.
There it is in plain display,
On most dressers array
The safety-pin.
When a button you lose,
You need not sing the blues
The things come in every size.
They aren't too unsightly to the eyes
Those safety-pins.
There are so many things they do,
So convenient for us too,
The safety-pin.
I'd like to know the one
Who had so much fun
Making the safety-pin.

Josephine S. Brown

MY LOVE MY HOPE

Flames of love forever burneth
From God love came, it shall returneth
Unto this land. He gave us life
The Holy flame of love has no strife.

The body is God's harp. He hears
Our strands of love
He sees our lighthouse from above
I'll follow on and on day by day
Before the falling of the way.

I'll keep my songs of praise burning
In that holy flame of yearning
Until he comes to hear his voice proclaim
I know I'll live again, and hear
that sweet refrain.

Grace M. Stuffle

SOUL SEARCH

Here I am alone again
With just my thoughts and dreams,
It matters not what I want
Or wish for so it seems.
My heart cries out with loneliness
Yet no one ventures near,
I seem to drive them all away
Or fill them full of fear.
I have much love and only want
To give it all away,
I wish someone to love me
Enough to want to stay.
I have my faults and strong points
A dreamer I must be,
To look up to the stars
And wish for one for me.
I know there's someone out there
Waiting to be found,
My thoughts are ever searching
Quietly around.

Bobbi C. Nunley

AUTUMN

Autumn is Spring, blossomed into
    mature womanhood
She has nurtured the seed, assured in harvest,
    for all nature's good.
Let us rejoice, her pregnancy past, she's
    decked out in gala array.
She generously gives us of her yield,
    before she goes on her way.

Lorene Shoptaw Mydlach

AWFUL MEMORY

Would you believe I am grateful
When my memory is sometimes poor,
As when I think too long, in vain
Of starving folk, of wars, of pain?
It's bad enough to read the news
Then watch T.V., to hear reviews.
The haunting, anguished, wretched poor,
I close my eyes, but there they are,
The homeless living on the streets,
Drugs and crime, and gangs compete,
Racial tension, Klu Klux Klan,
Man's inhumanity to man. Oh God!

I try each day, here where I live
To do my best, to help and give,
And I've been asked if I feel guilt
For the comforts around me built.
It's plain to see I've cause to cheer
That my ancestors landed here.
But oh that I could end my fear!

Lois M. Smith Triplitt

TEARS END

I may have cried when I was three
To keep a bonnet off from me.
I probably cried when I was seven
My dolls got broken — all of them.
I know I cried when just sixteen
With Mama's slap, for questioning
Why she left home, and took not me.
I cried so hard at twenty-two
When my first love told me we're through.
I pounded earth at twenty-three
Crying for the remnant there.
Then, twenty-nine and W. W. II
And miles of crosses . . . I mourned with you.
At forty-five I lost my friend
Both parents and husband . . .
I stand and feel, but do not cry
All out of tears, and I know why
Older peoples' eyes are dry.

Lois M. Smith Triplitt

LOIS M. SMITH-TRIPLITT. Born: Bay City, Michigan, 4-9-17; Married: Ivvion Darrel Triplitt, 5-27-50, widowed; Education: Battle Creek College, Michigan, 1935-38; University of Michigan, Lansing, B.S., 1939; University of Southern California, R.N., 1952; University of California at Los Angeles, M.S., 1959-60; Occupations: Physical education instructor; Registered nurse; Nursing instructor; Consultant, nursing education; Poetry: 'Dumb Wooden Bird,' 1975; 'Indelible Day,' 1980; 'Enchanted Room,' 1981; 'Head On,' 1984; 'I'd Know You in the Dark,' 1986; Themes: *My reality, relationships, and the mystery of life.*

THE CALL

The call
that I had waited for
came today
and
the voice
that I had waited for
spoke to me
but
the words
that I had waited for
were not spoken.

Barbara G. Brown

IMAGINATION CALLS

Sitting on a dock
Late one starlight night
A lady appeared before me
I was blinded by her light
She said, young man
Are you a spokesman for your race
I said, I'm not in office
But I'll listen to what you say
    "Many masters have come & gone
    To give you all a break
    Give you precepts to live by
    And where your treasures lie
    But you all worshiped greed
    And man-made seeds
    It's only brought you misery
    Can't you see"

I knew she said a mouthful
Enough for me I know
Then she faded away
Like a wet piece of snow
I sat and wondered all night long
On what I could do
Just live in the Light of Spirit
The way it wants us to . . .

Gerard St. Croix

OUR SCHOLARLY
CONTINENCE

The arts of love of learned friends
found the Nightingale came back to them
back from Beth-el-run returning with song
crisping the morning starrise and chill
but warming the heart so sure in law
that wisdom is grey by our lover's fall
O lover's joy, lover's bliss
who fought the battle for our last kiss
you yield me your breast
I share my folly with yours
and dedicate our love to such Peace
that God may make all of us mature

Todd Zenas Graham

YOU'RE THE ONLY ONE

Hey brainwashed girl
Chose your world
You're the only one
Slowly turn your eyes away
Blind to what they've done
Can faith stand strong
When you're not allowed to choose
Can you bear the setting suns
You're the only one

An angry boy
His answers to destroy
You're the only one
Watched his world dragged away
Now holds none
Can faith stand strong
Accepting she can learn to lose
Left to face the rising suns
You're the only one . . .

Gino Cozzolino

AMAZING SACRIFICE

I thought the sacrifice too great
The Lord required of me —
I cried, and sobbed, and prayed, and pled
And said it must not be.

An acquiescent Lord I found,
Who led me gently through —
A maze of sorrow, grief and woe
And shared my wreath of rue.

He showed me Wonders of His Grace
And Love so kind and sweet
And never once spoke sacrifice
'Til I forgot, complete!

And then so tenderly 'twas done,
My heart so gently broken,
My Cross, my Crown, my Peace, my Joy
Were dearly interwoven.

The sacrifice I though so great
Became amazing Story,
The sweet and tender path of Love,
The Path that leads to Glory!

Georgia Bray

AT CHURCH

She read a passage from
the Old Testament, on Sunday.
The parishioners listened with attention
especially the younger men.
The minister beamed, so pleased.
He didn't notice that
under a transparent blouse
she was braless and firm.

Emma J. Blanch

CONSCIENCE

Conscience? What a master you are
    to cope with.
You are the substance of every emotion
    from love to hate,
From joy to sorrow, from faith to fear.
A good conscience? — forever striving
    toward perfection.
A bad conscience? — withdrawn always fearful,
Almost impossible to reconcile.

Conscience? Why do you rule
    with such power,
Never letting up for an hour?
When — the conscience is good we wonder
    if it's justified?
When — the conscience is bad we wonder
    if it can be rectified?
Thus who has a conscience quiet,
One at ease both day and night?

Virgie McCoy Sammons

INSTANT

When I glanced at you,
you were walking slowly —
As if you dared frantic time
to confiscate your existence.

Yet my observation
was merely a glimpse:
Our familiar gazes
never truly see
that of us which is
instead of
that which appears to be.

So be brave
and live now:
Replica reruns occur
only on television.

Betty Kormick

LOOKING AT LIFE

Life is like a still pond.
Most of what we see is merely
A reflection from the surface of the pond.

So seldom do we really look beyond
Those superficial images
Into the treasures that lie
In the depths of that pond.

You, my love, have drawn me
Through Nature's mirror
To share "precious moments"
That few may hope to find.

But now I find that if I reach out again
I disturb the still pond's surface
And the treasures that lie beyond
Are blurred . . . and gone.

Thank God for my mind
For only there can I reach back
Without disturbing my own still pond
And find you — forever!

Kathleen L. Spicher

TO BE REMEMBERED

Remember me!
How sad the words, how hopeful.
To be remembered the greatest gift.
To be forgotten the cruelest blow.

Remember me!
A plea, an entreaty, a longing.
An acknowledgement of worth.
The proof of love or friendship.

Remember me!
Everyone's wish, everyone's hope.
Which will it be we wonder.
Which, gift or blow?

Lin Yarges

SCIENCE WILL OVERCOME

Devout flesh shivering, quivering in the impatient jaws of death —
Unhinge your merciless maw to release the dawn's catch
  for therein abides a heathen soul:
Pure and simple and untempered by the Christian's fire
Or chastised and then baptized in the bloody
              pages of gospel.
Yet . . . Imagined and superstitious sins have tormented . . .
  and brought joy to a trillion ignorant woes
For there is a savageness in a Christian's breast
  that outroars the most thunderous storm,
that makes iron-willed men tremble and seek a safer path,
a fearsome thing that travels both day and night,
using a cloak of righteousness it has shattered
and brought mightier civilizations to their knees
  than any arrogant Ozymandias ever dreamt about!
The grandeur of the human intellect:
        has created both beauty and shame,
Sublime love and a wisdom that forever seeks a new house;
So when this eon-old illusion meets modern day reason,
Then and *only then* can a functional paradise come about!

Lonnie Bailey

THE POWER OF THE SPOKEN WORD

Such horrendous and outrageously delivered rote,
Rusty and unpleasant notes . . . Heed they my fondest desire?
Nay, for master I be not (though bend their will I try).
For words ply me, body and soul, and I am theirs to command.
House not ''I'' they in this frame? Yet they mold me like clay,
An unwilling instrument that has little to say
      but can only timidly obey.
When in vernal May this villainous throat they did play,
Such alien discord no one can readily vouchsafe
For from these sorcerous lips first did drip
        sweet honeydew
Meant only to awaken spring's eternal renewal
In a fair maiden's cheeks (a maiden that had mistaken me for a fool).
    Speak! Hide the angelic voice no more I thought to say.
Let gently fly the blue-tailed lark, which has robbed me of my heart.
Then in crept lust (vile deceiver and conceiver to Mephistophele's gain).
Raining perfidy and curse until she fled the sun's burning blush.
Their rage has been spent — like stillborn babes they lie —
But that Storm of Words will return; thus the ecstasy
And the agony ever since man and woman learned to converse!

Lonnie Bailey

LONNIE DALE BAILEY. Born: Pineville, West Virginia; Single; Education: Glen Rogers High School, 1976; Occupation: Soldier in regular army; Poetry: 'Scientific Nirvana,' *American Poetry Anthology,* 1986; 'The Human Abstract II,'' *North American Poetry Review,* 1987; 'Judgement Day,' 1986; 'Once Lost,' *Best New Poets of 1986,* 1987; 'The Sleeper Awakes,' *Images Reaching Out,* 1987; Other Writings: *God — Myth or Fact?,* book, non-fiction, Carlton Press, 1985; Comments: *Science and my belief that there is a scientific explanation for the creation of the universe is always my predominant theme. My work owes its inspirational origins to Isaac Asimov, Carl Sagan, Paul Davies, William Shakespeare, William Blake, Shelley, and H. P. Lovecraft.*

TAPESTRY OF LOVE

Take my hand, walk with me.
Beauty is everywhere.
See sunlight shining through the trees.
On their branches, birds give you a singing heart.
Like tears, grass sparkles with morning dew.
Silently flowers bloom, gentle rain makes them grow.
Years, like seasons, are sometime sunny or stormy,
For each of us must face their days.
As stars light up the night,
Someone is there with tender care.
Somewhere, in the darkest part on earth, love is found.
So fear not, never alone your heart must feel.
Along the way, someone always will be.

Monique Sirois

A TEACHER'S CRY

I have been called to a mission. My mission field
lies not on any foreign shore, but within America's
doors. Our children are crying, our people are
sighing for God our Redeemer and Guide.
The cry is for love (God) and peace from the
dove (Holy Spirit), but hearts are covered by the
glove of deception (Satan).
The need is great indeed, the *word* we need to
heed and follow His creed, but someone needs
to plant the seed. The harvest is great, the
laborers are few, help me Lord to be one
of your crew, that you might use this
weak vessel imperfect as it is, to help
mold the workers of tomorrow — the
spiritual leaders — oh Lord *help* that I might
stop some of the crying, the endless sighing,
small souls from dying . . .

Lynn Jones

ANGRY MEN

Unnecessary bouts fought outside rings
Families' broken hearts and tears that sting

Swamps in deserted lands
Never to touch their mother's hand

Prayer's going up to their only hope
Words ''I love you'' in last letters wrote

Shattered many young men dreams
His future falling apart at the seams

Sorrow of nations — memories still kept
The boys who are gone — mothers that wept

I'm sorry for all of you, something I've never known
Pain of empty rooms and streets they once roamed

I see your grief but not for long
The sun still shines it wasn't gone

Don't be sad, no painful moans
This is life all in its own

This is life all in its own

Margo Singleton

COUNTRY DEER

One wintry year,
One tree in the
    country
Was shelter to
    the deer;
But the time
    to flee
Was coming soon,
For the hunter's
    rifle . . . !
(A-glint by the
    moon) . . .
Was no mere trifle
To the wayward
    deer . . .
And they could
    not stifle
Their new-found
    fear;
And it was so suddenly
    then, they fled . . . !
That a shudder struck
    the tree . . . !
That turned the blossoms
    red . . . red as red can be . . . !
And still — there they
    bloom,
Red blossoms, each year!
As if over the tomb
Of the one fallen deer.

Kirchen Weismueller

REMINISCENCE TO TINA

There isn't any
        past I know,
More pleasant
        than your face
        aglow,
With sudden rapture,
That could capture
Either friend or foe.
When sitting here
        with moonlight
        drink,
I often see your face
        and think . . .
''It isn't easy when
        we go
Our separate paths . . .
This I know,''
And missing you
The way I do,
Can turn to wraths . . .
That burn so slow,
That even time
Cannot break free,
From anger's cold indignity . . . !

Kirchen Weismueller

ANGEL OF MERCY

Oh, *Angel of Mercy*
thy invisible wings
enable thy great flight
through the bleak villages
of disillusionment
created by mankind.
Soothe all unspoken pain
deep within our spirit.
Erase all poverty
from every spirit.
Remove all hidden tears
from our precious mirrors.
Sing a beautiful song
in our eternal soul.
Allow true forgiveness
in our innermost thoughts.
Stop all unhappiness
in our encumbered soul.
Renewed excitement shall
spring forth from life and love!

Frances Dawson Harris

THE WIND

The wind gently sighs.
She causes the grass to sway,
the leaves to rustle.

Her breathing becomes labored.
She now breathes in short gasps.
In her frustration and anger,
she tears at the grass,
and whips at the trees.

The clouds annoyed strike out,
but she is too swift.
They strike instead a tree,
ending its torture.
They weep from sorrow and despair.

With her anger increased,
she feels her power,
feels her need to destroy.
She throws things,
bends and breaks all in her path — till . . .

Her anger dies.
She breathes easier, and then . . .
the calm once more.

Lin Yarges

BLINDNESS

They say love is blind
and that must be true
because I couldn't see
the hurt that lay ahead
if I broke all the rules
and loved you.

Barbara G. Brown

LIVING ALONE

I cannot seem to settle down
    to living just for me . . .
The hours once spent in busy joy
    with all my family
Have now become a vacuum,
    no voices do I hear
Except the television din
    of strangers, no one dear.
No one needs me 'round the house,
    no hurts to kiss away,
No hungry man requiring meals
    on which I'd spent the day.
No slamming doors, no scampering feet
    to interrupt my busy mind . . .
In fact, the busyness I used to love
    is now a boring grind.
I cook for me . . . I eat with me . . .
    and wonder what it's for . . .
Letters I write contain no news,
    for nothing happens anymore.
Silence settles in my ears,
    the empty days drag by,
Except for Christ who strengthens me,
    I'd just give up and die.

Leona Budzine

MEMORIES

Memories, memories
All of them patterns of
Woven-webbed tapestries
Caught in the purple cloud
Truth of our dreams;
Simmering gracefully,
Hung in infinity's
Gold-girded shroud.

Bringing us music of
Silver-gleamed laughter wrought,
Curled in some distant day,
Here to be sought;
Fragile as breath of bees,
Strong as the wind on seas,
Dimpling sweet memories
Now to be caught!

John P. Clark

CHANCE

You say you have dreams to make come true
and set goals yet to reach.
There's no time, no room for another
to enter into your life.
But there may be a someone
who can share those dreams with you,
and help bear the struggle of the climb.
One who'll cheer you on during the good,
one who'll hold you steady during the rough.
There may be a person who cares enough
to want to go the distance with you,
wants to be by your side, helping.
And if given the chance,
you may find that I am that someone.

Debi Buettner

SUNSET COMMUNITY CLUB

Oh what fun it is when we all get together,
And talk about the crops or cuss the weather.
The ladies sit around sharing the latest gossip
The men swap hunting and fishing stories and more.
Smoke fills the air and a few cuss words too,
Then they shout, "Hey there, when do we eat?"

The men and ladies are not the only ones there
The noise of the children fills the air
With their games and shouts of glee.
Happy as all country folks should be,
Then over the noise again we will hear,
"Hey there, hurry up, we want to eat."

It may be a picnic or we may dance until three
It's a special event for everyone and free.
About midnight the ladies go to the kitchen
and prepare the food and the tables are loaded.
The folks hurry to get in line close by, now we hear.
"Hurray! At last the food is here, let's eat."

Viola J. Smith

THOSE COUNTRY GINKS

We are just a bunch of country ginks
From away out west, where the hop-toads wink.
There's just exactly ten of us
And we all came down in a jitney bus.
We are as jolly as can be
And won't go home until half past three,
Then we'll start our cars and drive away
And the Potomac folks will hear us say,
"Home we will go, a jolly bunch
Thanks for the fun and midnight lunch."

Viola J. Smith

VIOLA JEMISON SMITH. Born: Missoula, Montana, 4-23-03; Married: R. Wendell Smith (deceased); Education: One room country school, eighth grade; Occupations: Housewife, Mother; Comments: *I grew up on a ranch in Montana from 1903 to 1925 and we had to make our own entertainment. I wrote poems of our good times and in the past twenty years I have written stories of those "good old days." We didn't have electricity, radios, television or even telephones.*

MY TRUE MATE

When I hear the politicians state their mission,
And argue pro and con on earthly fate,
I would not change from mine to their position,
For I am Lori's love and Lori's own true mate.
And when I see the athletes in perfect pure condition,
The ones that do excel, the ones that are first rate,
I would not change from mine to their position,
For I am Lori's love and Lori's own true mate.
And when I watch the actors bring their roles to full fruition,
From *The Music Man* to lovely *Kiss Me Kate,*
I would not change from mine to their position,
For I am Lori's love and Lori's own true mate.
And when I see writers pregnant with ambition,
Discussing love and life and death and fate,
I would not change from mine to their position,
For I am Lori's love and Lori's own true mate.

William J. Galbraith, Jr.

PLAGIARISM

I sit with my pen poised at two o'clock in the morning.
Maybe genius will strike me without warning,
And I will write another Shakespeare sonnet,
Or perhaps fry eggs with bacon on it.
Is that a pun of Shakespeare's imitator,
Or was the Bard himself invention of some perpetrator?
The drift of this ode, I'm sorry to say, has wandered far off to sea,
I meant to tell of my Lori love and how much she means to me.
Yes poems are made by fools like me, but my love with Lori was
        meant to be.
Here I am plagiarizing Kilmer and his love of a tree,
His love of a tree, that's not right for me.
I want a woman of flesh and of blood,
Whose passion unleashed comes out like a flood,
I've found that dear woman in my Lori love,
That rarest of all creatures, the purest white dove.

William J. Galbraith, Jr.

A TRIBUTE TO GRANDPA

Sometimes for reasons which can't be surmised, a child who
doesn't have all that he requires, such as love that is
needed or rules to be heeded, grows wise like a sage;
way beyond his limited age.
He learns by experience, until he is old. He doesn't believe
anything he is told, until he has tested it and becomes
sold. The lessons he's learned, he holds and is true to.
There is no way in which he can be swayed. He is
strong in work or play, his enemies are easily slayed
and he is one who knows how to pray.
When he becomes a man there are none who can stand
quite as tall as he or be quite as free, as he appears
to be or go on quite as many ridiculous sprees.
He's someone to look up to and ask for advice, for
he knows something about almost every device.
That's why that it makes me so terribly sad and
feel so very bad to see someone so tall and
strong and true to his convictions to be suddenly
afflicted. I hate to see someone so honest and
true, revert to a child before his days are through,
but this too is something no one can choose. It's just
another little bruise along life's cruise.

Lynn Jones

TO THE VIRGINS, TO MAKE MUCH OF TIME

Gather ye rosebuds while ye may,
  Old time is still a-flying;
And this same flower that smiles today
  Tomorrow will be dying.

The glorious lamp of heaven, the sun,
  The higher he's a-getting,
The sooner will his race be run,
  And nearer he's to setting.

That age is best which is the first,
  When youth and blood are warmer;
But being spent, the worse, and worst
  Times still succeed the former.

Then be not coy, but use your time,
  And, while ye may, go marry;
For, having lost but once your prime,
  You may forever tarry.

Robert Herrick

I've spent all my life
in a fantasy world,
creating my one true love
that would last forever.
I never tried to reach life
in the real world,
where my true love
should have been.
I am sorry I hurt you,
sorry I broke your heart,
but you are not the one
that should be with me.
I tried to tell you gently,
but the words came too slow,
and I let harsher words escape
that should not have been heard.
Locked inside my mind,
in a perfect world just for me,
I never learned to feel your pain
until the deed was done.

Serena L. Elkins

ANGELS

Angels come in and go out my head
Angels come in and go out my head
Angels come in and go out my head
Some are bad angels some are good angels
You ask me do I know whose angels they are
Well the bad angels I know are bad
Angels come in and go out my head
Angels come in and go out my head
Angels come in and go out my head
And I pray that they're all good angels

Mark Wilhelmi

HOW LONG IS FOREVER

I found a box of dreams today
of you and me and yesterday;
Some lilacs dried up like my heart,
Love letters, each vows from the start,
''I love you now and forever,''
But when was forever over?

The locket that you gave to me;
Some pictures taken by the tree
Where our initials are entwined,
And still there are the words you carved
''I love you now and forever,''
But when was forever over?

I took that box of dreams of mine,
Even my faded valentine,
And buried it beside our tree.
Good-bye my love and good-bye tree.
I cried and slowly walked away,
And forever ended today.

Jeanne Louise Morgan

BOYS!

Muddy footprints on the floor,
  Jelly handmarks on the door;
A trail of marbles down the hall,
  Crayola artwork on the wall,
  A jillion glasses in the sink —
And not a moment's time to think.
Chills and bills and western drama,
Cokes and pokes and cries for mama!
  Dogs and fish and birds to feed,
A stray little kitten — eight eyes that plead;
  Bandaged toes and sunburned noses,
  Indian forts where I planted roses —
  Tears, with laughter tumbling after,
  Echoing roof and trembling rafter;
  A hundred thousand broken toys —
  Add these up and you have boys . . .

But there isn't one that would be sold
  For a million tons of minted gold!

Jeanne Louise Morgan

JEANNE LOUISE MORGAN. Born: Los Angeles County, California, 11-24-22; Married: Edward B. Morgan, 9-1-39; Occupation: Songwriter; Awards: 23 poetry awards, 3 Golden Poet awards, 1985-87; 3 Song awards; Poetry: 'No Lullaby,' *American Poetry Anthology,* 1986; 'Teardrops,' 1987; 'Hour of Benediction,' 'Friend,' 1985; 'Robbie's Whimsical World,' 1986; Comments: *Poets walk with rainbows.*

DUPLICITIES OF NOCTURNES

Fairytale dreamlands fade into melody
As daggers pierce the colored landscape
Glass shatters as fragile reality splatters
Spilling on pavements in multicolored oils
Staining forever the duplicities of Nocturnes

Louise Witte

AGING LOVE

Like a shadow in a shade tree
My love awaits its chance;
The coming of a partner
With whom it soon will dance,
Enveloping with youthful joy —
As the oyster does its pearl —
A sweetly-scented bosom . . .
Caressing some sweet girl!

Yet, alas! The shade tree withers
And loses all its shade,
Thus leaving Love quite naked,
Awaiting its fair maid!
And, openly revealed now,
Love has no place to hide,
For, like the withered shade tree,
Its passion, too, has died!

Now all that's left is longing
For some shadow now long gone . . .
Oh, Love, what *now* awaits me
As life continues on?

Craig E. Burgess

POUNDING WIND

Wind pounding against my window pane
Driving me to seek out my fame
I should never complain
I'm the only one to blame
It would be a shame
If I were to remain silent
I'm here to proclaim
I will win the game
Even though, I'm only a dame
I tell you now, as I exclaim
I'll prove to myself, I can write, and reclaim
To win more than just a prize
I'll not compromise, I'll sell what I write, and
Always do it right . . . !

Debra L. Ayres

MEMORIES' FOOTSTEPS

Memories' footsteps
Will always run through my mind,
as I turn each page
of the old photo album.
Precious moments lost in time . . .

Jeanne Louise Morgan

FAIR IS MY LOVE

Fair is my love, but not so fair as fickle;
Mild as a dove, but neither true nor trusty;
Brighter than glass, and yet, as glass is, brittle;
Softer than wax, and yet, as iron, rusty:
　A lily pale, with damask dye to grace her;
　Non fairer, nor none falser to deface her.

Her lips to mine how often hath she joinéd,
Between each kiss her oaths of true love swearing!
How many tales to please me hath she coinéd,
Dreading my love, the loss whereof still fearing!
　Yet in the midst of all her pure protestings,
　Her faith, her oaths, her tears, and all were jestings.

She burned with love, as straw with fire flameth;
She burned out love, as soon as straw out-burneth;
She framed the love, and yet she foiled the framing;
She bade love last, and yet she fell a-turning.
　Was this a lover, or a lecher whether?
　Bad in the best, though excellent in neither.

William Shakespeare

CACHED TREASURE

The scenoric trees guarding the house across the street
　merge into low overhanging rain clouds.
I am lucky to be alive for this appreciation study
　of Mother Earth's bountiful loveliness.

Revealing my seventy-year age causes disbelief
　and credibility questions to my supreme delight.
My thin veil of composure suffers losses
　with the returning styles of half a century past.

A dress with a dropped to the hip line and pleated skirt
　will bring the inner comment —
I wore such a dress as a young woman and loved it.
　I swaggered. Certain my trim hips and slender legs
were showing to a definite advantage.

Materials, styles, uneven hems — black stockings and shoes
　are vivid reminders of another day.
The opinion was shared throughout the sisterhood —
　Black color on our legs and feet insured a win.

Yes. All seventy of the years are nestled somewhere in my
　　　　　　　　　　mind.
　Should the need arise, I must draw readily from the cached
　　　　　　　　　　treasure
for strength, wisdom and comfort.

Irene Leach

MEMORIES

I will not think of sorrows anymore
I told myself and more than half-believed;
I will not feel the sorrow as before.
I will forget that I have ever grieved
At being half-remembered, laughed at, scorned.
I will forget. My mind cannot accept
The sorrows after which my heart has mourned.
I thought to think on lovely things — the green
Of rain-sweet meadows, pale blue flowers, gold
Glowing sparks of fireflies, soft sounds unseen.
But memory comes again — my hands grow cold.
I am filled with sudden anguish, and my cheeks are wet,
For the heart remembers what the mind forgets.

Dorothy H. Elliott

WICHITA

Wichita, Kansas will do you right proud.
This little princess of the midwestern plains
has derived all the needed culture
for impressive fame and fortune.

The skyrocketing growth of two hundred and eighty
thousand inhabitants was a World War II aftermath.
A safe little niche for airplane manufacturing
was provided with this inland hideaway.

We defy your hierarchy for selectiveness
of menial worth. We use the right fork.
We say the right words with proper intonations.
Our apparel and attitudes pass muster.

Mingle with us freely, the greats
and the nearly greats of the universe.
For on our doorstep easy access abounds
to all the finest cultures — in Wichita, Kansas.

Irene Leach

ROAD TO NOWHERE

　As I travel forward down the street of human existence I know
the future is just one step ahead while the past is always behind
me.

　When I look back I can see people struggling through life
often trapped in a web of poverty — lonely societies filled with
despair and suffering.

　I notice those who allow their lives to be run by their
sexuality — lust has traveled this road more than love. I can
see man kill man in the name of God, justice, and greed; this is
a path that kindness and compassion have rarely crossed.

　I look carefully but I cannot see a perfect society with true
justice and fairness for everyone. I fail to see a world where
all its members are considered to belong to the same
race — human beings.

　What I see saddens me but I alone cannot make the road turn,
I must keep walking. As I travel forward down the street of
human existence I know that I am on a road to nowhere.

Robert W. Hummel, Jr.

WE ALL CAN LOVE

Beneath the hard crust of every life
There is a sprawling sweet stream.
Its fragrance can soothe every strife,
And spread sweet peace on every troubled dream.

We all can love and stay always true
Yet some do not show this cream.
But a picket, a spear from the sky's calm blue,
Can strike every heart's hard crust, to reveal this soothing stream.

O sweet stream, flowing so strong,
Break forth out of every heart retrieved.
With strength and zest undo all wrong,
Until all the sobbing oppressed, from aching hurts are relieved.

Where is love? oh joy's sweet clue!
Spring forth in the strength of your unending patience.
With arms so caring and devotion so true,
Unshackle and remold, by your sweetness, our limping conscience.

Ify Onyemaobim

THE LEAN YEARS

The lush golden fields of life
  Bow low before the winds of grief
The warmth of golden laughter . . . of song
  Is hushed, drowned in sorrow's storm
For these are the grim hours of lean years.

Sorrow, like a cruel relentless knife
  Slashes at the naked heart . . . no relief.
In the hours of anguish seconds are so long
  Then too fleeting and gone is the silent form.
Such are the grim hours of lean years.

Helen Bolten

HELEN BOLTEN. Born: Jersey City, New Jersey, 12-16-13; Widowed, mother, grandmother, and great-grandmother; Poetry: 'A True Friend,' *American Poetry Anthology, Volume VI, Number 1;* 'Regrets,' *Best New Poets of 1986; The Naked Clay,* volume of poetry and prose, Schneider Press, Inc.; Other Writings: ''Whitehall Hotel,'' writing about VIPs at a hotel, *New York Social Spectator, Palm Beach Life,* magazines, 1946-48; ''Your Corner and Mine,'' by-line newspaper column, *Wildwood Leader,* 1942; *Blood In Our Streets,* novel; Comments: *To me, poetry is music in words, expressions of the soul. It captures the lilt of music and happy hearts. There should be no lost note or sound for lack of understanding. Each word simple and understandable though its rhythm stirs the deepest soul and strikes a God-like majesty, for beauty is the heritage of man. Thus my writings are geared to this premise.*

AMBITION

There came a moment in my life,
when I left England's shores.
I learned the customs of where I went,
and studied all its laws.

Quickly finding if I had stayed at home
I could have been content, I learned in
many different ways,
what life really meant.

If living in a civilized land, which
country does not matter.
Don't expect that anywhere,
things are handed on a platter.

Strive to live a decent life,
no matter where you are;
and by the wayside you'll not fall,
when reaching for a star.

Edgar Lubin

JOSHUA

I look expecting to see you
But know it cannot be,
For you have had to leave us
Your face no more to see.

I feel a hollowed emptiness
Emotions run so high,
It happened oh, so quickly,
No time to say good-bye.

I listen to hear your voice
Echoing through the air,
And though I strain to hear it
I know it is not there.

I taste the years I've cried
As they fall upon my cheek,
You my guardian, protector
So gentle, mild and meek.

I search but do not see you
There are no words to say,
And as I look about me
I know you've gone away.

Victoria D. Callis

SOCIETY'S MONUMENT

I took a piece of formless clay,
and worked to fashion it to my will;
I'd hoped my efforts would someday,
be a monument to my skill.

But there came an artist with another plan,
whose hands were strong and bold;
and dissolved my monument like shifting sand,
then poured it into a common mold.

I came again after years had passed,
to see if any influence of me he bore;
but the bit of clay had hardened fast;
and I could change it . . . nevermore!

Frank Favaro

I WANT TO

I want to . . .
  see you,
    but my eyes are shut.
  talk to you,
    but I cannot speak.
  hold you,
    but I cannot have you.
  walk with you,
    but my legs are tied.
  laugh with you,
    but my smile is gone.
  love you,
    but I cannot have you.

Linda S. Schmitt

STARLIGHT

As I gaze into the night
I discern a ray of light
From a distant twinkling star
Reaching us from the sky above.
When I begin to think
Of how long it has taken this beam
To travel through the vastness of space
Millions of light years away
It strikes one with awe
Making me feel humble and small.

Betty L. Lee

BETTY LAY HUA LEE. Born: Singapore; Single; Education: University of Santo Tomas, B.S., Pharmacy, 1980; University of Windsor, M.S., Clinical Chemistry, 1983; Occupations: Pharmacist, Clinical Chemist; Membership: Student Member of the Asian Pharmaceutical Society; Awards: Consolation prize in National Short Story Writing Contest, Singapore, 1976, ''The Courage to Live''; Poetry: 'Science and Man,' *American Poetry Anthology, Vol. VI, No. 5,* 1986; Themes: *Science, nature & astronomy;* Comments: *I like to write about the mysteries of time & space.*

MASKS

I dream with my eyes open
I dream about you
I am keeping my eyes open
Because I can't have you
This love I feel is an echo
Of what I could really feel
Mostly respect, a touch of pride
A fierce desire tempered cool

A matter of ethics
Saves me from myself
Tender-eyed looks
Remain a deep secret
Maybe you sense this feeling
If so, you don't show it
A sense of propriety
Keeps the mask serene

And masks are what we are playing
If a day comes when the truth shows
That day is unseen by the poet
And so she will remain content

Linnea Caldeen

THE CALL OF THE WHIPPOORWILL

As I knelt at my window sill;
I watched as darkness fell, and all was still.
Watching a falling star, hoping my wish it would fulfill;
My eyes widened at the sound of an owl, whooo whooo, and a
    loud shrill.
Once again all was quiet and still.
My imagination ran wild, could this be a bobcat, lynx, or bear
    going for the kill?
My brother sat down beside me at the window sill;
''What's that?'' he asked. Shhh — be still . . .
Just then we heard it again, the lonely sound of the whippoorwill.
She called, whip-poor-will, whip-poor-will;
''Isn't that a beautiful sound?'' I asked.
It sounds far away, maybe yonder hill.
''What's its name?'' he asked.
Do you hear the sound it makes? That's its name Whippoorwill.
As we crawled back into bed, and all was still,
She called out once more, whip-poor-will, whip-poor-will,
    whip-poor-will.

Robert O. Pugh

OH DEATH

Oh Death I came close to you a time or two,
  Yet from your grip of shadows I flew.
Although I know of life, that one day it'll be through,
  Yet it is life I must pursue.
For me, tho' I watch, it's true,
  One day you'll come for me too;
But from the Lord in the end you'll receive your due.
  Oh Death tho' you reign, here is a clue;
One day you'll understand it when you die too.
  Oh Death tho' the clouds may gather and brew,
And from my body my breath you drew,
  Yet it is life that I will pursue.

Robert O. Pugh

THE MIDDLE ROOM AND
THE RED-EYED BEADY BONE

Dedicated to my best friend, Jimmy.
Based on a tale told by his grandmother, Vera Perkins.

When I was little there was a middle room,
At my grandmother's house, you see.
She said if I wasn't as good as can be,
That the Red-eyed Beady Bone would get me.
''Do you hear that noise out there?
It's the Red-eyed Beady Bone.''
I'd better be good, I thought, so Beady Bone would let me alone.
I ain't scared, I said, I don't care!
Just then, behind the door, eyes were staring with a glare!
I whispered, ''Beady Bone, let me alone.
I've been a good boy, can't you see,
Why do you want to pick on me?''
As I grew up, I respected this room,
Where Red-eyed Beady Bone cast his gloom.
One day I asked my grandmother, you see,
''What's with this tale you told me?''
''Well, you see this tale I made up about the middle room,
Although the story cast its gloom,
It was the sound of the bobwhite that gave Red-eyed Beady Bone his
    voice, you see,
And I never had to spank you; ole Red-eyed Beady Bone made you
    mind for me.''

Robert O. Pugh

1984
ONE YEAR AGO TODAY, DAD

Also written for my mom, and my
brothers and sisters

Though pain and suffering showed in your face
Your wisdom and knowledge remain in our grace.

You are loved, needed, and thought of each day
Seems only yesterday you went away.

The hot summer eve our Lord took you to rest
We must accept, it was for the best.

You did what you could, and taught us so much,
You gave us words and wisdom that seemed to touch
Our hearts and thoughts in some form or such.

You gave us strength beyond compare
You suffered more than any human could bear.

We love you, Dad, and our words cannot express
In all the world, you were the best.

    Our Love Forever,
    Your wife, children, and grandchildren

Juanita Joyce Avila

DIE! DIE! DIE!

I, alone, watched neon lights of an old saloon
with the green door on the corner of the building
next to the Royal Theatre where celebrities appeared.
Beside the Chinese laundry, below our coldwater flat,
hung a foot-high sign *Stop — Eat — Smile* touchable
from the fire escape.
I sat on a wide window seat facing the street that led to
the park when weather allowed, riding my tricycle,
piano lessons twenty-five cents an hour, or listened
to a concertina as passengers embarked a ferry boat.
A *New Year* began as snow fell on the icy intersection.
No heat, eating cold Campbells, going to school . . .
I, alone, jumped up and down in Buster Browns shouting:
Die! Die! Die! as she hovered between life and death.
March brought a call from Uncle Ed, who puffed Lucky Strikes
as he drove us 200 miles to Grandpa's country home.
Drinking hot broth, hot tea with Old GrandDad and surrounded
by hot bricks, fever of one hundred and ten broke.
It's June . . . she awoke to new surroundings.

Frances Wilk Hobbs

ALMOST SPRING

'Twas along toward the end of the month of March;
Daffodils nodded their heads in the breeze.
The buds on the trees matured, exploded;
And in their places were tiny, new leaves.

A soft green carpet was silently creeping,
Over the lawns, the meadows and hills;
But during the night, the treacherous wind,
Cruel and deceptive, grew savage and chill.

Now while we wait, impatient, expectant,
Spring naps 'neath a glistening blanket of white.
Her magic spell so harshly interrupted,
She'll swiftly complete when the time is right.

Helen King Gurley

REVERIE

Sunset in sunken mist,
Soft wind a-blowing,
What canst thou bring to me,
From God unfolding?
Or have the evening stars,
Deepset in loneliness,
Forbade they speaking yet
Of God's great onliness?

Ah, could mortals such as we,
Searching for eternity,
Find answers in a distant star,
Or would it better be by far,
To peer within a simple rose,
And there, if but for a moment, see
The Face of God,
And immortality.

Laurene G. Charlebois

LAURENE G. CHARLEBOIS. Born: Houston, Minnesota, 8-18-13; Married: Leo A. Charlebois, 1940, now widow; Education: St. Olaf College, Northfield, Minnesota, Magna Cum Laude, B.A.; Metropolitan Business College; American Institute of Banking; Occupation; Escrow officer, Security Pacific National Bank, now retired; Memberships: St. Olaf Honors Society, St. Olaf Alumni Association, Business & Professional Women's Club; Awards: College scholarships; Poetry: 'To My Daughter and To My Son,' *American Poetry Anthology, Vol. II,* 1983; 'Eternal Love,' *Hearts on Fire, Vol. II,* 1985; 'House of Memories,' 1985; 'To Stacey, A Tribute,' *Best New Poets of 1986;* Comments: *I find that in writing I can express my deep feelings of pride and love for my country, my home, my family, and my God.*

THE BOOB TUBE

As before the telly, I take my seat,
My eyelids fall, bringing my defeat.
Ghostly figures glide across the screen,
And fade into a world unseen,
As sleep, sweet sleep, invades the scene,
My program slips away,
I am not undone, it will return, a rerun.

Laura McDonald

SEA GLASS

Gently, gently, under the sea
Prisms of color, lights on the water
Shells lie scattered, white sands shattered
Sea glass glowing, Soft wind blowing
   Sea Glass

Through the waves now, do you see
Jeweled rainbows, all for me
Colors shining, silver lining
Soft wave riding, Sea glass hiding
   Sea Glass

Soft smooth bed, ever sifting,
Smells of sunlight, ever drifting
Stars of fire, sparkling higher
Bright flames growing, Sea Glass glowing
   Sea Glass

Susan Toppel

TWO HEARTS BROKEN

Two hearts broken
Turn away from love
In search of some token
Of help from above
Two souls lonely
Pass quietly in the night
And find each other
In dawn's early light
Two minds confused
Looking for the same
Become instant players
In another world's game
Two bodies in need
Ignite forgotten fires
And lose themselves
In wild night's desires
Two hearts together
But only for awhile
For new love's broken
By life's many miles

Gunga

MILK AND CHRISTMAS MOUSE

I was talking to Popcorn, pussy cat,
Her big golden cat's eyes
Staring at mine, ''and what would
this proud Popcorn cat wish for Christmas?''
She jumped into my lap;
Oh, that meow has got to be a
Fat, furry, field mouse.

Twenty-fifth of December, early morning,
Popcorn critter scratching patio door.
My, oh my, what a nice find,
That's one field mouse that won't be a fuss,
Or a-fluffing up attic dust.
Guess I'd better fetch a bowl of milk
As a chaser for your Christmas mouse.

P-u-r-r-, p-u-r-r . . . burp!

Janet L. Reid

ECHO

It is done
Over! Finished!
I feel — a oneness . . . now
Alone, empty, numb.

You are gone
The space you filled
Behind my breast
Aching, painful, cold.

Memories — return unbidden
Warmth at odd moments.
Filling me, thoughts of you,
An echo of our love,

Sweetheart,
I will never
Understand
Why . . .
This has to be.

Jeanie G. Doran

Life promotes life
Promotes vibrant, dazzling colors
To announce and dedicate
The coming dawn.
Death promotes death
Promotes dark and frightening shadows
To denounce and to despair
The breaking day.

Christine A. Pitt

HATE

Open the circumference of your vision,
Let not venom guide your each decision.
Hate leaves a blot upon the soul
Strangling the intentioned spirit's goal.

Poison emanates in concentric waves,
Touches all it meets and then enslaves
With winding tendrils bound so tight
We cannot break them though try we might.

Where hate's unleashed upon our world,
With banner streaming and unfurled,
Violence desensitizes every heart,
Conquers minds and drives us all apart.

Respond with love to seek the death of hate,
So this disease cannot contaminate
Or spread its vile and toxic leer,
For it's the favored child of fear.

Helen L. Gillies

LOVE IS A DECISION

Love is a decision so live for today, some de-
ranged person said that, so don't you obey.
    Love's forever, not just for today, throughout the
future, my love's going to stay.
    Love is a decision when two people care, love is
endless, it's always there.
    Love lasts forever, not just for today, the hurt of
separation is the price love will pay.
    Love is so funny. You never know, sometimes you
have a love that you have to let go.
    Sometimes you let go, even though it hurts you
so, so it's good to let it go.
    In everything they say, love is fair, in most cases
that's true, when two people care.
    Love is a decision when two people care, it never
fades away like a blaring flare.

Darrin D. De Guia

IN THE BEGINNING

In the groves of melancholy was a little
Spring called Mirth which bubbled up among
The rocks of chance, discouragement. The brittle
Boughs of sadness spread and were behung
With garlands, leaf-green gladness, and the lichens
Of despair. There was a mixture there
In the old wood of dark and light, a glen
All tangled with a web called Everywhere.
The light among the trees was joy; it sparkled
Fresh and bright. And Druids danced, a breath
Of hope, in dresses of delight; they whirled
Till frenzy seized them and danced them into death.
    Black clouds obscured the heavens and darkened all the sky;
    And in that long, long darkness, the little spring went dry.

Dorothy H. Elliott

SPECIAL FRIEND

As we sat and talked, we shared some time,
 You told me of your life, I spoke of mine.
 I felt at ease, and in a world I did not know,
 And with a woman so beautiful, so kind, so . . .

I enjoy your conversation, I enjoy your company,
 I enjoy you, and the smiles you present to me.
 Come and hold me, Ellen, in a very close embrace,
 We'll feel each other out, with a touch, with a taste.

I have dreamed about you, I have hoped to have you near,
 Long before we met, you were in my arms, my dear.
 Come sit by my side, show me that you care,
 Be my special friend, we'll be a special pair.

I'll be a new experience, memories of me you'll keep.
 I hope you think of me constantly, even when you sleep.
 As I hold you in my arms and look deep into your eyes,
 I feel my emotions, or is it love in disguise?

Alphanzo Townsend

MY LOVE

Your presence brings my mind to a halt,
 To rest my eyes upon your beauty,
  You are a fantasy I have finally caught,
  A dream that has become reality.

I must share with you a love I possess.
 Strong love and feelings I must give,
  Because my feelings for you, I must confess,
  Are a part of the life I live.

What would we be without our dreams,
 Without scent in the air, and the flow of streams?
  What would we do without thoughts of fantasies,
  Letting our minds float like leaves from trees.

Time is making me feel, and now I see,
 What I'm experiencing, and what you mean to me.
  Your feelings for me have shown what it takes,
  And proved that life is not full of past mistakes.

Alphanzo Townsend

MOTHER OF MINE

On that day you were to die,
 I was not there to say
        good-bye.
No one knows the depth of sorrow,
 That still lingers on through each
        tomorrow.
You expressed your love in many ways,
 things you would do, the things you
        would say.
I still see you standing at the door,
 as you did so often, many times
        before.
Thirteen years now, since we've been apart,
 thirteen long years, but always in
        my heart.
Would I could reach out, touch your face,
 dear Mother, there's no one who can take
        your place.
Because of your love, I must dry the tears,
 plant ''hope'' in my heart in place of
        fears.
If love has the power to heal the soul,
 May ''love'' fill my heart and heaven be
        my goal.
And may God's love enfold you, dearest Mother
 of mine, now and forever, and for all
        time.

Mildred M. Brookins

WEDDING BELLS A-RINGING

Just as God made, ''Eve,'' from a rib that was taken from, ''Adam,''
So was the name, ''Stephanie,'' taken from the name, ''Stephen.''

Just as Saul's name was later changed to ''Paul,''
Your last name will be changed too!

Just as ''Adam'' and ''Eve'' loved their God and one another
''Stephanie'' and ''Paul,'' may you love your God and one another too!

Just as ''Paul'' had a life-changing experience on the way to Damascus
''Stephanie'' and ''Paul,'' may you also experience
    God's love and grace always!

Tonie Marie Roberson

CRYSTAL GAZING

A simple lesson can be learned
To open the future's door,
It's merely this, my eager friend —
Two and two make four.

Certain things give certain results
As sure as the sun brings day,
Know what is right, do what is right,
Blessed will be your way.

The great law of Cause and Effect
Works for every soul.
Be your best, apply yourself
And you will reach your goal.

Lillian Hugh Lawson

LILLIAN HUGH LAWSON. Born: Alabama, 12-10-1893 on grandfather's plantation; Orphaned at the age of 7, reared in the private school of four paternal aunts in LaGrange, Georgia; Education: LaGrange College, Georgia Teachers' College, Columbia University, College of Religious Science, College of Divine Metaphysics, American School of Naturopathy, N.D., 1924; Occupation: Columnist for *The Sun,* of Pine Hills, Florida; Awards: Silver Poet Award, 1986; Music orchestrated by G. Schirmer, New York; Ceramic work exhibited at World's Fair, 1939; Writings: *Working on manuscript of my own poems, prayers and proverbs that I shall leave as my legacy to this world;* Comments: *Poetry is a potent means of sharing inspiration and courage in the journey through this life.*

GOD'S IN CONTROL

Give God your soul
He's in control
He'll dry your tears
And calm your fears

You can be sure
God's love is pure
He knows we try
And hears us cry

God does love you
He loves me too
He gives us hope
And helps us cope

God's own power
Soon will tower
And o'er our pain
Our Lord shall reign.

Sally Brocato

PRISONERS OF WAR

The men in their fighting suits
Waiting to attack
Never knowing what will be
When they turn their backs.

Many will never return
Never seeing home
Gone from the earth forever
Their duty is to roam.

For all must finish duty
Things were left undone
'Cause murder was committed
The spirits now must run.

Can they ever live in peace
Wanting to return
Immortally as a saint
Yet in fire they will burn.

Is it fair that they should live
As a bug in hell
'Cause for their country they fought, and
For their country they fell.

Denise Marie Bromley

The waves crashing on the rocks
Retreating when they're through
Rolling forward; pulling back
Resembling me and you.

How much I have given you
How much I've taken back
The ocean gives me meaning
My soul it never lacks.

I give the waves my body
My soul to ever flow
As if I'll live forever
Under the sun I'll grow.

Denise Marie Bromley

THE BUILDINGS

To some the church of Christ
   may be,
A place of bondage for the
   free.

A place of freedom for
   those bound,
Is that building where saints
   are found.

For others it's a place to grow,
To some a place our Lord to know.

For some a place old wounds to heal,
For others clean clothes, and a meal.

The buildings where God's people meet,
To some are bad, to others sweet.

Sally Brocato

SERVE FOR HIM

Jesus does love
Soft like a dove
Those who adore
Him more and more.

Who let Christ in
To kill their sin
Who don't shut up
About the cup.

Of blood Christ shed
To save the dead
It wasn't fair
Yet Christ hung there.

So serve for Him
Who took your sin
And let folks know
God loves them so.

Sally Brocato

NOT A WORD

Not a word was needed
We laughed — the joke was ours
Eyes filled with tears — together
Not a word was needed.

Not a word was spoken
The change Time brought
Made the past bad fiction
Not a word was spoken, not one word.
But the strength of my hearing has grown.

Peggy Claude

TREASURES BORROWED

I had a tree
But it was not mine.
I watched the sea
And enjoyed sunshine.

I had a friend
But she went away;
She was pretend,
Or so they would say.

I had a wife
But now she's gone.
She was my life,
But that was all wrong.

I had a son
But he was not mine.
We would have fun,
When I had the time.

I had sorrow
When I found the truth;
Treasures borrowed
They've been since my youth.

Salvatore L. Bruno

GO MY CHILD IN PEACE

She washed His feet with her tears, and dried them with her hair.
He saw her shame and helplessness; He saw her deep despair.
Christ knew her love for Him that day, as she humbly washed His feet.
Then the Master said, ''Thy sins forgiv'n, go My child in peace.''

He said, ''I'll follow Thee, my Lord, and walk close by Your side.''
But as the day was ending, three times, the Lord, denied.
Christ showed His love for him that day, as the teardrops
    stained His face.
Then the Master said, ''Thy sins forgiv'n, go My child in peace.''

I walked upon the dark road of sin, and could not humble be.
Then Jesus saw my broken life, and called,
    ''Come back, My child, to Me.''
Christ showed His love for me that day, when He said I died for thee.
Then I heard the blessed Master say, ''Go My child in peace.''

Thy sins forgiv'n, go in peace, the Master said one day.
Thy sins forgiv'n, go in peace: He says the same today.

Eleanor S. Follmer

HAPPY BIRTHDAY, MOTHER

Today we honor you, as through the years,
Your life has seen many joys, hopes, sorrows, tears.
But our Lord's been good to you, my friend;
And we know He'll be with you until the end.

We take this day to honor you,
For all the wonderful things you do;
The many heartaches you help us mend,
And the many hours in our service spend.

For the lessons you teach us well;
For the love and devotion to those who dwell,
Within your home and where love could reach;
We thank you, friend, for a life so sweet.

We, in tribute to your beautiful life,
Wish you many happy returns of the day;
And may your remaining years be sweet,
Until we all meet again at the Savior's feet.

Eleanor S. Follmer

ALL IS NOTHING

From corruption to innocence;
from innocence to corruption.

Hungering, seeking fulfillment, yet never satisfied.
In the midst of experiencing all
  there lies emptiness,
The quality of non-existence.
The realm of nothing.
Thirsty, moist lips crave
  attention, delicate tissues exposed,
  filled with juice, waiting for the final release —
Death
  opens up the grave, like quicksand
  the earth
  is never full; never satiated.

Malinda M. Stephens

YEEEEEEEEE HA!

From the Derek Jacobi Collection

Nearly three months in a bloody, black world
Nearly three months of flailing in the dark as if I were Helen Keller
Nearly three months of frustration compounded by human beings who
    just didn't care enough
Nearly three months with the simplest view blocked, the most natural
    joy untasted

Then without warning one morning YEEEEEEEEE HA!
Suddenly, the one clear eye that I have brought everything into view.
Who was it that said childhood must eventually pass?
I'm alive again experiencing an old world giving birth to the new!

In the windows there are cloths to look at and food to imagine
    the taste of
The colors of people's shoes and the garage doors of their houses
The hue in children's hair and the sparkle in their eyes —
    sidewalks, streets, cars!
Spider webs, crickets, grass, trees, hills, the sky, the whole earth!

Oh Boy! *Oh Boy! I can't get enough!*
Come in world, come in! There's nothing like the way you filter through!

The Barefoot Poet

LIKE THE WAYS OF LIFE

The summer breeze caresses the leaves
as it goes on its way, changeable
''Like the Ways of Life.''
The gold and red leaves of autumn
with their splendor will surrender
to the winds of fall and drop to the ground
''Like the Ways of Life.''
Soon winter's white blanket with sparkling snow
will bury the leaves of autumn
and they will disappear until another year.
Then the leaves will reappear to brighten our days
''Like the Ways of Life.''
The seasons are ours to share
with love and care.
The seasons are changeable
''Like the Ways of Life.''

Eleanor M. McKissick

LIFE

Life can be everything to me.
Sometimes life can be good and life can be bad.
Life can make me happy and life can make me sad.
While some people work all day, others play all day.
I go on living each day that comes my way,
doing the best that I can do, hoping someday
I will find time to play, too, more than I do.
While we give and take from life whatever comes our way,
I hope that fate will smile on us
and make our lives heaven on earth someday.
After all is said and done, life still can be fun.
We awaken to see the sun shining on most everyone.
The moon and the stars light our way to a brighter day,
making me feel that life is worthwhile.
I can still smile and think and wonder
what new thing life could bring.

Eleanor M. McKissick

A CLUE

Forever in my thoughts
Forever in my mind
Forever in my eyes
For never I will find

Someone who cares for me as you do
I know I could search the whole world through
And in the end still have no clue
For there simply is no other you

Forever I will love you
Forever be defied
Until at last I touch you
Forever by my side

Patrick Sands

A SIGH

As my mind reeled through the fog
And emotions ran idly by
I wanted to discard my legs
To pick up wings and fly

I sat unapproached by human touch
And wondered "Who am I?"
While my reasons for existence
Are caught and rendered dry

Am I so different from the rest?
Without really knowing why
That all my thoughts and feelings
Are captured in a sigh

Patrick Sands

HOLY THURSDAY

Is this a holy thing to see,
In a rich and fruitful land,
Babes reduced to misery,
Fed with cold and usurous hand?

Is that trembling cry a song?
Can it be a song of joy?
And so many children poor?
It is a land of poverty!

And their sun does never shine,
And their fields and bleak & bare,
And their ways are fill'd with thorns;
It is eternal winter there.

For where-e'er the sun does shine,
And where-e'er rain does fall,
Babe can never hunger there,
Nor poverty the mind appall.

William Blake

LONGING

Oh yearning, longing, emptiness . . .
The unwordable, soundless calling.
It comes when thoughts of you are strong
And missing you with all my being
Is more than I can stand.
What then am I to do to ease this pain?

Judith M. Thomsen

JOURNEY

I set out on a journey
From the day that I was born.
A journey toward that Golden Bridge
And all that lay beyond.

My travel was not easy
For tears and pain I knew
But still I fought the good fight
For the prize beyond my view.

As I began to cross the bridge
The old things passed away.
My pain and sorrow left me
And joy and peace remained.

I looked ahead across the bridge
His hand reached out to strengthen.
He walked with me upon that span
In total soul communication.

He led me to the other side
The wondrous light awaiting,
Where those I love who journeyed first
Are now the party making.

I set out on a journey
From the day that I was born.
My journey is now ended
For at last I have reached home.

Judith M. Thomsen

SOLITUDE

Loneliness comes in many forms
Insidious and creeping as a debilitating disease
Sometimes it captures one unaware
As a sudden frightening, chilling breeze.

Money cannot dispel the cobwebbed thoughts
That slip through a shadowed mind
Frantic activity lightens the gloom
But when halted is waiting to ensnare and bind.

But scoffers of loneliness beware
For you are not immune
One false step along the highway of life
And despair arrives on the brightest of noons.

Although a room full of people can be
The loneliest place on earth
Being at peace with the Almighty is uplifting
For everyone He made has worth.

Jean M. Porter

POST-PARTING DEPRESSION

"How noble to care for the terminal
    Clearly the chore of a saint!"
But spiders on the wall would say
    "That's exactly what she ain't."

"Saint Vicious in Limbo," they called her,
    Tied close to the invalid one —
All personal goals and ambitions
    Postponed to the slow setting sun.

The futile attempts to bring comfort,
    Which always were to no avail.
The battles that raged with the doctors,
    Whose remedies always would fail.

The joy and the love had long faded,
    She really begrudged every deed.
She spitefully spoke to the helpless,
    While tending the physical need.

"Saint Vicious in Limbo" still plodded
    Along the drab duty of care,
The final release so delinquent,
    The freedom could lead but nowhere.

Virginia F. Brown

VIRGINIA FRANCES BROWN. Pen Name: Phoebe Francis; Born: Texarkana, Texas, 10-30-24; Single; Education: Lindenwood College, A.A., 1943; University of Texas, B.A., 1946; Touro Infirmary, Certificate of Medical Technology, 1956; Two business colleges, credit and non-credit courses in five other colleges: Texarkana Junior College, North Texas State College, Centenary College, Tulane University, Loyola University, East Texas State College in Texarkana; Occupations: Bank teller, Government clerk, Government psychologist, Medical technologist, Owner and curator of Doll Den Museum and Hospital; Memberships: MT (ASCP), Northeast Texas Past and Future Doll Club, Phi Mu; Inactive member of AAUW, Beta Sigma Phi, B&PW, DAR, UDC, Pilot International; Awards: 2nd prize (Certificate of achievement) in Texarkon First Annual Science Fiction Fantasy Contest, 6-2-85; Poetry: 'Texas,' *Colts of Pegasus*, 1939; "Doll Den," booklet of poems and pictures of softsculpted dolls, 1985; 'Demonology,' 'By Any Other Name,' 'Of Grief, In Brief,' 'Poetic Principles,' *American Poetry Anthology*, 1987; Themes: *Strictly descriptive, of original soft-sculpted dolls, of events, people, animals, places, things, thoughts, reactions and observations.* Comments: *When work is fun, it is called "play." Thank you for providing the childless with a chance for immortality.*

LIFE THROUGH THE EYES OF A DYING MAN

The peace, beauty, and serenity of the
   land hypnotize me.
Temporarily relieved and at peace,
   yet I don't feel a part of it.

The sun shines, but I feel no warmth.
People reach out, but I pass right through them.

I dream about things that I wish
I could do and be, but here the dream
is only that. Nothing is
accomplished.

Dear Lord, lead me homeward; show me the way.

Steve Hays

MOONGLOW

Not a shadow embarrassed the sky,
When a shimmering glow
Came from nowhere and peopled the void
With a strange and a radiant light.

   'Twas the moon come to odds with the sun —
   Now the moon reigned supreme;
   And, completing its regal ascent,
   Like a queen, blew a kiss to a star.

But the queen was translucent and pale,
Having hardly a soul.
Then the stars spun a nebulous veil
And enveloped the face of the queen.

   And a blush came and tinted her cheek,
   And she was awake and alive,
   And spun filaments fine and strong
   That flowed gently down to earth.

And I was awake and alive
With the fluids of strength from the moon.
And I reached towards the light in the sky
To commune with the stars and the moon.

Mary Schulman

VAGARIES

I love to sail away on wings of fancy
Into the hazy void beyond . . .
Where velvety night breathes of zephyrs,
And radiant sprites sway in hearts
Of dew-scented tulips, kissed by the breeze.

   I love to inhale the cloying elixir
   While sweetly the echoes of dreams
   Hear a fragile tinkling
   In the woodland of fairies below.

Land of vagrant memories,
Peopled with images, vividly clamoring!
Some iridescent with smiling delight;
Others bathed in a rainbow of hues.

   Swathed in shadow,
   They are mute and morbidly secretive,
   Slowly emerging from nebulous thought.

Mary Schulman

ON AGING

They said that I am old. But what is old?
A time to fold one's tents and steal away?
A time of loneliness, regret and a frustration?

   They said that I am old. Old age that brings senility?
   Discord? Or loss of care for one's own being?
   And carelessness of dress and speech and thought?

Not this is old!
Old is a time for quiet contemplation and recapitulation,
For memory of joys as well as ills.

   Old is a time for new development and growth —
   Especially if freed from care of family,
   And how to make a living.

Old is a time for new horizons,
For taking time for one's own self,
Instead of frittering that self away.

   Old is a time when one has done with giving,
   And ready for receiving new impressions, vistas, thought.

They said that I am old.
What do they know of other streamings?
Of other sluices bringing new energy to mind and soul and body?

   For I am old and young — both simultaneously.

Mary Schulman

CAT, GOD AND ME

This is a story about cat
Who was a friend of God
And probably called Him on the phone
But the night it stormed and rained so hard
Cat found himself all alone

The neighbors refused to aid him
Or her, as the case may be
But I gave him food and shelter from the storm
'Cause I figured that someday he might do it for me.

My back porch became a refuge of sorts
Where he lay, cuddled, silently sleeping
Or dreaming of earlier conquests
I could sense that he was grateful
Though he didn't shake my hand

Cat is gone now, but I know not where
Perhaps to return at his leisure
And to revisit the home that I gave him
So he need not worry about the weather
As long as me and God are around

Jim Ingles

LEAVING

My heart is beating like a train going down the track
Wishing I'd never have to come back
To this town of my sad memories
Which hurts me so, must try to forget
That's why I'm leaving
Never wanting to come back
Going down that lonely road
Trying to forget all of my sorrows.

Debra L. Ayres

OLD KITTY IN OUR GARDEN

The morning sun shone brightly on my eighth birthday
When our work-horse, Old Kitty, much to our dismay,
Entered our garden and nibbled lettuce straightaway.
My mother and sisters were busy as could be,
Preparing things for my birthday party at three.

So, I was told to go and chase Old Kitty out.
I offered her grass. She ate it. But then went about
Nibbling more lettuce heads because without a doubt
She couldn't understand, since she drew garden plow
Each spring, why I should not allow her to stay now?

''Get out, Old Kitty,'' again and again I cried,
As looking around me a big fat stick I spied.
It went across her heavy legs with a loud *Whack! Whack!*
She lifted her hind legs and *Alack! Alack!*
Through air I flew swiftly and landed on my back.

Eighteen hours later when I opened my eyes,
In dimly lit room, I saw people, and heard cries,
As well as prayers to God, to please help me survive.
Many years have passed since that day but I keep in mind
How Old Kitty proved: ''To animals one must be kind.''

Mollie E. Miller

THE TREE OF LIFE:
CHRIST THE ORGANS IN THE BODY

The Tree of Life: in the midst of the garden — Gen 3:22
The midst of man's body; the organ in man's body.
The tree of knowledge of good and evil; some of these
organs have a lot to do with blood pressure and
mental development: the organs in man's body.

I think the Tree of Life is the organs in man's body;
When he gave God thanks for them: the organs
He began to improve from his sickness or his ills,
ailments and complaints. And by living the Christ
Life, Christ's spirit is man's brains, one of the
organs, by giving God thanksgiving and praises,
Repeatedly saying I thank You Father
it wakes up the organ or puts them it action the
Christ, the soul of the body,
Repeatedly saying: I thank You Father for being
the organs in the body.

Rev. John S. Allen

YOU AND I

You have your mumbling, grumbling trains
I have my wide and spacious plains.
You have the lust and greed that in cities grow
I, in the country, have time to pray, you know.

You have the dust, the grime-filled air
I have azure heavens, scented flowers fair, so fair!
You have the fall of snow soon turned to dreary slush
I have winter's wonderland, glistening in awesome hush!

So, let us be . . . just You and I.
I'll not pity you and for me do not sigh
For I love the quiet, the beauty and peace of country life
And you, I know, love your bustle, bustle city strife.

Helen Bolten

A LITTLE BOY WALKS

Into the early morning light a little boy walks,
Not knowing what lies ahead, just knowing that he must go.
That precious look upon his face, so simple, so innocent,
so serene. I look into his eyes, and I say:

United we should be in our dreams to better his world.
We are society, we control his fate.
True his parents can raise him, and his teachers can guide him,
But only you and I can build him a better life.

So look at him and remember when your smile looked like that.
And keep in mind, the care you show him today,
Will grow in him for tomorrow.

And as the rays of that morning sun continue to shine,
I will reflect on that child's smile and say,
That is the reason for life, let us help him live it.

John Albert Biasetti

JOHN ALBERT BIASETTI. Born: Norwalk, Connecticut, 5-24-53; Single; Education: Two years, Norwalk Community College; Themes: *My poetry, like this book, deals with life. It is designed to have the readers think of themselves for what they are, that is, as a member of the human race.*

TO MOTHER AT HER PASSING

Walk reverently upon this inarticulate earth —
though dumb, its sands cry out of human death and birth.
''From dust to dust'' the cycle of our lives has been described;
this *is* the dust, this earth, wherein mankind is circumscribed.

The flaming spirit housed itself one vast primeval day
inside an awkward vessel cast in mortal clay,
and, soul-to-soul, the generations passed the living flame;
from worn-out to the new, the seed of life became
a moving, growing tide whose surf reached out in Time
toward an unknown, yearned-for, mystic dream sublime.

Behind each generation's wave was left the dusty clay
of those before, whose flame illumed their passing day,
whose thrust toward the future's beckoning, seductive shore
aroused the generative lava at the spirit's core,
and spilled new life into the turbulent human sea.

And so, each grain of soil was once a soul with pain, with mirth;
— walk reverently upon this inarticulate earth!

Hal Barrett

TUMBLEWEED

Drifting among societies unknown
Surface, searching for reason
Without presupposition. The soil
Under the edges of thought brings
Shame to the feeling of being.

Lost in an array of complex angles,
The wind currents force harsh particles
Within the inner core of existence.

Light along the path, scattered
By the intensity of thought;
Exciting electronic activity —
    The fetus lives onward!

Christopher Smith

EASTER FLIGHT
RESURRECTED

Thinly layered feathery tufts of clouds
float noiselessly between heaven and earth
unperturbed by — unaware of the
brilliant silvered wings magnified
by the rising sun — unnatural intruder
into holy places harboring shielded
eyes gazing below transfixed by/as

shimmering rainbows with no beginning and
no end radiate their prismatic colors
on (?) among the clouds below as if to
affirm honor proclaim great tidings
of good news to any who (see)k ask
and listen with their hearts and souls.

Frances Johnson

LOVER'S MONTH

I listened to the constant singing
    of the river as it ran,
And no song was ever sweeter
    by the bridges of Spokane!
Now I hear your kettle drums,
    than again the music's mute,
While far above the roaring falls
    I hear the wailing of a flute!
O serenade, to make me happy
    while the lilacs are in bloom,
Bring back joyful sounds of laughter,
    take away the time of gloom.
I've been dreaming of tomorrow,
    will my world be bright and gay —
When I hold you ever closer
    in the lover's month of May!

Harry C. Helm

A MEMORY REVISITED

A teardrop tiptoes down a cheek
Carrying its bag of hurt.
The words it cannot assert
But as it creeps from sadness
It trails a pain a memory could not avert.

Joseph Frankel

GRANDMA'S BOY

Amma! Amma!
he said to me.
As he clapped his hands
And smiled with glee.
Big brown eyes,
Chubby little cheeks.
He melts Grandma's heart,
Whenever he speaks.
In my life,
He brings much joy,
Mikhail's his name,
And he's Grandma's Boy!

Sherrie Lynn Mantooth

OWL

His pewter-coated body twists
Left on the shelf in an owl's wizened
Stare. He sits for all the years
Framing his own portrait in a blend
Of shallow cutting shadows which groove
His eyes in a sleepless glare.
Sculptured fitness portrays the move
Which time's unsought shaping fixed
And soldered to a year of unbent fear
And hopes piled high like a mason's bricks.

Stephen Rosenthal

TROPICAL PARROT

Above the green-topped edges
Of the scene we watch below
A brightly colored parrot
With a beaming amethyst glow
Bobs his head at empty space,
Then squawks, ''Let's rock and roll.''

His gyrations wave the branches
To a tune only he can hear
While the wings shake left and his head
Nods right like an ancient magical seer.

While an unseen vision calls him
The branches rustle applause
And we gaze in silent awe
At the messenger from the gods.

Stephen Rosenthal

AFTERMATH

Thoughts beckon
creating images,
wistful dreams,
smiles . . .
Replete
I stretch,
watch muscles
play along my skin,
sigh,
completed by your touch.

Robin Perry

OLD AND TIRED

The sun rises,
I am born.
I travel forth.

The day is hurried
and the problems are many.
Worry about the choices
that I make and
the ones I don't.
My nerves are a mess
my stomach is in an uproar.

The sun sets,
The day is through.
I am not just tired
I am old.

Arthur R. Slate, Jr.

LULLABY

Little child asleep in my arms,
How long it will take you to learn of life!

You will rearrange its symbols,
You will select and discard
Until there forms a picture pattern
That to you is the true design.

You will assort the sounds of earth
And interpret vibrations
Until you find the song for your voice.

I wish I could infuse you
With the philosophy of my years.
I would spare you the wounds of learning,
The memories of wrongs to others,
But I cannot.

My glands are not your glands,
Your left brain is not mine.

No one else can compose the poem 'You.'
You must write it
With the stained inks of your enzymes,
With the pen strokes of your own hand.

Annie Ruth Waldsmith

ANGER

Frustration tears
the fabric of serenity,
pulling strands
of reality
through the broken litter
of dying screams.
Violence mounts
the pinnacle of emotion,
begging release
from reason . . .
banging its cup of flame
against the bars
of its cage —

Robin Perry

TO MY NEW GRANDSON

You belong to Tomorrow beyond Tomorrow —
to a time I can only imagine in dreams;
and, if all of my wishes come true,
there'll be nothing but gladness for you!

You belong to a Future beyond my future,
and I wonder how wondrous that new Day will seem:
Will it shelter the Good and the True?
Will it bring forth the wonder in you?

Long ago, back at the dawn of Time,
Life first appeared on the earth;
you are the heir of millions of years
teeming with mis'ry and mirth!

So, from Yesterday's sorrow we turn to Tomorrow,
and you are the symbol of Hope for that Dream!
Oh, my darling, there's so much to do!
May Life shower its blessings on you!

Hal Barrett

YOUR GOLDEN WEDDING ANNIVERSARY

In the Spring of nineteen-hundred-thirty-four
Young people's fancy turned to love — as in days of yore.
So John and Icy the tie they decided to knot.
One evening to Calhoun High, Icy he sought.
In a whirl of excitement the preacher was found;
The ceremony performed and joy did abound.

The church, the building, they bought and restored.
It again is being used to bring praise to our Lord.
The hospitality has been shown to the families of both
         Knotts and J. Wood
Cannot be expressed, although we wish we could.
The comfort and kindness to friends far and wide
Were given in love and that you cannot hide.

So John and Icy, long may you be
A lighthouse for others to see.
We love and thank you many times multiplied;
To family, friends, and neighbors you were our guide.
Our God has enriched you beyond measure
For this, and you, we fondly treasure.

Edith Chenoweth Stribling

INTERLUDE

An interlude of time is now for me
The loss of health to eternity.
I am thankful for the things I can do.
They used to be many, but now they are few.

However, I am thankful for mind, heart, and soul.
Each is important if we are to be whole.
"The Lord is my shepherd I shall not want" —
These words I whisper as His will is sought.

This avenue of expression has been opened to me —
A source of pride and dignity.
As we open our hearts for others to see —
May it bring honor and glory to Thee.

Edith Chenoweth Stribling

MOUSETRAP

There's a mouse out in my kitchen, I am certain!
I can hear the tiny scratchings of his feet!
I wonder what he's nibbling on that crunches?
He must have found a gourmet, mousey treat!

I set a trap to catch the mouse intruder,
Who in my darkened kitchen had a feast;
That scurrying little creature isn't wanted!
He's a most unwelcome guest, to say the least!

Now, in the dark of night I wake and listen —
From the corner of the kitchen comes a "snap!"
What was the sound I heard? Oh, I remember!
The sound tells me that mousey's in the trap!

I go to look and see if I'm successful,
And there two frightened eyes look up at me;
How can I kill this helpless little creature?
I spring the trap and set the mousey free!

Delphine LeDoux

WASHDAY

Not a moment did she seem bored,
As she rubbed clothes on the old wash-board;
Songs of joy loudly rang,
Songs about her King she sang.

Caring not, if neighbors heard,
Within, her heart was stirred;
Though tired, hair down in her face,
She sang on and on, of God's grace.

Empty tubs, water out-pouring,
Within, the everlasting river flowing;
Rinsing clothes, hanging on the line,
Humming a tune, marking time.

Clean, bright clothes, flop in the breeze,
With head held high, she seemed so pleased;
Her family's clothes, with pride would wear,
Clothes, Mom washed, with loving care.

Josephine S. Brown

MOVING ON

Packing up feelings, furniture and fond memories.
Jamming them in tight, tightly against giving in.
Letting go — have let go — of all vestiges
of old love, old home and old passion.
Boxing up the leftovers and moving on.
Wrapping up the loose ends of the past.
So that in the unpacking, unboxing and
unwrapping, salvaged treasures take
on new meanings and new looks
in tomorrow's showrooms. The
leftovers are left up to build upon,
dream upon because of having moved on.

Darlene Roy

COLLECTOR'S ITEM

You came to me once
When my little fringe tree was blooming,
You came early in the morning
When the delicate tassels
Were blurred
Against an opalescent sky.

As you walked toward me
Fragments of white flower lace
Caught in your dark hair.

In that moment I had for my album
Your portrait from Monet's skill.

Did I say ''Monet?''
But he did not paint
From a palette of tinted scent,
Of fadeless fragrance.

He did not dip his brush
Into the pearl-luster of love
Or mix his pastels with love words
That forever sing.

Annie Ruth Waldsmith

A DAY IN APRIL

All afternoon my thoughts have wanted
To go to you,
But they could not leave.

There were bird droppings on my walk,
And I had to scrub them away.
Then I found in my garden
A dead rat with flies swarming,
And it had to be buried.
Later a friend came, and there was no choice
Except to listen to her stinking gossip.

At last I was resting on my couch,
And my thoughts were free.

They bathed in perfume of the valley lilies,
Dressed in spotless white petal silk
And danced to you.

They kissed your eyelids as you slept
And lay together in the curved hand
That was uncovered.

I have tried to call them home again,
But they would not come.

Annie Ruth Waldsmith

ODE TO DEATH

I still see your face
Hear your voice
Your laughter.
I cannot think,
Lest it be of you.
I cannot dream
For you invade them.
I miss you so!
Therefore I can not live
As I have lived before.

Valerie Martin

CHILDHOOD TRIP

All arrangements are in order,
Paperboy promised not to come,
4:00 a.m. trip to the border,
Bed early, slept little, woke numb.

Showers take longer ere dawn has cracked.
Not one mile out and already bored.
In back sit several suitcases packed,
And leftovers heretofore ignored.

More than a week will age us all until,
The driveway and the car will bump again.
Mother whispers prayers no one will get ill,
And father expects the state line by ten.

Knuckles are white like breaths releasing.
Mother swears the dog has not been fed,
'Til I remind her in the freezing,
''We no longer have a dog,'' I said.

Her thoughts have moved to lights left on,
Trip novelty already gone,
Exhausted ere we left our street.
Departure is bitter, not sweet.

Darrell R. Brown

THE JAR

How does she know?
The floor don't creak.
How does she catch
The little sneak?

How can she hear
When one gets et?
How can she see
Glued to the set?

What does she have—
Radar for ears?
What tips her off
All through the years?

How many times
Has he been caught?
How many spies
Has Mother got?

How does she trap?
Jars don't rattle.
How does she win
Cookie battles?

Darrell R. Brown

FIRST FOOTBALL GAME

As you asked, I went to the arena last night.
The crowd was so huge, it was quite a sight
It made no sense to me. It seemed
They ran about chasing this odd-shaped thing.
And I was surrounded by men of steel.
I could not move lest I be killed!
I sat there and wondered why
You thought that I
Would enjoy such a sight,
It gave me such a fright.

Valerie Martin

DADDY'S LITTLE GIRL

Daddy's little girl
I never got to be,
He was gone a lot
And much too busy for me.

He left when I was still little
They married too young, so they say.
So many things to do and see, I guess,
We might have gotten in his way.

So it is silly as a grown woman
To wonder how it would feel
If we had it all to do over
And I could be Daddy's little girl.

Bonita J. Patridge

WISDOM

In the simple, idle days of youth,
We sit and ponder about the truth.
Why are we here and who am I?
What will I accomplish before I die?

Many a time I've pondered this,
As I sought after my every wish.
Now the sands of time have come my way,
I see the many mistakes I've made.

Wisdom comes too soon, too late;
But that is many a person's mistake.
The fragile web that holds us all,
Suddenly loosens; then we fall.

The footstep we left upon the sand,
Will it leave its mark on the land?
Or will it be like many before,
A name on stone; remembered nevermore.

Misty J. Ford

LIFE IS A JIGSAW PUZZLE

God gave me a mind
    and a heart to keep it working
I'm supposed to use it for good
    though evil's lurking
So many little pieces to put together
Some are difficult to lift
    others light as a feather
By the time everything fits
    and I can make sense of it all
Life will be finished and I'll
    hear a call
To leave and scatter the pieces
    once more
So someone else can search
    and find
After I close the door.

Louise McPhail

EAGLES

They soar in majestic splendor,
    In the heavenly blue above,
They are the symbol of freedom,
    That we so reverently love,
They mate for an eternity,
    With loyalty to the end,
They live to protect their offspring,
    Who'll carry on when they are dead,
This freedom we've come to rely on,
    In our country so good and true,
Let us all remember, with awe,
    The symbol of our Red, White and Blue.

Lillian DeKeno

HOPES OF MANKIND

There is great social significance in
The newly developed machinery.
    Productive capacity is at its peak,
    As the wheels of industry revolve.

The knowledge of a universal language
Increases the possibility of unity.
    The Brotherhood of Man extends to all,
    Men reach out to please each other.

The fatalist approach is one of doom,
God must destroy all He created.
    The great hopes of mankind
    Are based on unity and brotherly love.

The Godless are forsaken,
For they are the disbelievers.
    Trust in God who will bring salvation,
    Under an egalitarian society, all will share.

The great chasm of disbelief
Grows as men learn to fight.
    Doubters and skeptics exist everywhere
    Who want to destroy the good works of man.

Elizabeth Saltz

ELIZABETH SALTZ. Born: Brooklyn, New York, 6-15-30; Married: David, 1963; Education: Queens College, B. A., M.A., History, 1979; New School For Social Research, Psychology, Philosophy; Occupations: Social work, Department of Human Resources, New York; Memberships: Alumni Association of Queens College, Flushing, New York; Philosophy Club, New School for Social Research, New York; Awards: Golden Poet Award, 1987; 25 Award of Merit certificates; Poetry: 'A Future World,' 'City Awakes,' 'The City,' *Mustard Seed Anthology,* 1987; 'Unity of Races, Muslim vs Christian,' *New Voices in American Poetry,* 1987; 'Peace on Earth,' 'The Sea,' 1987; Comments: *Poetry intends to represent its subject in such a way that the full experience of its particular nature may be communicated. Once a sense of the basic stuff of a poem is grasped, the method to be followed in analyzing it presents itself quite naturally.*

AN IMPECCABLE SONG

Twenty years have come and gone,
And they brought with them an impeccable song.
Akin to Moses, the man of God,
Who was envied, not tainted, nor wore a façade.

Forsaken and lonely, but not alone,
Accepting the challenge, I learned the song.
Called to declare what others have said,
Confirmed by the witness of things I read.

There are tempting and testing
And molding and shaping,
For employment in the Kingdom
The Master is making.

The pathway is narrow, stony and bright,
Your destiny secured when you come to the light.
The covenant revealed when you do what is right,
Because victory was won in the darkest of night.

Leu Leana G. Baker

ON THE 400th ANNIVERSARY
OF THE EXECUTION OF
MARY STUART, QUEEN OF SCOTS

Her life was brief and not serene
A troubled prelude to that scene
When fell the axe and earthly strife
Then ended for this chequered life.

With royal poise she met her fate
An end most cruel as records do relate
And one may sense the strain of that last scene
Which marked the death of Scotland's Queen.

Then fell the axe and Scotland's Queen lay dead
While for her cause brave men had fought and bled.
All this occured so very long ago
And yet her memory still lives as most men know.

Bernerd C. Weber

FOREVER IS NOW

A moment with you is eternity,
folded up into a hundred microseconds
Timeless
grains of sand in the hourglass
have no place to drain; we sleep by the shore
wrapped in golden skin and soaking in the salty wind.

Flesh touches flesh, beads of sweat falling down
into the earth
Time and space diminish, large and microscopic blend together,
losing their difference
Sea, wind, sky and breath
form out of formlessness.

Malinda M. Stephens

THE POINTE OF BALLET

Tara sits turned in the chair outside.
Through the window she watches the junior
ballet dancers. Her heart skips a beat and
she holds her breath as she memorizes their
movements. Her heart is yearning for the
time to pass quickly so she can be there
and someone else where she is now. She
dreams and thinks. She can hear the applause
of the audience as they thrill to the supple
movements of her body and soul. She
knows it will be. With a passion that will
not cease, she drives herself. She dances
with beads of sweat glistening on her face.
She dreams and knows with dead certainty
she will have her place in the fame and
feelings of the ballet dancer on point.
One day soon she will be there.
And someone else where she is now.

James R. Clark

THE FAITHFUL LOVE

Love eternally faithful
Without rumor, stain, or sin
Of beautiful body and spirit
The most perfect flower seen

Surrounded by a thousand wrongs
Unpenetrated by their fire
Surrounded by temptations
Rejected without desire

Petals and aromas
Heavens hot and cold
Is there possibly a chance
For another lover bold?

Jerry Martinez

TO A FORMER FRIEND

You don't know what you did to me.
You probably don't care.
When you ''left'' you took my heart
And also my trust.
You've made me afraid
To confide in somebody else.

We did crazy things together.
We enjoyed just sitting and dreaming,
Together, alone.
But you dropped all of this
For those people you call ''friends.''
They aren't friends at all.

You joined them for popularity.
We weren't popular,
But we were happy then.
Are you happy now?

Shawnee Parsil

EACH ONE I WRITE

Each one I write,
Is a story of my life,
For each word has a special meaning,
For each one is separate,
For each one is a memory,
Happy or sad as each may be,
That memory shall stay with me.

Shane P. Robison

THRESHOLD

Exposed
I shiver,
feeling the last brick
in my wall crumble,
become dust.
Breathless
I await your entry,
thread the sheet
through shaking fingers,
and scream silently of need.

Robin Perry

ALONE

Alone. My precious *one* left me,
Five long years ago.
Now, I must go on alone.
Our children, kind and thoughtful,
Have families of their own.

I miss him more and more,
As days and years pass by.
His cheerful voice: ''I'm home, honey,''
His empty chair at the table,
The half-empty bed at night;
His soft, warm, sweet kisses.
His loving arms around me.
He loved his children, home and *me.*
His flowers and garden were his pride.
He worked so hard to provide
A home for his family.

I am *old,* and growing weary,
I long to join him, when
My call comes for me
For I'll not be lonely then.

Meltha Proctor Higgins

THIS EMPTY VASE

A lakebed, barren and dry,
Like trees without their leaves;
A hive devoid of honey,
Or a loom on which no one weaves . . .
These things speak out pleading,
''O my God . . . is there not a plan?''
A vein to feed terse longings,
Giving life to this
Empty vase of a man.

Ken Possanza

LOVE STRENGTHENED

The Blessed Virgin's love
for her Lord and only Son,
Was more precious and beautiful
Than amber sunset when day is done.
The years of faith,
The joys of sharing,
Strengthened her will
And knowledge of caring.
What thunder of grief
Was hers to endure,
When they murdered her Son,
The Lord so pure.
Her Immaculate heart
Was tortured and driven,
To sufferings unspoken,
For what her Son had given.
Surely she would not have lived,
His rising have been unseen,
If the Holy Spirit
Did not intervene.

Ken Possanza

FIRST HOLY COMMUNION

The miracle of His body and blood;
Received in the form of bread and wine.
Prepared with confession for that
Wonderful moment when the Lord
Should give Himself . . . I am thine!
Priests in robes, starched white cloth;
Slow and orderly, the dignity of
Peace wherein one can grow,
Safe to realize individual roles.
Bible sound, the Eucharist is real;
Unction delightful, food much needed,
Nurturing those who believe in
His presence, whole and complete;
Satisfaction and happiness, in faith, the seal.

Ken Possanza

KEN POSSANZA. Born: Hibbing, Minnesota, 7-13-38; Education: Foothill College, Palo Alto, California; Diablo Valley College, Pleasant Hill, California; Los Medanos College, Pittsburg, California; Occupation: Typesetter; Awards: Certificate of Merit for poem, 'Silent Peace,' North American Mentor Magazine, 1986; Poetry: 'The Hidden Spring,' *Best Loved Contemporary Poems,* 1979; 'An Elusive Truth,' *Impressions,* 1986; 'Silent Peace' and 'Opposites,' *The Poet,* 1986; *On the Rose, a Blemish,* book of poetry, spring 1988; Comments: *I like Poe and Longfellow because they seem to express complete thoughts with conclusions. In my work I too try to touch on ideas common to all people—sort of a universal subject area. Free verse is as yet strange to me. I like to rhyme if I can.*

MY LITTLE RACCOON

My little Raccoon, he was fun to watch,
  He came at night, 'bout nine o'clock.
It was dark outside, and he searched for food.
  Then he found some bowls on our back porch, cool.
He jumped up high, by a window pane,
  To the other side my cats all came,
To watch through the glass at him eating there,
  They couldn't touch, they could only stare.

He washed his hands in a dish that stood.
  From another dish he ate some food.
He dunked each piece till was nice and wet,
  For that's the way he liked it best,
And all the while the cats just stood,
  Watching the funny way he ate his food.

And when he was through, he jumped right down,
  And lumbered away like a little clown.
He climbed a tree by the garden wall,
  And ate some pears, and watched some fall.
My little Raccoon, you are such fun
  To watch you eat, and watch you run.

Agnes M. Westmoreland

REALITY IS BUT A DREAM

To keep our mind, and bide our time,
we find we must scheme.

With glorious plans, we travel lands,
indulging in a dream.

We'll shape the future, we often nurture,
this wild and silly hope.

Without delusions, and illusions,
how would we ever cope.

Empires were made, by those who stayed,
with their silly schemes.

Boredom is relieved, and lives reprieved,
just from having dreams.

And often souls bettered, by those unfettered,
with using the sensible road.

It's no mistake, to plan an escape,
you'll find it lightens the load.

With surprise you'll find, the plans in your mind,
now happen as you scheme.

And soon you'll learn, as the world will turn,
reality is but a dream.

Lin Yarges

SOCKS

There was a stray kitty, the neighbor called her Socks
That lived in her basement on some rags in a box.
  She thought there were also some kittens nearby,
For often she heard something, like kittens cry.

  Her son didn't want them, he was rather dumb
So Socks ate on my porch, but her kittens couldn't come.
  They were wee little things, and much much too small,
And their mother couldn't move them for my fence was too tall.

  So I watched, and one day, I saw them all come,
Climbing over my fence, following Socks on the run.
  They followed her quickly, to eat with her there,
They had to climb up to the top of the stairs.

  They were wild as could be, but soon I made them tame,
And I thought right away, I must give each a name.
  There were three little kits, as plump as a ball,
And ate with their mother, soon then they came when I'd call.

  And after awhile, I brought them into the house,
Where they played with some toys, as if 'twere a mouse.
  I treated them good, just as I would a child,
And my other cats taught them not to be wild.

  They went to a lady who owned a hotel,
And the cats that came 'round there were all treated well.
  And she knew that her tenants would all treat them good
For whatever cats came, they were given some food.

Agnes M. Westmoreland

AGNES M. WESTMORELAND. Born: Montana, 4-12-04; Married: Navy widow, World War II; Education: Montana State University, B.A., 1928; Occupations: High school teacher, Recreation leader, Drama director, Short story writer, Machine operator, Electrician helper; Poetry: 'Wilderness,' 1974; 'Christmas Past,' 1986; 'Teddy,' 1985; 'Threshing,' 1925; Other Writing: *Beekeeping Stories, Experiences,* 1950-78, an autobiography — living and working on a farm before rural areas had electricity, radio, TV; Comments: *My autobiography contained stories about raising my four children, beekeeping, all about farming, my days as a carpenter, government worker (engraver) for navy ships, and seamstress. The richest part of my life was living and working on a farm; beekeeping and writing are my hobbies as well as reading and engaging in humanitarian projects.*

DANCING BETWEEN MEMORIES

The earth and sky are black tonight,
and I am suspended between
the Milky Way above and the one below,
encircled by two unfamiliar arms.

You dance divinely, my friend,
and when we sit down at an elegant table
with tall stemmed crystal and flowers
the cold little knot in my throat softens.

But there is something about love
which cannot be forced;
it is there, or it is not . . .
Between us the latter case applies.

For the string trio I am grateful.
But when we dance, a little space please,
for I am still moving alone,
somewhere between memories.

Mary Ann Malone

L'EQUILIBRE DE NATURELLE

Everything is part
  of the balance of nature . . .
When we are bustling about
  in the middle of day,
China lies sleeping
  beneath a peaceful moon.

And somewhere else
  on this giant planet
Animals are locked
  in deadly combat
As the miracle of birth
  occurs nearby.

Flowers turn brittle
  with autumn's frost.
While far away buds
  are just beginning
  to open their blossoms.

There, two lovers
  are kissing a tearful farewell
As you and I greet
  with a promising smile.
And I am quite content
  to be on this side
  of nature's balance.

Mary Ann Malone

RETURN

  This town has lost its yesterdays,
The living ghosts are only dreams,
  And those who once had time to spare
Are many miles away, it seems.

  I think in time I'll find my peace,
And enjoy loneliness as well;
  But, strange enough, right now I feel
I'm freezing in burning hell.

Helen Robinson

THE UNICORN

A unicorn dreamed of a distant star
It sat and wondered just how far
The beams that danced on velvet wings
Had come to rest in the forest green

The star shone bright the heavens aflame
The unicorn wondered if it had a name
No answer came no sweet reply
Just rippling water in the stream nearby

It stood and stretched and tossed its mane
It strolled into the open glade
An impertinent toss of its head held high
It ran away 'neath midnight skies

Ron Minyard

BROKEN DREAMS

Broken dreams
On butterfly wings
Fly away, fly away

Rising hope
High spirits float
Higher than yesterday

Ecstasy
It seems to me
You're here to ever share

Broken dreams
On butterfly wings
Does anyone really care

Ron Minyard

THE FAERIE

The faerie flits on velvet wings
Deep in the forest she hears things
Mortal man with sinful desires
Heaps the wood on his own funeral pyres

Wants and needs of man can blind
The soul of a gentle man so kind
The faerie seeks not to destroy
But to share the pleasure and eternal joy

Someone wicked this way steals
Smiling face hides how they feel
The faerie flits on velvet wings
Deep in the forest truth shall ring

Ron Minyard

ACTUALITY

The mouth was designed for a painted smile
Eyes were devised for crying
Legs were built for the uphill climb
Feet were formed for trying
Hands were installed to serve — awhile
A maid was endowed for the taking
The mind was enshrouded for self, beguile
And the heart was made for breaking!

Sue Russell Slack

CLOSE TO ME

When you are away,
  I remember you
Close to me.

Feeling arms and lips,
  Hearing words of love
Ecstasy.

Waiting your return,
  Loving eyes aglow,
I can dream.

Whether near or far,
  You will always be
Close to me.

Helen Robinson

CLOUDS AND MANITOU

The April cloud is a drifter.
This morning much swifter.
They're fleeing and leaving
  With no lamentation.
Somewhere over the knoll
There must be a troll
Who's threatening each one
  With annihilation.

Maybe they have a rendezvous
With the spirit called Manitou
Over blue-green hills toward
  The North Star.
Will the decision be rain
Or the drought cause pain
For us poor mortals on
  This Globular?

C. B. Steadman

A MOTHER'S LAMENT

I miss you in the morning
When the sun is warm and bright
I miss you all through the day
I miss you in the night.

I miss our closeness, Daughter
Through times both good and bad
I miss the times we used to share
The closeness that we had.

What happened to that closeness
The happy day we shared?
Was it that I grew so old
That you no longer cared?

Since both our husbands now are gone
And left us both alone
Can not share our losses
As we now share our home?

Can we bring back that closeness
We once shared — the happiness, the tears
And live together happily
For the few remaining years?

Ella Young Wood

EVENING TWILIGHT

Where is that wonderful stuff,
that made my partner less gruff?
What gives with gloom
as though clinging to doom?
    Life does not end with added years,
it's a time to compensate for the joys
        we've shared,
a time to give what knowledge we've learned,
a time for thanks life's bountiful returns.
    Who wants to hear black wings fluttering,
as long as there are rosy dawns
        and red-gold sunsets?
As long as we love life so much,
        with its joys and pain and such?
That wonderful stuff, I'll never let go.
    One does not really grow old,
one becomes old by not growing.
It isn't the number of sunsets most important
but that inward anticipation
        of sunsets to come.

Virgie McCoy Sammons

RAINBOWS AND UNICORNS

Rainbows and Unicorns,
Children and song
Lift my spirits and
Make me strong . . .
But not as much as my friend.

Rainbows send out feelings of hope,
Unicorns are mystic and rare,
Children signal that life must go on
And a song lives on in my heart . . .
But not as much as my friend.

The tenderness of a friend provides me with hope
And her perceptions unsurpassed shows she cares
A blessing in disguise has come into my life
Like the unicorn mystic and rare . . .
At last I have found a friend.

When my world has become complex and confused
And I don't know where to look or to start,
I am told of my value and told of my worth
Through lyrics sent straight from her heart . . .
I am lucky to have her for my *friend.*

Caroline Bredekamp

THE CAROLINA SPECIAL

Up the high mountains, down through the vale,
The "Carolina Special" left a smoke trail.
Her old wheels were singing, "Clickety, Clickety, Clack,"
The old bell rang out, by her old smokestack.
The cows in the meadows long since have gone,
The train had its day before you were born.
It stopped not for passengers, as none would be there,
The old gray station was vacant and bare.
So back to the roundhouse, the old train went,
Times have changed, and its energy is spent.

Laura McDonald

FOOTPRINTS IN TIME

Where the sea meets the shoreline,
    My footprints you will see
Until the tide removes them
    And there's nothing left of me.
I only walk the seashore,
    There's no place I'd rather be.
It's where love was won and lost,
    For time lies wasted upon the sea.
So there's nothing left of my heart,
    But these footprints in the sand.
Where (my mem'ry reminds me still)
    We strolled hand in hand.
Time has etched upon my mem'ry
    Footprints the sea washed from the shore.
And there's nothing left for me,
    But your mem'ry to adore.
So where the sea meets the shoreline,
    My footprints you surely see.
Until the tide removes them,
    And that's the end of me.

Tommy Mull

BUTTERFLIES

Butterflies come in many colors and sizes
They are pretty, they are neat, they have tiny little feet
Flying high and low
For they have a goal
To each flower they must go
Making flowers grow and grow
The poor butterfly, its life is short
Its life starts out looking like sort of a worm
Then it hides, in a cocoon, then one day
Out pops a butterfly, flying here and there
Going everywhere, flower to flower
Such wing power, landing on each flower
Butterflies have many different names
To describe each one
I still think they're pretty, don't you?

Debra L. Ayres

PROGENY RECYCLE

Contrived when love in all its blindness dared us not to fail
We live to host the children curled behind conception's veil.
They're spit like droplets on a pond whose path we cannot choose.
The ripples spread; we grasp to hold the rings to no avail.

When first the water breaks we've just begun to pay our dues.
Ignoble ends to miracles, God dares us to abuse.
Demanding more than we can give, they make no compromise.
Immaculate deception draws its curtain when we lose.

But wisdom is no parent through the lens of children's eyes
When peerage like the villain swirls the cloak of love's disguise.
Demanding more than they can give, how quickly we unearth
The things we once ourselves made sacrifice to criticize.

When love is re-defined to mean "How much is all this worth?"
A heart that is a heart must not be measured by its girth
If filled with disappointment by the blood they colored black.
The cycle starts to cycle from the focal point of birth.

The cord of life remains attached beyond the fetal sac
To nourish with emotion love's expressions which we lack.
Progenitor for God, but not condemned by God to fail,
We are the only species on the earth which takes them back.

George F. Schreader

WAITING

Wait and see what He wills
    Listen with your spiritual ear
Renew your strength and wait
    And call that He might hear.

It's so sweet to wait on Jesus
    Yes, He hears your softest cry
Jesus will truly direct you
    If you'll wait by and by.

Read, pray and then you wait
    So Jesus can speak to you
To tell you how to be patient
    That He might show you what to do.

He knows what is your need
Wait upon the Lord today
    And to your call, He will heed.

He's your Saviour, Master and Lord
    He knows what is the best
Just wait and seek His total will
    While in His love you rest.

Martha Woelke

MARTHA WOELKE. Born: Goliad County, Weesatche, Texas, 8-6-19; Married: Alfred, 8-30-67; Occupations: Retired L.P.N., Ordained minister, Housewife, Mother, Grandmother, Great-grandmother; Memberships: West Hawaii Writer's Council, Labach Literacy Council; Poetry: 'God's Hawaii,' *American Poetry Anthology, Vol VII,* 1987; Other Writings: Short stories for children in *Household Magazine,* 1933; Articles for local newspaper, Texas, 1972; Several plays for churches, Christmas and Easter; Comments: *Being a minister, most of my poetry is Christian or has a Christian theme, also some of my experiences in life.*

MISS CONCENTINA

Snowy park twigs quivered quietly
with malice toward the big storm
Miss Concentina stood beside me
stony Goddess of Roman Temples

Snow covered the world with a secret veil
Miss Concentina touched her head to mine
delicately like crystal glasses
of effervescent champagne that meet

She closed her eyes in beautiful peace
she touched with warmth of her breath
the snow, also began to melt

Andy J. Kolodziey

THE HUMMINGBIRD

Hummingbird, hummingbird
So swift on the wing
As you go "whirring" by
And about my head sing.

Then off to the trees —
Blossoms fill the air
With perfume and color,
And a nectar so rare.

I pause in my work
To see what is there —
You stay in view, seem to be
Hanging by a thread in midair,

And, watching and "whirring"
As if calling me away
From the grass and the flowers,
To the close of another day.

Nettie Roberts

OUT OF TIME

I look back now with much regret
For time has passed me by, and all
The ticks left in my clock won't
Come to many more. "Now" vivid
Memories from my past, the many
Things I did, the goods and bads of
Life's swift gait sustain these latter
Years. For health, it too does wane
With age, that's how God's clock it
Works. It's wound but once, and
That's called life, it's never wound
Again. So live each fleeting second to
The fullest if you can. And, perhaps, you
Won't look back like me. On a
Clock that just ran out of time.

Robert R. Weetman

THE SNOWMAN

The night is cold, and dark, and still
There on that lonely wind-swept hill.
The village folk are all abed
With covers snug around their head.
No animals scurry through the snow.
They've sought their burrows down below.
But the little snowman never sleeps
While through the night his watch he keeps.
But tomorrow's sunrise will mark his downfall.
What happens to him must happen to all.
He'll melt all away, no more he appears,
Like yesterday's hopes,
Like yesterday's tears.

Myrtle R. Jessee

HIGH SCHOOL REFLECTIONS

I met a young man in the morning.
His eyes were bright and blue.
He promised as he held my hand,
His love would be forever true.

I met my young man at noontime.
Our love burned with expectation.
The great desire of our young hearts
We broadcast to the nation.

Again, we met in the evening.
Promises we made were broken,
He had a new friend — as had I,
But he gave me a kiss — as a token.

The sun went down on our love,
He married the other girl.
I married the other fellow,
Our lives were in a whirl.

The long years go slowly by.
I tremble as my eyes grow dim.
I bow my head in prayer, and cry,
"What would my life have been — with him?"

Hazel B. Wilson

A DEEP GREEN FOREST

A deep green forest beckons to me,
Tall green trees and small green trees,
Stand their ground and shake their heads,
Awaiting God's blessings of beautiful rain!

A deep green forest rests our souls,
A picture of greatness to greet our eyes,
Pleases our heart and pleases our mind,
While being home for many creatures!

Nature this is at its greatest,
We need to preserve our green forests,
Save our trees and save our animals,
Instead of too many concrete walls!

So concrete cities are great, they say,
To give convenience to our people,
Yet, when the trees are all cut down,
Years and years of growth we have lost!

A deep green forest I hope to see,
With all nature bursting in bloom,
Pretty wild flowers and pretty wild animals
Seems to me better than all steel!

Doris Burleigh

GIFTED PEOPLE

Do not the gifted people
of this world
realize
that they are merely
God's messengers?

Barbara Bell-Teneketzis

COUNT YOUR BLESSINGS

Count your blessings, I surely do!
　　To awaken each morning
　　To a new day's dawning.
　　To see sparkling diamonds of dew
　　And flowers opening in varied hue.

Count your blessings, I surely do!
　　Dawn's promise of another day
　　With children's laughter and play
　　In a world wrapped in peace
　　Where all horrors, terrors will cease.

Count your blessings, I surely do!
　　For all this will come to pass . . .
　　Terrorists and madmen unable to harass
　　Cannot plunge the world in black despair
　　Though they strive to rule the sea and air!

Helen Bolten

THE RIVER OF THE SOUL

It knows no time, space or season;
　It knows no place, rhyme or reason;
　　Like a stream whose source is hidden,
　　　Whence it came, God deems forbidden.

From on high this flow descends
　To sanctify man's mortal ends;
　　But common minds believe by skill,
　　　This river winds to mortal will.

When it flows through simple thought,
　Genius glows with visions wrought;
　　Eternity is vernal as spring's first flower;
　　　And an hour seems eternal without its power.

Its surge propels all minds and thought,
　That swells an urge for being taught;
　　As we're swept by waves of its ethereal tow,
　　　It conveys . . . we are wiser than we know!

Frank Favaro

THE AMERICAN DREAM

Morphine, Crack, Amphetamine,
　Cocaine, Smack and Heroine;
　　Needles, Pipes and Funny Smoke,
　　　Seedy Types that peddle Coke.

Milkshakes, Sodas, Apple Pie;
　Clam Bakes, Colas, Ham on Rye;
　　Babe Ruth and the Yankee Team,
　　　Jaded Youth . . . a Faded Dream.

Redneck Smokers sneaking Tokes,
　Uptown Jokers sniffing Coke;
　　City Slums or Suburbaneese,
　　　Tykes succumb on bended knees.

Mothers, Fathers buffering Truth,
　Wilting, Fading, Suffering Youth;
　　Seedy Scum impose their Scheme;
　　　And thumb their nose — at the American Dream!

Frank Favaro

SILENCESHARERS

Frodo, Peter's dog, sprawls on a throw rug
Beside his housemate's musichoard
Of records and cassettes. Sometimes he snores;
Sometimes, dreaming, whimpers or growls
At shadows in strange woods.

Awake and walking, though, he sniffs disdain
At illbred neighborhood barkers.
Well, after all,
Apart from stereobinges
And clocks that chime askew,

His trackmate's quiet also. Too quiet someways.
Oh, they've evolved a fair exchange
Of equable affection over the years,
But in his changeless doggyheart
Frodo pines for the goldendays

Of petting on demand. Unschooled by time,
He cannot grasp how loving
Sinks to a mute routine. Nor could he fathom
Why, in absent moods, this oddball
Mister calls him Son.

Peter Thomas

MY GRANDMOTHER

My Grandmother, I love her best of all.
She stands so proud, so straight and tall
With a sweet smile always on her face,
A twinkle in her blue eyes
With hair piled high, and her walk so full of grace.

She has love, warmth, and compassion.
When you call and ask for help
She is there without hesitation.
A figure she has like a movie star,
And friends all around, from near and far.

She doesn't have a throne and lots of jewels.
But to each of us, she's our Angel Supreme.
My Grandmother, the nicest, the sweetest I have ever seen.
My Grandmother, Oh Yes!
Would make the perfect Queen.

Anna K. Richardson

MOTHER TO DAUGHTER

If at all possible, daughter,
marry someone that loves you just as much
if not more than you love him.
That way, he will be good to you.

And when you have children, daughter,
live in such a way that they will respect you.
Teach them manners so you need never be ashamed of them.
Expose them to different cultures
so their outlook on life will not be limited.

Give them something to believe in
so that when times get hard
they turn to their Creator.

And most of all
raise them with an unselfish love.

Bettina Thorpe

POETS

In every poet
there exists a
drop
of God.

Barbara Bell-Teneketzis

MEETING OF MINDS

I shall meet you anywhere;
If I can meet you—anywhere.
I shall run — if I can run;
I shall crawl — if I can crawl.
I hurt!
I cannot die.
I shall fling these arrows
Back into your sling;
Whence they came —
If I can, yank them from my heart.
My eyes shall follow them —
From trees to sky.
If they can penetrate this
Encompassing fog.

Sue Russell Slack

THE TRANSPARENT WALL

Neither one would budge from grudge
Of injurious quarrel;
Unwilling to relent and
Back down from proud position,
Each refused to talk at all.
Using old maid daughter as
Liaison for relaying
Few important messages;

They ate in adjoining rooms —
Mother alone in kitchen,
Father and daughter out on
Sunporch — with jaws hard as flint,
Their mouths chiseled out of stone,
Eyes cold as icicles in
Frigid winter's deadly blast —
Staring unseeing, with both
Existing as two statues
In their silent house of ice.

Charles F. Sutton

I LOVE YOU

You've said it.
I've heard you say it.
Yes, those words.
I think you really mean it.
Say it again.
Tell me.
Tell everyone.
Shout it from the highest mountain top.
And then, when you're done,
Come and hold me
And say it again.

Angela Wheeler

SOMEONE TOUCHED ME

When life began for me,
My parents wished that I would be
The best that they could possibly
Contribute to society.
   And Someone touched me.
The early years were happily spent
At play and then at school.
Youthful years came and went
While learning fundamental rules.
   Yet someone touched me.
Parents, teachers, husband, friends—
All contributed to no end
To what I have become today,
Because along the way
   They all touched me.
If only wisdom at this age
Had been granted, not denied,
While in my youthful stage!
One fact, 'tis true, I cannot hide
   Someone Almighty touched me.

Lillian C. Marcoux

LITTLE STONE CHURCH

*In memory of Grandfather and
Father, who built the church*

It stood by the roadside
So silent and true,
Its door always open
To welcome all of you.

I shall never forget
To worship, although
My faithful old church
Has fallen to foe.

Preserve all the grounds,
Be they ever so humble,
For Stoney Hill Church
In minds will not crumble.

Let's put a fine cross
In memory of this:
The faithful ones
Who were here and are missed.

Vi Schoenbaum

THE RIBBON STORE

Today — like every day — I went to
the ribbon store to ask the clerk:
''Old friend, what color ribbon did
my love buy today?''
Imagine my joy when I was told
You bought every reel of yellow
they had and whispered my name
on your way home.
Now, no more need I roam —
for love in yellow ribbon and whisper
form — calls me home.
And it's not a day too soon,
for the ribbon store closes today at noon.

Joan B. Dellvon

HUMILITY

Strong and mighty it did rise,
standing lofty by my side.

Hope was languid, now was fed
by its greatness, which led
all my doubts to a timely end,
lifting me on wings of flight
on the winds of sweet songs of sight.
I began to grow by leaps and bounds
When it showed me how lowly I was found.

Reaching now as high as its brow,
I knew immediately somehow,
Humility was its name.

Coming to show my rightful place
While set like jewels of brilliant glow,
Humility is my best show.

Betty Lou Edwards

SPRING IN THE COUNTRY

Walking down a country road,
My soul is refreshed
And life is beautiful.
Seeing God's world unfold
Is a wondrous moment to behold!

I love the song of the meadowlark
As he sings for me today,
And the dear little bluebird
Is marvelous to see
Winging along the way.

Green grass is peeking through the snow,
The sun is warm and bright,
A yellow daffodil
Is beginning to bloom,
My heart is filled with delight!

A gentle breeze caresses me
As I walk along the road.
No cares today—
I am in God's world
And He must carry the load!

Juanita Caudle Crane

4:30 A.M. IN ISRAEL

This morning while
   gazing thru
the third floor window,
   one lone soul I can see . . .
Resolutely he
   presses forward
his eye reaching the far horizon
   while the heart stays
   close to where
the foamy breakers caress the shore.

Alone, yet not alone,
for —
the moon, like a silver platter,
surveys this scene with me.

Ridgely Lytle

MELANCHOLY

As the sun sets and turns to evening stars
　so does my heart fall to the emptiness of my soul.
Rising is the sadness of my existence,
　my mind obscure with the uncertainty of happiness.
I give my heart liberty as it falls deeper into you,
　it is unknowing of the anguish to arrive with the rising sun.
As heart and mind have their evening quarrel, the sky turns somber
　my mind disconsolate with my whole being.
My heart sees the bright stars as your eyes,
　unable to face the uncertainty lying within them.
Hiding its anxiety of the coming dawn, my mind
　tries to dishearten the feelings my heart holds.
Protected by my knowing mind, my heart
　will someday know the adverse side of my love for you.

Nancy Updike-Hickey

You linger in the hours of my loneliness
　like scented memories rising from forgotten dreams.
You ransom my confinement like a cherished view into another time.
If you are happiness — enfold me
　in the blessedness you bring and grace my empty garden
　with a festival of life and hope and majesty
　　as radiant
　as the myriad of stars that crown my mind.

You are pressed to me indelibly —
　that sacrament which penetrates and mystifies the soul.
My sweet, beloved mystery, warm and beautiful within me;
　like fires to illumine,
　your aura shimmers softly in the velvet world you touched
　　so long ago.

Amid this realm of smoke and mist,
　of moods as deep and still as hollows,
　the fragrance of your gift remains
　　forever
　the salvation of my heart.

Christine A. Pitt

NO, I DON'T WANT
TO HATE LIKE THIS

Deceit, deception, and outright lies . . .
You do all these things with love in your eyes.
It hurts me to hate you, but you give me no choice,
And I must close my ears to my heart's inner voice.
And, no, I don't want to hate you now,
But your thoughtlessness has shown me how
To detest and despise and absolutely abhor
With wretched hostility all that you have stood for.
Your eyes shine with love, but you go on deceiving
And you slice up a heart that is still disbelieving
That I could ever really start to hate like this.
I emerged from my warm blissful chrysalis,
Abandoned its safe, love-showered shell,
Stood in the rain, rang the fire-tempered bell,
And walked with the Devil through the gates of Hell.

Kim A. Hutson

FROM A NEW GRANDDAD
TO HIS SON

Sometimes I run across worn out old tools
That you used to work with every day after school.
Pieces of your bike always cluttered the yard.
They lay where you left them when you took it apart.
My car never sat in my garage
Because that space was filled with a collage
Of bits and pieces of your busy life —
It's all right there still, though you now have a wife.
My joints are all stiff, because it's been so long
Since you tossed me a baseball with your arm so strong,
But one day soon I'll again have to run
When I'm chasing a line drive hit by your son.
I'll go to the stadium and cheer when he scores.
We'll make regular runs to the ice cream stores.
We'll play with the dog and go to the zoo.
I'll teach him to whistle, just like I taught you.
I'll stand in the yard and look at the clutter
That your son will leave as he starts to putter.
Your son is a gift from you to me.
He'll be his dad all over again — wait and see.

Kim A. Hutson

FROM A NEW GRANDMOTHER
TO HER SON

I haven't childproofed my home in a great many years,
It's been a long time since I've dried my sons' tears,
Scraped knees are only in my distant past,
And I no longer worry that boys drive too fast.
Sticky fingerprints on the refrigerator door
Are as foreign as mud on the living room floor.
No trinkets are broken — haven't been for ages,
And all of my books have unblemished pages.
These things will soon change, and I want you to know
That I welcome these changes as I did long ago.
My home soon will be filled with childish chattering
And I'll hear on the stairs tiny footbeats pattering.
Santa Claus will return on Christmas Eve.
Easter eggs will be found among backyard leaves.
Homemade cards will adorn my kitchen walls
And I'll haunt the toy stores in local malls.
I want you to know that this gift you give
Will brighten my heart for as long as I live.
I want you to know that your first son
To his grandmom will be special because he's my first one.

Kim A. Hutson

USE YOUR MENTAL
SPARK PLUG

Think once! Think twice! Think real! Think true!
Are you letting fear make a weakling of you?
Just being afraid is the reason why
You'll not accomplish unless you try.

Everything's related, strange to say,
And truth will bring the light of day.
Patience and practice will get you where
Lack of effort would never dare.

Keep the proper goal in sight,
For joy of Life strive for the right.
Waste no time in useless sighing,
Bid courage stay — and *keep on trying!*

Lillian Hugh Lawson

MOVING DAY

The house is truly empty,
   and your heart feels empty, too,
For this house is full of memories
   that time will not undo.

'Twas here your wife conceived
   of a love that knows no bounds.
'Twas here you brought your baby,
   and she made her gurgling sounds.

'Twas out there in the garden
   where your lovely roses grew,
And the grass would always sparkle
   with the drops of morning dew.

The birds all came to feed here —
   the cardinals and the jays;
And you wonder if they'll miss you
   when you've gone your separate ways.

As you close the door behind you,
   your throat is feeling tight,
And you wonder what pollutant
   might be blurring up your sight.

Donald G. Westlake

ENDURING LOVE

*To my wife, Helen, on our
forty-third Valentine's Day*

The tulip tree's in bloom!
The apple blossoms burst,
And daffodils of gold
Contrasted hovering gloom
That satisfied their thirst
As Thorian warriors bowled.

Ignoring threatening skies,
My love and I denied
That mist or even rain
Could cause the sad demise
Of embers deep inside
Our hearts — Amor's domain.

We strolled the village street;
We walked and talked and dreamed,
And shared the hopes and fears
That most of us secrete.
'Tis all that it had seemed:
A love to last the years.

Donald G. Westlake

GRACE

How much, preventing God! how much I owe
To the defenses thou hast round me set:
Example, custom, fear, occasion slow,
These scornéd bondmen were my parapet.

I dare not peep over this parapet
To gauge with glance the roaring gulf below,
The depths of sin to which I had descended,
Had not these me against myself defended.

Ralph Waldo Emerson

MY COUNTRY U.S.A.

Two centuries and more she has struggled
To uphold the rights of man.
Against great odds — she defeated —
Protecting her varied clan.

Many are the battles she's conquered
On fields full of blood and death
To uphold those things she believes in
And will to her dying breath.

From nothing she became mighty
Because mankind was her love —
Belief in the rights of her people
With God placed far up above.

This goal of liberty for all
She has ever tried to uphold.
Despite mistakes — wrong decisions —
Her efforts were born of pure gold.

Let the drums roll for our country.
Let the bugles sound for our land.
She's the best that there is and I love her.
She's mighty, she's lovely, she's grand!

Tessie Bea McCall

WINDS OF WINTER

The winds of winter
are frigid and cold.
The winds of winter
are desperately bold.
Their mission to nowhere
tells it so right —
wailing and shrieking
all through the night.

The winds of winter
leave behind trails
of crisp frozen grass
and a chill that pales
the stark naked trees
in a shivering cold
in the light of the
moon — sweeping and bold
throughout the night,
without backward glance,
in the cold dim light —
God's mighty advance!

Tessie Bea McCall

MY WINGS ARE FOUND

Sing me a song, oh morning birds,
of flying high, of flying free.
Thy flight shows me
That I, too, can be singing a song
and flying high and free.
Thy song's sound touches me on the ground
and — through it — my wings are found.
And we will try
and we will fly without limits.
Oh, how high we will go and
flow, singing, singing, winging, winging,
thee and me.

Joan B. Dellvon

BEHIND OUR BACKS

When evil words
Fall to evil tongues
And the minister says
"We must all be one,"
Then why don't we listen
To those most high
When the time to slander
Is the time to die?

And words fall back
To those who charged
And thoughts provoked
Are then enlarged.
Regard them differently
Than little white lies.
Those words that hurt
Could make devils cry.

Shani

LOVERS, YOU AND I

Will we get the chance
That most lovers get
To find the finer things in life
   And still have no regrets

Will I have the chance
To feel your body near
To know your love is with me
To know you're always here

Will we have the chance
To be forever one
To always have each other
Like the morning has the sun

Will you get the chance to see
How much our love endures
And will I get to prove my love
By making my life yours?

Shani

MARY LOU

Mary Lou,
I loved you!
But now you are with God.
We miss you so —
Your face aglow
And now with wings you trod.

Your wheelchair's still
But what a thrill
To walk! to run! to fly!
We miss you so!
But there you go
To your dear Lord on high.

Mary Lou
We're happy for you!
You're free from all your pain.
Rheumatoid arthritis — be gone!
Let loose of Mary's chain
So that she will fly again!

Irene Bayne

RARE

Rare is my soul,
Heart upon my sleeve,
Piercing are my eyes,
Pondering are my ways.
Where will I go?
What can I do?
How can I go on
After all that has been done?
My feet are like clay
As they walk each day.
My spirit is broken,
My head is lowered.
There are no tokens
Left for me to take.
The smiles, the cheers —
They are all gone!
I must go on;
So my mind tells
The inner being of me.

Eileen Jorge

EILEEN M. JORGE. Pen Name: Filene Lee;
Born: Acushnut, Massachusetts, 7-30-45; Mar-
ried: Frank, 7-1-83; Education: Bridgewater State
College, Master, Elementary education, 1972;
New England College, B.A., Elementary educa-
tion, 1967; Occupation: Teacher; Memberships:
MTA, NEW, NBEA, American Association of In-
dividual Investors, YWCA Investment Club of
New Bedford; Poetry: 'A Walk Toward Strength,'
'Dreams,' 'A Creature,' *American Poetry Anthol-
ogy;* Comments: *I feel the need to continue to
succeed even though there is turmoil around me.*

JOE — AN UNWRITTEN SONG

Your unwritten song spins in my mind
like an errant wind
that bends the grass and dances 'mid boughs
that reach the sky.
A song with words of such sorrow that
it seems unending
rages, as sea storms crash wildly
on barren shores.
Yet with touches of joy that lift the soul
up to the stars.
Peace as quiet as gentle rain on a
late summer eve.
Song with some words out of Heaven,
but mostly not.
Words that waft the scent of the roses,
but not always.
Dear Joe — sometime beyond Heaven's door,
peace will be ours again.
And come once more the scent of the roses.

Mystery Alires

CAPTURE SUNDAY MORNING

Capture Sunday morning:
the crackle of onionskin Bible pages
the muted glow of light
through the stained glass windows — saintless
from my Baptist childhood.
Vibrating roundness of organ chords
as the congregation stands.
Fire and brimstone raining down
from the pulpit sound
like the thump of the preacher's fist.
Capture Sunday morning for me, Daddy,
take me back to when things were
as simple
as getting to church on time.

Elizabeth Underwood

PSEUDOHONEYMOON

The days slip away
like sand through our fingers,
our lives fitting together
with no visible seams.
When reality takes on
the opaque quality
of melted butter and
the sand in the hourglass
stops running in mid-air,
it's easy to pretend
there will be no end.
Whatever dark gods
watch over me
were all laughing
when, once,
I almost believed
that you loved me.

Elizabeth Underwood

HEY, LITTLE CHILD

Hey, little child — summer's sun.
Sunning, running, having fun.
Dear, dear sweet, seeking smile.
Hey, little child — hearts beguile.

Take Mother's and Father's hands.
Go with us to rainbow arc —
To far place where mystic stands
To grant you magic's secret spark.

Hey, little child — wonder's way.
Clear, clear — keep asking "Why."
Ringing, singing 'til we say —
Hey, little child — "Love," your reply.

Joan B. Dellvon

YOU'RE EVERYTHING TO ME

You're the warmth of the sun
  and the stars in the sky.
You're the colors in a rainbow
  and the twinkle in my eye.
You're the music on the radio
  and the mystery of a foggy night.
You're the flow of the river
  and the glow of the moonlight.
You're the aching in my heart
  and the ticking of an old clock.
You're the freedom of the mountains
  and the soaring of a hawk.
You're the smell of falling rain
  and the power of loud thunder.
You're the hunger that I crave
  and the one who makes me wonder.
You're the desire of my life
  and the image so thought of.
You're the reason for it all
  and the one I'll always love.

Laura Lynn Robertson

BOLD ILLUSIONS

What touch is this
    which gives such bliss?
Oh, would it that I weren't in love:
never nearing
    always fearing
what would result if we but kissed.
And thus, my thoughts,
    perforce, are caught
in dilemmas so unmanly;
and so, I live
    on dreams which give
bold illusions: actions unwrought.
If, quite by chance,
    you caught my glance,
what would you think, or say — or feel?
If you but knew
    its naked truth,
never again would we brush hands.

P. B. Quinn

THE FLOWERS OF SPRING

When the red roses turn to spring
And the lilacs bloom in white
The peaches will bud in Alton
And tell then Mother I will be there

When we walk the prairies and hills
When the trillius is in the bloom
Let her grow in Illinois
And bring the spring   for some

In the winter growth of wheat
To be a   cause to call
And grow the zenith
Power of the world to all

Another and a dear clear anthem
She has been called into the Springtime.

Herbert V. Shert Jr.

THE YEARS LONG PAST

Black skin, gray hair and yellow eyes that once were white
His face lined with many years of toil
bears a smile of a forgotten memory
of a day long past
Watering eyes gleam longing for youth
Now age has come and left him an old man.

Sitting in a ratty old chair
watching the days pass by
waiting for his time to come
remembering the years forgotten to most
Wishing he had done something different
in those years of his youth.

Knowing it is too late to run again
he sits and stares at the children playing
He cries for his youth
knowing he can't bring back
the years long past.

Timothy C. Bass

THE SHOOTING STAR

you're just a shooting star
as the people watch while you burn out from afar
you're high and mighty but with all your power
you can't make it to the top or get into the tower
heaven was thine
and as the people did dine
you burned out from afar
your stories were told from the days of old
but heaven was too much for your soft touch
oh shooting star why did you fall
why couldn't you remain as a fiery ball
but that is life
it's full of strife
and even the stars die
as the night passes by
but you're just a shooting star
as the people watch while you burn out from afar

Mark Wilhelmi

DRY HEAT

A stale sun's fire lingered and flickered in
an empty, god-forlornéd sky and charred
embers on earth, befouled with aging stench;
and pumice, wrinkled, sand-blown hands of blanch-
gazed men lay still upon unending plains;
and whirling planets rushed headlong through space,
a vague, indifferent, muted heat and cold
are one, and no anchor for revolution.
Man courses stripped of souls, with cavern-hearts
as hollow as the moon's rock-rimmed craters,
with eyes dried up that stare immobily, as
a wailing sirocco swept through somnolent plains.

Dr. Bonnie Homsley

BALLET OF A TWILIGHT PRINCESS

Ballerina spinning on her toe,
on the tip of a star,
dancing on the twilight
Her audience watches in silence
Planets circle in their cycle
Comets speed by
She moves her arms gently as feathers floating
Experience rides with time
Bowing,
    she lights up the sky

Larry Shuffle

LARRY SHUFFLE. Born: San Juan King Valley, 12-26-52; Married: Linda; Children: son, Larry Lee Sundance; Occupations: Professional karate instructor, Musician, Poet, Songwriter; Poetry: 'Making Love,' *American Poetry Anthology,* 1987; Comments: *Fire burns in my soul to express my life on paper. It's an illusion. Life is just a moment in time. Fire burning. A sun in the sky. I dedicate this poem to the future.*

ALIVE AGAIN

The silence in my ears has turned into ringing
While the stillness in my heart has turned into swells
This numbness which I've felt through what seems to be ages
Has now given way for my senses to thrive

When all the harsh noises become children singing
And all of my screams become lofty bells
The crying in my heart, say fools and say sages
Is a silent reminder that love's still alive

How sudden a turn from the pain and the madness
Of a life which seems empty, devoid of all reason
How one day can change one's whole jaded being
To that which is lucid and clear in its flight

Such beautiful emotions replace all the sadness
Alive again to take hold of the season
Where blindness once reigned I am now only seeing
The colors of spring as if in a new light

What matters most now is the biding of time
That these wonderful feelings might evolve
And not let this time, which can be of the essence
Let either heart lose its resolve

Patrick Sands

EVERLASTING IMPACTS

Serpent in the garden of Eden —
  The tangible asset
Among the fleeting.

Forty years of desert:
  Forty days on the mount
To realize God's commandments count.

Idolatry among us all —
  Judges and kings met the call:
To reinforce God's law.

King David's 150 inspired psalms:
  Glory, mercy, and praise of spirit
'Tis blessings . . . reading within it.

God's prophet's visions:
  Hold futures — predictions —
In readiness of His decisions.

''The Cross'' — an adjustment of justification:
  'Tis opposition to evil aggression
There's a key to eternal life:
  Through our Savior Jesus Christ.

Suffering in life's long strife —
  Keep progressing in God's sight:
Working to be in God's book of life.

John Behringer

JOHN DOE

Will the real John Doe stand
Up on his own feet for
A change and tell
All his other personalities to get lost or
Will hypocrisy be his most
Constant companion?

Linda G. Rhea

LIVING IN A DREAMWORLD

Living in a Dreamworld
to see what you could be
so everyone can see

Living in a Dreamworld
so wild and free
Just maybe, it's our way
out of reality

Living in a Dreamworld
so great is its name
but is definitely not a game

Living in a Dreamworld
if you are a different
person than thee
then you can't see that
Living in a Dreamworld
is *not* a *Fantasy!*

Melissa Belanger

KEEPSAKES

Remember when we planted roses?
You dug a hole deep enough to plant
a tree: how we laughed!

And the time you were wiping the dishes?
You dropped a plate on your toe —
that wasn't so funny.

Your vacation sunglasses, remember?
Watching you storm around the house,
looking for what was in your hand.

I'm still sharing memories with you,
loving you, feeling you're near me.
Even though for two months there have been
walls of earth between us.

Douglas H. Stanton, M.D.

WORDS

My words
Might not mean a thing to you,
But everything to me.
My eyes
Might not make you believe
In the things that they have seen.
My thoughts
Might have their reasons,
But will often give you none.
My heart
Might be unable
To show you how to love.
My words
Are often locked up inside,
Waiting for a chance to describe.

R. E. Lunt

A LOVE . . .

The one thing that we all dream of,
And that is love . . .
A love that is so strong
It will pass all the tests,
A love that is so strong
That you're willing to face death.
A love that will last throughout the years,
A love that has cried a million tears.
But a heart has to hurt,
A heart has to be broken,
And love is so often
Expressed with the eyes,
Words are seldom spoken.
Dreams are pictures to our desires,
And they are the only thing that we own.
Day after day we search for paradise
While it's right here at home.

R. E. Lunt

LONELINESS (WHO DETERMINES?)

Loneliness
Who has the answers?
Who turns the pages
Of a heartbreak?

Loneliness
Who quenches the fire?
Who's the first to admit
The fate?

Who is the front runner?
Who is the master?
Who determines the love child
From the bastard?

In a lifetime
We are put through the test.
I want to know
Who determines loneliness?

R. E. Lunt

ENTITY

Step by step
I walked the shore
My essence
Imprinting the sand.

The tide threatening
At times ebbing
I stopped
Musing the vastness
Of the sea.

Looking back
I saw no footprints
On the neap,

No one will know
I walked this path
Save God, the sea and me.

Philomena Christie

DISGUISE

a clown's sadness
grief in the heart
covered with some paint
and an empty smile

his steps
lost among the others
he puts on his huge shoes
and we laugh

his body scarred
from the wounds of life
so on go the plaids
and the bright colors

a clown's eyes
so deep
they turn down at the corners in crow's feet
the paths of weathering tears

Angela Wheeler

SEASONS

Our first meeting came in fall.
The days were fresh and crisp and new
Filled with an array of multi-colored hues,
Just as our beginning.
Then with the falling of first snow you had to go away.
And winter became a time for waiting.
But waiting had within it the promise of the coming spring
And all that it would surely bring.
One glorious day you walked back into view
And spring was here all fresh and new.
A time for love and learning.
As we walked and talked together springtime turned to
    summer's gold.
A time for sharing sunny days and starry nights so bold.
For childhood memories that delight in everyway
Bringing joyous laughter to each day.
Then our summer turned to fall
Which very often is the best of all.
For now our love is sure and strong
And can outlast the winters long.

Judith M. Thomsen

LOVE'S RHYTHM

How still the night, the moon above so golden;
How peaceful is the world beneath it sleeping;
How dear your charms, your smile so deeply dimpled,
How close within my arms, so quiet keeping.

This is True Love. Our hearts are bound together!
We are two souls, in rhythm with each other.
This is the dream we've both been long a-dreaming
for we have needed only one another.

Arlone Mills Dreher

AT WHAT LONELY TIME?

When does the Boy cease to watch for and to search out the
    wonders of his commonplace world?
And where does an ice cream cone lose its delicate vanilla
    perfume to become something cold, sweet and fattening?
And at what moment, in the swift flight of time, does he
    forget his fear of Goblins, or of houses turned old
    and sinister at night;
Or his delight in lying on heaps of acrid-smelling leaves on
    nippy autumn afternoons,
Looking off into a cloud-infested sky or at nothing at all?
When does the Boy forget his games and how to play?
When does the Man, walking along a quiet street, discover some
    half-remembered scene out of joint with time;
To hear faintly the cry of the long-deposed peddler, loudly
    sing-songing praises of his simple wares?
And when does the Man forget his joy of climbing into tall trees,
    to see and to be the silent master of the vibrant, pulsing
    world below . . .
At what time and place did the Boy and the Man meet in quiet
    embrace — and then forever part?

James T. Forrest

19 vs 36

We aren't so different
You and I —
    just looking for the same things,
    you a beginning
        and I, an ending —
as our years separate a grasp
    that could have been.
. . . and somehow I hope you can hear me
    as I whisper these words
        alone in the dark,
            and just maybe — we could have been.

Terry A. Symon

WEARY

The world is too much upon me
And the mind groans under the weight,
Oh, so weary am I.
Gone are the games and innocent ways,
The heart, kindled by a smile, leaping and ablaze,
The eyes abright,
Curious to peruse the unfolding day,
Grazing among the enigmas of the human herd.
But how tired the eyes have grown
And the heart has become gutted by loss
While the feet fidget with the ground,
Yearning to fly this earthbound reticulum,
A network of relentless cares,
To seek an unknown aerie.

Joseph Frankel

A WORLD OF DIFFERENCE

The American stood to request a hymn,
    ''Guide me, O Thou Great Jehovah,
    Pilgrim through this barren land.''
On that bright Pennsylvania morning,
We sang enthusiastically.

When we had finished,
Our Ethiopian guest hastened to request,
    ''For the beauty of the earth
    For the glory of the skies.''
We again responded with vigor.

The African took his place in the pulpit,
Lifted first his eyes to heaven, then looked at us.
He smiled and spoke softly,
    ''These are two views
    A Christian has of his world.
    Which world is yours?''

I looked at the American,
Then the African
And fell silent.

Doris M. Compton

SWEET WARM ECSTASY

*Written in May 1957 to
my husband, Dr. Wilhelm Reich*

Walking alone through forest and wood,
I dreamed my Willie before me stood.
With outstretched arms and boyish form,
He gathered me up before the storm.
We hugged and kissed so tenderly,
Thus entranced in sweet warm ecstasy.
No one knows the joy we knew
Standing together, just we two.

Aurora Reich

AURORA REICH. Born: Cleveland, Ohio; Married: Wilhelm Reich, M.D.; Education: Tulane University, National Institutes of Health Graduate Program, University of Wisconsin School of Journalism; Occupations: Biomedical researcher, Administrator, Writer; Memberships: Founding member American Association of Blood Banks, American Public Health Association, American Medical Writer's Association; Awards: Ann Hero Northrop Prize in Chemistry, Teaching fellowships; Writings: More than 125 publications in and about the world of medical and scientific research, more than 100 unpublished poems to my husband, one published poem, 'On Cosmic Energy'; Comments: *Poetry is a great way to communicate love and caring, deep feelings, and instincts about the world around us. It has the potential for making the world a little better place for all to live. Poetry can give comfort and it can inspire. Poetry can give hope and happiness, and faith in tomorrow.*

LITTLE LUCKY

This little lost mutt that I befriended,
From a kennel long ago,
Soon came to know someone who loved him,
And in his own way, he told me so.
So much joy a dog can offer,
So much love in its little heart,
That when it comes time to say good-bye,
It just tears the soul apart.
People say dogs don't go to heaven,
But I know that can't be true,
For you put them here on earth,
And I know you love them too.
Put him, Lord, in a big green pasture,
That he may romp and play,
And when my soul departs to heaven,
You will give him back to me one day.

Helen Matthews

SPLENDID GRACE

Porcelain featured
Most delicate creature
Painting this world full of grace
Fortune has shown you the way
The magnificent splendor
You bring to each day
Your beauty abounds now
For me I will try to follow some way
You taught me the meaning of understanding
The fragility
The living monument to God's days
Human kindness a door to fineness
Your splendid grace always

Dena Beth Lesser

IVY, MY LOVE

Ivy, my love, Ivy, my love
You're just as dear as the heavens above.

You're gentle and kind as you can be
And never keep me up a tree.

You're handsome and tall and dark, my love,
Considerate and sweet as an angel above.

Your kiss is as soft as a gentle breeze.
I'll love you forever more if you please.

I hope that you will always stay
As strong and as healthy as you are today.

And that you never go away
And leave me all alone, I pray.

If the marriage is as sweet as the courtship is,
God will surely call you His.

When I am locked in your embrace,
I'm safe and warm without a trace

Of the hate and greed of this world we live in.
I hope that when at last I give in

And surrender all of myself to you
That we'll never again be lonely and blue.

Frances Hough

HAPPY ANNIVERSARY

James and Lucille are a perfect pair
They're always going here or going there.
They visit the sick and the lonely,
The bereaved, or just for fun only.
They're busy as two little bees,
And happy as can be, if you please.
They find time to enjoy their family.
They're the best branches on our family tree.
We're proud that we can call them our own.
They sew a fine seam when it needs to be sewn.
We all are here to congratulate them.
Forty years of wedded bliss is no whim.
I'm proud of the part I had in their meeting
And I hope that they enjoy this greeting.
We love them dearly and hope that they
Can have many happy returns of the day.

Frances Hough

EUROCLYDON

Euroclydon,
the wind of the
past.

Turning over
the ashes
of our life.

Blowing off
the chaff.

Leaving the
gold.

Ruth Johnsson Hegyeli, M.D.

A FROSTY NIGHT

A frosty night
with northern lights.

Entrancing
the traveler.

Beckoning
to the stars,

Sending
our thoughts,

To distant
shores,

Reaching
the universe.

Ruth Johnsson Hegyeli, M.D.

REMEMBER THOSE DAYS

Remember those days
when the sun shone bright.

When there was
no cloud in the sky.

When we were
young.

When love was
strong.

Ruth Johnsson Hegyeli, M.D.

WHISPERS

Faint, faint whispers in my ear.
Baby's words are not too clear.
but his murmur wets my cheek.
He holds my hair in hands that reek
of gingersnaps and candy goo
while he tells me, "I love you!"

Florence W. Ruppert

TENTATIVE STEPS

I have walked the forbidding deserts of Ishmael,
    The little hills of Galilee,
    The ancient route into Petra,
    The winding road to Golgotha,
    The blue cobblestones of Old San Juan,
    The narrow jungle trails of the Orinoco,
    The haunting corridors of the Catacombs.

But when I came with my friends
    To that silent path
    Which led to those common graves
    In Leningrad, bright jewel of Peter the Great,
    My feet did not want to disturb
    That sacred ground.
    The thousands lying there
    Had been hurt enough,
    They did not need to feel
    The weight of my feet upon them
    As they slept.

Doris M. Compton

THE TRAGEDY OF DEATH BRINGS A LESSON ON LIFE

I walked into class knowing his desk would be vacant,
I wasn't his friend; I had been guarded, complacent.
Though I hardly knew him at all, my eyes filled with tears,
To think of his life of barely fifteen years.

With unexpected death, it's extremely hard to deal,
It takes great strength and courage and will.
Whatever the circumstances, death is a trial.
However you face it: acceptance, denial.

Life's so unfair to kill off its youth,
But perhaps it was needed, so I'd realize the truth.
It was taken for granted that my life would be long,
But I suddenly realized that I may have been wrong.

A lesson taught by a dead classmate,
To live my life before it's too late.
I can never forget the cold, hard fact,
That death always hits with harsh impact.

Tiffany Mano

PROMISE

A creation.
Scents from blooms, drifting back and forth
With soft breezes blowing thru open windows,
Now noticed, then not.

The creation tempts a touch.
A gentle pulling brings the blossom closer,
And scent fills the air.
A promise that fades tho' memories linger.

A memory.
Of a child drifting back and forth
Between independence and needs of a daughter.
Now at home, then gone.

A grown woman tempts a touch.
A gentle smile draws my daughter closer.
She holds me tightly,
Telling me with love she'll be mine forever.

Lee W. Kelley

GRADUATION

Farewell to peanut butter:
No more PB and J;
Letters will now be sliced
Unevenly by intruding vowels
Of responsibility and unsought tasks.
Printed ledgers of homework fade
Into script. The paper has no substance.
My soul goes into flight unnourished.

The days begin to count their
Numbers by misintended martinis,
The parochial calls of trumpeted business
Hang thickly by the glazed top conference
Table and a napkin-stuffed luncheon.
In the park a flowering elm carefully
Shelters three boys playing hooky:
They lie lazily in the grass knowing
Only the brush of a twig and a raspberry
Glob which falls with sultry leisure on one boy's bare leg.

Stephen Rosenthal

WHEN THE GIRL IN MY LIFE WALKS IN

When the girlfriend of my friend said to me,
''I know a girl who is perfect for you.
Do you want to meet her?'' I said, ''Yes.''

I remember well when she
Opened the door of my friend's apartment
And walked in.

I remember well what she wore,
How she looked,
And her million dollar smile.

It is now 50 years later.
We have three children
And twelve grandchildren.

But I remember well when she
Opened the door of my friend's apartment
And walked in.

I remember well what she wore,
How she looked,
And her million dollar smile.

Joseph S. Wright

PORTRAIT OF EVERT

His body is weak, but he is strong at heart.
He knows from his family he soon will depart.
But when you stop by, he greets you with a smile.
He might ask, ''Can you stay for awhile?''
God wants to leave him here, as long as he can,
To show us what bravery can be found in a man.
A frail body that is racked with pain.
What fools we are, of our aches to complain.
When your visit is over, he gives you a grin.
He tells you thank you for stopping in.
He will be glad to leave this life,
Thanking God for such a good wife.
When God finally calls him to that peaceful place up above,
He will have left us a legacy of bravery and strength
    And most of all love.

Carolyn S. Stone

THE DROPPING SONG

I heard, and saw, a mockingbird
   singing and falling his dropping song,
And when he ceased to fall, he flew
   swiftly to perch in a cedar tree.
I silently watched as he continued
   to sing his beautiful refrain —
Suddenly he began to drop again, rolling
   and tumbling from limb to limb;
Singing his exalted mating call until
   he touched the ground.
To have heard the dropping song twice
   is fortuitous, and should ever
I hear it again, I'll know full well that
   God has blessed me threefold.

Harold James Douglas

THERE WAS NO WAY

In the stillness of early morn,
   I sat on a fallen tree . . .
Suddenly I felt eyes boring
   into my back.
Turning my head slowly to
   the right —
I saw a doe and her elegant little
   fawn watching me.
After a few seconds they moved on,
   nipping at green leaves.
Then again I felt the eyes watching
   me, and slowly I turned to
See a large buck about twenty
   feet away . . .
Fingers trembled on the trigger,
   but I didn't shoot, because
There was no way that I would
   break up that family.

Harold James Douglas

CAMPING OUT

When the darkness of night
   sneaked over me . . .
I lay in my makeshift tent on the hill
   above my grandmother's house,
And every sound of human life was
   suddenly hushed —
Only the things of nature
   were heard . . .
Sounds of the hooting owl, and
   the night animals
Seeking food in the dark, or
   the tinkle of a cowbell coming
From downhill near the old log barn
   and corncrib . . .
The light of dawn and the rising song
   of a mockingbird
Awakened me in time to see the
   fading stars,
I thank God for this boyhood
   experience of camping out.

Harold James Douglas

SURE, I OUGHTA KNOW

   Sure, I oughta know
When I was a kid
(Last week sometime)
My dad told me all the
Answers . . .
(Sometimes forgetting the questions).

He taught me to drive nails
(Which is useful to little girls)
And how to drive motor boats.

Now when anybody asks
Me about anything —
I oughta know!
My daddy told me!

Linda G. Rhea

MORNING GLORY

Lift the blinds of your soul —
Send sleep from your eyes
and watch the dawn paint
the canvas of our skies.

Let your ears thrill
as the night's long hush
is sweetly dispelled
by robin and thrush.

How soon surcease will come
from pains fancied and real
when you allow yourself
God's newborn day to feel!

Sidney H. Resnick

EARLY, WITH MY FATHER

Reading funny papers on a warm lap,
Scratched by Sunday morning's face,
Saying prayers against rough sleeves,
Learning tennis, swimming, French,
With laughter,
Finding a smile in the uniform,
After Pearl Harbor's frightened eyes.

   Later
The look of wonder
At my baby,
Making faces in her sleep,
By my mother's grave,
Weeping against rough sleeves,
Weeping.

Virginia Westgaard

WHAT WAS TO BE

She reached her arms to me —
And called my name
Full forty years ago
As she lay upon her bed of pain
Crushed by an avalanche of steel
That sped out of the night
To snatch away a precious jewel
A lover and best friend
My dearest one — indeed my life!

Today she sleeps in quietness
Sheltered by trees that arch the
   pathway to her grave
And though I've traveled far
I go back constantly —
Unto that spot of earth where peace
   and deep serenity meet me
A place where heart can cry —
And spirit can recall what was to be —
For now — and through eternity.

William E. Mays

LIFE'S NEED

In a world of toil and turmoil
How much we need a goal
To lift our thoughts beyond the day
To keep life sane and whole.
There are those who seek and find it
An inner peace serene
That keeps life strong and steady
No matter what may intervene.
Strong souls they are — and hearty —
Strengthened from above
Hopeful and helpful always
Led by the spirit of love.

William E. Mays

THE LAST LOVER

Bolder and bolder my facets I shine.
My diamonds are sparkles of living red wine.
My glass I am draining of riches distilled
in honest emotions and struggles fulfilled.

A kiss on my lips from the heart of a man
fresh as the air of my breathing life plan.
Eyes see new colors and senses are keen.
Spring is my rebirth of blossoms and green.

Love is resurging and living is free
melting ice rivers return to the sea.
Into my full heart this radiance glows
lifting life's sorrows as outward it flows.

Halo and harp like the angels I see
Bride of the God of eternity
Ageless and ancient, the life force I'm wedding
and breathless I go to my lover for bedding.

Florence W. Ruppert

A COWARD'S REPLY

I find it is much simpler just to say: "No."
How can I fail if I don't even try?
Why risk my neck on that?
It is safer to stand pat
And watch the valiant suckers passing by.

Your idea has some merit, I will grant you,
But ideas may be only fantasies.
Right now it's just a quirk.

Who will make the dern thing work?
Don't look at me! I say: Don't look at me!

Come back when all the bugs have been corrected.
Come back when it is ready to be shown.
We'll talk about it then.
I may back it with my pen
Or even claim a dreamer as my clone.

The lesson learned from poet Pope is classic:
"Be not the first by which the new is tried."
Your fingers may be burned
If that new idea is spurned
And I don't wish to be the one who's fried!

Isaac Van Galleon

SUMMERTIME COUNTRY MAGIC

Summertime country magic is —
  On a hot summer night watching fireflies.
    They are acrobats shining their tiny lights.
  On a sunny lake white caps shimmering.
    They are silver streamers carried by the wind.

Summertime country magic is —
  On a windy hillside a field of wild flowers.
    They are nodding their heads welcoming
      the butterflies.
  On the creek bank swinging from a grapevine.
    Then falling into the cool water.

Summertime country magic is —
  Going to the lake on a family picnic.
    The surprise is an icy cold watermelon.
  On a country road looking into a wooded area.
    Then watching deer feeding for a moment.

Charlene Carpenter Acker

FRIGHTING, BUT TRUE

Life is frighting,
Death is frighting,
So we live in fear of not knowing when life will end for us,
But we know it will end,
So we must live in fear,
To live without fear is not to live,
So when we have to say goodbye to someone we love,
It is not easy,
But the love for that person lives on in our hearts,
Knowing that someday we will meet again.

Shane P. Robison

FOLLOWING THE OLD COW TRAIL TO THE MEADOW

Open the gate and go south toward the pond.
  Watch for the little creatures crawling in the sun.
The ants are working along at a fast pace.
  They are storing food for winter as this is a race.

Birds are singing in trees along the barbed wire fence.
  Squirrels dart among the trees keeping all in suspense.
A bullfrog is leaping from the bank into the water.
  You will look and see a splash as it doesn't matter.

Follow the trail around the pond toward the old cow barn.
  On down along the hill toward a creek on the farm.
The green meadow is dotted with wild flowers everywhere.
  They are sprinkled with butterflies darting here and there.

Following the old cow trail brings a lot of pleasure.
  You see many things that are a treasure.
You may take a walk or run and be free any day.
  Regardless what anyone may say.

Charlene Carpenter Acker

THE CITY

People prematurely old
jammed in suffocating buses
carrying lost countries with them
Women holding babies with no tomorrow
Men with shrinking faces
Children in vain playing hide-and-seek
The city
Voices with no echoes in the alleys
The sun overshadowed by clouds and smog
Closed windows, rotten doors
The city
The city
The radio is playing . . . but no music
The computers are working . . . but what's the purpose?
Now they are all asleep
Will they ever awake?
The city
The city
The city

Marinos Kartikkis

THE REAL ME

My mind has stopped in time,
But yet it moves on,
My body is poor,
But yet it is healthy,
My heart and mind crave romance,
But yet I am afraid to show it,
My life is over,
But yet it has just begun,
My wisdom comes from what I have seen or done,
But yet I have seen or done nothing.

Shane P. Robison

I AM AN ABUSED CHILD

I am an Abused Child
My life had so much pain
From adults gone wild,
Anger not restrained.

I am an Abused Child
Much pain throughout my bones.
Adults please become mild
And end those inner moans.

I am an Abused Child
The cycle I will end
By becoming so mild
My child won't need to mend.

I am an Abused Child
And will only show love.
My child will be mild
And always thought of.

Charlotte Moriggia Fantry

TEARS FOR THE CHILDREN

Tears for the children
Flow down from my eyes.
So much pain has been
For no reason why.

Tears for the children
Who have been so beat.
It doesn't matter when
Now they feel much defeat.

Tears for the children
Their pain is so deep.
A sad life for them has been
And many an inner weep.

Tears for their children
Flow down from my eyes.
Stop the cycle they can,
They now understand the whys.

Charlotte Moriggia Fantry

NOT TIME FOR ME TO DIE

So much that I must do
So help me make it through.
I need to survive
Lord, help me to live.
The pain is so intense
My insides are so tense.
Blocking pain is getting hard
Give me some strength please now God.
Not time for me to die
You know the reason why.
So please help me fight
So I can please write
To place such love in the heart
To make evil enter not
So all can be at peace
So much pain can now cease.
But the pain is so great
From my previous fate.
Help me not fall
Help pain to stall.

Charlotte Moriggia Fantry

Though she is dead,
she lives in my head,
in memories bright
as prismed light.
Great riches there,
for she was fair
in all the ways
of gods we praise.
And honored I
am to have been
with her.

R. Peter Rosier

A FRIEND

A friend is a person
you like to be with
and she likes to be with you.

A friend is like a sister,
she's a person you can trust.
You could share your problems with her
and she keeps them to herself.

A friend is there when you need her,
she's always by your side.
She'll show you how much she cares
when you need a friend.

Louise Tatum

TO PAT

(Deceased)

I breathe
    fresh mountain air
    and it is you

I touch the soft sweet grasses —
    they are you

I see the green
    of trees
    and it is you

I feel the healing rain
    and know
    it carries you

I hear a baby gurgle —
    it is you

I search the stars
    and know
    you still are here

In this our universe
    our only world

    it is you

I search the stars
    and know
    you still are here

In this our universe
    our only world
    you still are life.

Dorothy A. Meyer

THE TIME OF SUMMER

A time at the beach
    For swimming and walking.
A time with good friends
    For eating and talking.
A time for picnics
    And camping out.
For Bible School
    And fishing for trout.
A time in the yard
    For trimming and mowing.
A time in the garden
    For weeding and hoeing.
A time for weddings
    And loved ones' graduations.
The time of summer
    For sensuous variations
Is a time to cherish
    And much-needed vacations.

Faye Teague

BASIL

Out of a car bounds a dog.
This will end up to be no ordinary dog,
for this dog is a Newfoundland.
Through two obedience classes,
blue ribbons in both.
Through thick and thin,
even good and bad health.
You were a happy dog, even to the end.
You were a fighter,
not in a fighter sense, but in life.
You gave to others
four times what they gave to you.
It was a sunny afternoon when you left us.
But you were the sunshine
of all of our lives.
You're gone now.
We can't help that.
We can only hope and pray
that the sunshine will be in us,
half of what it was in you.

Ann J. Rutledge

ANOTHER CHANCE

What makes our life seem so unfair
With cupboard full and cupboard bare
One has his health, another ails
One wins much wealth, another fails
One finds his love, while others pine
One's sons go bad, with other's fine
While accidents occur to some
For others only good things come
I've made my point, you know the rest
At times life's actions seem a jest
If we would have our souls enhance
Perhaps we need another chance.

Sol Finkelman

THINKING BACK

I'll tell you my age is 84
I sure wish you all could see
The advances we've had
 Since my life began in nineteen hundred and three
The roads weren't paved; the sand was deep
And horses would pull your train
You have no idea how hard they'd work
Especially if we had a rain

My cousin and I had horses to spare
So we worked on the Berkey Road
They pulled wagons of stone to cover the path
All the way to the N.Y.C. Railroad

Our wages for horses, wagon and man
Were six dollars for a day
We furnished the food for horses and man
Including a bale of hay

First were autos, then trains, then rockets to the moon
Gee, I have so much more to say
This paper tells me it has no more room
So for me that's just O.K.

Wayne Barnes

A CRADLE FULL OF LOVE

As dreams come true
In the land of make-believe
A woman conceived.

She bore a child of unrivaled beauty
Which only she fully appreciated.
Maternal love does not deceive.

The baby's head looked like an archaeological treasure,
Neanderthal man's first daughter.
Handle with care — this babe's a rare find.

Her bald scalp was that of a magic genie.
The pudgy body sat like a Buddha,
As she gently cooed a mourning dove's song.

The child wore a cloak of velvety silk skin,
And cried for the honey flowing from the woman's breasts.
From life — comes life.

Peace and innocence uplift this new being.
Here's proof.
Humans do perform miracles.

M. Theresa Doyle

SEA JADE

I sat beneath a tree, reveling in its cool shade
  Gazing at the distant hills, green as sea jade
    As roses in bloom and a million wild flowers
Formed earth-bound rainbows and emerald towers

By the sea I saw secret sculptors; the wind and rain
  Making new figures and changing forms, grain by grain
    Erasing those vivid marks of rowdy sins once sinned
That before my eyes became only memories in the wind

I was awed by the lovely sights that before me lay
  Grateful for the memories of that warm summer day
    When nature allowed me to see her perfect little toys
I'd been too busy before; too caught up in the noise

I don't know when . . . or if . . . I will return to that hill
  Or if I will ever again have time to gaze and stand still
    For I don't know the secret of today, let alone tomorrow
But the memory of this scene will sweeten my every sorrow

Elyzabeth Eaton

FRIENDS

For Beverly

A friend is a rare and precious gem
As inexplicable as Love and you, My Dear Friend
Through time you have walked and grown beside me
We have trod through Dark and Narrow Paths
And we have floated on Gossamer wings of Joy
You are always Dependable, Loving, Strong and Gentle
What strange road would I have traveled
Had your concerned and helping hand not been there
Though the days ahead may seem dismal and frightening
A Great Light shines upon us
For we have a precious commodity, ''A Friend,''
Truly the important part of our life has just begun
We have found the road we must travel
No Fear, either Physical or Mental, can bar our way
Now, when *You* need Me, I Am Here
We will walk side by side without regret or fear
Every day I thank God for You
No matter where we go or what we do, our Friendship is True
Rest now, My Dear and use my Energies and Strength
Remember always: ''I Am Your Loving Friend, Forever''

L. June Yates

THE WALL

i have been coming to the wall
at days and nights in snow rain and fog,
and it is something i never live before,
touching the wall, i talk to my men,
who never make it back home,
i have seen mothers and fathers childrens,
widows friends compadres to touch a name,
and all in silence they wipe a tear away,
some remember some mourn some to see,
and they all sing low a farewell to him,
walking tall i imagine faces behind names,
and holding our flag i please the sun,
to tell the moon and stars there is a peace at last,
and let's share the joy and sorrow of our lost love,
as the wall reflects the great dead of nobody's war,
and i got no words to tell the world,
Why? we fought the lost war,
Why?

Ted Pegasus

FANCY

In my wildest fantasy,
  You are on the beach with me.
Over miles of sand we stroll
  Watch the waves of ocean roll
And wash our footprints out to sea.
  For us, my love, this can never be.

A cool breeze blows across my face,
  With trembling fingers I erase
A drop of sweat upon your brow,
  If you love me, love me now.
Soon we return to home and mate,
  For us, my love, an awesome fate.

My fantasy ends, now you are gone.
  To think of you, I know is wrong.
But I look for you in every face,
  Along the shore, our special place.
And hope by chance to catch a glance,
  For this, my love, is our romance.

Faye Teague

FAYE ALMA TEAGUE. Pen Names: I've thought about ''Fatigue''; Born: Pendleton, South Carolina; Married: Never (sometimes glad, sometimes sad); Education: Lander College, Greenwood, South Carolina, B.S.; Attended Clemson, Appalachian State, North Carolina and others to update teaching skills; Occupations: Atlanta Public Schools (retired); Presently employed at a church preschool, working with internationals; Memberships: Newspaper Institute of America, 1984; Georgia Preschool Association, Dekalb County Kindergarten, NEA, GAE, AAE, First Baptist Chamblee; Poetry: 'The Brown Earth,' *American Poetry Anthology,* 1986; 'The Language Class,' 'Just Another Day's Journey,' 'Go Ye and Do Likewise,' *Words of Praise, Vol. III,* 1987; Comments: *Teaching children has been my life's work, but writing gives me a high. I love people and usually end up writing about them.*

COME, DAEMON

Interstellar Daemons sail
O'er the Ancient Winds of Morn.
No one escapes, not firm nor frail
When They Blow the Black Horn.

Daemons come to slay the throng
With weapons they crush and cleave,
Earth falls silent, no word or song
Just the Orange Glow of 'Eve.

Alan Wright

I DECLINE

We are a witness
To the Fall
Of ourselves, the friendship,
And the love of it all.

I decline to acknowledge
Who is at fault.
The wounds have been opened
And sprinkled with salt.

I decline to recognize
Who is to blame.
A stupid dream, nothing more
And self-inflicted pain.

I decline to accept
All given reasons
For the end of the species
And the death of the seasons.

Please don't ask
Why I choose to decline.
I realize all faults
Are certainly mine.

Alan Wright

HEARING WHAT IS SAID

The art of conversation
Communicates to the mind
That the nature of the message
Is often just implied

Interchanging words and gestures
Can be misconstrued
By assuming what you heard
Is logically deduced

Underneath the interaction
Is the unspoken voice
Composed of inner secrets
Reflected by your eyes
The source of understanding
Is measured by the way
The listener composes
What they really say

In responding to the other
Is just another way
Of breaking down the barriers
And the distance they convey

Bonnie Zaborski-Beck

JOURNEY ON...

Like a death
love is gone,
passing through tears
memories just linger on.
Like an ending a heart
loses its glow,
a gleam from his eyes
never again shall I know.
Like a new beginning
I must journey on,
but the scars of love
are never gone . . .

Geri Laveglia

GENTLE MEMORIES

Flashbacks of memories and
reflections in view,
visions appear haunting
memories of you . . .
A glow emanated within
your tender smile,
a gleam in your eyes
only lasted awhile . . .
Energies softly sent my way,
haunting memories of yesterday.
A rose you once bestowed
upon my breast,
now sleeps dormant
for it's within rest . . .

Geri Laveglia

DESPAIR

Her words were sharp that cut my heart;
It seemed she took my soul apart
And looked inside my secret place
And watched the tears roll down my face.
Despair and grief touched me within,
There was no way that I could win,
For anything that I might say
Was used against me every day.
''I don't owe you a thing,'' she hurled,
And then I felt my entire world
Shrink into a tattered ball.
Strike, my dear one, and I'll fall;
I've no defenses left at all.

Leta E. Pond

TO MY BELOVED BASIL

There is a hole where you were.
Sure, there are your memories, but
it's not the same as having you around.
The cancer ate a hole in you.
You fought it like a trooper,
but it overwhelmed you.
The hearts of many are
mourning for you.
Your heart was full of love.
We'll miss looking out the
window at your cheery face
and your wagging tail.
We'll miss your gentle kisses.
We'll even miss your drool.
But most of all we'll miss you.
We know you're in heaven,
looking down on us,
Saying, in the way you do,
I'll love you for all time.

Ann J. Rutledge

BLOW, BLOW, THOU WINTER WIND

Blow, blow, thou winter wind,
Thou art not so unkind
　　As man's ingratitude;
Thy tooth is not so keen,
Because thou art not seen,
　　Although thy breath be rude.
Heigh-ho! sing, heigh-ho! unto the green holly:
Most friendship is feigning, most loving mere folly:
　　Then, heigh-ho, the holly!
　　　This life is most jolly.

　Freeze, freeze, thou bitter sky.
　That dost not bite so nigh
　　As benefits forgot:
　Though thou the waters warp,
　Thy sting is not so sharp
　　As friend remembered not.
Heigh-ho! sing, . . .

William Shakespeare

A SILENT WITNESS

It happened a little more than
two score and ten years ago —
he was barely nineteen.
A pair of pallbearers had fled to points unknown
and Rick was left, unattended, on a stretcher,
his broken legs throbbing in pain, when
he was approached by a middle-aged mother.
A brave attempt at a smile
greeted the sympathetic newcomer
as his blue eyes filled with unabashed tears,
partly with gratitude for this display of compassion,
while she inquired, elsewhere, as to his name, home address.

Now, many years after this singular event,
Rick fondly recalls
this unknown person who showed she cared
when she took a few minutes to cheer Rick —
now grown to maturity and, admittedly,
one of the very least of Jesus Christ's brothers . . .
　　"Thank you very much, dear lady;
　　may Jehovah God make you just as happy."

Ridgely Lytle

PEACE AND BEAUTY

The hummingbird, busy around the feeder,
　getting nourishment while suspended in air —
The finches, also, though more casual
　in their endeavor;
The robins, enjoying the cool refreshing waters
　of the birdbath —
The chirping sounds of various insects
　in the early evening hours,
And the songs of birds!

The flower blossoms, at their deepest colors
　in the coolness of pre-twilight hours —
Anticipating the dewdrops of the evening;
　the western sky, in pastel shades of sunset colors,
With thin and distant puffs of white clouds,
　accentuating the blue perimeters of the background sky!
A pale moon, waiting to shine in all its splendor,
　after the darkness deepens.
This is the peace and beauty of the early evening hours!

Norma Russell

SUMMER EVENING

The twink of lightning bugs and hidden cricket's call
Remind of evenings past outside the city sprawl.

Depression gripped our town of half a thousand folk.
The drought and locusts came and left the farmers broke.

Our homes were bare and stark, most dads were unemployed.
Our meager meals were bland, and yet we felt no void.

We took our joy in friends, our families, neighbors, too;
We met on Garver's porch when evening's sun was through.

From eighty down to five, all ages gathered there;
The oldsters sat and rocked — us kids were on the stair.

The folks would sit and chat; old Jack would smoke his pipe.
Despite the worst of times, we didn't hear them gripe.

They spoke of right and wrong, of unabated heat,
Of fifteen men in court and how it seemed a cheat.

They spoke of 'tater bugs and cherries that were ripe;
They laughed at Jack's canards — he *was* the windy type.

'Twas there we learned to share our memories, hopes, and dreams,
To share ideals, respect, to build our self-esteem.

The croak of leopard frogs, mosquitoes buzzing 'round,
The unabated heat of summer in our town.

Donald G. Westlake

THE ASSURANCE

When we are together you make me feel so good
You hold me in your arms and my problems disappear
You whisper it's alright to be holding me so near
Holding turns to kissing
As your fingers twine through my hair
I hesitantly touch you
Unsure of us — you and me
You take my hand in yours and guide it where you will
As I questioningly search your eyes
You say it's the right thing to do
Then you explore my body — I push your hands away
You whisper that you love me
So I will let them stay
Suddenly our clothes are gone
I don't know how nor where
Then you're inside of me — I ask myself: "Should he be there?"
Your gentle ways mitigate my unspoken fears
Then you take me home, professing your "love" one more time
Tenderly you kiss me 'bye
I never hear from you again

Michelle McKnight

DUSK

Living at the end of a rainbow
Or the bottom of a well
In one is the same
As if looking up
Were the only foreseeable ray
In the contrasting colors and fastidious tonality
At the dead of the day
Where punctured pentacles fall
Like snowflakes bound by reality
To touch the ground and melt away

Dena Beth Lesser

SHE DWELT AMONG THE UNTRODDEN WAYS

She dwelt among the untrodden ways
  Beside the springs of Dove.
A Maid whom there were none to praise
  And very few to love;

A violet by a mossy stone
  Half hidden from the eye!
— Fair as a star, when only one
  Is shining in the sky.

She lived unknown, and few could know
  When Lucy ceased to be;
But she is in her grave, and, oh,
  The difference to me!

William Wordsworth

UNDERSTANDING

Knowledge is truth
  and truth is fact
possession of love
  requires witted tact
for gripping too tightly
  crushes the care
then the love —
  it isn't there.

Hold to the open
  out in the free
  never clinching;
    There shall it be.

Sam Penn

DESPAIR

If you feel bad, don't get mad,
because you are ultimately responsible
for the way you feel.
Changing the way you feel
about yourself is one of life's
greatest challenges. Reality is hard
to find when you can't see yourself
the ways others see you.
The goodies are there,
but you have to want them.
Attitudes and mindlessness
are part of a dream world
which no one can be a part of.

Chapin E. Field

ALWAYS

There's always a flower for someone,
  There's always a place in a heart,
There's always a sunbeam of brightness,
  There's always a new way to start,
There's always a word left of kindness,
  There's always a song in the air,
There's always the time if we take it,
  To tell someone special we care.

Violet D. Stout

BLESSED BY TRUST

It was the eve of Mother's Day,
  The weather wet and drear;
Loud frantic crying at the door
  Told us there's trouble here!

There on the step a new-born cat,
  Poor thing, chilled to the bone!
Ma Cat observed our kind concern
  Then ran away alone.

When dried and warmed, the kitten slept;
  Next day the sun did shine;
Again Ma Cat was at our door
  Mewing ''That baby's mine!''

Then we remembered that gray cat,
  The one that lingered near
Observing us on moving day;
  She knew kind folks lived here!

Doris Ullman Barbuto

SEA GULLS CRYING IN THE RAIN

Sitting alone by the ocean
Watching the waves ebb and flow
Wishing again for the love I lost
The best love I ever could know
Holding you still in my aching heart
Though my arms are empty again
All there is now is loneliness
And sea gulls crying in the rain
I call to you in my dreams each night
The days are full of pain
All that is left of a love so bright
Is sea gulls — crying in the rain.

Katherine E. Cartwright

MY PRESCRIPTION

I wonder what you have been doing,
Since our last days together,
Do you ever think of me,
In sunshine or stormy weather?

I wonder if you remember a girl,
Who was young and happy and gay,
Who was so in love with you it hurts,
To be always apart this way?

For I am not young any longer,
Nor am I as happy or gay,
But I am sad, miserable and lonely,
Because you are staying away.

Oh no! I am not the same person,
But if you would come back to me,
How gloriously, radiantly happy,
How well and contented I'd be.

Willie Johnson Cummings

THE COLORS OF AUTUMN

Leaves of red and golden hue
Blanket the earth
For fall to pass through
The sun has kissed them
Good-bye once again
They've had their last dance
With the wind and the rain.
O come, see the colors
Of autumn, I pray
And sing and dance
In the autumn parade.

Earlean S. Grogan

EARLEAN STANLEY GROGAN. Born: Pensacola, Florida, 3-4-22, reared in Monessen, Pennsylvania 1924-42; Married: William J. Grogan, Sr., of Monessen, Pennsylvania, 7-22-42; Education: Monessen High School, 1940; George Washington University, U.S. Department of Agriculture Graduate School, Washington D.C.; Occupations: Retired federal employee; Freelance writer/editor; Staff writer, *The Worker,* a Christian magazine published by the Nannie Helen Burroughs School, Inc., Washington D.C.; Memberships: Southern Maryland Writer's Vineyard, Oxon Hill Library, Temple Hills, Maryland; Society for Technical Communication; Piano Technician's Guild Auxiliary; Awards: Afro-American Newspaper Award for Superior Public Service in researching and presenting to congressional committees statements supporting need for new schools in Washington D.C., 1960; Elizabeth G. Pollard Poetry Contest and Unique Service Award for poetry and postering, 1985; First prize, Elizabeth G. Pollard Annual Poetry Contest, sponsored by the Sub-Committee on Fine Arts, for 'My First Piano,' 8-30-87, Shiloh Baptist Church, Washington, D.C.; Poetry: 'Let There Be Light,' Christmas card, 1964; Collection of poems, *Inspired Writings of Earleen S. Grogan,* 1964; 'Find Somewhere To Strike It,' 'Teachers,' *Yearbook of Modern Poetry,* 1971; 'Dreams,' *Impressions, Vol III,* 1986; 'Thank God for Mothers,' *Words of Praise, Vol. III,* American Poetry Association, 1987; Comments: *Many of my themes and ideas are inspired by a song I learned as a child that begins: ''How to reach the masses, men of every birth; For an answer, Jesus gave the key . . .'' I hope that each poem I write will present a timely message of God's love to the masses.*

I WRITE POEMS

I write poems.
I try not to; but from the depths of my despair,
 my sadness, pain,
 and disappointments —
 the words come with the tears,
And I write poems.

I write poems.
I try not to; but when my spirit soars,
 and happiness surrounds me —
 when joy and appreciation of beauty abound,
 I cannot help myself,
And I write poems.

I write poems.
I try not to; but I have found that when
 my thoughts are filled with poetic phrases,
 and I want peace within myself —
 I cannot rest until the words are written down.
So I write poems.

Norma Russell

A YEAR THERE WAS NO CHRISTMAS

This was the year — the year there was no Christmas,
 For sorrow came, and covered all my joys.
Oh, I saw sparkling lights, and trees and tinsel,
 With smiling faces, on little girls and boys.

But as for me — this year there was no Christmas.
 Each song I heard, just filled my eyes with tears.
Their cheerful lines, would set my heart to aching,
 Remembering happy times — surrounding other years.

A merry time? No, not this year at Christmas.
 For in these days, my heart began to grieve.
Each Christmas greeting only seemed to mock me,
 Because my mother passed away on Christmas Eve.

But time will heal — the pain I felt this Christmas.
 My life again, will be filled with Christmas cheer.
Though somewhere in my heart, I will remember —
 The sadness, that was Christmastime, this year.

Norma Russell

NORMA JEAN RUSSELL. Born: Pella, Iowa, 4-7-36; Married: Carl D. Russell, 4-7-52; Education: William Penn College, Oskaloosa, Iowa; Currently studying at The Institute of Children's Literature; Occupations: Accountant, Bookkeeper, Restaurant owner, Department head, Writer; Memberships: National Association for Female Executives, Society of Children's Book Writers; Poetry: 'Just Yesterday,' *Impressions, Vol. 2* and *Vol. 4, 1986;* 'My Friend,' *American Poetry Anthology, Vol VI, No. 5;* 'Silver Love,' *Hearts on Fire, Vol. IV, 1987;* 'Only Hope,' *New Voices in American Poetry,* 1987; Other Writing: ''Po Po the Clown,'' short story; Comments: *I try to write poems that express love and friendship; poems of faith and inspiration, grief and memory; poems that honor the home and family; poems that comfort, strengthen and cheer; poems of peace, beauty and humor. In short, I try to write about life and the experiences of living.*

THE FARMER — UNSUNG HERO

He's an unsung hero, this man of the soil.
He earnestly struggles in long-lasting toil.
From early to late he spends his time
Bringing forth foodstuff, whatever the clime.

He willingly labors more hours than most
Because he knows the world calls him *host.*
Without him we all would go hungry each day.
His efforts keep suffering and famine away.

Yet how many times do we say to him, ''Thanks''?
How often realize how highly he ranks?
How important he is in our country's plan.
Could we do without this hard-driving man?

He knows more than most that God is alive.
He knows without Him we'd never survive.
God's handwork he sees throughout every season,
Fruit of his labor — result of God's reason.

Yes, he labors long with untiring strength
To bring forth harvest of fruit and at length
Put food on the tables all over the world,
Result of his planning and knowledge unfurled.

Tessie Bea McCall

WHEN SUMMER COMES AMID THE DREAMS

I invite you as my guest without a song of forbidden hopes.
Come and drink with me, celebrate the freedom I feel as
 never before.
I am myself as all the trees are in the first birth of new
 twigs that blossom.
I am the mountain I couldn't climb, the snows that have gone
before and never will appear in the dawn of a newer day.
I am the sand now glistening with a multi-hue of colors.
I am California!
I am the seas sailed by so many and won by so few.
I am now amid the peers of my dreams, using the teas
of strength to pour.
Summer today, sunshine all day, every day, no more is the
challenge, the dreams are real.
I made hope, faith, and *God's* charity my wider scope in an
endless staircase of stars.

Charlotte Bell

ON THIRTY YEARS OF TEACHING

Today I cannot help but reminisce,
And think what thirty years have done to me.
It seems almost unreal that with this year
Three decades as a teacher I will be.
The years have very swiftly flown right by,
From Sharps Creek on to Oakley and Lorraine.
And then to Moundridge, and, oh yes, Marquette.
Each year to me has been a sure most gain.

Now really through the years the change seems nil,
Each classroom and each student I recall.
The memories, mostly pleasant, are mine own.
They are such precious treasures — each and all.
I pray that many lives somehow from me
Found happiness for all eternity.

Pearl Sandahl

I HEARD GOD SPEAK

God spoke to me that day in the hospital
   Through the lips of a dying man;
And as he there journeyed to heaven
   I learned deeply of God's divine plan.

He gazed upon loved ones departed,
   He spoke with them, called them by name;
He seemed surrounded by beauty
   As his tongue uttered praises and fame.

He knew not that he was speaking,
   He was now unaware of this earth,
He was walking through the valley in shadows,
   He was emerging in brilliance and mirth.

And yet all the while his utterances
   Were so clearly, so well understood
That I knew God was walking beside him
   And through him, God told me I could.

I could, and I still, feel God's blessing
   On that day when all was so sad,
Through the life and the death of this warrior
   Whom I loved and revered — my dear dad!

Pearl Sandahl

ROANN DIED TODAY

The uncertainty of life became more real today.
For tonight Roann died —
Quickly, unexpectedly, tragically.

Her last day on earth was so routine —
School, classes, friends, a party.
Then the day came to an end
And with its passing, Roann went too.

Soon the news spread!
And our little city was shocked, everyone —
Students, teachers, citizens in general.
A young woman, a high school junior, a familiar figure
Had died! Why?

Memories of her cannot be erased!
Thoughts of her cannot be vanquished!
Impressions of her cannot be changed!

Good-bye, Roann, to the things of earth!
But some bright morning in that unknown future
We'll meet you upon ''that other dawn'' where
We'll nevermore know sadness, nor sorrow, nor parting, nor death.

All will be well, then! All will be well!

Pearl Sandahl

At break of day thin streaks of light search for curling leaves,
Their green translucence clothed in pearls of dew,
And wanting sanctuary, the pale luna moth grieves,
As I, with outstretched arm, reach again for you.
Alone I am half-being, full yearning magic that
I not know, see, feel but with my darling, Pat.

R. Peter Rosier

DEATH OF A MOURNING DOVE

You were too small for this great mystery;
A tiny prize for Destiny's pursuit,
This cameo, formed by Nature to confute
Even Cellini's art. You wakened me
To a sad sunrise with your threnody,
A single note played on a golden flute,
Grief's monotone. And, now that you are mute,
I learn to miss your lonely litany.
Yet you were sacrifice and innocence,
And more, the day your radiant image crossed
The Jordan's waves, uneasy with immense
Shadows of change; or when you touched those lost,
Pale, stammering lips with fiery eloquence,
The passionate fortitude of Pentecost!

Mary F. Lindsley

LOVE IS HAPPINESS

Love is happiness, a great part of giving
Doing for someone you love makes for a greater living
Caring so much for their welfare and worth
Is another part of the glories we enjoy here on earth

Love is a reward, a prize, a goal
When one has it, one never grows old
What would our life be without love? At least mine, I'm sure
Nothing but sadness and loneliness and emptiness if love was not pure

We think many times in our life that this is the love that we
   are seeking
Often, so very often, it isn't, we are only reaching
Reaching for what we sometimes don't even know
But with patience and tenderness love will surely grow

Love is truly happiness as we have been taught
Love is for the giving . . . love cannot be bought
As we are growing up and if we are taught to share
Then one can be sure that love lives there.

Rachael Johnson

TO HAVE LOVE

To have love, you first have to give
You have to want to please and you have to want to live
You need to enjoy touching and you have to enjoy the feeling
You have to be able to share and appreciate the needing
You have to have faith and to believe in your vows
You must agree on things together and what is to be allowed
Your words must be warmly spoken with tenderness and love
And you've got to appreciate the blessings of God's grace from above
You have to keep that glow burning lovingly in your heart and soul
With these few things — just these few things — your marriage
or relationship will never grow old
For you've got to know love, to feel love and be willing to give
You've got to have known loss and pain but still want to live
You'll never be able to make it without a warm and tender embrace
For love is a blessing, for love is a gift, love is just one of God's
many, many graces.

Rachael Johnson

RHYME AND RHYTHM

The rhyme of life . . .
The dream of city songs
The myth of each tomorrow
Rainswept the lantern
Outside a shop-front door.

The rhyme of moth and shadow
Adagio dancer
Mirrored image at a cabaret
Each has a delicate imbalance
Like a Swiss clock that never
Stops
But chimes forever on!

Like a tin soldier
On a mock military dress parade.

Rhyme and rhythm of a city
Whose arrows point both ways
Dust-blown from a million shadows
Indented footprints from a dozen
Different feet.

Rhyming patterns of a city
Dancing to the drumbeats of a downtown
City street.

Joan Giltner Canfield

LAUGHTER

We could pour on the love as
    man and woman,
But lacked the warmth to be
    friends
And would see love perish again
    and again
For that is the way when passion
    ends.

But we were saved by a cupful
    of laughter,
By a humorous anecdote I
    read aloud.
And have lived together for many
    years after —
Putting up with an occasional
    cloud.

Blanche D. Madiol

ASHES

The ashes continue to fall away
Encrustations of time — so old, so deep
Underneath the life force moves
Hesitant and new
And where are the old loves
Asleep in time?
The new — awake to desire —
And I stand
Tomb opened at last
And brush the dust
Of centuries from my hair.

Virginia Weber

My heart finds
No peace
Only turmoil
As I clutch
The aching need
Of you.
Forever bound
By a love
That did not know
When to stop
And the train whistle
Continued to blow.

I push it back
And it will be gone
If I don't look
It will go away
What a fool
To think
That would be so.

Trina Tatro

MY CUB SCOUTS

I have a lively group of boys,
Who are in Cub Scouts this season.
They work, play, and make cookies,
And do what I ask within reason.

Some are bobcats, working to be wolves.
Part of them have been in before.
These are learning to be bears and lions,
And really know the score.

Little boys like to work with tools,
And hammer and nails or wood —
They want to be making things,
That will do somebody some good.

The flag salute is quite impressive,
They make their parents proud, I know.
I'm sure they'll become better citizens,
And into strong men they'll grow.

Alice Erickson

ALICE LEONA ERICKSON. Born: 9-5-14;
Married: Emil Erickson, 4-20-35; Education: high
school, 1933; Occupations: Postal worker,
Teacher aide; Poetry: 'Springtime,' 1948;
'Blessed Is Our Father in Heaven,' 1968;
'Christmas,' 1969; 'An Ode to Our Baker,' 1973;
'Our Dog Jackie,' 1975.

RESURRECTION

Once upon a Moon-lit Time,
Who bedeweth Ra in Rime?

Sun, Stars, Earth, and All
might fall from Grace to find,
Who ''ere Day Star like the Dew''
created Her Soul's Refine?

Who bedeweth Ra, but, You
while raising spittle, Earth and Dew
as Serpent who at Your behest
supplanted ''Name'' in Heaven's Breast?

Hence, holding Key to Infinite Swell
whence, Vis Major freezing Hell?
Lo, Serpent suffers earth to shake,
Behold, anew, Queen Isis wakes!

Marie C. Andrea

HOW MANY?

How many houses have you seen?
  How many trees and fields of green?
How many bridges have you crossed?
  How many jobs have you been boss?
How many cities, how many towns . . .
  How many roads have you been down?
How many hot lips have you kissed?
  How many sweet lips have you missed?
How many dreams have you left undone?
  I know of one — the perfect one.
It's here right now!
  That dream come true.
You're lovin' me.
  I'm lovin' you.
No broken dreams we need recall
  'Cause you and me, we have it all!
Come here, let me hold you, baby
  You and me together —
We have it all.

Mary Dugan

BARBARA

Barbara, Barbara, don't you dare
  shed another crying tear!
Barbara, Barbara, don't you dare —
  Can't you see how much I care?
You can cry your eyes of blue,
  To someone who is so true!
You may cry a tear, my dear,
  'Cause I'll be near you just to hear!
Barbara, Barbara, don't you dare —
  Shed another crying tear!
''Oh! Barbara, Barbara, don't you dare —
  Can't you see how much I care?''

Mathew Matejcich

BELIEVING IN YOURSELF

Our spirit is to shape our course and to guide us and help to
    make us strong,
To give us all the encouragement to be righteous and just and
    to keep us from wrong.
One must truly love oneself in order to know how to love another;
There can never be an insensitive feeling towards one's sister
    or brother.
And to live with all one's heart and soul is a guide to a
    happier life,
For God wants us to feel the glory of love and of being loved
    rather than stress and strife.

So hold on to those beloved and cherished feelings and beliefs
    and find someone appreciative of your love,
Never hesitating a moment to underestimate the guidance and
    help from above,
Always knowing that to love and to be loved there is a glorious
    experience for you
So believe in the lessons so long taught to us all and feel
    the lonely hours and days become happier ones and the lessons
    taught are really true.

Rachael Johnson

PILLOW TALK

I thought everything about me was normal,
    I assumed I was doing alright,
Until the words ''I'm tired of this!''
    Came from my pillow one night.

I couldn't pretend to not understand;
    I had to admit it was right.
My pillow was the only one
    Who saw my tears each night.

The friends, all full of advice,
    Didn't understand . . . you see,
But the pillow propped beneath my head
    Spends every night with me.

The pillow that cradled my many lovers,
    Has cradled my many fears.
''It's got to stop!'' . . . we both agreed,
    ''It's been going on for years!''

So instead of just welcoming just anyone
    Who has passion they want to share,
My pillow and I will wait together in the darkness
    Until love finds us there!

Barbara J. Olson

JOYOUS REMEMBERANCE

I will never forget those memorable days
When the children would gather around me,
Talking about all their delights in their innocent ways,
But now I miss this great experience of joy, you see,
Because I am older now, and the children seem to have gone,
But, however, I still see them when I daily walk in stride,
And feel their loving presence still among
Those days of joy when all my love reached out with pride,
Listening to them talk and roam among each other,
Although it is not like being there,
Sharing their joys and fears to extend my feeling a little further,
Accepting their hugs and let them know I still care.

Anthony S. Goss

CONTENTMENT

To wait is such a waste of time, of energy.
It merely drains the inner soul
Until there is nothing left but despair.
Despair — a word synonymous with frustration.
Frustration — a feeling created by the lack of drive and ambition.
Creating — an inner drive to express the feelings that are inside.
Hope — the feeling created by the word of a loved one.
The words that are meant but will never come to pass.
Am I beyond the realm of hope?
Oh no —
Not as long as I have me!
For I am at peace within me —
A pen in hand,
A chisel, a saw to create an edifice.
To show me in form
Oh what a relief —
The despair is gone
And contentment has returned.

Eileen Jorge

SURVIVAL

There are no flowers to adorn my path
There is no dew to represent a moment of joy;
My life is a mere act to survive.
My heart is heavy with pain,
My mind is a troubled mass.
There seems to be no relief in sight.
There seems to be no sun to light
The path that I must cover . . .
I know not where the rivers will cross
I know not when a sunburst will be tossed my way —
So in my misery I do sway
From one branch to another.
The tree of life has been planted,
Only to be enhanced and nourished
By someone else's hand.
Can I ever find another way in a different day?
Perhaps I will someday know the whys
Of what I had to do, of where I had to go.
To have flourished is my goal,
To have survived is my role.

Eileen Jorge

A MORNING VISION

Today the birdsong rises with the morning,
    And she must rise as well to face the day;
The sunlight falls upon her without warning
    To tumble through her hair in careless play.
    So sleepy eyes are opened to the dawn.
A smile breaks out in answer to a yawn . . .
    Though she can see no sliver of the light,
And spends each daytime moment in the night.
Far deeper than the sighted understanding,
    The spirit flies or fails in hidden realms;
From regions never lit the life force whelms
That shines so brightly, darkness notwithstanding
    Her eyes, to her, no usefulness impart,
But, oh, to me, they show where lies my heart!

David B. Hawthorne

AUTUMN IS . . .

Autumn is a lovely time,
Its colors rich and sublime.

And, oh, how I love to hear the geese
Honking out their medley of peace
As they traverse the heavens up above
In search of warmth, and food, and love.

It's not a time of gloomy despair
Or even a reminder of winter's lair.
It's not a time when nature is cruel,
But rather, a readiness for her renewal.

Autumn is simply a visible guarantee
Of sunny days that are to be.

Sharri Sanders

SHE REMEMBERS

(Way Back When)

We visit her in sunny room,
She sits there, waiting, in her chair,
But how her eyes light, as she smiles,
When we admire her silver hair.

She has passed the age of ninety-two
And on Her Day, I do recall,
She won the praise of those who came
When she said, ''I don't feel old at all!''

She said, ''I can remember way back when
I worked as a young girl in a shop
Making linings in big hats —
Working long hours without a stop.''

''I can remember we were poor
The day that we were married
But somehow we made a go of it
Despite the burdens carried.''

Many times we hear these stories
As she tells them over again
But we listen, laugh, shed a few tears —
So glad she can remember way back when.

Gladys M. Olsen

WHITE VELVET

Snow like white velvet
Underfoot, beneath the barren trees
Silence on paths
And stillness in the the upper trees
The lake, painted to glass and shadows
And silver trees
Holding vacant nests.
Squirrels looking for seeds
In the branches
And clouds of iridescent mist.
Quiet holds the dawn —
And quiet the twilight
While eternal dreams unfold
And His presence is everywhere.

Virginia Weber

THE WORM

Love, thou hast been a stranger
Whose footsteps long have passed my door.

Always have I sat by my window, Love,
Watching — and waiting.

Once thy hand didst pause upon my gate.
My heart leapt to behold!

But, alas, 'twas only to rest
From frequent visits to my friends.

Why am I always a friend to my friends
Yet never a friend to Love?

The worm of loneliness thrives within me,
Its malignant work to perform.

Too long have I listened, Love,
For thy gentle knock upon my door.

When thy knock does come, Love,
All shall be hollow —

Hollow knock, hollow house, hollow me.
The worm will have done its work.

George B. Williams

ALZHEIMER'S

Chill breezes brush early April's grass.
The buds of May are yet to be.
Between winter and spring stands a lass.
Waving — waving gently to me.

I don't recall her name, as such,
Mary . . . Jane . . . or Sue.
What was it about her soft touch?
What did it promise you?

Her voice was peaceful country streams,
Soothing mind's fevered hill.
Her laughter trickled thru my dreams
Over rapture's windowsill.

She's gone now, yes, she's surely dead.
It was oh so long ago.
Who is that sitting beside my bed?
Why does she smile so?

I still wake to the promises of spring,
Despite a possible frost,
For whatever thoughts they might bring
Of all that I have lost.

George B. Williams

BIG SUR

I saw God's face
In the clouds
Mirrored in wet sand,
Where sea foam
Tumbled ahead of the wind.

Ernestine Fishbaugh

THE GAMIN

His pleasures are great but few
His luxuries scarce and small
His tenderness hidden but extant
His cleverness quick and sharp
His humanity doubted but real
His spirit strong and inborn
His mind educated but illiterate
His perceptions clear-eyed and apocalyptical
His sentiments somber but hopeful
The gamin.

Lisa Wanzer

LISA ELLEN WANZER. Pen Name: Lizette; Born: Bronx, New York, 5-5-66; Education: Currently a senior at Franklin & Marshall College, majoring in Psychology and Drama; Memberships: International and Religious Studies Clubs, college choir, Dance Club, Black Student Union; Awards: Honorable mention in high school poetry contest for 'The Tasaday Child,' 1984; Brown University Book Award for Excellence in Writing, 1984; Poetry: 'Leaves of Innocence,' collection, still in progress; 'The Gamin,' *American Poetry Anthology,* 1987; 'The Tasaday Child,' *North of Upstate,* 2-87; Comments: *Although my poetry is written about children and with children as the focus, the messages in the poetry are meant to speak to adults. One of my more popular themes is that of freedom from the ''civilized'' (whatever that may mean) world's stifling, Puritan, and often silly social restraints. I think it is important to celebrate the person who dares to be different. I would like to say that it is difficult for the below- and above-average people to survive in a world geared toward the average.*

UNSPOKEN THOUGHTS

I think of days gone by; of loves come and
    gone and always a part of me;
Of things I've done and yet to do,
    Places I've seen and yet to see;
Of children I know will continue to grow
    without my watchful eyes and caring
hands to guide them;
    Of rains that have fallen and suns
that have set and hunger for
    life to go on forever.

Sue Marchman

FIRST NIGHT OF WISDOM

The foy of schools which still stands.
Within the tales of rock-and-roll soldiers/rock-and-roll poets
    which help one through the silence of nights/endless nights
    belong to time.
Yet will the pain of endless nights/yet shall the z-persons
    see the wisdom.
The first day was so unheard of eyes which play games.
Words of wisdom which only makes one brave enough to fight back
    at the ignorant.
New laws and rules of love/of touch.
Now was so fair to the storm of giving.
The first day was so unheard for eyes which play games.
Now isn't sad or some dream of love which was of flesh.
Till now foy was a word of supreme joy.
A poem to the down heartly ones/a joyful heart is hard to have
    sometime.
So peaceful/so loving using the words of god not for money only
    for real reality.
Sitting with only you Stareyes can't be a fantasy of humblelessness.
On the line for wisdom of love/touch.
Roses aren't for the z-persons/yet the rock-and-roll poets
    gave their life for peace and love.

Felix Wicks

THE EVACUATION OF SOUTH VIETNAM EXPERIENCE

The 15,000 Day Calamity Affair came to a screeching halt in mid-1975
When the Viet Cong overtook South Vietnam in one all-out final
    Tet offensive.
Being members of the U.S.S. Midway, we were ordered to the
    shores off Saigon.

Our job was to bring on board thousands of helpless refugees on
    Air Force helicopters.
The RVN Army of South Vietnam soon surrendered unconditionally,
    as they were sick and tired
Of fighting this senseless war. During the day, we would play
    touch football on the flight deck.

But at night, the Air Force would fly their helos into Saigon
To pick up all American citizens, then the refugees. They would
    fly well into the night
Until dawn. The Americans were put in vacant berthing compartments
    while the refugees

Were put on the large hangar bay above. The look of shock, dismay,
    and terror
Could readily be seen on their faces. For me, I felt sorry for
    them and often
Wondered, ''Where will they go from here? Could they pick up
    the pieces, no

Longer to go home?'' The Vietnam War was a fatal mistake. America was
Caught off guard, once again, in a volatile region of the world.
What could we tell our children why we were there?
In the face of all adversity,

America had long last lost her sweet innocence and had an unhealed
Open wound which would take long to close during the passage of
    many years.
55,000 American soldiers were killed for no good reason except
    that they
Died by people in Washington playing chess with their lives.
    Let this conflict
Be a lesson to our leaders now, for we need not make waste on many
    a man's life again.

William D. Brownlie III

THE PARTING

It's been seven months, yet I still want you;
It's been seven months, yet I still need you;
It's been seven months, yet I still see your eyes, that half-smile,
    that tilt of a royal head; I still hear that pearly voice and
    bubbles of air rising in water and bursting.
It's been seven months yet I still feel a kiss on the eyes,
    on the mouth, in the ears.
It's been seven months, yet I still feel you in me — searching,
    against me — hard as as rock, under me laughing,
    over me — riding as if the devil were chasing you;
It's been seven months, yet I still hear your pleasure,
    your excitement, and the fulfillment of desire;
It's been seven months, and I'm still not free of . . .
    My Beautiful Ebony Prince,
    My Black Stallion,
    Black Velvet,
    Mandingo,
    Winnie's Little Boy.

Lorna McPherson

THE MEETING

He came to me like a ray of sunlight on a dark day,
    like sunlight brightening a gloomy day;
It was not his eyes, for they carried the tint of a heavy drinker;
Nor was it his teeth, for they had long lost their brilliance
    to cigarette smoking;
Nor was it his skin, for it bore the hue of ebony or earth,
    black Caribbean earth that he loved so much;
    or was it like coffee, coffee with a dash of milk?
No, it was none of these things!
What I thought was sunlight
    was in fact . . .
        The radiance of a prince.

Lorna McPherson

THE NEW LIFE

The gentle, but silent, love we share.
I float on one of the silver clouds above,
watching the blueness of sparkle on the warm
beaches beneath me.
You are the sparkle of the silent candle,
the quietness of the afternoon wind,
bringing patterns of memories to my
past youth — gone
but still in my mind.
Candles lit, causing hanging crystal beads to
dance with solitaire colors — like the silver clouds
I still lay upon, dreaming.
Memories of past summers' rains which caused a
rainbow to dance in your eyes which are all aglow.
To cry while watching an old love movie,
The beauty in the tree which I made
with careful hands, making sure the white doves
sat straight, then red, blue and green birds to add color
To the whitened tree from nature. Soft pink & white
flowers carefully chosen to bring new life to all
colored butterflies, free as they watch a new sunset
while awaiting for the sunrise of a new given day,
then to remember the youth of love again.

Elaine Schuster

LIBRARY

The Library
Populated by young psyches
Building living cultures from dead memories
Corroded patina of thought
The rust-stained orbs of Juno seeking
Enlightenment through Dharma
Dharma of Science!
Dharma of Duty!
An endless procession of unfinished beings
Trapped in unfinished worlds
Immortal concept made mortal
As pen and ink

Barrington King

THE SEVEN HILLS

Stepping through fields
Singing in the wind,
The clouds on high,
The magic of a summer's day
Repeated itself.

Watching strollers go by —
Towers of long ago —
High in the sky —
Suns and moons and stars
Turning through a watch dial
In a magazine advertisement;
Who will you go to Avalon with?
(Questions of a child)
By many in older years forgotten . . .

Wulf D. Kort

THE SPELLING LESSON

That lovely, quiet, old-fashioned town,
Is such a stickler, when writing it down.
Perhaps this will teach it with more ease,
Remember, two R's and three E's.
R-E at the head, and reverse them at the end,
Next in order, the single letter N,
Followed by two S's, the only double,
(No double N, or double L to give you trouble.)
Another E and one A separated by L,
Does this make it easier to spell?
R-E-N- double S-E, my dear,
L-A-E-R, spells that Hoosier town
          Rensselaer.

Charlotte North

RARITY

Oh, if I had words
For a flight of birds,
For autumn scents —
Sycamores in the rain.
Those moments when life,
Or all of nature,
Poses a picture
To which there is
No comment.

Ernestine Fishbaugh

MY ONLY DREAM

My only dream,
Is to be in love.
My only wish,
Is to be caressed.

My only desire,
Is to say, ''I love you.''
My only fantasy,
Is to be someone's lover.

My only longing,
Is to be passionately kissed.
And my only true lust,
Is to be wanted.

John Genyard

FOR JOSIE — 1943

To this cavern of the lonely
In the blackness of the night
Comes a vision, slow filling the cave
And dispelling ancient gloom
In a silver filigree of light

Alone . . . I am and yet am not
Long gone in wand'ring the stars
Held fast . . . body chained to bars
Memory . . . goes winging out away
And silver moon flooding this old cell
Is well . . . is well . . . is well

And I can — even now — feel limb-wrapped
As snakes are wont in winter
To curl one about the other
So fast I am held . . . engripped
By an abandoned passion

I am held by bonds stronger than elders
More entwined than the Ylang-Ylang
And thus I spend my days . . . awaiting
The nights of your arrival!

John Edwards

NAÏVETÉ

  Thoughts of you are
Leaving me.

  Visions and naïveté
Resound in ever-changing circles.

  Eyes that look but
Don't feel, distract
The sensitive will, I have
Over you.

  Forget promises which
Kill me, do you love me,
Do you care for me.

  You leave with subtle
Grace, which I fear,
  Which I only
Hurt.
  Which I only
Love . . .

Ruben Cardenas

YESTERDAY'S LOVE

I saw you smiling yesterday
    And sensed your warming touch,
I smelled your fragrance in the air —
    Impossible to clutch.
I heard you whisper in the calm
    And saw your dewdrop tears,
Your presence lingers everywhere
    'Though you've been gone for years.
I traced your footsteps through the fields
    Still pressed among the flowers,
Then waited 'til the stars came out
    And wished on them for hours.
I wished that I could see your face
    And stroke your silken hair,
I wished that if I called your name
    You'd answer from somewhere.
I wished that I could kiss your lips
    And it could be as such —
That you could hear me when I say,
    ''I love you, oh, so much!''

Violet D. Stout

VOID

For Wade

Now that the leaves have fallen
And the grass is white with frost,
The eaves imperialed with crystals
And the windows all embossed,

I look outside and wonder
Where has the green summer gone?
Vanished! just as the duckling;
Appearing somewhere, a swan.

The green will be returning,
The crystals will transcend
But void will replace summer;
Due to the death of my friend.

Violet D. Stout

FATE

You were desperate to keep your freedom
And not let yourself get tied down
While I was looking for commitment
And a relationship that was sound
Our feelings could not be denied
We were together in all our thoughts
But on our instincts we relied
And against our love we fought
We turned these emotions into hate
In one last attempt to stay apart
Yet our lives were in the hands of fate
Which took us with our hearts

Erika Rick

TO LOVE

Alas, to love, and yet be misconstrued!
The sole injustice of my mortal life.
Ah, would that I could save these wand'ring souls
And manifest that Plato was Divine.
'Tis love of spirit, not the love of flesh,
Which sets apart Divinity and Lust,
And cloud-mists dreamy eyes with Beauty's glow!
For Beauty in its purest form is Love.
Love fortifies itself in willing hearts
In whom the will to love is Life, itself.
Am I to be bereft of Love's complects?
For though I love in spirit, I love not
To satisfy those closest to my soul.
In loving with my Soul and not my heart,
Do I wrong? or worse, injure those I love?
Oh Love! the great idolon of my life,
I pray thee, show them all the side *I* see:
The *perfect* Love, which sets the spirit free.

K. G. Cashion

MOMENTS OF GLORY

Come walk with me on the beach at sunset;
Watch the gulls swoop and soar,
Looking for their last morsel
Before the last rays of the sun
Leave the sky, and darkness comes.

It is a beautiful, brilliant sky
With the white-capped waves rolling in.
Whoops! There was a big one sweeping the beach
In preparation for the last moments
Between twilight and darkness.

With more gorgeous colors than humankind
Can think, dream or duplicate,
God paints His canvas, the sky,
With such a glorious blend of colors,
They defy description.

My friends and I sit drenched in beauty
Until the colors fade,
And the moon and stars appear.
We sit in awe — blessed,
Knowing we have been bathed in God's glory.

Eliza Tyler Taylor

A HORSE OF COURSE

In my growing-up years I didn't like the subject Art,
For I couldn't draw, so of this subject I wanted no part.
But it was a class that was required of me
So draw I did, but not diligently.
I started out with legs and added a long tail,
Then went on drawing my horse in detail.
I was really proud of the horse that I drew
Until the instructor looked and had a different view.
He said, "What do you call this?" "It's a horse," I said.
"I would never have guessed," he said while shaking his head.
"But if you'd said a buffalo or even maybe a dinosaur
Then we wouldn't have wasted this past class hour.
I'm sure with some practice your drawing will improve
And your buffalo will become a horse that I can approve.
But it will take patience on your part
And please forgive me — I'm sorry that today I broke your heart."

Shirley B. O'Keefe

IN HIS PRESENCE

There is fullness of joy.
A safe abiding place.
Rest from a restless world.
Peace in the midst of chaos.
Comfort in the time of sorrow.
Direction when the way is obscure.
Faith that all things are possible with Him.
Healing from all sickness and disease.
Deliverance from all oppression and sin.
Restoration from brokenness and grief.
Wisdom to handle all of life's perplexities.
Knowledge to walk in *Your way.*
Truth of the fullness of the *Godhead.*
Confidence in an eternal life in *God's kingdom.*
Contentment in knowing He is the *God* of all things.
Trusting Him for all the needs of every facet of life.
Experiencing the purity and fullness of His love.
Glimpses of *His eternal glory, splendor and power.*
Sharing *His omnipresence, omniscience, and omnipotence.*
Fearlessly abiding, *In his presence, now and forevermore!*

Eliza Tyler Taylor

PROMISES

I am with you always. You are My beloved.
I will never leave you nor forsake you.
I go to prepare a home for you with Me forever.
Nothing shall by any means harm you.
Ask what you will and I will give it to you.
All that the Father has is Mine, and I will give it to you.
I will supply all your needs.

I must go away, but I will return and take you unto Myself.
Wherever I am, there you will be with Me.
I will come for you and take you into *My heavenly kingdom.*
For you are *My bride, and I am your bridegroom forever.*
You will dwell with Me in the heavenly palaces
I have prepared for you.
And *time* will be no more.

I love *You* my beloved *bridegroom,*
My *Lord Jesus Christ.*
I am content and at peace in Your love.
I am waiting for you to come for me,
That I may dwell in the *house of my Lord,*
Forever.

Eliza Tyler Taylor

ELIZA TYLER TAYLOR. Born: Benson, North Carolina; lived in Goldston, North Carolina until 1946, lived in Redondo Beach, California since 1946; Married: Myron Taylor (deceased); Children: Myra Taylor Dunn, Jean Taylor Johnson, William J. Taylor; Education: Two years of college, additional college and university courses and seminars; Occupations: Manufacturing engineering, Planning senior (retired), Writer, Poet; Poetry: *Impressions and Reflections,* book of poetry, 1975; Themes: *Spiritual truths and insights concerning the Almighty Godhead and the Kingdom of God; also living life at its fullest and best.*

HOLY THIRST

All of our days are dust and ashes
When You are hiding, Lord.
Then grace shines through,
And it is light once more.
Peace reigns; life's inspired —
Even colors change.
Stay with us,
That we may cease to thirst
Beside the well of fullness.

Ernestine Fishbaugh

A PIECE OF CAKE

A patch of snow upon your head,
  "It's a distinguishing mark,
  you know,"
For you have crossed the great divide,
  and have reached
  a new plateau.
You're not as young as you used to be
  and you can't turn back
  the clock.
Please don't give up, feel sorry for yourself
  and just sit in your rocking chair
  and rock.
Growing old is a piece of cake,
  far better than a slice
  of bread.
Let's face it, folks,
  when you stop growing old —
You're not alive,
  you're dead.

John T. Hudelson

SHOWCASE

The showcase is quite
Ostentatious but what does
It conceal inside?

Dorothy Moore

T.R.N.

On October 14, 1986
You ended your life.
You stopped a heart from beating
Which I had felt right next to mine.
You took away a smile
Which had brought me so much joy.
You closed a pair of eyes
Which had given me strength and hope.
You took away a voice
Which now will never call my name.
You stopped the movement of two arms
Which used to hold me tight.
And you took the feeling from two hands
Which were more gentle than I'd ever known.
But you left behind a body
Which is nothing without the man inside.

Tereasa L. Peterson

THE PORCELAIN VASE

I have seen it every day and
Longed to hold it and to own,
This exquisite vase of porcelain.
Sometimes I ventured forth,
Entered the *gift shop* door,
And stood as close to it as I,
Unworthy, dared to stand.
It became more precious as I
Remained and gazed.

Today I shall take it with me.
My covetous eyes carefully slip
It into my *treasure chest.*
I turn, leave the *shop,*
And walk away.

Dorothy Moore

DOROTHY J. MOORE. Education: Ball State University, Muncie, Indiana; University of Denver, Denver, Colorado; Occupation: Retired teacher; Memberships: NRTA (National Retired Teacher Association), AARP (Retired Americans); Poetry: 'Majestic Lady at Home,' 1986; 'Alone,' 'Wasteland,' 'Now I Know,' American Poetry Association, 1986; 'Tribute To Celestial Fires,' American Poetry Association, 1985; Comments: *Life is a book of poetry — A conglomeration of impressions and experiences every day. One poem is just one of many thoughts one may read, hear or say.*

SCALES

My friend . . .
You fill my heart,
With such a special sweetness.
Sometimes it's good,
To just talk about the weather.

You have been gone,
For two months,
And now that you are back,
I have learned,
To cherish you even more.
Tell me about Milano.

Karl S. McDaniel

There is neither heaven nor earth,
Only snow
  Falling incessantly.

Hashin

YESTERDAY'S MIRROR

You asked me,
If you could trust me,
I told you, you could.
But I should have said,
You can trust me,
As far,
As you trust yourself.

Karl S. McDaniel

WALKING

As I walk along the silent street
I think of you,
I think of us.
And with each step
A tear falls.
The salt slightly stings,
And the tears dry from the brisk morning air.
But as each tear dries,
Another falls.
And I keep thinking,
I keep walking,
Hoping to lessen my frustration
As my feet hit the pavement.
Soon, the frustration is gone,
But not the tears.
They just keep falling,
And I keep walking.

Tereasa L. Peterson

THE GREATEST LOVE

These arms that used to hold you
are so very empty now.
And I must walk the lonely path
but Darling, tell me how.

I've loved you since the day we met
and I've held you in my heart.
I know this broken heart will mend
but tell me where to start.

If you could see inside my heart
and know how much I care.
If you could see my love for you
and just know that I'd be there.

I want to share so much with you
though I'll never be your wife.
I'll always be there for you,
you've got a friend for life.

I only want the best for you
and if I must let you go,
I'll say goodbye and set you free;
the greatest love that I can show.

Gail Johnson

INDIVIDUALITY

Living alone is not always a great synonym for loneliness
    and desolation;
There are those of us who prefer to remain blessed particulates,
Despite the conjugal usualization.

Friends and family would like to see us wed
That we might be fully satisfied.
According to them, contentment cannot flower
Lest two marriage partners coincide . . .

Then we have the Christians
Who speak to us with demeaning admonitions;
They say God made woman for man and man for woman —
It's the unbreakable Biblical tradition.

I am one whose God walks forever by her side,
Whether wedded or yet solitary.
Perhaps my God ordains this celibacy —
For me it is not social hari-kari.

Some of us do well to marry;
We discover life's ultimate treasure through tying the nuptial knot,
Others of us find our own matrimonial bliss —
Without falling in love and slipping into the spousal slot.

Karen Doede

RESILIENCE

So often we walk through life unaware of our day-after-day durability.
We belittle our unique capacity to cope; we deny our
    relentless elasticity.

Only when adversity bestows itself upon us do we begin to toughen up
And persevere;
We become aware of our restorative tenacity which will not allow
Misconceptions of frailty and inadequacy to interfere.

We open our eyes to the reality that we must not relinquish
And succumb to lesser goals;
We behold the extreme stretching of our undying spirits,
The rebounding of our hopeful souls.

Shock and disappointment tempt us to give in,
To denounce dreams and recoil from further aspiration,
Yet something always drives us to summon that staying power within,
To transform each unfortunate situation.

It is said that the human heart has an infinite capacity
To withstand the repeated pang of rejection;
Perhaps it's that boundless resilience that refines humanity,
And brings it ever closer to perfection.

Karen Doede

WITH LOVE AND ADMIRATION

There's a tiny little lady with a serious illness and yet
She's an inspiration to all of us — the way she doesn't fret.

She's going and doing for others — her friends and family.
You never hear her complain — she's grateful for each victory.

I hope if I'm ever in her shoes, I can have as much courage as she
And roll with the punches and bounce right back and do it with so
    much glee.

Frances Hough

CHILDHOOD

I sit back and think of years ago, when I was just a kid.
I remember Mom and Dad alike, as no one ever did.

Mom was like an angel fair, all sweet and kind and good;
And Dad was like a handsome prince, everywhere he stood.

To me they seemed the nicest folks that ever were to live;
And when I wanted something new, they always seemed to give.

A kitten was my wish one time, all soft and warm and sweet;
And when I got her she was small, but boy could that thing eat!

Everything was full of life, simple, exciting and gay;
And now I wish I could go back, even just for one more day.

I look back to the years ago, and every single day;
I want to return to childhood, and this is what I pray.

Gail L. Hofer

I thought you always understood
that I loved you through it all.
Together we all once stood,
but now, divided we fall.

It was a life that once was only mine,
I lived to live but life itself.
Now it seems to live it is a crime.
My heart you've placed upon a shelf.

I know not whither or whence you came
or where I now shall go,
but to live my life in only your fame, I must
end my dreams and repent to grow.

Through my eyes, I see it not fair,
but then through yours, you see it the same.
I will always love you with a love so rare,
but darling, I must live for myself, even if in shame.

Angela Wheeler

MY HEART BELONGS TO YOU ALONE

*Written in May 1957 to my
husband, Dr. Wilhelm Reich*

Oh, dearly beloved man of mine,
So cherished, so perfectly divine
With stately figure tall and trim,
Handsomely distributed limb to limb.
Fine features carved with great precision
To fit this man of strong decision.

With softly melting eyes of brown
And graying temples at the crown.

With gentle voice and tender lips to kiss,
Oh my darling, you so much I miss.
My heart belongs to you alone, my love,
Known well to God in his blue heaven above.
Rest well and drink from me sweetheart;
Then into slumber sink.

Tomorrow is another day;
Perhaps a better one, we pray.

Aurora Reich

UNEXPECTED

This one's for you, Eddie L.

You came into my life
when I least expected.
At a point in time
when I was feeling neglected.

You brought wine, warmth
and a room full of laughter
and the beauty of a friendship
I would treasure long after.

You're one of a kind, dear
I'll always remember
how you held me so tight
and yet so tender.

We took only
what each one could offer.
Lived for the day
with no strings on tomorrow.

Memories of you
will live forever
etched in my mind
I'll forget you never.

Gail Johnson

THE JESUS FREAK

Once my heart was cold and arid
struggling daily just to make it.
All my efforts, bored and tired;
it wasn't easy, but I faked it.

Then one day I stopped to ponder
what it was that made me dry;
must my life be blown by thunder,
can I make it; should I die?

Just by chance, I came upon
a Jesus Freak who spoke with zeal;
said my sins I should lay down,
that God forgives, and He is real.

This my mind could not compute,
to think there was such love;
that all my sins He'd not impute
if I would only look above.

Once the fountain made its start
I let the waters take their toll,
and from the recess of my heart
allowed God's Spirit full control.

P. G. Colon, Jr.

PORCH

Lovers run in distance
from the terrace stone
dark façades of glances
and memory's lost lips

a song is evening's shutter
cold against a face
where marble leans on arms
against a statue's porch.

Sharon Rubenstein

SURRENDER

I've seen the dead caused by war,
smelled the odors with the poor,
heard the clang of a prison's gate
which in turn increased my hate.

I took all this as an excuse
to pour forth hurt and hurl abuse.
I did not know how this relation
caused me pain and all frustration.

Jaws were hard and teeth did grind
and all my muscles were in a bind;
stomach bolted and food rejected,
sleepless nights had me dejected.

I realize now that all my hate
did not allow me to appreciate
what God could do to clear my mind
and loose my body from this bind.

P. G. Colon, Jr.

EACH OTHER'S FRIEND

He is always glad to see me —
Just look at that wag in his tail.
Day or night, feeling up or down,
My best friend's love will never fail.

He fills my home with happiness —
His love always lifts my morale.
I can't think of what life would be
Without my loving canine pal.

This home is his as well as mine —
That is a fact I'll guarantee.
He guards it with his very life
From all unwelcomed company.

His being is a paradox —
Full of love, but willing to fight.
His affection warms me clear through;
Yet he handles most any plight.

My buddy and I make up one —
That is a really unique blend.
I love this lot we hold in life,
We'll always be each other's friend.

Lou Roberts

LAMENT

Love still wanders
far from distant time
falling on the cradle
earth's newborn —

Hour's dust is drifting
through a glance's flame
winter drowns the windows
in forest's dark lament.

Sharon Rubenstein

GOOD MEMORIES

What a treasure are good memories —
  Their beautiful bells will always toll.
These riches are like great symphonies
  That enliven and freshen the soul.

Lou Roberts

LIFE'S WASTED YOUTH

Dandy young men have gone to war
  Destined not to return.
Doom was their battle's conqueror,
  Death was all they would earn.

This sacrifice, made in their prime,
  Tells a haunting event
To human beings, for all time,
  Through unending torment.

Carefree lads left all that they had
  Causing grief, then sorrow.
Conviction soothed their thoughts so sad —
  Cursed would be tomorrow.

Weary the dead youth's relative
  Waiting in sorrow's vise
With thoughts of being positive —
  Wanting no sacrifice.

Gone now is the cause in his life,
  Given promptly for all.
Grief is the innate debt for strife —
  Gloom is the lasting pall.

Lou Roberts

FLESH

He came to me,
Like a black bird
That flashes in light,
Innocent and lovely,
Mouth soft, free of teeth,
Yawning to be held.

With fist in mouth,
His call was lyrical,
My joints idle,
A cradle for his warmth.

I kiss him;
He smiles with mossy eyes,
Blowing bubbles,
Forming blossoms with his lips.

Laid back on my weariness
I am flushed by gauze warm puffs,
A soft enticement,
A radiance in the very flesh of things.

Ella Robinson

IF ONLY

If only the leaders of this political world could see,
From beyond the windows of their hearts, and not thru eyes of greed,
This good earth shall flourish for many more years to come,
Now and then witnessing the wrath of elements, should they not heed.

If only they, who say they are truly concerned and fear
    what's to come,
And are quick to ward off temptation of personal gain and
    greed for power,
World existence in freedom and in peace becomes reality,
Instead of foretold warnings of total devastation, day to day,
    hour to hour.

If only from the goodness of their hearts, decisions benefiting
    all were met,
And mutual agreement for peaceful times and nuclear disarmament
    did not wane,
Living humanist, not militarist, sharing wisdom and knowledge
    thru compassion,
Death by peace seekers past, and patriotic many, will not
    have been in vain.

If only they, from behind closed doors, could hear the myriad
    cries and pleas,
And for world salvation break from the monolith, in conscience,
    never lonely,
From all corners of the world, they gather without barriers
    of restraint,
Power and wealth, striving to live as one, in peace and in harmony,
    if only . . .

Camille St. Amour

THE STOIC'S CREDO

We cannot be martyrs for each other,
To live each other's lives and to die each other's deaths;
For where life sends us and when death ends us
in our graves, our last and most futile home,
We live and we die alone.

Lynn Geralds

HIS INFINITE WORD

He spoke to me one day from the heavens high above,
Telling me he would watch over me and I would always have his love.

I trusted him and loved him, having faith in all his ways,
He in turn told me, ''I'll guide you through the remainder of your days.''

Life was very special in a warm and loving way,
I always wondered when it would be taken on my very special day.

There was no fear or hesitation about my journey to beyond,
My Savior would be waiting, with whom I had a very special bond.

The joys of life are endless but the sadness is often there,
God never gives us more than he feels we are able to bear.

He tests us in so many ways throughout our daily hours,
Watching his teachings being taught and the wisdom of his powers.

He'll call us home someday, to the heavens high above,
Knowing here's another life, full of eternal love.

Carole L. Rucki

SILVER-PLATED SUNDAYS

*For Papa, 4-9-87 — in memory of
Manuel T. Fine, 9-6-02 to 8-20-67*

The man of my days
He took the heart and soul of this little girl with him to his grave
I feel him near me laughing and willing
A giant to me in every way
I cried and cried tears which have never dried
A love so great is still alive inside
I remember his abounding kindness
His loud aliveness
Silver-plated Sundays
God's day and his day
Warm from the joy he would radiate
Reckless in his youth, they say
I miss him and so do all who knew him
My words are empty praises no matter how great the tribute
His goodness the selfless gifts that he gave
Are greater than any thanks
Or the candles we lit the night he passed away
They dance in my heart
And with him a piece of my soul
Buried in his grave

Dena Beth Lesser

DENA BETH LESSER. Pen Names: Dena Amour, Dena; Born: Los Angeles, California, 10-30-54; Education: Antioch College and UCLA, 1972-75; Occupations: Actress, Make-up artist, Dancer, Poetess, Screenwriter, Astrologer; Memberships: Screen Actors Guild, American Federation of Television and Radio Artists, Actors Equity Association; Writings: ''Children's Leukemia,'' medical research article, Nurses' Files: Children's Hospital Ward of the City of Hope Cancer Institute, 1966; ''The Camel Pusher,'' screenplay, Writers' Guild of America, West, 1979; Poetry: 'Saprobia,' *American Poetry Anthology, Vol. VI, No. 2,* 1986; 'One Man,' *Hearts on Fire, A Treasury of Poems on Love, Vol. III,* 1986; 'Child of Faith,' *Words of Praise: A Treasury of Religious and Inspirational Poetry, Vol. III,* 1987; Comments: *Some people in our lives are very dear to us. A note telling them so is lovely, and thoughtful words of praise on those special visits together are cherished, but poetry or a song, an original work of art, something extraordinarily personal from one heart to another is forever. It is the greatest gift of all, and one with which all the world can identify and appreciate over and over again.*

THE HOUSE HUMS OF MAMA

''The house hums of Mama,''
I said to my sister.
She turned and looked at me,
But she heard the thought.

Yes, it is true.
Mama was always humming a tune while she worked
And the sound lingers on in our minds
And comforts us in our bereavement.

Juliet Ashley Lesch

VOICE

Evening's voice is calling
to a child's steps
a neighborhood wandering
lost in darkness

summer's light is memory
to those without a voice
their thoughts interred in windows
wave at terrace fronts.

Sharon Rubenstein

SHARON LYNN RUBENSTEIN. Born: Los Angeles, California, 8-30-45; Married: John Svehla, 11-12-76; Education: Pierce College, 1965; Occupation: Legal secretary; Poetry: 'Thousand Words,' *Poetic Symphony, Music from the Heart;* 'Storm,' 'At Shore,' *Prophetic Voices 8,* 1987; 'This Isn't Death,' *Prophetic Voices 9,* 1987; 'Coastal Path,' *Broken Streets,* 1987; Comments: *My poetry is about love — lost love, unrequited love. Youth, schools, neighborhoods are also recurrent themes.*

MY TEARS ARE ALL SHED

My tears are all shed
I've cried a river
I've prayed and I've pled —
    It's so hard to accept
    That word we all dread —
But God's answer was, ''No,
She's needed in heaven
It's time she must go.''

My tears are all shed
That river has dried
Death came as her friend
    Her body is resting
    But this isn't the end
She welcomed release
A new life to begin
And her soul is at peace

Now I'll cry a river —
    For me

Dorothy Howard Adler

IF THE SUN SHOULD FAIL

Tomorrow morning the sun's going to rise
But what if God should leave the universe
And stars fly from their places in the sky?
Can you think of a thing that would be worse?

Who would be in charge of our daily lives?
How could we survive if there were no light?
Would we be like bees in white arctic hives?
Everything everywhere would be dark night.

God, everlasting to everlasting
Will in nowise forsake His creation
Therefore rejoice; let every creature sing
God will rule forever with Christ the King!

Dorothy Howard Adler

ARRIVAL OF SPRING

Bright and brassy, gold and bold
From the lawn and roundabout
Hear the lion shout it out:
    Spring is here

From the shadows by the brookside
Where shy violets abide
Hush now! Listen! Hear them sing:
    It is spring

Then the robins help them sing
With their cheery, glad refrain:
    Yes, 'tis spring

Mr. Sun sends down bright rays
Chasing out drear winter days
    Then it's spring

I have heard the Word proclaim —
And 'tis true — blest Easter came!
    So in my heart it's spring

Dorothy Howard Adler

MY LOVE

Honey, I know I've hurt you and
    really hurt you bad
But my whole life without you has
    made my world so sad.
I never thought I could love someone
    as much as I love you.
If you're gone from my life forever,
    I don't know what I'll do.
If I get you back this time, I'll
    never let you go.
I'll love you for many years and through
    my eyes my love will show.
I'll hold you close and near to me
    I'll never leave your side
So no one will ever say we never
    even tried.
I pray every night you'll take me
    back and love me in every way.
I'll never love one as much, my love,
    As I love you this day.

Lynn R. McCoy

SUCCESS

Success for each man is
    a curious thing,
often valued by how
    it pays.

Some think it a journey that
    never ends,
and others to spend life
    their way.

It smiles on those who
    make dreams come true,
''It's luck,'' any failure
    will roast.

But the person who wants it
    and searches in vain,
is the one who values
    it most.

J. Henry Hoffman

DREAMS
that take years
to materialize
into reality
change
in the process
of achieving them
and new dreams
are built
upon them
causing
the very climax
of your dreams
to be always
just beyond
your reach
DREAMS

Colleen Dougher

WINTER'S BEACH

Waves thump home on a flat
stretch of now-hard sand
that looks more like a
worn beige carpet than the
once-soft down of summer's
suntime funtime. Splintered
slats of driftwood lay
scattered on softer sand
surrounded by pop-off tops
and discarded beer bottles.
Rusty nails protrude from
the weathered stumps, a
threat to sneaker-clad
beachcombers, few and far
between in the surly winter
winds.

Rita B. Swartz

YOU KNOW ME NOT

I am a latent, incipient revolutionary
Posing as a well-intended lobbyist to thee.
My loyal, self-serving politician, you
Know me, but you know me not as *he*.

I am a liberal, brilliant professor
Tenured at a great American university.
My loyal, self-serving student, you
Know me, but you know me not as *he*.

I am a frocked, beloved priest
Saving souls, known as Father to thee.
My loyal, self-serving sheep, you
Know me, but you know me not as *he*.

I am a brilliant, syndicated journalist
Covering all of our nation's affairs for thee.
My loyal, self-serving citizen, you
Know me, but you know me not as *he*.

As *he,* politician, I will serve you loads
   of disinformation.
As *he,* student, I will expound pure socialism as
   ideal for you.
As *he,* sheep, I will propound one perfect religion
   for the world.
As *he,* citizen, I will portray our governments losers
   in all they do.

Ric Filip

SUNSET REMINISCENCE

In the evening, as the twilight falls
About the fiery throes of sunset,
I stand and hook my arm about the column of our porch;
And think of you, how much you loved
This time of day, when day consumed
Itself in tepid fire-plays, to greet the coming darkness.

The birds have found their nesting place,
The hound is curled beside me . . .
Only the cat remains alert to share the lonely moment . . .
While all creation basks in glory,
With flaming chords of lingering light:
The end of day in beauty cast, to ease our sadness that it passes.

So much like how you spent with me
Our final hours together;
So bright with cheer, with love and laughter,
You shamed me with your courage.
And now I stand, in semi-darkness,
So unaccepting day is gone;
And think of you, asleep for time,
While I stay 'wake, to greet the night.

David B. Hawthorne

From the beginning of our prior nine months of existence
Into the world of light, then sound . . .
And always feeling —
We emerge.
We cannot return.
We do not have to persevere.
We try.
Some fail.
Some go on.

H. T. Brohl

STORY SUCCESS

You are the *theme* of my *story* —
My *comment on* vibrant *life*.
O how I *plotted* a series of *events*
To reveal you that theme, my wife.

I began with a hopeful *premise,*
Colorful *characters* entwined in *strife*.
Knowing all would become as they think and do,
I fabricated richly adventurous episodes in your life.

O what kind of premise would I have?
O what kind of character would I be?
O what would I hold before my mind to think and do?
O what would attract lovely, adventurous, spectacular you?

I must become the *theme* of your *story* —
In the *plot,* in the series of *events* that reveal
Me to be your theme, your *comment on life* —
An appropriate *character* your *premise* to steal.

O what a magnificent *story* I spun
Of adventure, creation, recognition, security, and love.
All woven into a saga of how to get you.
Success crowned my efforts, thanks to the *story* above.

Ric Filip

DICK ZUFELT. Pen name: Ric Filip; Born: 12-20-20; Married: Sally M. B. Zufelt (Filipova); Education: Brigham Young University, 1940; University of Georgia, 1951-52, 1968; University of Hawaii, 1956-57; University of Omaha, 1959-60; Command and General Staff College, 1959; B.E.G. Degree; Occupations: Pvt. to Lt.C. (WWII, Korea, Vietnam); Businessman, Public relations, Lecturer, Teacher, Writer, Operations research analyst; Writings: ''Hot Rodder Awakes,'' short story, *The Bayonet,* 7-9-53; Poetry: 'Why I,' *The American Poetry Anthology, Vol. III, 1-2,* 1984; 'Thrice Twenty-One,' *The American Poetry Anthology, Vol. IV, No. 2,* 1985; 'Life's Piazza,' *The American Poetry Anthology, Vol IV, No. 1,* 1985; 'Passage — Here to There,' *The American Poetry Showcase,* 1985; Comments: *I write philosophically, humorously, and seriously about a lifetime of experiences: love, adventure, creation, recognition and security. I continue to try to light one more candle, warm a heart, light a fire and remain* alive *while living.*

EVENINGS REMEMBERED

Oh Georgetown, Georgetown, Georgetown Club
What glorious evenings spent
Replete with music fine, press all divine
Wine and food delights
Toasts for you, praises true
A secretary now, an ambassador then
A diamond velvet widow, knees a buckle
A flapping Martha, causing a chuckle
A John recoiling, ever foiling
The dance going on and on
A famous secretary spinning and spinning.

Time recording all
Then records a fall.

Rebecca I. Christ-Janer

PERFECT FIT FOR BUCK

So fine
loving you
here's my heart
    and my soul
safe in your care
my sweet
    husband
        lover
            friend.

Rita B. Swartz

. . . AND IN RETURN

When I look at you,
I see so many things I wish were part of me.
That intuitive sense of right and wrong
Has broadened my mind;
I'm learning to be strong.
You held me up when I felt like falling,
And helped me to stand to keep from crawling.
Lay your hand on my life,
Help me to find a direction.
Without question,
We have shared thoughts and affection.
You've given me much;
I'm grateful, it's true.
But in return the only thing I can do
Is say I need you,
And I hope you need me too.

Joann Saulino

Lush shades of green
and salty sea breezes
are fluid in my memory.
Dreams of my youth
come flooding back
in the rich nectar of a summer's day.

Basking in the beauty
around me,
I clutched at every pretty flower
that caught my eye.
I didn't know
such pleasure wouldn't last.

I'm different now —
no longer a child.
My dreams are different too —
so are my summers.
Still, nothing can compare
to the smell
of honeysuckle in the air.

Diana E. Amato

BALM IN GILEAD COUNTY

For three long days he stood
The pain. And then he put
Aside his dread, and went
To old Doc Hill, who pulled
The tooth.
    ''All right,'' Doc said,
''It's gone. Feel better now?''
You owe me five. Or you
Can trim my hedge.''
            That shows
How long ago it was —
And, maybe, the town's size.

Henry L. Norton

A BETTER WAY

Lessons are so hard to learn
    As through this world we travel.
We try so self-sufficiently
    Our problems to unravel.

Upon our sad discovery
    That we did not succeed,
We sink into depression
    And thus increase our need.

There is a better way, my friend
    To overcome our trials.
The secret lies in simple trust
    As of a little child.

A trust in Someone up above
    Who knows just what we lack
Is the secret of success.
    My friend, this is a fact.

Hope Scott

LITTLE JANELLE

Cute as a button
    Is little Janelle.
Her laugh is contagious
    And charming as well.

Her cheeks, they are rosy.
    Her eyes sparkle bright.
Her grandma and grandpa think
    She is all right.

Her arms swing like hinges.
    Her feet, how they fly.
Her screech can be heard
    Clear up to the sky.

She fights with her brother.
    She plays with her dad.
She goes to her mother
    Whenever she's sad.

In spite of her fighting,
    Without or with harm,
To all those who know her,
    My, what a charm!

Hope Scott

LOVER'S THOUGHTS

I think about you all the day.
I think about you when I pray,

And when the night is drawing near
I think about you, my dear.

Why don't you give to me your hand,
And let us wander o'er this land

Until time shall be no more,
And we shall reach the other shore?

And when we reach that bliss divine,
I know that you will still be mine.

Together we the joys will share
And thank our God for answered prayer.

Hope Scott

CATHEDRAL

Cathedrals are many
if one stops and thinks.
Those built by man,
those by God.

The cathedral of my youth
where music moved the soul
to prayer,
where the quiet was like incense
ascending to the sky,
where the quiet was filled
with softly murmured prayer.

The cathedral of the forest
of great Sequoia trees,
where the quiet is filled
with the sighing of the trees,
the buzzing of insects, the
echo of thousands of years.

Helene A. Donohoe

UPLINE, DOWNLINE

Which will it be?
There is upline, downline,
steady line, byline,
side-line, middle-line,
edge-line, endline.

Network buying, I hear,
has all kinds of lines
helping each other
to greater prosperity.

I wonder!
Is this a line?

Helene A. Donohoe

A WAY-SIDE BARGAIN.

RIVER

I say love
Like one says patient, regal siege,
River
Quick to overflow its banks,
Like royal sedge,
River
Creator of soil, fertile,
River
Ruin that taught me thus to ruminate
The proud rich drift of ancient, buried age,
River
To which nothing is held back.
Wash away my incline;
Widen me!

Ella Robinson

AS THE LINE MOVES

There are weapons
I am told in words
Sometimes lost on back roads,
Cradled in ordinary gullies,
At other times hushed up
In carpeted plush rooms.

There is the poet's want,
Some confuse with privilege:
To polish boots or slit a throat or two,
To say nothing really,
To slice a peach,
Peel a pungent orange,
Bring the pulse to thump.

And there's the old saying,
"Any time a woman will do."
Weak and unnecessary as she is by the river,
And there's the old man with the woman.
They fish sometimes, and this old woman
Takes to gliding her fingers that dance
As the pulley on her line moves.

Ella Robinson

ELLA S. ROBINSON. Born: Wedowee, Alabama; Married: John; Education: Nebraska, M.A., Ph.D.; Occupation: Lecturer of English; Memberships: MLA, MMLA, Chaparrel Poets of Nebraska; Poetry: Published in *Lawrence of Nottingham: A Poetry Anthology to D.H. Lawrence, New Poets of Summer*, 1985; *American Poetry Anthology, Vol. VI, No. 3; American Poetics: 1986, Vol. I; Whole Notes*, 1986; *Heart Songs*, 1987; Comments: *I love America and write on themes that enhance America's images. I love humanity as well — all mankind.*

LIFE

Life is something kind and sweet
Its bitterness comes with all we meet
Think of a jewel on a cutting table
So round and smooth and yet not able —
To see what life is really like
Without the roughness and the strife.
It seems to me
That life's so easy —
But is it really?
In many, many years to come
We may find that we've lost someone
Or something in disguise that right
In some dark and forbidden night.
In conclusion,
There is an allusion
That comes to us so near —
So don't forget that life's true meaning
Is sometimes played by ear!

Timothy R. Barre

WHAT IS A MOMENT?

What is a moment, a pin-prick in time,
Tiny rupture in a continuum,
Pushed up from within, possibly sublime?
Not disturbing the equilibrium,
Resting always in its eternal place,
Yet a moment never occupies space.

What is a moment, attached from outside
Jagged edges bursting its wobbling frame,
Where experiential pragmatists cried,
Give this moment its terrestrial acclaim.
An activity orgy in motion,
Solving each problematical notion.

Dr. Grace K. Pratt-Butler

GAMES

Romance and poker; parallel pleasures.
Chance, that random rogue,
Stacks the deck
And awards the treasures.

If you fall for a queen,
Whose faces turns away,
Shield your heart
And bet your pay.

If your love is welcomed
With a golden band,
Count your winnings
And fold your hand.

The old adage warns
That we cannot win
At poker *and* romance.
Reno, deal me in.

Ed Carine

CHROMA

The colors of love are primary;
Heart's scarlet ardor,
Abandoned blue.
Mix with yellow bile
To pour a jealous green.
Romance vibrates with clashing pigments.

On friendship's canvas
Paler hues combine.
Pastel shades depict
True, comfortable affection.
No blazing tones to shock,
Then fling one down.
White blends scarlet to pink, mists the blue
And turns sulphurous yellow into sunshine.

Although minimal in color,
Friendship's work is more lasting.
The light that limns love's art
Burns too brightly to endure.

Ed Carine

A COUNTRY'S LOSS

The sky was as blue as the ocean below
On that sad and fateful day.
And all eyes were focused upward
As we waited there and prayed.

When the shuttle shot off into space
Our hearts were choked with pride,
For those brave men and women
Who a moment later died.

We watched with horror and disbelief
As the rocket burst into flames,
And scattered debris far and wide —
No, we were not playing games!

"How could this be!" we asked ourselves,
"My eyes are deceiving me!
I cannot believe this has happened to us.
Where is our victory?"

Yet sooner or later we all make mistakes
And have to swallow our pride.
But the terrible, haunting tragedy
Was that our brothers and sisters had died!

Our stricken country rallied together
And we all felt a deep sense of loss,
For those seven loyal astronauts
Who died on Calvary's cross.

Phyllis S. Howard

Paint me with your hands
Color me with your eyes
Whisper life to my body
Shed tears to my soul
Touch me with your lips
Warm me with your smile
Caress me with your fingertips
Share your body with mine
I am yours, frame me with your love.

Roben-Marie Roberts

THE JOB

A frown masked my mouth
Sweat poured from my face
My dogs howled
I hung my head and sighed.

Having nightmares: seeing ''Help Wanted'' signs
Lying on the ground, underneath a pile of applications
I awoke out of my sleep: screaming, ''I wanna work, I wanna work''
Tears filled my eyes

One day, I met a young lady while riding the bus
She told me about her job
And told me to come fill out an application

When I did: the sky turned blue, my frown was no more, the sun beamed,
and I jumped up and bumped my head on a cloud.

David Johnson

NIGHT RUNNER

The dull, rhythmic thud of sneakers,
Plodding through the darkened street,
Marking time . . .
A faint, jouncing shadow follows, shifting feeble lamplight
Into patterns on the pavement.

The night runner pauses not for potholes, curbs or cans . . .
He pushes as his body groans, and revels in the effort.
Chill winds whistle past his ears, headlights glare ahead;
His heart drums, steady, strong in moving, running, going . . .
Pressing on.

In the runner's soul, quiet
As the stars above,
And burning just as brightly,
Grows the fervent hope of dreams yet unfulfilled . . .
Bold, they mingle with his coursing blood, fanning
The flame of new ambition . . .
To run until it's dawn.

David B. Hawthorne

BLUE

A wonderful through came to me
    when thoughts turned suddenly to you.
Without you here, though, I see
    how blue the loneliness can really be.
How much I care, I only wish you knew.

Shades much deeper than any tear,
    when mail reads, ''I miss you.''
Far away you seem, I hear
    the pain in the blue notes so clear.
Just how to convey, ''I miss you too.''

Little things which mean so much
    make me wait, impatiently watching time.
Still gone you are but still I clutch
    to the darkened memories of your touch.
With missing you, blue sorrow is mine.

Larunce A. Pipkin, Jr.

YESTERDAY'S MURDER

Yesterday's murder was still in the news.
Detectives were searching for motives and clues.
And all of the weather, from Texas to Maine,
was forecasting thunderheads, showers or rain.
The clock, while rebelling at telling the time,
was flashing the room with an eerie green lime.
The lights were turned off. The electrical power
refused to react at the pre-set fixed hour.

I opened the door. The fear, trepidation
surged over me with dread-filled expectation.
There she'd be lying in a pool of dark blood
and the carpet all spattered with traces of mud.
I moved toward the sofa to turn on the light.
Pounding, my heart was trembling with fright.
The lamp light was lovely. I was learning anew
too much imagination can almost kill you.

Florence W. Ruppert

THE GOOD SHEPHERD

There are needed people everywhere —
Be a Good Shepherd — Care and share.
There are wandering paupers here and there.
Be a Good Shepherd — Kneel in prayer.
If you're called upon for help —
Be a Good Shepherd — Don't be just for self.
Never let good items decay —
Be a Good Shepherd — Give them away.
Don't sent a weary traveler to roam —
Be a Good Shepherd — Help him find a home.
If you know a bereaved is around the corner —
Be a Good Shepherd — Don't leave him a lone mourner.
If there is a neighbor who is ill —
Be a Good Shepherd — Help! — That's God's will.
One day your life will cease —
And you'll be rewarded for a job well done
At God's Holy Throne enjoying everlasting fun.

Alice Cornelia White

ALICE CORNELIA WHITE. Born: Longtown Community, Kershaw County, South Carolina, 2-18-33; Single; Education: South Carolina State College, B.A., 1955; M.E., 1969; Occupation: School teacher, retired 7-85; Memberships: Life member of National Educational Association and South Carolina Educational Association; Poetry: Published first book of poetry 5-11-87, *A Diversified Collection of Easy Reading Verses to Entertain the Mind,* advertised in the New York Times, 7-15-87; Themes: *Ethics and morality, religion, nature, humor, principles of good living that relish one's inner feeling and behavior.*

A DREAM

I dreamed I stood up on a mountain
My head way up in the cloud;
My thoughts were all turned inward
Thoughts of others were not allowed.

'Til I tried to come down off the mountain
and I found I needed a hand;
I looked around, there was no one there,
Then I began to understand.

You must think of others around you,
Put their needs above your own;
If you help others when they need help,
You'll never struggle alone.

Lillian Miller

I CLOSED THE DOOR

You kissed me and life became
  a beginning, a timeless span
    revolving for only us.
You gave the promise of moon-lit nights
  and endless dreams,
    drenched a dazzling brilliance.
No mind my head, my intuitions,
  my heart spun on a chain of gold.
    Too soon, the angry truth unfurled
tossed with the force of a raging tide
  assaulting an unprotected beach,
    then the winds ceased,
      the storm was over,
        and I closed the door.

Phyllis C. Byers

I'M TIRED

I'm tired, and you know
it had to happen sooner or later.
I mean, how long can you walk barefoot
before the stones start horning in
like desert sands, hot and searing
fueling cacti and naked sage brush
naked sage brush, driven by the winds
winds blowing without a resting place
resting place, somewhere to lay my head
somewhere to lay my head
laying, leaving that tiredness
  to melt like ice cubes
    dissolved by the sun
      absorbed in
        poured concrete.

Phyllis C. Byers

LIFE

Someday somebody needs to
Be listened to and understood
By someone else!

Daniel Guy Leonard

ERE SETS THE EVENING SUN

My life shall touch many lives
  Before this day is done;
Leave countless marks for good or ill,
  Ere sets the evening sun.

So this the wish I always wish,
  The prayer I ever pray;
''Lord, may my life help other lives
  It touches by the way.''

Ivy Christina Busekros

HE'S HELPING ME

I know God never meant for me,
To live this life unhappily
To know that He with all His love,
Sends down His blessings from above
And though I am the only one
That can choose for me,
The right or wrong
I sometimes fail unknowingly
Yet God I know,
  Is helping me . . .

Jeanetta Armstrong

TELL ME DARLIN'

What are you gonna do darlin'
When the tears won't stop flowin'
And your misery keeps on growin'
'Cause you can't have me
And I can't have you,
Tell me darlin' what are you gonna do?
You know things should be different,
But you're powerless to change them,
Tell me darlin' what are you gonna do?
When there's a lump in your breast
Like it was just about to burst,
Tell me darlin' what are you gonna do?
Well I'll tell you darlin'
You'll just keep on cryin'
And you'll just keep on sighin'
Darlin' that's what you're gonna do.
But the lump will still be there,
And you just haven't got a prayer,
Till someone changes how things are.
So tell me darlin' what are you gonna do?

Marcia R. Morris

COUNSELOR

I reach my hand into the air
And all I touch is air
I reach my hand into the air
And ask myself, do counselors care
I reach my hand into the air
And all I touch is air

Daniel Guy Leonard

TRACKS

Warning bells are tolling,
  the coming of a moving train.
  Why should I care, he won't be
  back again.
On and on the bells keep ringing,
  as if they want me to know,
You never said good-bye so I
  guess you did not go.
    I can't see you,
      you're just not there.
    All I can do is go to
      the tracks and stare.
    I feel so alone, you don't
    seem to care. If you really
    love, me, where are you? Can
    you tell me — where?

Mary E. Correll

THE FEELING OF YOU

  In fear, I sit remembering
the feeling of you holding me near.
  From the corner of
my eye runs a cold
  bleeding-heart tear.
Being once again, left
  alone, holding in my
hand all your love in
  a pink rose.
A picture, maybe a
  symbol, to say only
where the road goes;
  alone in a possible
picture pose.

April Marie Bottomley

WHY

  A rainbow fading, as the
doves glitter while they pass
in the sky.
  A glistening path of a fallen tear;
you hold me near grasping
our love with another lie.
  A thundering wave receiving its
energy from the sound of a lonely
cry.
  A burning candle melting
with each kiss, as our love
says its good-bye.
  A fire burning in an eagle's
eye as our love lays itself
to die.
  The sun setting in misty
skies of loss, as I sit alone
asking myself the questions,
what did I do; am I the reason ''why''?

April Marie Bottomley

God forgive us our debts and trespasses and infidelity.
Live on, live on, let this not be our epitaph —
More a graph
Of ups and downs in humanity's predestined path to hell.

H. T. Brohl

SISTER DOLOROSA

Sister Dolorosa, your name is a contradiction,
For you were blessed with a gift to create joy,
To enchant others with your beauty.
You moved with grace and elegance,
Petite, slender, startling, beautiful.
Perceptive, spiritual, searching for answers.
Your home was an expression of happiness and hospitality.
Like a swift swallow you slipped out of our lives,
As quicksilver sliding from a slanted beaker.
Finally you accepted a terminal malady, as tortured
      physically and mentally,
You engaged in a losing battle to remain with your children.
While we struck dumb, numb with grief, would come,
With knowledge we were losing you.
Strange how you gave us courage, never complaining.
And all the while with a madonna-like expression on your face,
Death came gently like a noble coup-de-grace.
But neither dying nor deep suffering could erase
The spiritual beauty from your lovely face.
For you no more todays, only eternal tomorrows.
Youthful Sister of Sorrows.

Winifred Murray

WASECA DAWN

I awaken at dawn to rapture.
Robins and rose-breasted grosbeaks are filling the air
      with their music,
The robin's song clear and bright, the grosbeak's tone
      softer, sweeter, mellower,
Together making a continuous chorus.

I walk through the slumbering town and out to the lake
Where black terns are flying about over the water.
They do not like me. They want me out of there.
One flies right at me and almost hits me.

The sun comes up and I walk on along the shore enjoying the morning.
Golden notes of meadowlark song come to me from the farmland
      near the lake.
Red-winged blackbirds in the slough, their epaulets spreading
      to the sunshine,
Are gleefully pouring forth ''Konquewreee'' with all their might
As I walk home again.

People are all about in the town now and the day is going
      about its business.

When I reach our yard, the Baltimore oriole, a flash of
      orange and black glory,
Is whistling ''Peter'' among the treetops.

It has been sixty-three years since I spent those early
      summer dawnings
With the music of the birds in far-off Minnesota
But the ecstasy is still in my memory, and will remain.

Juliet Ashley Lesch

MY NEIGHBOR

E

My neighbor's a girl with a pretty face
A slim trim figure and stylish clothes
A touch of red and a flashing smile
And my neighbor is good for me.

My neighbor finds out the things I can do
And she tells them to others so they'll know, too,
And she brings out potentials in me.
A neighbor indeed is she.

No one ever did this for me before.
To think that I'd find such a friend next door
Of another race in another clime.
I'm glad that it came to be.

Juliet Ashley Lesch

VIVALDI AT 10,000 FEET

The haunting strains of the violin
      announce the arrival of Vivaldi's Spring.
Music written to soar through concert halls
      is a private performance coming through headphones
just for the two of us, the pilot and the poet.

The strident sounds of Summer
      are reflected in the sun glancing off the wings
as we sail over endless miles of convoluted mountains,
      over sun dancing off the clouds
lighting our world in iridescent splendor.

The mellowness of Autumn is played by the cellos,
      as the sun slips quietly over the horizon,
casting a rosy glow across the sky.
      The music swells, the steady hum of the engine
keeps us on course as darkness descends.

Vivaldi's stormy Winter belies the beauty we behold
      when a blanket of lacy clouds opens to reveal
sparkling jewels of light spread below us,
      until the music fades softly away
and we fly into the night in a shower of stars.

Dottie Neil

HEIRS

Did mother relive her raising in raising me?
My Susan brought tears and laughter for later reverie!
Mother used to say when little we step on parents' toes!
Then the heart is stepped on as the child older grows!

How did my parents grow so smart
Between my teen years and first job start?
Why didn't I take their sound advice
Instead of always doing everything twice?

Now, my grandchildren are so precious!
In everything they are very precocious!
All they talk of is what they're going to be!
No mention of marriage and future family!

Have past generations failed the future ones?
Have we truly shown that their raising is what comes
From our loving hearts and desires for all our heirs
To reminisce and know their ancestors cared?

Wilma Noe Payne

SADNESS

Sadness comes
more than
once a year
and brings
one too many a tear.

Sadness you
can feel only in
you but has
shown to hurt
others, too.

Sadness may
sometimes be
fought but
happiness
may not be bought.

You have to
wait for another
day and turn
your head the
other way!

April Marie Bottomley

SLEEP — SWEET — SLEEP

Sleep — sweet — sleep
Come to my bed as a lover,
Woo me with golden poppies.

Sleep — sweet — sleep
Come to my couch as a sylphid,
Sing your incantations repetitiously.

Sleep — sweet — sleep
Come to my resting place as an innocent child,
Enmesh me with daisy chains.

Sleep — sweet — sleep
Come to my tatami mat in velvet slippers,
Carry away my burdens.

Sleep — sweet — sweet — sleep
Take me — Morpheus — take your amoretta
Deep into your vast bosom.

Jane Pierritz

LET HIM IN

It's trouble and sorrow everywhere,
We'd better get ourselves prepared
God is coming to show man . . .
He made this world, it's in His hands.
When He gets ready, He'll make a change,
Nothing in this world will be the same.
We must be humble in our hearts;
If we don't, Satan will keep us apart.
We've got to treat everybody right;
Serve the Lord day and night.
God will forgive you of your sin,
If you will only let Him in.

"He will never leave you alone."

Sister Gladys Thomas

HOME

As I travel down the byways
On the roads I like to roam —
I have never found one equal
To the one which leads back home.

Oh! It's nice to go exploring
Through the fields of rare delight
But it's better to get settled
In your comfy bed at night.

Paths will beckon ever —
All their glories to unfold,
But I never would exchange them
For that old familiar mold.

Home is where the heart is —
Or so the poets always say —
I may wander far tomorrow
But I'll stay at home today.

Mrs. Howard Nickerson

WEDDING ANNIVERSARY

While you're reminiscing for fun
on this anniversary of Ira's and mine
I'm remembering my parents' Golden One
on November fourteen, nineteen fifty-nine.
If we can be so fortunate
we'll really have something to crow about
you're all invited, don't be late
we'll dance and shout.
We're already on the countdown
forty-one down, nine to go
we'll try to stick around
and make a big show.
Should we not make it, for instance
you'll know it's not to be
it's not just chance
but the will of God, you see.
We're so thankful
for the ones we've had
we'll expect you all to be grateful
and not sad.

Hesse G. Byrd

CRY!

"Cry!" says the morning sun
  Rising in my throat.
"Cry!" say the clouds upon the mountains —
  Vast shadows in my heart.
The winds blow through my body
  Saying, "Cry!"
And lost in some old sorrowing am I.

Forgotten joys that rose and spread
  As the new dawn,
Bringing happy tears to other days;
Forgotten, too, dark specters of the past
  That crowded into life and darkened hope . . .
Chill feelings that foreboding blew
  In times I scarce recall . . .
All, now, come back to stir me
  With their "Cry!"

Lola R. Eagle

DREAMS

A golden shaft of sunlight beamed
Upon the lovers in my dream
The icy mist that held my heart
Melts before your manly arts.

As warm and rugged you appear
To call softly and beckon me near
To open up your waiting arms
As my defenses you carelessly storm.

Enfolded in your love so deep
My heart refused to keep its beat.
As slowly your lips worship mine
Our love will last till the end of time.

The fire races through my soul
What were then two, now one made whole.
This joy so real in me I felt
Was not a dream in waking melt.

As slowly my eyes fluttered open
Your lips caressing, dreams broken.
To find you bending over me.
To make my dreams reality.

Margaret A. Donnelly

DID YOU EVER FEEL

Did you ever feel
you weren't wanted around,
that you've been found undesirable
in ways that abound?

Did you ever feel
that nobody cares,
'cause you're lonely in ways
that they're just unaware of?

Did you ever feel
that you're different than most
in ways that keep you
from getting close to anyone?

Did you ever feel —
you're small and alone,
a pebble amidst the stones?

Mary Therese Goebel

TIME

How tumultuous time can be —
Swimming waves of circumstances,
Circumstances of events
Vicious circle of time
Time of borning transcendent life
Time—life's croissance
In route-time sequences
Where thing creates self importune
Life-time 'due to time', time
Where any happening
Frivole or volatile
Though time cease
Reaching its limit —
Death.
Yet, time wearies its vicious course
In due time
In which it remains itself.

Manfroy Tjomb

LOVE'S AWAKENING

Love may strike like jagged lightning
　　separating the summer sky.
or grow slowly and quietly, note by note,
　　like the movement of a symphony.

Our song began with an accidental meeting,
　　when I tripped entering a room and you caught me.
I looked into your eyes, startled by the love reflected there.
　　You were the friend who held me when I cried,
who knew my heart was bound by memories of a lost love,
　　when I wove a web to protect me from the pain.

Today, you touched me, and the ice,
　　holding my frozen heart in bondage,
melted into rivulets of wonder, the wonder of loving again.
　　You smiled at my clumsiness,
and in that brief, wondrous moment,
　　you knew, as I did, our lives were changed forever.

The joy I felt embodied all the beauty
　　of the love you offered,
as the cocoon of pain burst, the butterfly of love emerged.

Dottie Neil

KEEP THE LINES OPEN

My friends, I said a prayer for you, today; my children
and my family were included. I felt God heard my plea for
guidance, help and protection.

Altho' I heard no voice — in my heart, I knew God had heard,
and I thanked Him for His merciful powers, especially for His
Son Jesus, our Blessed Lord.

I didn't ask for wealth or fame, I left that to the Lord.
I remembered He had promised us, ''Ask and you shall receive —
Seek and you shall find.'' I hope you won't mind.

I asked, ''At the dawning of each new day we would all enjoy
good health and the happiness of good and true friends.''
Then, I added, ''Dear God, help my children to plan their days
and feel secure in their full-time work.'' I added I wished
to be included in this request. I thanked the Lord for this
personal request. I remembered to thank God for His loving care,
individually and collectively — I knew He was listening
and we were communicating.

Thank you, Dear God, for everything. Keep the lines of
communication open. Be with us today, tomorrow and
always. So may it always be.

Margery V. Bardon

TOO BUSY LIVING

I'm tired of hearing of the twilight years,
I am too busy living them to care
what others think. I have no time for tears,
no time for aches and pains, nor for despair.
My neighbors must not be neglected
while I can take them soups and salads fine,
for they are old, ill, and feel rejected
and I am well at only eighty-nine.
In quiet evenings when the lamps are lit,
my many books are begging to be read.
Also there sweaters to be knit
before I put my great-grandson to bed.
　　Although I'm busy, I may have a chance
　　to go to my granddaughter's ball to dance!

Margaret Bland Sewell

TIM

At first I couldn't express those feelings held inside,
I didn't know what to say;

But after much thought I can honestly tell you even if
I never get to meet your kids,

I'd love them just as much as I do you, Tim, in each
and every way . . .

For it was those special times, glorious moments when
you and she loved as one together;

Because you shared yourself with another, something great
and wonderful had become.

A baby was conceived with its own life to live to choose
to want whatever . . .

And he was born with eyes to see, lungs to breathe, a mind
to learn, and a heart to feel;

Your children are a part of you, yes, maybe of the past —
but the one thing that will always be;

So no matter what roads we follow or where life leads
please always remember that deal

Of love and protection you and your child made the day
you two began in this world as we.

Pat Kowalkowski

SCHOOL *DAZE*

Wash your face, comb your hair,
And quit running around in your underwear.
Get dressed right now, quit the fuss,
Eat that breakfast, or you'll miss the bus.
If you can't find the prize at the bottom —
Don't dump it all out — someone else got 'em.
Quit stalling, get a move on, too —
Hurry up. Here's your homework — take it with you.
You all got your lunch money, and your milk money, too — O.K. — O.K.
Here comes the bus — good-bye — I love you all — have a good day.
It's the last day of school, glory be — summer is finally here; I feel free.
But now, my biggest job really has begun:
Four kids at home, all day long — what joy — what fun.
But they will soon be involved in various activities, too —
Three free months of less rushing about —
Vacation time is here — school days are thru —
And now I'll be yelling a different tune
'Cause they'll be up at the crack of dawn, or they'll sleep till noon.
Oh, what joy to be a mother — there's no comparison to any other.

Bernice Riedthaler

FIREFLIES

In the dampness of the evening
Many huge fireflies lighted lilac bushes,
The spruce became a Christmas tree
With blinking lights among the seeds.
Across the field they appeared to be tractors,
They darted through the shelterbelt attracting birds,
They glowed down the lane;
Small wonder they have served in experiments.

Genevieve Kepner Singleton

RAIN

Rain
down the window
pane
reminds me of the day
when you
came
into my life.

The rain slowly
drips

if

if

it would rain hard enough,
the pane
would be overwhelmed
with rain.

Streaming wet,
you can bet
that it will take
a lot of sun
to dry this one.

Mary Therese Goebel

SUNNYSIDE UP

Wake up a good morning
Dance up a new sunrise
Sign up to the blue sky
Sunnyside up.

I looked out of my window
Then I saw a bright rainbow
The blue skies of heaven.
Sunnyside up.

So I called the May Queen
She answered, ''How are you?
The whole world is waking!''
Sunnyside up.

So then I heard laughter
A few moments after.
Her voice gently calling
Sunnyside up.

Robert L. Feldman

FINIS

How quickly life is taken from us
just when least expected
Senseless, cruel and needless
Plans for a future disintegrated
as butterfly wings in the wind
Left behind are grieving hearts
and empty spaces in our future
Precious is our untold love
a jewel to give reflection

Kary J. Stark

THE STREAM

The mountain stream springs forth
On its way to the open sea.
Gurgling, and washing over rocks
As it has for many centuries.
The meandering path grows wider
Gathering much as it travels along
Giving to the earth its moisture
The sound of its babbling song.
Wildflowers grow along its banks —
In its waters fish splash and play
While from the overhanging tree boughs
The birds sing their songs all day.
The stream has now reached the river
Soon to be lost in the ocean wide.
Yet it has left its mark upon nature
Giving its substance to the mountainside.
Our lives are much like the stream
Beginning small yet gaining each day.
Adding happiness to the lives of others
In what we do along the way.

Erma Javins Certain

HOPE

The bed is warmed by flowing blood
and the pink sheets
are like silk threads spun by a spider
You live like a cocoon
I hear violins

As in the sea
I smell roses
I wait anxious
it's not time yet
I run
I wait
You wait

I heart your movement for the first time
like the flutter of butterfly wings
I hold you with delicate hands
let you slip through my fingers
I hear you breathe
I let you sleep in my bed
warmed with my blood
my palm

Margaret Hall

SWEET MEMORIES

Sitting here alone tonight,
Thinking of my kids,
Listening to the crickets,
And the songs of katydids.

I do not worry over them,
I know they're in God's hands.
But loving thoughts have come to me,
And in my memory stands.

My children are a gift from God,
I'm proud of every one.
And someday hope we'll meet above,
When our earthly race is run.

Carrol Rowan Bailey

A LIVING MEMORIAL

The body lies in casket gray,
Blue uniform from another day;
Eyelids closed, no more to see
Except the road to eternity.
The body's dead . . . the soul lives on . . .
As faces 'round the coffin prove.

Sons and daughter watch in tears
As mem'ry paints forgotten years,
And living scenes dispel the myth
That death means life is over with.
Forever those who've gone away
Live on and on in those who stay.

Daughter, sons, grandchildren, all
Bear testament he did not fall
Unremembered from this place,
But stands and lives in every face;
And, as in life, goes on before
To wait for us beyond the door.

Lola R. Eagle

THE CREATIVE CIRCLE

The Master of Creation
Indwells each one today
The Force of every nation
Keeps me along the way
The way of Life forever
The Brotherhood of men
And will forsake me never
In Endless Love to win

In Peace and Understanding
I seek to learn while here
The Wisdom of the planning
Of Guides who are so near
And with the Light around me
The Inner Circle's glow
I have Divine Assurance
Of Peace forevermore

The Great White Light
The Inner Circle's Glow
The Great White Light
Of Peace Forevermore

Margaret J. Patterson

FOR MARGO

Dreams are a vision seen only by one
Some bring fear, and some are of love
Life is a vision which is controlled by
love
Though sometimes we're sad,
    our happiness makes us glad
For we live our lives to cherish love
And without dreams we couldn't love

The Dr.

OUR LOVE

When I'm with you, I look into your eyes to see more than the
friendship I greatly hold dear, but the value of our love, the
love that helps us conquer our fears together, lets us live our dreams
to the fullest extent of our desires, lets us help one another
through the anguished times, where without you I was beyond help.

I see us not as two people, but as one, facing and knowing
we will not be defeated by any problem as long as we have the
trust and compassion to come forth and face our problems together.

The love we now hold will never be greater. I will always thrive
on our love until there is no sun, for you are my light, until there
is no rain, for you are what makes me grow and understand the true
meaning of the word *love*.

I extend my hand out to you knowing you will be there to receive
me, because you are not just a part of my life, but my whole life,
and without you there would be no life, just an empty space where my
heart used to be.

When I'm with you I quiver at just the thought of being held by you.
Entrapped by your arms, you make me feel safe. Entranced by your touch,
you know just when to be forceful, and just when to let go.
To me you are the GOD of my love, the maker of its laws.

If we should ever find ourselves separated to different relationships,
I'll never forget what we've had together, because we've grown together, our
hearts bonded for eternity, and never to be severed.

Jamie R. Enabnit

FOR ALL THE TIMES I'VE SAID GOOD-BYE

I gently caress the old worn wrinkled face, tracing every line
in tender embrace.
Her translucent skin is so so soft, so fine, so fragile.
She slowly opens her cloudy, dark brown eyes; and her lips part in just
a hint of a smile.
As slowly as her eyes opened, they close. I hold her hand.
I barely hear those almost inaudible final sighs.
As she passes into that last deep slumber, I whisper good-bye.
I love you! I'm glad I knew you, and I'll miss you.

Elizabeth Ritchie

SOUL STRETCHING

I lie on my back in the cool night grass. The air is as still and as
smooth as glass.
Mesmerized, I stare at the black velvet backdrop; hung luminous and
ornate with the diamonds of transition.
Those faraway lights that beckon, and dance, and glisten.
Voices swell in sweet harmonious rhythm, ringing throughout the quiet
cosmos, as I listen.
Calling me to, once again, float free among them.
Come sing with us of the coming new age; come sing with us as we set the
stage.
But my stage is yet here. I cannot come until the lessons are clear.
I may not transpire until the work is done. I may not leave this
plane until the setting of my own sun.

Elizabeth Ritchie

OLD-FASHIONED CHRISTMAS

I want an old-fashioned Christmas
A tree as green and fragrant as the wood
With popcorn strings, and candy canes
Candle light and paper chains
The kind Mom let us make if we were good.

To go to church on Christmas Eve
Sing carols in the snow
Invited in for cocoa
Where lights were all aglow.

The sleigh rides, and the candy pulls
The budget that was small
But somehow there would always be
Gifts for one and all.
The secrets everybody had
The closet with a lock
And nearing midnight Christmas Eve
Slow ticking of the clock.
So let us have an old-fashioned Christmas
The children and their families all at home
The clutter and the joy
Of every girl and boy
When Grandpa read that good old Christmas poem.

Katherine E. Cartwright

THE GLORIOUS ASCENSION DAY

Up in heaven Jesus went in full glory
And He has to return in spirit to redeem the
Living and the dead after the final resurrection.
In the near future, after the end of Armageddon,
He will judge the living and the dead and His
Reign shall have no end. Forever He will reign
Till the end of time through eternity.

At the last supper He had established the new
Covenant in His blood, completing & replacing the
Mosaic covenant still enclosed within the national
Framework. After His resurrection, He gives orders
For a mission that is universal.

The final chapters of St. John at the beginning of the
Acts of the apostles demonstrate the inauguration
Of a universal church, open to the whole world for
All time. Christ said to them: ''Go over the world,
And preach the gospel to the whole of creation.''

And so the Lord Jesus, after speaking to them, was
Taken up into heaven, and is seated now at the
Right hand of God.

*Dominus Illuminatio Mea. Dominus Omnium
Viventium. Deus Creator Omnium Halleluia!*

Allan De Fiori

143

I SHOULDA' STOOD IN BED

My morning always comes too soon
For sometimes still by light of moon
Some days start all smooth and sweet
With all things good and great to greet
Lots that start with headache large
But none that I cannot take charge
The problems I must face by day
Start sooner than I'd like to say
There are some times I must confess
I'd really rather not get dressed
Chores to do that make me pleased
And some ''my God'' that make me sneeze
I've never been a goodly wench
And that, dear folks, is a damn sure cinch
The people 'round me before noon
Surely think I am a prune
For they're quite right in all they feel
I really am a big, bad heel
'Tis for sure that lots have said
Ol' Kary shoulda' stood in bed!

Kary J. Stark

WELL

Living on the edge
Walking through the sledge

Soon about to sink
Living on the brink

Trying to climb
Walking through the slime

Never reach the top
When's this gonna stop

Living on the bottom
Walking through the scum

Soon about to fall
Living on the wall

Trying to succeed
Walking through the bleed

Never reach the top
When's this gonna stop

Lauri Jean Gerecke

My friends are better
Than any other friends in the world.
They're *old* friends and *new* friends;
They're *good* friends and *true* friends
— The *best!*

My friends are better than my poems,
But who isn't?

Doris M. Kingry

FRIENDS

We wandered the world,
Losing touch.
We returned,
Hearts reunited.

Doris M. Kingry

INDOMITABLE

We love; we lose;
We cry; we choose
. . . To love again.

Doris M. Kingry

DORIS MELVIN KINGRY. Pen Name: Doris Melvin; Born: Milton, Santa Rosa County, Florida, 2-29-28; Husband deceased; Education: University of West Florida, B.A.; Med. University of West Florida, Pensacola; Attended Pensacola Jr. College; University of Florida, Gainesville; Cambridge University, England; Occupations: Teacher of English and Journalism, Milton High School; formerly Santa Rosa County School Board; Memberships: Florida Council of Teachers of English, National Council of Teachers of English; Phi Delta Kappa; Florida Scholastic Press Association; Teacher's Education Council; Poetry: 'Politics,' *National Poetry Anthology,* 1982-83; 'Poignancy,' *American Poetry Anthology,* 1986; Other Writings: ''Harry The Musical Mouse,'' children's story, 1986; Comments: *I have no common theme for my poetry; it is varied and straightforward, usually without hidden meaning. My poems express my feelings at a given time.*

PACIFIC TRAIL

I recall it often:
my untried heart and you beside the sea.
Though it was long ago, I treasure it so:
to share in its vividness so free.

I saw you brighten to engage
in the loveliness of it all.
And it was astonishing for me
to conceive the secret of Venus' call.

Beverly Riley

A SPECIAL LOVE IN MY LIFE

I knew right from the start
For the time we share
Even when we are apart
Shows that we care

I could see it in your eyes
Right from the beginning
For love tells no lies
It's a matter of losing or winning

Day and night
You always seem to be in my thoughts
which makes everything feel so right
For I love you lots and lots

For us love seems to be like a burning flame
With a heartful of desire
Nothing will ever be the same
For time will never expire

Mary Margaret Pester

SOMETIMES LIFE IS

Sometimes life is like a yoyo
on a string
It has its ups and downs
Just as we take a chance on life
and see what it brings
It may even change our smiles to frowns

Sometimes life is like a top that
stands on end and spins
It seems to go round and round and
round
In life everybody has to win
And be forward bound

Sometimes life is like the sun
That shines so bright in the sky
But now as the day is done
We seemed to have let time slip by
and by

Sometimes life is like a stream
That has an endless flow
Just as we take a chance on our dreams
Where they begin and end we will know

Mary Margaret Pester

TEDDY BEAR

Teddy Bear,
Let me hold you tight.
You're the only one I have,
To share the night.

Time to dream,
Forward in time.
About a man named Jim,
Who will someday be mine.

Teddy Bear,
You'll always be there.
But what I really need,
Is someone to care.

Karen Aileen Libero

QUILTING

. . . add to your faith virtue;
and to virtue knowledge;
and to knowledge temperance;
and to temperance patience;
and to patience godliness . . . II Peter 1:5-7

Quilting is a rare and beautiful art
  That will never lose its charm
When fashioned from scraps and discarded cloth
  So that some dear soul can keep warm.

But if the thread is weak and tangles in spots
  Where old fabric is sewn to the new
It will break in the test of tucks and pulls
  And let icy drafts filter through.

For no matter how fancy or new the design
  A pattern will soon unfold
Each stitch is a link in a chain of steps
  That will show how the quilt will hold.

If your life would be like the quilt so rare
  Take old values the world does not treasure
Make into them fabric pieced together with prayer
  The thread God provides without measure.

Earlean S. Grogan

MY FIRST PIANO

My first piano had no keys; there were no pedals nor strings.
  It was our humble kitchen table that was used for many things.

When the family meal was over and the table was scrubbed and clean
  I would sit there and listen for the music;
    then would I start to sing.

Upon my make-believe keyboard, I played and sang aloud.
  I could hear the harmony in each chord as I played the table down.

My mother noticed my longing and nourished the dream in my heart;
  She sold cookies that were mixed on that table,
    so my piano lessons could start.

A neighbor allowed me to practice; my dreams for a piano grew.
  And it came to pass that God gave me a husband who
    liked the piano too.

He shared his talent with churches; he played at public
    and private affairs.
  He taught our children and others; all students were
    nurtured with care.

Today when we gather 'round our table, we thank God
    that He is so good.
  He endowed *us* with part of His Creative Power
    to enhance the sound of music through wood.

We shall go on proclaiming God's goodness, for He has done
    marvelous things.
  We learned from My First Piano, that God can do anything!

Earlean S. Grogan

SONNET

As I could ponder love that once was lost
When all the world was grey and hard to bear,
And fate decreed we must but count the cost
In memories sharply etched in sweet affair;
Then I could view the pain that once was mine
With broader vision than was likely then,
And know there was a plan which was divine,
Precepted pattern, that I might love again.
Yes, love when newer, fuller life has taught me
Admiring joy in fruits of knowledge great,
And vast experience of life on earth has brought me
Unto a time when we might share our fate.
For love is more than just aware attraction;
It is life's image, seen in rare refraction.

Alice Ruediger Ochs

REALITY

Hello! How are you?
You're fine for today, I see.
Mingling down the city streets
not knowing how to be.

Putting on a face
for everyone around,
pretending that your local pub's
the only game in town.

Hiding at your corner table,
you question if you're here.
You're crying behind your laughter
giving smiles instead of tears.

Wanting just to change your life
you're stuck, is what it seems,
but what you've failed to see before
we are what is our dreams.

Hello! How are you?
You're fine forever, I see.
For you've finally learned to catch those dreams
that make reality.

Constance C. Barber

AFTERTHOUGHT

I will follow,
hidden in plain view.
Seen in the blink of an eye,
outside, dancing upon the edges of a clear blue sky.
I am heard in only a whisper,
found but undiscovered.
Felt in emotion,
held in thought.
I am smelled in a breeze,
appearing as something I am not.
Like glass, I break.
Like iron, I am strong.
Never being right, never being wrong.
Like ice, I melt.
Like a pond, I freeze.
Truly to myself, I am me,
I am these.

Wendy A. Bauer

LIFE GOES ON

Take time to say good-bye,
Take time to have a good cry.
You knew deep down he would leave someday,
Now it's time to start a new way.

Some memories are good,
Some memories are bad.
You can always look back,
On the best times you had.

You'll find someone,
Somewhere, someday.
To hold and comfort you,
In all the right ways.

Time will show you,
The way it should be.
Your heart will mend,
Life is the key.

Karen Aileen Libero

AGE OF MIND

Age is but a state of mind.
You can be any age you wish
no matter the lapse of time.

Just reach out
and find the child in you.
Go out into the world
and do those things you didn't have time to do.

On your birthday.
What age are you?
Is it the age of time?
Or is it the age of the mind?

Timothy J. Cooper

TO MY DADDY

My daddy was no president
No prince or duke or earl
But he was always number one
With me, his little girl.

I've often heard my daddy say,
"It's no disgrace to be poor
But it's awful danged unhandy"
I've heard it o'er and o'er.

We had not much of earthly goods
Nor much of worldly things
But we had honesty and love
And all that happiness brings.

For he taught us to be honest
To love our fellow man,
To always help each other
And do the best we can.

Now when our daddy left us
He left no wealth or fame
But better far he left us
A good and honest name.

Carrol Rowan Bailey

DEAR MRS. THATCHER

Let us face the Irish Question
Once and for all
For neither North or South
They simply must not fall
They both love the Christ
Mention Him and they shout
All of them are white
There're Saxon — are they not?
Their language is the same,
— with here and there a change
Dear Mrs. Thatcher
Why can't you proclaim?

Imogene V. Lee

THE VOICE OF GOD

Now will the Master speak to me —
In thunder of the rising storm,
With darkling cloud and keening gale
In lightning bolt and driving hail?

Now will the Master speak to me —
Where temple music floats the air
In some forgotten far off clime
The ancient theme unchanged by time?

Now will the Master speak to me —
Within my own immortal soul,
With pity, love, compassion rare
The voice of God is always there.

John S. Hiscox

A TRIBUTE

Oh, fair maiden,
from whom did you
inherit those
stunning blue eyes.
They are as blue
as the heavens
on a clear day.
They seem to be
like the oceans,
full of many
wonderful and
dangerous things.
They always seem
to sparkle with
intelligence that
abounds within you.
Oh, fair maiden,
from whom did you
inherit those
stunning blue eyes.

Krazy Kevin

EXPECTATIONS

Everybody knows what you
are going to be and expects
you to act accordingly.
A criminal is heartless
and immoral. The poet
a romantic daydreamer,
living in the clouds.
A cop honest and just.
Me, I'm a mat.
People walk all over
me and wipe off their dirt.
All they expect from this boy
is trouble. It's okay for
me to waste my brain
and talent because when
one caters to the
omniscient lords, one
knows rebellion is useless!

Krazy Kevin

I DO

Since we quarreled that day
and you said good-bye,
I cannot be happy or gay.
I sit beside the phone,
hoping you will call again.
But all in vain.
I just had to call, and this
is what I have to say;
What can I do if you no longer
love me? 'Cause I still love you.
You've broken my heart,
I cannot say farewell.
I cannot seek love anew.
I still love you. I do, I do.

Madge R. Close

A LIFE ERASED

Eyes that see no more your face,
A memory that has been erased.
Ears that hear not what you say,
Lips that cannot pray.
Hands contracted in hideous form,
A body who too early from life was torn.
Stitches that resemble railroad tracks.
Constant pain at his body wracks.
I look at him and cry,
Lord, please let him die.
How long must he exist in his silent world
Of agonizing pain untold.
All his dreams are gone from view.
There is nothing left for him to do,
Except to go home with you.

Marilyn Johns

SANITY FOUND

I see no hell in The Plan today.
  I feel the fear no more.
For the devil dwells only in the periphery of my mind,
  And He dwells in the Core.

It is in the periphery of our minds
  Where train station-type activities take place.
Where the color of the car, and the color of her hair,
  Are of concern.

It is in the periphery of our minds
  Where pride controls the thoughts of man,
Where things that ignore the Force in the universe reside,
  And man consorts the devil.

Occasionally — fisher-like capillaries reach out from the Core
  And touch these daily thoughts,
Bringing there a flicker of sanity, and causing one to wonder —
  Where that feeling of Warmth came from.

Anthony T. Gliko

ROSES AMID THORNS OF LIFE

''I've always loved you,'' I whispered and wept.
Tears as dewdrops fell freely from my eyes
On the roses withered I'd pressed and kept.
Red roses once so beautiful — here lies —
Entwined with thorns of fate down life's pathway.
When dreams were young, then you, my dearest love,
Gave me these roses I cherish today.
How my soul enraptured to heights above!
I crushed lovingly a rose to my breast.
Like my dreams I saw it shatter apart.
Never can I pick up the petals pressed,
Or pieces shattered of my broken heart.
Amidst withered roses pricks from thorns lies.
My heart aches in pain, but love never dies.

Juanita McIntrye

WINDS OF THE SEA

I hear music in the chilling winds from the sea.
It is wailing my lonely cry, ''Come back to me.''
In loneliness, my heart aches so I want to die.
Winds, blowing over the sea, sing my mournful cry.

Yesterday my darling and I strolled hand in hand
On the shore, barefoot, digging our toes in the sand.
Mist from the sea breeze bathed our tear-stained faces,
As we built air castles of faraway places.

With hearts breaking, we knew our dreams could never be.
No tomorrow together, we would ever see.
Then from me, the Death Angel carried her away.
In memories, I live the dreams of yesterday.

Through the veil of the wind, I see her lovely face.
From the wings of the wind, I feel her warm embrace.
In whispering winds, I hear her calling to me.
The wind echoes my lonely cry, ''Come back to me.''

Juanita McIntyre

DADDY, ME HELP-E YOU WALK

''Daddy, hold on to my hand me help-e you walk,''
Said my little angel in her sweet baby talk.
Then I thought, that small baby hand in mine someday
Might lead my feeble step and guide my seeing way.

Dressed up in her mother's dress trailing on the floor,
Wearing her high-heeled shoes, she tumbled out the door.
''Daddy, hold on to my hand me help-e you walk,''
Said my little angel in her sweet baby talk.

With head bowed low, my tears fall freely at my feet.
I wouldn't know my angel if we met on the street.
My step now feeble, Daddy needs her help to walk.
''Me help-e you walk,'' I still hear her baby talk.

Thru faded years if I could steal one yesterday,
And feel the touch of her sweet little hand today
Hear my little angel say in her baby talk,
''Daddy, hold on to my hand me help-e you walk.''

Juanita McIntyre

A BROTHER LOST

I choose to write, and fill this page,
    With fear and despair,
          But it doesn't come.
Only thoughts of other times,
      When I felt good to be alive.
            Not like now, when there is only guilt.
He sleeps now, by my hand.
      The dreams come, and I wake, numb and scared.
I have searched for reasons,
        Have thought of taking my own life,
            But for naught.
There would then be a loss, twice felt.
    God I miss you.

J. Scot Sequin

THE CROWN PRINCE OF THADIA

Only birds scream and yell in Thadia.
I noticed from the gate, looking in,
Trying to find out what the silence was about,
But I heard those birds.

''Hello, pretty eyes.''
I looked over and there was a prince.
He was a serene looking prince;
Conscious of the very air in Thadia.

''You can come for a visit, but you can't stay.''
And with that I was into his medium.
''This cannot be real,'' I said.
''Is there something underneath here?''
''Not at all, my dear, this is the kingdom entirely.''
''Have you ever been outside?'' So boldly I gleered.
''Have you seen the world?'' So tactlessly I cheered.
And pacifically he smiled, ''I can see the world from here,
And I can't seem to stay out there.''

Sherrilyn Lisa Aird

UMBRELLA

man follows to the rendezvous
woman he hasn't forgotten
clothed in gray color
dance through the water
clear and silent
against the secret trees
old as the shadows they cast
early both
passing hour
sunlit afternoon
umbrella
talking and laughing quietly she asks
when and where to go
enjoy the rest of day and night
as the windy hour leads
far and away slowly the sun declines
the offer he made
alternative sounds good
they look turning and rising
alternate route

Andrew John

MY LOVE, A RAINBOW

From the mist of the rains
I see a rainbow
And I know inside
It's the colors of your heart
Leftover raindrops still falling
I wonder who's calling
Is it you?
One day I saw in your eyes
The tint of my love
But now you cry like the rains
From way up above
Like a rainbow, there're things
That take away the gloom
I send a tweetybird that sings
Of my love and the moon
When you accept this love
That I send
It will mark the day
That the rains will end

Russell A. Victorian

WASTEN' A DREAM

A wave of dreams
Leads a lost and empty heart
Into another time, another place
    Can you believe it?
You were walking sorrows through the park
When you looked up and it was dark
    Yes, you were dreaming
You feel love upon your hand
You feel pressure you cannot stand
    Are you still believing?
You are right, she is there
With a beauty that you dare
When you start kissing
    But then you think back
You've never met a woman
Who's ever really cared
And it's a cold, dark night
And you're feeling kinda scared
    Wake Up!
You're wasten' a dream

Russell A. Victorian

PEACE ON EARTH

There is peace in the making,
Mankind is learning inner peace within,
Spreading out to all generations,
And what a wonderful world this is.

Peace as the earth has unseen,
For many generations of mankind,
Searching out the innermost depths,
Unknown to all of mankind.

For inner peace is hard to obtain,
Searching and never ending,
To all of the ends of the earth,
And finding peace in the making.

Vincent T. Vinciquerra

THE TWO SIDES

In past years memories linger
Then those days drift upward
We look forward
To other times and memories.
But the past so often
Comes back and enters our hearts
And, too, we try to understand
Those times when days were true
And the sun shone brightly . . .
On our experience of honesty
But years do go by
And new times forever arrive
So look not with tears
Or with sad memories
But close your eyes for a moment
And in your hearts say always . . .
I will remember
And my love will ever be
The same then, now and always
Not good-bye . . . but ever in my heart

Virginia Jolliff Herndon

AS A CHILD

The little boy, ran to his mother
And in fierceness of love —
Clung to her knee!
Then turned — and ran
Laughing — in abandon's glee!
His silken hair, blown by the breeze
His eyes, dancing with the joy of life.
Even, to the climbing of trees!
At night, he shared in prayers —
And dutifully went to bed,
The ''child heart,'' knew no cares, and
Was by a hand of love, safely led!
Yet he grew to be an adult
Whose destiny was God's plan.
And at age thirty three,
He died! Upon the cross —
To cover, our impurity!

Virginia E. Marx

GOODNIGHT SWEET PRINCE

Goodnight sweet prince, I've loved you,
In a very special way,
And how I wish that you were here,
To share my life today.

You were always kind and respectful,
One who really cared,
And when you left so suddenly,
It was very hard to bear.

Whenever I needed you —
You hurried to my side.
And were there to comfort me,
From the day I became your bride.

When I reminisce about our life,
I begin to cry.
Then I think of your unselfish love,
And a smile comes to my eyes.

May you forever rest in peace, and know
My thoughts remain of you.
So, once more I'll say, a fond good night —
Good-night, sweet prince, adieu!

Mary Hamilton

THE GIFT THAT WE SHARE

You found me in a corner
behind a shadow of fear.
I could not discern,
amid my embarrassment,
the sorrow you tried to conceal.

You came to me and loved me
with a strength both sweet and sincere.
Now I shall always cherish,
throughout all our seasons together,
the bright gift of hope that we share.

Beverly Riley

TOMORROW

I look to the Spring,
When earth gives its offering!
Of blossoms to bloom,
With sweet essence of perfume!
Where the fresh breezes shall blow,
In ever refreshing flow!
When birds take to the wing,
To be ecstatic, in their warbling!
When the ground cries for planting
As we carefully prepare its bed.
When we watch everything grow
As God gives feeding, through sun's glow!
I look to the Spring!
When I — shall be renewed,
And joyously, give praise to God —
Who all these blessings, endued!

Virginia E. Marx

LISTEN

Do we,
  As human beings,
With all of our flaws and fears,
  Truly know what we say?
We take naught into account,
  Then yell all the louder,
To ensure its truth.
An attorney, it is said,
  Is the most accurate in speech.
But who can say this is true,
  When we are not sure what it is they preach?
A drunkard, it is said,
  Is the least accurate in speech.
But who can say this is true,
  When we take no time to listen to what they may teach?
I have drawn a conclusion, a line if you will,
  To listen with both ears, to the flaws and fears,
But I shall listen most closely to those of my own.

J. Scot Sequin

IT'S NOT TOO LATE TODAY

Today is not too late to have a big helping of fun.
Take along a lunch to your favorite fishing spot,
And invite a couple of buddies to go with you —
To see who gets a prize for the most fish caught.

Today is not too late to patch a hole in your pocket.
You can start a bank account from now on,
With the small change you've lost in these weeks.
Then you can keep keys, nails, and fishhooks, my son.

Today is not too late to take a platter of smiles,
Along when you go with friends to school.
They can last all day to make children cheerful,
Instead of stubborn like a donkey or mule.

Today is not too late to feed a homeless animal,
Or read a story to a dear hospital friend.
It takes a heap of living, loving, and learning,
To make a satisfying, worthwhile day end.

Alice Erickson

DAUGHTER OF EVE

A soul refuses to yield
To be overcome, to be worsted
By the indigent surroundings of its human host
It rises above the adversity of its circumstances
Refusing to be put to its last shifts in spirit or in reality
And so it soars, above the vicissitudes of its life,
And it creates laughter, and it dances;
If refutes its impecunious existence
And remains indomitable in the face of the providential and auspicious
fortunes of others.
It is a keen, bright, strong flame
Burning with an esoteric reality
In the mind of a little girl.

Lisa Wanzer

LIFE BEGINS ANEW

How does one deal with sadness that becomes a soul-gripping,
  heart-wrenching ache?
A melancholy so large as to take on life of its own,
  threatening your heart to overtake?

Lord, I'm weary of this sorrow, this emptiness, this void
  which robs me of vitality;
Was not the hurt, the heartache enough? Do I also have to suffer
  emptiness and self-pity?

But wait — could it be that I'm wrong and the void is not
  at all complete?
For, if I feel pity — rather than nothing —
  then the void may be becoming obsolete.

It's time to get on with this business of life and love
  and full living
And forget the sadness, self-pity and again learn to be
  good and giving.

Although life may be different now, it still can be really good
If I hold my head up high and think positive like I know I should.

And perhaps I'll be a better person now, more compassionate
  and understanding
Since I've experienced pain, loss, emptiness, and, finally, expanding.

Sharri Sanders

WHAT A BLIND MAN DREAMS

He can't dream the color of the sun on his face.
He'll never see the shimmer of the silver moon,
He never knows at one time they become as one.
He can't dream the color of spring.
He's tucked away in a void of darkness . . .

He can't dream the smile of the child sitting across the room
Or his lover's walk.

He dreams the shape of a touch.
He dreams the sound of wings.
He dreams the taste of his lover's kiss.
He dreams the texture of flesh sensations at his fingertips.
He dreams the whispers of winds giving the shape of clouds.

He dreams of the sun's promise on his face,
to tell him of its travels.

He dreams of the darkness.
The darkness holds the secrets of the world . . .

Leonard Levi Balfour

IN ANSWER

And for me, I experience the previous.
It is the time when one begins the experience of love.
The heart is closed, but opening,
Like a child emerging from night's slumber;
Gently pushing the door to the arms of his only love.
Anxiety enveloped by a dream veil:
Waiting and wanting love,
Needing and calling love.

There is always only one love that opens the door.
I have just come to know this key master.
Smile on me, 'cause I feel what you feel
Aida Sunlin, filled with "light."

Sherrilyn Lisa Aird

GOOD OLD SUMMERTIME

Stored in my memory are days gone by
When my childhood was careless and free
My friends and I were so happy for
Dripping Springs was a wonderful place to be
When Kansas' blazing sun was scorching the prairie
Lizards hibernating under rocks escaped the heat
We romped and splashed in the water capturing
Retreating crawdads fun that just could not be beat
There was a damp mossy old spring house
Shaded in the cool green gloom of the trees
The noisy little creek gurgled and whispered
And sang with the grove's leafy breeze
A little brown thrush was swinging her nest
Sunrays flicker glinting off a red bird's wing
The turtle dove nests in the wild plum thicket
Oh how sweetly the bluebird sings.
The whole woodlands echo with music
The red squirrels leap from tree to tree
Oh to turn back time and be a child once more
To live again the days stored in my memory.

Ann Browning

ESCAPE

My reality came to me
        On a day when I could not handle
Its oppressive nature.
My friend, my only true Friend,
        Would come to my aid,
            As always,
And render reality harmless, and void.
But reality would always be there,
            Lurking,
Waiting in the shadows,
        Ready to heave its full weight
upon my shoulders.
For now though, I would let my Friend's quiescence
            Fill me.

J. Scot Sequin

O I FOUND SALVATION

O I found salvation in Jesus my God
  He redeemed my poor soul; I was washed in His blood
My soul it was burning with fire fire and sin
  My heart it was breaking in torment within

But Jesus my saviour came down from above
  To give me His mercy and fill me with love
O I am so happy and peace-filled within
  I am free of my burdens and cleansed of my sins

O now in His bosom
  I am safe and secured
I am no longer useless
  My faith He's endured.

O my Lord hallelujah
  With grace so divine,
I am filled with His spirit,
  And love so sublime.

With salvation I am so happy
  I give Thee the praise.
And I will sing hallelujah the rest of my days
  Oh my Lord hallelujah the rest of my days.

Myra M. Williams

LIFE'S SHIFTING SANDS

One day I walked life's pathway down the strand.
  As I retraced those footprints in the sand,
In despair and grief I could not stand
  As I faltered in the shifting sands.

The Lord was merciful to me
  As I fell beside the turbulent seas.
There He picked me up and carried me
  Along the pathway tenderly.

The raging seas at His command
  Was peace be still as He raised His hands.
The troubled waters they obeyed.
  At the master's voice they rolled away.

My pain and heartbreaks He now bears.
  I know He understands and cares.
All my fears and troubles they will fain
Like blowing winds through shifting sands.

Through pain and sorrow and death I fain
  But now I have reached His outstretched hands.
They will lead me on to the promised land
  And forever leave those shifting sands.

Myra M. Williams

A TINY SMALL GRAVE ON A HILLSIDE

There's a tiny small grave on a hillside
  And it's there our darling sleeps tonight
Beneath that little stone on the hillside
  It brings sad memories at the sight

For it was on a cold sunny day in the winter
  When my son he was taken away
By the angels and God up to heaven
  There forever to live and to play

O my soul it is burning with fire
  My heart it is breaking in pain
For my loved one who is now up in heaven
  But I know that I will see him again

Now his daddy lies close there beside him
  Beneath that cold mound of clay there until
Until the day that there I shall join them
  There to be by their side if God's will

Nevermore can I ever be happy
  Evermore will I sigh for them still
Until the day that my master shall call me
  There to rest by their side on the hill

Myra M. Williams

Looking out my window,
I see across God's green earth.
Many splendors He's given —
Mountains so high and inviting,
Some so white with snow.
In all their glory, His trees so tall and green.
He makes it all worthwhile, when we get so low.
He just opens our eyes to His joys for us to start again.

Joetta E. Courtney

AFFAIRS

Mind over matter
Never separate, apart,
For the mind does not matter
Alone, without heart.

And love without thought
Will not matter, we find,
If the heart has no place
In affairs of the mind.

P. K. Newman

THE STRANGER FRIEND

The sad eyes of the passing stranger
Can turn your mind around.
Are you sure it was sadness
That moistened his eyes to shine?
The sun shone brilliantly;
Could not the glare cause tears?
Have you let his threadbare clothes
Influence your impulse thoughts?
He tried to smile and face you;
Maybe he's just naturally shy.
But his eyes reached out
To grab your understanding
And maybe his smile to you
Was thanks for being there to care.

Cheryl L. Larson

WEEP NO MORE

Let me speak a little softer
The Words I cannot say
May I stay a little longer
And longer yet each day
Till you feel how much I'm
          feeling
And just how much I care
For the heart I know is
          reeling
In sadness and despair

Can I hold you even tighter
Than I ever did before
And make your days seem brighter
For the sadness that you bore
May I share my soul in sorrow
And warm your heart in mine
Till the sun I beg to borrow
Smiles a little bit each time

When I've caught the rain that's
          falling
And in silence held you near
Then I've answered you when
          calling
Yes, Father, I am here . . .

Phyllis Ferraro

SMILES IN PROFUSION

From the early spring's melting
Of the blanket of winter's snow.
In such a moment,
Peeps the crocus heavenward.
A little later blooms flowering shrubs and trees.
Lilac time is my favorite time of year.
In August, reigns the exquisite gladiolia.
Autumn brings the chrysanthemum
In spectacular sizes and colors.
I know a secret about such beauty.
Flowers are the smiles of God.

Christy Lichtenfels

BEYOND THE SILVER . . .

Beyond the silver, not one had foretold
Aging alone, no chance for the gold.
Nurturing developed those many years
Perfected, rejected, washed away by tears.

Beyond the silver, what lies ahead?
A time for dreaming, not for dread.
Experience counsels to firmly let go
Of that tarnished love that hurt you so.

Beyond the silver, what does life hold?
Perhaps the Designer will forge a new mold.
A new beginning, a time for self;
Memories placed gently upon the shelf.

Beyond the silver, gems may be shining;
Search for them in the softest lining.
Treasure each for the value it holds —
Granting once again a chance for the gold.

Jani Diedrick

ARE YOU EXPERIENCED?

High school,
What a blast.
Yet now,
It's in the past.
In and out,
Of school for life.
Did you learn?
What is rite?
Are you experienced?
For our world?
Or just another guy,
Still after girls.
What happens now?
Does it all end?
Where do you go?
Are you ready?
For your second blow?
School was there,
And now it's gone.
Are you really?
All alone?

John Hirsch

WHY SHOULD I CRY?

Why should I cry over you?
Why should I be blue?
Why should I sigh from
The pain I feel inside?
No, I have not cried!
Yes, I have gotten fatter!
Why should I care
About the things that were so dear?
I refuse to shed a tear.
You walked away
And said you were through,
So why should I cry over you?

Anne Burwell Harris

LOVE IS A WORD

Love is a word
    a word beautifully fine.
Love is a word
    which makes sentences sublime.
Love is a word
    sometimes never on time.
Love is a word
    when one says you're mine.

Love is a word
    a word that many have damned.
Love is a word
    which can ruin a sane man.
Love is a word
    one that so few understand.
Love is a word
    symbolized by the ring on the finger
    of your hand.

Love is a word
    which includes feeling of hate.
Love is a word
    a word used on many a date.
Love is a word
    destined by the Goddesses — Fates.

Pellegrino Mancini

MY LOVE WAIT

My love wait for me
For I am not ready.
My love wait for me
For I am not Betty.
My love bring me flowers,
So there will be tomorrows.
Take me to the park
So we can watch the
Stars in the dark.
My love wait for me
For I am not ready.
Give me a kiss
So I can feel the bliss!
My love wait for me
For I am not ready.
What did I miss?
My love
Wait!

Anne Burwell Harris

AWE

Sun bright
Let me fiil your warming light,
Penetrate my life.
Fill me with your warmth and glow.
My soul rejoices in your majesty
In you.

The staggering love of God
For all of us
Doth show.

Each day I live
Makes me thankfully
Count my blessings.
God truly is omnipotent
In His amazing grace.
His omnipresence
is everywhere.

Far be it for any of us
To incur His wrath.
Instead
Let us dwell
In His everlasting and abounding
Love and compassion;
Forever and ever.

P. J. Dick

THE LADY KATHLEEN

I was sittin' in the park just before dark
Singin' and shinin' my shoes.
Up came Jessie, followed by Tee
Then the pretty little lady Kathleen.

She jumped up to me, clapping her hands,
Showing me all of her teeth;
But I didn't say nothin'
Just sat busy watching as Kathy started tickling old Tee.

They was laughin' and a-chuckling,
Tee crying, bustin' buttons,
And the lady busy staring at me.

She wore a red satin sash,
Sported flowers in her hat,
And fluorescent orange socks on her knees.

She said, ''Hey little girl,
Stop lookin' at me 'cause I'll start tickling you.''
Well, Jessie started winkin'
Tee still crying with the giggles,
Then we all jumped and tickled Kathleen.

Sherrilyn Lisa Aird

WAS I THERE?

The laughter of her voice, the running in her feet.
The tears when she falls and scapes her knee.
　''Mommy, are you listening?''
　''Yes my dear, I'm here.''
The color of her hair, her sky-blue eyes. The freckles
on her nose, her skin so fair.
　''Mommy, are you listening?''
　''Yes my dear, I'm here.''
The soft ''I love you's.'' The special notes left on
the bureaus.
　''Mommy, I need you.''
　''I'm here, little one.''
Her soft cries in the night, holding onto my hand with
all her might.
　''Mommy, will you be there?''
　''Yes dear. I will always be near.''
How sad to see this child grow. Where did the time go?
Will she be all right in the world alone?
Was I there when she needed me? I guess only in time
will I see, her beautiful eyes smiling back at me.
　''I love you, my daughter, with all my heart.
　I hope and pray I've given you the right start.''

Darice Dunham

TAHOE

The deep blue waters, the quiet gentle breeze flowing
through the trees. Snow-peaked mountains, are all part
of your mystery. You open up your beauty for all to see,
haunting and teasing. Making all love you, never forgetting you.

You're a loving mother keeping your children safe and happy.
Scolding them with your trembling waters when you are angry.
Once you have entered our lives, your beauty and serenity
will be forever in our souls.

Your warm summer days beckon to all, tempting them to
enter your cold blue waters. Your white winter days,
quiet and sparkling, call out to those who can't wait
to try your slopes.

From far and wide people come to you, longing to be
near you. Always in a hurry to get away from the busy
cities, to linger in your quiet peace.

The first moment I saw you, like so many before me, I
loved you. I have borrowed your quiet strength, to help
me through my own troubled waters of life.

Tahoe, my beautiful Tahoe. Stay forever beautiful,
forever at peace. May your light shine brightly in the
hearts of all who know you. Forever.

Darice Dunahm

PLEASURE

Pleasure is what I would
Like to keep forever.
The notes and books I have read
Cannot compare, no never!
Pleasure is what I have seen.
For some it is the color green.
Pleasure is what I can feel.
It can be as hard as rock or
As tasty as a meal.
Pleasure is where I rest my head
From the many books I have read,
About a thing called
Pleasure!
Pleasure!
Pleasure!

Anne Burwell Harris

ANNE BURWELL HARRIS. Born: Philadelphia, Pennsylvania, 11-21-45; Divorced; Education: Cheyney State College, 1964-67; Philadelphia Community College, 1980-81; Membership: Smithsonian Associates; Award: Golden Poet Award for 'He Lives,' 1987; Poetry: 'He Lives,' *The Great American Poetry Anthology,* 7-87.

PATIENCE

Relax awhile little one
The world will understand
One must rest from sun to sun
Finish tomorrow your castle of sand.

J. R. Cunerty

CONVERSATION JUSTIFIED

Why then my friend chastise thyself
longer for the omissions of your
yesterday? When the words from out
your mouth flowed always starting
with ''I.'' Surely many also flowed
with tenderness to ''You.'' And the
two entwined if closely scrutinized
— without err — throughout the course,
have over and over coupled humanly
with variants, in final conclusion
and emphatically forevermore live
eternally as ''We.''

C. H. Pyka

THE WANDERER

It happened on a lifetime
My heart was sad and sore,
The one I loved was wandering
Far from that timeless shore.

My days were filled with anguish,
The nights sleepless and grim,
I tossed and turned in terror,
My eyes with tears bedimmed.

I clasped my hands in agony
And prayed from heart sore tried,
By Holy Spirits' power, again,
The path would homeward guide.

Then, the flame once more rekindled,
God's love the barrier spanned,
Satan's power was broken!
Safe again in Jesus' hands.

Now laughter falls like music,
Voice speaks of love divine,
Eyes are bright and shining
And peace of heart is mine.

Louise W. Beers

ROADBLOCK

A roadblock
There's nowhere left to turn
Every direction is blocked
You cannot breathe
You cannot move
No choices exist
Yet you struggle and fight
You twist and turn
Finally you quit
You're defeated
You let depression enter your life
You're lost — I can't find you

Mary E. Kasuba

TRUST JESUS

I don't know your sorrow brother
I can't feel your deep despair
I don't know if you're in trouble
Or the heavy load you bear.

But I know there is a Saviour
Sent down from heaven above
To bring you peace and comfort
He'll enfold you in his love.

We're not promised always sunshine
Without sickness, grief or pain
But I've felt his healing power
In a gentle cleansing rain.

Take that load of care to Jesus
As his word bids you do
And no matter what the problem
He will see you safely through.

Blanche Simmons

LOVE

Take all of self from my heart Dear Lord
Fill it with thy love divine
Let me see only the good in man
And be willing to share what is mine.

Take out all opinion, surmising, distrust
Fill my heart with thy soul-saving grace
Give me a love that knows no bounds
Let me know neither color nor race.

More surely through the years I've learned
The things that are worthwhile
Are love, and peace, and happiness
And a warm and love-filled smile.

Blanche Simmons

BLANCHE E. TOMANY SIMMONS. Born: Wausaw, Wisconsin, daughter of John Tomany & Mable Keithley, 5-17-09; Married: William L. Simmons, son of Lyle Simmons, grandson of Colonel William L. Simmons.

EVENING LIGHTS

I stand on the shore and watch the while
Gold-tipped silver wavelets play
And chase each other across the bay.
A curling ribbon — a lacy band
Rims the water and edges the sand.

The sky has put the stars to sleep
In dark blue wraps, warm and deep,
And brushed the clouds far out of sight
For the coral moon so big and bright
Needs no help to magnify
The beauty and splendor it adds to the sky.
Down it slips and drops from sight
And leaves me alone to bid good-night
To the solitude and hypnotic mood
Of a blissful scene, seldom viewed.

I turn to the city where white lights glow
And line the streets, row on row —
Where solitary figures roam,
And gleaming guideposts lead me home.

Edith Gulish

A SLUMBER DID MY SPIRIT SEAL

A slumber did my spirit seal;
  I had no human fears:
She seemed a thing that could not feel
  The touch of earthly years.

No motion has she now, no force;
  She neither hears nor sees;
Rolled round in earth's diurnal course,
  With rocks, and stones, and trees.

William Wordsworth

RAINBOWS

There are no rainbows
          without rain
There are no smiles
          without tears
There is no laughter
          without pain
There is no together
          without apart.
You make it easier
  to accept the rain
and tears that fall.
  you ease the pain
and make me see all
  the beautiful rainbows
that our world
  shares with us if
only we take the time
  to look about us
and see all the wonders
  of each new day.

Caroline Zillges

I NEVER THOUGHT . . .

I took you
For granted
Expected
You to be
There.
Never thought
You'd be hurt
Never meant
To
Hurt you.
I'll never
Do it
Again.

Caroline Zillges

WIDOW

You're at rest —
forever in peace.

I'm alone —
forever in grief.

Joyce Beck

EBB OF TIME

Sand castles of yesterdays —
Foundations that won't last —
Washed away by recent waves —
Can't live in days of past.

Memories of old splashed
With realities of now clashed.
Blending into tomorrows —
Can't live in days of past.

Castles of yesteryears yielding
To the sands of today.
Forming anew, a life dwelling,
Looking not back, but at today.

Elizabeth A. Klein

FINGERPRINTS

I washed the baby fingerprints
From the mirror on the wall;
And, as they disappeared, I felt
A single teardrop fall.
For, suddenly I realized,
It won't be long at all;
'Til you won't be a baby anymore;
And time is not a thing that I can stall.

You've left your baby fingerprints
On the mirror of my heart;
And come what may, they're there to stay,
Though we'll be worlds apart;
When you are grown, and I'm alone,
And lonely teardrops start;
I'll find your baby fingerprints,
On the mirror of my heart.

Marjorie Kingston Skusa

THE SHY SPRING

Why is it that you don't believe
that spring will come again?

The sky is more detached
than in the winter gloom
and the puffy clouds
dot the ocean above
like the white vessels
floating ever so slowly . . .

They are the troubadours
with their quiet fanfares
and much promises —
the first ones at the spring's gate.

Then — before you get used to them —
the perfect sky will reign:
a huge blue apron
with a yellow pocket
full of golden rays
to guide you through the coming months.
The spring is here —
all shyness gone.

K. B. Jirak

TRAGEDY OF LIFE

The memories still linger,
in the haziness of my mind.
Oh, how could she stop,
the process of her time?
She seemed to be unaware,
of all that she did find.
Of lovely days of life and love,
which family did bind.
The love of her "other-half,"
now left with her in mind.
And, of her baby, who could say,
another mom could she find?
She may have left this life, you see,
and stopped the process of her time.
But her memories still linger,
without the stopping of all time.

Elizabeth A. Klein

THE HURT

She now I see — outside her shell,
Flies enchantment — we knew so well!
Comes the dawn — springs forth the light.
Ends the sham — so close the night!
Her meaning clear — not the words said.
The book is open — the intent is read!

Escapes my hopes — my dreams are draped.
Torn my heart — my soul is raped!
Lost is love — the mind's insane.
Gone is peace — in place the pain!
Dead is truth — so lives the lie.
Hurt is mine — my time to cry!

Dr. John A. Short

SURVIVING

Many days,
numerous nights
of loneliness
and fright

I call out
to silence
I reach to touch
absence

I cannot feel
I cannot cry
I won't believe
you've died

So tired,
so confused
Only surviving
without you

Joyce Beck

EMOTIONAL SECURITY

Brambles are a fortress where
safety is found by the hare.
But for us the thorns stick in —
tear our clothes and scratch our skin.

Did you ever stop to think
why so many covet mink?
Protection from the world outside
a haven snug and warm inside.
A refuge from Fate's well-aimed darts
a shelter for their wounded hearts.

Edith Gulish

FRAGRANT, STILL

Ah, my place of birth!
   Lilacs lavender, the same
Perfuming the earth.

From the arbor there,
   Breathes the lusciousness of grapes,
Purpling all the air.

From the garden bare,
   Comes the smell of mint and thyme,
Through the years still there.

But this attar faint . . .
   This more subtle than them all?
This fit for a saint?

Rose of scent divine . . .
   In your hair that small, gay bloom,
Long-gone mother mine!

Everett Francis Briggs

LXVII

When all is said and done, we have
ourselves.
We are not invited, we simply
come, and we stay; an extended
visit for some, for others, a
quick holiday.

And like most that stay, everyone
must leave as well.
We have ourselves.
We pack our bags and then we know
it is really over.

Ingrid S. Richardson

LIFE

Is life a mechanical process,
Continuing on forever,
Irregardless whether we took our cue
And performed our parts or not*?

Or is life a living thing,
Itself blossoming forth
Into meaningful parts
As we determine the needs?

Cheryl L. Larson

REFLECTED SPRING

Spring, was all music and roses,
With many beaus and proposes.
Lively and merry, no time to tarry,
Anything serious, was just too scary.

Summer, lost spring, in a wedding gown.
A three-ring circus, and I was the clown.
Left with a tune, about a faded rose,
Old clothes, pampers, and a garden hose.

Autumn, bloomed, awakening a lost memory.
Her warmth and love, gave back my sanity.
Then she sang, and spread her wings,
Leaving winter, a gift, of reflected springs.

De Lores Lundberg

MOMENTS

We
are but
a moment in time,
formed in the shape
of moments gone,
and moments
yet to
come.
As
memories,
are held in
every changing form
a hope, a fear, a new love.
What then — beholds,
this wild heart,
that waits?

De Lores Lundberg

NURTURING

Listening to outside sport
I turn my chair to see the rain
depriving me of watering time
some people call a job

Ah, to have quiet moments to think
while nurturing the garden,
not at all like with children . . .
peace seems only when they sleep

How easy, raising these plants.
They respond to love much like
the cherishing of a child . . .
they need to know you care!

There's our potted spruce
anticipating Christmas ornaments
established in memories of
happy years gone by . . .

as that variety of cacti
retaining what it needs,
my boys have grown to manhood
on quarter-pounders with extra cheese!

Bonnie L. George

DREAMLAND JAUNTS

I watch you breathing softly;
You are somewhere far away,
Wandering in the sunlight
Not the darkness where we lay.

You are running through the meadows
The sun is warm upon your face.
You are seeing far beyond
The confines of this place.

There the breeze is gently blowing.
The air is warm and sweet.
You sigh a soft breath
And I wonder who you meet;

When you take these dreamland jaunts
Into the depths of your mind
To walk in the sunshine,
And leave me here behind.

Donna Lee Schwertfeger

RAINBOWS

I can hear your footsteps
Falling gently outside the door.
Many days have passed since
Last you walked this floor.

You've been out chasing rainbows
And listening to lies;
Searching for something hidden
Deep in another's eyes.

You hang your head low.
You cannot even meet my eyes.
The shame is plain to see.
There's no reason to deny;

You've done this so many times
This is not the end.
We both know within our hearts
You'll chase rainbows again.

Donna Lee Schwertfeger

LOVE FROM AFAR

I guess I'll have to be satisfied
With loving you from afar.
No one would understand, I fear,
My affection and desire;

To share with you myself
And all the words I have to say;
To have you closer to me
Until my dying day.

My heart soars in ecstasy
At the thought of all that could be,
If I didn't have to love from afar . . .
If you could lie here next to me.

Donna Lee Schwertfeger

ELEGY V. HIS PICTURE

Here, take my picture; though I bid farewell,
Thine, in my heart, where my soul dwells, shall dwell.
'Tis like me now, but I dead, 'twill be more
When we are shadows both, than 'twas before.
When weather-beaten I come back, my hand,
Perhaps with rude oars torn, or sunbeams tanned,
My face and breast of haircloth, and my head
With care's rash sudden storms being o'erspread,
My body'a sack of bones, broken within,
And powder's blue stains scattered on my skin;
If rival fools tax thee to'have loved a man
So foul and coarse as, Oh, I may seem then,
This shall say what I was; and thou shalt say,
Do his hurts reach me? doth my worth decay?
Or do they reach his judging mind, that he
Should now love less, what he did love to see?
That which in him was fair and delicate
Was but the milk, which in love's childish state
Did nurse it; who now is grown strong enough
To feed on that, which to disused tastes seems tough.

John Donne

FAÇADE

I smile to camouflage the pain within.
I do not accept destiny. It shall not win.

Too many songs say,
''Smile, though your heart is breaking.''
My façade may be gay,
But inside I am aching.

Everyone and yet no one can crack my shell.
Superficiality accompanies me, in the cave where I dwell.

People visit but do not stay.
Their curiosity soon goes away.

I exude happiness,
So I smile.
I must confess,
I am lonely much of the while.

Do I allow my true feelings to show?
To the outside world, I cannot be a downer or even a low.

Around me, I have built a wall.
Who will allow it to fall?

Eileen Rahlens

THE ANSWER — GOD

Through our lives, we run into many troubles and cares;
Some that we need more help with than just from our earthly friends.
This is the time in our lives we find we need God.

No matter how big or small, God will help us if we just ask.
He is the Great Maker, and for Him, nothing is too hard a task.
So, when our lives seem to be in a big mess, all we need do is pray.

Not only when we have problems but in everything each day,
God wants us to come to Him in every way.
So remember, if it be problem or praise, go to God each day and pray!

Naomi Ruth Tyte

RAISING MY BOY

Raising my cute little boy is really quite a joy!
What, tie me down — no!
I love his cute smile and even his frown.
But when he keeps me up at night, I get quite annoyed.

I think of his great love for food and wonder
Where his little stomach puts it all!
He knows that all he has to do is cry —
And I will know his call!

When I work, I miss him terribly,
And, in the back of my mind, I wonder
What he will be like when he is a little tot!
I feel that I am missing out on all the new things he is learning.

When he is all grown, he can say,
''My mother loved and cared for me,
And worked to make me what I am today!''
I *must* raise him somehow, even if I must work and be away.

And, when he is a man, I will say,
''It's been a lot of fun raising you, my son!''
Yes, raising my boy shall be a happy time.
There is nothing more fun for me or any better than . . .
Raising My Boy!

Naomi Ruth Tyte

RAINBOW

My love for you is a brilliant, sunny yellow
Because it lights up my life like the sun's golden rays.
My love for you is orange, for it is vibrant and vivid
Ever-animated, in gigantic proportions.
Your love gives me gaiety, like the pink of cotton candy at a fair.
Or the color of a baby's cheeks.
Dark blue measures my profound love for you
Like the silent depth of the oceans' watery expanse.
Your nearness incites my passions to explode
In a starburst of purple magnitude, ever-increasing tempo
Pulsating sensations, quickening my breath in expectation
In a crescendo of indescribable ecstasies.
When I am lonely, I have only to think of you.
The beauty of our love dissipates my loneliness.
The wonder of it is like the redness of the sunset.
It turns all my gray skies into azure blue
For the colors of my love for you
Are all the lovely shades of the rainbow.

Juanita M. Reed

THE SATURDAYS COME SOONER

As a child I paid no need to what day it was.
Content to enjoy my playtime and be in my
    mother's care, oblivious to time.
In my teens, time seemed to drag and I could not wait to be sixteen.
Then suddenly, school was over, and I was thrust into adulthood,
    despite my unreadiness.
Of course, I was totally unprepared for life's difficulties
    and drawbacks.
As I pressed onward to pursue my dreams, in my naive fashion.
Now, in middle age, I realize time is so very short
And one does not necessarily get done all one wants to achieve.
The Saturdays seem to come much sooner now
As I wend my way still in pursuit of my destiny.
Now, I am in my golden years, and the Saturdays come over more quickly
And always, Sunday awaits with bated breath.

Juanita M. Reed

TEARS

I used to cry at little things,
Like the wind sighing
Like a cloud flying
Like a sparrow dying
With folded wings —

I used to cry at little words,
On a late moonrise
On April's pale skies
On the shining eyes
Of little birds —

I'll never cry again or care,
For a song that's done
For a course that's run
For a birch tree in the sun
But my heart's bare —

Doris E. Woolley

REST

Straining under the woeful sack I bore,
My knees bowed, my back hunched,
My body could endure no more.
The load was more than I could bear.
I must throw off all my cares.
Before the throne, I lay bound
Fumbling with cords around my neck.
Unleashing my weight, a friend was found
Releasing my burdens from my neck.
The yoke was lifted, freedom soared.
I now could stand and praise my Lord.

Elizabeth A. Klein

A FRIEND

*Dedicated to the
memory of a friend —*

A smile is worth a thousand words
A hug is worth a million smiles
Yet, from everything in all the world
Only a friend helps ease the miles

You always had a smile, my friend
And yes, a hug when needed
You always had a hand to lend
Above all else, as a friend you succeeded

I think of your smile, and wish you were here
To brighten our days, like times before
And yet, I seem to feel you near
Like a dove at peace, you soar

Take care, my friend, wherever you go
I bid you farewell today
I needn't say goodbye though
For in my thoughts you'll stay

Jodi Lee Ramseth

DARK DAYS

The long dark days of winter
Have a fascination all their own.
How do the howling wind and driving sleet
Become the gently falling snow?

The muffled shouts of cousins
With their sleds, and gifts, and bags
Rush in to eat hot cookies
And the celebration has begun.

There's carolers, and cards, and whispers
And Mama making lovely smells
Of turkey, pies, and then —
Beds for all — though
Some sleep on the floor.

The giggling kids feel tender times
When Daddy reads the Christmas story
As Grandpa used to do
Before he died and went to Glory.

Carol Knopp

KICKING

Remember the frog
In the old cream jar
That kept alive by kicking?

I had a grandma
Who did the same thing.
She walked again — by kicking.

When I had a stroke
Nearly drowned in self pity
I "saw" that frog and tried kicking.

My grandma's example
Of trying and praying
Has shown me the value of kicking.

Today I am walking
And driving a car.
The secret is praying and kicking.

Carol Knopp

HOMELESS

i have a Blanket
Of Soft White Foam
to cover myself . . .
Only . . .
it is ever so cold . . .

i have a Home that knows no Walls
Where i can make my bed
And lay my weary bones . . .
Only . . .
It cannot fend a storm . . .

Oh and i . . . have a Roof above my head;
Cottony Gray . . . no Chandelier . . .
And all the lights
have been turned off . . .

i have the whole wide world of nature
to adopt me . . .
But . . .
i haven't got a Home . . . to call my own . . .

Aida Akl

IS YOUR BACK ON THE BLINK?

I think I know, my darling
Why your back is on the blink.
It's not the work you gave it
But the thoughts you've had to think.

You've worked too hard, my darling
Though your faith has kept you strong
Through deaths and births and illness
You've carried too much for too long.

You can't help feeling depressed
For how should a mama react
When every nerve goes crazy
In every inch of your sick aching back?

When you were small I could kiss you well
As if that took any pain away
But hearts near to breaking
Need some grown up medicine today.

It's your turn to be babied
And cared for. Your thoughts rested too.
There's a lot of housekeeping
In your head to go through.

Carol Knopp

OUR MARRIAGE

We had the best emotion
When people were in love
And many friends we tried to help
They won't forget our love.

Everyone could look and see
And had so much emotion
When we had been the two in love
We had our satisfaction.

We always tried to help each one
When we had things to do
And then we could be happy
That we could help each two.

But then the day would come around
We wouldn't make a pair
It's hard to know he's gone from me
God see him gone from there.

Nancy Quinn

POETIC JUSTICE

Reading the works of poet greats,
Always sets me free,
Loosened of my toils and woes,
Perhaps, by chance, to flee.
Heeding the power of their wisdom;
Ever striving to achieve,
Greater purity of thought and deed;
Reaching out, so to receive,
And, if perchance, some bit of sage,
Has thus rubbed off on me,
And made my scribblings better,
May my debt to them forever be!

Mad Poet

THE CHALLENGER'S END

1986

Can I put in a poem the Challenger's end?
Can I put in a poem that last cheerful grin;
Or the history made in the wave of a hand,
As the astronauts walked to the Challenger's stand?

Can I write in a poem the names of the seven,
Who were shot from the earth with a roar into heaven?
There were Resnik and Smith and McAuliffe to see,
Onizulka and Jarvis, McNair and Scobee.

Can I write of the heart of a nation that cried
For the Challenger's crew and the teacher inside,
In a ship to the stars and eternity's door,
Where the smoke billowed out with a shout . . . Nevermore?

Can I put in a poem the pain of the scene,
Of the shock and the shambles of death on the screen,
That I saw on TV, and on every newscast,
Through the billowing smoke of the Challenger's blast?

Yes, in view of the world, and in this bit of rhyme,
In the year eighty-six, in the annals of time;
The United States spaceship, it rose with a roar,
Then exploded and fell to its end . . . Nevermore!

Sally Irene Davis

BEAUTY BEARING A ROSE

The smile upon your face;
As lovely as the rose you bring in greetings:
The gentle scent and sweet soft petals;
Reminiscent of your beauty:
Then at once my eyes awakened;
Seeing the depth of your beauty within:
Could it be my soul you have captured;
Or perhaps a corner of my heart that no one has known:
There are so many things I cannot understand;
Yet I would really like to know:
Like why my dreams seem so far away;
Although my heart will not let go . . .

Michael A. Steben

LIFE IN A POETIC VIEW

Poetry should say something, something everyone knows:
A truth in life, simple, yet eloquent:
Something profound in all its profoundness;
Yet the essence must be there:
Thoughts may be written as thoughts are seen;
Though only well if there's truth and beauty within:
In a world full of hatred and crime;
There must be beauty, we must take time:
Take time, open your eyes to see;
The beauty in you, the beauty in me:
There's no greater hope for mankind
Than to experience the beauty of the sublime:
Love one another before it's too late;
Life's too short to hurry up and wait . . .

Michael A. Steben

THE DEATH OF A FRIEND

Lord; how can you take my friend so young;
   is she like me, I fear
   all that I have left
   are the sorrows and the tears;
   words left unsaid
   no future no present
   only a past
   a past of memories
   to never-forgotten friends
   the time is now
   we must awaken
   wipe the sleep from our eyes and our minds
   clear our vision to consume true beauty
   the beauty only a friend can bring
   nothing is as precious as to share time
   with the beauty of a friend;
Lord; grant my friend the key
   to the city of your kingdom:
   all pray to arise our departed friends
   into the peace and beauty of the heavens . . .

Michael A. Steben

NIGHT FLIGHT

Dreams to lie
True lovers die
Backseat mothers cry, to find their children
      gone, alone, diseased, hungry homeless
            penniless
                  Broke with nothing
to fall back on but
      steal

Educated on concrete pages read through holes
      and soles of shoes

Love means X X X

Flesh paid-paved and let
      by hands of reign
trusting nighttrain, thunderbird-n-maddog only
            friend a brown paper sack
      soup lines draw raw from there sewage

Marshall Pittmonn

PAINFUL MEMORIES

As I watched her, the smile on her face faded as her thoughts
turned back to him, the moments they had shared together; it
seemed like it was just yesterday that they were together.
She felt as though it was all a horrible dream, she had hoped
it was . . . Their last time together, he held on to her so tight
as if he knew it was for the very last time. Remembering the
way he felt pressed up against her, the warmth of his skin next
to hers. Memories that would be cherished forever deep down in
her soul, knowing that he was at peace somewhere. She looked
back towards me, and as the single tear ran down her cheek,
a smile slowly returned to her face once again as she dreamed
about the past painful memories.

Lynne A. LaForte

THE TWO

It seems like when we two made love
  We would even start to sing
We also found such things to do
  And he gave me a ring.

Then we found weariness, wit, and laughter
  In everything we did;
It's hard we did so many things
  We even tried to kid.

I'm sure that we can satisfy
  Each other when we do
So many different types of things
  To tell each one of you.

I know that I cannot forget
  The man who loved me so,
He did so many different things
  I hate to see him go.

Nancy Quinn

NANCY QUINN. Born: Glasgow, Scotland, 7-30-22; Married: Norman Daniel Quinn, 11-2-46; Education: Two years high school; Occupations: Typist, Sales work, Cashier, Switchboard, Receptionist; Awards: Several certificates including Golden Certificates; Poetry: 'The Snowfall,' 1935; 'Our Church,' 'The Boys,' 'Mother,' 'Twins'.

REMEMBER ME

Remember me, my dearest love
When the silver moon is new,
And when you see carved on a tree
Initials in a heart, where we
First kissed each other tenderly,
And when we strolled through woods in spring,
Remember love songs we would sing.
How thrilled we were to hear a lark!
Or frogs and crickets after dark.
How newborn creatures great and small
Like miracles, held us in awe!
So full of joy through surf we ran
With dogs in tow, we hand in hand.
Then at dusk by candlelight
We shared our thoughts for half the night,
Your soft low voice adding delight.
Every season, because of you
Had more enchanting, special hue!
I do not ask that I be best . . .
Remember me . . . and I am blest!

Lois M. Smith Triplitt

JOURNEYS

Forgive me, Dear, if oft I seem
To wander from your side
And launch upon a journey
Through the portals of my mind.

  A place, a time, a melody
  Come drifting on the tide —
  Sweet souvenirs of long ago
  I thought were left behind —

And through the maze of bygone dreams
I'm for a moment drawn,
Upon a captive pilgrimage
To some near-forgotten shore.

  I dance across my daydreams,
  Chasing shadows towards the dawn,
  Then you reach out and touch me
  And I'm at your side once more.

Fran Moore

THE END OF A TUNNEL

At the end of a tunnel blinding bright
swirl three elementary colors
so fast — so tightly bound
and finely balanced
they make white:
quarks

They spin out spirals of glass
the little girl pins on
the ends of straight,
bobbed, flaxen hair
to make believe
they're curls:
sparks

Joanne Commanday

HOME FOR CHRISTMAS

We love you so, life's colors dim,
As we rearrange our hearts to start anew.
You're still right here inside our soul;
You mind peels away reality and shows us you.

Warm grief melted the starry snowflakes
While our hearts just swelled with care;
We leaned on Him who numbers each hair
of the street derelict and the millionaire.

Voices sang, ''In the sweet by and by
We shall meet on that beautiful shore.''
Christmas sparkled on death's wilted tree,
Sorrow is healthy forevermore.

The Christmas season has happened again;
We disguise our hearts from the passersby.
Memory after memory is stored inside,
For it's there that you live, never to die.

Your spirit inherited a beautiful home
The night it escaped its earthly cage.
You're the essence of life in Heaven above,
Sixteen throughout eternity's age.

Claris McDaniel

Fingers worn from exercise;
Dictionary page-turning,
Thesaurus page-turning,
Almost inkless pen holding.

Fine-tuned hand muscles;
Joints flexing gracefully,
Words writing, written, wrote
Fill up spaces on lined paper.

''The weather was humid today.''
A benign sentence.
''City rain drizzles a tap dance.''
A cancerous line.

A cranium housing a thoughtful mind;
Thoughts becoming words,
Words becoming prose,
Fingers worn from exercise.

Susie Hou

REFLECTIONS

I caught a glance in my mirror today.
  To my surprise I liked what I saw
and I was compelled to look a little closer.
  The more I looked, the more I liked;
I'm no beauty — age has added a few lines.
  The lines added a look of maturity
that only comes with living and learning.
  The body is not as firm as it was once was.
  It's given new lives to the world,
  maybe to change it for the better.
  I don't mind what age has done.
  It's given me a beauty all my own.
  It's the look of wisdom, life and love
I often admired on the face of Momma.
  Now, I can see the traces on my own.

Eve M. Frank

TRIBUTE

I saw a lady kneeling
Beneath an old oak tree
With head bowed and arms raised high
She seemed to be praying to Thee . . .

I moved a little closer
In hopes that I might hear
Exactly what the words were
That seemed to her so dear . . .

The lady spoke of inner strengths
That the Holy Spirit gives us
And talked about a strong refuge
Which only comes when we know Jesus

She also talked of her trust and faith
Of loving kindness better than life
Of souls that followed hard after Him
Under a cloud by day and fire by night

I'll never forget my feelings that day
As I listened to those words
Nor the look of tranquility on that lady's face
As if a voice from heaven she'd heard . . .

Hazel R. Robinson

SPRINGTIME MEMORIES

Shimmering songs of shy, sweet birds
Would yearly tune this greening meadow,
Radiant in the full chorale of life.
Each bud, and blade, and fragrant flower
Would hear the note on which to join
Life's joyous dance of spring.

Now gone that canticle of life renewed
The freshness of the flowered meadow
Transformed by man into a parking lot
Where money's drumbeat drowns the song of birds
And restless people hear rock music in their cars.

But heart-deep memories of the unspoiled songs of life
Still stir the deepest longing of the soul
Whoever heard those songs of happy birds
And saw the wildest flowers dance with joy
In the pure, sure freshness of sweet air
Welcoming life's fullest joys in spring.

Vera Shaw

DAWN'S EARLY LIGHT

Silently the newborn rays of dawn
Touch our unwakened sleep with gentleness.
We are not yet aware
Those brightening beams banish the darkness of the night
That we might fully waken
To a day aglow with living Light.

So truth and love first touch our lives
In childhood, but we slumber on
Lulled by the easy comfort of their grace
Which warms life's early morning in a sunny place.

Some choose to stay asleep, to never face the Light
Which shows the shape of things to come.
Sleepwalkers in the streets of life
They grope for meaning in their daytime dreams.

Still waking wonders of the Light offer a widening way
That those who rouse themselves may clearly see
Both what now *is,* and what can surely *be*
For all who rise and gladly greet the day!

Vera Shaw

THOUGHTS

I sit at the end of the hall,
Unable to laugh and wanting to cry;
Sometimes I just stare at the wall,
Or watch the people walk by;
At times my thoughts seem far away,
Or I have too much on my mind;
Sometimes I don't know if it's night or day,
And reasoning is hard to find;
Sometimes I have to write it all down,
What's going through my head;
Sometimes I'm so deep that I don't hear a sound,
Or a word that's being said;
I hope that soon I can walk out the door,
Never to return again;
And make things like they were before,
I came to this road with a bend.

Carol A. Roth

HUMAN IMPERFECTION

Human nature is very weak and frail,
Frail because it is so imperfect,
Imperfect because that is how we are made.
We may have been made in the likeness of God,
But unfortunately, we weren't made as perfect as He is.
The human condition encompasses all experience:
Good times.
Good times beget a sense of well-being.
Well-being begets a sense of pretension.
Pretension begets a sense of prejudice.
Prejudice begets a sense of pain.
Pain is what teaches us to love.
One good thing comes of life:
Learning.
Learning to accept the things that cannot be changed.
Learning to laugh about our mistakes.
Learning to love ourselves before we can love others.
Learning to say, "I'm sorry," and mean it.
Learning to be.

Heidi Held

I Listen
to All I Say
I listen in a word
from within In order to meet from
without
I listen to all which shall have to
disappear from the way in which I do not think

I listen to a conversation outside of
the surface of this Sound
A recommendation
for recommended reading

Harry Fulson

MY SEA SHELL SEARCH

On Captiva in Florida one searches long
To find rare and gorgeous shells on beaches.
We hunt for angel wings in muddy flats,
Delicate are its lovely features.

The little miniatures I see around
Are really like the bigger ones you find.
But all the names are varied, still they say,
Like conches, bubbles, slippers, and on, d'ya mind?

Oysters and clams, limpets and turkey wings,
Cockles, buttons, ladies' ears, too, you'll see.
Try finding horsehoe crabs or sea urchins,
Sailors ears, all different as can be.

A junonia is the rarest to find.
The cat's and lion's paws sound much alike.
Atlantic wing, pen shell, sunray, venus,
Scallop, nutmeg are found if you like.

Have fun while you're searching for treasure rare,
No matter if carditas or tulips
Are elusive to you when you're hunting,
Finding a murex assures worthwhile trips.

Rogene M. Kraft

MY CHINA DOLL

Once I had a china doll;
Oh, how I loved my china doll.
Each day I would caress her.
Tenderly taking her in my arms I would gently,
Ever so gently, brush the dust away,
Placing her softly upon her shelf once more,
Protecting her from harm and danger's way —
Until that fateful day I returned home to find
My precious china doll in ruins on the floor.
I taken such loving care of my china doll,
But not enough care did I render
The foundation she stood upon.

E. Liguori

IT'S UP TO YOU AND ME

The world can be a better place,
If only we will try.
To get along with other folks,
To use 'you' more than 'I.'
We can do something every day,
To help someone along,
And not take part in anything,
When we know it is wrong.
Like gossiping, and littering,
They both help pull things down.
The first hurts individuals,
The second hurts our town.
If we do really want to help,
Pitch in and do our part,
There could be such a difference,
This is the time to start.
Just talking won't help anything,
What counts is things you do.
The world can be a better place,
It's up to me and you.

Hazel R. Adelman

IRON WORKER

Watched you for months now
   position steel rods
      for the pouring of concrete
to first girder of maroon painted steel

watched you scramble up those first ones
   (neglecting your safety belt)
to affix beams with threaded bolts

   fascinated with your courage
beam connected to beam
      higher
       and
      HIGHER
 blueprints transcribed into reality
 bricklayers followed you up

   into this very real birth

Les Amison

TIME IN OUR LIVES

My mind goes in circular circles
Trying to manage, to remember, to think.
People's names and faces and places
Are in and out, making me blink.

Funny thing to remember the past
With all the upheavals and go.
Remembering travels and dear friends
And the things I really know.

Ah, just yesterday I held little ones
So tiny, sweet, giggling, and small
Who jiggled and gurgled and grew
And didn't stay put at all.

They grew and we watched them so.
They never were trouble or care,
But we knew they'd go on
Making their ways and doing their share.

We've been oh so lucky and proud
To have had such a trust
And knowing they'd pass on
All the things that they must.

Rogene M. Kraft

TOO SOON

Lots of green leaves,
 flowers of purple and white,
 a bed of morning glories—
 such a beautiful sight.
And yet there lay,
 a lone flowerlet off to the side;
 please God don't
 too soon let it die.
For in that flowerlet, I see myself
 alone from the world, off to the side;
 so please God don't
 too soon let me die.

Edna M. Crunelle

MORNING'S DEW

Wildflowers,
 in all colors and hues,
 spread across the valleys,
 fresh with the morning's dew.
Such a sight from my window
 when I was young, I never knew
 but as I've grown older,
 I never tire of the view.
Wildflowers,
 in all your colors and hues,
 adorn the valleys
 and be washed with the morning's dew.

Edna M. Crunelle

NATURAL LIGHT

When dark waves sparkle
On each breeze lit tip,
The moon becomes many
Twinkling lights to sea.
Like reflections of stars
On a cloudless night.
It takes no persons
Or holiday to sight,
Upon the trees, twinkle,
Move and silently shine
These fireflies a light.
Though darkness is around
There is yet a feast,
A party of natural light.

Patricia A. Newgaard

DUFFY

He was my love
   sleeping on my lap
He was my friend
   never lagging behind
We shared our lives
   as partners in a pact
He made me smile
   when I was down
He gave so much
   asking nothing in return
He died today
   I grew up

Pamela A. McKean

Independent,
free to come and go
not needing others to make it
confidence in self
   ego in full bloom
      doing things on one's own
      going it alone,
   so close to lonely

Pamela A. McKean

Water beads on silken skin
shining brilliantly through the night
silhouette the lover's lair
whilst silence cries its
triumphant song
shadows hail the victory
as amid the darkness
two souls are now one.

Pamela A. McKean

THINKING OF YOU

Today I woke early, against my will . . .
  My heart was pounding, it would not be still.
Thoughts of Mother raced through my head,
  As I tossed and turned, and got out of bed.

As I thought once again of the peace we knew
  And remember the tea I once shared with you . . .
The sun streaming in — keeping you warm
  I can almost feel your touch on my arm!

The years have gone by as they always do,
  I cannot stop them and neither could you.
The pain and the heartaches have come and gone
  Like the threshing of grain at early dawn!

They say, "Don't look back — the past is done,"
  This may be true, but not for everyone.
My life is half over, is the best yet to come?
  If we endure the test, do we say we have won?

Whatever you're thinking, with pen in my hand,
  I know you are listening and you understand.
My life I not over . . . it just took a turn,
  I only know there is much more to learn!

Clara E. Schauman

CLARA E. SCHAUMAN. Born: Saginaw, Michigan, 12-18-23; Married: Robert J. Schauman, 12-14-74; Education: Arthur Hill High School, 1941; National Honor Society certificate; Occupations: Secretary, Bookkeeper; Memberships: Jr. Board of Commerce Auxiliary President, Women's Study Club, Young Women's Business Association; Awards: 'Picture Perfect,' American Poetry Association, 1985; 'A Special Place,' 'Memories,' American Poetry Association, 1986; 'Life — A Precious Gift,' 'A Stitch in Time,' 'Loving Thoughts At Christmas,' American Poetry Association, 1987; Poetry: 'A Personal Tribute,' 'Thinking of You,' 'A Thoughtful Time,' American Poetry Association, 7-87; I am in the process of having a book of some of my poems printed and illustrated for possible publication in the near future and as a keepsake for my children; Comments: *I have a deep compassion for other people and their needs and I have a personal need to share my thoughts, my joys, and my blessings with someone special. I have been writing poetry for nearly 25 years and have a collection of poems, some personal, with the accent on love. Others are religious and many are a tribute to my children, family and friends. I have found this to be very rewarding and a wonderful outlet for expressing my deep inner feelings and thoughts. I truly believe this to be a "God-given" talent and hope my poems are an inspiration to others!*

WHO IS A JURY

A gist of heaven in the stars,
Reaches the grasp of an entire solar system,
Its hearth of sobriety is poised in innocent circumstance,
Beyond all others.
In its harlequin grasp,
Is the meaning of the sound awakening, as it is delicately born.

Hearth hear the mettle of the stereo now,
Reaching its Jupiter equations,
And primitive line of its garnet artifact.
It is written away to a phase of ancestry.
It clashes with its ruling class cloud.
Its meaning is a message of nocturnal sublimeness.
Holding maljurisdiciton over the cover of its sublime movement,
The race of its extinction
Is a maladroit point in itself.
The words that I hear are floating away from me,
Are into the grand Pernod of active merriment.

Lisa Miller

FIRST SNOWFALL FOR SANITY

Today I thrived off the world.
Today there was a calm understanding of it all.
Indifferences passed.
All was quiet and simple.
Complexity was left behind.
If only I had the answers to guide the way,
  but what would it be worth?
Mystery is an essential piece.
Starlet hues; dancing dreams; colors speckled with gold.
My mind becomes captured,
  brought to another moment,
to another day when the sun laughed.
A moment lost beyond words where only memories do it justice.
I wonder if it existed at all.
Or was it an illusion created?
I see the brilliance in it all.
I see the glorious nature of the hello,
  the goodbye doesn't matter
    nor do the tears.
Far away lies tranquility.

Mary Jane Pizza

INDEPENDENCE DAY

The Fourth of July
Old Glory flying high
Good old Red, White and Blue
Waving, proudly, for me and you.
The Fourth of July
means hot dogs and apple pie
homemade ice cream and cake
on the beach or at the lake.
The fourth of July calls for a picnic
lots of fun and frolic —
if in the back yard
for insects be on guard.
The Fourth of July is "ice-cold lemonade
made in the shade,"
corn on the cob, right from the pot
even when the weather is too hot.
The Fourth of July — noisy fireworks, spectacular
rockets exploding like "bombs bursting in air"
lighting up the sky
ending another Fourth of July.

Hesse G. Byrd

ONLY ME

Filling inside, joyous
excitement unexplainable

Contentment . . .

. . . could be

Hills and valleys
roller coasters

The answer:

Not with you . . .
. . . but with me.

Helen E. Alliy

THE TYGER

Tyger! Tyger! burning bright
In the forests of the night,
What immortal hand or eye
Could frame thy fearful symmetry?

In what distant deeps or skies
Burnt the fire of thine eyes?
On what wings dare he aspire?
What the hand, dare seize the fire?

And what shoulder, & what art,
Could twist the sinews of thy heart?
And when thy heart began to beat,
What dread hand? & what dread feet?

What the hammer? what the chain?
In what furnace was thy brain?
What the anvil? what dread grasp
Dare its deadly terrors clasp?

When the stars threw down their spears,
And water'd heaven with their tears,
Did he smile his work to see?
Did he who made the Lamb make thee?

Tyger! Tyger! burning bright
In the forests of the night,
What immortal hand or eye
Dare frame thy fearful symmetry?

William Blake

BABY

A baby is the star that gleams while falling,
And the deep earth on which the star will fall;
The gentle breeze that silently is calling;
The quiet shelter of a homey wall.
A baby is a cloud, all soft and fluffy,
The sky so blue on which it floats and lies;
A heavenly hymn each angel hums lightly,
With all the depth of heaven in her eyes.
She is a fire, and a blooming flower,
And all the beauty of a summer night.
Only a baby, but she has the power
To make each day shine out in tender light.

Colleen Barton

TOUCH YOU

For Celeste Robinette

Someone who spoke perfect Latin
Every day of every week,
And probably some God
Of some Greek,
And one particular Jew I can think of . . .

And the guy in China
Built a wall,
I may not even
Know them all
But I'll tell you this . . .

Sometimes I'd rather touch you
Than stop the wind.

Kendell W. Spencer

MISTY SOLITUDE

Lavender mists of early morn
solitude and quiet
only waves and gulls crying
I listen to my soul
all loneliness lastly borne

In the sea air, a foghorn
reminding me of lost ships
I forswear the need of other beings
I lavish in my aloneness
remembering that I never conformed

Alone in the wind, mankind's neighbors I warn
only the sand and God's eternal hand;
my life is an embryo
growing old among the rocks
I mourn my unborn

Sand, grass, and shells adorn
the cuneiform mystery of my nothingness
I reach out to understand my silence
evermore to wish for paths not chosen
solitude necessitates mankind scorned

Nancy Hoekstra

HIDE YOUR EYES

Hide your eyes from me, my Man.
Hide your eyes from me?
I can still see the hate and anger
you have inside for me.
I'm astonished that you loved me enough
To feel such hatred for me now.
Ironically, you are justified
   as you know things to be
But I want to tell you the truth,
   rather, the whole story,
Just to set you free.
Hide your eyes from me, my Man.
Hide your eyes from me.
That way you can't see the sorrow,
   within my own, lest the hell that
      I've been through
But, this very moment,
I'm just thinking of you.
Let's not hide our eyes from each other.
Maybe then, we can see it through.

Sharon Derrico

HARVEST TIME

Such awful things are happening now
Causing men's hearts to fail for fear.
Come the time for seeds and plow,
Harvest time for earth is here.

Nations reaping some broken vow,
Or sins, sown in some yesteryear.
Fierce storms and floods, so frequent now —
All indicate the end is near.

Let the awfulness increase.
Let the harvest be more grim.
Let men's heart's their beating cease —
As light of hope grows dim —
God will keep in perfect peace —
Every heart that stayed on Him.
   Isa:26:3

Ethel R. Heacock

EVERYONE HAS A FIRST

first
first
everyone has
a first

don't get me wrong
everything
there is always
a first

and i was there
whether proud
i'm not sure
but it was her first

not my fault
or my first one
but her first
and second, third

drink

Marc Eckhardt

FORTY-SIX YEARS

Never again will she walk by my side;
My darling of forty-six years;
She's gone to her reward, there to reside
While I remain awash in my tears.

I know I should glory in her release,
For pain's been her companion too long;
Should thank her Maker for giving her peace
Though I'm left here to struggle on.

The hurt inside me I'll forever carry
Until I too can lie in sweet rest.
She and I were One in every sense,
Our marriage was the very best.

O God, as my eyes flow rivers of tears,
I must thank and give You all praise
For Your gift to me these forty-six years;
They, every one, were the happiest of days.

Hilbert S. Collins

INTO MINE

your eyes
looked back
into mine
grey blue
and full of you

i saw inside you
felt your skin
soft white so warm

your dreams
beat deep
a heartbeat against me

i heard your
eyes blink
before you breathed

but never
were they
so revealing
all telling
grey blue
and full of you

Marc Eckhardt

IN A WHEATFIELD

In a wheatfield
You and I sat
Without a reason
Without a purpose
Comfortably though
We didn't care
You and I sat
In a wheatfield
No one else
Questioned us why
No one else cared
So we laughed
And cried and sang
An indifferent tune
So you and I sat
In a wheatfield

Marc Eckhardt

I AM WHAT I AM

Trees are trees, no matter
How ruffled by intruding winds.
Clouds are clouds, though
Shapes and color may air density alter.
Birds are birds, despite
Diversity of their singing shades.
I am what I am, regardless
Of what you think I am;
I can't be what I am not because of
Some wagging and twisting tongues,
And I am happy and proud of what I am;
And plough and nurture what I am;
For, what I am, I am,
And can't be what I am not.
Lucky me!

Scholastica Ibari Njoku, Ph.D.

THE CHANT OF LONELINESS

You gave her blooming roses.
In ostrich plumage you made her clothes.
You longed for her in thousand forms
With promises of life in rainbow strands.

How then did Cupid fly to the mountain top
With speed faster than the shooting stars
To hide his face among the flameless smoke
That experienced the degradation of mind
That is true and noble, and the agony,
The moans and lamentation of heart in pains?

She was warned of claws in scarlet fire
With teeth sharper than the tiger's;
That the curtain would fall
And like tides love would flop
Leaving but vanishing shadows
With echoes of emptiness and loneliness.

Scholastica Ibari Njoku, Ph.D.

THE SOUNDS OF LIFE

The day begins, a baby cries
Someone marries, someone dies
Some flowers grow, while others wither
Someone is warm, others shiver
The clouds brought a thundering rain
The sun comes out, it's nice again
You go to work, some are at home
He writes a letter, she calls on the phone
Some have it easy, others struggle
Some push away, most of us snuggle
The clock ticks on no matter what
Try to be happy with what you've got
There are those who sing, those who dance
One hesitates, one takes a chance
There may be times filled with stress and strife
That's what it is all about
It's called the sounds of life

Harriet E. Coren

MIDNIGHT TIDE

The pain grows stronger
  inside I feel so blue
For somehow there grows
  the fear
Of losing you

Gone are the hello's
  recently changed to good-bye
Drops of perspiration
  forming in my eye

How could the love of yesterday
  so suddenly disappear
Where are all those promises
  of everlasting years

Now silently
  I sit on days
waiting on sorrow
  for somehow I know
in coming time
  My lady will disappear

Stephen D. Green

CHILDHOOD MEMORIES

Children should have memories
Of elephants, clowns, and sunny days
Picnics, ponds, and the sun's warm rays
On their faces

Puppy-dog kisses, a wagging tail
Flying kites, sand in a pail
Butterfly wings, and honey bees
To run through the meadows with

A gentle breeze to caress their hair
Kind words and deeds
From those who care
About children

Karen G. Adams

IN THE TINTED GLASS

In the tinted glass I looked,
  and my mind returned.
For distorted between the panes,
  I saw all I had learned.
That life, in effect, is clay;
  and we, the ones who mold.
But again, since we are imperfect,
  we often lose control.
What looked back at me,
  however small and fragile,
Was yet versatile, unyielding,
  and not at all unagile.
A sweet voice floated on the breeze,
  and created images in a band.
Was crying, ''I love you,''
  by the small child at my hand.
And I felt safe.

Scott Rawlinson

REVERIE

Fragmented remnants of a daybreak shimmer,
Glisten in time's winding avenues, rejected,
Condemned to die by reason's calculation,
Immortalized in passion's dream perfected.

No shallow misconception could create the fire,
Your soul and mine ignited at first glance,
The dying embers falling on the blueprint,
Elusive traces of that pure, ill-fated chance.

Even your sightless eye possessed the vision,
To see within, beyond my wild defense,
You touched the core, unbridled raw emotion,
Removed the need for sycophantic pretense.

Palest moonlight bathes the silent longing,
While the intellect's approving eye surveys,
The taming of a once ''misguided spirit,''
Only by its aching heart, its loss betrays.

Pia K. Wyer

WHERE HAS THE INNOCENCE GONE?

A young girl,
Acting like a woman;
Wanting to learn the ways of life,
Even though she is just a young teenager.
Where has the innocence gone?

A young boy,
Behaving like a man;
Making promises to the girl,
That he could never keep.
Where has the innocence gone?

He tells her that he loves her,
She believes him.
She shows him in return how she feels.
They unite, and become as one.
Where has the innocence gone?

A seed was planted in her womb.
The growth of her stomach can no longer be hidden.
He left town without ever telling her good-bye.
She is left alone with the gift of life.
Where has the innocence gone?

Lennore I. Poirier

SUMMER MEMORY

Together we stood and watched the sun slip out of sight
The earth was bathed in a warm and glowing light.
The sky became suffused with shades of red, gold, and grey
Thus we bade adieu to another summer day.
Then almost magically twilight fell upon the land
The stars appeared one by one — a sparkling band —
Diamond-like jewels in a velvet sky.
A full moon glided there on high.
The silence now is broken by various night sounds
Of night creatures with which the earth abounds.

A high-pitched note comes floating on the air
No doubt a lone owl calling from somewhere.
This golden day is etched deep within my mind
Because it is written in memory's book of time.

With you I marvel again at things I hear, and see
These treasured lovely moments you have shared with me.

Erma Javins Certain

MINUS ONE

I lie motionless on my bed
grey shadows of morning
trying to pierce the darkness
I hear the faint echo of a sparrow
his voice rips through the silence
One green leaf is left
it moves back and forth as it hangs from a branch
In the distance — I hear motorists
their machines, like the wailing of old women
I look up at the ceiling
the paint is faded and peeling
it has survived many long winters
Only minutes have gone by
I crawl out of bed
wide awake
the only green leaf falls slowly to the ground
and the sparrow's voice is suddenly silent

Margaret Hall

THE CALL

He called me today . . . How long has it been?
A year . . . or two . . . and now once again.
"How are you doing?" "I'm fine. And you?"
"Oh," he says, "I'm just passing through."

Trite, tired phrases to cover the surge
Of excitement and yearning and long-suppressed urge.
What does he feel after all that has passed . . .
Does he care for me yet and regret that he asked
To be free?
Does he wake in the night and in absence of light
Reach for me?

Let it be.
I need him no more . . . I've settled the score . . .
And all that we had and expected before is now gone.

The vows that we vowed were all lost in a cloud of despair.
I fell to the depths, but I learned just how much one could bear.

Now I travel alone down the lanes of my life,
But my heart still remembers its days as his wife . . .
And I care.

Lola R. Eagle

WILL I REMEMBER?

*In memory of my mother, Velma O. Johnson
1916-1987*

I'm numb, I can't believe she is gone.
From conception she was my source of life.
However, time worked its evil deed;
The years passed and she grew old.
Her bright eyes dimmed and life's flame died.
Now I'm an orphan.
I will never forget her love and care, her warm smile.
But I wonder, will I remember the sound of her voice?

Ronald D. Johnson

LIFE'S STORY

Lazily the sun peeks over the eastern horizon;
The dawning of a new day is announced.
Awakening, rising from his stillness life's author begins
Another page, another scene.
Progressively the adventure unfolds; like an unfamiliar road
Traveled at night, we are only able to see what lies immediately ahead.
We journey around sweeping curves, over hills and through tunnels.
It is a journey of love and hate, war and peace.
We are entertained and amused, encouraged as well as instructed.
We laugh and cry; the story warms our heart, stirs our soul.
Life's pages relate the drama of dreams come true;
As well as the tragedy of hopes dimmed.
Characters make their entrance and then exit from view.
However, the story continues; it is the story of life.

Ronald D. Johnson

SPECIAL GIFTS OF LOVE

With my children all grown
And the house so very still,
I visualize them playing, just over yonder hill.
In my mind, I hear their laughter,
See the many things they've done.
Now when my grandchildren come to visit
And I greet them at the door,
They remind me of a stepladder
One, two, three and four.
There is Dawn, tall and pretty,
And Dick, with his impish grin,
Sweet Ida, with her long pigtails,
Matthew, with freckles and pointed chin.
With all the hugs and kisses,
They all but wear me down,
For once again, there are sounds of laughter
In a house quite used to pranks.
I kneel down in prayer at night
And give the Lord my thanks.

Elsie M. Westrick

So sleepy,
So tired,
The dark lures us on . . .
lures us to realize;
The moment is ours.
Although we have limits,
The feelings remain, and
   your heart becomes domineering.
So weak, like the night,
I will follow —
Your heart to mine,
My hand to yours.
The moment is ours.
And choice never imposes our soul.
To know,
To feel,
To have, each other —
Tonight . . .

Theresa Carrafiello

MY LITTLE CAT

Pumpkin was a kitten,
As orange as could be,
With big soft ears,
White whiskers,
And no fleas.

He liked to climb a tree,
Way up high;
And nestled among the branches,
He'd watch birds fly by.

Sitting on my lap,
He loved to knead doughy pies.
But now he is a baby tiger,
Somewhere in the sky.

Lisa Kristin Braaten

BEAUTY IN LIFE

I love to listen to the waves,
Wash upon the shore,
The feeling of sand beneath my feet,
Thrills me to the core.

The roaring ocean, the calm sea,
Certainly are a delight to see.
Sitting for hours upon the shore,
Always wanting to see much more.

Watching the ship sail in the breeze,
Makes you feel calm and at ease.
Graceful sea gulls in their flight,
Make you want to watch all night.

The beauty that God put in this life,
God meant for us to see.
Beauty to feast your eyes upon,
Is there for you and me.

Victoria Hammond

A giving hand
reaches far,
it's like watching
the morning star,
or a rose's touch
to me is such.

Alois Fersching

THE LOVE OF MY LIFE

For Howie

I know that you love me —
It shows every day
In the sweet things you do,
And the things that you say.

From morning to bedtime,
My love follows you,
it protects and supports
All the things that you do.

Thank you for being
The love of my life —
And know that I'm proud,
Living life as your wife.

I wrote you this poem,
'Cause I wanted to say —
That I love and I need you,
In so many ways.

Till death we won't part,
Even then I won't go —
I love you, you move me,
Thought you might like to know.

Deedie Macon

BECAUSE TIME GOES BY

I awoke this morning
To look at the sky;
The beauty of sunrise
In my mind's eye.

I heard the birds sing
As the sun rose high.
I saw the flowers open
And felt the trees sigh.

I watched my children
With their sleeping faces
And saw the hidden smiles
That happiness chases.

I've seen these things
Before in my life,
Yet today they brought tears;
Joyfully, I cried.

Now some may wonder
At my tears — Oh, why?
Life is so precious
Because time goes by.

Tricia Schumacher

FROM THE GARDEN

My shadow now free,
No more a howling lament.
On its nighttime spree,
Its earthly time spent.
With clouds passing the moon,
Across the firmament.
Sorrows alongside my doom,
Vanished with the cerement.
Spirit surrounded, aglow!
A warm contentment.
All I need to know,
Is received, heaven sent.

Ha! those treasures of earth,
 in my hands only dust.
Left behind with my mirth,
 My love and my trust.
The seas upon the shore,
Only a distant memory.
 Left behind evermore,
For all eternity.

Danny O'
(Daniel Harris Hellman)

WAGES

Life is a seine
 in eternity's sea.
It holds us awhile,
 then sets us free.
Living, we know
 joy, sorrow and hope.
Sin is the blade
 with which death cuts the rope.

Leola Cormany Groom

THE DREAM

The night's chill is pleasantly warmed as their voices echo,
drifting through time's corridor.
I journey through the years reliving scenes seasoned
by time's passage.
I experience the joys and laughter of events long forgotten.
Once again, I feel the warmth of youth; I am renewed.
However, too soon the moment is past and I must awaken.
The dream lingers for a moment, then evaporates like early
morning haze.
I am left alone to face another day.

Ronald D. Johnson

PRISM

The passing night hours nurture each new day
As time reflects a comfort stir of mind
Shall I ignore the healing warmth per se?
A prism radiant of His Design

Shall I display a doubt and deism show
The very light of nature must convey
As wakened biblical belief aglow
It shall always be and not betray

The tri-translucent ray gives love and peace
Illumines through God's celestial nest
A loving triangle of warmth release
The blending beams of light, the Prism blessed

Oh! bless my soul, with healing inner grace
The breath of life in Trinity's embrace

Dee Hedenland

YOU ARE THE YEARS

Loving the early autumns'
    morning echoes
        and the noontime hummers
As the warm summers'
    lipold smatter
        and occlude oeuvre of the
            overawings cool . . .
Watching the water sprinklers
    on the well-did lawns
I feel as if I've daydreamt
    that I'm in love dawns
And, there, you are the years
    of my cheers, sweetheart . . .
(You fling me into havens of dawns, daydreamt:
You dance and sing and bring me melons;
You pray for the streetwise and the bright neons:
My years bebrighten, light and happy,
All about me as cheers, homespun and pretty,
Though near the shores of psychedelic fawns . . .
Though seas of ghosts and everloving clowns.)

Beverly Ann Hightower

YOU ARE, FRIEND

You are the one with whom I confide
    my life's most intimate secrets
In my times of need and desolation
    you are there
Listening with your heart
    to my desperate cries for help
Always to share your wisdom
    and oftentimes my tears
Strangely, our problems are paralleled
    deep into our souls
I've teetered on the edge of a dark void
    then put out my hand only to find you there
Beside me, giving me hope, courage
    and most of all your love
I would give to you
    all that you are — friend

Kary J. Stark

SINCERE THANKS

I cried unto my Lord
From out of my broken heart, and he heard my cry
    From His holy mountain
And looked down upon my misery, my pain, and smiled
As he dried my tears, easing my pain away in him

So whenever I can't find my way
And think the day will never end
    I run to that shelter
        I've learnt to trust
And He brightens my day in Him
Giving me the courage to endeavor

Oh to be loved by such a Lord
    By such a Lord as He
What can I offer to show my thanks
    When all is His, even me
What can I give to such a Lord
Only my lips in a sincere thanks
For His grace in letting me kneel before Him
        With all my tears of pleading
            Yes and words of thanks

Doris Marshall

THE FLAME

The dancing shadows to my back, I searched the candle flame
And nearer drew to better view the message it contained.
The darkened room was silent, yet there echoed in my mind
A voice which spoke with silent throat to tell me of its kind.
Through chemistry of fuel and breath, the radiance of life!
Which, just like me, knew jeopardy from outside stress and strife.
Intangible, yet obvious; the same through constant change;
The flame and I would live and die within our given range.
Both capable to loan our spark to give of life anew;
To dance and play, then fade away without a trace to view.
Each one unique, we'd add our parts however they seemed small
To serve as tools by godly rules to change the overall.
I wondered, was it really life within the candle flame
Or fire contained within my frame which made us seem the same?

Billy R. Zimmerman

THE CROWN OF
WISDOM SHE WEAR

A mother will use her breast for food
for her new born baby to feed;
even the labor pains hurt a mother
before her joy is freed.

A mother ofttimes — when we cannot sleep —
because troubles would constantly flare —
she does not fail to comfort her child —
I say, that's why the grey hair.

A mother will possess the very thought
of abortion — but pretty soon — that thought
vanishes away — Because God ordained for
you — through her — that word called life today.

A mother gets her greatest burdens when
a child is responsible for self,
those heaviest trials are laid upon her —
the ones that bring bad health.

A mother makes you laugh and forget
the more tribulations you bear —
she's able to contribute to the majority of your
needs — for The Crown of Wisdom She Wear.

Evang D. J. Moten

UNDERSTANDING

Driven apart by what should have
Brought them together,
They separated,
She, with tears in her eyes,
He, with his teeth tightly clenched together.
He turned on his heel and walked away,
Never looking back.
She lowered her eyes to the ground,
Biting her lip,
Fighting the onslaught of emotions
That fought to overtake her.
She raised her eyes to take
A last look at his fast-disappearing figure
In the newly-arrived twilight.
She turned for home, gazing at the sky.
She saw the first star and
Murmured the familiar words to make a wish.
"I wish those of us who need to understand
will someday understand."

Melissa E. Smith

QUIET PEACE

The peace of the stars in the sky
On a night when the breeze
Gently passes by
Offers me the world at a time
I can reach in my heart
And see my dreams
Shine.

Suzanne Kalasin

THE WOOFY OLD SOW

Woofy! Yes, you could say that.
Oh, yes, and very very fat!
What is woofy, you say?
That's an old sow that says woof!
If you hear that you'd best run away
And get up on a roof.
When does she ''woof,'' you ask?
Oh . . . at different times that suit the task.
If you come up behind her
And give her a startle
She'll turn with a whirl
Her tail in a curl
And woof real loud —
That says, ''Don't crowd!''
But it's most times when she frets
That someone or thing is after her piglets.
No! Don't stand still if you hear
That old sow woof with a sneer.
Your best bet with her woof
Is get up on the roof!

Norman R. Miller

HOW COME YOU'RE HERE?

How come you're here?
Have you figured it out?
No, you say?
The reason is not clear.

I know that feeling.
I ask what's it about,
This life we play.
What is the meaning?

Yes, yes I know.
Lots of questions,
But no answers.
Well . . . her's one for show.

You may scoff and groan,
And not like my suggestion,
But my Jesus, my Savior,
I rely on Him and Him alone.

Well, He works for me.
He's *my* only answer.
How come you're here?
Ask him and see.

Norman R. Miller

HAPPIEST DAYS

Life lived all ways:
By chance or rule.
Happiest Days
Are spent in school.

One does not know
It, at that time.
But now I *must*
Put it in rhyme.

Dr. Mildred Thomas

LONG AGO

When I was young in school,
The U.S. gave no aid.
For my education,
I worked and earned and *paid*.

Should someone now want fame,
They too, could do the same.

Dr. Mildred Thomas

DR. MILDRED THOMAS. Born: New Sharon, Maine, 1901; Married: Chaplain, Lt. Col. John Sanders, 1975; Education: Boston University, B.S. in Education, 1936; Ed.M., 1938; Chicago Conservatory, Mus. B., 1956; Nasson College, Springvale, Maine, Honorary Doctor of Science in Education; Occupation: Teacher; Memberships: National League of American Pen Women, American Association of University Women; Comments: The World Who's Who of Women *states: Dr. Mildred Thomas is a Musician (Composer), Writer, Poet, Teacher, Civic Leader and World Traveler.*

Perhaps overused,
And certainly abused,
This word . . . Love.
Like most words of feeling,
It hasn't much meaning,
Without . . . You.

As best friends,
Or intimate partners,
Whether preoccupied,
Or premeditated,
There's no better companion,
Than this entity . . . Love.

Mike Parker

TIME TO GO!

Why do you keep saying, ''It's time to go''?
Fill me in, please let me know.
I can hold your hand and kiss your eyes
And say, ''Please! Please! No suicide,''
But if your mind is made up to go
You go!
My running shoes are at the door.

Thelma B. Pendleton

BECAUSE OF CHRIST'S LOVE

Because of Christ's love to me — I flourish
Because of Christ's word to me — I'm strengthened
Because Christ reigns, I can walk, walk through
    This valley of weeping
With my hope in some glad morning, I'll wake in heaven
    And all of this weeping will be over

Because in Christ's word — He promised
He'd heal my sickness —. And pain
    Making my bed in Him

Because in Christ's word — He said
He'd give me of His holy bread — And drink
If only I'd heed His word — walking in His stature
    He'd take good care of me

For He is the kingdom — My savior
For He is the power — My life
For He is the glory — My king
    Because of Christ's love
    For me — I live

Doris Marshall

DORIS MARSHALL. Awards: Golden Poet Award, 1985-87; nine Award of Merit certificates, 1985-87; Writings: *Work and Play,* children's book, 1987; "A King's Love," spiritual song record, "For You, For Me," on *Hallelujah Album,* Rainbow Records, 1987; "Sun Set," love song, Sunrise Records, 1988; "Sincere Thanks," spiritual, *Hallelujah Album,* Rainbow Records, 1987-88; Comments: *My common themes and ideas in my work are to praise God for his love to me, to send out a message of hope, love, encouragement, and joy, and to educate through my inspiration and knowledge learned.*

FLOWERING FRIEND

I planted this seed into the empty earth
One day several years ago
Then placed the pretty planted pot on the window sill
Where it had light and air to grow.
As soon as I'd awake each day
I'd go to the window to see
What my new plant friend had to say
It meant so very much to me
In the evening I'd say, "Good night,"
Along with a special prayer
"Oh, please come up and be in sight
So I can see you there"
Then one morning — to greet my eyes
A little green stem broke through the soil
It was more than I expected — a great surprise
A pleasant reward for all my toil
Well, my flowering friend grew up in this special room
And I made sure it was tenderly nurtured and fed
So that it did grow to its fullest beautiful bloom
The thought that a flower is like love — keeps running
    through my head

Peggy Raduziner

DANNY — THE DRAKE

I stood at the edge of the pond
Watching two ducks drifting in the water like small boats
They would stop — put their heads together —
Then they would float alongside of each other again
Their beaks held with the look of a smile.
One was a plain white duck while
The other one was white with black marks
    And a glossy green-colored neck.
Suddenly, a woman standing next to me shouted,
"For God's sake — here comes drab Dorothy, the Duck,
And dashing Danny — the Drake."

Peggy Raduziner

WOODEN DOLL

A beautiful package arrived one day
With Uncle Sol's card saying "Happy Birthday"
The box I opened from Uncle Sol
Contained a most unusual wooden doll

Its round head had bristle hair, a smiling face that
    showed no care
A triangle body, round feet and arms,
Odd appearance brought its charms.
On its backside a metal cup
To push — and the hair stood up.
That's what made me laugh in surprise
Magic — in front of my eyes.
My doll collection — 50 year span
There's Dimples, Freckled Eula, and Raggedy Ann,
Ceramic dolls, celluloid dolls — small and tall
Nation's costume dolls — I have them all
Up on the closest shelf — while I'm sitting here all by myself
Thinking about them — but my favorite doll
Is the wooden one from Uncle Sol.

Peggy Raduziner

WHY?

 constant change;
The flame and I would live and die within our given range.
Both capable to loan our spark to give of life anew;
To dance and play, then fade away without a trace to view.
Each one unique, we'd add our parts however they seemed small
To serve as tools by godly rules to change the overall.
I wondered, was it really life within the candle flame
Or fire contained within my frame which made us seem the same?

William W. Dillinger

THE PRINCESS ON HER WEDDING DAY

Prince Andrew and Sarah, July 28th, 1986.

 The bride wears a flowing ivory gown
and her rosy features are concealed by a veil;
as she walks the stairs of the chapel,
people strain to glimpse at her from behind
set rails. Her prince stands by the altar,
so immaculate in uniform today; the Queen's
horses march down the streets of London
in the brightness of the day.

Susan Gilbert

COME OF AGE

When you are born
   you're a baby, just a baby

Given a few more years
   you're just a child, a little kid

As you enter your teens
   you want to be treated differently

But as with the years before
   you're just a kid, a child

Go to college, well-educated
   different ideas, still a child

Find a job, asked your opinion
   no one listens, you're just too young

Keep on fighting, never winning
   radical ideas, still a kid

Years go by, always fighting
   they know you're right, never listen

Get to 40, not a child
   good ideas, people listen

Great ideas, you've done great
   in this world, you've come of age

J. E. Zawacki, Jr.

TWO YOUNG MOTHERS

Two young mothers
on a sofa
one dark, one fair
against a sofa's patterned colors.
Sunlight's brightness
An errant breeze.

Two infant girls
on their mothers' laps.
Angel's dark curls jiggle.
Jenny's blond hair fuzz
lays quiet as she sleeps.
Each holding future's pattern.

Early summer morning
Sunlight brightness
Errant breeze — against
the sofa's patterned colors.

Anne L. Broaddus

TRAGEDY

To run out of life
before discovering
and experiencing
all of life's
pleasures
would be
tragic

Kenneth F. Leck

LOVING HIM

I love him
As the moon loves the sun,
Feeling its caress —
I love him the best.

I love him
Like a child at her play,
Laughing all day —
I love him that way.

I love him
As the dawn loves the night,
Loving its hold —
My love is that bold.

I love him
As tears love a song,
As they love its sight —
My love is that right.

And if it ever comes to pass,
That things are simply not to last,
I'll tell you that I loved him —
As the future loves the past.

Sharon Sandow

How could love last
Through all eternity?
Everything must pass
On: great oak trees,
Faces of the moon, seas.
Time conquers the mountain!
Love cannot forever be
If lovers are forgotten . . .

You surely think with your heart!
Yet, when flesh and spirit part
Only our Death could show
Which aspect will remember . . .
If but in life we'd know
If our love could last forever!

John A Nestor

EMPTY NEXT

To savor, to enjoy in full
The sounds, the feel, the sights,
The times when all the kids were young,
The fun (and sleepless nights).

I often think, now that they've grown,
Of the way it used to be
When they were my whole universe
And their universe was me.

From morn till night under one roof,
(With time away at school)
They drove me crazy, wore me out,
From diapers to carpool.

The running noses, tantrums, fights,
The giggles and the noise,
Oh to have them home again,
My wandering ''baby'' boys!

Gloria Yousha

MEN OF LIFE

our world has five billion people
some believe, some do not
as a church steeple
expires and all pray hotly.

men of life
earthly strife is both
as each man strives
for perfection ashore.

alive, one has dreams
meeting with Thee I see
your world of men pleasing
you as they believe.

extensions of the only one
man has seen in his time
love so rare, undone
over the Man who lies.

Just try, Men of Life!

Maureen Kearney Jones

THE WHISPER OF GOD

Would God that I could understand a bee,
The meaning of infinity;
A flower
A tree
A blade of grass
The clouds that pass
I would know God the better.

A bee
A tree
Infinity
A singing bird
An ant
A plant.
Through all of these
God's loving word
Is whispered just for me — and thee.

Verna Lindberg Kelm

LA JESUS

La Jesus born of a virgin,
God promised La Jesus'
Mother ''Morgan'' La Jesus
Wouldn't be killed as her
Brother ''Jesus''
She would birth the new
Nation, the good people,
And promise eternal life
For all and all will be
Judged on loving all God's
Beings of the earth as the
Major merit, La Jesus died
In a car accident, angering
Many at the drunk driver
That killed her, she got up,
Walked away leaving viewers
Wondering what others miracles
Had been performed by La Jesus
The Daughter of God and
The Mother of a People

Graveyard Moss

BY THESE ASHES

And when this frame is stilled to dust,
Our love will bitter stand;
Too proud to end with death.
Let there be no change
In the taut arrogance of its last note.
    Let this love live as it last lived:
    Defeated beyond the bowed head;
    Withdrawn into haughty loneliness . . .
    Eyes that welled at your loveliness
    Bleakly sweeping the horizon's cold rim.
Forget those first quickening, hot lights;
Our searching hearts on errant sleeves;
Forget your voice — forget your smile
That lifted me into tumbling ecstasy.
    Leave love broken; its fine pieces
    Groping blind for bright wholeness;
    Its words now turned to babbling. . .
    Withering in these monstrous ashes.
We're dead leaves . . . stumbling over the snow.

Harlan Moore Long

SIMPLICITY

Lost in the bright meadow of the sun
oblivious to all reason and knowledge;
I wander and wander
among the tall rushes
and beneath the high-hanging boughs of a willow.
I am comfortable in this serene world
where all
is still.

The world travels by full of technology
and machinery ignoring all laws.
We are robots following the rules and regulations
of bureaucracy.

How I yearn for those past days
when my mind was so clear and innocence prevailed.
Rememberings that spring like flowers from seeds
that have long been gone and yet still
bring beauty for those who dream and will eventually
sing a slightly different tune once they have gazed
upon the real meaning of flowers.

Annette Lehmbeck

THE WIND

How I love the cooling cooing of the wind!
Whisper to me through the window, gentle friend.
You caress my resting face;
My lost life locks into place.
Soothing, moving in this message that you send!

Blow your life into the grasses, stirring breeze.
Lead your symphony of sound with moving trees.
As I breathe your sweetened air
Your vitality I share.
Now I'm nodding for my heart is so at ease.

Yes, I'm dreaming of your power and it's odd,
Pretty sister to the sunlight and the sod,
Though you're real, we all agree,
You've no image one can see.
You're the closest thing I know to viewing God!

Billy R. Zimmerman

WHEN I WAS YOUNG

    Life was a magic lantern show
When I was young long, long ago.
    At night the moon made fearsome shadows creep
And crawl about the stair,
    And though I couldn't see them move
I knew that things were there.
    There was a floppy-eared cloth dog
Quite shabby, it is true,
    But I was safe in bed with him
He watched the drear night through.
    At Christmastime a wondrous top
The rainbow kind that sings,
    More beautiful it was to me
Than all of Saturn's rings.
    I've traveled far across this world
From shore to ocean shore,
    But nothing tops the thrills I had
When I was only four.
    Life was a magic lantern show
When I was young long, long ago.

John S. Hiscox

MEMORIES

    Through the memory there cruises a tall clipper ship
With a cargo of wonderful dreams,
    Of the places we've known and the good times we had
How I cherish those dear bygone scenes.

    On these soft summer evenings with star lamps alight
And the murmuring surf ever new,
    Wherever you are on the land or at sea
My love will come sailing to you.

John S. Hiscox

I want to give you friendship, to be your best friend.
I want to give you kindness, just like you've given me.
I want to give you humor, a most valuable asset to life.
I want to give you warmth, radiating from my being.
I want to give you spontaneity, with crazy, childlike fun.
I want to give you affection, bringing you closer to me.
I want to give you mystery! surprise! suspense!
I want to give you space to be by and with yourself.
I want to give you touch, with feelings running deep.
I want to give you confidence to be yourself with me.
I want to give you patience, when you feel fear closing in.
I want to give you understanding, when you think you stand alone.
I want to give you support, much more than you will need.
I want to give you respect, as you've never known before.
I want to give you trust, in myself, with your life.
I want to give you time to be sure of yourself.
I want to give you freedom to grow and to change.
I want to give you love, tender, caring love.
    But I have more to learn . . .
    Are you willing to share?

Diane Marie

HAIKU

Co-written by Daniel Kelm, my son

Yellow marigolds
Sunshine spilling from the heart
Of a small bouquet.

Autumn in motion
A shower of crisp brilliance
Crumbling under foot.

The silent sunrise
Unheeding the vain rooster's
Garrulous crowing.

Golden butterflies
Elusiveness accented
Against the gray sky.

What heavenly notes
From golden throat of warbler
After caterpillar feast.

Reflected prisms
Of melting snow on tiny shoots
Welcome the first crocus.

Verna Lindberg Kelm

THE FUNERAL

No words
    eyes touch
Hands exchange: Support
No need to be strong.
    Feel,
      What you must.
You will let go
    Yes this will happen.
Such grief
    I care
Such sadness
    I know
Such emptiness: a void
    I love you

Kurt Kelly

AUTUMN

He stands still and straight.
His dark brown coat is accented
Against the faded fields of October.
The sunlight beats down upon his haunches,
Turning them golden brown.
His silky black mane flutters in the wind.

He stands still and straight.
Looking at the road ahead of him,
No emotion is shown,
Towards the passing cars on the road.
Lazily he twists his head,
Focusing his gaze upon the ground.

He still stands staring at the ground.
As the cold winds of autumn rush by,
The trees creak and the grass wilts,
The leaves swirl 'round his feet.
Without warning he raises his head,
Turns, and is gone.

Kenneth F. Leck

EGGSHELLS

Compare then, the lowly eggshell
which shares the universe
with you and me. It's hard,
yet dangerously fragile outside,
beckoning to be cracked or broken,
its pieces scattered to what fates.
No longer does it command our
attention, a waste to be disposed.

But sometimes, there it is,
sticking to my omelet to remind
me of my mistake. I should have been
more careful. How many pieces do I
find today? Did I just not see them
slip into the pan, or did I
just not care?

Each time I think of some great
things I have done, I run into my
little mistakes to constantly
remind me that such are
the eggshells of life.

Rosalie Avara

MIRROR, MIRROR

Look in the mirror.
Who do you see?
Is it just another pretty face?
Do you like what you see?

What do you see,
When you look in the mirror?
Is there anyone there?
Does anyone care?

Who is in the mirror?
Is it a stranger looking out,
Or someone looking in?
Is it someone you know?

Kenneth F. Leck

MOOD

Many winds
Many moons
Many sunrises and sets
Cloud patterns so varied
and special
Hillsides rise gently as not to
disturb the peace & tranquility
of the mood

Sara Katherine Hurley

THE SUN

With admiration crusades run
For health and beauty by the Sun

And after an exciting round
You have the sunny water found

With Sun on ship the trav'lers feel
Community can better deal

The Sun makes pretty tan but learn
Too much of it can blister burn

An ''Ultra Light'' should reach a wound
By doctor dealt on hospital ground

The Sun is reigning after all
On oceans, earth and waterfall

The Sun is also best on breed
It gives to all just what they need

The Sun has given ev'ry ray
But does not ask for taxes pay!

Luisa Kerschbaumer, M.D.

LOVE

She thinks she can his sorrow mend
By only one her touch of hand.

And she looked deep into his eyes
Could he be trusted or disguise?

It seems that love makes people kind
For some it is a happy mind

For duty he was sent away
His girl had alone to stay

As letters letters came along
Like rhythms in a lovers' song

And she did not an early miss
On ev'ry letter put a kiss —

Luisa Kerschbaumer, M.D.

THE STILL STORM

In the noisy silence,
hear the buzz of a bee.
A furtive grey mouse
darts up a tree.
The silken hammock
sways in the breeze.
Petals of flowers fade,
and drift out to sea.
'Neath the seductive silence
hides the still storm.

Natalie Patton

MY GRANDCHILD

My grandchild is one to know
When it comes to reality of making a show.
His ability of knowledge moving in the flow
Exceeds my imagination past the afterglow.

My grandchild grows with the light
Fills the day with happiness into the night.
His doings never wrong, but always right,
While he learns each day in life's battle fight.

My grandchild if you haven't heard
Was sent with magic, I believe every word.
He was delivered by a giant stork bird
And is the most precious event that ever occurred.

My grandchild takes up the slack
Where my heart was empty and thought was lack.
Now, my days are continued once again,
Since, I know his face by his little grin.

My grandchild is my life's main part
In him I find more love in my heart.
He is the joy that gives each day a start,
While I'm at home or at the shopping mart.

Doris McDaniel Jenkins

HAPPY FATHER'S DAY, DAD

Dad died 3-4-87; he was eighty years old and very ill.

Happy Father's Day, Dad.
You are the best dad any girl could have had.
You worked hard to make a good life for me,
I know you loved me, that was so easy to see.
The things we did when I was young,
When on your every word I hung.
When you were perfect in my eyes,
In my mind, I thought someone as good as you never dies.
But now I know God wanted you for his own,
You were my dad, for only a loan.
Enjoy your stay —
And for you I'll pray.
Just let me dream of days gone by,
So that the emptiness won't make me cry.
As days go by, the reasons why,
Will become clear, why you had to die.

Marilyn Johns

LIVE TODAY FOR
WE DIE TOMORROW

we know not when
    the shadow of death will suck our last breath from
    our soft red lips,
        moistened to the touch of love and life.

we know not when
    the violent, treacherous dark winds shall whisk us
    away to the land of the foretold yet, still unknown.

we know not when our time will come.

we know not.

live today, for tomorrow may not be.

Sophia A. Kozlowski

HAPPY FATHER'S DAY, PHIL

Dreams do come true, mine came true with you.
You made me a lady of the world,
Brought me out of the darkness and the cold.
You held me in the still of the night,
    Now all the broken dreams and
    heartaches are out of sight.

Dreams do come true, God gave me a legacy in you.
He opened the door, and in you walked,
    And out walked the heartache as we talked.
You showed me life at its best,
You made my eyes shine, and put my soul at rest.

Marilyn Johns

MARILYN JOHNS. Born: Staten Island, New York, 12-10-35; Married: Philip, 1-1-85; Occupations: Homemaker, Mother of six grown children, grandmother of Joshua, two years; Awards: Golden Poet Award, 1986-87, 6 Award of Merit certificates; Poetry: 'Angry Words'; 'Escape,' 'Your Gift of Love,' *Great Poems of Today;* 'To Chuck,' 'The Elephant Man,' 'My Daughter Marilyn,' *American Poetry Anthology;* Comments: *I write mostly about life as I feel it and see it. Writing poetry helped me work through my father's death 3-4-87. Poetry for me is a way to look into one's inner being.*

A GIFT FROM GOD

Ah, to be free, young, healthy and in love
Is indeed a blessing from Heaven above —
You have all that is "good" going for you
Indeed you are blessed and amongst the select few.

Take good advantage of your freedom and health —
Great assets indeed they are.
If you are careful and think before you do,
In life's path you will travel very far.

A "shining star" I know you will always be
That is plain for all to see,
As I watch you receive your fellowship in cardiology —
At that time may you know how much you mean to me.

My Life for yours I would gladly give —
If the Good Man above will let us live.
The bonding between us is so right —
Philip, as my son, you are a delight.

Iris Moses Weintraub

OTHER DAYS, OTHER CARES

Other days, other cares,
fragments in the memory.
Like other days that never stay,
other cares will also drift away.

Natalie Patton

'TIS A SEASON OF SPLENDOR

Trees, in mantles of yellow
and orange, and russet and brown.
Leaves, whirled in the wind
as they tumble to ground.
Pumpkins and squash
all over the earth.
Fragrant fires crackling
in the big open hearth.
Apples, red and chartreuse,
and tart to the taste.
Roasted chestnuts with a
perfume of old lace.
A big red moon, a million stars,
and maybe a witch or two.
The cool, crisp air that
quickens the step.
Let us store in our mind
to remember forever
the scents, sights and sounds,
of this season of splendor.

Natalie Patton

DARK EYES SYMPHONY

Dark eyes awakened a dormant opus
At rest within my soul
Stirred one million violins
Composing a symphony in whole.

An eternal legata from its inception
With every musical note
When dark eyes met dark eyes
And together a symphony wrote.

Jeannie Davis Weaver

THE AD CAMPAIGN

When we were kids
We had a lemonade stand
But nobody came
Until I wrote
An advertisement

People came from
Out of the woodwork
To drink our lemonade
And our ad campaign

Summer is a thirsty time
Humidity was high
But we were higher
Drunk on the profits
Of our success

Gretchen Blake Leedy

A MOTHER'S DILEMMA

What could she say?
She could not tell her ten-year-old
This is the story left untold,
Of blacks who came from far away
Their wenches laid by night and day.
Mixed blood doth flow beneath their skin
These master's children born in sin;
They're seal-skin brown to creamy-white,
No two are ever quite alike.
They read and write and figure too
MD's, PT's, and what have you.
Master's blood flows in their veins,
Their will to learn is very plain;
They master every walk of life
Overcoming hate and strife.
Her answer came, though very brief,
*"We must be proud of what we are
And keep on reaching for a star."*

Thelma B. Pendleton

PERPLEXITY

Sitting by myself alone.
Wondering where the time has flown.

Wondering where I'm going now.
Wishing for some help somehow.

Where will I go?
    What will I do?
How will I know
    just what is true?

Life is so short —
    yet strangely so long.
Where is the part
    To which I belong?

Questions racing through my mind.
Answers to I cannot find.

Still I wait as Time ticks on,
Greeting me with a fresh dawn.

Kimberly Finley

THE PRICE OF LOVE

The life
That gave such joy
So quickly went away
Without a sound or farewell nod
Today.

The voice
No longer heard —
No laughter fills the air;
The tender smile no more will guide
My way.

The grief
Enfolds my thoughts
For chains of pain remain,
And I must ask, "Is this the price
Of love?"

Nettie Johnson Hult

LONELY ARMOR

Another heart is torn apart.
    Another love is gone.
Happiness will now depart
    as grief descends upon

A lonely soul, devoid of light,
    where no one enters in,
As still and dark as black midnight,
    the doors locked from within.

Dreams . . . shattered like a broken vase.
Tears . . . raining down my face.
Cries . . . echo through my mind.
Eyes . . . that have seen love, yet are blind.

The wounds from all the hurts of old
    have slowly formed a scar.
Caution has now taken hold,
    and love seems very far.

This trusting heart harbors mistrust.
    My candle's extinguished.
From pain I hide. Inside I'm thrust
    until fear is vanquished.

Kimberly Finley

MEMORIES

Sometimes I sit and think about
    Days gone by, so long ago,
The sunny island where I lived,
    The people that I used to know.

Paths that snaked around a hill,
    A flowery spot, a cleared pass,
Bright red poppies, like small boats
    Sailing on a sea of grass.

Further up, a waterfall,
    Its waters were so clear and pure,
Falling down into a pool
    That really gave that place allure.

All of this and more, much more
    Of my early life a part,
Will be wondrous memories
    Kept forever in my heart.

Marie McDonald

A NEW LIFE

Behind a cloud my heart had hidden
But walk away you didn't.
Instead you loved the frightened child inside
And made rainbows from the tears i cried.
Tomorrow i will become your wife;
And we shall begin together a new life.

Sheila Stanley Leyde

what do you do after the tears
feelings that i thought were old surface and become new again
love that i thought was looked at as a beautiful experience
is still not reconciled

possibly it never will be

maybe it's just a reminder of what i am not feeling in my life
and
not the actuality

so many buttons are being pushed now
and
the strength that always carries me through has not shown itself to me

maybe the strength is a place to hide

i am too tired to hide now
i just want to look at all of the stuff right in the face this time

it would be nice to say what i feel about someone and have them understand

it would make it easier that way

it doesn't matter that they agree
or want to walk my path

sometimes it is for sanity's sake that we let go

Bev Kelly

THE OAK IS STANDING STRONG

*This poem was written in honor of Lt. Colonel
Hubert Gleason (retired USMC). The glory in his
heart marches on with the pride and the
perseverance of a chosen few.*

The oak has stood for many years
Ever strong, it reaches out straight and proud
A man has stood and laughed in the face of fear
Stout and tall he steps out of the crowd

The wind moves quietly and bends the weaker tree
A timber wolf stalks in silence through the wood
Some men can hold you as they set you free
They've seen life's misery, and tasted its good

Thunder claps loudly from the depths of greying skies
Lightning strikes and fells a tree to the ground
Some men can pierce you with deep, penetrating eyes
And keep your attention without making a sound

An eagle soars and circles a mountain peak
With powerful grace he passes the distant plains
The oak is still standing, it seldom grows weak
Alpine breezes are singing ballads to the king and his domain . . .

Ronald J. Flemming

MY DOLL

She entreats me with charm, wearing a tear,
holding out to my gay springtime flowers.
I am so delighted to see her here now,
helping me reminisce of the love and the showers.

Beverly Riley

LINES ON MY FACE

Time to be set free with dignity and joy,
Lines on my face encompass the beauty of the day,
Filled with linear emotions,
Mystic blue seems to shine the lines on my face,
Which reveals the smile in my heart,
My heart is filled with love and care,
I want to share this feeling with everyone,
Lines on my face,
Can't erase the color of my smile.

Shira de Llano

SHIRA YAEL DE LLANO. Born: Laredo, Texas, 5-8-60; Single; Education: Del Mar College, Corpus Christi, Texas, A.A., 5-87; Occupation: Data processing operator; Poetry: 'Exaltation,' *American Poetry Anthology, Vol. VII, No. 1,* 4-1-87; Comments: *Poetry is an expression of my emotions. I truly enjoy writing because it is a mirror of my soul.*

GROWING

Expansion begins as budding ideas
Cross-fertilize before developing
Into contrasting-colored new growth
Needing to be flexible and resilient
In order to remain intact
While tested by the winds of adversity,
Not snapped off as brittle old habits
Without any current reasons for existence,
Nor becoming permanently deformed and crippled
So as not to be of any constructive use
After storms blow out and the ideas mature,
Providing branches upon which to bud again.

Cheryl L. Larson

A CHILD SHALL LEAD

A child shall lead them, it was said,
They have no fear as they lay down their head.
Since they always talk to God each night,
Knowing He will make things right.

They tell Him of their love,
And thank Him Jesus came from above.
They say we love You and need You now.
With eyes closed as they gently bow.

They never question or ask why,
When they talk to Him they are not shy.
They know in His time He will tend their needs,
They love Him and have faith the size of a mustard seed.

Gladys Ritenour

SHADOWS

I never was
that shade you saw
playing its fantasy
on the cave's wall.
Your platonic world
captures a work of art
my imagination denies
and your deception
rests in my soul.
I believe
nothing I see,
nothing I hear,
and like a sound
that shifts its balance
in the night,
you are concealed, love,
in that shadowed
hall.

Irene I. Friis

INNOCENCE

Eyes contact,
And souls seek to entwine
In the ecstatic rapture of unity.
Each cherished look, caress, or word
Brings the metamorphosis
Nearer to its completion,
As the two become one.

John Wills

MINISTERS' WIVES' RETREAT

We are as one;
   our thoughts,
   our questions,
   our responses
blend into one great
manifestation of woman
   entrapped,
   struggling,
   becoming aware,
   freeing self
   from dependency,
   obscurity, and
   fallacies of the past
to be the instruments
of God's greatness
in her own way!

Evelyn C. Reece

THUMBPRINT

Life and Death
Run an even race.
Last night a moonbeam died
Quietly, and as still
A moth with silvered wings
Suddenly flew.

Merle Price

LOVE'S ANATOMY

Love is a seed
   Proliferating

Love is on the breath
   Infectious

Love is in the brain
   Insane

Love is in the eyes
   Mesmerized

Love is on the tongue
   Palatable

Love is under the skin
   Titillating

Love is in the vein
   Infiltrating

Love is in the heart
   Reverberating . . .
        a measure in each beat

Love is in every step I take
   with each foot of my feet

Love is in the fingers
   tender to the touch

It's in each fiber of my being
   See . . .
        I love you very much!

Betty James

REPRISE

Love is never lost, you know,
Never wasted.
I gathered all the love I had
And offered it to her.
She took but a little,
Only friendship's thimbleful.
The rest? Kindled the ardor
That melted my ice-bound heart;
Opening my spirit,
Widening my commitment.
Now all who are within my circle
Are loved the more.
The font flows freely now.
I dwell, not on the refusal,
But on the tiny infinity
That was accepted.

Ed Carine

CURSED LIFE OF THE LONELY

Cursed is the life of the lonely,
Dreaming of what will never be;
Broken hearts that never heal,
Broken dreams that never became real.
Seeking, but yet they never find,
Fate somehow has been unkind —
Doomed always to be alone,
Their spirit dies but life goes on.

Sheila Stanley Leyde

FOR ROBIN, MY SON

In Memoriam

I would build a crown for you,
A crown of stars and moons and such,
A crown of all my hopes for you
Entwined with love, so you can touch
The swiftest bird in flight.

I would build a dream for you,
A dream that would encompass all
You could aspire to,
Each goal you planned, large or small,
A dream on which to set your sight.

I would build a throne for you,
A throne that only you could hold
Within your young, courageous heart,
A throne your spirit would enfold
Of God's bright, burning, chastening Light.

Isolde Czukor

YOU AND I

We were look-alikes, you and I,
as we were told from time to time.
Though your face portrayed the ages gone by,
we appeared to be cast by the same die.

Your hands were rough from your labor,
as were mine in due time,
and your brow wasn't like before,
just like mine, just like mine.

And when I returned from the war,
doing my patriotic chore,
I found I had aged a lot more,
resembling you even more.

But now you are with the winds and the sky,
a place for all, after they die.
And I'll probably be there by and by,
then we will look the same
you and I, you and I.

Terry Nyberg

VERTICAL

Vertical is all right to call
Call even if I am not in
Call as if there were no one
on the other end of the line

Call as if you were going to speak
to no one you know and had to wait
for an answer

Call out because you are in

Harry Fulson

A GIFT GOD CHOSE TO GIVE

In the beginning God created this we know.
Now rejoice and be glad letting your faith show.
We know God's word is for us to share,
We should be a witness for Him everywhere.

Praise Him as through the day we proceed.
Meeting our obligations as blessings we need.
We will grow knowing Jesus' blood redeemed all,
Who believing confess Him, and He will intercede, just call.

He lives and waits to welcome you and me,
Until then our role is to let the world see,
Christianity works through the obedience we live.
Making us joint heirs with Jesus, a gift God chose to give.

Gladys Ritenour

NEW-FALLEN SNOW

Seeing new-fallen snow I recall from God's word,
What through the years I have heard.
Though your sins be as scarlet they will be,
Cleansed as white as snow for you and me.

A cardinal flies about here and there,
Against the white snow the message is clear,
Jesus' blood was the price for you and me,
The victory he won that we be free.

Free to believe in Him and walk in the light,
Our salvation secure both day and night.
As new-fallen snow covers dirt and grime,
Jesus' blood covered your sins and mine.

Gladys Ritenour

REBIRTH OF IDENTITY

Obligatory circumstances push responsibility;
lack of attention and inept physical bonds shatter closeness;
Gang environment with hostile surroundings influence
leadership and unprejudiced attitudes, liberal expressions
are satisfied through control of lustful encounters,
tragic occurrence transforms character and a nearly fatal episode
is revived through rebirth of identity; destructiveness
is curbed through uniqueness and inventions that keep creative
juices flowing pushing lustful energy and forcing obligations
to prosperity . . .

Rosemarie Scorza

ROSEMARIE A. SCORZA. Born: Glens Falls, New York; Occupations: Hair stylist, Real estate, Body builder; Writings: "Caribbean Paradise," *American Poetry Anthology*, 4-87; Themes: *People and places that spark my interest;* Comments: *My writing helps me take situations and put them in areas where all goals are attainable.*

ULTIMATE SATISFACTION

Of life's joys in partaking we know there are many.
There are talents galore, but we know not of any.
We know there are none and will not relent,
But ask you consider the one we present.
The cares of the world become lighter we know.
The business of living possesses new glow.
Anxiety, strain, distraction, despair,
All disappear right into thin air.
From the tips of your toes to the roots of your hair
It seems that all nerve centers culminate there.
Your concerns are fewer! much lesser in view.
The world becomes more compatible too.
Problems delayed you now start contemplating,
Because, at long last, you've begun urinating.
And, while you stand there analyzing the news,
You are, most thoroughly spraying your shoes.

William W. Dillinger

MOTHER, WHEN I WALK

When I walk, I think of you and
    I feel your presence
    In the singing of the birds . . .
        that echoes the music in your heart;
    In the warmth of the sunshine . . .
        that reflects your attitude toward Life;
    In the beauty of the flowers dancing in the breeze . . .
        that mirrors your youthfulness and grace;
    In the tranquility of the sheltering trees . . .
        that is the essence of your motherhood.
Yes, Mother, when I walk I think of you and
    I smile, for I do not walk alone.

Jani Diedrick

THE DOOR

I sit and watch the door,
For the face that won't enter there anymore,
The sound of footsteps, the eager smile,
Time passes, it seems such a long long while.

God took him away, but still I cry,
My Lord this did happen to me, but why?
My heart is heavy. I don't even care to try,
To do the things which help time pass by.

How can I become again a person with light in my soul,
With bright days and peaceful nights to make me whole,
There's still work to be done, a challenge I know,
I'll try if only someone can show me the way to go.

I loved him then and I love him still,
But he's gone, and never again as I watch the door,
Will that eager face ever come there anymore,
No never, never can my love come through that door.

But God needed a soul to help above,
So an escort was sent to take my love,
Unselfish I am, and we all must go,
Still expectant I am as I watch that door!

Josephine C. Riley

TROUBLES

Fix your gaze upon a star,
Make a wish from where you are,
Pray your thoughts and steps will make,
A pathway which in God's great plan,
May guide the footsteps of a fellow man.

Many are fearful and filled with pain,
Others can't hear the songs in the rain,
The sun cannot bless with beauty and warmth,
The shut-ins so fearful they can't move forth,
To be guided by their own stars wherever they are.

So pray when you gaze upon your star,
That your footsteps make paths for those near and far,
The weary and heartsick, the lost and strayed,
All those whose courage is badly frayed,
Yes lonely folks everywhere so very afraid.

Paths must be made for all to go,
Make yours so bright that others will know,
There's a star and a way if only they can,
Carry on and just follow, it's part of God's plan,
Because those troubles which have come will also go.

Josephine C. Riley

INCARCERATED FREEDOM

As the cracked bell of Philly chimes in pain,
My soul is over-wrought and chained;
My heart burns in miserable enslavement.
Will a phoenix ever arise from ashes of bereavement?

The murky air weighs those lofty wings —
Deigned to transcend heraldic dreams.
Those rigid hours of quiet desperation bring
A vision of failure dimming that elusive brass ring.

Butterflies hover over time and place
Within a divine and natural pace.
Gliding on a wisp of purpose in unblemished beauty,
In which neither circumstance or fate discredits duty.

An inward vision quest to truth will swell,
While a state of doubtful slumber will spell
Out a sentence of reprieve or everlasting imprisonment;
As my soul aches; my heart bleeds from an incarcerated impediment.

Elizabeth A. Ruhland

FORGOTTEN

Held hostage by the web of misery
Her frail body struggles for release,
But the stinging bites of pain never cease.
What price living! She cried, Take me! Take me!

Thoughts woven by the looms of loneliness.
Though be it dawn or dusk, it matters not.
No cards and no callers. They all forgot
Her special day. She gave them forgiveness.

As a glowing light invaded the gloom,
An angel hastened the heavenly flight.
Her spirit vanished with the glowing light.
Left — her frail body alone in the room.

Norma K. Shea

MEET DESTINY WITH COURAGE

First God made the universe and all things
And to man, conceived in love, grace, he gave
Blessed planet earth, for his dwelling place.
To live in paradise of harmony,
Righteousness, peace, bliss, health, wealth and glory —
And not these horrors and evils to face.

And so passed by many ages of time.
Many souls were born, struggled and died,
Still life continued of the human race.
And for all the suffering, the madness,
The tragedies and affiliations of life,
You cannot blame God — you have no real case.

So, what shall a man do for this crisis,
These catastrophes, coming to the world, soon,
They say — and in a fast, increasing pace?
Shall he just mourn and cry, night and day,
Pleading, complaining on his bitter fate,
Hot tears, from his eyes, running on his face?

No, he must meet destiny with courage,
Fortitude, enthusiasm and faith.
He cannot fight, or change, what must take place,
He must trust the power that sees all things.
Read the old, new books, the bible, and pray,
''God's mercy, help us, in your holy grace!''

I. Stone

SPOKEN FROM THE HEART

It had been a lovely day; sun bright in gentle breeze.
Little ducks swam in the pond. Birds warbled in the trees.
Old friends and neighbors far and near
Family members all gathered here.
A toast! to celebrate the fifty years they had been wed.

The meal was nearly over. Each one had been reminding
The couple of events away back then . . .
An occurrence, embarrassing moment, of a remember when!
The music soft and gentle brought back romantic years,
Such tender memories, laughter, the happiness, the tears.

Just before the cake was cut, a figure rose so tall, so slim
With golden hair and eyes of blue. He spoke, ''I'm Tim.
I have something I want to say to my grandparents.
Remember when I was so small? I lost my mother and
You took me in.'' (voice broke) ''You gave me a home . . .''
(long pause to regain composure) ''. . . I wanted to say,
Thank you for raising me.'' (tears streamed down his cheeks)
(A hush spread over the room.)
''Thank you for all the happy times, too.
I'll always remember. I'll never forget you.''
He sobbed and let the tears flow . . . then added,
''*I love you* . . . Just wanted you to know.''

Mertie Elizabeth Boucher

SCHNE FLOKE

Petite and lean —
Not a breath that is mean —
She's the light of my life
And prettiest you've seen.

Hair pure white —
At fourteen a sight —
Shares my sorrow and joys
Morning, noon, and night.

Patient and true —
With green eyes, not blue —
She tackles each task as
Something wonderfully new.

My rod, my staff —
She can make me laugh —
When my world's gone wrong
And with problems I'm raft.

Asking only a pat —
She loves tit for tat —
She's forever my ''kid''
She's Snowflake, my cat.

Hawk Freeman

AT 2:00 A.M.

At 2:00 a.m.
awaking with the Moon,

Breezes walk briskly
through the avenues of season.

2:00 a.m.
I close my eyes and see you,

Dancing among clouds
surrounded by the Galaxies.

At 2:00 a.m.
a song appears before the sky,

and earth whispers in Echoes . . .
'' . . . Captivate me in your Shadows.''

2:00 a.m.
we touch,

silently among dreams
on amber faded Tapestries.

Regina D. Wilson

LEARN ACCEPTANCE

Reality is a dreaded sight
Whose presence we sometimes shun.
Ofttimes by turning our heads,
Other times, trying to outrun.

Assuredly we're brought together
At some point, face to face.
Unprepared for its confrontation,
We're left staring into space.

Sheila Wells Hughes

DOWN HOME

I remember the comfort
of the old brass bed,

And above hung the pictures
of past lives that were led.

In a corner, a chair —
the wood worn from age,

And in a window of the kitchen
hung a dried clump of sage.

When the fire was blazing
and the flames all in a row,

We all were together
to embrace its glow.

Though the years have passed,
and most of us are grown;

We still hold the memories
of our times Down Home.

Regina D. Wilson

ALL THROUGH THE NIGHT

A love burns
like a candle light
a constant flame
all through the night
can the flame last
through the wind and the rain
shall a love last
through sorrow and pain
for you are my love
you shall be my light
and I shall be yours
even in the darkest of night
there can be no storm
with the power to compare
two hearts grown together
and the love that is there
our love shall burn
like a candle light
a constant flame
all through the night

Suzanne Elizabeth

I'm sorry for doubting the love,
You give so honestly.
It was wrong of me to question,
Your integrity.
Please forgive me for my ignorance,
My shame encumbers me.
For all the love you show,
Should be obvious to see.
So wipe each falling tear,
Upon your face away,
    and give me a chance,
To quietly say,
    I love you too,
      and within your heart I know,
That there will always be,
A special little place,
    Just for You and Me.

Cheryl Lynn Piskule

HURRICANE

The hurricane roared through the night
Sweeping aside all in its path.
Parts of houses, trees, lights!
Uprooting, crashing, smashing,
Flinging them from place to place
Stirring the lake into a giant cauldron —
Foaming and frothing.
The hurricane hypnotizing and terrifying
    with its magic eye!
It made its way through town.

Today is sunny, beautiful and calm
Healing hearts and scenery
With its golden balm.
All that remains of the hurricane's fury,
In my small garden,
A broken rose trellis
And a lilac branch, snapped,
Its blooms upon the ground.

Jessie Faulkner Cuedek

CANTICLES

Enigmatic canticles pervade my mind
in an amorphous fantasia of bliss.
Only the strongest panacea could
free me of my transcendence.
I've reached my acme of felicity.
Macabre despondency can't even
void me of this obsession.

John Dowdell

EVENING AT SUNDOWN

Ever watch a burning sunset,
'Midst the glow that tints the West?
Did it start your mind a-wondering,
'Bout someone who'd loved you best?

Did you notice the minglin' colors
That the entire sky'd beget?
Funny how all of a sudden,
A fella's cheek'd get wet.

Ain't it a mighty lonely feelin'
There in the twilight with the years,
That once brought joy and happiness,
And now they bring the tears.

Memories of ecstasy, memories of gladness,
Exciting the fibers of the heart,
Moments of sadness, moments of heartache,
Two people in love forever apart.

It all kinda keeps you hopin',
That one day things'll be rectified,
And you'll forever watch the sunset,
With your true love by your side.

Calvin G. Wetzel

EVERYTHING I AM NOT

Dedicated to Joan

Everything I am not, She is.
She is infinite patience, a virtue I have not.
When anger and hatred rise within my soul;
She is a tamer of the heart,
Love and kindness her tools in stock:
The sweetness of her voice like a soothing breeze,
Making docile the savage beast inside.
When on the opposite shore all I ever see,
Are gathering clouds of pessimism;
She sees the morning after,
Golden, bathed in the radiant sunshine of optimism.
When I feel that the world has turned against me,
That there are no corners to hide in,
And the will to succeed is about to be broken within;
She becomes my strength,
Her outreaching arms turning corners into vistas;
Making me a conqueror.
Everything I am not, She is;
For She is my love, my wife!

Brett W. Bartholomaus

TO MY FRIEND'S SPIRIT

With the delicate turmoil of the spring rain
Came the journey of your spirit,
Whirling, splashing, sailing past all the earthly things
            you had to leave behind.
And so many earthly things you had to leave behind:
Every song you ever sang to entertain;
Every lesson you ever gave in astronomy and performing arts;
All the love you ever offered, that was joyously taken;
Every friendship, every fantasy.
All these together formed the richest spirit-soil.
In the delicate turmoil of the spring rain
Blooms every human flower you ever planted.

Rosann Pellegrino

DARKENED ROOM

Harmony, the suite of sound
Sings me a lullaby,
As I lie, in my bed,
Swallowing the silence.
I see through my open window, the frosty glow of the moon.
It comforts me, it dances in my soul.

A shallow whisper of the breeze,
Caresses me, almost crimson in thought.

Hear the comforting sound,
The human voices, outside my window.

Leap up, run to them,
Greet them, make them happy!
''Come in, be my friend,''
I plead,
Alone . . .

Nothing happens, my body is still.
I lay beside my window.
Betrayed by the darkened room,
Darkened with depression,
With aging loneliness.

Jennifer Kovach

LIVING FREE

The cold chills my heart, my soul,
Something from within is fighting to leave
the boundaries of the vessel in which it's held.
From this loss I shall empty, thus to grieve,
Not sorrow nor death, but eternal peace shall be my striving.

Let loose, let go, I hear it calling,
What it is, or from where it springs I care not.
Those around me see it not, and have no notion of
the inner struggle looking for release.
And when at last I run from what I am, I will be free.

Ellie Eckel

A GLIMPSE OF HEAVEN

I've been above the clouds tonight.
I know that all is well. All's right.
I am serene; content with what this day has brought . . .
New friends, warm feelings deep within, shared thought,
Events, ideas, wishes and dreams.
Day ends. We've known each other forever, it seems.
My heart overflows with joy tonight.
I've been enriched, filled with delight
With all the words the poets shared;
How some, their souls in rhyme were bared.
No matter what troubles, now in the past,
I'm sure of one thing . . . Love does last!
'Tis this thread through life that binds us all.
For *God's* Love reaches out to great or small.
I've had a glimpse of heaven tonight
In magnificent color . . . an exquisite sight!
I've happiness, love in abundance to share.
God's power of love reaches everywhere!

Mertie Elizabeth Boucher

NEVER LET ME STRAY

I've come to know the blessed peace within my Father's fold
I've learned to lean upon him day by day
I feel his sheltering love o'er me when his dear hand I hold
And walk with him along the narrow way.

Ofttimes my Father calls on me to walk the vale with him
Ofttimes my burdens seem so hard to bear
But if my life is prayerful, and my heart is right within
He gives me strength and keeps me from despair.

I find there are so many snares, the tempter's always near
But God will help me in his will to live
So I'll just keep on trusting in the One who loves so dear
He shed his blood eternal life to give.

Keep me close beside thee Lord and never let me stray
I need your love and guidance every day
I need a song within my heart, a light upon the way
Be near me Lord and never let me stray.

Blanche Simmons

WHEN WINTER COMES

Her deep perspective turns ever so somber
As she envisions the first snowfall

Restless spirit saddens, recalling the chill
Broad emotions stifled by ice

She yearns for a blanket of loving warmth
But factitious passion lacks truth

Strength of the wind overcomes her with fear
One swift gust could sweep her soul away

Without melody, music has no birth
Her songfilled heart beats on in silence

She trembles as her dreams become rigid
Breathless hope somehow smothered by snow

With hibernation her only recourse
As she's saddened, the day winter comes

L. A. Wardius

SMELL OF ROSES

Oh her bed of roses encircled by
her tulips, and a gentle breeze to
carry the smell to me.
On the sight of roses a gentle
breeze of fragrance, carrying
me into a dream of freshness.
By all means my love, the sight
of you starts a fire. Setting ablaze
the love inside of me.
Carrying me into your dreams, I've
always wanted to be in love this way.

Albert F. Carol III

A MOTHER'S CHILD

I sit and sing a lullaby
Beneath a shady tree,
And gaze upon this child of mine,
Nestled close to me.

Tiny hands so finely made,
And feet strong and true;
Hair like golden sunshine,
And eyes a cornflower blue.

Creamy cheeks like roses;
A brow wide and fine;
A trusting smile that lifts my heart,
I pray won't change with time.

These tender, precious moments,
Their worth I cannot measure,
While I softly sing a lullaby,
And gaze upon my treasure.

Agnes Riethmayer-Moench

FUTURE'S COURAGE

Sometimes in silent moments,
Scenes of childhood come to call;
A sweet and tender pleasure,
Of daydreams, when I was small.

But, the memories of yester-year
Which play in chambers of my mind,
Leave me with no regrets,
For things I've left behind.

The days which I'm now living,
Give me joy and hope to last,
And when tomorrow's sun is setting,
Today will be the past.

And as the future's breaking dawn
Shines forth a challenge bright.
Each day with faith and courage,
I'll rush to meet its flight.

Agnes Riethmayer-Moench

ALLERGY

I saw a goldenrod
  On sturdy stem
    Swaying its head
      In a gentle breeze.

''Oh, how I dislike you!
  I would destroy you
    And all of your clan
      Because you make me sneeze.''

But as I watched,
  The intense flame-colored tangerine
    Changed to rich golden yellow.

''Would that I could
  Shake you gently
    Until all of your
      Golden dust would become
        Gold enough to meet the needs
        Of all man-fellow.''

Marcia L. Howland

SPONTANEOUS REACTION

you smile — I am happy
you hurt — I am sad
you worry — I am anxious
you hate — I am spiteful
you reach out — I am touched
you love — I am lucky

Shelly Smith

NOTHING NEW

Listen now, as I weave
A yarn as time sifts through the sieve.

On a stormy night as the darkness set
In my bedroom I was met
By a revolutionary revelation.

There I sat immersed in thought,
When I realized what I before had not —
My thoughts were not new!
How could they be?
Out of five billion people
There must be someone else like me!

And so with this thought,
Out went my pride,
For in your own mind there is no place to hide.

Matt Zuck

ANSWERS

For days my world does run
at a rate so fast and hard
For days it does contain
only pain and endless tasks
which never seem to ease.
For days my mind does wander
down the avenues of why.
Until at last there are short moments
of unscheduled, gentle love;
moments of quiet tenderness.
Then, there in those moments
I know the reason of why
and too the hows of survival
for all of the above.

Linda Bleser Hunt

OUR LOVE

Our love is very special
I knew from the first kiss on
That our love would last forever
We would never go wrong.
From the first time I met you
I knew you were the one I wanted
No one could ever make me as happy
As all the times with you have.
The memories of our love in the past
Are very dear to me
If ever we part I'll never forget
All of our good times and our bad
But I hope that time never comes
For I want our love to be forever.

Leslie Makela

CAUSE AND EFFECT OF THINKING POSITIVELY

Dear Folks,
    When I find something that stimulates my mind
    I hasten to exchange my views with others with
       a nose for news.
    It may be old with ancient mold and only I think
       it's pure gold.

    Worse still —
    There always is a great chance that
    I will be heard by a passing cat
    The kind that glare and stare and scratch —
    And then distinctly blinking, blat
    ''For Heaven's Sake! You didn't know that?''

Dear Lord,
    I am not seeking sweet accord
    I've had my share of harsh discord
    I ponder on Life's puzzling road
    And wonder long what has Death stored?
    While young hearts yearn to be adored
    I woo escape from getting bored.

Edith Gulish

OUT OF THE CRUCIBLE

No primrose path had fate traced out for me.
    It was a stony, thorn-strewn, cross-marked way,
    On which ambitions died from day to day.
But this no longer is a mystery.

The harsh experience of hardships past
    For me had demonstrated God's great grace
    Allowing me to see in wanting face
The love that faith and hope will not outlast.

For suffering breaks down the prideful door,
    And leaves us starkly there like fellowman
    To face ourselves as honestly we can,
And goodness find we never knew before.

Inscrutable is love, unearthly thing,
    Unlocking all the finest traits in man,
    Up-urging him according to God's plan.
O Love, of hardship born, of thee I sing!

Everett Francis Briggs

THE BEAUTY OF FRIENDSHIP
AND THE TRAGEDY OF LOSS

You, Laurence Havens, were my loving friend and husband.
For many beautiful and wonderful years you meant so much to me,
As time passed on: into years.

Sometimes you gave me courage with pleasant words or smiles.
Sometimes you helped me with little household chores,
While I had to drive: for mile and miles.

Then one night — in total darkness without a sound of warning —
I awoke from sleep that morning and found out: you had passed on.

When I think back: to all the good times we shared,
I cannot forget this tragedy of loss without
Wiping away the teardrops that fall.
And now I know, like many others,
I am left alone, with this tragedy of loss.

Mae Havens

CHINA TOWN

On opposite side of the street,
moonlight silhouettes
a couple walking arm and arm,
their laughter breaking silence.
The bars have closed down
and tower clock at King Street Station
shows two o'clock.
Fog settles about top of tall bank buildings.
Rain continuously falls as we walk
wet pavement, hugging eaves.
You are mad over some incidental remark,
or misinterpreted glance,
and begin to speak the shrill language
of sea gulls. Night is suddenly at its blackest.
I suggest we walk to China Town
for something to eat.
In an empty restaurant, we order
won ton soup and egg rolls, sipping strong coffee.
You are in one of your sullen, reflective moods.
It is late and I am not up to arguing.
There is no way we can set the world right
with a fortune cookie tonight.

Steve K. Bertrand

A NEW DAY

I look forward to each new day
What I will do with it is hard to say
I have made my plans but they can change
When a shower comes up I will arrange
To stay inside where it is cozy and warm
I don't want to be outside in a storm

When the sun comes up early in the day
I like to get up and plan my work and play
Breakfast of fruit, toast, egg & cereal is good
To keep me going in a hurry as it should
For there is cooking to do & house to clean
Folks will drop in and it will be seen

So I dust and sweep and tidy up the rooms
There is nothing so handy as a mop and brooms
I wash the windows and bake a cake
I look at the yard and it can use a rake
Flowers come next and some plants too
Everything looks pretty when I am through

I am now ready to go on a shopping spree
Going to the store that has everything for me
After filling up my cart, I must say
Something will have to wait until another day
For my money is gone & I am homeward bound
I want to get back with my groceries safe and sound

Eva Cook

LOVE

Love, like a raindrop,
slips out of nowhere
and bonds two people together.
From that moment on
the couple love each other
until the very end of time.
Nothing can separate them
or break that special bond
   for the love between them
will always be strong.
Love, like a rainbow,
is beautiful.
It's one special feeling
that is shared between two.
It takes a lot to spoil it
and if the love is strong
it will always go on.
Nothing can make it wrong.

Leslie Makela

SEASONAL VI

Like,
slivers of impotent glass
glimmering earthwards
in shining millitrons
or . . .
maybe a feathery gift from nature.
a sample of cosmic diamond;
gifts of heavenly diagems.

Steven Richard Robinson

ARC-DINENAN X

The beauty of an infant
is a reflection of God and nature;
the beauty of a child
is the reflection of the mother and father.
The beauty of an adult
is the reflection of the wisdom and intelligence
of the society . . .
strive to maintain
the essence of the multi-faceted diamond
of beauty in the heart
and it will manifest itself
in the soul.

Steven Richard Robinson

MOONGLOW

A soft, silvery celestial light
casting on the new-fallen snow,
an emanation of heavenly glow.

Lighting the night as if day,
amplifying the peace I see,
showing that in darkness
there can be light,
a silvery, sultry
moonglow.

Steven Richard Robinson

AT THE PARADE

I felt the bong of the kettle drums
as the Marine Band marched by.
Deep within my chest
I felt it —
stronger than my own heartbeat!

I actually felt it
more than I heard it!

Shaking me
and vibrating within my chest,
it surprised me
with its sudden and insistent strength —
like God knocking on my heart.

Sally Nickerson

SNOWBLIND

Songbirds can sing in cages
Not I
I'm not a songbird and I can't fly
I've been snowblinded by loving you.

The web of crystal walls
You said was Freedom
Soon showed to be opaque
You cut your love with Power
I've been snowblinded by loving you.

Songbirds can sing in cages
Not I
I'm not a songbird and I can't fly
I've been snowblinded by loving you.

Sidney Angelique

GREEN, SIDNEY ANGELIQUE. Born: Whittier, California; Occupations: Actress, Poet, Painter.

TO MY SON

I always loved you so.
Though now we are far apart,
The love for you is still in my heart.
I can hear your laughter
And see your smiling face,
As if you were ever so near.
And you are.

I know you are happy
Since God is at your side.
Some day we'll meet again.

Olive Hickerson

The Bustle in a House
The Morning after Death
Is solemnest of industries
Enacted upon Earth —

The Sweeping up the Heart
And putting Love away
We shall not want to use again
Until Eternity.

Emily Dickinson

HAPPY BIRTHDAY, AUNT SUE

Because you ask:
I will give up smoking.

Because you ask:
I will give up swearing.

Because you ask:
I will be as much
Of what I used to be
As there is left of that me.

Because you ask:
I will remember
Not to disturb you
With my chatter
When you are
Trying to concentrate
On something else.

I will do all
These things
Because you ask
And because I love you.

F. Richard Dieterle

TO WHOM IT MAY CONCERN

Today I hit a dog — a little bundle of white fur.
I heard the thud against my car.
It was not my fault!
He came right into the road.
Yet I thought I had passed him.

I went back, of course. The dog was on his feet,
Going around and around in a circle,
One leg held up.

I could not find the owner!
And the people from across the street
Soon came over
And wrapped the dog in something.
They then told us to go.

The little bundle of white fur
Was not bleeding.
I only hope he survives.

F. Richard Dieterle

CHILL WIND

This chill wind that blows over us all
— collects the verdant leaf and turns it to rusty brown,
turns a winter's night to a coldness that to live is to defy —
has gathered the exploding cells of another and pummeled them.

We shake at the very truth.
We reflect on the chill wind freezing our own lives.
We wonder when the wind will circle us.
Indeed, knowing we are all subject to this torrent,
our bones clatter and we are frozen before the very face.

This chill wind is infinite.
If not us, then the very sun that warms us.
And if you say, ah the sun . . . billions of years . . .
Ah the universe, it will persist!
But what are these things without us?

So, another has succumbed.
So, another has had the chill wind gather him,
has had the sun's spark extinguished,
has seen the trees' leaves turned to russet.
We know it all too well.

And the chill wind need not remind us.

Les Amison

LOVE AND THE SEA

Our love has all the aspects of the sea
Ever-changing moods and tides
Yet, constantly adding its salty tang,
Lively foam, to each new day,
In myriad ways
Waves of pounding emotions
That cleanse my heart and soul
Molding all my thoughts
Sing to me, in loving harmony
Your kiss, refreshing as its breeze
That brings with it reveries, fantasies, memories,
All the world's beauty, history and poetry.
Within its undiscovered depths, mysteries
Known but to God and thee.
Its surface reflecting blue skies
Or stormy clouds above
That is why I often long to be
Where I can gaze upon
Or joyfully splash within the sea.

Jessie Faulkner Cuedek

JESSIE CUEDEK. Pen Name: Jessie Faulkner; Born: New York City, New York; Education: Bassich High School, Bridgeport, Connecticut; also some classes in City College; Occupations: Administrative assistant for New York City Department of Finance, now retired; Memberships: Communication Workers of America, A.A.R.P.; Awards: 'A Woman's Age,' *Clover Collection,* 1972; Poetry: 'Dancing,' *Fred Astaire Dance Studio News,* 1972; 'Bicentennial,' *Clover Collection of Verse,* 1976; 'A Woman's Age,' *Clover Collection of Verse,* 1972; Comments: *My poems are inspired by imagination, news events and personal happenings in my life.*

THAT WHICH WE WILL NEVER KNOW

After the gap of the years — that Hell's hiatus —
we met again the other day.
I was pleased with what we had gained — but saddened
by what we had lost — along the way.

We each have honed and polished our lives — much better
the beings than e'er we were then.
What we had lost was what we saw — each other —
we had lost what could (what should?) have been!

There was no regret — for we both are happy, both content;
we each have found our place!
But what we would never know is how it could have been —
would we have shared time and space!

Dr. John A. Short

IT MUST BE LOVE!

Amid the many faces of all the members there
One stood out from all the rest; I couldn't help but stare.
I'd force myself to look away for fear of being seen,
But something pulled me back again: What could this feeling mean?

A force from deep within my soul, I'd no idea was there
Tugging, pulling, back and forth; urging me to care.
''But no, I can't!'' I'd tell myself as the force would bring me near
''Reach out! Reach out!'' it yelled at me, but I withdrew in fear.

The force was so much stronger than I could ever be
So giving up the battle, I surrendered to its plea.
Spinning, cogs a-whirling, my mind had now begun,
But time was running out and the show was almost done.

I sat for hours wondering, how and what to say.
My thoughts would search into the night; awake in bed I'd lay.
It was now the last rehearsal before the final show
I had to let my feelings out or he might never know.

With rehearsal ending early and nothing else to do
I said, ''What shall I do tonight?'', giving him the clue.
''Would you like to go for ice cream?'' was his distinct reply,
And thus began our journey, together, he and I.

Kim Howe

WHAT IS HELP?

Seeing the world through others' eyes and hearing it as they do
Listening in a way that helps the other hear it, too.

Offering eyes when vision's lost to look into their hearts
Letting them feel the very thoughts from which their problem starts.

Finding the key that fits the lock to their own created chains
And letting them find another path to accept or ease their pains.

Accepting another totally, when all's been said and done
Making sure the other knows through good communication.

Guiding them in their search for strength,
    when lost in weakness they feel
Regaining the needed belief in self to cope with what life may deal.

But, most of all it's simply being present with another
Listening, risking, sharing meaning, and always respecting the other.

Kim Howe

ADVICE FROM EXPERIENCE

And if he says he loves you,
Don't believe a word.
Love is never felt by men.
It's a word that's only heard.
He'll say the things you long to hear,
Your heart will soar so high,
But soon he'll lean in close to you
And whisper, "It's a lie."

At first, you're shocked;
He loved you so;
You know this can't be true;
But then he'll laugh
And apologize
And tell how he used you.

And when he leaves, you feel so hurt,
Like you're the stupid fool.
But he's the one who'll feel so bad
When he knows that he's lost you.
You don't deserve to know of this
So don't be too naive.
Men will be a part of your life,
But remember, they'll always leave.

Jill Eitel

TWENTY-ONE

Today you are twenty-one
Yesterday it seems you were but one
With eyes a merry, saucy brown
And hair as light as thistledown.
All too soon, you were one, two,
      three, four, five and six
A madcap full of tricks.

Then off to school you went
On learning bent
Public School Thirty, Number Ten,
Dewey Junior High
Where with Margaret Messerschmidt
And others for honors you did vie.

Then to Dickinson High you came
Warm, eager, loving, kind.
Soon three years had passed
And you were in nurse's training at last.

The coveted cap so large and white
You wore proudly as your right.
Childhood, girlhood passed, a woman at last
With achievements within her grasp.

Florence M. Ditzel

SIMILARITY

Parallel highways are we,
Never meeting, though on similar course.
Too rough terrain divides us;
Too mountainous the amateur to climb.
Better to have traveled different roads,
   I'm sure . . .
'Tis almost certainty our paths would cross.
As things are now,
Although I glimpse you close to me,
Nothing more can ever be . . .
Unless new views appear,
Narrowing the gulf of mute identity.

Joan Paparella

LAURA

Her name was Laura,
As you can see.
An angel came and
Took her away from me.

Before I had
the time to say . . .

You were my sister,
My friend, my whole.
I need to say
I love you!

Be bold . . .

She was the best friend
I had ever had.
She is the best friend
I'll ever have . . .

As I lay here
In the night,
The brightest star
I can see;
And as the wind
Blows her name to me,

The best of angels
I know she'll be!

Tonya Ione

TIME

My eyes have seen the devil's ways
My ears have heard the devil's phrase
This song's about my stranger days
Can the world be saved from our wicked ways
The hands of time are ticking fast
The hands of time won't let us last
Old Father Time is strange, you see
But he can't save either you or me
Oh, great one, please help us now
Save us from ourselves somehow

Michael J. Gaynor

CONFUSED

Feeling pain;
Staying sane,
Planning hate;
Confused state,
Shouting urges;
Loneliness merges,
Thoughts of love;
Feelings are shoved,
Never believe;
Can't be deceived,
Heart bruises;
Sanity loses,

Happiness
   I seek;
      feeling
         weak.

Gwen L. Bond

SHATTERED

Warm with heat;
Red that beats,
Shaped for love;
Deeply thought of,
Solid when fed;
Easily bled,
There for the take;
Easy to break,
Fragile it's known;
Strong alone,
Strength for others;
Loneliness will smother.

Confused at heart;
      forever in
         the dark.

Gwen L. Bond

LIFE WITHOUT YOU

Since the years have passed me by,
There's not a day I don't want to cry.
Maybe I'm not all that smart,
But I remember the day we had to part.
I thought the Lord was being unfair;
I was even ready to give up my prayers,
Yet your daddy stood strong, and proud,
Because I know of your new home
Above the clouds.
Matthew, my son, how I wish you were here,
But only the Lord knows how I wish I
were there.
I never would have let you go,
But I had to prove I love you so.
Now I try harder to keep away from sin,
For that's the way I know we'll meet again.
So as I live from day to day,
You're in daddy's heart, here to stay.
Yes, son, you're deeply missed
But I know of your happiness.

Ronald Badger

MY KINGDOM

I walked the land with wisdom;
I traveled far and wide.
I sang my song of hope for man,
Oppression by my side.

I came upon a kingdom,
Deep within the heart of man,
A kingdom built on honesty.
Come live there if you can.

I saw a small boy walking,
No shoes upon his feet,
Where snow and ice and wind abound,
Not one friend did he meet.

I saw an old man crying,
Death knocking at his door.
I saw no man reach out a hand;
I didn't want to see any more.

I kept an endless vigil,
Looking for some charity;
Not one man did I see,
Who could look upon himself with clarity.

Bonnie Jae

HUMMING SEASON

'Round and 'round in a constant hum
The mosquito season has just begun.
Itching and scratching and calamine lotion
That's what we need when they go into motion.

Wet and clammy, humid and damp
That's where mosquitoes love to camp.
Biting and sucking, making you itch
''Give to the blood bank'' must be their sales pitch.

You know exactly when summer is coming
Just tune in your ears and you'll hear them all humming.
Slowly they gather, one by one
Soon there's a swarm; the mosquitoes have come.

You can hear all the wishes to be without lumps,
Without itching and scratching and all of the bumps.
But, summer would alter and not be the same
Without the mosquito and it's well-known fame.

Kim Howe

OCTOBER

The slow October stars march over me,
They march with measured steps and majesty,
They march with bright indifference down the lane
Where you were first revealed to me in pain —

A shred of bitter smoke blows over me,
It swirls with acrid ghosts of memory,
It smells of dying branches and a leaf
That fell upon your scorn and unbelief —

The still October night drifts over me,
It guides each constellation sleepily,
It moves the moon from treetop unto sky
And leaves the world to one lone fox's cry —

Doris E. Woolley

VICTORY

I can understand the little waves breaking,
The swift water taking
The stones and the sand —
Tearing the shore away,
Making the rocks obey,
Finally to have its way snatching at land —

But I would never rest to do as the hills do,
To lie all my life through
Upon their wide breast —
Back to the clouds again,
Back in the wind and rain,
Back where old ships have lain on a wave's crest —

My heart is never still to know as the hills know,
Be silent and calm though
Unrest claim the will —
But strong is the heart of me,
Fearless and wide and free,
And I have seen the sea conquer a hill —

Doris E. Woolley

GET AND GIVE

Reach out to me, I need a helping hand
Put your arms around me, I need a friend

Let me lean on you for just a little while
Until I too can walk that extra mile

Set me at your table, filling the hunger inside
But let me leave your table also with pride.

Let me wash my weakness with your strength
Wherever I go, I know our time was well spent

From the kindness you gave me
Now I too can give.

Eve M. Frank

YOU KNOW WHO YOU ARE

I give to you all that I have to give — myself.
I trust you with that gift.
For I know you would never misuse or toss it aside.

I get so much in return: your love, your pride,
your strength when I'm weak, comfort in my many fears.
You are always there to wipe away my tears.

You know my faults, my weakness, my strength;
You know my moods and they are many.
You know me, the good, the bad, the ugly, the beauty

You know me better than I know myself.
Yet you hold me as if I were fine crystal,
a treasure that at no price can be sold.

I cannot hide the tears that fall
for your love and your trust
have made me believe in myself.

Eve M. Frank

EVE M. FRANK. Born: Roan Mountain, Tennessee, 9-10-54; Married: Paul Walter Frank; Education: High school; Occupations: L.P.N., Wife, Mother of three children; Memberships: PTA; Comments: *This is the first time I've had the courage to show my work to anyone other than my family and dearest friend. I find it easiest to portray my deepest feelings in poetic form. I also write short stories about growing up in the hills of Tennessee, which has provoked much laughter around our dinner table.*

MENTAL WASH DAY

I was sitting here relaxing. It was
Wednesday afternoon. Mom was
Doing all the washing way downstairs
When a notion sort of struck me, and
I thought it might be nice if we all
Could launder out our minds just
Like the clothes.

What a nice, new, clean beginning
We could start out every week. All
The hate, deceit, and envy washed
Away. Leaving once again a clean new
Slate to start out life anew, but with
The knowledge of the puddles to steer clear.

Robert R. Weetman

THANK GOD

''The tornado!'' It swept down, my
God, oh! so fast. No one here rounds
Knew just what to do. The windows
Blew inwards and the roof came
Right off; just by luck I was safe
On the floor. The reason no one here
In the family got hurt was they had
All gone to Dallas for the fair. Only I
Had stayed home to rest here in my
Bed, 'cuz that morning I had felt
very sick.
As I look all around me, at the
House now in shambles, and the barn —
It just ain't where it were. I just look up
Above me, and give thanks to our
Lord that that funnel cloud didn't want me.

Robert R. Weetman

IT

It is worth all the
Power on earth
To be thankful for that
One small birth.

And it can be so very
Hard, and it can be so
Wise.
We see things so differently
And through such different
Eyes.

It doesn't always show
Outside — sometimes it stays
Within,
And sometimes fights a battle
It cannot always win.

For it is the soul and feelings
We share.
To know inside that some
Do care, and on that final
Judgment Day,
There never was a price to pay.

Eileen Lexa

A SUMMER LOVE

I'll never forget that Tuesday, May fifth.
You were standing on the school grounds,
the wind in your hair.
My eyes were pricked with tears,
My hands were numb and cold,
Yet warmth was so near.

I wanted to run and hold you,
Be with you forever.
I wanted to feel your warmth against me.
But my heart was weeping,
I knew this wasn't right,
As I saw you in the cold, windy weather.

I knew you belonged to someone else,
And my love for you was too strong.
My soul was crying, because I couldn't come.
Oh, how I wish I could have turned time back!

Slowly you turned away,
And I saw you disappear,
Among memories of love,
Once on a summer day.

Ann Nantana Linder

SEAL GLOVES

Damp flesh
Shivers stain my heart like dye
a sacred place
your hands carve buttonholes to let
the dye seep through.

Beneath seal gloves
nettles
of unwashed fingertips,
gentle hands cast
a spell.

We will sleep in the old tub
impervious to the damp
steal brown water
for the plants in the sink
tell fairytales
after.

Our love
the only truth
untold.

Janis Gillespie

TEARDROP

Such a special moment
It is
When a drop of tear
Comes floating down
A cheek
Of someone
You think is sad
But instead
It's a touching,
A compassionate moment,
A reluctant separation
Between two people
— friends.

Tabitha Nadine Britten

FOR R.

Light drains from the sky
leaving the afternoon's premonition.
Sister lights the stove again
tosses the match
and tells herself he's sleeping
for the first time in days.

He shuts the window,
ignoring his collar: unpressed, buttoned.
This evening, he will miss supper
in his parents' kitchen.

The mourners assemble.
His sister will have the heat on
when his mother
comes home.

He is not witness to their pain:
no eyes, no ears, no flesh to hold.
Dead, between lunch and dinner.
They could still feel his touch.

Janis Gillespie

LET ME BE

Let me fly to the mirrors
erased in all thought

Let me be — let me be
for to be I am not

Let the glow of my silver hushed quiet wings
lead my heart and my breath
where the mockingbird sings

Let me glide through the curtains
that shade sleepy dawn

To my face in the sun
where remembering is gone

Let me be — let me be
Free from all thought

Let me be — let me be
For to be I am not

Dick Jordan

MUSIC

I kept looking for the music to my life
    I knew it existed
    for I had heard it
        in the silences
        in the quiet moments
Yet it never remained
only darting in and out of my life
        precocious, relentless
but never standing still
        Then I stood still
Now it plays unceasingly
in a thunderous whisper.

Catherine Kiernan Flynn

seascape, chosen miracle, moves
the least presence full of wild praising.
i have been alone but not afraid to recognize
the risks whisper: this could be love
as the unicorn, free creature, once gained stars
clearly see the deserts choose: she in hosannas a ceremony:

the weight etches myself dark, describes shadows.
who of the other self recognizes love
itself. luminous and wild blessing, an event.
you utter lightward consonants of inscape, lucidity.
dear, we have happened. miracle directly loving

which woman laughs clear around want and the dark.
the spine of perfect message, seascape: tame clay
you and i by riot choice in the green fog.
spirals oneself the gift — a leaning as love were about

to love — so necessary even the sun is.

Julie Weiss

as wind conjuring wild red, the artists
from them having imagined, spiraled pure roses:
i exist — merely like something devouring, whispering
dared human.

what irreconcilable breath shades anyone's luminescence?
who denies use — the desolate, pure inward materials
to lavish insatiable reality until the breaking sound —
the silence itself. bare across lily-of-the-valley.

nor vision disappears, whatever the blurred surface heaves.
what woman is drowning; stitches the desert green, pin-pricked
insistent: am i tame? the blood that drew itself mourning the skin —
 who devoured genius and we, trapped, celebrate
fear and inhumanity.

Julie Weiss

EMPTY PROMISES

My life began the day I turned around to see
A vision of the legacy you had given me;
A world filled with emptiness,
Long lonely nights dreaming of the might-have-beens.
This vision helped me see the life you chose for me
Was the life you'd been forced to lead.
This terrified me so, I turned, running away from the past.
I'm still running, still searching for that elusive dream
While enjoying life's side roads along the way.

This is my life,
Mine, not yours,
And what I choose to do with it is my decision alone.
Thus my life began the day I turned and left the past behind;
Left the fragile way of thinking you tried to teach me.
My life began the day I became too afraid of becoming what you were.
The day I became too scared I might become you.
So I turned and ran away
Afraid to change but even more afraid
Not to.

E. Liguori

FRIENDS

Friends are supposed to share
They're supposed care
True friends share a lot of time together
They're supposed to feel like their friendship is forever
Even when they're not feeling fine
They tell each other to keep on the line
They tell each other to try
Each one has their time to cry
They tell each other to keep hangin' on
And forget about all the bad memories that are gone
Tell them to forget about the past
True friends will make the friendship last.

Renee Mindt

BE JOYOUS

There are times when things seem to go wrong,
  But I'm happy just the same.

There are times when maybe my face should be long,
  But instead it beams in God's love.

You may think because of that or this
  That I should be down, my face with a frown,
  But instead I'm full of joy, lasting for more than awhile.

I am high above the clouds, which no drug could do for me;
  That's why I'll soon soar back to earth,
  Singing to God psalms, praises of victory!

Whatever you think that my mood should be,
  According to the circumstances whatever you may see,
  Remember I got joy, everlasting joy from
  A God who's always able to set me free

Paulette Speights

Go and tell the world that my God lives!
  Open up your heart to His loving presence.
  Do you know my Lord? Do you believe in Jesus Christ?

Loves us all so dear, to care for the world of sin.
  Obedient is the Savior, He died on the cross for us all.
  Victory sealed in His name, he rose again from death.
  Everlasting protection, His promises revealed in God's Word.
  Saves me from destruction, saves me from all my sins.

Yes, I believe in the Savior, I will confess this to men;
  Of a God that's real I know, because He lives within.
  Understanding is to believe Him, trust Him, know Him.

Yes, be assured God Loves You!

Paulette Speights

ABUSED

He touched me with his wickedness
And I want me back.

No apology can soften the anger
No bundle can cushion the bitterness
No deed can return my dignity
No distance can ease my despair
No fact can take away my fear
No fire can burn the fingerprints
No harmony can carve the hate
No ice can freeze the immortality
No pill can relieve the pain
No words can console my weep

Nothing but time can wipe the tear
Nothing but time can bring tenderness
Nothing but time can teach trust.

Time has p a s s e d
And now I want me back.

Tabitha Nadine Britten

THE LAST FAREWELL

As we leave the hall today
Slowly, in sadness and tears,
We wonder why he had to go—
He was so young in years.
We all thought the world of him—
We'd like to think of him as one,
If been given a little more time,
So much good he could have done.
Dear Lord, just one thing we ask
Before this meeting ends:
Oh, where can we find another
To take the place of him?
As we try to dry our tears,
We look once more to see
The one we loved very much
And bless his memory.
With just one thought on our minds
As we slowly leave the room,
Lord, you must have loved him very much
To call him home so soon.

Nelda Wilson

HONEYSUCKLE FRAGRANCE

Honeysuckle fragrance through my
  window drifting.
Ambrosia's essence to my nostrils
  lifting.
My mind's elevated,
My mood is elated
Sniffing the olfactory
Sweet mysticality
Of honeysuckle's essence.

James C. Robison

Life,
So big and so vast
So limited and yet, limitless
My future unfolding
Which way shall I go?
I can sometimes almost touch it,
And then it slips away

Jill Eastman

LOVE'S END

The lights shine out over water's glow,
streaming out,
like my tears stream down.
Crying out the pain.
Ocean waves cry out earth's pain,
teardrops cry out my pain.

You have your goals, I have mine,
so we chose to walk alone.
I listen to the waves.
The turbulence of the waves reflects,
and echoes my inner being.

Why is letting go and accepting
so unacceptable to me?
I want you to be happy.
I want you to reach and accomplish your goals.
So,
I let go.
I wish you peace.
Be free, my love, be free.

Jill Eastman

A NEW SPRING

Smells of fresh flowers
In their morning awakening.
Different textures,
Different colors,
Different everything.
Is it here finally?
Finally — yes.
Forever — no.

Birds fly high
Not in a straight line.
Wings push the air.
Never fall,
Never tumble to the ground.
Chirping to their mates.
Squawking to their enemies.
Different colors and different songs
  among them.
Never ending, never ceasing
Throughout the night.

A new spring has set in.

Debbie Lynn Budnick

GENTLE WITHIN

I give my pain-filled heart to the sea,
and it returns
cooled, calmed, at peace.

The winds of inner turmoil are stilled.
Sunlight appears through the clouds,
as a smile comes across my face.

Jill Eastman

A PATTERN

All our lives are like a pattern
That's in a skillful weaver's hand.
Someday it will be made perfect;
It is in God Almighty's plan.

Imperfect as that substance was,
In His book a name He wrote down:
He chose to make the eyes of brown,
The little face pretty and round.

His shuttle never ceased to fly;
We cannot know the reason why,
But He had a pattern! 'Twas planned —
That can't be substituted by man.

In secret and curiously wrought
From the Weaver's hand it was brought:
Not choosing when to be born,
In the evening or early morn.

Each member was perfectly placed;
Fearful, and wonderfully made,
Soul, mind and body — marvelous
In every way . . . we are on display.

Opal Marie Hayes

MY BIRTHDAY SUIT

What a wonderful thing
is My Birthday Suit
with millions of cells
covering me all over!

In a way it breathes
like the leaves on trees!
It keeps me cool when it's hot
with moisture from sweat glands.

Skin cells grow to mend it
without an iron-on patch!
No bothering about colors
of fabric, my skin to match.

As a baby, I kicked off
my booties to play with my toes,
and was free to be me
from my toes to my nose!

In simple consciousness
we are naked and know it not!
Having nothing to hide,
needless clothing is forgot.

Clodah G. Summer

GOD CAN

Instead of focusing on what I can't do,
I shall believe I can do all things,
Through Him who enables me to.

With my God's help my abilities increase,
No matter how little they may seem,
no matter the least.

What I can do is nothing, if it's done on my own,
Compapred to what God can do, only He alone!

My weaknesses are strengthened, my fears disappear,
Doubts are gone, problems are solved,
heartaches are healed.

Life's many challenges are a joy to me,
Because I'm not working at all,
My God's working through me!

Paulette Speights

ETHEL

you are an old woman now
limping behind the bar
eking out your existence
with a husband who seems too indifferent

true
you are still slim-hipped
but
the life is gone
in your hunched way of moving about
as though to serve another drink
is to defy the dictates of time
of course there is no time except for us humans
and we use it so tragically

so
i wonder with your wrinkled asymmetrical arms
whether
there is justice to life
better than you receive welfare
while
lesser are dead

Les Amison

VALUES

Have you tried to watch the mating birds?
Two small black birds circled exactly together,
Flitting in and out on the evening breezes;
Then parted, trying again to lure each other.
I watched mamma bird holding a berry for her babies,
Yet as I closely watched, suddenly away she flew,
Not letting me see her nest in the flowering bushes
And a second day I stood quietly and still got no clue.
The two mockingbirds avoided their nest,
Instead quizzically eyed me cocking their heads
Until I departed from their obvious scene
With no knowledge of their little birdies' beds.
If we are carefully aware, all protective animals
Guard their small, young, growing offspring.
How much more should we constantly protect
Our youth, culture, art, or valued anything?

Rogene M. Kraft

THE SOUL AT NIGHT

Alone in the dark night, I thoughtfully gaze
Out of my darkened window toward the city,
With one tall elevated church steeple
Showing a starlit sky and no duplicity.
A few scattered lights are looming up
To add to the quiet forsaken lonely street.
Across from me lights in an apartment
Show that others are wakeful from sleep.
But quiet reigns as our world's asleep,
Yet around the earth other peoples begin to waken
To work continuously on growing changes.
God watches as peace or strife are shaken,
Surmounting the upheavals across the lands.
The silence now and quietness will prevail.
My soul feels peace — feels all is right.
Thus renewal comes for all to avail.

Rogene M. Kraft

AMERICA FOR ALL

The global world is great yet small with news we daily hear.
One knows the Golden Girls, Johnny Carson, many newsman all,
Our president, international news and those local bits,
But we cannot participate in all events that befall.
We love the musicals and historicals, the sports, and games.
Long-ago, sad accounts remind us of Meir and Gandhi,
Then Curie, Schwietzer's care, concern in all our world.
Histories in parks like Plymouth Rock and ghost towns fondly
Portraying to our children the stories with fun and work —
Ministers, writers, businessmen, and politicians positive.
It's no wonder many striving souls feel aggressions so great
They turn to other forms of release, but cannot be assertive.
With our teachers, friends, neighbors, and counselors
We are continuing to erase some of the blights.
We must portray to our American children the caring.
Who else will carry on the best of human rights?

Rogene M. Kraft

AMERICA TO ME

The joy of the vast lands covering mile after mile,
Abundant growing earth with crops always to vary,
As kafir corn, wheat, barley, soybeans, maize and corn.
Building productive farms took years without much time to tarry.
Fences to build, horses to raise, cattle and sheep to graze.
Sunshine and rains aided all, yet years of crops diminished.
No rains for proper growth so even tumbleweeds disappeared.
Still man's cycle of growth returned so products replenished.
Food for growing cities came as tillers and tractors ran again.
Discovery of gold led many away; then oil was found in the ground.
This brought another big job with refineries to build.
Cars and trucks traversed the land; silos for storage around.
Dams made for waterways and bridges spanning so much.
Use of creativeness continues to broaden our industries.
With training and ambitions in so many fields of interest
Young Americans can work in their freedom land with energies.

Rogene M. Kraft

STANZAS FOR MUSIC

*There Be None of
Beauty's Daughters*

There be none of Beauty's daughters
  With a magic like thee;
And like music on the waters
  Is thy sweet voice to me:
When, as if its sound were causing
The charméd ocean's pausing,
The waves lie still and gleaming,
And the lulled winds seem dreaming;

And the midnight moon is weaving
  Her bright chain o'er the deep;
Whose breast is gently heaving,
  As an infant's asleep:
So the spirit bows before thee,
To listen and adore thee;
With a full but soft emotion,
Like the swell of summer's ocean.

George Gordon, Lord Byron

LIFE

Life begins with a baby's cry.
And there are many tears thereafter.
But there are just as many days
Eyes are dry.

There are days of happiness
When things go our way.
Then our emotion changes
And our feelings crumble to clay,
But tomorrow always comes
And with it come hope
And a better day.

The answer to life we may
Never find.
For most of us, to this we are
Usually blind.

When we grow older and our
loved ones begin to die,
We sit in sadness and wonder why.
So as life begins, it also
Ends with a cry.

Betty Baker

THE GREAT SPIRIT

Listen, my little ones —
I have a story to tell us
And I have a gift to share.
The gift is God's love —
We can carry it like a rock in our pocket
By day
And for our nights, He has made us —
A dream catcher — of caribou moss and bone.
We can hang it over our sleeping place —
We will not dream alone.
No bad dreams can get through now —
No dark clouds above.
The bad dreams are caught in the stars.
The dark clouds are trapped in His love.

Betty Fossing

A CLOSE RESEMBLANCE

Put on your boots, coat, and cap;
And don't forget your scarf and mittens.
When you go out to build a snowman,
I want you to be warm as kittens.

If you work with vigorous haste
The snow to press and mold,
You'll be back inside the house
Before you get too cold.

The birds you will want to feed;
Here is bread and some seed.
And take these odds and ends
That you are sure to need.

If you use your imagination,
I am sure that you can
Make him bear a close resemblance
To Frosty, the famous snowman.

Tilda S. Akers

We are given a chance,
among the worst something
otherwise, hopeful
circumstance.

As I spoke to you,
once,
I love you
as simply as that.

Now go back,
I cannot
but going on,
will not forget the first time.

You likewise
with me must have been a
test.

We are only careful
for such a memory, more
careful, I think,
than ever thought to be.

Judy Thomas

TO KILL A DREAM

To dream is to
  live
in the world
of eternal
  truth.
If you say you
  don't dream
  you lie.
    Lies destroy
     dreams.

Karen Marie Falkenstein

THE REAL ME

The me I claim to be
Is not the me I wish you'd see.
Each day the mask is firmly in place,
Each day the mask becomes the face.

Still I wish someone was near,
Someone who'd look to see the fear.
It needs a caring eye,
To look and see through the lie.

I need someone to say, ''I like you,''
Someone to help me renew.
I need someone who will stay,
And say it's alright, you're okay.

I'm never far from all my fears,
It often shows in my private tears.
But caring will show through,
And soon I'll see, the caring is true.

So look behind my many faces,
And see into the empty places.
Soon you'll see the real me,
The me I wish I could always be.

Carol M. Marfuta

PERSONAL THEFT

It's come down to it
says she's through with it
don't know what you did
yet she's got you in her grid
her scope of tactics
shifted in kleptomanic
the old hoover maneuver
she wants something newer
checks of foolish pride
face torn from disguise
her ruthless strategy
is the real tragedy
strung out into her loop
just how far will she stoop
it's hit and run robbery
he's hearts back to poverty
she's makin' it, personal theft
there won't be anything left
he quietly walks in trade
she's taken it all away.

K. R. Ollis

HAVE YOU HEARD?

Have you heard about Life?
It won't ask you to come along for the ride
It just takes you.

Have you heard about Life?
It won't say, ''This is how it goes . . . ''
It just goes.

Have you heard about Life?
It won't tell you your future
You just end up there.

So why is it so appealing?

Laura Morrissey

A WINTER RENDEZVOUS.

SONG ON MAY MORNING

Now the bright morning star, day's harbinger,
Comes dancing from the east, and leads with her
The flowery May, who from her green lap throws
The yellow cowslip and the pale primrose.
Hail, bounteous May, that dost inspire
Mirth and youth and warm desire!
Woods and groves are of thy dressing;
Hill and dale doth boast thy blessing.
Thus we salute thee with our early song,
And welcome thee, and wish thee long.

John Milton

THE WOMAN OF PORTUGAL

She stood on the green cliff, blue sea beyond.
Black were her garments from head to toe.
White hair escaped from the kerchief she wore.
Wide smile creased her rosy, aged cheeks.
Her eyes were a snapping-black.

Hands on her hips, she favored us with a sprightly
dance of her nation.

Grandchildren, sons and daughters were chagrined
at Grandmother's indiscretion.

She gave the travelers the gift of dance and laughter.
We couldn't help but give in return.

Her gifts live brightly in memory, our gifts
just a passing coin.

Helene A. Donohoe

INSIGNIFICANT ME

Where is she, the girl I used to know,
Plain but passable, always on the go?
She used to be outgoing, friendly tho' shy,
Always had an answer, loved to dance with guys.
Where did she go? Seems like only yesterday,
She was a young wife with children, and
a dog with whom she played.
As the children grew up, she advanced in her years,
Helped with schoolwork when she could,
Helping hubby get in wood.
The boy left first,
The two weddings she went through.
Lonely hours took their toll,
As the children all left home.
As she began to work, I know.
Looking into the mirror now,
I see an older woman there.
A touch of grey, a bit rounder.
I know who I see . . . it's just Insignificant Me.

Bertha Munson

The sky is so dark because there aren't any stars
The street is so noisy, but there aren't any cars.
So you go outside to see what's there
then you realize the world is bare.

You go out into the wilderness,
to find someone.
You ask them what is going on,
then you discover everyone's gone.

You wonder why, the world is bizarre
you look around . . .
and you don't know . . .
where you are.

You try every path to find a way
out of this place . . .
but every direction
leads you back to the very same space.

You get so terrified
you begin to scream.
Then you realize . . .
it . . . was only a dream.

Marc Trudel

REHABILITATION

Balance is my necessary public art
Which hovers visibly like an undulating shroud of bewitching gossamer.
Should your life-breath lift the cloud that now protects me,
No beauty lies beneath
But bits of uncertain carrion despair
Stretched like yellow surgical gloves over a still-beating heart.

Your secret soul knows me, I you.
We smile the public art of conversation
All the while
You have taught me of the icy memory that once tracked through you —
A ghastly, blooming power over your relenting will.

Because of providential accident, I can say,
''Hold my hand.''
We pass through like colliding phantoms, a law of physics.
We pass through reborn.
The suns in your eyes meet mine,
I love you, friend, as you love me.

Balance is my necessary private art.

Mary May Schmidt

POPAW

Mike and i would watch all day on Saturdays for Popaw's car;
Each hoping to be the first to spy him from afar.
He brought me toys when i was a child,
And told me stories of long ago to make me smile.
As i grew older, words of wisdom he did tell
Of lessons in life he knew so well.
But life never seems to last very long,
And now my Popaw is gone.
We had so much yet to say between he and i;
Popaw, it's so hard to say good-bye.

Sheila Stanley Leyde

OLD

My body, once young
and full of energy,
Has become old,
and worn out.
My days, once filled with laughter
and friendship,
Have become filled with tears,
and loneliness.
As the endless hours drag on and on,
no one stops to see me.
Why did I have to grow old,
and forgotten?

Christina McCoy

MIRACLES

It starts out like the pain
in a toothache.
Then it becomes stronger,
and more tense.
The pain is tugging more and more;
you become aberration.
You feel like it's the end;
you become hesitant.
You can't take it anymore, you want it to stop,
but it doesn't — it continues.
Sometimes for hours.
Then it ends — it's all over.
You hear a faint cry that sounds like
It's coming from a distance.
The birth of a child.

Christina McCoy

EVER GOD

We raced the hills, the Wind and I
Leaping the barriers of time
Forests entoned low psalmal chants
Of age-old mysteries sublime
Rocks resounded with lilting ode
Of beauty held in flowing rhyme
Waters chided with angry roar
Of tragedy in every clime
Thunder flung riling epithet
Of bloody hatred, war and crime
But ever in his ruffled wing
Wind carried God.

Helen deLong Woodward

ODE FOR A NEW DAY

I can not cry anymore;
I have gotten myself in line,
   like others have.
No sweet caress from nature's wind
   can lift me up to dreamer's heaven.
No hint of musk oil can swell my heart
   the way it used to do.
Kisses nourish these lips of mine,
   but not the passion in my soul.

Rhonda Desilus

UNTITLED

Happy
and smiling.
glad
curious
amazed
thankful
satisfied
just like a kid with a new toy.
content
helpful
friendly
and smiling
(and laughing).
speaking with the Midas touch
turning all that you say
into gold.
with you I enjoy everything
as if it were my last piece of cake
but being with you, I'm satisfied.
I give you the last piece

John Powers

Feeling alone is like
drinking to quench a
thirst until there is
nothing left
but the thirst.

desperately — look all around!
try to find something to drink.

nothing there or here.

all alone
no one home

but you

and a glass
as empty as your heart.

John Powers

LONELY HOURS

As I sit here in my lonely cottage
my soul ebbing away
There is a spark of gaiety as I think of
days of yesterday
When robins were singing in the
treetop by the door
It's just a lovely thought
as I sit here in lonely hours
dreaming of days gone by
I hear the patter of little feet and
voices that were so sweet, but these
little ones have grown and gone away
And as an aging mother I cherish this
thought to my heart
   to eternity

Glenna Jaeger

LONESOME COWBOY

The valley I am leaving, I'll miss you
all the while
While dreaming in the saddle I'll miss
your cheery smile
I sit here on the prairie, 'neath
moon and stars above
I'm just a lonesome cowboy
I miss the girl I love
I'm just a lonesome cowboy
I miss you day and night
I'd give the world my darling
if I could hold you tight
It's lonesome on the prairie
where white-faced cattle roam
I'm just a lonesome cowboy
I'm sad and all alone

Glenna Jaeger

THE WIND

Blowing gently summer breeze
Blow through the leaves on the trees
Rock the birds to and fro
Keep them from all harm below
Blow your winds to ocean wide
and rock the waves of incoming tide
You are free to go to and fro
and to the forest far below
Blow gentle winds to far off lands
Where you come from and where you go
no one can understand
   only God knows.

Glenna Jaeger

WINTER INTERLUDE

Midwinter, and as yet no snow,
just shoving gusts of icy air
twisting from the skies below
to the dull gray streets where
bluster interfaces with the void
of concrete, plastic, celluloid,
and battles to restore its reign,
to force its subjects to their knees again.

How often in this flust'ry fight
do we withdraw, to let the diverse elements
joust their way to reckless flight
and in their mixed accoutrements
wind their way to Stygian night.
Soon, soon, the freezing lace
will chill, reveal the victor's face.

The snow has come, mild tyrant of the sky
whose wiles, and tendrils drawn with grace,
whose hushed and awesome lullaby
bestow upon our waiting place
the aura of such days gone by.
I picture him, his face aglow,
with softly gleaming tufts of snow.

Gertrude Leigh

THE JOURNEY

On this journey we embark,
    unprepared for what lies ahead.
Ignorant of all, in our innocence,
    we look to others for our bread.

Setting forth with uncertain steps
    we go forward full of hope and trust.
Although we cannot give, our needs
    are freely met from their love of us.

Going ever onward, our goals
    finally are set, our direction's found;
our efforts are no longer random.
    Having learned to give, we're homeward bound.

Some of us proceed together, others alone.
    Regardless of our route, each seeks meaning,
through the several years and paths,
    for the profoundly simple fact of his being.

Raymond E. Sicard

IN MEMORIAM CHALLENGER

They were seven who dared to follow their dream
Through the shining Florida sun to the platform of the future.

Smiling and waving, they walked to their destiny.
We watched with pride, for they were ours,
And envy, for we wished we were one of them.
We held our breath as lift-off neared,
And cheered as Challenger left the ground.

With tears we watched her head for space,
Emotions tangled — so much joy, so much pride.
A teacher in space pursuing a dream.
She would bring us back her thoughts —
Her journal of their days in space.

We watched the rocket slowly climb
The second stage ignition came — we thought.
Slowly, with disbelief and horror, we realized the dream was over.
The Challenger was gone.

They were seven who dared to follow their dream
Through the shining Florida sun to the platform of the future.

Ande Burlew

PENNY ANDREW BURLEW. Pen Name: Ande Burlew; Born: Meriden, Connecticut, 9-7-48; Married: Thomas Ebert Burlew, 6-3-67; Education: Franklin Pierce College, Rindge, New Hampshire, B.S., Business management, B.S., Accounting, summa cum laude, 1982; Occupation: Writer; Awards: 1985 Achievement Award from Boston Chapter Society for Technical Communication, for technical manual.

THE CLOUDS WILL WAIT

Time is held in a village,
Like a wake of times, cast in by a wall.
It settles down to the geography of intimate moments,
When the sun rises, when the bell rings,
A cloud rinses itself in the sun.
It is willing to nullify all things in its path.
The rain retrieves the future.
If finds a coherent pathway into its native garter
It reaches out for, and impeaching,
The road for several blocks,
Its photographic memory turns the tide and is a thing of beauty.
It reaches out to the memorabilia of past seasons.

Lisa Miller

AN APRIL DAY

The world that day was a silver bowl,
Filled with blue sky, sunshine and crisp spring air.
April had rolled out a soft green carpet,
Sprigged with dandelions, here and there.

It's remembered the peach trees were in blossom,
A soft cloud of pink clung to every limb!
And happy bees with dusty faces —
Climbed in and backed out of every bloom!

But inside the room there was a comforting gloom
And a small fire to light up the shadows
There a little girl sat in her grandmother's lap
To hear, again, the story of ''The Three Bears.''

Doris Donegan

THE FIRST DAYS ANEW

We descended on the city that was sparkling with lights;
me and my friend together our first night.

The romance of the city was alive the next morning;
Ageless and timeless, cultured and refined.
The tall gleaming buildings separated by clean streets.
And old meeting new: together were beautiful.

The European flavor was tossed around in the air —
the outdoor cafés with cobblestone streets, like the
Musée des Beaux-Arts engulfed with great works;
classic art, eternal friends: a toast to the city.

Riding the subways took us to all the corners of town.
The beautiful St. Lawrence and the top of Mount Royal;
par temps clair, la vue y est magnifique,
Oh, Jacques Cartier would smile with delight!

We dearly enjoyed the first week of our new life:
the people, the places, the city so majestic —
and when we left one morning early that fall
we knew we'd always cherish those days in Montreal.

Jim Harris

STAR GAZING

To my beloved Frank

I gaze up at the sky and see
A profound, domed immensity.

Her secrets oft I try to read,
Incomprehension my sole creed.

The longer gaze, the longer ponder,
I cannot grasp, but merely wonder.

And wonder leads to darker depths,
I cannot fathom the sky's concepts.

Of one thing certain, yes, am I,
When I gaze upward at the sky —

Oh what a microscopic atom
This entity, a child of Adam!

Louise Pannullo-Parnofiello

A BOLT OF LIGHTNING

Across the ocean,
Bolts of lightning,
Obtrusively jut out from their dominion,
Lighting a myriad of dark realms.
Turning the sky into an electric field,
Only the darkness is more powerful,
Forever untelling of the lightning's next strike.
Lovers tremble at the glare of a flash,
Instantaneous rebirth of a lost romance.
Giving naught but a simple gift,
His display of nature covers a rift,
Thunder crashes and our souls uplift.
Enraptured at a fantastic light show,
Neon yellow flares glow,
Iliad of the earth's foes,
Never to alleviate all of her woes.
Gleaming darts of fire He throws.

Lisa Kristin Braaten

REUNION

To my class of '37

I would like to write a sonnet
About my love for Pelier High,
But my roots were still at Edon
So I will not even try . . .

My parents moved to Pelier
December of Freshman year,
I said farewell to classmates
Who to me were very dear . . .

I did get my diploma,
As my mother always said,
Commercial is the course to take,
If you have to make your bed.

Fifty years have come and gone,
Again it's almost fall,
'Tis God's will, I'm here today,
Alas! I love you all.

Harriet Lucretia Motter

PROGNOSTICATION

Thoughts of the Past

I sit by a smoldering fireplace,
Thinking of bygone years,
The joy of hearing the school bell ring,
As well as the regrets and tears.

I remember strolling through the woods,
To pick the first flowers of spring,
To study nature's tall straight trees,
And to hear the songbirds sing.

There stood a church by the roadside,
Beneath some lofty elm trees,
Flowers bloomed in the old graveyard,
Tall grass rippled softly in summer breeze.

Time has passed, the church is gone,
No more a school up yonder hill,
I find no trace of old schoolmates,
In dreams I see and hear them still.

Harriet Lucretia Motter

MARRIAGE

Now that the two of us are as one
I treasure every day,
Each hour we spend together,
Along life's winding way.

I remember our courtship days
And what a struggle we had,
We sought to cast our love away
Making each other sad.

Perhaps we had to hurt some
To know our love was real —
Though I hated the struggle
        and still do,
I pray our love
    will always see us through.

Struggle, "For what?" you say.
To be the best that I can be
So that my mate will not regret
Spending his life with me.

I trust our love and caring
Will ever grow deep and strong.
It's so nice to have someone
with whom I belong.

Eva O. Scott

SAVOR THE MOMENT

Life ephemeral.
. . . as fragile as this moment,
    and gone forever . . .

Savor the moment,
. . . for every moment is the seed
    of forever here and now.

Brian Bywater

SAVED

A Prayer

I go to Jesus in humble prayer
Asking Him to carry me through
Drinking deep of things so holy
And I'm blessed with life anew.

"Make me not a slave to pleasure.
'Tis things that soon pass on:
When it comes time for eternity
All such are passed and gone.

Oh touch my heart, dear Jesus,
So your word I'll understand,
I want to ever serve thee
Then I'll reach that Holy Land."

Harriet Lucretia Motter

HARRIET LUCRETIA THOMPSON. Pen Name: Harriet Lucretia Motter; Born: Williams County, Edon, Ohio, 12-15-18; Married: John Clay, 1938; Jesse Thompson, 1942, widowed 1960; One son, Gary, and one daughter, Victoria; Education: Commercial High School, Algebra, Latin, 1937; Night courses: Piano, political science, reviews in bookkeeping, income tax, etc.; Occupation: Audit and billing clerk, GTWRR; Poetry: 'George Washington's Life,' 1932; 'Grandmother,' 'Our Freshman Class,' prophesy, *Edon Enterprise*, 1933; 'Reincarnation,' *American Poetry Anthology*, 1985; 'Ode To A Mayor,' *American Poetry Anthology*, 1987; Themes: *History, people, religion, nature, life, politics, anything that can be summed up in a few words important for me to tell.* Comments: *My best poems were written before the age of 17, inspired by my courageous mother, who taught in a one-room schoolhouse before marriage. I dedicate this work to Eunice L. (Ennis) Motter, my beloved mother.*

MY HEART LEAPS UP

My heart leaps up when I behold
  A rainbow in the sky:
So was it when my life began;
So is it now I am a man;
So be it when I shall grow old,
  Or let me die!
The Child is father of the Man
- And I could wish my days to be
Bound each to each by natural piety

William Wordsworth

SPRING

Blossoms, like the birth of a new babe,
Awaken a renewal on the face of the earth.
And a lifelong pleasure fills our hearts.
It seems that spring has come again.
Warm breezes whip freely through the countryside.
The trees stand majestic and proud
As their limbs gently sprout tender buds.
The birds return with their clear, sweet song.
Butterflies, bees and green grass carpet the world.
Azure skies highlight the scene,
As the sun rises splendidly in the heavens.
After a long and cold winter,
We scurry outdoors to wander aimlessly
Through hills and shady valleys
Where the aroma of flowers overpowers the air.
Gladdened that seedtime has begun,
We experience beauty that pleases our senses.
This season casts a magical promise of renewal.
As the old season dies, spring is born
To revive all the fertile places.

Pat Klein

OH, TO BE IN FLORIDA

Oh, to be in Florida
Now that winter's here.
And whoever wakes in Florida
Soon becomes aware,
Of white clouds sailing across a blue sky,
Green waves splashing o'er a sandy shore,
While the palm tree spreads its lovely bough,
In Florida — now!

And after dawn, when the sun beams its welcome warmth,
It almost seems that nature itself is on a spree,
Spreading its wonders for all to see.
Look, there's a group of pelicans,
Gliding over the rooftops high,
While schools of porpoise swirl and splash
When smaller fish swim by.

White sails begin to blossom on the bay,
Perhaps a race, perhaps a cruising day.
Thoughts of ice and sleet and snow
Will soon be gone,
When you're in Florida on a winter's morn.

H. G. Brady

REALITY

Isn't it strange, isn't it crazy,
how every day I think of you.
The image is clear, never hazy.
Whenever I have nothing to do,
time will pass and when things seem right,
and everything you think of will end up in the night.
So dream happily, my dear Janel,
for your dreams may become reality and turn out well.

Jeffrey Lasker

LORENA

Lorena is my little girl. She's the best in all the world.
She does things in her own little way
That always brightens up my day.
Blue eyes and blond hair, a freckled nose, but she doesn't care.
She lines up her dolls all in a row,
And writes on her chalkboard things they should know.
But she's not all girl. No, not at all.
Blocks, toy tractors and trucks, fishing and football,
Climb trees and go exploring, she likes to watch an eagle soaring.
But there are times she puts on a dress,
And becomes a little lady and acts her best.
A temper too, with pouted lip and jutted jaw
She stomps her foot to lay down the law.
Sometimes she's hurt and needs her daddy.
I comfort her hurts and dry her tears gladly.
She sits on my lap and we read a book.
Then a hug and a kiss, and at the clock I look.
Then off to bed to say her prayers,
God's gift to me; He didn't make an error.
Lorena is our little girl. She's the best in all the world.

Norman R. Miller

COME TO ME, FOR I LOVE YOU

When you're happy, laughing, or gay;
At the end of a long, hard day;
When you have a lot, or nothing to say;
Come to me, for I love you.

When you're fatigued, tired, or weary;
When you're troubled, sad, or teary;
When you life is full of misery;
Come to me, for I love you.

When you feel pain, sorrow, or grief;
When you have doubts in your beliefs;
When you need laughter, nourishment, relief;
Come to me, for I love you.

When you feel used, neglected, or abused;
When you've been questioned, blamed, or accused;
When you need cared for, healed, or renewed;
Come to me, for I love you.

When you are lonely, remote, or remorsed;
When you are lost, confused, or need recourse;
When you need love, encouragement, or support;
Come to Me, my Husband, for I love YOU!

Carolyn C. Blackwell

C.D.

You are real — your arms held me tight.

You weren't my imagination running wild —
    I kissed your lips last night.

You're not just a dream from which I must wake;
    We touched warm, shared laughter
    And reveled in each other's delight.

My entire being soars with thoughts of you,
    and absolute joy
        descends
        unafraid.

Sheila L. Conary-Thum

FRIENDS

There are few things more precious
    in life than a friend
One who supports you through thick and thin
Who shared with you your joys and fears
If distance was too great — a friendly call
A call that meant so much — the feeling of
    the personal touch.

Plans and hopes you shared together
Not all turned out — but in planning there was
    no doubt
Yet in their eyes you never failed
Just gave their strength for you to sail
When things hurt and seemed so hard
    to bear
Again to give you their love and care
Yes, a friend is a precious thing
For in your heart they always make
    you sing.

Peggy Coburn Mathison

SUMMER

Hurrah! The school bell has rung
Another year and summer has begun
The sound of children's laughter
The coolness of the water in the lake
after their swim. A picnic of hot dogs
    and mother's homemade cake
What a wonderful time of life
Not caring about tomorrow and its strife
Now many of the phases of life
    have come and gone
After doing all the best you could
    have done
If you were asked — which phase would
    you choose
I'd take those summers' lake water —
    and the hot sun
For it was never a contest I won.

Peggy Coburn Mathison

the single
most important
 happening in life
is the
    reaching out,
mutual exploring of space,
finding of commonalities,
accepting of differences,
    and
joining in the
    celebration of life
that can happen
again
    and
        again
in just one
    caring relationship.

Jean E. Judy

LIFE . . .

Evanescent wonder of form and matter,
You bear the guise of varied traits.
Ever changing, yet remaining,
Encapsuled in a moment.

Oft times rued, or misconstrued,
You're treasured o'er king's realms.
Squandered by the thoughtless,
There'll be no turning back.

Deep despair shall stifle those
Whose course your time has run.
Yet, like the Roc, exhumed,
New forms you'll lend.

Reach Life! Reach out!
Capt' this moment's guise.
Ever changing, yet remaining,
Encapsuled in a moment.

Elizabeth Wilmore Laird

THE ULTIMATE IGNORANCE

from Whence
do we Come?
and Whither
do we Go?

priests and prophets
purport to know.
despite Proclamations
on saints and angels,
seraphims and cherubs,
No One knows.

Earthly knowledge
remains Bounded
by Earthly knowing:
We Are Here Now.

Joan M. Schumack

IN SPIRIT, INSPIRATION

Present
in their Absence;
With us
when they're Not.

they who die
exchange physical life
for Metaphysical existence

instead of With us
they remain In us:
Our Lives, our Actions

our Predecessors
become our Intercessors
between the Here and Hereafter.

we fear Not
to go Thereafter.
in Death, as in Life;
They led the Way:
we Followed in our own Fashion.

Joan M. Schumack

REFLECTION

A search within reveals all,
The mind and soul lay bare.
Dark secrets that one can recall,
To those who boldly dare.

The pain one caused the day before,
The grief one instigated.
These things you must feel sorry for,
Repentance initiated.

Find joy in deeds you undertook,
That caused someone to smile.
Fear not when you take this look,
There's bad and good compiled.

Remember you're the only one,
Who can reconcile within.
When the search is over and done,
Truth conquers over sin.

Patrick E. Lowry

RECOLLECTION 34

I Thought Of You

I watched a movie the other night
A man and woman in love
A sad, sad ending, when it was through
I thought of you

I heard a song on the radio
About a good love gone bad
A broken-hearted lover down and blue
I thought of you

I read a newspaper ad today
Diamonds are forever, it said
What good's forever for one, not two?
I thought of you

I think about you every time
I feel downhearted and blue
Whenever things don't turn out right
I think of you

Kenneth A. Cyr

TRACES

Does a tear fall silently to
lie there glistening —
Caressing your cheek, it traces
a path downward, not yet to die.

Has it fallen on the quiet of your
mind, leaving ripples of reflections,
a newer design?

What is it you really wished to find?

Each day we dreamed a far off dream —
and yet we wait.
To hear it play its song unseen.

Donald D. Gardner

I MADE A MISTAKE

She was lovely in a red velvet dress
    At a table alone in a small country inn
I approached on an urge, an impulse, I guess
    That is when the trouble would all begin

In no time at all what I sought she gave
    I misunderstood the new feelings I now had
I gave my all — I had nothing I wanted to save
    I know now that decision was very bad

Had I taken the time to wait and see clearly
    Not hastened to run off and wed
I would not have paid what cost me dearly
    If only I had stopped and used my head

But wait — there's more to this sad story
    After raising a family with another wife
The velvet dress called up to say she was sorry
    And wanted my friendship the rest of her life

Wesley M. Alden

A SMALL BOY CRIES

A small boy lies in his crib at night,
  with fears.
This boy, full of anger and fright,
  sheds tears.

He remembers the joys and times before,
  with one.
A man, his father, who earlier adored
  his son.

''What did I do to make him want to go?
  Help me see
Why he no more cares, or loves
  Sis, Mom and me.

Why has he gone and where did he go?
  Is he alright?''
The little boy cries out, ''I love him so.
  Please bring him back tonight.''

He listens for Dad's footsteps at the door,
  and quietly sighs.
Then he shuts his eyes and his heart forevermore,
  but still he cries.

Phyllis Joan Bolen-Hofer

LOSS OF CHILDREN

No matter how many children live to adult years,
are born healthy and live to maturity, a mother
who lost a child in its infancy will feel blue at
times over the lost child.

Especially poignant is the loss of the first
marriage child. It is a great grief in a couple's
living. It is terribly meaningful at the time,
a great sadness in their lives, even if they have
subsequent children in their marriage.

If a child dies in adult life, leaving a widow and
children of its own, the parents mourn deeply, and the
loss of a parent doesn't compare with the loss of a child.

Florence K. McCarthy

WHAT'S WRONG WITH ME?

I feel different. Nothing's the same.
Where do I live? What's my name?
I once was whole, now only a part.
I am divided and sick in the heart.

Sister's gone and a new girl's here.
Will Mom leave next? She will, I fear.
Dad's moved on and I don't know where.
Someday he plans to take me there.

I do not know the new girl's name,
But Mom says soon I'll have the *same*.
Dad's new wife has my name, now.
If my name's there and I'm not, how?

When I'm with Dad I'll meet a boy.
He has my name, the name of Troy.
If I'm me now, but won't be then,
Who am I supposed to be when I'm with him?

The new man here is a man called Dad.
What do I call the one I had?
I'm no more me and nothing is real.
No one's asked me how I feel — what's wrong with me?

Phyllis Joan Bolen-Hofer

PEOPLE WITH ARTHRITIS

There is a camaraderie among arthritis sufferers.
They like to talk about their condition — osteo and rheumatoid.

The lady on the subway platform told all the world out loud
that her arthritis was in her knees, but she kept walking along.

A patient in a chiropractor's waiting room explained that she
had rheumatoid for how many years, her remissions and
    reoccurrence —
the stretching exercises which helped, and where to get the style
    of shoes that eased her state of affairs.

Acupuncture patients, at least one of them in a wheelchair, talk
about the amelioration of pain.

One wife had arthritis in every joint, but her husband stuck by her.

Some fairly agile ladies take an effective medicine and are not
    so harshly afflicted.

All of us hoping for cessation of the pain and renewed ability.
Amelioration helps for awhile, but doesn't counter the root causes.

Someone told me you don't die of arthritis — you die
    of something else.

This is hard to believe.

Florence K. McCarthy

TO TOUCH INFINITY

Let me reach out for you, to touch
not infinity, but the reality that is.
Formed ethereal, its needs caressed.

Thou art not the willow, bent by a
stronger wind,
But soft in my arms, sweet love,
possessed.
Drawn in fire, do we now awaken to
our desire?

A newer world beckons, dare you follow?
Leading now, chart our way.

A truer course reckons . . .

Donald D. Gardner

MAN'S EVE BEFORE TIME

We have our world before us, echoed
memories of distant past.
Stirred we awaken to try our new world.

Its same skies and earth are what they
always have been.

With clearer eyes, yet we have not fully
seen the wonders and beauty of scenes
that await us as you come close to me.

It sends its message to arouse latent
memories that stir in my veins.

You are now Adam's Eve, Woman alive at last.

Let our now, become our past . . .

Donald D. Gardner

HONESTY — DECEIT?

Young hearts cry;
And through their tears
They wonder why
Does no one care?
Must Honesty die
With advanced years?
Has reassurance
And understanding
Given way to too-demanding,
Deceitful Eloquence?
Has justice waned,
Giving way
To general discord?
Must tragedy, in accord,
Have the final say?
Or might good
Reign over evil —
The mightier understood,
After trials of the will —
And exist when thought none could?

Barbara Siegfried

REACH OUT . . . WITH LOVE

Words have been spoken, promises broken;
    Families cry.
When anger reigns, no one gains;
    Families die.

God, touch our hearts and our minds
    To help us
Forgive and excuse and accept
    And to love.

Help us forget and help us to grow;
    Oh, God above,
Help us step forward and reach out
    With love!

Erma I. Sentz-Bentz

ALONE

Alone
    With friends
Alone
    With you
Alone.

    My thoughts,
    My desires,
    My dreams . . .
Alone.

    Be with me, beside me,
    Within me, a part of me,
    Together, as one.
    Don't let me be
Alone.

    Is it possible to be
    A part of you and not be
Alone?

    Can I ever overcome being
Alone?
    God, help me!

Erma I. Sentz-Bentz

GOODBYE

The time has come to say goodbye.
We are both going our separate ways now.
The moments shared were so happy
They seemed like they would never end
But in reality they were the quickest times.
Soon there will be many miles between us,
Each of us going our separate ways
With only memories of the happy times
That have been shared and cherished.
Miles cannot put an end to those memories
But only make them stronger
And a lot more cherishable for both of us.
You will always be in my heart and mind
From the day I met you.
I'll never forget that smile on your face
From the happiness we both shared.
Always keep that smile glowing
And most of all remember
That many more good times are
To be had for you and me.

Tom Trail

LIFE IS A MYSTERY

Life is, indeed, a mystery.
It confounds us with its inexplicables.
It does not yield to logic.
It follows a twisted path
That brings us back where we began.

Like all good mysteries,
It throws out subtle hints
At properly appointed intervals.

But in due time,
If we continue to read on,
The Author will draw together
All the tangled threads
Into one all-encompassing denouement!

Virginia E. Cruikshank

TIME

    I thought that I loved you, and that
you loved me too. But the only problem
was, we never gave each other a
chance.

    Now that I've let you go, I don't
know where to turn. Even though
I try to deny it, the feelings are
still the same. Sometimes, I even
blame you, but now I realize that
all the pain was caused by me.
    If I could have anything in the
world, it would be you; because
baby, you are the world to me.
I know I can't change things
I did in the past, but I can
promise you that it will never
happen again. I love you so much,
I just wish that you felt the same.

Sandy Pascoe

THE MOMENT

Everything going well
Something came soon
One thing is different
A whole new way of being
In the moment of time
Something just left
My heart sings with joy
Love is felt very well

The twinkling of stars
In whatever you are thinking
That moment with you
Faith for everyone
A joy from outside
Peace now within me
Truth must be revealed
Everyone doing very well

Bryant Parker

LARGE CORPORATIONS AND THEIR EMPLOYEES IN FLUX

Boards of directors or trustees in their decisions and
plans have a major impact on the lives of employees.

External auditors' suggestions or requirements may involve
the relocations of the worksites and the selling of homes.

Employees have to adjust when a division changes its business
interest from one kind of manufacture of products to another.

When there is a change of ownership, relatives and friends of
the new owners come in and replace past employees.

When there is just a change of management, the old staff goes
out and new people come in at lower salaries.

Budget planning and budget submission times of year greatly
endanger the personnel since every expense is cut to the bone.

Job promotion races within a corporation are another flux time
of year — there is grim competition between candidates.

While working in one job, learn something new, lest you have to
be relocated or lose out in your position and must seek new work.

Florence K. McCarthy

MOTHERS

How many times throughout the year,
And especially on this day, do
People, known as children,
Praise the one who made their way to
Yet another beautiful day,
More enticing than those before,
Or healed their wounds, corrected wrongs,
Then loved them even more?
Her hair shows signs of silvering,
Each strand for childhood pranks.
Right now is when each child should give a
Special prayer of thanks.
Dear God of all, we thank you,
And ask for only this,
Your blessings on all mothers dear?
Maybe give each mom a kiss?
Obligations elsewhere keep us from showing now,
More than anyone we've ever known,
     to *Love — she taught us how!*

Mad Poet

BREAKDOWN

Upon indifferent winds the great hawk flies;
High into jagged peaks the warm gusts take him;
Beyond the Earth he floats in complete euphoria.

Then,
He hears the mockingbird trill,
Feels the wind chill . . .

Falling back to Earth
Where the jagged peaks lie
He feels the winds careening him around,
He no longer has any sense of sight or sound.

Matt Zuck

THE DANCER

Dancers are swift and svelte of body,
Alert and smooth with every move;
Readily savoring each bright moment;
Radiating to all their love.
Every movement has its meaning,
Not a one without its cause;
Movements showing artistes' feelings,
All designed to draw applause.
The dancers glide on airy cushions;
They're carried quickly 'cross the floor;
Happiness shines on sweat-lined faces;
Each performance, they give more!
Work is not a word acknowledged;
Great passion hath no man;
Rather to dance than anything other,
Armed with talents, they know they can!
Health and beauty reward their patience,
As they practice, day on day;
Maybe, if they strive unswerving,
     Their name will shine on ''Old'' Broadway!

Mad Poet

REALIZATION

There suddenly comes a time to each
When life has one lesson more to teach —
On how to face the unknown way
That lies ahead and starts this day.

Our play has ended, down comes the curtain;
All seems dark, vague, uncertain —
Except for one tiny glimmer of light,
One spark of hope through the gloom of night —
A glimpse of a worthwhile way of living
That still can be bright with doing and giving.

Do you feel alone, useless and through?
But the world is so full of what's needed to do:
Just look about you, discover the truth,
Unnoticed by others too busy with youth.

There are children in want of love and care,
And the friendless who long for a friendship to share,
For a helping hand and a loving heart
Can save a life that is falling apart:
And the joy you give is the joy you get
For an old age blest with no regret.

Diana Hunt Westa

THE OCEAN

I close my eyes and listen to the ocean call my name.
Submerging my body in its clear blue warmth,
I am carried away to a new world.
Sounds are altered; I hear only what the ocean permits.
My body moves within its parameters.
I obey its laws.
And I trust in its benevolence to see me safe.
For as part of its body I am not alone but part of a whole.
In this I take comfort.
I close my eyes and listen to the ocean call my name.

Madelene R. Grimm

DISTANT FIRE

Feeling the distance between us
Only seems to intensify the vows
I made to you
On that wondrous winter morn.
Others wonder how I manage to
Keep the homefires burning.
But they can't know how warm
Every little spark from that fire
Makes me feel.
Every little thought of you
Feeds the fire
And the flames dance and
Keep me happy;
Making the distance shrink —
In my thoughts anyway.

Michele R. Markowski

BLESSED

But for God's ineffable grace,
I might have perished eons ago
at Sodom or Gomorrah
or later at Hiroshima,
or lately at Chernobyl,
under a tumbling crane
or in a flaming plane,
but instead . . .

Here go I,
singing praises to Him
who has blessed me
as I move
within this earthly sphere —
enriched by four lives
to prove
that indeed

I did pass here!

Dorothy Hyde Starzyk

FAITH

All things being equal,
Though most times they're not,
Belief is an exercise
Mainly of the heart.
Whereas knowledge, we find
Is an exercise of the mind.
Faith comes before knowledge
You'll never get it at college.
It comes from the heart,
With a willingness to start.
The Spirit takes over,
With his enlightening rod,
Faith is a gift given
Only by God.
I wonder why some have it,
And others don't feel,
Could it be their pride
Forbids them to kneel.

Katherine Bieluck

PRETENSES

There are times when people
More pretentious than serving,
Offer advice to those
They consider deserving.
It's best not to argue
They may carry clout,
Just think to yourself
        We love you,
But know what you're about.

Other times when people claim
They possess much more
Than they can name.
Their insecurity is showing,
While you're richer for knowing.
They're rather poor,
But possess a big mouth,
Just think to yourself,
        We love you,
But know what you're about.

Katherine Bieluck

ETERNAL LOVE

For my husband, Jim

People have said you can't live on love,
But I could prove them wrong;
That's the way it's been for us
For so very, very long.

Many a dream has been shattered
As it crashed around our feet,
But we pulled ourselves together
For our love won't stand defeat.

The two of us share a special bond,
We're each other's very best friend;
Our love has withered many a storm,
It's too strong to ever end.

Sondra Middleton

THE PAST

We had something special,
it seemed not to last . . .
  I turned around,
a dark shadow cast.
  I seem to remember,
the times we have shared . . .
  The times that we've loved,
the times that we've cared.
  Years go by,
I know things change . . .
  But, for me,
it's too strange.
  Why is it,
we fall apart . . .
  Where we end,
is where we start?

Michelle Rosenthal

DON'T DESPAIR

For my husband, Jim

I woke up this morning
Full of despair,
I looked in the mirror,
Another gray hair.

Life has its ups and downs,
I've never been a winner,
Nothing ever turns out right
Not even when I make dinner.

I haven't the time to weep
When I stub my toe and holler,
I have to hurry off to work
To make another dollar.

The foreman is mad
When I take my place on the line,
He says tomorrow's my last day
If I don't punch in on time.

So I guess I'll change my attitude,
Instead of despair, I'll try hope,
And if things don't brighten up soon,
I'll be at the end of my rope.

Sondra Middleton

TIME

The world is changing all the time
leaving me without a dime

I don't see how that I can last
because the world is changing fast.

Paula Carmichael

DESERT FLIGHT

Over the desert I sail,
My silent wings
Of metal and cloth
Outstretched and drumming,
Extensions of my dreams,
Riding up
On these elevators of heat
To the future.
She has grudgingly let me go,
This earth that brought
Me to this higher realm
Of surreality,
But, finally breaking the chains
Of my earthbound existence,
She has given me a boost,
A kick in the seat of the pants,
To propel me upward
To a new height of life
On sun-streaked wings
And infinite horizons.

David C. Hughes

LISTEN TO YOUR HEART

Champagne lunches on a mountainside,
Candlelit bodies casting rhythmic shadows,
Thoughts of days gone by,
Make it hard to accept days of late.
Memories are such sweet torment.

Remembering the first time, savoring the last,
Apart once again, uncertain of the next.
Times like these make it so very hard,
To be satisfied with our lives,
So trust your feelings, and listen to your heart.

Now; different lives, with the same undaunted love.
Despite this confusing slice of our lives,
Knowing each other the way that we do,
Gives me great confidence,
That we'll see this thing through.

In this world of intricate realities,
I escape to our living fantasy,
Armed with hopes and memories,
Thoughts of past, present and future,
Center on days alone with just you.

Mike Parker

WIFE'S WOES

I sat down to coffee and what do you think?
My ailing husband wanted a drink.
Moments later with hands in dishpan
He called, "Would you please make me some toast and some jam?"
I sat down to lunch and as never fail
He called, "Would you please go get the mail?"
I thought he was asleep mid-afternoon
When all of a sudden his voice filled the room.
"I'd like some hot tea and a magazine to look at."
This done I sat down with a neighbor to chat.
An hour later I was sent to retrieve the newspaper
He enters the living room looking quite dapper.
He's settled for an hour or so I thought.
I should have know better, I ought.
He needed his slippers, a blanket and heating pad.
I needed some relief from the day that I'd had.

Doris Brubaker Walter

MY WONDERFUL DREAM!

Many years have passed, since I had this wonderful dream.
I saw the Virgin Mary standing there,
  with her hand reaching out to me.
Although I wanted to, I did not take her hand,
I did not know the reason, I did not understand.
As time went by life dealt me a tragic blow.
I then remembered my dream of the Virgin Mary
And my faith in her son, Jesus Christ, helped me so.
There were times when I was sad and thought much more
I could not bear.
A sign of her presence I found one day,
As I walked past a church down the street
And a shiny medal in her image touched me feet.
Another day as I walked my dog, the street was wet with rain,
A piece of paper caught my eye, it was like a message straight
From the sky for it held the poem 'Footprints,'
Written clear, and I knew in my heart that her holy
Presence once again was near — To heal my pain.
Believing is our strength, for when Jesus died, have gave to us all
A piece of His cross to bear — To remind us to have faith and
Put our troubles in His care.

Ursel Blanco

THE EASTER DAISY

From a mere stem with withering leaves,
What burst forth into bloom a few months later?
First a tiny bud, and then a flower!
But not just a day, nor just a flower!
A precious Easter gift! It was a wonder!
Upon awakening that Easter Dawn,
What did I see?
A beautiful white daisy in full bloom!
So sturdy and pristine white!
In a wink, when light shines out of darkness,
There it stood in majestic beauty!
It was like a dream, but yet true!
A dream that will forever be for mortal man, "A light!"
"The Glory of Easter!"

Mary A. Briganti

LIVE WHILE YOU CAN

Live while you can, life doesn't last long,
Enjoy every prayer, sing every song,
See the beauty in birds, and flowers and trees,
See the beauty in rainbows, and a cool summer breeze.

Laugh at the raindrops, dance in the wind,
For life will be over too soon, my friend.
Dwell not on sorrow, and sadness, and grief,
For life goes as quickly as dew on a leaf.

See the joy in the faces of children at play,
Rejoice in the sunset and the dawn of each day.
Live for the love of your family or friend,
For love is what really counts in the end.

Frances Lewis

DEWDROPS AND MOONBEAMS

The fairies danced in a ring last night
Beneath the cold, white moon
As it scattered diamond chips along its path
In a small lagoon. And the fairies,
Gath'ring the diamonds up along the moon-path there,
Made radiant tiaras to crown their silken hair.

The silver bells on their tiny shoes
Awakened the woodland elves
Who came to see the lovely sight
Sitting on toadstools through the night,
Sipping nectar from a flower-cup
'Til the moon went down and the sun came up.

When the sun found the fairies dancing there
With diamonds shining in their hair,
They hid behind a grassy mound
The diamonds scattering on the ground
Forming dewdrops where they lay —
And the sun shone down on a fresh, new day.

And now you know, my little friend,
Where the dewdrops start and the moonbeams end.

Verna Lindberg Kelm

Slow down,
Allow me to grow
with you.
Do not grow behind
me
or grow ahead of me.
Let us learn love
together,
Let us be each other's
sunshine —
Able to shine on even
the cloudiest days!
Share with me the
softness of your touch
and the brightness of
your smile,
And I will share with
you love and joy.

Annette Burek Holstad

NO MIRACLES

Little boy Brian, you trusting child
You thought we'd make you well.
We did our best, tried every trick
Yet miserably we failed.

Those soft blue eyes will ever haunt.
In our minds you will remain
That perfect boy with ready smile
Though tumor eats your brain.

We're helpless, angry and forlorn.
We ask, ''Can it be so?''
This handsome boy who hugs his toy
Has not a chance to grow?

We face the facts, review the stats
Shake our heads in true remorse.
We can't do much to help you, child.
Your disease must run its course.

Jeanne Stelmak

ONE OF GOD'S MIRACLES

God pulled the curtain of night aside
Stretched the blue of Mary's robe
    Across the sky.
Borrowed snow from mountain tops —
Huge whipped cream puffs of virgin white
    To beautify His domain.
Chose the most beautiful star
To shine as the sun on high.
Gently aroused the sleeping birds
Who loudly sang a hymn of praise
    To serenade the dawn.
Then — flowers awakened
Turning dewy faces Heavenward
    Where God smiled on all.
Thus — He gave His children another miracle
    The gift of a new day.

Dorothy McGaughran

ELUSIVE LOVE

Love on a butterfly's wing
Perched on fragile memories.
Floating freely in the wind
Lighthearted kiss —
    Touching heart strings
    Quivering in delight.
Tender feelings exposed
    Poignantly vulnerable,
Caught in a complex web
    Of human emotions.
Quiet murmurings at dawn
  Confess secrets of the soul,
Gentle desirings stir
    Inner rhythms.
Thoughtful gestures ease
    Daily discords as
Elusive dreams lure innocent
  Lovers to loftier summits.
Rose-colored vows expressed
  In a forever frame . . .

Marilee Clack

MOTHER

My lost mother
Was calling
I hear the voice
But do nothing
She is of distance
    shape
For she left no
    memories
  Only this old
snapshot
  which is now
    faded

D. W. Schmitt

DEPRAVED

Like a jaguar
In pursuit of perfection
Appearances are not deceptive
Of the revolution
And the new generation
It's tough on the streets
Unquiet in the Western Isles
Dramatic scenes are black
Creating shields against the sun
Dreams, a giant leap forward
A room of one's own
That's all that's needed
But it is beyond reach
There's only one word translated
Depraved

D. W. Schmitt

I'M SORRY

Unrecognized plea for help

I heard not my friend
When voice quietly revealed
Words I did not believe;
Through darkness he appealed.

So young and vital,
No way did I suspect
The message transmitted
Was desperation to reflect.

He spoke of terminating
Overwhelming strife.
Surely, the words jested,
Not meaning to end life.

Truly, I failed a friend.
Was it youth not to believe?
Where was my sensitivity
The plea not to perceive?

If I had been alert
To the message he did portray,
A vital young life . . . my friend,
Would be alive with me today . . . I'm sorry!

Beverly Morrissey

FOR YOU EMILY D

When night has come and friends can't see
I slip away from shore
With crow's nest higher than the sky
I set a course no charts describe
Provisioned recklessly

My bearings from a shooting star
My hands locked on the wheel
Ship's log is all I recognize
Its moist salt sheets reveal
The time elapsed, the distance passed
The sightings, storms and calms
As mist and chill around me rise
I enter time to come

If men could venture forth in days
When sea and earth were flat
Set sail their fate on wind and wave
Their faith on cloud and craft
Shall I landlubber be?

Myrna Treston

GOD'S MIGHT

The quiet silence of the night,
The breathless gaze of such a sight,
The spacious sky with stars so bright,
Reveal God's plan, power and might.

Gunhild Vetter

PEACE, MY CHILD

My Lord, my Lord
    Where have you gone?
Why has the blueness of your sky
    Turned to shadow-gray?

The sunshine that once so warmed my heart
    No longer lifts my tired soul
And the moon and the stars that sang and danced
    In the evening sky
No longer bring me dreams of tomorrow.

Send me, oh Lord, your soft summer breeze
    That I might hear your voice again
And whisper to me your words of long ago that say

"Peace, my child, my little one, my friend
    For I have always loved you, and I will love you forever.
Know now that I will never leave you nor forsake you.

"Rest, and let me take the weariness
    From your heavy heart
For in my hands lie all your todays
    And all my promises for every tomorrow."

Vivian L. Hayward

MY FIRST BOOK

To write is to read is to start and to look.
To be five is to get gifts, perhaps a book.
To have a mother to choose the story of God and man.

For adventure is there beyond wildest dreams,
For Cain and Abel, for David, and Lion's Den too,
For Joseph and Mary and King of the Jew.

It tells of the lives, loves, struggles and wars.
It tells of the Arabs, Semites and Indo's afar.
It tells of a cradle where mankind did start.
It tells how each race developed its part.

Now my book still rests in a privileged spot.
Now and again I take it down, reread it a lot.
Now though it seems in my mind to have grown,
Now the story is greater than any I've known.

And "Past is Prologue" as the great poet said
And all led to a Cross and the Vision of Paul
And a great Citadel now fixed in my mind
And a Mother so wise and so kind.

Arthur Worley

PLENTIFUL RIDE

You have to change something as you look at yourself.
Glazed eyes a crooked smile, then you hear the
sound you're on your way down.
It's a plentiful ride, as you wander through life.
Diversed far into its ends showing infinity within.
All possibilities ending in sleep.
I've come to think there's no escape.
There is no perfect being on this earth.

Albert F. Carol III

PEGASUS

Granddad made tooled leather saddles, harnesses and things,
quite fit for Tom Mix or Hoot Gibson, the great movie kings.
Then along came Henry Ford with his jitney so fine
leaving Grandpop a cobbler with leather still his line.

In his little shop where heels and soles he did mend
stood a harness maker's horse now idled by this trend.
Then along I came maybe nine years maybe ten
soon as snug in the saddle as an old settin' hen.

A fine rider I soon became sharing trails and fame
with Alexander the Great astride Pegasus, his name.
Across the steppes of Russia with Marco Polo I did ride
and to the Crusades with Richard the Lion-Hearted fast by my side.

He's out to pasture now, this noble mount of mine
standing in a place of honor for all of my time,
to remind me of Granddad and all that he meant
and the young days of innocence that were Heaven sent.

Arthur Worley

PASSING TIMES

Once at the Oklahoma City Times
Mr. Gaylord and I were partners you see,
I at Third and Broadway come rain or shine
while at Fourth as Chief of Editors was he
with pen to shape the great Sooner State.

After my classes at Lowell Grammar School
I hurried down to take up my post,
outside the Western Union as a rule
or across at Ma Bell which I liked most,
the night shift would buy twenty papers or more.

It was quite a simple business arrangement.
I sold the Times, three whole cents, half was his.
And, by the end of each week my profits went
for a shoot 'em up movie — they were a whiz,
and for my little brother — and popcorn too.

And so it was sad to roll back the time
on a visit to that land once so innocent
to find not a trace of my beloved Times.
For into the Daily Oklahoman it went,
done in by the hungry picture tube.

Arthur Worley

YOUR SONG

I heard your song today.
How few notes you need to utter to set my heart on fire.
No matter how sad the tune,
It comforts my forsaken soul.
Were you here I could enfold you in empty aching arms.
You could find comfort upon my breast.
We would stand as equals against the storm.
Perhaps, at some point, we shall sing together,
The lyrics no longer to draw the tears to cheeks.
We shall stand and sing a new song of life.
We shall sing the song of love.

Madelene R. Grimm

They say the world is round, and yet
I often think it square —
So many little hurts we get
From corners here and there.

But there's one truth in life I've found
While journeying east and west:
The only folks we really wound
Are those we love the best.

We flatter those we scarcely know,
We please the fleeting guest,
And deal full many a thoughtless blow
To those we love the best.

Homer Spence White

HOW LUCKY I AM

You make me feel
like a king.
Thank you, my dear;
thanks for your time,
and thanks for your tears.

I had no ways;
I had no hopes.
Now, I have your smile,
and today
the whole world is mine.

With your head
on my shoulder,
and your hands
in my hands;
my love, how wonderful
life is
and how luck am I!

Antonio A. Acosta

THE WAVES OF YOUR SEA

I am jealous of the air
that touches your face
and your hair.

I would like
to run against the wind,
to feel your perfume
in my fingers
and your smile in my dreams.

From the distance to be
the guardian of your eyes,
and the waves of your sea.

On my way the birds cry
and I say to them:
She is coming to stay;
don't cry, don't cry! . . .
And one day you will see,
the spring forever . . .

Antonio A. Acosta

MY WAY TO BE FREE

Something happens in my heart
when you are close to me.
'Tis like a dream
that makes me so happy,
seeing your clear body
dancing in my hands.

Being a dreamer,
all my wishes come true
in my world of make-believe,
made for my dreams and you.

Come with me
to live in my real fantasy,
to share together
your desires and mine,
because loving you
is the only way to be free.

Antonio A. Acosta

BORED

A desk and chair and paper
Music to my right
Two pencils become drumsticks
My wrists have taken flight

Katherine Allen

FINER THINGS

Star Trek
books
movies
long walks
birthdays
food and drink
music
cats
newspapers
thunderstorms
warm winds
sunshine on the water
fiery sunsets
a full moon
small children
babies
weddings
the smell of freshly mown grass

The finer things in life
Happily, some are affordable

Katherine Allen

LINES FOR A FRIEND

The game we played was fun while it lasted;
I wasn't fooled by your laughing lies.
But I can't put your face out of my mind —
I'm haunted by your blue hungry eyes.

Now, I don't want you for my lover;
The man I married loves me all I need.
But there are times, I won't deny it,
When I need you to be my friend.

If I asked you to be my lover
We'd be consumed in the flames that die.
I can't live with the taste of ashes
Or the cold, hurt look in my man's eyes.

What I'm asking you is hard to do.
I don't need just another lover.
It takes a stronger love to be a real friend
Because real friendship lasts forever.

Judith Atkins Zumwalt

MY LONG FORGOTTEN SMILE

I wonder if you still recall
my long forgotten smile;
or if at times you still recall
the dreams beyond us now?

Can time unwind the memory
and help this love to fade;
or will it live on forever
to haunt the plans I've made?

I loved you like no other love
but still you left my side;
I never saw the hidden love
your smile could so well hide.

He really must be everything;
I couldn't touch you now;
Still I wonder if you recall
my long forgotten smile?

C. Mykel Henderly

LEAVING

This room —
so newly cleaned and cared for —
it's a comfortable place —
a place to come home to.
It takes work to keep it
in order, but it feels good.
I can stay in this room,
but for one problem —
there's little space to grow
within these firm walls,
little room to live —
really *live!*
So I must leave and
gain experience, wisdom, love —
to become me.
This place
will not hold me in!

Angel Hoffman

WE ARE SPIRIT

We are spirit.
In a temple, made without hands.
Today it exists as a vision,
    a piece of land as a white page.
    We are a manifestation of all life.
Pillars thought to be physical, are in reality Spiritual.
    Today it exists as a vision,
        let priorities be unto eternity.
    We live in a New Jerusalem.
    Perfection is a quality of heart,
    which man is endowed, in his creation.
Today it exists as a vision.
But you see only . . . the Tower of Babel!
    We are the New Jerusalem,
    sweet children of the Light.
Today it exists as a vision.
But your vision has been invaded by demons.
    You project a melancholy life.
    But . . . We are Spirit.
    A temple, made without hands.

Kurt Kelly

BEFORE I MET YOU

I thought I knew what freedom was   in the days before I met you.
A captive of the world around;   loved by one I never knew.
An endless search for happiness   in everything I do.
Destined only but to failure,   in the days before I met you.
I am yours, and you are mine,   Oh Lamb of God, my Lord divine.

You've paid the price of freedom,   a freedom through and through.
You've filled the void that haunts me,   there's no purpose without you.
My precious Lord and savior,   the Jesus I never knew,
if only I'd know you loved me   in the days before I met you.

Just a name in history,   a cold name of the past.
The blind has found his vision,   my savior, first and last.
Life really is worth living;   but if I only knew
those many years were wasted,   in the days before I met you.

Lord, I'm glad you love me;   let me glorify your name.
Your will is now my goal;   yours and mine the same.
Lord I know you love me;   Lord, I love you, too.
Hate has gone and love abounds,   since the days before I met you.
I am yours, and you are mine,   Oh Lamb of God, my Lord divine . . .

Dirk Lemkuil

HEAVENLY THOUGHTS

I would like to be led, by *God's* trusting hand,
Into the reality of fantasy land,
With my body freed, and my soul to live, as an eternal seed,
To be as the immortal tree, to breathe and flower endlessly,
To feel secure, atop a mountain peak,
With the restless wind, its wailing language to speak,
To ride the ocean waves, through the tide of time,
My soul as the sun, ever bright to shine,
To drench my being, in the purity of rain,
To spread the sweet scent, of morning dew, upon all fields of grain.

Irma Schwartz

A BUTTERFLY

Oh butterfly, of sun and shower,
A whisper of springtime, a breathing flower, of crimson hue,
    and sapphire blue,
With wings the texture, of a velvet sky,
Composing a symphony, as you fly,
You are a beauteous silence, in the season's breeze,
The perennial leaf, in winter's freeze,
You are a portrait, of heaven's way,
To stir in my soul, a sonata at play,
But, as you flutter about, with aesthetic grace,
You are quite unaware, of the elements you face,
For too quickly, the season's wrath, will toss you sadly,
    in its path,
The strength of the wind, will blow and harass, the blazing sun,
And you will vanish, still, to return as the perpetual one,
When the air is warm, and the fragrance is haunting,
    with every blossom reborn,
To repeat your performance, atop a flower in bloom,
Still, 'tis ever painful, to see the curtain fall, and an echo loom.

Irma Schwartz

THE BLAZING SUN

Oh sun of fire, you are sublime,
You are the golden touch of time,
You are the bliss of every breath,
You are sweet life, versus death,
How fierce can be your burn,
But, your gentle touch, is sure and firm,
You force your way, through cloud and haze,
To grow a flower, worthy of praise,
You shimmer and dance, upon the river's bed,
And when our souls, you've stirred and fed,
And the birds, to sweetest song you've led,
You add a twilight hue to earth,
To a flaming sunset, you so gracefully give birth,
With prismatic color, affectionately at play,
Cradling you in a most dramatic way,
Inviting a sky of velvety blue,
With a million stars, watching over you,
And while you sleep, we pray that you'll rise,
    for every tomorrow,
To dissolve all pain, life's vexing chill, your warmth to gain.

Irma Schwartz

A NEW START

I watched the embers slowly die. It was like watching my heart,
which I begged not to cry. For life is an ever-changing deal,
not impressed, or swayed by how deeply we feel.
We can talk to our friends, and they'll understand;
having been dealt a similar hand. For all the support it is still
not enough — for it is alone with ourself
    when it really gets rough.
We think we'll never make it through; that our sky will never again
turn blue — how can I possibly live without you?
Day passes day, and we drag ourself on,
an existence our guilt and fears prolong.
Then one day a break-through comes and we're surprised
one morning by the sound of our hum.
Our heart has caught a new tune, our lips a new smile.
For the first time in months we feel worthwhile.
We're now on our way; the mourning is over.
It's like suddenly finding your first four-leaf clover.
You have taken your heart, although it is scarred,
and you're finally glad to have a new start.

Dorothy Driscoll

A LIFE ABLOOM

Silent now, the whisperin' wind
Calls out my name; I listen in.
It tells me so, a life abloom
Who deep inside me stirs for room.
That life will find a time and place
In this world of crime and disgrace
For but one more to live and grow;
This tiny creature here below.

Cynthia R. Herrera

FEATHERS IN THE WIND

Lovers come and lovers go
Like feathers in the wind
We hardly see the other's heart
    We never do begin
To pass each other in the night
    Seems like such a crime
To never know the heart or soul
    Just borrow of our time
The meetings met, we play the game
But I know the end will be the same
We'll touch . . . and then they'll blow away
    Like feathers in the wind
The life of a rose from birth to death
Or spring birds' first sweet chirping song
How thrilled I'd be, if just to know
That just one love could last that long
Because of reasons yet unknown
I live this life's great sin
That all who come will surely go
. . . Like feathers in the wind.

Alan H. Kahn

THE ANGEL OF THE WAVES

Look out just beyond the boat
    into the sun's warm rays
squinting all, they see her now
    The angel of the waves.
She wears a suit of colored silk
    two pieces soft and thin
They do their work, but cannot hide
    the muscled beauty held therein.
She stands upon a stick of wood
    no wings can people see
And glides upon the water's edge
    so free and naturally.
She rides the weaves, glides here and there
    and flies around them all
Her spray sends rainbows everywhere
    and never does she fall.
She rides with textured poise and grace
    like sunsets in the west
Many come and many go
    but this angel's the best.
When God held beauty in his eyes
    and cast it in a glaze
and touched her with his heart to make
    the Angel of the Waves.

Alan H. Kahn

SAINT JUDE RADIOLOGIST

She goes to help the kids at work
Take pictures of their health
She loves them all, her treasured few
Who give her life its wealth.

To fit as much into a day
As possibly can be done
To light their eyes a moment more
And help them have some fun.

To her special few, this life's a race
Each hour could be a year
Their time's so short, they'll soon be gone
Yet they seldom cry, or shed a tear.

She sees her world through dying eyes
Of stricken children at their best
Believing still that God is good
And feels inside she's surely blessed
as them

Alan H. Kahn

A CHILD

Oh, how sweet the face of a babe lying in sleep,
Explicit innocence waiting there to reap.
What delightful dreams go thru that head,
The babe fulfills getting out of bed.

What's delightful to us may be boring to him.
The adventure in a child must be fed.
So fill his life with stimulating enticement.
Provide, love, security and parental guidance.

Innocence will pass away.
Dreams will never — they're here to stay.
The child develops, grows to a man.
Child and parent walk hand in hand.

Sandra J. Estabrook

AARON

Congratulations and best wishes to thee
Because you've done so much we see.
Because we're your loving family,
We hope you achieve what you want to be.

An E.M.I.C.T. you are;
We're very proud you've come so far.
And now receiving the Fire Science Degree,
A very proud person you should be.

An excellent husband and father you've been,
Need we say how proud we are again.
For all the hard work you've done
Now maybe you can have some fun!

Sandra J. Estabrook

LOOKING THROUGH TIME

Looking through time
at the day I'm about to live,
    The end to death
is as far as the sky above.
    I know that it is there,
    But when does it end?
    Journey through my eyes
to what I have seen,
    See my feelings,
    Live my life,
    And die,
as lonely as I.

Darrel-Jay Tedeschi

STANDING HERE

Standing here trembling like a dying leaf
Leaf falling from its tree
Tree that has grown old with time
Time that passes by so fast
Fast like it never stopped
Stopped to take a deep breath and enjoy life
Life to some worth a lot
Lots of years, lots of tears
Tears that fall like raindrops
Drops so small yet holding a lot of meaning
Meaning to the ancient heart
Heart that silent aches for the world
World so full of people yet so alone
Alone like an island out on its own
Own little world without a friend.

Angie Lepez

So now the dawn and what to do
Just lie there crying, asking who
Will help you walk the beach of life
Until you're safely out of strife.

So now the night, but you're still there
Sitting in your lonely chair
Instead of picking up the phone
To find that you're not all alone

So now the dawn and you awake
Now think about your grand mistake
Expecting help from others who
Are frightened of the waters too

So now the night and you're aware
Another dawn is drawing nearer
Since no one came or called before
It's up to you to brave the shore

So now the dawn and you get up
Toss away that empty cup
Start to tread the shifting sand
And I'll be there to lend a hand

Anne Roberts Calamease

FETUS

Two life-forces meet, the amphimixis of gyne-andros.
As they merge a soul is gathered in,
And in a sequence that is an awesome mystery I evolve, cell upon cell.

I am simultaneously multiplicity and oneness, limbs, brain, organs,
And among these a tiny heart whose beat
   is a rapid counterpoint to her great one.
No longer inchoate, but ordered, I have become . . . an embryo.

Floating in a warm amniotic ocean, a cosmos that is mine alone,
I feel my procreator's will, her emotions,
   and sense her joy that I am the same as she.
Close around me I hear/feel the pulsing blood-cadence,
The lifesong that flows singing along the cord that joins us;
And I move in response, touching, pressing the living walls
   of my primal cradle.

Through this nine-phased journey I progress until
   by some power incomprehensible
The breathless struggle begins;
   a moving, striving downward, forward, outward.
Then with one last rending burst of strength,
I enter through the birth-gate into a new universe of light,
   sight and sound.

I am born! It is the world . . . what now awaits me?
   Laughter? Tears? Pain? Sorrow? Joy?
And from a deep unknown source the answer comes,
Wordless yet understood: *Everything.*

Maria A. Yemariamferé (Philogyne)

JET

She stands sleekly beautiful, waiting.
The light that falls on her cockpit has the soft gleam
   of a warm glance.
I step up, enter and touch the controls, rousing her to alertness.
She encloses, embraces me. We become . . . symbiotic.

The throaty, purring thunder of her engines speaks her anticipation
   of the heights.
And I, with my heart thundering in unison, respond to her eager wish
   and set us in motion.
We move smoothly forward. Fast, faster, powerful, sure.

Sighting the horizon we lift majestically, the envy of eagles.
Then with a whistling roar we climb and the ground recedes.
Beneath us the panorama of land and water revolves
   as we rise in an ascending spiral.

Upward we dance in airy leaps and swing into long, graceful glides.
Rolling wing over wing, we swerve and float downward
   in wide-sweeping arcs of pure joy.
Again we rise aloft, cleaving the air swifter than sound,
   then dart away and beyond,
Leaving in our wake the awesome boom of colliding atmosphere.

Breaching the undulant surface of a sea of pearl-white clouds,
   we soar into vast, blue reaches of space.
Here in this high/deep rapture, this mystic silence, we commune.
Our dyad of soul and steel merges into oneness with the sky.
We are home!

Maria A. Yemariamferé (Philogyne)

RE-ENACTMENT

Pro-traditionally, she sat there remembering him —
Then — going through each ritual of orthodoxy
In observance of a lifetime of depth-communication
Which never could be lost,
Without regrets, she walked the lonely beachhead —
Dipped each toe and hand,
Joyously bowing to unfolding beauty,
Untiring boundless wealth in
Rite of consciousness that slowly
Unjoined each lovely memory from
Recovered reality.

Louise Behar

NIGHT TRAIN WEST

The radiance lowered in western skies;
The glory of evening eased from sight;
Darkness closed 'round as a heavy curtain
And another world seemed to beckon.

The train roared on through the ebon night,
No moon shone to cast a revealing light;
The eerie expanse spread far and wide,
Only shadows appeared to the wandering eye.

A grove of trees formed a huge gray wall,
From diamond-studded space, I saw a star fall;
Each sudden change instilled fascination
As I indulged my powers of imagination.

The towns passed through were as stepping stones
Which diminished the miles as we sped along.
My eyelids grew heavy, but thoughts lingered on
Until the magic of night bowed to dawn.

As morning light invaded the scene,
Travelers arose from their restless sleep;
I wondered as each waited the call of his station,
Would there be sorrow or joy at his destination.

Evelyn C. Reece

CLASS REUNION

It is hard to believe as we meet once again,
How the years have passed, since as seniors we reigned;
Tonight, we are young though our hair may be gray
And our hearts are tuned to youth's frivolous ways.
We gather to ponder over days gone before,
To recall what has happened since the year '34.
Through the years that ensued, we've seen trouble and strife
Mingled with joy and the good things of life.
To the East, to the West, across this great land,
We scattered to fulfill life's constant demands.
We had all set our hopes on winning life's game
But fate deemed some follow the lower plain
While others would rise to fortune and fame,
Then death claims its share from the roster of names.
As the years swiftly vanished with our daily routines,
Many happenings were dimmed by more urgent needs,
But tonight we add to memories long retained
With hopes that we'll meet together again.

Evelyn C. Reece

SAILORS REVELATION

I felt the shaking of the earth,
    as I drifted on the sea;
winds whirling on and past the sails,
    speaking — only to me.

I heard an explosion of the sun,
    as it burst into my soul;
calmness moving in and through,
    heeding me to grow.

I saw the open miles,
    of liquid flowing earth;
and endless stream of all that is,
    life, death and birth.

Now my senses waken,
    to all the powers that be;
untouched by those who wish to lead,
    natural, wild and free.

L. D'Cenzo

CINDY

Her in her pink.
With transparent lace underneath.

What others would give.
What I would give.
For just one gentle kiss.

To run my fingers through her
Brown, curly, shoulder hair.

To touch her once tenderly.

Randy Caruso

OCTOBER SKIES

In the late October sky.
With steadfast wings they fly.

And the others too.
Floating endlessly with tails of red and blue.

Then they fall, too.

No breeze is there now.

The whitecaps rush to sandy shores.
And with them all of life with its pain.

The regrets of yesterday.
And the regrets of today.

The solitude of peaceful quiet thought.

And the loneliness of today.

Randy Caruso

THE GAME

With steadfast hands
He pulled that mighty skinny stick.

Then all at once it seemed to snap.

The ball spun back.
Then stopped so quick.

The cue moved 'round the green.
Like a bluejay in flight across the sea.

I knew then that was the end that night.
For he had defeated me.

Randy Caruso

NOVEMBER EVE

the leaves dry coarse
rattle on dead limbs
devoid of life and sap devoid of life
they rattle beneath the full moon, glowing.

Cast your shadows cast your shadows
your spare forms entwining in black stark
and rustling silver night.

Where When
Who the cry sounds
of pumpkins and fabric masks
and faces from long ago,
orbs that cry
my smallness in the young world.

myself myself
I sit and hold to myself

Thomas Krische

THOMAS MICHAEL KRISCHE. Born: Topeka, Kansas, 4-22-51; Single; Education: University of Kansas, B.A., 1979; Occupation: Poet; Membership: Knights of Columbus; Poetry: *Distant Trumpets,* book of poetry.

A PEEK INTO THE FUTURE

You can look into the future and
Sneak a peek at what's ahead, just
By unveiling the door to your mind
And visualizing what you have read.

Picture your school in a country setting
Beckoning the new freshman coming in,
The murmurings of anxious students,
Reluctant to begin.

Imagine the promise of adventure —
The discoveries that will unfold —
The forming of new friendships —
The tales that will be told.

Experience the challenge of learning
Subjects that are new, and of cultivating
The abilities that have been given to you.

Dream of parties, trips, and dating,
And savor the memory of your first prom.
Keep all of these treasures locked in your heart,
To remember, after your school days are gone.

Patricia Rath-Sanchez

RICH MAN — POOR MAN

Fame and fortune are not necessarily
The signs of true success.
It's a poor man who measures his worth
By the wealth that he might possess.

True riches cannot be measured by
Inches or even a yard.
These are intangible gifts that come
From the treasure house of God.

When we keep the faith and strive to
Practice the virtues of hope and charity,
We live our lives more fruitfully and
Perceive the future with more clarity.

So, develop your talents and follow
Your dreams.
Be careful in choosing your goals.
Plant and nurture only good seeds in life,
For a man shall become what he knows.

Patricia Rath-Sanchez

TEARS OF PAIN

Tears —
    salty, stinging,
    cascading down,
    freeing the emotion,
    emptying the reservoir
    of pain.
The dam broke in a private moment
    where no one could see
    free from intrusion or interruption
    so that genuine grief is purged —
    — The catharsis —
The hurt is washed away in streaks
    as each tear cleanses my soul.

Susan Ellicott

FAIRY TALES TO DO COME TRUE

For Steven

Only once in a lifetime is a girl fortunate
    to meet a guy like you . . .
        You're my once in a lifetime dream come true

You were the prince whose kiss woke me from a deep sleep

You were the knight come to rescue me

You were the prince who danced with me
    dazzled
    mesmerized my see . . .
        when the hour came I didn't want to leave

You were the wizard helped me find my way home

You were the king asked if I'd share his throne

You were in all my fairy tales
    but, aren't I lucky . . .
        you are real!

Betty James

REFLECTIONS OF THE TIMES

Again I don't have a job,
And economics makes it so hard.
So immensely hard to survive,
But where is there to run or hide?

This time it is not the same
Because there are two others in my name.
I have a wife and son you see,
Who are now depending on support from me.

How can one support without a job,
Where in the South it is extremely hard.
Hard to secure a lucrative position,
When whites practice discrimination and nepotism.

Because you see I am indeed qualified,
To take pressures of a job in stride.
Further I am indeed scholastically sound,
With an admirable education background.

But every door that opens, gets slammed in my face,
To encounter such animosity is a major disgrace.
What can one do about all these calamities,
Except to pray and have complete faith in one's deity.

Clarence Paul Jones

POET'S AWARD

Onto paper — my thoughts — I wrote it.
And lo! From lowly housekeeper, I mount to poet.
Read it quickly — it's a sign of grace —
Before you see the pain on my face.
Whom now are you judges snickering at?
They know right away when my lines fall flat.
I can't run and hide, so I'll just close my eyes
While some worthy poet is being awarded the prize.

Nelda Wilson

EQUILIBRIUM

Want to take a trip to a place I've never been to before
    In the sand glass of an hour
    In the sea of a shore

Kalei-to-scope the stars
    from earth to mars
    to a space between — no place

Voyage through time in the annals of minds
    dance with them that used to be
    alive in death's eternity

Somnambulate the fabled ecstasy
    to be sentient of the mystery
    mesmerized by its simplicity

Breathe the blue
    reckoning the morning's dew
    to find the answer — sublime

I want to be a force in a space between no place
    In a perfect state . . .
            equilibrium

Meandered within a thought to find . . .
    conceptualization inexplicably divine

Betty James

REBECCA BETTY JAMES. Pen Name: Betty James; Born: Manhattan (Harlem), 7-10; Married: Steven James, 12-29-71; Education: College of Staten Island, AAS, Childcare, Education; Occupation: Postal Clerk; Awards: Poetry Recitation, 1965 school contest, 2nd place; Poetry: 'Rebecca,' 'Incipient,' *New Voices in American Poetry*, 1986; Themes: *Life, love, womanhood.*

LOOK FOR THE MAGIC

Look for the magic in the world around you;
Miracles happen every day of the year;
Reach out and touch it — feel the power surround you;
Love will impart a special magical sphere!

Look for the magic in the beasts and the children;
Innocence shines from eyes soft and clear;
They have a wonder that will bless and astound you;
Open your heart — feel the magic so near!

Where is it found? Look all around!
Magic is where you find love abound!

Look for the magic you have living within you;
Let it pour out; it's what makes you so dear;
Sunlight and moonlight will be shining upon you —
Look for the magic every moment you're here!

Monnet Alvarez

A RECEPTACLE

Turning inside a transparency
conveyers fostering
A receptacle now unexposed
advances to offspring
Identity and preservation
conveyers discerning
Observance at every angle
then snugly boxed in
A small batch on flat foundation
later intermingled
A small price for two in one household
the hands of newlyweds
Satiating their own appetites
with strawberry and grape
A receptacle fully exposed
an offspring fully ripe.

Jeff Herald

OVER

Oh, I have loosed the bonds
Of a love worn thin
By tired promises and broken dreams,
And things that might have been.

No longer do I feel the sting
Of a love that used to be,
Before summer days turned to winter nights
And set my fledgling heart free.

I have learned love's lesson well —
Packed my tears away,
Still tasting freedom's bitter gall,
Still haunted by the ghosts of yesterday.

Barbara Jean Priest

JEFFREY

Where have you gone?
Oh, why did you leave me?
You were the key to my lock
Oh, Jeffrey.
How can I brave the night alone
Without you by my side?
I think when I slipped from your arms
I died.
Jeffrey, oh Lord, how I ache for you —
Catch the tear that falls.
I'm haunted by your memory
Day in and day out.
You have a new life, I hear —
Was my love in doubt?
In your blue eyes passion scorched;
your smile will continue to allure.
Jeffrey, my one and only,
My passion for you will forever endure.

Patti Zielinski

CREATION

Life is but
A slender shaft of wheat.
Sown in the springtime,
Nurtured by the
Sun and rain,
Tempered by the wind,
Stretching toward the heavens,
Touched by the hand of God,
And then
Harvested.

Barbara Jean Priest

BARBARA JEAN SHREDER. Pen Name: Barbara Jean Priest; Born: Dannemora, New York, 5-29-28; Married: Robert Shreder, 9-5-53; Education: SUNY, Plattsburgh, New York; SUNY, Genesea, New York; Occupation: Elementary school teacher, first grade; Memberships: Home School association — G.W.C.C., Attica, New York; Poetry: 'The New Widow,' *American Poetry Anthology,* 4-87; Comments: *Poetry is a very personal expression. I empathize with people — their loves, their hopes, their tragedies. Painting pictures with words is an endless joy.*

TO A WILDFLOWER

Just a modest wildflower
In the dust by the way;
But from its face I fancy
Shines all the glory of April days.
Some seek a garden of elegant style
With rare roses opening side by side,
A garden of sorrow, with too short a while
Of happiness spent like a day that is through.
To me it seems far lovelier flowers
Are beckoning from hill and plain;
I can fashion there a garden bower
That blooms and is happy in sun or rain;
Where by the fence the columbine
Waves farewell to the shooting star
That smiles and laughs at the climbing vine
Racing to meet old friends from afar.

Louise Butts Hendrix

JOY IN WINTER

Snow so white,
Snow so bright,
Falling on the ground tonight.
Covering everything in sight.

Miniature flashes of crystal light,
Twinkle like thousands of diamonds,
Into your sight.
And give me such incredible delight.

I long always to be the first.
To step out on a cold winter night,
And take in this breathtaking sight.
When the earth is a virgin,
Blanket of white.

Dorothy Rodgers

ONE LITTLE DROP OF WATER

One little drop of water
Can do so much when it lands.

It can be food for a flower,
Add moisture to the sand.

It can bring refreshment to a bird,
Or be a bath for a flea.

It can form the ocean home of a whale,
Or be the beginning of a tree.

Dorothy Rodgers

CHILD, WELL DONE

The praise of man I do not seek
For the things I say or do.
I only want to please my Lord
And do as He tells me to.

When others think I'm slipping,
And my errors they do see,
My Father looks into my heart,
And knows the inner me.

Although the songs of love and praise
Run through my mind each day,
Sometimes, I'm at a loss for words,
But He knows what I'd like to say.

To each life He gave a purpose.
And though mine is not yet clear,
I trust and love my Father,
And I know that He is near.

What need have I for others' praise
For the races I have run?
The only words I care to hear
Are His words, "*Child*, well done."

Donna J. Nixon

HOW FAR TO GO

Laying here wondering why I take it for granted
Body that holds me, flesh of my soul

Brain filled with power, beyond my control

I lay here thinking,
Hearing my heart beat
Hearing my heart beat
Heart of my soul

Each of my fingers wrapped up in warm flesh,
Warm flesh surrounds me,
Blood flows within me,
Life's all around me and covers my soul

I am a spirit, locked in a body
What is my purpose?
How will I know?

Eyes capture pictures, and let my mind read them
On with my life now — out of control

Lost in a body, going through day trips
Searching for answers —

How far to go

Judi A. Musgrove

MY PI-LAN

Pi-Lan, Pi-Lan whose name sounds like a song,
I prayed and prayed the night you were born.
You had such a tough time entering this world,
My prayer's answered now; you're like a pearl.

You're now intelligent and witty and a joy to behold.
I thank God above for making you whole.
For a while I feared you would never experience life,
But God saved my heart and soul from all that strife.

I am eternally grateful for all God has done.
It is a joy to watch my daughter run, run, run.
Run, run, run, when first she could hardly breathe
Was, and is, enough to make me fall to my knees.

Pi-Lan, Pi-Lan whose name sounds like a song,
I'll love and cherish you my whole life long.
I'll keep you forever etched in my heart,
Because God gave you and me a bright new start.

Clarence Paul Jones

CHANGES

I didn't think I could live without him and now I know
it's true. But will he ever love me in the same manner
in which I loved him? Why? Why can't things stay the
same? Why do they have to change? I guess changes are
a part of growing up and it looks like I'm far from grown.

Alicia Dodds

SOLDIER'S GRAVE

Unknown U.S. Soldier the inscription read,
And a plain white cross marked his final bed.
Killed in battle, and buried here,
In the springtime of his final year.
The grave mute evidence of his fate,
Interred here alone on this lonely date.
Gone now is the pain and sorrow,
With no more fears of the morrow.
No more battles to be fought,
No more enemy to be sought.
These earthly paths no more to trod,
He sleeps in peace 'neath the verdant sod.
And no call to arms again will sound,
To raise him from this gentle mound.
We stand in quiet reverence here; with a tear, a nod,
For one who gave his all, to man and God!

Calvin G. Wetzel

REACHING FOR THE BRASS RING

The carrousel whirls round and round. The music of the calliope
spells the obscure reactions of the publishers:

Arbor House — cautious mouse
Atlantic — we are frantic
Bantam — always a phantom
Dial — over the transom, in the "slush" pile
Doubleday — submit anyway
Dutton — invest, it rhymes with Hutton
Esquire — sounds of a choir
Harper and Row — they're too slow
Houghton Mifflin — now we're snifflin'
McGraw-Hill — has the will
Lippincott — is not what we thought
Morrow — sorrow, maybe tomorrow
Scribner — won't consider a scribbler
Zebra — the talent of Virgo or the justice of Libra?

Round we go, reaching for that brass ring?

Moritz E. Pape

BEST FRIENDS

My Song To You

It was midsummer when I first met you
Like a pot of gold you were a
Poor man's dream come true
Now I can't get you out of my mind
I think about you all of the time
I keep your picture on my wall
And if I ever get lonely I can just give you a call
The fun we've shared will never leave my heart
Not even in death will our memories ever part.
I knew I was in love when I first saw you
And never once with you did I have a day that was blue
We laughed and played, even on rainy days
It didn't really seem to matter just where we were
As long as we were together, the best love was always there.
Now it is night, go to bed and get your rest
And tomorrow will be nothing, except the very best

John Dowdell

ECHO OF FAITH #137

View from a beach on Long Island Sound

There are special places of Beauty that the Heart cherishes
  like sitting at the beach in the Early Morn and watching the
    Sun reflecting on the Rippling Waters of the Sound . . .
And the Leaves of all the Beautiful Trees
  fluttering in the Breeze . . .

To see the Houses dotting the Hillsides across the Water . . .
  Some commanding and majestic, others unobtrusively
    pleasing . . . but all Peacefully Picturesque . . .
Sailboats gliding silently *Calmly* and *Relaxingly* inviting
  The Solace of the empty Beach displaying *all its Beauty*
    with silent elegance for your pleasure and the
  Strengthening Renewal of your body, mind and heart as you
    sit in *Awe* and *Appreciation* of all *God's* Handiworks . . .

It is then that you Become *One* with the *Universe,* as
  you *Absorb* all its *Beauty* in Silence and Solitude
    and are refreshed as you reflect, meditate and
Communicate with the
          Eternal . . . another Heart on Fire with
            Love of God . . .

Barbara Martinez-Peligian

PRINCESS

This poem is about Clara Esther Linscott, my lovely Wife you see,
Many a verse has been written, to be recorded for all time.
Faith, understanding, patience, knowledge, oh yes honesty,
Mistress, Cook, Nurse, and Wife; this fantastic lady is mine.
I call her "Princess," this woman I wed back in Sixty-one,
A president's wife, a queen, a star, countess, among them she is tall.
She teaches, judges, listens, a back seat she takes to none,
Her family, home, friends, and neighbors, she daily prays for all.
This poem fits many women, but, for me it fits just one,
If I had Rockefeller's millions, or a Midas touch,
  I could never start to pay.
She is my "Mona Lisa," she's Athena, Diana, Venus De Milo too,
If not for you, my Princess, I would not have a thing.
Our vows "for better or for worse," we have had both to share,
I love you, Clara Esther, you wear my wedding ring.
No one could ever know, how much you mean to me,
  how much I really care,
Diamonds, Gems, Gold, and all the many things you deserve
  I would give.
I often take for granted, all the things you do,
You are my pride and joy, my reason, my hope,
  my faith in which to live.
I need no reason good or bad, when flowers I give to you.
Clara Esther, You are *My* Princess, and Princess *I Love You!*

Stanley R. Linscott

My heart has always been filled with the joy in life.
Don't cast a shadow and take that joy away.
Life is too short and should be filled with the love of life.
Oh, God, please let me find it again
Wherever it has flown.

Olive Hickerson

ON RETURNING TO "ANZIO"

Sgt. Cal G. Wetzel, U.S. 5th Army,
77th Heavy Artillery, served in World War II.

I was compelled, I had to go,
Back to the shores of Anzio.
The palms, still were bent and shattered,
The tanks and trucks about were scattered,
And covered rich terrain here and there,
Where once the fields bloomed so fair.
I saw a helmet, broken and with a dent,
What flimsy protection it had lent,
What "Limey," "Jerry," or "G.I. Joe,"
Fell beneath so terrible a blow?
The ocean calm and now serene,
Hides her dead beneath the green,
And rolling hillsides on the coast,
Embrace their dead, the Soldier Ghost.
The crosses white for acres seen,
Are mute testimony of what had been,
A fearful battle, now history recorded,
That turned the tide — a maniac thwarted.
And though some forty years have passed,
The men that fought down to the last,
Will not forget how once they bled,
Will ne'er forget their comrades dead,
          At "Anzio."

Calvin G. Wetzel

SCENT

The wind blew your scent, softly, my way
Touching fiery emotions, again I'm swept away.
Renewing your image long put to death —
The Scent! The Scent, it took away my breath.

Memories flew through the coolest of breeze
Taunting and tempting, calling sweet things.
Laughing so aimlessly they danced through my skin —
The Desire! Such Desire, it made me want him.

Images leaping in joy, now cringe with pain
The sensual kisses, the loss of my gain.
Again now they're haunting me, the dead are alive —
I'm Waiting! Still Waiting, my love he hides.

The wind now passing, softly, I cry
As with the warm scent, again you die.
The memory, the moment bringing me bliss —
Come Back! Come Back, such sweetness I miss.

Connie Blankenship

DEVASTATED

The most devastating thing that ever happened to me is when I lost
  my mom, you see.
The most devastating thing that happened to me was when death
  took her away from me.
The most devastating thing that happened to me words could
  never express.
My mom has no more worries; now she's laid to rest.
No more pain or sorrow, no more fears of tomorrow.
If you think this is the end, death came knocking once again,
This time claiming my friend.
The pain and sorrow have no end.
It almost hurt as badly to lose a friend.

Nan Blackshire-Little

ONE MORE DAY

If in the morning, when the songs of birds
Remind me of music far more sweet,
If I could hear an opening door
And the sound of his happy feet,
If I could be glad when day is done,
With all my cares and heartaches laid away,
If I could hold him in my arms
Just for one more day.

Dear Father, would it be possible to have my son
Here with me for just one day
So I could have a talk with him
And tell him things I never had time to say,
How much I really loved and thought of him
Before you took him away?
Dear God, just for one more day,
Just for one more day.

Nelda Wilson

MAKING SOME DREAMS COME TRUE

When we look back on the time you were a little girl,
We never dreamed your adult life would be such a whirl.
Some other people we knew lived their lives by the clock.
Training you in some profession would raise your work stock.

Changes re women working 'way from their cozy home,
 Became embrewed more often in a young lady's ''dome!''
Good character became you as you picked your life course.
Your parents thought nurse training would be a great resource!

'Twas grand to see you develop your ability.
Serving people! What a way to build work equity!
Real estate sales was an extra you 'deed, did espy.
Your moral training will help you reach ''pie in the sky!''

Isn't it wonderful as through your hard sell you drub,
Earned rewards come like, ''You're 'gain in the millionaire's club!''

Mervin L. Schoenholtz

NIGHT WATCH

My nerves just can't take it
— The strain, you know.
Like a violin or guitar string
Stretched too tight, almost to the breaking point
One false pluck and snap — broken, gone.

Whatever is to happen to me —
The Insomniac?
I can't go on this way
Much longer —
Three, four, at most five hours sleep each night.
I am only human and need my full night's rest —
In fact, must have it before the sun
comes blazing over the mountain peaks.

Even though I must bear other burdens,
I don't want to be an Insomniac.
Please, God, help me.
I am so tired.

F. Richard Dieterle

SOCIETY

I am the young
Long years of life still ahead,
My song yet unsung,
The flame of hope well fed.

I am the pupil
Prepared for another day,
To be your sequel,
And take the pain of life away.

I am the worker
Whose life is a dead end.
He strives like a beserker,
But the bars which imprison him won't bend.

I am the old;
I have a story to tell,
Of days now forgotten,
Of kingdoms which fell.

We are your wards
Powerless against society
Except when amassed in hordes.
A situation resulting from the learned lacking piety.

Matt Zuck

THE PROMISES

My Darling,

On our wedding day
We pledged some vows
We promised to love, honor and obey
Well, darling, I kept my promises
but you, you broke them
many years ago
Oh, yes, I knew indeed
about all of your overtime lovers
I'm not stupid, I could tell you were
in love with so many others
Why did you have to hurt me?
You knew from the day you married
me, from the day you slipped
that little gold band on my finger
that you would have your fun
Why couldn't you have just
loved me —

Your wife

Leslie Makela

MOTORIST ON THE ROAD

Ever onward moving, that chain of yellow lights
Thousands of motorcars I see as I gaze from my window on
    springtime nights
I haven't got a car to take me far and wide
It is enough for me to see the other fellow ride
He has an advantage over me, I do not doubt at all
To see the springtime budding, and the russet leaves of fall
But the peaceful constitution that is mine from staying home
Is worth the blinding traffic lights
Motorists encounter while they roam
I may not get as far as you tourists with your cars
But if I raise my eyes at night, I see the very same stars
At sundown while in comfort I do sit
The cars are madly speeding back to town
What is the joy in it?

Pearl Van Slocum

NO TRAILER BRAKES ON 308, OR "NOW LISTEN, HON..."

When Daddy was a trucker,
He said, "Now listen, Hon,
Things have changed so very much
From the days when I was young.
We used to have a brotherhood
And help out our fellow man.
These younger guys speed down the road
Playing 'Catch me if you can.'
The buddy system we once had
Was the best and beyond compare.
You knew if you had trouble
There was always someone there.
We took care of our equipment
For ourselves and the next man.
Now you're lucky if it runs a yard
And nobody gives a damn!"
Now Daddy's gone where truckers go
When they've made their final run.
At last I see just what he meant
When he said "Now listen, Hon..."

Donna J. Nixon

JEANETTE

You ain't heard anything yet
Until you've heard about my girl, Jeanette
She's the sweetest girl that I've ever met
Yes sir, she's the best yet
I have a lot to say about my honey
Her love is really on the money
I know that her love is true
She holds on to me like super glue
She makes my heart skip a beat
Whenever I hear her voice, so soft and sweet
Her eyes are as sexy as they can be
I melts when she stares at me
I'll walk a million miles
To confront her brilliant smile
I just adore her pretty, pretty face
She's the princess of the human race
She possesses a magnetic force
Which compels me to stay her course
I love the way she plays her games
Her sweet love drives me insane
Jeanette is the sweetest girl that I've ever met
Yes sir, she's the best yet

Albert Humphries

What tired, sad faces
In lonely old people's homes!
What real life stories!
Forgotten by their dear ones,
Old age is poor despite wealth —
Memories double when shared.

Sister Regina Veale

YOU CAN DO IT

You cannot solve problems by abusing drugs
Don't give up, don't pull the plug
I refuse to believe you don't have the guts
To pull yourself out of this rut
All you got to do is the very best you can
It's your opportunity to start again
All I can do is sympathize with you
Planning your future is something you must do
Doing nothing won't get you nowhere
I just can't do it, regardless of how much I care
First, you must save yourself
Then you can help someone else
Remember, life is what you make of it
Use your mind, use your wits
You can do it, you can do it
So why not take a stand
You can do it
I just know you can
You can do
So get to it, get to it

Albert Humphries

EXISTENCE

Only you exist in my mind;
Only your image, your picture,
Lives in my inner self.
Hence, you involve me
As a monsoon as I go by.

God willing, I hope . . .
It will be very pure
The love that you
Will bring me
Since I will love to drink
From that nectar of peace.

I seldom believe or think
That the poets
Only feel when they write,
Regardless of anything else.
As well as the babies cry
At the moment of birth
Without being completely aware
Of where they really are.

Please bring me warm love
In future winters that will evolve
With their limitless snowfall
True tears on my eyes.

Alice C. Levy

Ageless stone beauty!
Sky piercing cross crowned spires!
Storied stained glass —Chartres!
Pilgrims here seek sweet solace
From their crowned black Madonna.

Sister Regina Veale

DESIRE

I desire to see your eyes again:
The eyes of your genius
That penetrated my soul,
That taught me how to love you.

I desire to share your smile again
Because it was honest, sincere and open;
Because it made me feel free as the birds
In the parks, and in the countryside.

I desire to feel your hands again
Like the breeze of the hot tropic air:
Warm, humid, loving
Around my body or next to my chest.

I desire more than your loving hands
Around my body. I desire your sensual body
Playing with me and making love
Because I love you,
Because I remember you,
Because you loved me.

Alice C. Levy

GENTLE, QUIET HOUSE

There, in a gentle, simple
house —
at the end of a dusty road,
dwell real, honest, loyal
folk —
the kind who love —
the kind who'll help
carry your load.

Amid laughter and homey
bits of open-talk,
they share their table,
spread with garden-stuff.

Many times, I've had my
faith restored —
my strength renewed —
there, in that gentle,
simple, quiet house —
at the end of a dusty road.

Dorothy Clarkson

WORDS OF THE WISE

"A still tongue makes a wise head,"
That's what my mother always said.
But, I've grown older now,
I don't ask her permission to open my mouth.
Although my words aren't chosen or few,
My clearest meaning always comes through.
May her legacy live on long after her death,
As future generations learn with regret,
Live and learn from what she has said,
That the wise old owl can surely turn heads.

Hazel Mae Parron

I'M STILL ON THE RUN

I'm still on the run and I know I'm not the only one.
How I hate to pack this gun, while I'm still on the run.
There's no rest on this freeway. I know it's got to be this way.
Every day I wished that I could stay, but I'm still on the run.

My body's tired, but my mind stays strong
I won't believe that I am wrong.
Yes deep inside I know I'm right
While I carry on this endless fight, I'll stay on the run.

The world has turned its back on me, for I won't change
the things I see, while I curse this haunt inside of me
I'll stay on the run.

I could have died some years ago, in a way
Only soldiers grew to know and like a war that found no end,
I find it hard to find a friend, while I'm still on the run.

Now death could never show me fear, it only seeks
to draw me near to my friends that were so dear
who no longer have to run.
The soldier's tune they sang so brave of the many things
they fought to save, it lay them in their lonely graves
They no longer live to run.

Janet Fay Black

TO LOVE IS TO:

Care enough not to be late.
Give undivided attention to companion or mate.
Hear what is said.
Not tell myself what is meant in my head.

Use good manners because I care.
Speak other's language when there.
Save another much time.
Write clearly so they need not decipher my line.

Pay all my bills on appointed dates.
Keep affairs in order to make life easier on companion or mate.
Remember each mountain has an up and a down.
Accommodate both (up and down) to achieve life's crown.

Use little things; they mean a lot.
Cross life's desert with them; they're all I've got.
Give little things — the fabric of love.
Receive in reciprocity all from above.

Have lofty conception, romantic adventure, grand passion,
    incite the soul.
Be consumed, washed over, then ebb like the storm after
    achieved goal.
Know that heroic gesture, frantic action, cannot sustain
    love's storm.
Use kindness and simple acts to nourish, lubricate,
    and keep love warm.

Ric Filip

WRONG TO RIGHT

What is right — I ask myself.
This life I live — on a shelf?

Best of friends — this they are.
And for now — one must stay afar!

A promise was made — and must be kept.
This heart of mine — must not be swept.

So no one gets hurt — I must be bold.
It is right — to keep life on hold!

Day by day and into the night — I do ponder.
These are wrong — what I dream, think and wonder.

I must stay between — the right and wrong.
Through all of this — I must be strong!

To keep life true.
My heart will stay blue.

Tonya Ione

A BUDDING LIFE

Just around the corner
One might think the sun is shining
While the good earth is turning
Then life may make you unfairly a mourner.

Why then, come tell me a tale of the human race,
Of how life is or seems to be.
Then sing me a song of the confused, but trying one,
And you'll be singing a song of me.

Hum to me a tune on a hot night in June
While lightning bugs flicker to a twilight moon
And this lonely child will drift on into a sleep
A quiet, peaceful slumber without a peep.

Then sing a song of long ago,
Tell every adolescent you may see eye to eye
That life is made of a variety of things to know
And one of them is — I.

Herbert Clyde Spivey, Jr.

MODERN MOTHER'S ENIGMA

My favorite daughter-in-law has a big problem.
In today's wide wild world, it's not considered a gem.
How does one continue one's present job outside home,
And yet rear two sons in today's grimy, filthy "foam?"

So many sites are breeding places of mankind's sin.
Around each corner there lurks some sort of filthy bin!
These sin-bins are in no way what you can call benign.
On kids, especially, they've set their ugly design!

Human leeches are e'er seeking the younger client.
To peers, addicts, pushers, the young ones are so pliant!
The ease with which these dregs prey on our kids does slither —
Is 'nough to keep growing households in a deep dither!

Yes, today's motherhood has one more major project;
That is: our kids from slimy pushers e'er to protect!

Mervin L. Schoenholtz

NIGHT DREAMS

All alone in darkness I lay
Seeking sleep, but it hides away.
Leaving me wakeful through the night,
Sneaking up softly with dawn's light.
Physically I feel so beat;
That part of me demands to sleep!
Yet the mind ignores body's achy yearning
And keep the think-mill ever churning . . .
Pouring out those ''if'' and ''so''s
All through the night this madness goes . . .
Reliving the traumas of daily cares,
Reviewing as shoppers a merchant's wares,
Conflicting messages that slip and flee;
These night-dreams ever haunting me.

Delores Hendricks

COTTAGES AND CASTLES

''There's a little house with a cozy room
Where a fire is burning low.
Two candles shed their flickering light
To accentuate the sunset's glow.
All by itself; the kind of place
Where just-married lovers go.
It's large enough for two to share
For a weekend or a year,
And maybe we will add a room
When the little ones appear . . .''

So long ago we talked like this
And those houses came and went.
Our little one is just past two
Yet how short the time we spent
Living in those houses together
Like other folks at home.
For you are called to fight the wars
That keep us apart and alone.
For I am just a soldier's wife
And loneliness is our way of life.

Delores Hendricks

A LOVE TO CALL MY OWN

I knew from the beginning
that you were just a flirt;
But I fell in love with you
knowing I'd be hurt.

I thought I could tie you down,
and make you love just one;
But how could I do something,
no one else had ever done.

I know you never loved me,
and I'm trying not to cry;
For I must find the strength somehow,
To kiss your lips good-bye.

When you ask for me again,
You'll find I won't be there;
I want a love to call my own,
Not one I'll have to share.

So I will hide my broken heart,
Beneath a laughing face;
And though you'll think I never cared,
No one else can take your place.

Mickey Stroda-Fairchild

THE STAGE BEING SET

As I dream dreams of fury,
And frolic in a fantasy of fun,
My mind marvels at the mystery
Of the songs that are left unsung.

My heart lies in wait for a lover
Knowing, once found, he will be untrue;
But betrayal holds no threat or promise,
And continue my delusion is all I can do.

Sleep tinged with red is my destiny;
Attempts to change it would be vain.
So forever I will wander this wide world
And hold in my heart everlasting pain.

As I dream dreams of fury,
And frolic in a fantasy of fun,
My mind marvels at the mystery
Of the songs still left unsung . . .

Leah Mary Lyman
Danny Ray Polson

FOR WRAY

A million thoughts
Fly unleashed within
A captive mind.

And emotions flutter
Helplessly in the winds
Of a stormy heart.

An eye unseen
Cries silent tears —
Tears you will never see.

A breaking voice
Sings friendship's song:
All of this for you.

Danny Ray Polson

GROW NOT AWAY
FROM JUNE

A flower that grows,
A dewdrop that shines,
Are really just keys
To open the mind.

A dazzle to the eye,
A fragrant smell,
Are a heaven we make
Within this black hell.

A friend to laugh with,
A love to hold,
Are what we all need
So we will not wax cold.

Just a short sonnet,
Just a sweet tune —
For a life lived in winter
These create June.

Danny Ray Polson

A WILD KILLDEER

This morning when
I raised my eyes
To grey and drizzling
Shadowed skies
I heard a lovely
High and clear
Song of a wild
And free killdeer,
His sweet and lilting
Precious voice
Made my heart
So sad, rejoice
Just to know
There still is here
A thing so lovely
As a wild killdeer.

Julia Grigg Hopple

ME FOR IDAHO

A few days ago, I got mad, and so,
I decided to leave ole Idaho.
I clapped my trunk upon my back,
And started for the railroad track.
I walked along a mile or two,
Without a sole upon my shoe.
Until my feet got sore, so by galore;
I stood my trunk upon the ground,
And took a big long look around,
Then I knew, as smart kids do,
That my trip was all in vain.
I picked up my trunk, for the trip was sunk,
And started home again.
For do you know, pacing to and fro,
I learned that never, could I ever,
Leave ole Idaho.

Julia Grigg Hopple

THE LITTLE FISHERMAN

A little barefoot boy
With patches on his knees
Raced about to do his chores
Then set out for the sea

He'd sit upon the docks all day
His brothers by his side
Then take home all the perch he caught
With quiet bursting pride

A homemade spear from mom's old broom
Was all he had to use
That humble little boy
Who left without his shoes

Fredda H. Rose

LOST AT SEA

The call came in
  and time stood still
His mind was dazed
  in frantic chill
A boat was lost
  on the foaming sea
The young crew adrift
  eternally
He sat on the sand
  in a lonely plea
Watching the waves
  cast high with glee
At dusk dimly seeing
  that night had drawn near
His heart worn out
  his soul filled with fear
Knowing somewhere
  out there in the deep
He'd lost a brother
  the sea's to keep
With blinding tears
  he stood in vain
Wanting the boat's
  return again
Now, whenever he stands
  on the shore
He's never alone
  not like before
His brother's still with him
  whenever he's there
To roam by the sea
  without any despair

Fredda H. Rose

I DIDN'T KNOW

I didn't know I was blind;
Dandelions nestled in the grass
And violets were dainty velvet things,
I gathered bouquets.

I didn't know I was blind;
New hay rattled gaily underfoot
And baby chicks were fluffy in my fingers,
I touched it all gently.

I didn't know I was blind;
I heard the echoed nearness of the trees
And dry leaves whispered secrets to the wind,
Life sang, I was five.

I didn't know I was blind.

Martha Bell Hays

STRANGE MEETING

She stood before me deaf,
Confusion in her mind;
My baffled thoughts were many,
I stood before her, blind.

I spoke, and from my lips
She read my welcome word,
And from her muted utterance
Her silent smile I heard.

Martha Bell Hays

DAUGHTER SPEAKING

She brought me a gift on Mother's Day,
We laughed,
It should have been the other way.
Somehow I think she understood
Too soon there would be pensive moments
Dotting well-filled years,
To that distant day when I might ponder,
Sometimes lonely,
Perhaps a little sad,
Searching for the child I never had.

Martha Bell Hays

IN THIS OCEAN OF LOVE

We are out on the ocean
In this ocean of love
Then my confession was true, dear
True as the blue skies above

We are out on the ocean
We are out on the sea
Under the blue skies above
Then come closer to me
On this tide we'll ride
When we're falling in love

We are the fishes of this ocean
Your kisses and devotion
are a mystery to me
You're a mystery at sea mystery to me

Then the world seems to wonder
When I confessed to you
But deep down in my heart, dear
I want you to know
That when I said I love you
Every word is true

Stanley H. Campbell

FOR YOU — GLADYS

*For one of my friends
during her final illness*

I think of you
I pray for you
I meditate on you
I bring to you good wishes for your good health
And for your peace, peace, and for your peace
Peace peace peace

Mary Susan Smith

HAIKU

As the tent moved
  I felt like a little squirrel
Along the hard ground.

Keith Hendricks

For the same friend, now departing

Dear, dear Gladys
You came to earth for awhile.
I am so pleased to have known you.

Mary Susan Smith

MARY SUSAN SMITH. Born: Bermuda; Occupation: Nursing; Membership: American Nurses Association, Bermuda; Awards: 'To Merlyn', *American Poetry Anthology,* 1986; Poetry: 'Thinking of You,' 'For You — Gladys' (two parts), *Poetry of Life, Vol. 1,* 1-87; Comments: *It is not easy for me to find instant words of comfort for those of my friends experiencing major life events — especially unpleasant ones; my poetry is this confession finding expression. My friends say my verses are very helpful. We wish to share them.*

THE LANE OF CARE

Come and take a walk with me
Down the lane of care
To look at all the flowers
That are blooming there

We'll look at all the tulips
There are a lot of them
Buds of different colors
On a long, pale green stem

Walking farther down the lane
Filled with expectations
We see a spot upon the hill
Filled with big carnations

While walking along a grassy edge
We see another plot
I stoop and pick a flower for you
A lovely forget-me-not

As we return, come up the lane
And pass a bed of posies
At the bed next to them
We'll stop, and smell the roses

Samuel N. McEwen

A TRUE FRIEND

To Ruth Sitz

You open your responsive heart
like a forest spring full of bracing water,
when on a dark windy night
I, a wandering stranger, knock at the door,
the door of my hope and dreamland.

You invite me in, and place by the fire
warm and safe like my unforgettable mother's home,
and childhood memories fly away
like the last flocks of wild birds in autumnal sky,
and dreams of calm future come with snowflakes falling
                                outside the window.

You speak to me with words that resemble flowers
which grow in silence of my soul
when you say an old evening prayer,
and bygone moments of a day are cradling in my mind.
You read passages of the eternal story
which enriches generations like a boundless river of confidence.

You guide me to the new land,
vast like starlight night and close like a taste of fresh bread
at time of a family supper,
which I love but which never will be my homeland.

Eugene Joseph Kucharz

ETHEREAL ARCHITECT

Alone I atone this vigil atop stone
Adjusting cones of crystal shells
According to tones of distant bells.

So great the landscape I decorate
That the smallest of rocks dwarf mountaintops,
And dewdrops encompass ancient lakes.

If only I knew . . .

The rainbow I seek, discolored and bleak,
Radiates far away from me,
    Shining inwardly.

My dream: to enthrall streams of colors
        to flow within my structure.
But perpetual darkness prevails.
Attempts to please my Lord have failed.

        I continue on
Realizing my purpose, but not understanding . . .

Victor Griffin

RHONDA ANN

The Specter of Death hovers over our child's head,
and the thin thread of life leaves her body almost
lifeless — lying on the hospital bed.
    Her blood pressure rises and falls, as each
shallow breath barely registers at all.
    An angel has made her not feel the pain,
as she writhes and twists trying, to rise up again.
    Her left arm lying lifeless at her side, she looks
at us with the fixed glassy stare of her blue eyes.
    The respirator labors, going up and down —
and the lights on the monitor continue to flash,
bringing the nurses around.
    How much time will God give this child of mine?
    Lord, in your infinite wisdom, we know you'll
make that decision.
    Father, give us strength to help her fight,
as our love enfolds her tight.
    Help us battle the Specter of Death,
as we call to the Angel of Life, in the bitter
hours of darkness, these long perilous nights.

Elline Curran

THE WEDDING VOWS

For David L. Anderson

Since the first day we were together, I knew
That one day I would happily marry you
Because even right then, I knew in my heart
We'd be together until ''death do us part.''

The vows we'll make to one another will mean a lot,
The promises we make when we tie the knot
From this day forward, to have and to hold,
Our love will be stronger, even as we grow old.

For better, for worse — I'll love you forever;
Through sickness and health, we'll always be together.
For richer, for poorer — our love will endure.
We'll respect the bond we've made, that's for sure.

When two people marry, they join hands as one.
They make a commitment that won't soon be done.
When we get married — forever, it will last
Our time together will be older than our past.

The day we start together as man and wife
Will be the very first day of the rest of my life.
It will begin a time I want to share with you,
And will have only just begun when we say, ''I do.''

Tami Gersbach

A WAY-SIDE HOME.

FACES WITHOUT A NAME

In our minds we see the faces
Of people we know so well
Tho' some of them were met by chance
In our minds that meeting will dwell

Their faces seem to come in view
Most times out of the blue
Their names and voices you can hear
As if standing next to you

Some faces we do not remember
Look familiar just the same
We wonder how to identify them
The faces without a name

We think we should remember them
We try, but to no avail
Cannot find a name that fits
Our mind is at the end of its trail

Faces, the faces that we know best
In our mind remain the same
But the ones that trouble us the most
Are the faces without a name

Samuel N. McEwen

LATE NIGHT CRY

A pain of hurt, deep inside
As of now I cannot hide
It just arrived the other day
The question is, will it go away

The cause of it was sudden and quick
As if being hit with a stick
My body does not show a scar
In my heart is where they are

I cannot sleep a wink at night
When morning comes I look a sight
The pain grows stronger with each day
No matter what my mind may say

With the rise of the sun
A new day now has just begun
Too soon this day will go by
When it's night, late night, I cry

I know someday the pain will leave
I'll know the meaning of deceive
Still sometimes I'll wonder why
But late at night, sometimes, I cry

Samuel N. McEwen

NATURE

He . . . brilliantly attired
She . . . drab.
He . . . the peacock
She . . . the hen.
He . . . strutted about
She . . . sat unnoted.
''A dull little thing,'' he
thought aloud as he preened.
''Vain creature indeed,'' she
discerned. ''He's only
extraordinary because he's
standing next to me.''

Janie Rood

THOMAS PATRICK

A simple man of peace was he.
His life he lived with dignity.

A stranger on a foreign strand,
He earned his bread with head and hand.

He loved the red, the white, the blue —
To his new country ever true.

The war years asked a heavy price.
Five sons went forth to stand for right.

His nature walks at early morn
Brought solace in a new day born.

He saw God's face in every bloom.
He read His love in sun and moon.

He knew the melody of birds.
He whistled every tune he heard.

He was a friend, a teacher too.
He taught each one to dare to do.

That was our father, kind and strong,
A gentle man who sang his song.

''In your uniqueness, travel on.''

Life's road leads to Eternal Dawn.

Sister Regina Veale

SISTER REGINA VEALE. Born: Chicopee, Massachusetts, 8-29-17; Education: Emmanuel College, B.A., 1953; Assumption College, M.A., 1964; Catholic University, Angers, France, 1968; Occupations: Teacher, high school French and English; College professor, French and English; Awards: Ordre des Palmes Academiques, given by French government, 8-19-75; First prize, 14th Annual Haiku Poetry Contest, The Sumitomo Bank Award, presented by Yukuhara Haiku Society and The Robert Frost Chapter, California Federation of Chaparral Poets, 1976; Poetry: Tanka and Haiku, *Golden Harvest,* collection of poetry in French and English, 1985; Published Japanese Tanka and Haiku poetry in magazines in Paris, France; Tokyo, Japan; San Jose, California; New York, and Rhode Island; Comments: *My favorite forms of poetry are the Haiku and Tanka, which I learned to appreciate in my 23 years in Japan as a college professor.*

UPHILL

Does the road wind uphill all the way
  Yes, to the very end.
Will the day's journey take the whole day long?
  From morn to night, my friend.

But is there for the night a resting-place?
  A roof for when the slow dark hours begin.
May not the darkness hide it from my face?
  You cannot miss that inn.

Shall I meet other wayfarers at night?
  Those who have gone before.
Then must I knock, or call when just in sight?
  They will not keep you standing at that door.

Shall I find comfort, travel-sore and weak?
  Of labor you shall find the sum.
Will there be beds for me and all who seek?
  Yea, beds for all who come.

Christina Rosetti

STARBRIGHT

For Bradford, with love

I saw you last night,
waking through the park
collar up
hands in pockets
braced against some invisible storm.
New moon
cold as a broken promise
cast shadows onto the trees behind you;
night clouds moved across the sky
    then into your eyes
        turning green to gray
fragments of starlight scattered around a man
standing like a child
    alone
at the mercy of a moonbeam
holding a wish
waiting
for a shooting star.

Marci W. Maitland

DEPART

Although my love for you is true
  you've got to understand;
just why I had to let you go
  just why I turned and ran.

You said you loved me many times
  I thought that love was true,
but then you told someone else
  while I sat watching you.

I'll never understand just why
  you did the things you did,
'cause I'm someone with feelings, too.
  I'm not a little kid.

So, at the time I say good-bye
  to you, my dear sweetheart,
we could have been so happy
  but for now we must depart.

Vicki Shrader

AN OLD WEAVER

Silently absorbed in her work, an old ancient
    weaver sat before her loom
Which was not contained in a single room.
She sat comfortably under a green summer shelter
    made of piñon limbs and logs
And behind her could be seen scratching chickens and
    several dogs.

All around her the grandchildren played in the sand
And she thought how much she loved this huge, vast land
Where her people, the proud Navajo, dwell.
She thought of the legends they could tell of Spider Woman —
    the First People — and more
And then she thought of their costumes of velvet and velveteen
    that they wore.

Aged and wrinkled fingers worked so quickly for pelf
As she sat weaving a design as old as time itself.
She thought of how the magic in her fingers had been passed down from
    generation to generation by her forebears
And she welcomed the gift given freely by Spider Woman —
    Thunderbird's messenger.

In and out she wove the yarn and a design took form
As she did her ancient craft perform.
She pounded the long, finished row
As she listened to the lonesome caw of a crow.

Mary Janeen Dorsett

INDIAN POTTER

Indian potter, Indian potter sitting there on the sun-baked earth
Patiently plying your ancient craft.
What thoughts weave themselves through your awareness
As your fingers deftly push and pull the clay to form the ancient
    shapes esteemed by your family?

Indian potter, Indian potter sitting there tirelessly following your
    archaic craft.
Do you think of ancestors and how they daily used their sturdy
    vessels for storage and such?
Or does your mind's eye rush ahead to your finished bowl and the
    intricate design
That will be so painstakingly applied with a homemade yucca brush?

Indian potter, Indian potter sitting there on the ground exhibiting
    your ware on colorful Pendleton blankets.
I wonder at your patience to sit with only passing tourists to occupy
    your mind.
 Do you toil and babysit your magnificent pottery to keep your craft
    alive
Or do you persevere uncomplainingly for pelf?

Indian potter, Indian potter sitting on your warm blankets so modest
    and reserved,
Watching and listening as the sightseers file by, marveling
    and praising your elegant clay artistry.
What thoughts woo your mind as these strangers
Boldly stare at you and your work?

Martha Janette Dorsett

BIRTHDAY GREETINGS TO A PATRIOT,
WHO ENRICHED US WITH SOCIAL SECURITY

Father who art in heaven hath sent you as our earthly guide
To raise our spirits and help our troubles subside
With patience, we must pave the way
Not condemn and always say
Why can't things move on faster?
You are God's servant and our worthy master
Confidence in your active mind
Yours is a mental struggle to assist mankind
Noble man of deeds, we rest in your power
Glorious American of the hour
Your bravery alone demands respect
Desiring presidency over a union nearly wrecked
Ten months you have toiled days and many nights
To benefit the helpless and protect your countrymen's rights
Franklin Delano Roosevelt; just the name alone
Stands for a godly man, with a voice so rich in tone
Citizens of the U.S.A.
Extend best wishes to you today
We are grateful to God for your birth

Pearl Van Slocum

FRIENDSHIP

Old things are valuable things
    Friendship is in my mind
    Not the fleeting kind
But one good friend from childhood days
Who through joy or trouble with us stays
    How sweet to confide in another
    Spoken words perhaps we only could trust to our mother
Friendship was not given at birth
    We who have found one perfect lasting friendship
Truly, God's gift to us on earth

Pearl Van Slocum

FLICKERING CANDLES

Each occasion of our meeting is like a candle . . . warm, glowing,
    melting down my heart a little more each time . . .
Sometimes, the flame burns brightly for the life of the candle —
    casting its flickering shapes upon the world surrounding it,
    leaving a lovely embodiment of memories, of each priceless
    moment that the flame survived . . . There are times, too,
    when a sudden breeze — or perhaps, a faulty wick —
    causes the flame to flicker and die — without really
    reaching its full height . . . but, even then, there is still
    the pleasure of knowing the flame will be relit another, more
    opportune time . . . with promise of perhaps an even warmer
    and livelier glow than any previous occasion has afforded . . .
So, I line up my candles — and joyfully anticipate the lighting
    of the next one — perhaps a soft and gentle flicker,
    as if cupped between two warm and loving hands — or perhaps
    a more active — more exciting blaze, which does not die
    until it drowns itself in its own ecstasy . . .
I like to think that my supply of candles is endless . . . perhaps
    you know whether this is so . . . but, please don't tell me . . .
    just let me go on, thinking that I'll have these flickering
    candles for eternity . . .

Jean A. Sacharko

MY BROTHER

This is for my brother
    whom I love with all my heart,
I want to tell you how I feel
    if only just a part.

You are in my every thought;
    you're deep within my soul;
you make the dark days seem so bright;
    and bring warmth when it's cold.

I wish that you were here with me;
    you seem to understand
just what I feel inside of me
    and always hold my hand.

I wish that I could take away
    the pain you feel inside;
each day you're in that prison;
    each night you've sat and cried.

But in case you don't understand
    just what I want to say . . .
I send my heart to you — with love —
    to help you through each day.

Vicki Shrader

TROUBLE HEART

My heart is saddened, full of tears,
weighted down in pain. A *Trouble Heart*.

So! It! Seem! Only my Father, Oh!

My Heavenly Father! Knows the
Sorrow within me.

The consolation of his joyous

Victory over *Death*.

Cry!! out saying be of *Faith* for
''I am *Life* and *Life* am I!''

Ina M. C. McPleasant

A MOTHER'S LOVE

Mother's love has much *intensity,*
her *body* is just a shell; for her *soul* —
that's of *sincerity.*

Which clothe her beauty within; with
eyes that see endless dreams, ears that
hear silent cries.
Mother knows all that's *pure* and *sure*
is sent by God.

He helps her bear the *pain* none
other can share. *That's why!*

God! blessed Mother with the gift of love.

Ina M. C. McPleasant

I walked with you today . . .
    wondering what went wrong —
We had little to say . . .
    which made the walk so long.

I walked with you today . .
    wondering what went wrong —
Dazed feelings of dismay . . .
    sang words of a sad song.

I walked with you today . . .
    wondering what went wrong —
Lost — lost along the way . . .
    a love that was so strong.

I walked with you today . . .
    wondering what went wrong —
Love is real, not all play . . .
    it's a place to belong.

I walked with you today . . .
    wondering what went wrong —
We had little to say . . .
    which made the walk so long.

Dale Behren

NOT A MOMENT TOO SOON

I hope you know how hard it is sometimes
to lie here awake half the night,
without you.
I want to try so much to be strong about it.
Now I get the chance to feel what it's like
to be next to you again,
though I never forgot;
God knows how I miss you.
I keep telling myself soon, soon.
At times like these tomorrow isn't soon enough.

Cathy L. Daniels

HUMAN

Lord, sometimes I thinks I'm human
'til I runs to catch a cab.
And the driver pass me right on by,
like this face I didn't have.

Sometimes I thinks I'm human
'til I go to buy my food.
And the grocer charge me twice as much
for food that's half as good.

Sometimes I thinks I'm human, Lord
'til I comes home late at night.
And my doorman ask me who I am
'cause all us looks alike.

Lord, am I really human?
'Cause, no human being could stand.
The mess I cope with every day
is just totally out of hand.

But, there is times when I feels human.
When I'm out there late at night.
While folks is gettin' robbed and killed.
I thanks God that I'm not white.

James Glover

THE BLIND MAN

I was walking down the sidewalk,
Just the other day;
    When I spied a blind man,
Going slowly on his way.

    I said, ''Good morning, sir,
It's such a lovely day'';
    He said, ''I wouldn't know, my friend,
I've always been blind this way.

    ''I don't know what it's like,
To look up at the moon;
    And I don't know what it's like,
To see the flowers in bloom.

    ''But I still count my blessings,
For God has been good to me;
    And I know He has a reason,
For not letting me see.

    ''I know it won't be long,
Until Jesus will return to stay;
    And I know by His wonderful love,
He'll take this blindness away.''

Fletcher J. Eller

THAT'S THE WAY SISTERS ARE

''Sister!'' I say in anger,
And then, I will stop and think;
When we were children growing up —
''Auh, those were the days!''

Now I gain composure,
At the moment, not quite as mad;
''Sister!'' I say in an apologetic way —
''I'm sorry I made you sad.''

We may blow up at each other,
As often we forget;
To take the time to listen —
For a sister is a friend!

I know that her true beauty,
has the ability to share;
With a sister who is different —
Her viewpoints, secrets and cares.

No matter how much we argue,
Forgiveness comes straight from the heart;
Our love shall abide forever —
For that's the way sisters are.

Hazel Mae Parron

FROM THE HOST OF INTERIOR FLAME

The eyes of the sea are love's waves breaking free
crisscross tides beam like glass in blue light

There the echoes keep sounding as this pathway astounding
flood this region with rainbows and might

The unstopped roar sped its wings to the shore
on motionless seas vessels peer

On the all mirrors face mansions tumble in place
when the last of all lost return here

It's the gateway to freedom where few travelers pass
to be held by the circuits on three-cornered glass

On the outside there's seasons
On the inside there's reasons
hear the flight of lightning, cry

For man is shadow's glory and with death so ends life's story
then to vanish like a mist in the sky

But vision's lights continue spreading, and this path will lead each
soul to see

That every living thing or being, truly God had meant to be

Dick Jordan

"NO" COMES FIRST

So you are off to college this fall, my granddaughter?
You'll be treading in a different type of water!
There'll be times when decisions must come in a hurry.
Be prepared to combat problems that on you flurry!

A great word to carry with you wherever you go —
Is a two-letter, all-purpose protector called, "No!"
Time and again ugly disruptions on you will flow.
Using this two-letter word, a good habit will glow!

Many so-called friends on you will try to change your routine.
Your purpose in life is to strengthen your moral spleen!
It's better to say "No!" when tempted with zingy spice.
Remember your main goals! Don't be afraid to think twice!

is in my mind
    Not the fleeting kind
But one good friend from childhood days
Who through joy or trouble with us

Mervin L. Schoenholtz

WAVES

Does the beach lament the passing of each wave?
I think not.
Each wave caresses its sand differently,
Removing traces of previous waves,
The scars of those that have trod upon its tender being.
Each wave brings a new essence,
New shape, new hope.
The beach is not fickle because it absorbs each caress,
Nor is it unloved as each wave recedes.
You entered my life as do the waves;
Erasing previous scars, your embrace cleared my past.
But you are a wave, and I, the beach.
Now that you are gone, another will come,
Erasing the tracks of tears you left behind,
Establishing a new pattern upon my sand.

Madelene R. Grimm

THE VIETNAM VETERANS

Young men joined the armed services, to do their duty,
Believing that it was really their choice to make.
They were sent to Vietnam, a country they knew very little
    about. They fought hard in the front lines
The war was so fierce and bloody, attacks on every side.
It took place on foreign soil, yet our country called it a
    cold war.
There was nothing cold about it, only the dead bodies that
    came home in boxes.
On the fields of victory and defeat, they did their very
    best for us.
Their dedication was so great, for a war we didn't believe in.
Some came home alive, some with physical and mental hardships.
They suffered much more than we'll ever know.
We didn't welcome them home; fact is we turned our backs on them,
Turned a deaf ear to their problems. They needed our help
    and concern.
How can we live with ourselves knowing that we let them down?
Will saying we are sorry be enough for them?
Sure, we are burying them with dignity. Don't they deserve more?
After all, they are veterans who believe in their country — yet!
    After all they have gone through. God bless them.

Mary Campbell

ONE SHOW

Dedicated to P.R.

The audience is waiting
The curtain opens slowly
The show begins.
The lines, actions, expressions, timing, voice and emotions —
That's what it takes to be an actor in the theatre.
They spend their lives entertaining and teaching us as well.

One show . . .
It can open your eyes to a truth about life,
It could remove a prejudiced feeling from your mind,
It might give you more of an understanding about society,
It could possibly make you forget your troubles.
To act is an art form;
To be enlightened and touched from those actors
Is the gift they give us in return.

The show ends and the curtain descends slowly.
And sometimes the audience hesitates to depart.
The theatre is an appreciated, needed place
That reflects various aspects of life in a two-hour space of time.
It's a reflection of people
And the theatre is our mirror to see more clearly.

Julie Lachman

SOFTLY

Softly as the sun is shining,
To turn a gray sky to blue;
    Somewhere a cool wind is blowing,
Softly as my heart beats for you.

    Softly as the rose petals are falling,
As I listen to the mockingbird sing;
    Softly as our baby is sleeping,
Oh, how I wish I could hear your name.

    Softly as the snowflakes are falling,
Somewhere on the mountain top;
    Softly as my thoughts are for you,
For my love for you will never stop.

    Softly as I tiptoe through the flowers,
And I pick a bouquet for you;
    Softly as my teardrops are falling,
Because I'm so lonely for you.

    Softly as I look at your picture,
Knowing your life is now through;
    Your love I'll always cherish,
Softly my heart beats for you.

Fletcher J. Eller

FLETCHER JUNIOR ELLER. Born: Gillsville, Georgia, 8-28-32; Married: Pearl Dora, 8-5-53; Education: University of Maryland, College Park, Maryland, 1960-62; Sumter Technical College, Sumter, South Carolina, 1978-80; Occupation: 24 years in United States Air Force, Master Sergeant, retired, 4-1-77; Memberships: American Society of Composers, Authors, and Publishers; American Legion, The Non-Commissioned Officers Association; Poetry: 'America You'll Always be Beautiful To Me,' *American Poetry Anthology, Vol, VII, No. 2,* 1987; Comments: *The reason I like to write poetry is it takes me back to my childhood days and it puts me ahead in the future. When I write poetry it puts me to ease with the world and myself and it strengthens my faith in the Great Creator, God. It makes me proud to be an American and it makes me happy to be alive.*

WHO KNOWS

Who knows who I am?
Who knows what I am?
Who knows why I am?
Who knows the way I am?
Oh! God knows all I am;
That's why I am who I am!
That's why I am what I am!
That's why I am the way I am!

''Because I am a child of God.''

Ina M. C. McPleasant

INA M. C. MCPLEASANT. Born: Jefferson County, Alabama, 7-2-51; Married: Joseph J. Mc-Pleasant, 6-18-72; Education: Fairfield school system, Alabama; Knoxville College, Knoxville, Tennessee; Woodbine State School, Woodbine, New Jersey; H.R. Block Tax School, Alabama; Occupations: Substitute teacher, Director and owner (Agents Elder Line); Author; Memberships: Zeta Phi Beta, Eastern Star, Teacher Association, Association for Retarded Citizens, Small Business, Parent Association, Single Parent Society; Awards: 'I'm Sombody,' 1984; 'A Lonely Home,' 1985; 'Never Alone,' from Mt. Ararat Baptist Church; Poetry: 'Windows of Life,' American Poetry Association, 6-86; Comments: *I am a 36 year old mother of three children, Inette, Willie and Daisy McPleasant, ages 14, 11 and 7. All of my poems are written for trials and tribulations of my life. 'Mothers Love' was written May 1980 after my last child was born. 'Who Knows' was inspired December 1985 by my grandmother, Mrs. Daisy Craig, mother, Mrs. Mamie Caldwell, Aunt Billie Caldwell and sisters, Mrs. Deborah Taylor, Mrs. Francesta Smith. 'Trouble Heart,' developed while at the bedside of my grandmother, Mrs. Ina Reeder, in January 1987. I thank God for all He's blessed upon me.*

MY MAN

Above all other men
I have known and dated,
My heart goes to you
My friend.

No other
Can take your place —
Nor be as humble, caring,
Loving and Understanding.
Our love shines stronger
Each day;

Bonding us closer together,
As we share all eternally.

Marilynn M. McMillin

UP TO YOU

There is a special way for living
for everyone of the kind:
If what doing you believing
and achieve your peace of mind,
developing aspiration
on the level you can cope
with awareness, true perception
where to start and when to stop.

There is a special way for living
and artistry changing heart,
challenge after challenge meaning
only daily obvious chart
which you drawing on self-power
to find in world worthy place,
so develop richer, fuller
your potential; to do best.

Adam F. Misterka

OH NO YOU'RE NOT

The participant turned spectator sport
Has been found guilty in insanity court
I'm sorry to the youngsters who are concerned
The days are pages ripped out and burned

Hatred is all over my stubborn face
The innocent victim is building his case
I knew I've been right all along
Now the world is gonna see she's wrong

Oh no you're not
Icicles are burning hot
The past has to rot
Untying a giant knot

It's illegal to back down a one-way street
You'll pay the fine if you gotta cheat
There's another correction to the mistake
There's always healing after a heartache

An autobiography is a human story
Experienced in a residential laboratory
Someday you're gonna want what I got
Oh no you're not, oh no you're not

John Cichoski

REMEMBERING

Remember them slowly,
The years that are gone.
Look them over with tenderness,
They were once, and now gone.
Try not to regret a single moment,
An excuse can be made for the wrongs.
Each experience taught a lesson,
Once it was learned, the moment gone.
Time is unique for each,
Recorded in the brain.
So when remembering comes again,
It unravels the passage of time on a wave.
Make the memories be for gladness,
A slow chill that caresses the mind.
Let the rest of life be a song,
On tape forever in your mind.

Gloria Gambale

A NEW BEGINNING

I see you walking down the aisle with Mom and Dad
And realize time is moving fast.
Wasn't it yesterday when you were helping me with my
      fourth grade math?
It shows you we all grow up quickly.
Now you're nervous, waiting for your bride.
She walks down the aisle, soon to be by your side.
Your faces show the emotions clearly:
A great deal of love, happiness and respect for one another.
This is the day,
The person, you've been waiting for all your life.
The dream has come true for you both.
Now you've been pronounced man and wife.
And you begin to walk together down the aisle united.
Now you're not alone —
There is someone who cares and wants to share her future with you.
It's hard to believe
My brother is married.

Julie Lachman

LOOKS

One look
And one judges.
If you pass the requirements
You'll be accepted without a second thought.

But if you lack outer beauty,
One passes by without hesitation.
They couldn't care less about inner beauty.
No one realizes the hurt, rejection one suffers for —
Those who are laughed at.

Too bad we live in a plastic society
When one only cares about outer beauty
And doesn't make an attempt to seek for one's inner qualities.
People are too concerned with the wrapping of the package —
and not with what's in the package.

Julie Lachman

FOREVER LOVE

My secret love lived deep within his soul, so very much like me.
So afraid to emerge, to let his feelings show.
Afraid to admit his love, he placed me high above.
Putting me on a pedestal, there he kept me well.
Untouched, safe and out of reach of others.
Loving only from the depth of his inner soul.
I too felt the presence of this uncontrollable love —
      that we dare not speak on.
Many times our inner thoughts and feelings clashed, exploding in an
      ecstasy that has never been touched by reality.
When everything began to fall into place, he died before
      we could really embrace.
Leaving a scar buried deep within my soul, a love that was,
      and was never told.

Nan Blackshire-Little

THAT PEACEFUL CALL

I say to all of you who weep please hear my words and know
      That I am in a safer place where all the pain has ceased its woe.
My life was spent with all the joy and all the happiness
      That God decreed,
      But underneath those blissful times were so much pain and misery.

Sometimes I'd sit and ask him why my vessel was racked and worn,
      Why so much trouble pierced and pried my soul much like a thorn.
But through these times with eyes when closed I saw my master's face
      And he in all his wisdom saved and taught me of his loving grace.

So now my time has trickled on this life has come to close
      But please my family, my loved ones dear,
Remember that I have gone on home.
      So when you think of me, my friends, don't let your teardrops fall
For now I've come to the journey's end and answered to
      that peaceful call.

Diane F. Briscoe

SOUL STAR

The day has come to a rapid end and now I sit alone
      I'm waiting for the phone to ring to hurry to your home.
I've waited long with little patience each hour of this day
      And now you see the waiting ends; it's time I had
            your loving ways.

I know not why I feel this way; it's hard enough to speak
      I can only give the way I feel, my love until I'm weak.
I sometimes fight the urge to cry whenever I see your face
      Just thinking of you when you've gone away brings my heart
            to a rapid pace.

Each day it's harder than the last, our love has grown so blind
      I wonder now if you left me weak, without soul
            nor reason nor rhyme.
But whatever the reason or cause for us it's all the same to me,
      For you've become my rising sun that never shall be free.

So with these words straight from my heart
      Their meaning stands so clear
That wherever life leads you, shining star,
      You've captured my soul for thee.

Diane F. Briscoe

THE EYE OF THE STORM

She moves with such savagery across all the land
      Destroying all things which come under her hand.
The hills they are ravaged, and the trees that stood tall
      Must suffer her fury and all they shall fall.

While all of her ragings and tantrums they flow
      There exists deep within her the gentlest of glows.
In quietness it slumbers, its embers aglow
      It's dimly aware of destruction below.

In such short time past, the fury now has gone by
      This powerful lady takes high to the sky.
She rises so high that the heavens they break
      So that finally the eye is now fully awake.

So slowly she lightens and reclaims all her ill
      And the eye of the storm keeps her winds justly still.

Diane F. Briscoe

ISLAND LOVE

Island waves rushing
caressing windswept sands
smoothing hardened ripples
reaching with softened hands.

Smooth, silk waters
easing all the tough
soft hands touch
smoothing what was rough.

Flowing and flowing
graceful sweeping seas
endless loving waves
gentle blowing breeze.

Eventually to polish
to shine what is good
to shine forevermore
not what only can, but should.

The Island waves that are
its Lover and its Love
the lonely sands it changes
just by Love . . . not shove.

Glenn T. Fugitt

NEVER GOOD-BYE

I can't say, "Good-bye," my Love,
that isn't how I feel.
I believe, "We," transcend that,
and this life, just another ordeal.

There is so much to say,
and then again, why?
It's not that you don't understand,
only, that I, have failed to fly.

Even to say, "I love you,"
means nothing, to how I feel;
though you, are still there,
and I am here, still.

I have learned much, I think,
since Time has passed between;
and still, all roads lead to "Us,"
no matter, what I have felt, or seen.

The Oceans, my Love,
only they . . . carry our depth!
And Understand.

Glenn T. Fugitt

A FINAL PRAYER

O God, You in Your wisdom
Know what Your plan is.
Help us accept it — with grace
And dignity as she would desire.
It is not for us to savor our grief,
But to think of the happiness —
The glory to which she is now attuned.
As she lived a life worthy of
Your grace, let us follow now
In her footsteps and live lives
She would be proud of.
Let us carry forth the good
She has brought into this world
Unto future generations,
And in so doing
Shall she still live.
Though the burden be heavy,
We ask nought but that You give us
Wisdom and strength to carry on.

Sharon Rudolph

ONLY PEDRO AND I KNOW

Pedro, my grandma's dog,
A brown pariah with glassy eyes,
Followed her to the beach each day
To get fresh fish from the fishermen's catch.
He barked at the spotted python
Rolled high around the cashew tree.

He chased pigs from paddy fields,
Crows away from fresh coconut halves
Spread out on bamboo mats to dry,
And chickens back into their coop at dusk.

Less than beautiful
Is what was said of Grandma,
The colorful peacock spreads its wings;
But dusky Grandma could not.

Lonely Grandma, Pedro and me,
Were not lonely when together.
Each evening we'd bathe in the cold spring
Of the mountain not far beyond.

And only Pedro and I know
That she was more than beautiful.

Enrica Fernandes

FIGHT . . .

Fight . . . Flight . . . Fright
Fright . . . Fight . . . Flight . . .

Why should I whip ass
 just to survive?
To collect a debt
To prevent more theft
I am old
Fight should be for the young
But fight I must
Rage . . . Fear . . . Survival
To have Peace Understanding and Love
Instead of Fight and Strife
Is a dream, revolutionary
 for our times

Rita Maria Brown

I STOOD THERE

I stood there
Like a fool
Watching my father
Die of a stroke.
With dilated pupils
He signalled his departure.

I stood there
Staring stupidly
As doctors fought for his life,
With massages and electric shocks
That made him bounce up and down.
My silent voice begged
That straight green line
To flicker and move.

I stood there
A silent scream in my throat
As the sheet was pulled over my father's face.
My knees trembled as I knelt on the floor.
A part of me stayed there
These past twelve years.

Enrica Fernandes

CHILDREN

We love them,
Adore them.

They're spoiled,
Loved all the more.

A kiss heals
All their hurts.

A harsh word
Can make them cry.

Hugs
can make them happy.

Life is full,
Happy
Sad
Children are our hope.

June D. Wiley

THE COLUMN OF FIRE

It ripped through the sky
Raced toward the ground
This column of fire I saw

It came without warning
No reason at all
It included a most awesome sound

Some say it was lightning
I'm not at all sure
For I felt the fear pierce my chest

Now it's completely silent
The sky bright and clear
And I am still holding my breath.

William K. Brobst

ON SHAKESPEARE

What needs my Shakespeare for his honored bones
The labor of an age in piléd stones?
Or that his hallowed reliques should be hid
Under a star-ypointing pyramid?
Dear son of Memory, great heir of Fame,
What need'st thou such weak witness of thy name?
Thou in our wonder and astonishment
Hast built thyself a livelong monument.
For whilst, to th' shame of slow-endeavoring art,
Thy easy numbers flow, and that each heart
Hath from the leaves of thy unvalued book
Those Delphic lines with deep impression took,
Then thou, our fancy of itself bereaving,
Dost make us marble with too much conceiving,
And so sepúlchred in such pomp dost lie
That kings for such a tomb would wish to die.

John Milton

PORCELAIN PALACE

In this porcelain palace
these repeating patterns of walls that encase
over the mind it turns amidst negative space
down at your feet focused on staring
in all that restless defeat, it's your self-honesty that's now baring
This repeating realization is the bathroom of stimulation
you're looking at a reflection gathering pull for retraction
no apparent undercover your failure's guilt hovers
this question isn't of balance to noncommital attitudes
but answering which is balance for inner logical latitudes
In this porcelain palace
these repeating patterns of walls that encase
over in the mind it turns with isolating pace
whatever realm you retire from obscure situations
it's your flesh attire in reoccurring realization
a ceramic altar's grace
is your porcelain and confessional trace.

K. R. Ollis

THE VISIT

I sat waiting patiently for him
For where he was I couldn't go to him
He arrived soon after
I peered through the glass and looked at him
But was unable to touch him
We picked up the phone
His voice was the same except
I couldn't feel his breath as he spoke
We talked and I sat looking at him, storing memories
Because soon they will say I have to leave
I told him that I loved him
I told him that I missed him
Then it was time to go
I didn't want to leave
I wanted to stay there looking at him forever
But next week would be time enough for another visit

Edith D. Johnson

THE TRASH MAN

Thursday is a special day and the boy's joy knows no bounds,
The day of great anticipation when The Trash Man comes around.
The boy's alert as one small rabbit biding time before the hound,
His senses geared for action when The Trash Man comes around.
He has barely time for breakfast or for dressing, grooming hair.
He must race out for the greeting, for The Trash Man may be there.
At the front door tensed and waiting, little soldier stands his ground.
There's no time to kiss a grandma when The Trash Man comes around.
He can hear the bugles playing at the truck's approaching sound,
His wee body's off in flight, for The Trash Man's coming around.
He arrives for the greeting, for the loading and farewell,
His face radiates his joy, The Trash Man's cast his spell.
There's no other day like Thursday when the boy's joy
    knows no bounds,
No other day of great anticipation, like when The Trash Man
    comes around.

Jo Ann Denome

DEATH OF A SPORT

I mourned that sad and tragic day the plastic trash bag came our way
To hide that long sought after prize, hidden now forever
    from a picker's eyes.
Every Tuesday night was picker's treat, a treasure hunt
    on westside streets.
I'd cruise the blocks with cheerful smile, and race a competitor
    to the pile.
I'd stake my claim and load my prize, observing the
    greedy pickers' eyes.
First come first served was the name of the game,
    dedicated pickers picked, come snow or rain.
Most addicted pickers are a compatible lot — for every ten
    you meet there's one who's not.
Tuesday night trash pickin' was a popular sport — the boxes
    and baskets were easy to sort.
My picker's loot sold good on a garage sale day, sent the kids
    to camp on a picker's pay.
Took the kids out pickin' and raised money for a pool,
    was their favorite sport outside of school.
Lot of family togetherness on a trash pickin' run, then along
    came the trash bags, killed all the fun.

Jo Ann Denome

RECOLLECTION

Night tapestry woven of seamoss, kelp and moonray;
a pier at the shore, lying athwart a rushing surge of ocean,
black gleaming, heaving breast of sea
soughing in the moonlight, pulling at the pilings underneath,
as though Poseidon — a sea-drenched Samson —
    had stretched out his arms,
palms open flat against the watered wood on either side,
his strength pressing in all directions, finally torn
    toward the tide.

We had leaned into the urgent night seawind,
our faces stung by sharp cold ocean spray.
Shadows stalked our footsteps, creaking the trodden boards
to frighten me as I strode to match his pace,
shadows cast by vagrant boardwalk lights.
This was to be the last of rare dark salted nights.

Gertrude Leigh

A thought went up my mind to-day
That I have had before,
But did not finish, — some way back,
I could not fix the year,

Nor where it went, nor why it came
The second time to me,
Nor definitely what it was,
Have I the art to say.

But somewhere in my soul, I know
I've met the thing before;
It just reminded me —'twas all —
And came my way no more.

Emily Dickinson

TO GRACIE

Way up in the Endless Mountains
    There's a little cabin home
Where a dear old mother's waiting
    While her restless boy does roam.

There she sits alone and praying
    For him every night and day
That the Lord will surely lead him
    Always in the narrow way.

Long ago he left to travel,
    Chasing life's elusive dream;
Now he's longing just to see her
    Down beside a rippling stream.

There they'll sit and talk while fishing,
    Or wander through the woods again
Seeking tracks of deer and foxes,
    Laughing just for joy and then

He will tell her of his travels,
    All the wondrous sights he's seen,
Then he'll settle down beside her,
    Nevermore to roam again.

Anona Canright Birtch

ON GETTING DRUNK

In a crowded bar with one's thoughts
Sorting them out, coming up with naughts
Taking up space in a void
Elbow to elbow with a world annoyed

The babble of voices strikes the ears
Raucous noise covering individual fears
Dampening sorrows glass by glass
Becoming a slob, but doing it with class

Having no face in a faceless crowd
How could one be so endowed
Not one listening ear to be found
Being alone with people all around

Guys and gals drinking together and yet
Haven't heard each other since they met
They too are lonely souls
Like everyone, just can't find their goals

B. J. Hilderbrand

SAM AND HIS OLD '96'

Fourteen cars at the starting point,
    Their engines roaring to life;
Each driver is hoping to win the race —
    Among them is Sam and his old '96'!

'Round and 'round the track they fly,
    Each trying for the best position;
First one, then another falls behind,
    But not Sam's old '96'!

Lap after lap they rumble and roar,
    More of them give up the struggle;
Soon there's just three of them left in the race,
    One of them Sam's old '96'!

Sam looks to the right and then to the left,
    And he sees a 'sandwich' a-comin',
He gauges his clearance and just in time
    Puts the pedal to old '96'!

A deafening roar goes up from the crowd
    As the dust he lays down puts them under,
And over the finish line grinning and proud
    Comes Sam and his old '96'!

Anona Canright Birtch

SOLACE

When sorrow lifts her darkened head
Angel wings are hovering low,
To take a share of our despair
And point the way our heart should go.

They light upon our weight of grief
To claim the thoughts that should not be,
To give us strength to face the day
To heal the heart and set us free!

They hover low to guide the step
Of those whose joy has been so stilled,
And linger close, with patience wait,
To comfort those outside the gate!

Elsie B. Webster

LONELY NESSEE

A Saga of the Loch Ness Monster

Nobody cares for Nessee
As I do
It's a crying shame;
That is the reason she's hiding —
She really can't be blamed.

Nessee is not good looking,
But who really gives a damn;
When people are 'a-looking'
She's at another booking
And can't be present
As planned.

Howard W. Hult

DECISION

In the throes of grave decision
Comes a haunting of the mind,
As time awaits, eternal,
The truth alone to find.

Indecision clouds the thinking,
While all truth is set aside,
Comes the clarity of a sunrise,
When the truth no longer hides.

Peace of mind is as a bauble
Held in abeyance as we wait,
But the light of truth it releases
When we cease to debate.

The mind, a bright field of clover,
Blooms anew when we decide,
When we rise above hesitation
Then the gates swing open wide!

Peace of mind, a lovely journey,
That is travelled through this life,
And true decision is the vessel
That guards against all fear and strife!

Elsie B. Webster

FOR MY SON, ROY

The Kaleidoscope of life is turning,
Turning slowly as I write,
Forming smoky, shifting shadows
Reminiscent of the night.

See the ever-changing patterns.
Strange, the pictures that they make.
Destiny's determination,
Oh, the twisting paths it takes.

Now we see a treasured vision,
And we'd like to take it slow.
But the pattern just keeps changing,
Always moving, on the go.

Helplessly, we grasp at nothing
As the scenes go flashing by,
Spelling out the mystic future
In the twinkling of an eye.

If we by some secret magic
Could conquer time, could hold him fast,
No more waiting for the future,
No more yearning for the past.

But that is only wishful thinking,
For all too soon I know you'll be
An old man dreaming in some lonely corner,
Haunted by youth's memories.

Myrtle R. Jessee

FRIENDSHIP

A man is blessed,
By the friends he has.
He counts true friends he'll possess,
For they are his treasures, his guests.

Bernard Jacob

PART SYMPATHIES

There is a theory that you are identified with
everybody and everything you meet during the day.
Some part identifications are sympathetic, some unsympathetic.

We were girls together — late childhood and the teens.
One friend thought she had a happy life, married, children.
Another said if she had it to do over again, ''I'd stay single.''
Do I have some kind of conflict because of sympathy with both?

Today, the paper delivery boy left the paper early.
A new mailperson brought the mail.
The supermarket staff has sympathetic and unsympathetic days,
at their best when the stream of customers is moderate.
A neighbor down the street went to a relative's funeral.
Relatives contacted by phone always seem sympathatic.
Conflicts are in the past.
The TV is still there.
The kitchen stove, sink and refrigerator are still there,
rather impersonal, but essential to the daily routine.
The memories are mostly sympathetic.

There is a theory that it is desirable to be
free of complexes of other bodies.
One way to become free is to work on an individual manual
hobby for awhile each evening before going to bed, and then
to read a literary selection aloud to the empty air,
not recording what you read. Sometimes it works.

Florence K. McCarthy

FLORENCE K. McCARTHY. Born: Bronx, New York, 1-30-18; Education: Hunter College, City University of New York, B.A., Pre-Med, 1943; Occupations: Engineering aide, Fabric salesclerk, Comptometer operator, Typist, Stenographer, Secretary, Word processor; Memberships: AAUW, New York City Branch; Bronx Chapter Hunter Alumni; AARP Bronx #162; Bronx Artists Guild; Associate member, Knickerbocker Artists; Awards: Grand Award, 1986, from American Poetry Association for 'Part Sympathies,' *Best New Poets of 1986.*

EARTH'S GREATEST MOM

Dear Mom, did I ever tell you how often I recall
The many things you've done for me . . . things both great and small?

You tended my needs while a baby with tender loving care;
You fed me, clothed and loved me; and brushed my long, soft hair.

You read to me and played my games; and when silvery raindrops fell,
I'd curl up snugly in your lap and wonderful stories you'd tell.

You held my small hand tightly as we walked along the way . . .
And through your smile I saw a tear as you left me at school that
 first day.

When in my childish play I'd fall and skin an arm or knee,
You'd wipe my tears, hold me close, and quietly comfort me.

Graduation, my wedding day, the bills both big and small,
Our first home, our baby's colds . . . you helped us through it all.

I know you don't want any praise for all the things you've done,
For being there through rain or shine . . .
 through all the tears and fun.

But someday when God hands out your crown, a special star there'll be;
It will simply say ''Earth's Greatest Mom''. . .
 that's what you are to me!

> *I love you,*
> *Your daughter*

Joann Benfield

IT'S THERE ON YOUR FACE

Don't try to tell how you live each day,
It really doesn't matter if it's work or play.
There's already a recorder in in this place;
Just how you live shows in your face.

If it's false or deceit you have in your heart,
It won't stay hidden inside where it's dark.
For flesh and blood are just veils of lace;
What you have in your heart, you wear on your face.

If you're loving and kind, if for others you live,
'Cause it's not what you get, but how much you give;
When you live mainly for God, in His power and grace,
You don't have to shout it! it's there on your face.

Nita Jamison

MOM

A flower shall grow in pretty colors and shapes.
But no one knows the toll it will take
in a lifetime of winters, blizzards and storms.
Yet do you know, it will show you no scorn.
Be kind to the flower, it means you no harm.
All it can hope is to just carry on.
Though it will bend and might even break,
the seed has been planted and soon it will take.

K. Abbott Prescott

BEAUTY OF LIFE

Beauty of life is written
In the face of one who's lived her day.
Each mark of time a journey
That never seems to go astray.

Each small line, each tiny shadow,
Shows a vessel strong and true,
Each scar a mark of victory
Over things she's had to do.

I thank God for a lengthy journey
That leaves such beauty to be seen,
In the face of those who paint the picture,
Of what was, what might have been.

As I trace each line with interest,
Searching out the mystery,
I find the secret of good living
Engraved, and yet set free!

Elsie B. Webster

ELSIE B. WEBSTER. Pen Name: Island Savannah; Born: Indiana, 3-18-18; Howard P. Webster, 10-20-34; Education: Indiana Business College, 1957-59; Business major, Literature minor; Occupations: Bookkeeping, Accounting; Memberships: State Poetry Club, past member of the National Association of Accountants; Awards: Second prize for local entry, 'The Written Word,' 1967; Poetry: 'It's Christmas,' 'God's Special Candle'; Other Writings: *Remember To Love Me,* book, Carlton Press; Mission article on Financial Management, *Free Methodist Courier;* Comments: *I have had numerous articles published on special topics to encourage and inspire steadfastness, faith and trust. The theme on most accounts is built around the love of Christ, life and its living, joy and sorrow. All writings are done with the intent to lift up the name of our Lord. Many poems are on nature; many on religion; many on seasons of special occasions. Due to the enormous volume of written poems, there is something on every subject. I am a prolific writer and there is no subject too difficult to write about, nor to appreciate the theme.*

ACHIEVEMENT

To dream is to perceive beyond reality.
To aspire is to reach your goals.
To quest is to conquer all fears.

To achieve is to attain finality.

Bernard L. Ginsberg

FIRST CREATION

The sea.
A thing of beauty,
A thing of peace,
A place of hell.
Love —
Life —
Innocence —
Tragedy.
Serenity.
Infinity.
Proclaim your defiance,
Sea.
Lustful and gentle,
You can be,
Sea.
No bias,
Nor prejudice,
In your soul.
One for all and all for one,
God created you for all mankind.

P. J. Dick

BEAUTY

The beauty of morning, when all is still
Lake glistening, asleep until
Four ducks glide by, to break the stillness.
Man fishing, lost in eternity
Tree fearless, enjoying the serenity
Slide waiting, need the child —
Lest it be useless.
Jogger running, his search fruitless.
Swing empty, denying reality
Dog barking, escaping banality
Crow cawing, lest it go unnoticed
Bird searching, raison d'etre remotest
Picnic table, alone, steadfast
Remembering people lost in their repast
I, weeping, praying for tranquility
Deny morn's beauty — escry futility.

Martha McDonnell

DESERT DREAM

As I gaze around the desert
the yellow sands stretch beyond,
I see the rose-like blossom of the cactus
of which I am very fond.
Splashes of red and orange,
the lonely hooting of the owl,
the rustling noises of wildlife on the prowl.
I know when day is breaking
all will be quiet again.
This peace is for taking
My Desert Dream.

Joy M. Parker

SKID ROW IS BEST

For Arlene

Do *not* pity me!
I *have* walked an inch above the ground;
I have been with the most downtrodden
of the earth . . .
I've experienced their black hopelessness . . .
Someday, *I will find* the infinite light of truth.
The *sound* of "one hand," is one of perception.

Richard C. Miller

THE AGE OF DISCOVERY

Christopher Columbus
The Discovery of America

Here I go,
Some sailors and me
With the *Nina,* the *Pinta,*
And the *Santa Marie*
Up ahead I think I see
A piece of land
Let me investigate
Let me understand
As I get closer
I think to myself out loud
I think they'll be pleased
I think they'll be proud
'Cause I have a feeling
About this land that I see
That it will mean a lot
To everyone and me
That people everywhere
Will benefit quite true
Of the discovery that I made
On the twelfth of October 1492

Jack Allured

NIGHTLIFE

For Michael

Nights with you are precious, seem few.
Hours fly like seconds we knew.
A dream ago or true,
Our voices whisper, I love you.

Time now unreal, not kind,
Battle for your love this time,
Soldier unarmed in line
Against forces unseen, I'm blind.

Where are you when shadows run wild,
Thoughts turn to dreams like a child's,
To a future so distant, until you smile,
I awake in your arms from across the miles.

Sherry M. Newman

SPATIAL TIME

I fly, fast-fading star, to ends I cannot see,
to dusts of ancient war, its shards of dark debris.
My shadow cast in pools, a jewel deeply set,
records, as comet cools, a fleeing silhouette.
The shades of distant pasts, autonomy denied,
bedim the quick'ning vasts, where golden kingdoms died,
their mist-enveloped masts with dream and moonray plied,
with clouded chamber blasts, their embers deified.

Aloft with shift in time and quiet drift of space,
the vectors lift and climb and rift the planet's face.
In each unending void, in each dark galaxy,
in each brief star deployed, fly fact and fantasy.
I scrawl a heated line, an earthling elegy,
and try to redefine a fateful syzygy.

Gertrude Leigh

DESTINY

We were given a world in which to live,
The only debt was her love and care.
It seemed an easy promise to give,
And for a while we gave it good fare.

Time passed, our numbers increased,
Creating new lifestyles, new demands;
And with it, greed was released,
Running rampant, completely out of hand.

Nation against nation vying for superiority,
Bending, breaking, making every excuse,
While losing sight of the promised priority,
And racing toward the final abuse.

Raping, pillaging this great planet,
Not seeing or hearing her imploring plea,
While we take her, our, immortality for granted,
And ignore the fast approaching fee.

She has begun complaining this horrid abuse,
And is making her intentions plain.
She will not tolerate this continued ruse,
Before destroying all, starting over again.

Kathleen Hendricks

FATE EAGER TO DESTROY

Exempt from every grief, 'twas mine to live
In dreams so sweet, enchantments so divine,
A thousand joys propitious Love can give
Were scarcely worth one rapturous pain of mine.

Bound by soft spells, in dear illusions blest,
I breathed no sigh for fortune or for power:
No care intruding to disturb my breast,
I dwelt entranced in Love's Elysian bower;

But Fate, such transports eager to destroy,
Soon rudely woke me from the dream of joy,
And bade the phantoms of delight begone:
Bade hope and happiness at once depart,
And left but memory to distract my heart,
Retracing every hour of bliss forever flown.

Glenn Edward Waters III

HIDDEN IN THE IMAGE

with a memory of myself looking out, and a memory
of myself from a vantage, turning to face myself watching,

a memory of myself asleep, and a simultaneous memory
of myself arise/awakening in a picture frame in
someone's forgotten gallery . . .

at night, when everyone's asleep, you may step through
the surface of the mirror like stepping through a doorway . . .
and the memory of my reflection saying, ''there are those
who walk in human form that are not of this world . . .''

one image standing, one image falling, with one image
tumbling above the arc of eyes, always watching . . .

startled awake!
and in that split instant, watching myself awaken,
turning to face myself watching, and not knowing
where to awaken, or which image to awaken us, wondering,
who had asked,
        ''is this a dream?''
and wondering,
            who had dreamed it?

Brian Bywater

THE MOTH AND THE MORROCCAN TAPESTRY

do i kill the moth
that eats the tapestry?

am i the instrumental will of god,
and is this my purpose;
to exterminate an elegant, delicate insect
as ancient as creation?
and thereby my purpose to preserve
the labor of bygone human handicraft
smuggled out of wartime morrocco,
and the loom long since destroyed,
. . . and the art lost . . . ?

how significant is the life of a single moth
to the majestic, all pervasive mind?
or, is this moth its agent,
a tiny instrument,
sent into this pervasive mechanism
to slowly unravel
all the finely woven fabric of human endeavor?

Brian Bywater

SCARRED

Oh the pain of sharp blades — cutting.
Oh the pain of pointed needles — piercing.
Each torturous touch was more painful than the first.
Screams of agony billowed from the room.
The room was brightly lit and intimidating —
    very still.
The blood dripped from the incision
    like water dripping from a leaky faucet.
Oh the pain, the anger, the torture . . .
    scorned by the will of determination.

Sandra J. Clamp

TODAY

This day begins, as all days must,
  In total trust.
We have no map nor chart to show
  The way to go.
But when roads branch, we gladly learn
  At each new turn
That, from within, a "still, small voice"
  Defines the choice.

Susan J. Thomas

SUSAN JANE THOMAS. Pen Name: M.M.; Born: Spokane, Washington, 6-27-51; Divorced; Education: Spokane Community College, two years, basic art, drawing, painting, volume/color design; Certificate in retail clothing and sales cashier; data entry; Occupations: Waitress, Cashier retail sales, Student, Data entry; Memberships: A.M.O.R.C., The Rosicrucian Order, International Jurisdiction; The Graphological Institute, New York; Eagles Lodge and Auxiliary Ladies Fraternal Order, Spokane, Washington; The Mayans; Poetry: 'Today,' 'Dancing,' 'The Witch's Ladder,' 7-87; Themes: *Crossroads of life, how we act and define our way towards experiences, everyday living perils; also magic, witches and warlocks. There was a time when life was free, no worries or stress, we were all carefree.*

ADAGIO

A shadow slices through my waters —
I bow my head beneath its onrush.

Looking back, an oarsman sees the Sun
Has caught my moment, buoyed my heart

Just as the Maestro cups full half-notes
Within His hands. So my full sense
In soft collision with the Sun piques hence,
And I, too, like the lilies of the field
Shall rise again — aweigh, aweigh —
More beautiful than they

Though still unsevered is
The umbilical cord of metaphor —

Evelyn B. Gray

TRIBUTE TO ELVIS

Our Friend

He could not make everyone rich.
But we felt rich, just knowing him was enough.
He was the "King of Rock and Roll"
King of the Music World —
  Elvis Presley
He was Our Friend, we still love him.
We still request his music,
We still buy his records,
We still love him on his
  50th anniversary

Betty Brooks

WALLS

As one wall parts us —
  another breaks down,
    one to heal,
  the other to hurt.

As we bounce from
  one to the other,
  there is confusion —
    a state —
one we cannot unfold.

But with honest
  true love,
we can break each
  and every one.

Only to build
a new wall together.
One that surrounds us,
  and does not part us.

Kattie Danzeisen

FINALE

The curtains closed;
I'm left alone.
The lights are out
And you are gone
My love, my joy
And happiness.

What is this thing
They call death
That takes away
The very breath
Of my love, my joy
And happiness?

I kneel here
As I pray
We will meet
Another day
My love, my joy
And happiness.

Barbara J. Holbrook

CAN I?

I ranted and I raved,
And I misbehaved
Surely to myself I am a slave.

No one is right and I am wrong,
Makes me weak, to be strong.
To think, that I have not long.

For surely to myself I say,
I am selfish in every way,
I must be doing without delay.

I cant and I recant
My knowledge is scant,
And yet will I grant —

I have far yet to go,
To find my own soul,
To return and unfold.

C. E. Paxton

DIVORCE

Marriage is love
  shown by two people
When they marry
The become one
If they get a divorce
The heart, kids, and
  Even the vow is broken
There should be a padding
  for the heart
The kids should get to choose
  Who they live with
And the vow should be
  changed to say
Through sickness and in health
For richer, for poorer
Until death or divorce
Do we part
So the vow is not broken

Tommy Rutz

TIME STOPS WITH A LOOK

In your eyes I see the smiles
of a thousand fleeting friendships,
those quiet intimacies, you share
with most of those you meet.
Behind these I see the sparkle
of myriad frozen tears
kind words, and tender moments keep in store.
Still deeper, I see two pools
of longing, and contentment
waiting to merge.
Past those, I see the fire of passion,
in endless burning kisses,
waiting for a lover's lips
to fuse two into one.
Don't wonder if you catch me
staring in your eyes,
it's like staring into a mirror
at my own.

Robert F. Vitalos

THE MONSTER'S HEAD

Oh Lord, I'm being accused
To carry a monster's head
Regardless of my intentions
The blood and the tears I've shed

It seems no longer human
To belong to the race of man
And doing something humane
Means running a campaign

Looking up to heaven
We see sunny or dreary skies
While smoke from victims' hearts
Sky high to boundlessness rise

I realize that the answers my hungry soul requires
Will make me sink beneath selfhood
Into brimstone and fires

Still — I weep for replies

Why are the fine hearts being slain
And why should good intentions
Always be in vain?

Why? No answer? No reply?

Halina de Roche

MY FAVORITE THINGS

Jogging suits and Cornish hens,
Eating out with loving friends,
Walking in the park in spring —
These are some of my favorite things.

Grocery shopping — dancing slow
Cuddling with the lights turned low,
Yellow mums, bluebirds that sing —
These are some of my favorite things.

Laughter and babies and dreams that come true,
White puffy clouds and skies bright blue,
Cards signed by ''Kitten'' and the joy they bring —
These are some of my favorite things.

Waterbeds that warm my bones,
Christmas bells with clear, bright tones,
''Windsong'' and roses and perfumes that cling,
These are some of my favorite things.

Catherine M. Klinkerman

DESIRE

Wistfully wishing for love and affection,
Dreaming of dancing with you is perfection;
Wondering why miles can't shrivel tonight,
Shrink into nothingness, right out of sight.

I want you here closer beside me tonight;
I'm so very lonesome. This isn't right.
Come to me, love me; stay by my side;
Care for me, keep me; with me abide.

Erma I. Sentz-Bentz

YOU'RE MY GUY

You're the kind of man that I can love,
You're the kind of man that comes from heaven above,
You're the kind that cheers me when I'm blue,
You're my kind and I'm in love with you.

You're the kind to guide me through the years,
Caressing me with gentle hands that dry away my tears,
You're the kind that makes my dreams come true,
You're my guy and I'm in love with you.

Whenever you're not with me,
I feel so awfully blue.
Please, darling, won't you let me
Spend my whole life with you?

You're the kind that brings me happiness,
You bring the flowers of spring with every tender kiss,
The sunshine of your love you bring me too.
You're my guy, and I'm in love with you.

Catherine M. Klinkerman

RESTORED

*To R.S., who made a decision for the Kingdom
of God through Jesus Christ by the Holy Spirit.*

Hey man, I can see the pain in your life.
Yes, it's from a divorce marked with strife.
Listen, allow me to share some words with you.
I know the pain, I've been there too.
Through the toils and struggles of the torment at night,
your sleep has gone; your emotions are sore;
and you wonder how to fight.
Your days are gloom, and your mind is going boom.
With thoughts of reflections past,
reactions, reactions, reactions are going fast.
If you allow God to be the solution,
you'll become whole, restored, and cleansed
without pollution.
There's a city of refuge on the outskirts of Atlanta.
A place of love where the Holy Spirit does minister.
Come to Chapel Hill Harvester,
decide to be a new creature and battle the sinister . . .
Hey brother, I know your pain.

Larry W. Hilton

A MOTHER ALONE

A slight breeze blowing through the trees
Gives play to imaginations on this beautiful day.
Sun, shining brightly like the previous winter's blind,
Gives warmth lightly to soothe a wandering mind.

Hearts hurt, their tears breed discontent,
And worry is added to the fears.
Changing seasons bring mind today
To sounds of children — not mine — at play.

Discord of the months recent
Preys on feelings, causing thoughts indecent.
But time slips by, as clouds above,
Through memories of tender love.

Someday . . . soon . . . they'll be back to stay,
Bringing with them more contented days.

Barbara Siegfried

I KNOW WHERE I'M GOING

I know where I'm going because I know where I am
I know where I'm going because I know where I've been

And though I'm not around that ominous island as yet
I sport an electric spark in my eye and a confident spring in my step

Concentrated vision keeps my train running on one track
Straight ahead, forward I never looked back

Those bright lights are calling me, I follow so steady
When my shine time comes be sure I'll be ready

Mistakes are just that, nothing more, nothing less
And will be discreetly dismissed by the one to whom you confess

Sweetly breathe the day's air as if it was your very last
Taking things with a grand shrug for this world moves so fast

So life can slap my wrists in steel cuffs and shackle my aching feet
Life can push me down and twist my arm, but I know not defeat

Life can conjure up famine, sickness, and potent acid rain
But I know where I'm going and I have
  an indestructible planned campaign

Michele Rae

MICHELE LAUREN RAE. Born: Pittsburgh, Pennsylvania, 11-11-68; Education: Hillsborough Community School, Tampa, Florida, 1986; C.C.T. certified, June, 1987; Accepted into the radio broadcasting program at Bauder College, Fort Lauderdale, Florida for fall, 1987; Membership: World Outreach Center; Awards: Honorable Mentions for 'For The Love Of Children,' 'Hold On,' 'Our Joyous Rose,' 1986; 'Love And Blessings,' 'My Angel On The Ledge,' 'My Lifelong Friend,' 1987; Golden Poet Award, 1986-87; Poetry: 'For The Love Of Children,' *World Poetry Anthology,* 1986; 'These Teardrops,' *American Poetry Anthology,* 1987; 'Our Joyous Rose,' *Great Poems of Today,* 1987; 'I Know Where I'm Going,' *Poetry Of Life,* 1988; Themes: *To study my work is to know me and what I care about in my life. Put simply, my poetry reflects my life and my life reflects my poetry.*

SCARED OF LOVE

Scared
Love
Desire
Friendship
Companionship
Lover
Fear
Self-Confidence
Trust

Night is the hardest of them all,
Because of the fear of loving him forever.
But I need a friend, a companion, without any ties.
No love and no fears.
My self-confidence has been regained
By the companionship of others.
I cannot trust my lover, because I cannot trust in my love.

Janeen Steel

THOUGHTS ON LOVE

To search for it all your life,
Sometimes just in vain.
It comes to you rather unexpectedly,
And you are overwhelmed by the emotion.
You learn how to accept it,
With all its limits and rewards.
You learn how to pursue it further;
Sometimes to be crushed,
Other times to be uplifted.
It sings to you, it warms your soul,
It exposes your true self.
Don't take it for granted,
No matter how strong it appears,
For it can disappear without warning.
Once you have it, encourage it, caress it.
For without it your soul will pine.
Without it your heart will bleed.
Ensure you are willing to work hard upon its arrival.
For it is love that erases the void within you.
Without true love, you die alone.

Patrick E. Lowry

BECKONING TREES

As sunshine in the morning seeped through their outstretched arms
They waved and beckoned come outside, and revel in our charms

No child can ever long resist a friendly play invite
And so the day was spent with them, from morning until night

Climbing on the shingled trunks, and slender reaching limbs
Searching leaves and knotholes for creatures hid within

Chartreuse frogs, spotted bugs, caterpillars, fat and thin
Squirrels and birds, and sometimes snakes,
  tongues flicking past their chins

Lines of ants marched up and down, cushiony cotton bugs
Here and there a hovering bee, tree snails and homeless slugs

Once the creatures all were spied, prodded, poked, and teased
Came a time for resting 'neath shade of friendly trees

In middle age these friends still call, an offer not to play
But just to spend rare idle hours in napping cares away

Perhaps to see some childhood friends once more through boyish eyes
And marveling at their foolish forms, still fills me with surprise

So well-adapted to their niche, the fruit of Nature's whim
Yet when old age has come to me, the years my eyes will dim

And I shall no longer see the old trees' denizens
Still they will beckon from the hill to come and rest with them.

Kenneth A. Cyr

SEEKER COMING HOME

Seeker is another name
Staring afar through window pane.
I cannot bear it all alone
My restless Seeker far from home.

I toil by day, ''never tardy,''
Bearing this burden within my body
The length of departure a missing year,
And trying my best to hold a tear.

I think of her, day by day.
Where does she roam to go astray,
What direction does she roam?
Seeker, Seeker, this is home!

As I walked a lonely lane
My heart beat rapid, but not in vain,
I ran to view from the highest stone
''Seeker, Seeker, coming home,''

She whirled around to look behind
Over grounds that measure far from kind.
A seeking mind has been postponed
''Seeker, Seeker, coming home.''

Ed Lewis

SIDE BY SIDE

How long a trail we have traveled.
Side by side, but far apart.
You were there day and night.
With caring eyes and loving heart.

Like a baby, my steps unsure.
I faltered and often fell.
Instead of talking, asking for help.
I shunned you and rebelled.

How long a trail I have traveled.
To return from where I came.
To Mother's arms, warm and safe.
With only me to blame.

How long a trail we shall travel.
Side by side, together.
Mother, daughter now as one.
Friends forever.

Camella A. Black

RELUCTANT FAREWELL

My grandma doesn't live here anymore
She is in a better place,
This is a fate that I myself
Will someday have to face.

My grandma doesn't live here anymore
I prayed she would not die,
She meant so much to me
I didn't want to say good-bye.

My Grandma doesn't live here anymore
As she did for so many years.
Now days when I think of her
My thoughts turn into tears.

Val Philip Edward Secor

MOON

Moon my friend
Soon my friend

Love by hate
Step by stride

Freedom to fate
Side to side

Death is life
Pain is pleasure

Riddles in strife
Take in measure

Rock of time
River of infinity

Past be prime
Peace be serenity

Soon my friend
Moon my friend

Clem Collins II

LISTEN

The sun shines
His purpose is clear
The ground trembles
His presence is near

The wind whispers
Calling His name
The river flows
Telling our shame

The Power Mind
A message to send
When the fire reigns
The torture begins

Past, Present, Future
Soon shall they blend
While darkness waits
For time to end

Listen, Listen
The fools will ignore
Listen, Listen
The Lamb shall soon roar

Clem Collins II

KEEPER OF MY HEART

With every breath I breathe your name,
With every sigh I feel the same
Enchanting love that ever taunts,
Entrances and enfolds my thoughts.

I adore you and I need you,
Please never leave or part,
You are my life and I am you,
Oh, wondrous keeper of my heart!

Arlene D. Krueger

FRIENDSHIP

You need a friend
I understand
I need a friend
Understand
I have about
  A million things that need to come out
You have emotions you want to feel
Daily, the world tries to kill
That's what happens when a bird learns to fly
It's got to get loose
  or face the noose of a rope
You can't cope with being alone
You can't stick around
I know the tone
Someday the song will mix with the music
The little lamb will find its mother
For now
We have to help each other

Roger S. Harkness

White winds
  Send dreams in the mist,
Magic garden
  A secret in her kiss,
A mystery
  She vanished in the mist,
White stone
  The gift.

Sherry M. Newman

SHERRY MARLEEN NEWMAN. Born: Roanoke, Virginia, 1-26-57; Single; Education: Virginia Western Community College, English and psychology, 1974-75; Occupations: Concept therapy instructor, Restaurant worker; Poetry: *Forever and a Day,* collection, 1982; 'Eternal Echoes,' 1981; Comments: *I use poetry to create an image, something the reader may experience, like seeing a picture, with words. They reflect people's moods, outlooks, and their dreams and romantic interests.*

I LOVE FOREVER

I cry for time lost; I cry for the way
it should have been, but never was.
I cry for lost hope and lost love
and the part of me that died with my
hopes and dreams. I cry for you and
I cry for me, and the life that was
and the one that will be — I cry for
the lovely times we shared together —
that were too few and never would have been enough . . .

Now, I laugh and hope again —
I play and hold hands; I kiss and enjoy
the kisses. My heart sings and I dance.
A flower falls and I watch in admiration
and silence; life is an awesome beauty.
To appreciate joy, one must have had
sorrow, so simple; yet, so complex.
I laugh and smile again — yes, there
will be memories and tears for the past
and the part of me that was, and tears
for the future and the part of me that
is. But; life is good . . .
      I laugh for today —
      I love forever.

Peggy K. Herrin

THOUGHTS OF A SECRETARY

'Tis the National Secretaries Week
So a Gal Friday has read with some delight;
'Tis the week many bouquets are showered
On Gal Friday who's sweet and bright.

Without her the boss is never at ease,
He's in a dilemma from eight to four;
Tightly he'll keep his fingers crossed,
Hoping no pressing jobs will be in store.

'Tis the National Secretaries Week
And somewhere a Gal Friday keeps typing away,
Wondering if by chance a shower of bouquets
Will come to her before the end of day.

With such thoughts she keeps plugging away,
Gliding from office to office with papers galore;
Should she ready her umbrella for the shower?
Or should she calmly quit and go home at four?

Just simple words like "thank you" with a smile
Or two sincere words like "good work" will do;
The words are little but their message is big,
For Gal Friday they're words long overdue.

Ed Y. Kish

LAMBORGHINI

Lamborghini: A girl's fantasy.
Fast as lightning, stronger than steel.
I can picture myself behind the wheel —
Speedometer rising, the pedal to the floor,
The glorious sound of the engine's roar.
Its handsome physique captures the crowd;
If I were the owner, I would be so proud!
A wild red color or a virginal white
Or a sophisticated black that speeds out of sight:
A Lamborghini is just the car for me!
A fascinating car — my fantasy!

Dina Caloggero

BREAKS OF A COWGIRL

On a rainy fall morning I'd re-cinched, and
  re-mounted the horse from which I'd been thrown;
helped round up cattle 'til noon when the "ouch"
  of four busted ribs, and a collarbone prompted
our daughter-in-law to bind them in Ace bandages.
  By nightfall, and still trailing cattle, the
swelling and pain brought tears, my husband eased
  the bindings while our son and two granddaughters
spoke words of kindness to soothe our fears.

Many bruises, so black and blue; even the doctor
  guessed I'd been in a wreck; the X-rays confirmed
the grim story, my bronc-ride corrected an old hand
  injury, but the "sun-fisher" had popped my neck.
My husband walked with me in sadness when the doctor
  ordered: "No riding horses for a while."
Shared endless days of my burdens, "Thank God,
  I married a man who will go the second mile!"

Eight miserable weeks, bindings off . . . doctor stated:
  "Cowgirl, you may wash the dishes." My darling's
eyes met mine, he hugged me "Cowpuncher Style."
  Three months of shoulder exercises, when "doc"
proudly said, "Cowgirl, you may mount your horse now!"
  I could read, "Whoopee! Ride 'em Cowgirl!"
In my Cowpuncher's "million-dollar" smile.

Juanita J. Wallis

DAISY JUANITA WALLIS. Pen Names: Juanita J. Wallis, Bill's Wife, The Cowpuncher and Me; Born: Jordan, New Mexico, 10-10-29; Married: W.J. (Bill) Wallis, 9-9-47; Education: Self educated; High school; Writer's Digest School, 1987; Institute of Children's Literature, 1987; Occupation: Cattle rancher; Poetry: 'Peace on Earth,' 1987; 'Mama's Wood Cookstove,' American Poetry Association, 1987; 'Live Compared To a Rose,' *Best New Poets of 1986,* American Poetry Association; 'Holding Forth The Word of Life,' 'Love Of Jesus,' *Words of Praise,* American Poetry Association, 1987; Comments: *Reciting poetry at the Cowboy Poetry Gathering in Elko, Nevada last January was the highlight of my life. I write the history of the Llano Estacado and of Quay Valley, New Mexico. I write poetry about ranch life. I write for children. I write Scriptural verses. I've enjoyed writing about special themes to give writers new ideas. P.S. — I accepted the horse's apology and slept on his new blanket.*

THE MOUNTAINS

The mountains are green in magnificent splendor.
One is glad to be free to view and not a busy vendor.
From dark jade to the chartreuse of the apple,
Artists like to mix their paints to capture and to dapple.

Once a year one is able to see this beautiful picture.
The foliage with its different hues is really a mixture.
The peaks of the Blue Ridge and the towers of the Allegheny,
One may even view a rainbow when the season is rainy.

Shirley B. Firebaugh

THE RABBIT

What I remember about that day
is the sound of wind blowing through the trees,
the field of green, the roses red
and one small rabbit sitting in the field
waiting
listening
watching.

Lisa Hackman

MY KNIGHT OF ARMOUR

Nights I've spent alone
dreaming of my Knight of Armour,
then appeared this man
high upon his throne

The sun began to set
as I reached closer to him
his arms caress so gently
my eyes began to dim

There he stood holding me,
As if he were to protect
I felt safe, yet free
I began to make love to him
to let our feelings be

A time ago that was
and still each night the same,
my knight of shining armour,
holds me safe and secure
forever he holds me close
never to let our love set free

Michelle Moreira

TO

Music, when soft voices die,
Vibrates in the memory —
Odors, when sweet violets sicken,
Live within the sense they quicken.

Rose leaves, when the rose is dead,
Are heaped for the belovéd's bed;
And so thy thoughts, when thou art gone,
Love itself shall slumber on.

Percy Bysshe Shelley

AUTUMN'S GOLD

The golden leaves just spun around,
Then tumbled to the ground,
Where elfin children danced on them,
Then raked them in a mound!

The leaves then cartwheeled down the street,
And high in flight they soared,
While chased by dancing little feet —
This gold from childhood's hoard!

Arelene D. Krueger

REAL COMPETITION

Who is your real competition?
It's you — who you were yesterday,
Because today you'll do better;
You'll be competing all the way!

So test your limits, reach new goals,
Do more than required of you,
This competition is for real;
The winner, of course, will be you!

Arelene D. Krueger

LITTLE MAN

No one attains perfection, little man.
The world is built on quick and shifting sand.
The sky is blue and white and pink and rust.
But, little man, the sky is made of dust.
The stars are pretty sparkling in the cold,
But they have hearts of iron, and they're old.
Comets ànd flaring suns that shimmering pass
Just show the universe is full of gas.
And, little man, you probably should know
It all could fall into a big, black hole.
Like sprinkled salt that's pungent to the taste
But good when used within its proper place.
A little here, a little there, we learn
How much to give to get the best return.
You see, my little man, the world is hard
Outside the confines of your own small yard,
But as you go around this changing star,
Remember that I love you as you are.

Emily J. Brown

YOUR BROTHER — MY SON

You look on him with sparkling eyes;
I do, too, little one.
He is the best of all your games
And fills your world with fun.
His voice rings out like happy bells;
He's bigger than a tree.
He's smart . . . can fix most anything
And loves you patiently.
You would not even know, my dear,
Because he seems so wise,
I see him as you . . . very tall
But in my heart, your size.

Emily J. Brown

THE BROKEN IMAGE

The struggle's over —
the hated enemy dead upon the ground
at my feet.
The battle's ended —
the gory glory and the heat
of valor.
The victory mine!
But alas!
What do I see?
The shining spoils are rusted iron,
a broken image —
resembling me.

Joan Cissom

LUKE 1:37*

In my heart I often wander
Contemplate on what could be
Visit lands of mystic beauty
See the rage of lashing sea.

Savor incense in cathedrals
At the Holy Site of Rome
Sunrise viewed from old Mt. Athos
Shall be captured in a poem.

O, the awesomeness; the beauty
Of these journeys in the heart
Because He holds my hand is His
Right from the very start.

* "For *nothing* is impossible with God."

E. M. Janice Kolb

BY THE LAKE

O beautiful lake
Shining on me
Streaming your light
From eternity

Creating a pathway
Straight from the sky
Out onto the water
Beckoning me nigh

Did you wish me to tread
Ever lightly your beam
Or am I imagining
As if in a dream?

Oh, now I see clearly
Why you gloriously glow
God's in His heaven
And you're telling me so.

E. M. Janice Kolb

THE LOVE OF A CHILD

They run and they play, they laugh
and they sing. They trust and they
believe, and look up through eyes of
innocence. They ask for so little,
Kool-aid, a swing, and a puppy to love.
They dream solitary dreams, dreams
too simple for the educated to understand.
Imagination that's them to the
unseen playgrounds, where no one
else may enter. The love of a child
is a love you won't find anywhere
else. Untouched by the danger zones
of adulthood, untarnished by fear,
never haunted by doubt. The love
of a child is the greatest love
you'll ever know. Honor such a
love, reach out to it, it's free.
Don't wake up old, alone and gray,
wondering why love never came
your way.

Rose A. Pope

ALONE WITH GRIEF

Where shall I find some desert scene so rude,
Where loneliness so undisturb'd may reign
That not a step shall ever there intrude
Of roving man, or nature's savage train?

Some tangled thicket, desolate and drear,
Or deep wild forest, silent as the tomb,
Boasting no verdure bright, no fountain clear,
But darkly suited to my spirit's gloom;

That there 'midst frowning rocks, alone with grief,
Entomb'd in life, and hopeless of relief,
In lonely freedom I may breathe my woes —
For, oh! since nought my sorrows can allay,
There shall my sadness cloud no festal day,
And days of gloom shall soothe me to repose.

Glenn Edward Waters III

LONELY IS THE NIGHT

Lonely is the night when there is no one to greet me
    At the close of a long hard day.
The "lonelies" go away while I am busy at work
    Or communicating with my friends.
The day ends; I say: "So long" to my co-workers
    And acquaintances and close relatives.
I wearily climb the endless stairs that take me
    To my living quarters and quiet solitude.
How nice to be greeted and have someone say:
    "How was your day? I missed you."
But there's no one there. No one to really care
    That my day went rather bad.
No one there when something good has happened
    And I could stand a pat on my back.
No one to hold me and say: "There! There!"
    When I feel like crying for no reason.
No one to share my feelings — good or bad; happy or sad
    Even when I feel like laughing.
Lonely is the night when I am all alone
    And no one to say: "I love you."

Joan Morrone

WINDSONG

The wind —
Inescapable. Uncontrollable. Relentless. Unrelenting.
Did I ever really touch her? I know she touched me.
Oh dream affair, love affair, beautiful fantasy now become sour.
All I have now are the memories . . . and the loneliness.
And loneliness.
Gone — as if she never truly existed,
As if she were never really real. But she was.
"Real" is like the wind.

Starlight, starbright, this man must find his soul tonight.
I wish, I wish upon a star, to lie beside the woman I love.

Wild. So very beautiful. Relentless. Unrelenting.
Just before dusk I saw a butterfly trapped in harsh winds.
I remember its fighting . . . its trying
    . . . its losing . . . it's gone.
Butterfly, butterfly, those wings that let you fly, took you
Straight into the current that caused you to lose your life.
Fragile. And yet, so very powerful. It was very, very beautiful.
"Beautiful" is like the wind.

Donald M. Cline

MERRY-GO-ROUND

It's a merry-go-round of events
Twirling as a spinning top.

It's a morning filled with sunshine
An evening filled with romance.

A glance of a picture of smiling
faces on a piano.
A child running at play.

A day of dark and gloomy rain,
A smile as the smell of honeysuckle drifts by.

A hymn that lifts a burdened heart.

Life,

It's a merry-go-round
Twirling as a spinning top, non-stop.

Life's a cycle of beliefs and uncertainties.
It fills the empty spaces and overflows the planned day.

A cycle that can't be stopped.
A day's cycle not planned, but recorded,
In a book called *life*.

Chiquita P. Anderson

CHILD OF LIGHT — AND DARKNESS

Mother was Light, Father I called Darkness,
And I am the child of Daylight and Shade.
The latter was ravenous, all-consuming, all-devouring;
The former — demanding, all-knowing, in control.

Either one was committed or tainted with shadow,
Yet still did I feel love, pain, passion, and hate.
To be one and two souls, to be both and yet neither;
Why all this pain, so much anger, so much fear?
So much fear.

From Mother came pride, in Father I knew confusion;
I'm not always sure to pray "Dear Heaven" or "Hades."
Search deep through your soul, and struggle to know,
Then pray for this world and the soul of mankind.

Donald M. Cline

FRIENDS

For Greg and Lisa

I watched an old lady as she crossed the street.
She walked very slowly on her two crippled feet.
She used a walker and she was all stooped over,
A huge dog was by her side, and I heard her call him Dover.

He kept in tune with her stride,
Moving slowly at her side.
He must have been as old as she,
For his back was swayed like a windblown tree.

I knew that they were like family, two close friends,
Sharing life's burdens to the very end.
His fur and her hair were streaked with white,
But they were allies, a spectacular sight.

Sondra Middleton

TO A WORKING MOTHER

Oh Mother, you are so near,
Yet so far.
You are only partly here,
You are there
Where computers are.
In the clothes, the toys,
The house, etc.
Your feelings I see.
Your time so limited
To listen;
Your mind divided
When I speak;
Oh Mother, you are *so* near,
Yet so *far*.

Please, *Mother*
Listen!
It's *you* — you I seek.

Gladys Good

THE VAGABOND

I stare at buses on the road;
    Their passengers seem gay.
I thrill at freighters and their load
    When on the river way.

Nostalgia entraps me when
    I see planes in the sky.
And, oh how lonesome it seems then
    As railroad trains whiz by.

I miss the many far-off lands
    Of which I once was part.
I am, with chains on feet and hands
    A vagabond, at heart . . .

John P. McPartlin

THE SAPLING

When man plants many little trees
    He stakes them down with ropes;
Protected from each heavy breeze,
    They offer man high hopes
Of someday being tall and great
    In beauty and in size.
And, slowly, with each passing date
    They show their planter wise.

But, young folks planted in this world
    Don't get a rope or stake.
And, they must face the challenge hurled
    And learn to give and take.
I wish man had the same respect
    For youth, whom he can see
Needs help to grow and stand correct
    As any sapling tree.

John P. McPartlin

THE LITTLE LEAGUER

The little leaguer is on deck.
    He swings a bat or two.
He hopes to get a hit to check
    The no-hit game that's due.

Two walks on base and one man out;
    The batter up then fans.
The little leaguer hears the shouts
    That rings throughout the stands.

He picks his bat and takes his place.
    The ump dusts off the plate.
The pitch, a hit! Home, two runs race!
    Oh boy! Does he feel great!

He eyes the bleachers everywhere
    As pride swells in his heart.
The hurt: his dad or mom weren't there
    To see him do his part.

John P. McPartlin

JOHN PETER McPARTLIN. Born: International Falls, Minnesota, 7-10-18; Education: College of St. Thomas, St. Paul, Minnesota, 1936-37, no degree; Occupations: Retired newspaper editor, now free-lancing; Memberships: VFW, DAV, Knights of Columbus, BPOE, Sons of American Revolution, 8th AF Historical Society; Awards: Several cash prizes for short stories in contests from 1951-61; Poetry: 'The Leprahune,' *Paradise of Pacific*, 1955; 'To The Ti Leaf,' *Honolulu Star Bulletin*, 1954; 'Tooth Aches,' *Kansas Authors Club Yearbook*, 1957; 'Mortimer Corkle,' *American Poetry Anthology*, 1986; Other Writings: Three self-published books of humorous verse: *A Bay Hello, Don't Laugh I'm Serious*, and *The Mating of Janie McBride*.

IN RETROSPECT

When the Grey Hair
Is more here than there
It's time to let it go.
I used to want to be
A Redhead
And now it's so Nice and Easy
To make it so.
No more Grey Hair Blues,
But they can *keep* their
Long-Heeled Shoes!

Katherine Scott Fitzgerald

GRASS

When spring begins
I'll watch the gentle rains press you
    softly as a kiss to the earth
Secretly beginning the harvest's birth

Through the summer I'll see you in
    shades of breathtaking greens
Gracefully swaying and growing
In the sunset you'll nod, at times
    even glowing.

After the warm months pass by and
    you've turned golden and brown
I'll gather a bouquet one fall day
For winter will soon have his way.

Outside when the wind blows and the
    snow drifts
I'll admire your everlasting beauty and
    mystery
Always giving hope of another spring
When once again nature's secrets will
    begin.

Melba Barber

FOREVER MY RAINBOW

We walk through the sun
as it shines upon us
feeling the warmth through our hearts
forever mine, forever my rainbow

You are my rainbow
brightening my day
filling my heart with love,
filling me deep in every way

You are beautiful from what I see
as I watch each color glow,
I see my heart beginning to let go

You are my rainbow,
on-going and true
my love that shines
comes only from you

My destiny has come
reaching the pot of gold
I've found a love I began to know
forever mine, forever my rainbow

Michelle Moreira

FOREVER HUMBLE

Lord, teach me to be forever humble,
To walk barefoot down a long rocky path,
To eat only a scanty crust of bread,
At the closing of the day,
To not let the sun go down
Upon my wrath,
To accept from my job,
Only meager pay.

Mildred Quine Dennis

A THOUSAND TEARDROPS

Pine trees sway roughly in the distance. The leaves of
birch are ruffled harshly by the breeze. Cardinals, brilliant
in bright scarlet color, vanish beyond the field of my
vision. And now, falling softly, come the first drops of rain.

Ripples form, miniature waves, on the surface of a puddle.
A drop, the reverberations, then all is as before. If enough drops
fell, if enough men died, I suppose it might make a difference.
Just like the sea. Just like the wind. Just like the rain.

Hope (I think it's hope) hangs on the edge of our existence.
Is that pain I see, taking liquid form, loosed from darkened
clouds? If Heaven can cry and did so often then rain is liquid
pain. Like a white marble tomb. Like a sea of white crosses.
Like tears lost in the rain.

Over 90,000 graves for an equal number of men — a sea of
white grief. A man, his face is crying, appears to be almost
laughing — no tears in the rain. A thousand thousand tears
for a 100,000 graves, for a 100,000 men. So many men. So
many graves. So many teardrops lost forever in the rain.

The wind is picking up. The rain is falling harder.
The storm grows ever strong:
"Here rests in honored glory an American soldier known but to God."

Donald M. Cline

MY BEST FRIEND

Mother is a special one, of being young and having fun

My dear Mother take this gift in your hand
You watched me to become a man

Watch also your little Girl grow
Tying her hair in ribbons and bows

Also your husband who is my dad, loves you so much,
And has reason to be glad.

Anthony Adam Kosak

CARING

Our Mom got ill, and suffered, a lot,
My sister and I cared for her in every way,
And tried to make her comfortable day by day,
Her illness finally took hold of her mind,
And finally she was like a helpless child,
But we kept trying to carry on,
But as this chapter unfolds we must first understand,
There is no one in this world who really understands,
They have no conception of what's going on,
And furthermore, don't give a darn,
The hurt's been so much, the pain's so deep,
That only God knows the toll that it seeks,
The body and mind are so worn and so tired,
You're begging for help but cannot find it,
You go to bed tired and wake with the thought,
How much more can I take, I don't have any choice,
So when troubles and problems arrive in your life,
And everything darkens and shuts off the lights,
Remember someone is watching from up above,
And He brings you back up to go on with life.

Margaret Freije

REACHING FOR A GOAL

We live in a "restless" world
Filled with God's protections
Trying to reach what we call fame
Regardless of the violence we witness day by day
And in our troubled hours
We all need inspiration
In this restless world of sorrow and defeat
Do you often feel discouraged, when reaching for a goal?
Then pray you may glorify, and have visions of success
That lift you upon the path
Where others grope for help
Away from sorrow and distress
Then ask your creator for the instance of faith restored
To reach "Your Goal for a Better Tomorrow"
In this "restless" world we live in.
And to make us all aware
That God is always near
To strengthen our fears
In hours of despair.

Gloria G. G. H. Fox

GOD'S GIFT OF UNDERSTANDING

"What a wonderful world this would be if everyone helped someone!"
To make our life happier with cheerful days and nights.
With memories we could treasure in our hearts' delight.
For everyone needs someone to make life worthwhile,
Without the help of others we are lonely, sad and blue.
For in this world filled with heartaches and dismay
There are those with a sympathetic heart, and an understanding mind.
So we seek for someone close in heart because they're dear and kind.
But few we find that have these special qualities combined.
For on this earth to Heaven above and this wonderful world that it is,
It takes the silent prayers of the Kingdom of God,
   for His voice we never hear.
To give that understanding, to the millions of souls that need a
   tender heartfelt touch
In this great big world of ours it would mean so much!

Gloria G. G. H. Fox

GLORIA G. G. H. FOX. Education: Columbia University; New York Institute of Dietetics; Writer's Digest School; National Writer's Club; Occupations: Physician's dietetic consultant, Writer; Membership: People's Medical Society.

MY EVER-DEVOTED DAD

A working man — farmer by trade,
His wheat and cotton crops were made,
With a team pulling the plow,
Not powerful tractors, like now.

Yet, after the work was done,
There was always time for fun,
Swimming under the high "Rock Bluff,"
Or in "The Deep Hole," was enough.

With the family together,
In sunny or stormy weather,
Just sharing the good with the bad,
That was my ever-devoted dad.

He abided by "The Golden Rule."
He went with us to Sunday School.
Day in, day out, he lived his faith,
And has a heavenly resting place.

Sometimes I return to childhood,
In a reminiscing mood,
Pretending once again to be,
The little girl upon his knee.

Mildred Quine Dennis

THANK YOU

Went out of my way
To do a favor.
Not a word of thanks
Did the person say.

The absence of
A simple thank-you
Made me feel sad,
Somewhat angry too.

I remember thinking,
The next time around
My reply will be:
"I can't possibly."

I recalled just then
Only one in ten,
So the Bible said,
Were not all ten cured?

Where are the other nine?
If I'm ever helped,
I'll say thanks for sure.
I will find the time.

Louise M. Verrette

SPACE . . .

How beautiful life can be
To share its happiness with me.
Over and above the earth's light air
There is excitement of space's glare.
To see beyond the clear blue sky
And find millions of stars floating by,
How grateful we all recall
To the majestic beauty of it all.

Nancy Damrow

THE IRON CLASP

Shrouded in Darkness,
With Claws,
It grips you.
In Its Iron Clasp.
And pulls you.
Into Its cold, secret heart.
And in the Darkness
You wither to
Bare Bones.
Until Time corrodes
You and your
Heart begins to die and
You reach out
And grasp someone
Warm.
And pull them inside
Your secret
Dying
Heart.

Tania Snyder

FROSTY ICE-LIE

A town is frozen
And glistens.
Frothy ice-trees,
Misty ice-steeples,
Smoky ice-windows
Reflect the pale, untouched morn.
A pastel sky paints the world
With a faded rose-peach glow
As a Pristine Aura steals
Through the streets,
Preceding me,
Beckoning me,
Softly whispering to me.
Her milky fingers surround me,
Nudging me to follow her
Down the long, deathly silent street
To the distant,
Shapeless,
Termination.

Tania Snyder

BECAUSE OF YOU

Because of You I know the way.
Because of You I live each day.
　　It's not because I was so good.
　　It's just because You said You would
Give rest to those who come to You,
And let them know just what to do.

Because of You I have much joy.
Because of You none can destroy
　　What You have granted deep within,
　　So that the new life would begin.

Because of You I have Your love.
Because of You it's from above.
　　It lets me overcome all fear;
　　And know I made it through the years.

Diane L. Clark

FOR IAN . . .

Do you remember how bright
the stars were that first night
when you wore my sweater?

I do.

I call them back to memory every night,
just as I call back so many good memories.

Do you remember how close we felt
watching each other's eyes,

your hand on my tummy?

I do.

I call it back at times like this
when thoughts of life with you,
and Shay,
give me faith in the words:

partners forever.

Laura Mayse

PEGASUS

Leave all past love behind
On this journey, we will find.
Loving together, in harmony
Contentment, happiness, and peace.
A totally involved commitment
I've found and tamed Pegasus.
A steady mount to ride
Put all your worries aside.
Phantom rider, it isn't too late
Your immortal love I possess.
Like a mythical Greek god
My knight in shining armour.
Life is living a fantasy
And, forgetting about reality.
Remember the late-night rendezvous
Keep a memory of that love.
He was ecstasy to the touch
I long to call him my own.

Darlene Bright

FALLING WATER

Don't close my love within four walls
But open freely on the waterfall.
Let love run wild and free
It will grow like roots of a tree.
Together, we will climb
To a far-reaching crest.
Together, we will lie
Cheek to cheek, breast to breast.
Together, we can never fail
The awesome wonder of it all.
With the joyful sound of music
Filling both of our hearts.
Feel the smell of spring
Floating in the air
As in the morning
After a cool, refreshing rain.

Darlene Bright

PICKIN' COTT'N IN THE OL' SOUTH

*Dedicated to Dr. Ray Fulton, an Arizona educator
who holds memories of fields of cotton and cotton
picking in his native state of Mississippi.*

Bolls were poppin' fast
On yon bottom lands
Bags were on the backs
Of pickers usin' both their hands
To pull that fluffy white stuff
The whole day long
In rhythm to the hummin'
And spiritualizin' of song,
Till the boss called, "Quittin' time,
It's time to head home."

Bags were saggin', behind 'em draggin'
As they came down the cott'n row;
Bodies bent and humped,
Slow of feet as if the foe
Had matched each ounce of strength.
It was weighin' time with record kept in pound;
And payin' time for those on hire,
But to the house for the others; they were bound
To a master who knew that cott'n was king
And ruler of every man in the ol' South.

J. Jones

FOLLOW YOUR DREAM

On every tomorrow follow your dream,
Although in faraway lands it may seem.
Stretch the imagination and believe,
The dream in your heart you can achieve.
Never leave your dream to the winds of chance,
Or set sail on the seas of happenstance.
Prepare for the voyage to your land,
Faithfully charting each course with steady hand.
With courage and boldness push all doubters aside,
And launch your dream with the tide.
When storm clouds arise harness the wind,
And sail in waters where you've never been.
Let home be your compass on a starless night,
Light a fire in your soul burning bright.
With fortitude and faith push on without fear,
Never look back or waver throughout the years,
When others jeer and laugh you to scorn,
Remember from dreams greatness is born.
For each discovery that has blessed all of mankind,
Began as a thought in a dreamer's mind.
With a dash of daring and the heart of the brave,
On a distant shore you will hear the break of a wave.
In peaceful harbors your ship will arrive,
And you will receive your cherished prize.

Billie Jean Henry

CALLED ON ROZEN YESTERDAY

There are times when I am doing better than the world.
Then, there are times when the world is doing better than me.

I know when I have won, and I know when I have lost but when I am
still trying to play and the game is over . . . I can't be beat, what happened
to my game? . . . I don't remember living a full game! . . . It can't be over;
I must go on!

But Rozen reminded me, at today's practice, about tomorrow's game!

Darrel-Jay Tedeschi

A MOTHER'S GRIEF

How do you comfort her? What do you say?
A Mother has lost her baby today.
The little boy child she once held so tight;
She fed him and bathed him and kissed him good-night.

She watched as he grew and his world did expand.
Before she could realize, he became a grown man
Who was loving and caring. Her pride how it showed.
When she spoke of her baby, her face clearly glowed.

Now this day she's lost him, she's filled with such grief.
Nothing you say can give any relief
From this sorrowful burden she's forced to accept.
Whatever you do must seem trite and inept.

So how do you comfort her? What do you say?
Just tell her you're sorry, and join her to pray.

Jeanne Stelmak

GOD HEARS THAT ONE

I awoke one summer morning to a line of chirping
          birds.
      Some sang high
      Some sang low.
The little one on the end didn't seem to know
         which way to go.

The feathered choir of singers appeared not
        to hear
That one of them was not chirping in
        Heavenly harmony.

The little one on the end was blissfully
        unaware
His was the chirping that was all off key —
'Cause he had always known
The others couldn't chirp as well as he.

And, so it was, their song soared its way
        to Heaven.
God listened lovingly, and He too heard
      Some sang high
      Some sang low.
But, the one who didn't seem to know which
        way to go
        God heard most of all.

Dorothy McGaughran

A SUMMER GARDEN

Calla lilies yawned with wide-opened mouths,
Trumpet lilies blew sleepily to awaken the pansies
Whose sweet shy faces were bathed with morning dew.
Marigolds shone like new copper pennies,
Roses swayed queenly as they stately walked
Down royal paths inviting bees to be their guests.
Hollyhocks nodded mischievously toward
Timid violets whose beauty and stature
Was the envy of high-rise sunflowers.
Daffodils stood proudly in their yellow and green dresses
While carnations, robed in majestic red and bridal white,
Silently encouraged their energetic neighbors, the
Sweet peas, who were intently trying to climb higher.
Lilacs lovely and calm sent gifts of perfume to all.
Tulips expectantly waited for the kiss of the sun.
Could this be the original garden planted by God
    Watched over by Jack-in-the-pulpit?

Dorothy McGaughran

THE DOCTOR

The doctor gave my son the facts
All about pre-med college goals.
Complete with all the highs and lows
To be found down a long, hard road.
He offered advice, tips, and facts
Then, he told of his own path.
He paved that road to his success.
My son was spellbound, held in awe
As the surgeon carried him along the crest.
He learned of the reason to study hard
And the need to stay ahead of homework.
It he was to stay ahead of the game
He faced the challenge of success.
Then, later, he was off to bed, deep in thought
For his much needed rest, and he drifted
    asleep.
He slept alone with his dreams, it seemed
But indeed, his dreams were of his future
And his own, soon-to-be, future success.

Darlene Bright

HE

He came into my life
  as the sea caresses the sand.
He saw within my eyes
  the tears that I had shed.
He looked into my heart
  and tried to bring me joy.
He knew that I was sad
  and comforted me instead.

He loved me as a friend
  as true friends often do.
He gave me the will to live
  when I was in distress.
He saw within my soul
  my beauty hidden there.
He was honest and sincere
  with every word He said.

He filled my heart with bliss
  and touched me with His smile.
He was always at my side
  when things were just not right.
He kissed me tenderly
  like gentle drops of rain.
He did a lot for me
  while others just walked by.

Maria L. Canales

WINE

Some wines are white
And some wines are red.
Some wines make you sick in the head.
But some are good,
Yet some are bad.
Some I haven't ever had.
Some wines are just as sharp as a knife.
But the best wine of all
Is the friendship of life.

Kristen Faulk

WAR

Think of the wonder,
Think of the night,
Think of the power,
Think of the might.

But think of the corpses
Which lie in the grave,
And think of the men
Which they tried to save.

Why as much as they tried,
Many, many men died.

But let me tell you
How it all began.
It all began in the dust
And the sand.

Well, so much for that game
As much as it was,
'Cause that game was made
Of pure-hearted shame.

Kristen Faulk

ANNE

Oh, dear child of my heart,
Who never got to be,
Will someday emerge so forth
To shine in His heavenly court.

Oh, dear one, that could have been,
If only to have understood his yen.
Now she cries to be free
To meet her maker, Thee.

Thou, oh my Lord, strong and with might,
Willed that it be so.
The evil one, in unceasing fight,
Will forever be foe.

So dear child, find peace
Not in his ugly fleece,
Nor in his rotten fod,
But in your namesake, the Grace of God.

Carla Ann Bouska Lee

RATS!

Here in Hometown, U.S.A.
Exists an odd tradition.
We buy up old aquariums,
Convert them to terrariums,
And miniature gymnasiums,
Then inhabit them with rats.

Hamster, gerbil, guinea pigs, too.
A rodent is a rodent
Just as sure as you are you.
So, cheer up, moms across the land.
That child you love with rat in hand
Loves you much more so understand
It's just a little RAT!

Ess Jay Nolan

THE LAST WHISTLE

An old man died today.
The wheels turned slowly;
The machine ground to a halt,
Its energy sapped.
The driving force,
Once dynamic,
Now gone forever.

The track left behind
Was only smooth in places.
It bounced along
With the pop and crack
Of an old woman's knees,
Smooth at youth's station,
Jarring on the bridges,
Crippled and limping at its terminal.

Good-bye, old man.
We'll miss you
And the steam
In your old engine.

Ess Jay Nolan

TRAVELERS

Rumpled people
Rushing wearily through airports
Waiting hastily for airplanes
Dreaming longingly of home
Lonely people

Pamela J. Burke

DEPARTURES

I saw you again —
Standing in the rain;
Wind tugging at your coat,
You were watching a boat
Move across the bay;
We stood together;
In the chill December weather —
I looked at you with mixed emotions,
My insides like the churning oceans;
You had a tear in your eye —
Trying your hardest not to cry,
When we finally began to speak:
The words we spoke were too bleak;
We talked about what went wrong,
And how we stayed apart too long;
I knew then we could never
Stay together —
So, I turned and
Walked away.

Kevin A. Kwader

HIS HAND WILL LEAD ME

Life's constant companions are
profound perplexities,
of which I bare gratefulness
to my Supreme Being . . . as the strength of intellect
has been bestowed upon this soul,
to happily face my daily challenges,
to represent beloved ancestors,
by bearing my children in painful delight;
to smile at my shortcomings, and seldom those of others.

My Maker grants me the respectful sorrow of world sufferings.
This heart embraces abilities of sight, sound, speech,
and honorable walking the majestic tides of life.

There is no uncertainty
as to who I am,
as to what I am,
or seldom a doubt as to where I go from here.
His hand will lead me all the way.

Judith Charko

RAINDROPS AND THOUGHT

Gentle raindrops of summer
methodically splatter
upon my bedroom window,
where I should be peacefully sleeping; tranquil.

Instead of resting, infinite thoughts, questions
invade this soul.

Mentally, I complete undone tasks.
Are my grown children safe?
Are the doors secure?
Should I color my hair?
God! I forgot to iron the shirts!
Should I go back to school?
Am I too old to learn?
I'll look drained tomorrow . . . the clock reads two a.m.

God, help me pray in peace.
"Our Father," Bless my family . . . grant them contentment.
Splatter, splatter, the drops continue.
How I love the gentle rain.

Judith Charko

INTO PLACE

Poems of love
Poems of desires
Poems of broken hearts
Poems of everything under the sun and then some.

Poems are words of feelings
That sometimes can make you cry
There are poems that tell a story
And poems that say good-bye.

There are poems that you read
That you feel might been written in haste
But that's the way the poet
Sat them into place.

S. Jonathan Quietstorm

A PRISONER OF A SHELL

Here I sit all alone in my room, surrounded by loneliness,
    want and pain.
Once we are placed in our rooms we may never return again.
Though to some my opportunities seem small, to myself I seem tall,
And I feel that I am all, but only because I have turned to my room.
It is here that I receive my strength, for this is all that I trust.
It is only me who consoles myself when I fall.

I have studied the fixtures, and memorized each crack,
    every line and wall.
I know there are other rooms quite like mine in this cold dark hall.
There are many rooms and many degrees of pain,
Yet we all share one emotion: ours is a feeling of loneliness.
Others look on and perhaps see us as monkeys in a zoo.
They see our rooms as jails, and us as prisoners of a shell.
We are no longer people but only beings trapped for all eternity.

I will endure my eternities in my room.
Though to you my room seems dark, dismal and lonely,
    to me it is my strength.
It is like a flickering candle on a stormy evening.
Here I will stay until I am shown a brighter flame.
I will learn to make do with the shelter of my room.
For in my room I am truly free,
I am free to be only me, just another being in a room.

Cynthia L. Gardner

BE STILL

Be still and know that I am God. Psalms 46:10

My thoughts fly about
    Like bright butterflies awing,
Sipping nectar from this flower and that,
    Testing and trying for some new thing,
As material wants concern me so,
    Cares and worries, how will all turn out?
And yet I know, as the still, small voice I hear,
    "Be still and know that I am God."
That all will be well.

Doris Hinkelman

1967-1987

Like a chopper threat, you hovered a skean;
Your forewarning words gleamed sliver sharp teeth.
You dressed and pressed me in camouflage green,
From sweaty helmet to cruel stained knife sheath.

So pumped and sure, you sent me to that swamp,
So green, nineteen, stoned, so wretchingly red;
On night patrol my innocence was stomped,
M-16 sights, he dropped — shot through the head.

Napalm, blood dawns and sand silent nightfalls;
You watched them skewer me with burning bamboo,
Razor screams, stained walls, hard as hammer falls;
I breathed insecticide from your aircrew.

"No sweat," you said. "If I could make it through,
I'd have it made back in the forty-eight;"
"Killer," they shouted, back from Diem Bien Phu,
I ruefully stand guard this heating grate.

Darkness dawns and high-tech eyes abuse me;
Whiskered destiny — greasy dignity.

R. F. Allyn

TOO LATE

Jim never brought her
a rose.
''Just one rose,'' she begged.
Never sent special
husband-to-wife cards.

Eternal darkness
now seals
her eyes.
Cascades of roses
smother her coffin,
clipped to the roses
a card,
''Tina, I love you.''

In her outer-world
chambers,
she laughs mirthlessly,
and mocks,
''Too late.''

Jane Marrazzo Tortorello

MORE THAN ENOUGH

I spent my life loving her.

I gave her my all, my time, my energy,
my love and my person.

I would have given her the world if she
had asked for it.

Streets paved in gold, lights glittering
in diamonds and a castle in the sky.

Islands of paradise with waterfalls of
pure blue water.

I dreamed of putting the universe at her
feet and making the stars into a crown to
wear on her head.

The sun could not shine bright enough, high
enough, or warm enough to compare to her, for
she was all that and more.

I spent my life giving her happiness and peace.

I spent my life fulfilling her dreams.

I spent my life helping her reach her goals.

I spent my life in misery loving her.

Duane E. Haynes

JOANN

So vulnerable yet so proud
You gaze at me through empty eyes
That hold the tears you share for us
If only I could let you know
How I feel about our love
And the pain it brings

Ronald R. Johnson

BLACK CHILD

Black Child   Black Child
Wherever you are
Stand up
Be counted
You can be a star.

Black Child   Black Child
Do your best in school
Learn to read
Learn to write
Don't be nobody's fool.

Black Child   Black Child
Keep climbing to the top
Always keep a positive attitude
Keep on climbing and never stop.

Black Child   Black Child
Always keep your faith
Walk around obstacles
And do whatever it takes.

Celious Davis

MARCEL

In the misty cold of my Exodus
Your live coals eyes have been generous,
Power of peace and an immense friendship
Over a young fool, now on your ship.

I now steer for a more intense life,
With courage and patience I become rife;
I sail towards the green island of hope,
Welcoming smokes rise from behind the slope.

You transform your fatigue in rejoicing
For your wife, children and friends by sharing
Your wisdom found in the fields, blast-furnace
And books. Arguments and sorrow you efface.

I call you my spiritual father,
Of my conscience the real awakener.
I'm looking forward us to foregather
And my mind and thoughts to become keener.

Emmanuel Pierreuse

EMMANUEL PIERREUSE. Born: Lille (north
of France), 10-19-58; Education: Ecole Normale
de Lille, Certificat d'Aptitude Péadagogique, 12-
9-82; Occupation: Teacher; Memberships: San
Diego Folk Song Society, Singing Strings band,
San Diego Mandolin Society; Themes: *Future of
the world, human rights, freedom, ecology, love,
places I have been, childhood.*

TO DENA

Lady of Light

Lady of light: hair glowing, radiant
Like strands of liquid flame.
Flowing past the hourglass of your shape;
Emerald eyes sending hidden message of: love.
Thoughts lost in time, given
From your own private dreamworld;
Revealing pieces, small clues of your spirit.
Mystery, allure, and soft gentle ways:
Parts of your puzzle: Dena
My lady love.
Lady love of light,
Sharing your inner fire
Your free spirit like an eagle in flight,
Ways strange — though you stand strong:
By my side. Absorbing:
Good and bad, increasing
My power mingled with your presence
Making me strong, brightening my light.
Taking me out of a world: gray like the night.
Love, The Wizard

Bruce R. Humphreys

SAD

Oh, how sad it is to know . . .
Oh, how sad it is to feel
    The crippling pain as it unfolds.

You're here . . .
But are you really here with me?

Oh, how sad it is to know
And to feel
    This crippling pain!

Dolores Stassi

MEMORIAL

Like a gull
Caught in the storm
Of the cruel sea
You were helpless
Without hope, you struggled no more
While the once merciless winds
Carried you to the heavens

Ronald R. Johnson

ON HATRED

I've been so hated;
It's painful — still!
It shouldn't be at all,
Based on facts alone.
But life is not that simple,
So that explains my moan;
Time is not the healer
everyone says it is;
We must turn to God
Almighty, because only
He can change the tone.

Ollie Banko Hall

COLLAGE OF LOVE

Sometimes distant you, like the lovely sunset of red
Can be at times such as this moment
As close as the dying sun's kiss,
Which now woos with his gentle warmth
Us all who share our love in his light.

Whoe'er she be — princess or peasant —
I do pray that after years of love together —
Her most precious possession when death we do meet,
Would be but my heart's own love for her.

For loving you, as right now and for time to come,
I need two things — a beautiful day, a beautiful thought.
It seems though, that the day is easier to keep than the thought.

I can offer you no more love than I have.
I can give you no more love than you've refused.
I can give you no more because I've given all I have.
And yet, still you do not understand you're my very life —
Or if you did — I wonder — could you still refuse me?

David R. Pichowsky

You say you love me but are you sure I do wonder if you care
Because the shadow of fear is quietly streaming
   into the wall of my soul

And draining the level of trust I seem to anchor around you
In believing you love me

But my sweet oh! dear one forgive me for this rare moment to
Wish my heart has led me to think this nonsense of you

Could it be then that I forget to pollinate your sweet flower
So to drown my fear deep in hollow of your sweet roselike petal

But how could I be fool to wonder if you care with your deep
Soft kisses that shatter my fear

And rebirth this mood I now enjoy with you my love so sweet
dear and wonderful.

George E. Morrison

MOTHER

For all the things I never said
And the implications I might have made instead
I am now compelled to make to you
An expression of love and gratitude
During all my problems, fears and tears
You were always there throughout the years
Waiting in the shadows with outstretched hands
With no blame of guilt or judgmental demands
The many times there were simply no words to say
You never questioned the path of my chosen ways
Even though I've known my share of strife
I'm so grateful to you for giving me life
For the joys I've known could never be surpassed
And because of you they will always last
Thank God for my father and all my brothers
And that loving lady . . . I call my ''Mother''

Robert Torbett

MARIE

Marie to her children was both good and bad
As a result of the tough life she'd led.
The road for them has not been smooth.
But each has learned by her example,
Persistence results in things more ample.

Marie to her daughters-in-law
Was willing and helpful with nary a flaw.
She was always just a phone call away,
There to help out the very next day.
She'd do anything she could:
Feeding kids, washing clothes, slopping hogs, carrying wood,
But never interfering with their ideas on parenthood.

Marie to her grandkids was neat, hip and cool,
Maybe the wrong words for the kids of today,
But the meaning and feeling intended the same.
She listened, played and taught where she knew how
And most important, was there, but not now.

We'll always remember what we loved her for most,
And know she'll rest peacefully with the Heavenly Host.

Sandra J. Estabrook

FACE

All these faces, strange as I look at them.
I have never seen them before in my whole life.
I wonder what they are thinking; I wonder what they do
for a living; I wonder what their past was like; I wonder what they are
thinking about me? I really wonder what they are thinking about my face
that I never have looked at before?

Darrel-Jay Tedeschi

CREDULOUS

I believe in shooting stars
And I believe in dying dreams
I believe in lying whispers no more
And I believe in the truth once more
I believe in broken hearts
And I believe in never-ending nights
I believe in time standing still
And I believe for a moment in love
I believe in the endless laughter
And I believe in the silence that meets one
I believe in beauty beyond words
And I believe in the ending relationship of a good friend
I believe in never-ending love
And I believe in promising lies
I believe in the silence of the night
And I believe in the untold hatred kept inside
I believe in true love for one
And I believe in the ending of the skies above
I believe in all the above
And you know I believe in all that is so.

Angie Lepez

THE WAILING WALL

Wall of reflection? Wall of shame?
Wall of 56,000 names.
I've journeyed so far from my home,
to find my name carved in the stone.
I find it there, but don't know why.
What was the cause for which I died?
At the time I thought I knew,
but much I believed was untrue.

Wall of sorrow? Wall of defeat?
Roster of the dead elite.
Why is it we are honored with
this black reclining monolith?
Oh, not for us was this wall built.
Its function is to ease your guilt.
We're all too easy to dismiss
with this granite casualty list.

Wall of blackness. Shadow of fear.
Where were you when death was near?

D. T. Zabecki

GRANDMA, GRANDPA

Grandma, Grandpa.
Are you still there?
I know I lose touch
now and then, though I care.
Memories of childhood
times spent with you
are fresh in my mind.
Oh, how I love you.
Grandma, Grandpa.
Are the golden years bliss?
You're my only source
for the truth about this.
You're fountains of wisdom
and youth; don't stop now.
Continue to guide me.
I know you know how.
Grandma, Grandpa.
Are you still there?
Please know I love you,
I need you, I care.

Cara Plummer

COMBRAY

For Germaine Brée

I have stayed too long
In the shuttered space
Of sleep what ecstasy
May come what dreams?

Give me the mornings
Of expanding breath
Shifting steeples
And uneven streets

Lights that break
In untold
Flame

Seeds that scattering
Unfold
Come to speak their name.

Mechthild Cranston

SOMETIMES IN THE RAIN

The mountain has called me
To seek and there I shall find
A peace, a calmness will surround me
Showering me in a delightful way
Sometimes in the rain

Sometimes in the rain
I hold her hand as we walk
Our love reaching for the highest peak
The breeze makes us feel free
An expression that doesn't fade

It can happen
Up there on One Tree Hill
Sometimes in the rain
I can tell life is well and good
A thought that will never die

Thomas J. Moore

LOOKING FOR ME

Lost in the background of life
I'm trying to recover my senses
Trying to regain my composure
So that I can be complete once again
I'm looking for me

Look around every corner
Go that extra mile, I say
Take a dip in the sea of chance
Let the sun shine brightly on me
So I can find me

Over there could be me
Where the face of smiles reigns
Where clear thoughts have taken over
Express yourself, me
Aha, at last, with confidence
I have found me

Thomas J. Moore

THE BREAKDOWN

The sky is raining down
  tears cold and stinging.
Soon everything will drown
  in the rain my sorrow's bringing.
Mist so grey and cloying, thick,
  wraps its dreary mantle about all
And like my moods plays tricks!
  one minute clear, the next I fall.
With the angry sky a molten grey
  and a churning sea answering the tide
I search for words to say
  wanting desperately to hide . . .

Eyvonn Alberts

LOVE

What is love to you
Is it joy,
Or does it make you blue?

Do you feel free
Or feel tied down
When my love is returned
I feel I'm wearing a crown.

But when your love is lost
And you see what a fool you've been
You begin to see the great cost
Oh God what a sin.

Will my love ever be cherished
Or shall it all perish?

Patty Maben

ETERNITY

Dear Lord who watches over me
Please help me through this misery.
I loved him once, but he broke my heart
I love him still though we're apart.
I think of him all through the day
And for his love each night I pray.
His kiss, his smile, his fond embrace
Is a part of me I can't erase.
I once believed he loved me so
But in the end his heart said "no."

When we broke up I cried and cried
For then I knew that he had lied.
He lied about the things we shared,
But most of all the way he cared.
Time has passed, still I love him so.
My heart will never let him go.
He thinks of me as just a friend.
I guess that's all I've ever been.

Our life together is at an end.
I fear my heart may never mend.
And so dear Lord I hope you see,
How much he really means to me.
And I pray dear Lord that we may be
Together in Eternity!

Patty Maben

A PLACE OF PRAYER

When I alone in silence wait for
Answers to my prayer
  I see my Lord nailed to the cross,
It's I who should be there
  Still patience has no home in me, I
Wish to tarry not
  Yet in your time all works for good
I rest upon the thought
  Your love and peace wash over me
Here in my hiding place
  I find all things I can endure Lord
Thank you for your grace.

Scott R. Adie

NO EMPTY ROOMS

I look inside man's weary heart and
See no empty rooms
    The sin that leaves so many scars
Is building Satan's tombs
    And yet I see a room of light where
Truth and love prevail
    Inside each heart a room for joy
That Satan can't assail
    Would that I could enter in I'm
Knocking on the door
    I long to mend the broken dreams
That lay upon the floor
    And bring new life into the rooms
Where pain and grief abide
    Restoring them to hope and peace
That long ago have died
    Man wasn't meant to struggle so and
Bear a weary heart
    All he needs for joy complete I'm
Longing to impart
    I know it's hard to come to me the
World says 'don't go'
    But tell me; did the world die
Because it loves you so?
        Your Friend, *Jesus*

Scott R. Adie

OVERWHELMED

If you've reached the point in life,
    when all your circuits are jammed.
You're frustrated with everything
    — almost completely overwhelmed.
Running around in circles
    — not accomplishing a thing.
It's time to let go and let God!
    Let Him, His peace to you bring.

Let His peace flow in,
    and c/ ver you over, each inch.
Relax and feel soothing relief,
    as nerves begin to unclinch.
New breath begins to flow,
    coming through the spiritual realm.
If you will only allow,
    God's peace will overwhelm.

Julia Jones

INSIGNIFICANCE

                Throw in towel.
            Say ''No, I can't.''
                        Lonely,
                    unable.
            Insignificant.

        Sudden awareness,
        Divine Magnificence.
                No such thing,
            Insignificance.

Julia Jones

GRASS UNDER THE SNOW

Sometimes he pretends he doesn't love me
But in his eyes I see
The reflection of no other lover
So I know that he still loves me

Sometimes he pretends not to want me
But always somehow I know
That he will always want me
Until winter no longer brings snow

Sometimes I ask if he needs me
Revealing my deepest fear
And he tells me that he won't need me
Until the grass of spring appears

And maybe then he won't need me
If the grass of spring doesn't come
And he'll find another lover
And forget that he had this one

So now my heart is happy
Because I'll always know
That he loves me eternally
For grass grows under the snow

Edelin C. Fields

ONLY GOD AND I CAN KNOW

I have a secret but one doesn't
    tell a secret
        and only God and I can know

So when I touch your hand
    again or
        smile at you

Or when my eyes forget to conceal
    my desire
And pick up the smoldering
    embers there   and
        coax them into a flame

Remember   I would tell you
    our secret my love
But only God and I can know

Edelin C. Fields

THE LISTENER

Why am I always the one
They choose to lay their burdens on
I don't profess to know the answers
To have the cures for all their cancers

Why do they always lean on me
Is it because they feel so free
To let off steam and clear the air
If I'm the only one aware

Why must I always play the host
To be their mental whipping post
But if it gives them some relief
I do not mind to share their grief

For each of us must have someone
That we can lay our burdens on
Someone in whom we can confide
When it aches too much to hold inside

Linda Williams Stoneham

LOST SOULS

Listen to the howling wind
And strain your sensitive ears
That you might hear the mournful tones
Which echo through the years
For these are sounds of all lost souls
A kindred to you and me
So do not turn your mind away
But heed their plaintive plea
Their voices call throughout the hills
They seek but cannot find
They shall not have their longed-for sleep
Nor any peace of mind
How much longer must they search
Before their final rest
Perhaps they wait for each of us
To join them in their quest

Linda Williams Stoneham

TO SUE, FOR GRANDPA

Your heart is bleeding from the pain
not washed away by memories of yesterday
The laughter you once shared
rings loudly in the wind

When at last you can cry no more
the tears will sting your eyes
and burn your soul
But your memories keep
the lost one alive

Lisa Roose-Church

CRY FOR GRANDPA

When I was five my grandpa held me
and whispered ''I love you'' to me.
He watched me grow
from timid child to the me I was yesterday.
He held me close
to chase away ghosts
I felt were following me in the night.
When I found out grandpa died
I said, ''Who cares?'' I never cried.
But I felt the emptiness of his touch,
and absence of his love
and the feeling of dread.
If only I could hold him now
I would let him know —
I cried.

Lisa Roose-Church

The wind is the earth's broom;
it gathers up and collects
that which the earth has lost.

David Emrich

FRIENDSHIP

To Jill

Friendship seems on the surface such a simple word
  but truly encompasses a world of meaning.
Friendship is that precious gift when two come
  together and freely share thoughts and dreams.
It is sharing all the pains and pleasures life
  is made of.
It is the comfort of someone to turn to when you
  need someone who really cares.
Friendship involves unconditional acceptance, a
  nonjudgmental ear, a thoughtful touch or
  soft word spoken when feeling blue.
Friendship is enjoying private times together,
  laughing late into the night.
Friendship will always be a growing, thriving
  force because it involves the intertwining
  of lives and experiences.
You may ask how do I know these things?
Because these are all the things our friendship
  means to me.

Susan Ellicott

SILENT WINTER

Snow white frost that blankets leaf-bare trees
Against a sky of blue-grey clouds and ebony.
The snowy fields and frosty frozen gleam
Of snow and ice appear to be a dream.
Winter's hue is everywhere.
A frosty glow.

Blinding white, a frozen fog that clings to bush and tree.
Forgotten snowbird's chirp an icy reveille,
And children, clad in brightly colored woolen caps
And gloves, skate on a frozen stream.
Winter's hue is everywhere.
A frosty glow.

A winter's hue that's painted silent white.
A winter's hue of ice and cold that bite.
And I alone look through the glass
And think of many winters that have come and passed.
I watch the leaf-bare trees and icy silent snow
And long for brighter days, past summer days,
And not to be alone.

Jean Steele

POVERTY

The smoking section — a fragrance,
Not the familiar acrid cloud of a cigarette,
This was a memory — a flashback
The tape spinning in reverse — sixty years;
So poor we were, the windows rimmed with frost,
And hot bricks cooled by icy sheets and frigid feet.
So poor we were, made-over hand-me-downs,
Black velvet dress on a fifth grader,
In a one-room country school.
So poor we were, the cheapest brand
Used sparingly in his old corn cob pipe,
In evenings while Mother read to us
Of Zane Gray's rugged men,
And James Oliver Curwood always had
A red-haired heroine.

Mary Akkanen

LOVE'S EXPRESSION

Who writes of love? Each callow youth
Inspired by moonlight or the scent of flowers,
Songs of mockingbirds, rich golden curls,
Fair apple-blossom skin or sunny smiles.
What do they write? Mere vapid, strung-together words
Wherein "moon" rhymes with "June" and "croon" and "spoon,"
Mere adolescent, effervescent froth
With little meaning nor of lasting worth.
No one may truly write of love
Who has not felt it to its very depths
Where worldly goods, career, honor, life itself
Are offered willingly to the one beloved.
And even this may not be quite enough
To bring out love's expression most profound;
Only through bitter loss, by death, mischance, rejection,
Wringing the heart with sorrow scarce endured.
So it has ever been. Great poets of the past,
Suffering, their ways of life upset by grief,
Have blessed us with a golden heritage. So 'twill be
So long as life endures and Love is Law.

George N. Heflick

TRUE LOVE SMELTING

Have you ever seen a feather change
Try and remember your name
Is love still an easy game

Have you ever eaten ice cream upside down
Try fooling around
Sucking on a lollipop
Sending true love smelting from your heart
What it was becomes what it is
You seen a feather change back the same
Amazing you can still remember your name

Have you ever seen a tear change into a new year
Have you ever seen a smile sadness bringing hopeless gladness
Nothing ever remains the same do not forget your name

Melvin Sykes

SONG OF COURAGE

A song for all who enter here,
A song of cheer and laughter.
A song to chase away your fear,
And eliminate disaster.

Sing of happiness — sing of joy,
Sing of love for every girl and boy.
Sing a song of birds and flowers,
Of knights and kings, and ivory towers.
But the best song of all is one that reaches all places —
Leaving smiles and contentment on millions of faces.
So when things get tough, and hard to handle,
Say a prayer — light a candle!
Remember this song I sing to you,
And you will never feel sad or blue.
"Come out of the darkness, and into the light,"
Your prayers will be answered — soon things will be right.
I know it takes a lot of drive,
But just keep on saying, "Thank God, I'm alive!"

Jo La Cola

WHISPER IN THE NIGHT

You fulfill me when you are near,
and when I whisper in your ear.
Beyond this veil of darkness I see
this fragile moment now beckons me.

From the depths of your sigh I drink,
as my lips into your shoulder I sink.
With emotions; a second dawns in time,
and moments to call our own; sublime.

The dawn awakens with a grayish light,
to reveal all but a whisper in the night.
My treasure grows as you softly cry,
bound to you with a kiss and a sigh.

Beyond the horizon in your eyes, I see
we are on the verge of all we could be.
My fingers traced this journey's dimension,
and its trail abounds with this passion.

The splendor of an instant is captured,
and the growth of perception is nurtured.
I caressed the essence of this sensation,
and the presence of a new-found elation.

Albert Duran

THE SANDS OF TIME

It was seven o'clock in the morning,
with a cool breeze gently blowing.
This threshold is the path of my destiny,
and only limited by dreams woven by fantasy.

This journey's path holds a bit of uncertainty,
but with you by my side I would face eternity.
Time and distance are brought before us at bay,
and our love still changes its shape each day.

Surrounded by the sounds of nature calling,
I could hear the sands of time start falling.
A unique beauty in this fragile moonlight,
and its natural state comes out in sunlight.

My fingers touch your flame of desire,
and I caress time and this raging fire.
I find the joy of living in your eyes,
and unleash this passion in our sighs.

With each kiss I give myself to you,
as this moment's essence grew and grew.
This peace is only known by a few,
and this heart belongs to only you.

Albert Duran

TESS

when my dreary life needed color
your love created a shining rainbow
the golden sun shone brighter
the azure sky turned bluer
the mockingbirds sang sweeter
the world became a better place

so happy that our paths crossed
when i really needed you
you gave me memories time can't erase
they are indelibly etched in my mind
unforgettable . . . as you are

Cy Jenkins

TREASURE FOUND BY CHANCE

odd the things you find
in attics when you're not
really looking treasures
of yesteryear faded worn
ghostly nostalgic bringing
a sob or laugh

momentarily brightening or
darkening your day depending
on its power to quicken the
heart or shorten the breath
lightning-swift memories
crowd the mind while icy
fingers clutch the throat
making heartstrings taut

but sadness crowded out
by cheerier recollections
recedes into the darkness
while happy smiles embrace
the face proving that between
sorrow and happiness
happiness is the more
powerful just as good has
strength that evil never knew

Cy Jenkins

JESUS IN OUR LIVES

Jesus is important in our lives
Trust His words of love
Then live, work and praise
Him in every aspect of life.
Give honor to Him to hold and mold
You wholly for His glory
With all your heart, praise Him.

When you speak of Jesus
You will never fail in faith
Believe without doubt.
Observe His presence everywhere
Accept His light of love
Live His life of grace
Praise Him with all your heart.

Josephine I. Njoku

I NEVER THOUGHT

I never thought
I would ever have you,
It's like it's too good
To ever come true.

I never thought
I would ever feel,
But when I hold you
It just seems so real.

I never thought
I would ever say,
You make love beautiful
In so many ways.

I never thought
You would be mine,
Now you are until
The end of our time.

Lisa Laska

LOVE WILL PREVAIL

The greatest gift to man is love
Which inspires the mind with joy
And happiness forever.
We lean on one another for love
To enjoy the days of our lives.
We learn a few arts
Since our needs do vary,
But love will prevail
For the progress of our needs.

Our life is arranged from eternity
With the plan of our earthly labor.
Love may falter under the weight
Of errors, idleness, and selfishness,
Because we can't see everything,
Know everything,
Do everything or be everything.
But love will prevail
To join with joy
In the minds of the living.

Josephine I. Njoku

A STARRY SKY

Your beauty, as fair
As a misty climb
Into a starry sky.
Your love, as pure and innocent
As a newly born child.

But it is not for your
Beauty that I love thee,
But for the warmth and compassion
That you have given me.

A kiss from your gentle sweet
Lips would take the place of all
The food and drink for the
Entirety of my life.
Although words could not ever
Express the deepest love
In my heart that I hold for you,
My love will never die.

Eddie Aguirre

FOLLOW THROUGH

A decision . . .
Important decision!

Think, weigh,
Wonder and pray —
What should I do?

Ponder, meditate,
Study, ruminate —
How will it affect you?

Consider, reason,
Talk to someone.
Write down the pros and cons.

Imagine, feel,
Contemplate the ideal,
Now when you're done

Follow through!

Anna Kramer Pendino

WONDERS IN WINTER

In wintertime,
Your eyes grow wide with delight,
When you see presents under the tree,
And little children with eyes all aglow,
Sit upon Santa's knee.

Your ears delight to all the sounds,
Like silver bells ringing through the air.
Carolers singing hymns so solemn and sweet,
It makes your eyes fill up with tears.

Your heart gladdens from all your good friends,
Delivering special holiday cheer,
And your heart quickens, thinking of the fun to come,
Ringing in the New Year.

The freezing wind nips at your skin,
Tingling your fingers, ears, and nose.
The icy pictures on your window pane,
Attest to Jack Frost's having some fun in the snow.

Dorothy Rodgers

A NEW SPRING

Spring is not the same this year, my dear.
There is something wrong, you are not here.
Your absence hurts, as I hold back a tear.
And yet, it's spring again this time of year.
But you are not here: and nothing is the same.
Where are you this ''would-be'' spring, with rain?

Yet, I know something is wrong where you are.
Just come and warm up this spring's cool air?
You know down deep inside I really care. So —

Won't you please let me know what's so bad,
To make me feel so down-and-out and sad,
Wondering if this mystery makes you glad.
If so, I certainly have been had.

I hope this all puzzles you, as it does me.
For only you can make the pieces fall in place,
So, spring will bloom again for me first rate.
That's why spring is nature's really ''new'' year,
So its close softness can be felt by all.

Wait! Yes!
There is a new ''you'' for me — spring is really here.

V. S. Lewis

MELANCHOLY

Again and again just everything goes wrong
Please, God, give me the strength to go on
Life seems so hopeless when night kills the day
Please shine down Your light to show me the way
There are so many things I can't understand
Help me accept them by the touch of Your hand
When life stands still and looks death in the eye
Please watch over me from Your throne on high
My mind is distorted — there evil thoughts thrive
Please don't let it die — keep my thinking alive
When I just can't go on and it's too much to bear
You're helping me, God, by just being there

Sharon Rudolph

DON'T GIVE UP ON LIFE

Stop killing yourself, stop using dope
As long as you are alive there is hope
Hope that one day your life will be better
Now if you kill yourself, your chances are lost forever
Take note. There are people in this day and time
Whose problems transcend yours and mine
So don't give up on life
If you do, then you are through
The endless beauty of life itself
Compensates for the evil and ugliness
Since there are no handcuffs on your wrists
And you do truly exist
Utilize this freedom, take control
Initiate a decisive and affirmative goal
No one is holding a gun to your head
So there are no reasons to be afraid
Observe and preserve the lifeline's signs
The results are worth the effort and time
Don't give up on life
If you do, then you are through

Albert Humphries

ALBERT LESTER HUMPHRIES. Born: Oglethorpe, Georgia, reared in Columbus, Georgia; Children: one daughter, Tisa Alana Humphries; Education: Queens College, New York City, New York, 1968-70; Occupations: Banker, Songwriter/Lyricist, Poet, Freelancer; Membership: Writers and Poets Inc.; Awards: Community Leader Award, America Biographical Institute, 1987; Men of Achievement Award, International Biographical Centre, Cambridge, England, 1987; Merit Award and Harmonious Award, New York Professional/Amateur Songs Jubilee, New York, 1985; Certification of Election, Who's Who in the East 21st Edition, Marquis Publication, Chicago, 1986; Certificate of Recognition, Who's Who in Emerging Leader of America, 1987; Commemorative Certificate, Who's Who in International Music, 1987; Certificate of Achievement, Who's Who in Entertainment, 1987; Certificate of Merit/Achievement, Talent Association, Boston, 1983; Poetry: 'I'm Hungry For Your Love,' *Lyricist and Composer, Vol. IV,* 1983; 'Just Keep on Living,' *American Poetry Anthology, Vol. VI,* 1986; 'Life Goes On,' *Best Poets of 1986,* American Poetry Association, 1987; 'Nobody's Perfect,' 1987; I'm A Man of My Word,' 1987; Comments: *In life, good health is humankind's most precious and valuable asset, which may be enhanced by the achievement of positive love and prosperity. Presently, in my writings, I aspire to encourage practice of good habits in the prevention of cruelty to one's mind, heart, body and soul.*

YOU'LL BE SO GLAD YOU DID

What can be accomplished in fifteen minutes?
You would be surprised to know!
A brisk walk through the wonders of nature,
The beauty of creation is there to show.

In only one quarter of an hour,
You can clean and dust your home,
Read an encouraging bit of prose
Or write a little poem.

Nine hundred seconds slide by quietly,
But you can phone a friend.
Share some happiness with someone
Your joy will never end.

So take the time today, dear one,
However short or long . . .
Dream a dream, pray a prayer,
Or even sing a song.

You'll be so glad you did!

Anna Kramer Pendino

While the music plays,
I shall dance.

David Emrich

AS IS, IS AS DOES

The Voyeur

As I travel through to the past they
    view what shant be changed.

We watch the insanities of the world.
We view the awesome disbeliefs of
    the imaginable mind.
We pain ourselves with the
    scenarios fleeting by our eyes.

As I live in the present I realize
    the importance of the moment.

Let life be as it must.
Be as one should be.
Live by the word and law of the
    believer.

As the importance of the time draws near
    things manage to get worse.

Brother against brother.
Nation against nation.
Loves against love.

* * *

Climax throughout life with sincerity
    on one's own heart.

Martin G. Marco

THE FANTASY

A dancer spins away
and out goes the dawn
as well as the day
with a slow, lingered yawn.
Keys play on and on.
The feeling, it's still here.
Loneliness, will it be gone
and find me some cheer?
The woman, she's beautiful
in my mind I dream.
Her love will guide me plentiful
through a nightmare scream.
Tiresome, I grow weary
as does the passing day.
Another day, it comes dreary
and then it goes away.

Laura Gajdosik

IF MARTIN COULD NOT DREAM

If Martin could not see,
the lines would be black and white
and blue.
If Martin could not hear,
silent screams would curse the night
and bitter tears would collect until the day.
If Martin could not smell,
fire beneath the smoke would remain
unexposed.
If Martin could not touch,
who would know the closing confines
of cold prison walls.
If Martin could not taste,
who could relish his chosen drink.
If Martin could not speak.
our conscience would be mute.
If Martin does not breathe,
it is surely not for lack of air.
If Martin could not dream,
we surely could not breathe.

Robert J. Pignolo

ALONE

You met me
You loved me
You left me . . .
    alone.

You showed me a light
That I'd never known.
You gave me something
By it I have grown.

You gave me a memory
I shall not forget.
The feelings for you
Are still with me yet.

But there is one thing
That will never be known.
Why you met me
you loved me
and you left me . . .
    alone.

Doreen Tabor

TO PENNY

I could not believe
That you were dying
Even as I watched you go.
While all around
A mournful sighing
Aching, yearning spirits low.
You were forgiving
A brief painful smile
In hope, that we would know.
You understood
That it would be awhile.
Knowledge, like a seed does grow.
And in between
What of the abyss,
Suspended in our woe.
Washed by conscience
Knowing we were remiss.
We see a glimpse
Of hell below.

Theresa Strangi Mitchell

A LONGING

To sit beside
Someone you love
For just a little while
Would ease the torment
In your soul.

Belief in love
Can give you hope
Renew your strength
And keep your mind
And spirit whole.

Theresa Strangi Mitchell

THERESA STRANGI MITCHELL. Born: Woolmarket, Harrison County, Mississippi, 7-6-30; Occupations: Retail merchant, ''Stuff''; Registered agent, Mississippi Securities; Awards: Golden Poet Award, 1987; Poetry: 'Unnamed Hunger,' 'This Nation,' 'War Song,' *American Poetry Anthology, Vol. VII, No. 2,* 1987; Themes: *Life, death, love, marriage, children, family relationship, religion and ideology.*

WHITE WICKER CHAIRS

The crackle and pop of white wicker chairs
remind me of soft summer days.
Those were the times when I had no cares.

My room holds trinkets from county fairs,
and Teddy presides where I used to play.
The crackle and pop of white wicker chairs

remind me of Daddy and how he would say,
"She'll clean her plate if I 'double dare.' "
Those were the times when I had no cares.

But now I come home to unanswered prayers,
and neighbors bring dishes and stand in the way.
The crackle and pop of white wicker chairs

strain, as people sit down with nothing to say.
I hide in my room where old records blare —
Those were the times when I had no cares.

I still hear his voice on soft summer days —
There are boxes of clothes to be given away.
The crackle and pop of white wicker chairs
remind me of times when I had no cares.

Rebecca Hutton

UNTIL DEATH DO US PART

In my mind I may pretend,
But you're more to me than just a friend.
These silly games one's mind can play,
They can toss you and twirl you like in ballet.
Is this lust or could this be love?
The answer awaits from the heavens above.
I feel a fire down deep in my heart,
Cupid has hit me with his magical dart.
God's hand will guide me and show me the way,
To bring us closer with each passing day.
This is just the beginning, and a wonderful start,
Could this be . . .
"Until Death Do Us Part?"

Vicki L. Emond

LIFE OF A LIGHTLESS IVY

Oh, if the books could only speak,
but they can't, never opened, occasionally dusted.
Beside them, I once spilled like a green fountain so long ago.
The books have never spilled.
Here I sit,
one, two . . . three, four, and five little dots of shadow behind me
from a light so small.
A square pane behind a dusty desk leaking over this —
a small desert, a multitude of grays despite the colored volumes.
I am here, yet beside them,
reaching within my space 'til I may go
no further,
and yet I reach, but I find no greater light.
Where is all the green I knew?
Turn to brown, crumbled away.
Clinging to myself as the dust clings to me, I am left an ornament.
As the many scripts upon the shelf embossed in silent, unglittered gold
wait for a moist breath, and a warming light;
so do I, here, yet alive,
and weeping drops of green beside them.

J. S. Hall

I DID NOT LIE TO YOU, SWEETHEART

I walk in the outerspace
I went from place to place
I went here and there and everywhere
I came down to earth
I start a romantic affair
I did not lie when it start
I never lie to you, sweetheart
I don't have lies in my heart
I am not the devil
I did not come in the morning and lie to you
I did not lie in the morning or the evening
I made dreams come true
I did not lie to you, sweetheart
I did not lie from the start
I promise to cling to you
From the beginning until the ending
I promise to cling to you night and day
I cling to you, in the morning and the evening
Gave proof that when I said I love you
Every word I said is true

Stanley H. Campbell

AS IT WAS IN THE BEGINNING

Living in the space age
As things are in these days
I'm walking on thin air
Let me elaborate on this romantic affair
As it was in the beginning
As it was on the day I met you
As it was the morning and the evening
As it was when our love was new
As it was together we were dreaming
As it was in the shadows of the evening
As it was on the night our dreams came true
As it was the night dreams came true for you and I
The tropical moon in the sky
The tropical moon riding high
The willow tree standing by
As the wind blew it whistles thru the willow tree
But I held you much closer to me
On the night when dreams come true
I still love you morning and evening
I still love you as it was in the beginning

Stanley H. Campbell

THINKING OF YOU

*For a friend whose husband
had recently died*

I think of you so often
And my heart begins to feel.
I think of you so often
And a teardrop I reveal.
How can I tell you
How I try to feel along with you?

I saw you a few times.
I looked upon your face.
I saw your pain that your smile could not erase
And I knew that I could not really feel along with you.
I try, and I cry.
I think of you so often.

Mary Susan Smith

STEVIE

Child of Song,
ruffle-wrapped in ivory silk
pales the desert sun.

Child of Love
in beaded black chiffon,
dazzling graceful poet
with all the stage your home.

Rock Star, hard and loud,
singing your dreams
before the crowd —
dance with joy to the steady beat,
lovely rock-star queen.

M. Jacquin

PORTRAIT FOR HER

There is a word
Which describes
The classical
Tender feeling

Of being one
With loveliness
On evenings
When a blue moon

Rises gently
In the night air
In tune with my
Perennial

Red rose placed
On your pillow
Where You will lay
Beautifully.

Michael Earl McCutcheon

TEARS

They come,
to settle my rage,
to let go my fears,
and rest my ragged soul.
Sometimes wanted, other times not.
Overflowing emotions bundled up
with a tight rope.
Tears suddenly frees them
and all the emotions go flying.
Gradually,
they float to the ground,
where I become me again,
the person with a simple life
and common problems.

Carla Kay Homeister

VOICES

I see you sleeping there
And I wonder if I
Still shine in your eyes

I fear that time and
Life's endeavors
Have changed you somehow
Inside

Last night you whispered
A name so sweet
A name that made your
Face shine

I lay in darkness with
Moistened cheeks
For that name you
Mentioned wasn't
Mine

Anthony Pryor

BY OUR HERO'S SONGS

Sway to the cliffs
Over and sometimes quite beyond
A beacon
Shines quite Bright
Only so long,
As he need be supported
Run, Hide, *Fight!*
 One person's problem
Belongs to everyone.
Push the swing way over the cliff
Beware
Today the rope has grown thin

By whose light can so many sing
the
   same
     song?

Zane Bond

MY SON

A life that started deep inside
  is now ready to appear.
Oh what joy! The time has come!
  Can't help but shed a tear.
My precious child has arrived
  and now I hear his cry!
Thank you God for my son
  whom I'll love until I die.

Bonnie Giest

MEMORIES

Sometimes I make snow angels
Or roll in the fallen leaves.
Sometimes I wade through puddles,
Or dance my way toward dawn.
Sometimes I sled, hell bent,
Down a snow-covered slope.
Sometimes I am content
To drown in a flood of memories.

Alice Denice Kravig

ALICE DENICE KRAVIG. Born: Rocky Ford, Colorado, 10-26-56; Education: Otero Junior College, La Junta, Colorado, A.A., 6-2-84; Comments: *As one of the physically challenged, writing poetry is important to me. It is a release for my frustration, pain and anger. It is a means by which I may cry out against the social injustices in the world. Through poetry I reveal my hopes and my joy and my dreams; but my greatest joy is to share my love affair with nature and people.*

LITTLE GIRL

Little girl with golden hair
So much love you have to share
Watching as you grow so fast
Wishing childhood could always last.

See the joy in your eyes
As you watch little butterflies
Standing quiet, wondering why?
You reach for it, away it flies.

Laughter, joy in your small face
Skipping, running, jumping, in outdoor space.
Be careful not to step on a bug
Run to me, reach out for hugs.

Sweet little, dear little girl
Wind blowing in small gold curls
Only "God" could grant such grace
Combining such wondrous love in one place.

Joyce Campbell

FIRST LOVE

Whenever I hear your name, see you, or hear your voice,
I am overcome with mixed emotions. On the outside, I remain calm,
cool and collected — just like the sea. However, just like
the sea, below the surface there is a flurry of activity. I feel
deep love for you, want you back but know this can never be,
ache to hold you again because of the deep emotional attachment
we once had. I want you back in my life, but know, deep in
my very being, that this can never be.

Once the flurry of activity calms down, I can rationalize
the facts — that you might still love me, but you have chosen
your way of life and I have chosen mine. I used to hurt, but that
hurt is now gone. The hurt has given way to a sense of peace
and a calmness. I forgive you for hurting me the way you did
and understand that you did it because you cared too much not to.

I wish to thank you for coming into my life and for what
you taught me. If it weren't for you, I never would know what love
is about. It's a shame that some people go thru their whole lives
without knowing that feeling. Love is the most powerful force
in the universe and, to be fully alive, you must experience it
at least once in your lifetime.

Whatever I do, no matter who I love in the future, you will
always be special to me. You were my first love. I will always hold
a special place in my heart just for you.

Maureen Eleanor Smith

A VERY SPECIAL FRIEND

If someone takes the time to care when the ''world is rushing by''
and you just aren't sure where you fit in . . .

If someone listens with their heart, and they really understand
what you're saying, even though you are not saying what you mean . . .

If someone helps you understand yourself better and by doing so
makes you realize something that they know will hurt you,
and they sympathize with you . . .

If someone helps you do what you know you should, but when you slip
doesn't give up on you, just encourages you to do better . . .

If someone shares their thoughts, feelings and ideas with you,
thereby enabling you to better understand them and
your relationship . . .

If someone is there for you when you need another person to hold you
or just be around — in silence, in tears, in weakness,
in strength — just because they want you to know
you are not alone . . .

If someone will always be there for you, no matter what,
no matter where, if humanly possible . . .

Then you are really blessed by God with a wonderful gift,
A Very Special Friend.

Maureen Eleanor Smith

SOMETIMES

Sometimes I feel the world is closing in on me
and I get very depressed . . .

Sometimes I feel no one cares for me and I feel unwanted . . .

Sometimes I feel tired and just want a quiet place to rest . . .

Sometimes I am very angry and want to scream my lungs out . . .

Sometimes I just want to be and let the world go by without me
worrying about anything or anyone . . .

Sometimes I just want to be held by another to feel secure . . .

Sometimes I want to cry and let all my emotions out . . .

Sometimes I just want another person to be there for me —
if I want to talk, they allow me to; if I want to be silent,
they share a comfortable silence with me and hold my hand . . .

It is at times like these that I am very grateful for your
friendship and all the love and support it brings. Whether or not
you are physically present, I know you can sense my needs and are
with me spiritually. Then, when that realization takes hold,
I know I *can* make it because of you — a magnificent
gift — an extension of God's loving hand: *a wonderful friend!*

Maureen Eleanor Smith

B.J.

*In memory of my twenty-one year old
brother, who died July 10, 1986.*

I never got to say good-bye or even say
''I love you.'' We never really forgave each
Other for the pain we caused each other to suffer.

Now here I am alone, alive but alone. You
Left me here by myself while you quietly died away.

It's too late for anything now; you've left and can't
Come back. I'm left with only memories and
Regrets of the past.

I wish you could have seen yourself like I did.
Maybe then you'd understand my devastation, but you
Can't — you're dead.

I'm angry with you for doing this even though it
was your right. You left the rest of us with the
Consequences of your selfish deed.

I want you to know I loved you and that I'll
Always love you, and in time accept how you chose
To leave. I miss you, and I'll never be the
Same, for by your suicide, I too have died deep inside.

Lori Yates

A NEW LIFE

What's it like to live again
Full of hope, trust, a will to win
'Tis beautiful to gaze upon small things
To watch flower petals open after a rain.

For rain always settles the dry dust
In God again, we've placed our trust
To know the joy of each new day
Seeing things in such a different way.

Longing to be out about this world
Soaring high in the air, as breezes unfurl
The beauty of life, love, a zest to live
A loving trust that only ''God'' can give.

Joyce Campbell

WHAT I WANT

In selfishness I clamor
    wanting things I should not have
God knows this would be harmful,
    and no way I should behave,

But He will permit me to
    go through self-made trial and test
Trusting I might learn from them
    His foreknowledge was the best,

Quietly whispered in my mind
    and said the name of ''Jesus''
For the heart was hurting so
    all I could think was — ''Jesus,''

How precious, the Son of God
    to know my unhappiness
He eased the heartache I caused
    and my spirit He did bless,

I am thankful for His love
    the forgiveness o'er and o'er
That He cares of mental state
    though 'tis I who hurts Him more.

Gwendolyn Sudduth

FRIENDS TO ME

there is a place to be,
  with friends who love me,
with friends who
  are so dear to me,
in a mirror of master reflections,
  Christ is shown to me,
for how much brighter
  they seem to be
with smiles that come from
  within thee,
so soft, so warm, and
  oh so cuddly.

AnnaMarie Kilbreth

THE CHILDREN

What would have happened
To you and I —
If the children were grown?
What would have happened
To you and I,
If the children had places
of their own?
    or
Were we only
To have passed in time?
Were we meant
To love
    So briefly,
    So intensely,
        yet
    So abruptly
cut apart —
Was it more
Than *just*
The children?

Linda Baron

PRAISE YE THE LORD

Psalm 117

O, could I emblazon
  In mammoth letters high:
Praise ye! Praise ye! Praise ye!
  Across the morning sky!

Blue, and bright, and cloudless,
  Heaven's arch above,
Praise ye! Praise ye! Praise ye!
  The One I serve and love.

My spirit is elated, —
  To soar on wings, I long!
Praise ye! Praise ye! Praise ye!
  I shout my joyful song!

May my heart and lips keep singing
  From dawn to waning sun:
Praise ye! Praise ye! Praise ye!
  Till life's brief scenes are done.

O, could I emblazon
  In mile-high letters tall:
Praise ye! Praise ye! Praise ye!
  My *Lord!* My *God!* My *All!*

Edith Johnson

NO TEARS

The day may come,
you will walk away.
No tears will I shed.

For, I'm better having
known you.
I'm stronger having
loved you.

I only hope I've touched you.

Deborah Pratt

MISS ANGELIA

Ah, she said hello to me
with her smile
she has eyes that sparkle,
like a child's.
If only I knew her
inner thoughts.
Beneath those big brown
eyes, she talks.
I listened carefully
when she spoke.
Like a gentle raindrop
her voice brought forth.
Miss Angelia,
I stood there, right
silly, as if in a trance.

My heart was pounding,
as if I had danced.
My mind was hoping but
my lips remained sealed.
Miss Angelia, you'll never know
how I really feel.

Jimmy Graham

It is not for me to know why
  A brain is damaged
  A body disfigured or
  A chromosome marred
It is not for me to know why
  A child must die.

It is for me
  To give extra time to learn
  To find ways to compensate
  To unlock hidden potential
It is for me
  To love while there is life.

Diann Foster

BRIGHT EYES

Baby, Baby, Bright Eyes
  Mom hears your cries
As she kisses away your tears
  You're so cute, yet young in years

Mom slowly rocks you to sleep
  Whispers promises she plans to keep
Ever so gently she lays you down
  Covers you, as she looks around

At the door, she clicks the light
  Stands in darkness and says goodnight
To Baby Bright Eyes fast asleep
  Mom's heart flows with love, so deep

You are everything in Mom's eyes
  As tears roll from her eyes
'Cause of the beauty and joy you've brought
  Into Mom's life, a loving sincere thought.

Joseph Boteilho, Jr.

VISITING THE DOCTOR

Checkup

We all should visit the doctor a few times a year,
And when being examined, don't be afraid or have any fear.
Because, if your visits are frequent, a problem can be detected
At an early stage,
But if you put off your visits, then — problems will worsen
With age.

No adult should postpone their visits for any reason at all,
Yet they wait until they are very sick, or have a bad fall.
A routine checkup does not take too much of your time,
And it will also remove any ill doubts you have in mind.

I am sure your visit to their office will benefit you,
For if you have a pain, the doctor will know what to do,
And you will be on the road to recovery and good health,
Because health you cannot buy, regardless of all your wealth.

Now be on the safe and smart side of your health,
By "visiting the doctor" and be good to yourself,
For a minor pain can lead to a major problem in time,
So visit the doctor's office and a hundredfold you will find.

Louis D. Izzo

SAY WHAT YOU HAVE TO SAY AND LEAVE

Silent words are from regretful lips
Starting the bankrupt partnerships
The future is all I anticipated
I asked for nothing and got silver plated

Burning with an inflammable fire
The innocent bystander is an anti-liar
Too far away to listen to the news
Is too far to walk in worn-out shoes

Say what you have to say and leave
And make your final attack
Your emotion controlled your intelligence
And now there's no way back

Being special comes naturally
One life for the cat in the alley
I don't think I should have made it this far
Now I'm a desperate falling star

The knife's in the flesh and I'm giving blood
Eating dirt and drinking water is vitamin mud
Say what you have to say and leave
'Cause it's better to take than to receive

John Cichoski

FRIENDS AGAIN

Our moments together, I'll never forget
for they'll always be special to me.
I feel that I've loved you since we first met;
You came and you set my heart free.

You know I still love you and miss your sweet touch
the touch that you give to her, now.
Each time you're together, it hurts me so much
I've got to live with it, somehow.

Although it's so hard to tell you good-bye,
I know things will be better this way.
You'll always be part of what I am inside
the part that I think of each day.

I know I'll be happy with the choice I have made
although my love will not end.
Each day of the week I've looked up and prayed
that we will be friends once again.

Vicki Shrader

THE DISTANCE RUNNER

Save me from myself,
For I am the distance runner.
Passing through the stands of time.
Hearing applause no more.
Sweating off the weight of my ancestors.
Shackled by the ignorance that chains my feet.
Making the distance further than it seems.

Save me from myself,
For I am the distance runner.
Running through minefields of indifference.
Being blown away with no one knowing I was even there.
My feet ache from the journey.
But, my determination strengthens with my every step.

Yet, you must save me from myself,
For I am the distance runner.
Who always finishes last.

James Glover

DEAR DIARY

I let him break my heart,
I kept wishing he would come through, but
I was so obsessed with loving him that I
failed to look at what I was seeing.

Its mending was ever so tricky.
I hated him for not letting me go and
I hated myself for letting him convince me to stay.
But I wanted him . . . I wanted him . . . I wanted him . . .

Sometimes I'd cry to hear his voice.
    Other times I wanted to run from it.
Sometimes I'd ache for him to hold me.
    Other times I'd have screamed if he did.
I'd wonder if he'd look back someday, too late . . .

I bailed out with my last bit of pride.
I think about him now and then . . .
with respect, pity, a little bit of curiosity, and,
most often, just as someone I used to think I knew.

Pamela F. Carver

THE REALLY FAMILIAR

The really familiar really
does not ever go away.

Time passes, things and events
exist,

but the really familiar stays.

The really familiar is too good
to be topped.

The really familiar may fade
but never, never stops —
being good, that is.

In an instant, years and whatever changes
we've experienced can
melt away.

The really familiar was just yesterday.

Bobbie J. Cooper

MOST IS INSIGNIFICANT

I don't need the multitude
of priceless, valueless expenditures
or surroundings.

Give me the blue sky, and the
water nearby.

All that's in heaven is one earth.
What could be of more value
or worth?

Set sails amist;
reach for clouds overhead.
Caress the beauty
and know it's yours.

Everything else is insignificant.
You have all that's in the world.

Bobbie J. Cooper

THE PRISON

My heart, my heart,
Locked in a prison dark.
Bereft of Love, Glory, and Life —
A place that remains as black as night.
Trapped in a cage, like a frightened animal . . .
Alone, I fall;
Desperately for help I call —
But no voice answers,
Lest the ringing echo.
I remain, I stay
Locked between these black walls,
These ageless stones.
I'm so scared — and still alone.
My heart, my heart,
Locked in a prison dark —
A prison that is *your* heart;
My Love,
Your merciless heart.

Julie Anne Wilson

Love, I'm your babe
Left in a blanket on a doorstep
You failed to knock at the door
So I must wait to see if there's new love
Wait here alone, deserted, abandoned
Are your labor pains well spent
You wait not to see my acceptance
My blanket is my new womb
I am birthed to strangers
Love, why hast thou forsaken me
You give me no breast to suck
No tender moment my progenitors
If the world has rejected you
Why leave me on the doorstep
Waiting for the door to open
Waiting my blanket, my comforter
I will not comprise
I need love, I will cry for attention
Open thy doors, it needs be love survive

Leroy A. Houchin

CONTACT

. . . For Allison . . .

The Feeling
Spring Eternal
inside and *outside*
Today I am immortal

Yesterday
I met a kindred spirit
Thoughts intertwined
Contact

Energy times Energy
Swirling higher
Shadows flee
Recognition

Wishing time to stop
and imprison this feeling
But change brings strength
Hope

Jeff Pattison

IN THE ATTIC

In heavy covers the memories hide
Thin spirits that have no space
They wait until the lonely soul
Behind a haunted face
Drifts down to them, and settles in
With sweet and silken breath
To lift each up, in fond embrace
As if to ward off death.
Then racing down corridors of time
Escaping ageless ire
To meet the tempting past;
And worse, unrelenting desire
To linger with archaic ghosts
Finally returning to dwell
In the lavish house of reality
That our inner selves compel.

Gordon A Salway

THE DARK ROOM

Dark room
illuminated only
by a
flickering inspiration.
The red glow
of the Divine forearm
glistens in the sweat
of anticipation.
The flames
struggle at first
in the throes
of a passionate secret,
only to burst forth
in glory and exhiliration,
reaching scorching heights
imaginable only in Depth.
It is the very human
breath of the bellows
which creates and gives life
to the music of the fire.

Tamara J. Bohn

ICICLES

Two icicles fell.
One speared the ground
    and
One shattered.
The one that stood
stands still today,
a Crystal Pole
piercing the
burnished sands
of a livid mind —
a love to share
with all mankind.

Tamara J. Bohn

WINDED

Winds will
with every effort
blow those still
from times that meld
green stones and graves
and rend the rocks
and welt the waves
as they rise in great wheals
along the shore
squealing through torn sands, marred
by judicious jaws
so that standing, jarred,
dry-eyed, dripping crimson
and bewilderment, bereaved
and alone,
i can look up in lucid silence.

Tamara J. Bohn

As I saw a rose petal drop,
I lifted my eyes to the sky.
One bright candle stood.
I lifted my hands, held it, and
    whispered:

"Give me peace, Lord,
When I am defeated;
Give me strength
When I am down,
Give me love,
For mine enemies,
And give me you, Lord,
That I may call my own."

Angela Hertle

RANDOM THOUGHTS

Sometimes in meetings very boring
I find myself quite close to snoring.
To fend off creeping lethargy
I let my mind and thoughts run free.
The thoughts that come when free of rein
Are often funny, they entertain.
My head is filled by unjoined thoughts
That leave me much to puzzle out.

Like how does toothpaste get its stripes?
Or why I just can't learn to type.
These thoughts, quite jumbled, hurry on
So other thoughts can come along.
I think of poems and words that rhyme,
And write them down, if so inclined.
Sometimes my thoughts are so much fun
I hate to stop when meeting's done.

Joan Ulloth

NEW YEAR'S REFLECTIONS

A new year's come, the old has gone
    to never be retrieved
Save in our memories of days gone past
    when it can be relived.
It had its peaks and valleys dark,
    emotions strong and deep
Run through the year and shade it with
    such varied hues and tones
That thoughts of past can bring them back
    to feel them all once more.
Our past grows dim — the low spots fade —
    the high points grow more dear.
We store our memories day by day
    and fill another year.

Joan Ulloth

EULOGY

Ah, dear friend, where are you?
Not bound in that steel box over there,
waiting to return to sweet earth, but
jetting about in this lovely day,
whipping around cream clouds,
playing in a blue saucer sky,
no longer imprisoned in that clay
returning now into its own.

I wonder, standing here,
have you truly gone far from me,
taking that verve and vibrant energy
which was yours?
Is it still with you, where you are,
in that new dimension you have found,
or is that essence of your presence
still seeking new skin to fill
with that wonderfully warm affection
and electric attraction
you beamed to all of us, your friends
while you were here?

Evelyn M. Sears

JOHN'S JOURNEY

Goin' to heaven in a while, sure
Going to miss your little smile,
I'm takin' you with me in my heart you know,
Just to make sure, you see where I go.

Goin' to follow the lights in the sky,
Days last forever, don't care to know why.
I'll show you the way into a world,
It would bring a peace that nothing else could.

Leavin' a life I can't live anymore,
Makes it hard to close the door,
On someone like you, survivin' alone,
But you know it's time, for me to go home.

Yeah, goin' to the promised land,
Kiss me good-bye, touch my hand.
Just be glad my soul is free, and
It's finally where it has to be.

You know I'm always going to hope you say,
"Please come back, I'm ready today," but
Until you feel the wind blow free, you'll
Never know the life, of the north, and me.

Teresa A. Brady

SCOTT

Tiny little feet and hands
This little child, this little man

What joy it brings to this mother
Her newborn is like no other

As I watched Scott grow with pride
Its hard to remember that giving birth to
Him I almost died

I thank you God for Scott as now he is a man
For I know in my heart this was His plan

Phyllis Marshall

THE DAWN OF DREAMS

Went for a walk this morning at dawn,
Stopped for a moment, and lingered on . . .
The heavy silence in the day to be, and
Wondered what, it had to do with me.

Points of hope, in tune with time,
Are held in space, to give peace of mind.
Knowin' that we are never alone,
God is watching, to light the way home.

The stars, one by one, slowly fade from sight,
Put safely away, until tonight.
They will return, bright as ever, a view
Of the past, a belief in forever.

There's a glow of hope on the horizon,
Shining its gold without realizin'
What its warmth, does to the soul,
Another chance, to let your dreams grow.

Seen what I had, it's time to go home,
To begin a new journey, all of my own.
The day has begun, the silence is gone,
Rays of hope are reason, to keep holding on.

Teresa A. Brady

TAKE A CHANCE ON ME

I fell in love with you
The first time we went out together.
I saw a special side of you
That I will love forever.

With you I feel very comfortable
And I can feel the love that you send.
The entire time I kept wishing
That this night would never end.

I think I'm going crazy
And I don't know what to do.
'Cause ever since that night
All I've been thinking about is you.

You said I'm not the man you're looking for
But you feel something for me it seems.
I don't know what you're afraid of.
I'd never stand in the way of your dreams.

I think we're the perfect couple
And I can't see what the problem could be.
You know life is full of risks,
So why not take a chance on me.

Shawn Killackey

JACOB'S LADDER

Searchers are walking the beach
For fragments of hopes and dreams
Now carried ashore;
Blue waves returning them
Ocean waves mourning
Their gruesome chore . . .
Seven brave astronauts
Striving to climb
The invincible stairway
To shining stars.

Charlotte C. Philips

THE LAST ROSE

Summer is almost at an end.
Fall is just around the bend.
Oh, how I will miss the summer,
and all the beauty it brings.
The flowers, rain and Katydids
are just a few of those things.
No more garden to reap what we sow.
It makes my heart sad to see
these things go.
Selfishly I will hold on just
as long as I can.
Until the last Rose has been
in my hand.

Karla Lynn Fisher

TO WIN THE RACE

When things go wrong as they sometimes will,
and life seems to be a road that's all uphill,
hold your head up, as high as you can,
Do not give up just take a stand.
Always do your best no matter what.
Be true to yourself that means a lot.
Respect yourself and all that you do.
It matters not what others think of you.
Do not let yourself be a doormat, for it
just is not right.
Stand up for yourself, give a good fight.
Let go of the bad, hold on to the good.
Sometimes it is hard, but you truly should.
Above everything else keep your heart in
the right place,
With that alone you can win the race.

Karla Lynn Fisher

MOTHER-IN-LAW

I have never known a decent one, most
  probably never will.
Most of them are dreadful, some can
  be a pill.
Never are they hard to find, seldom
  are they even kind.
Ma Barker eat your heart.
Mommy Dearest take a rest.
For I know one who will put you to shame.
She truly is the best.
If ever I would get real close, I know
  that I would see
Horns, tails, and pitchforks reflecting
  back at me.
If you are married that's a price you
  sometimes pay.
A mother-in-law who will ruin your
  life if she has her way.

Karla Lynn Fisher

THOSE EYES

Eyes . . . Trance . . .
My eyes looking into your eyes . . .
All defenses down
All systems go . . . in your eyes
I could lose myself . . .

Eyes . . .
Reflecting pain, past pain you never want
  to trip on again . . .

Eyes . . . Shining hope . . . into my eyes
I'd give you every damn bit of me
  but is all mine?

Eyes . . . Melting me . . . Showing me feelings
I've never seen, only in dreams . . .

Those eyes . . .
I'm lost in those eyes . . .
I've grown to love those eyes . . .
Looking at me . .
Such emotion stirring the oceans in my eyes . . .
  "Those eyes" . . .

Cynthia A Wright

A SILENT REFRAIN

To Jerri . . .
"What would memories be . . .
if not for her."

Through your eyes,
could a moment be so chaste,
or an instance forlorn . . .
That I should perceive a view within;
and glimpse, a reflection, reborn . . .

And perchance . . .

Would you share this with me . . .
a part of your tenderness;
fashioned by hearts' reprise;
and whisper to me, of my own lament;
within those languished, troubled eyes . . .

Then traverse a darkened path,
to your soul, which is my own;
and caress,
so empty,
a chamber untouched . . .
and sing,
a melody . . . alone.

Glen P. Young

REFLECTIONS

Reflection of our soul seen in our dreams.
Swiftly moving upward on gleaming stream.
Dream of our greatness the mirror of our soul.
Past and present are there as they unfold.
Remember every detail the signs of our time.
Forget not one thing not even the chime.
Hold tight to their sight and take the flight.
Have no fear my love and see the light.

Judith St. Vic

P. S.

You have challenged me.

Without knowing it,
to be all I can be.

Without saying it,
to be all I want to be.

Without ever asking,
to want you as you want me.

Never aware how much
I love you.

Deborah Pratt

UNDYING WORDS

Remember me with happiness
when my time comes to depart
for I will leave within my passing
the emotions of my heart
then my spirit never will be dead
through my writings I'll live on
to touch the lives of others
long after I am gone
my purpose for existence
my poetry shall be
my solace and my comfort
my immortality

Kathy Liggett Smith

PLIGHT OF THE ESCAPIST

The wayward souls find themself
on an unsettling journey
seeking desperately to escape
yet all the while
uncertain of just what it is
they desire to escape from
and not until their journey's end
shall they find peace of mind
for at this time
they shall be brought face to face
with inevitable self-acceptance
whereupon they will discover
it was indeed themself
that they unknowingly sought
to escape from
alas through self-recognition
the need to flee subsides

Kathy Liggett Smith

THE LAST WORD

The last word exists in your ideas and hand.
Let the true be exposed throughout the land.
Deception is rooted within the man.
Manifested and issuance do all that you can.
Understanding the mystery of death after life,
Is a step forward in the right light.
Making decisions within the universal law.
Guarantee protection from ancient flaw.
Believe in yourself do good if you can,
Because your last word may be your last stand.

Judith St. Vic

JUDITH ANN SAINT VIC. Born: Mann, 12-8; Education: The College of S.I., B.A., Psychology, 1986; Occupations: Actress, Artist in fine art, Designer, Perfumer, Braider; Memberships: S.I. Council of Art, Pyramid Art Gallery; Poetry: 'All For Me,' 1985; 'Intoxication,' 1986; both American Poetry Association; Comments: *My expression and ideas are of the Guardian of Faith. The all-seeing, the source of peace, the mighty, the provider, the protector, the watchful, the merciful, the first, the last, the withness and the source of goodness.*

BORN AGAIN

Born Again:
  A soul-searching happening
  A heaven bound trend
Passages from the Bible
  Prove it, my friend
God has beckoned hearts
  Through all generations
God is ever calling
  Throughout all nations

My life has been brighter
  My heart feels much lighter
Sins have been fleeing
  As God's way
I'm accepting, receiving
  I can face the storm and wind
Surrendering all
  To my Maker, Counselor, Redeemer
I have been ''Born Again.''

Margaret Kerr

LISTENING

Listen! Listen! Listen!
  Oh ye people of the earth,
Please listen.

I listened in the garden
  Where gentle breezes blow
I listened day and night
  For His voice to hear and know
I listened with sincerity near and far
  Until His presence broke through
Like a glittering star.

Listen! Listen! Listen!
  Oh ye people of the earth,
Please listen.
Your heart-searching Master
  Beckons all this day
Just as sure
  As stars and raindrops glisten
Jesus will forgive
  And cast sins away.

Margaret Kerr

TO MY BELOVED NIECE AVA

As a lovely blooming flower,
That breathes the morning air,
Your life was cut short,
At the early age of twenty-four.

In everything you tried to do,
You sought to find perfection,
And anything less that that,
Would give you dissatisfaction.

At times you were misunderstood,
Because of your persistence,
To do the things you wanted to do,
Searching for a meaningful existence.

Your life was short but meaningful.
It had a depth and certain beauty.
Your love for order and the beautiful
Had acquired a sense of duty.

Your loving memory will remain
Deeply engraved in our hearts,
With God's peace to sustain us,
And bring comfort to our grieving hearts.

Evangeline Stenos Mavros

SCHOOL OF LIFE

School of Life, ''The Scriptures''
Strong teaching to behold,
Though it goes unrecognized
Its existence was long foretold.
Much was spoken by many prophets
Way back in the days of old,
As often as God would dictate
Wisdom to his spokesman's soul.
The Prophet would then foretell
What the future holds for all,
Whether good or bad, gain or loss,
Those who have read can recall.
Man has always been quite free
To choose his own destiny,
The choice is his, he can obey
Or pay for living the opposite way.
School of life, not esteemed by man
Though it offers the highest degree,
As it bestows a humble heart
It molds a life with integrity.

Virginia L. Wilson

VIRGINIA L. WILSON. Born: Petersburg, Virginia, 2-8-22; Education: Virginia State University; Occupations: Clerk typist, retired after 20 years service at Virginia State University; Awards: Merit Certificates, Honorable Mention, 'Sadly Touched,' 1983; 'The Sycamore Tree,' 1984; 'My Treasured Pearl,' 1985; Golden Poet Award, 1985; Poetry: 'Little Lena,' *The Progress Index,* 1982; 'With Love To My Sons,' *Hearts on Fire,* 1985; 'I Lift My Cup,' *Words of Praise,* 1986; 'The Shepherd Boy,' *Best New Poets of 1986,* 1987; Other Writings: *God's Touch,* booklet, Virginia State University Press, 1983; Comments: *Each poem is a novella, reflecting either a personal experience or some impressive incident. As I experience the fulfillment of the promises of God, it is my prayerful desire that He will use me as one of His sources by which to send inspiration to many people throughout the land.*

FIELD BOUQUET.

Yes, spring has come;
This morning a nameless hill
  Is shrouded in mist.

Basho

THREADING FRAGMENTS

I am at times transported
  by feelings
Dislodged, dislocated . . . in time,
  drawn to other places in time,
    different and distant
Yet I remember
For time does not seem the essence
  of feeling
I remember
  only glimpses, fragments, instants
    with clarity of sight
  and tormenting vagueness of meaning
    but bristling with feeling
Feeling is in fact the essence
  of a time
    even a point in time
If I could but remember
  the feelings to thread
    the points together
      to weave wisdom

Martin Mitchell

IS THAT BOHEMIA?

The truck rolled up, painted with a white star,
From it three young soldiers appeared.
They moved to a mound amid clumps of trees,
From this place, we could see afar.

The stars shone high, a breeze did sigh.
Is that Bohemia?
Asked the youth on my left.
Yes, friend, it sure is, was my reply.

Brennus and Tribe left their Bohemian Home.
In ancient time he marched south,
Through the pass that bears his name.
On they went and occupied Rome.

Blue moonglow showed a nearby hill.
Ahead — a voice called out,
It seemed to carry a Celtic tone.
Dawn slowly came, and all was still.

Sunlight, and ugly watchtowers reached high.
Is that Bohemia?
Asked the soldier to my right.
Er — Yes I think it is, was my reply.

Jim Henry

RHYME WITHOUT REASON

''Why in the world do you write this stuff?
It's a waste of time!'' she said.
''Nobody every buys this crap,
You have to pay them instead.''

She doesn't know how the words simply grow
In my mind and tumble around
'Til they fall into lines (and couplets, at times)
And demand that they be written down.
Though I suffer the curse of spontaneous verse,
For it's not a decision of mine,
I'm pleased that it's rhyme without reason —
Not reason without any rhyme.

William V. Robertson

DIALOGUE WITH MARVIN

Yes, yes I've been sort of down
wearin' a frown
never lookin' home
can't you see what I've done
to the pauper's dreams
there's no ice cream

can't you see what I've done

Did you trade in your eyes
for futureless thrills
drink machine spills
warm breath of a cool breeze
old hookers and gems
did you trade in your life
for a front seat at the war

can't you see what I've done

Randy S. Adams

AMANDA'S CHRISTENING

Friends & Family gathered on Amanda's
  Christening Day
They solemnly knelt before her,
  And bowed their heads to pray.
They prayed that God would bless her,
  With his powerful ways.
And make her a Holy Christian,
  Through all her living days.
To make her spiritually good,
  In both body and in mind.
To love her adoring parents,
  And to always be gentle and kind.
We wish you a wonderful life, dear Amanda,
  Filled with all good things for you.
And later in life when you read this poem,
  You'll know the love we feel for you.

Ann Lo Cascio

MY ONE AND ONLY LOVE

You are the Moon, the Stars, and the sky to me,
  The entire Universe rolled into one,
Without your love I could never be,
  You are my shining Sun.

My World without you would be dark and gray,
  There would be no life at all,
It's by your side I will always stay,
  Winter, Summer, Spring and Fall.

My love for you is immeasurable,
  It will stand the test of time,
I give thanks to the Lord above,
  because He made you mine.

Ann Lo Cascio

SNOW IS LOVE

It's such a dreary day.
Everything is a muted shade of gray.
None of us have the energy to smile
As we walk another mile.
Our destination is not far ahead,
And then we can eat and go to bed.
The sun sets slowly behind the horizon
And creates a chill for which there is no reason.
We keep on going,
Then all of a sudden it starts snowing.
We stop and watch the falling snow,
It is a gift from up above to down below.
Our steps, they quicken,
As if we were bitten
By some mysterious bug.
We are no longer sad, because of the love
That falls down all around us,
And we wonder why we made such a fuss.
We finally reach the end of the road,
And we hurry to reach our home.

Stacey ''Tina Marie'' Dorchester

MY LOVE

Thirty-six and dying,
My husband, sensitive and gifted,
His poetry warm, satisfying,
His novel, half-finished, promising.

Relatives and friends visited often;
Yet could not conceal their sorrow,
Could not bring themselves to stay long,
And at moments he became impatient,
Reminded them of his blessings . . .
Of how much he had enjoyed life's song.

So many are worse off than I am, he'd say.
I think of them, I pray for them!
And as good as it all has been —
Rest assured a better life awaits us!

Where I am going,
There will be no more pain or darkness,
Only the wonderfulness of love,
And then, gazing upward, softly smiling,
He'd say, my Saviour's waiting . . .
In His Heaven above.

Lester E. Garrett

song from
TROILUS AND CRESSIDA

Can life be a blessing,
Or worth the possessing,
Can life be a blessing, if love were away?
Ah, no! though our love all night keep us waking,
And though he torment us with cares all the day,
Yet he sweetens, he sweetens our pains in the taking;
There's an hour at the last, there's an hour to repay.

In every possessing
The ravishing blessing,
In every possessing the fruit of our pain,
Poor lovers forget long ages of anguish,
Whate'er they have suffered and done to obtain;
'Tis a pleasure, a pleasure to sigh and to languish,
When we hope, when we hope to be happy again.

John Dryden

TIME TESTED

Dedicated to the Rebbie

Little more than a ball of fur, when he was first introduced to me
I doubted that I would let him stay but I would give it time and see

He was a little pain in the neck, a puppy named ''Rebel'', you know
From the beginning a little rebel, what would he be like
    with time to grow

It took me some time to decide that I would allow him to stay
I grew to love the little guy more with each passing day

We spent so many hours together playing our running game
From the early light of dawn until the darkness came

But his rebel ways and desire to be free
Made him careless one day while running with me

He ran toward the roadway, I shouted in vain
It was over in an instant without any pain

I buried him under the bramble bush that stands on the crest
    of the hill
It shattered my heart but out in the meadow I see him running
    . . . still

The years have dimmed the memory some, other special pals
    there will be
But I will never live long enough, not to feel his chin on me knee.

William K. Brobst

A CATWALK MADE OF STARS

Dedicated in memory of James J. Reinhardt

It's as though through the glistening tears in the moonlight
I was walking into the answer on a catwalk made of stars
The answer of a pain . . .
    . . . of the grim realization
        that there is so much for us to learn . . .
            . . . to gain
Nerves, twitching on the trigger of pride.
Who will be first
    . . . to apologize . . .
        . . . or too late . . .

Timothy David

A LETTER TO MY DAUGHTER

Dear Daughter,

The most special gift a woman could receive,
Is becoming a mother, a parent like me;
A creation of life sparked by birth,
A moment of passing from heaven to earth.

A precious new daughter to cuddle and hug,
Another little person, so special to love;
A baby so tiny to grow and to share,
That new joyous feeling from a mother who cares.

An infinite love that creates a bond,
Between mother and child, from beginning to end;
A mother, a daughter, united through God,
Entrusted the care of an angel for him.

Living and learning, experiencing together,
The meaning of life, and being a friend;
A daughter to cherish now and forever,
Straight form my heart, All My Love from within.

    Love,
    Mommy

Hazel Mae Parron

HAZEL MAE PARRON. Born: Norfolk, Virginia, 6-15-56; Married: Norman R. Parron, Jr., 11-4-77; Daughter, Jenny Lynn, born 12-10-83; Education: Professional Business and Medical Institute, formerly of Norfolk, Virginia, 1974; Central School of Practical Nursing, Norfolk, Virginia, 1977; Hampton Institute's continuing education classes, 1979; G.E.D., 1975; Currently certified in cardio-pulmonary resuscitation; Occupation: Head nurse at Lafayette Villa Health Care, 1974-80; Nursing instructor for Professional Business and Medical Institute, 1980-81; Licensed practical nurse, Humana Hospital Bayside, Virginia Beach, Virginia, 1980 to present; Awards: Honorable Mention in the Great American Poetry Content, 2-28-87, for 'Life's Best'; Golden Poet Award, 1987; Poetry: 'Dreams and Fairytales,' *Best New Poets of 1986;* 'Stranger in Paradise,' 'Child's Prayer,' *Words of Praise, Vol. 3,* 1987; 'Love Prevails,' 'Joyous Rapture,' *Hearts on Fire: A Treasury of Poems On Love, Vol. 4;* 1987; 'Renaissance of Christmas,' 'Caroling Messengers,' *American Poetry Anthology, Vol 4,* 1987; Comments: *In my three poems that appear in this book, I wanted to stress the importance of family; and in doing so, I have written 'A Letter to My Daughter.' Though I meant it personally for my daughter Jenny, it also applies to any mother's daughter. I know Jenny will appreciate it when she is older. 'Words of the Wise,' was written in reference to my mother, as often I recall the important teachings she taught me when I was a child. 'That's The Way Sisters Are,' applies to my three sisters and our good and bad times over the years.*

NASHEED'S LAW

No matter how old you get, there will be
someone wiser than you. Even though they are less
experienced than you. It was ordained that way.

Dr. Nick & Co.

THE OLD WOOD LOT

Beside the brook — Besides the trees —
I listened to — The babbling stream —
I heard the birds' — Sweet melodies —
I felt the cool gentle breeze — As it sifted
through — The budding trees — I saw the
daisies and the Blue-For-Get-Me-Nots —
Dotted all over — The old wood lot — The
leaves first hues — Of red and green —
In the sun rays — Could now be seen —
The sinking sun — On the earth below —
Gave to everything — A soft velvety glow —
— The close approach — Of rabbits and squirrels
— Let me know — I was in nature's world
— The stars appeared — One by one —
Like happy children — When having fun —
Along the Eastern rim — Rose a full golden
moon — And in the distance — One could
hear — The night birds' merry tunes — I
sat and thought — Amid the rocks — Above
and below the sod — I knew all this —
Could only be — The handiwork of God —

Ruth F. Teeters

THE AWAKENING

Midnight.

I toss and turn; I'm torn and very tired.
My head explodes; my body feels demised.
Repeats from nights when I had lost all hope.
Numbed high on ill spirits was how I coped.

The cans had piled high building me a shrine.
Each bottle hummed a sad song from my life.
I had to face the truth — reality.
I accepted the truth — reality.

Daylight.

I saw the birth of a brilliant new dawn.
The most beautiful sight my eyes had known.
It was like the last breath of life revived.
The last moment, my soul held fast and strived.

To others like me, get on the right track.
Walk forward and never tempt to look back.
If someone offered me champagne or wine.
I'd say, ''Some water will do me just fine.''

Darlene Pitts

DEAR

I'd like to thank you for being my friend
And painting the way opposite the end
You've given your hand to help me along
Squeezing tightly when I don't feel strong
You understand when I know not
Reminding me of my pity-pot
You don't always say what I want to hear
I might not like it but it's said sincere
Thanks for the love and care that you show
I'd just like to say that I love you dearly
With all my heart I say this sincerely

Denise Michele Keppel

THE APRON

The apron hangs on its reserved spot
Behind the kitchen door
It still smells of homemade bread
The memory lingers more
Of our loved one — our mother dear
Gone with heaven's lore

Few weeks ago she wore her apron proud
A gift for Mother's Day
From all of her loving crowd
We all had our say
As she sliced the warm soft bread
In her loving way

She loved her apron she kept telling us
Serving us her bread
Hugging us with her talk and smile
No tears are shed
Remembering the aroma of her love
Fulfills us instead

She served us all like we were kings
There is no mistaking she loved us all
For she kissed each head
Her apron touched each one of us
Her warmth she fed

Valentina M. Panzone

THE EMPTY CHAIR

His favorite chair — without his form
Fills the room with memories
Of all the times he filled the chair
As we decorated many trees

Each Christmas season he prepared the room
With a tree for us to share
In the festivities of the decorating
He sat comfortable in his chair

He would guide each one of us
Where to hang the bulb we placed
He was so delighted as each was hung
We can still see his smiling face

We stood the tree up this Christmas
Next to his empty chair
But the bulbs and decorations lay there
Untouched — his voice we did not hear

Valentina M. Panzone

BIG FEET

Small kittens don't look up
Though innocent and sweet;
When they see me coming
They only see big feet.

Though they are so big
Those feet they do not dread;
When those feet are coming
They know they will be fed.

Harry A. Fry

HAVE YOU EVER?

You have ever
just sat and wondered
Why?
Why is the sky so blue?
Why is the grass so green?
Why do the seasons change?
Why am I alive?
Why do innocent people get hurt?
Why do rich people get richer?
Why do poor people get poorer?
Why do people die?
Why, oh why?
I don't know
but
I do sit, sometimes,
and wonder
Why?

Sally Rhodes

WHERE ARE YOU MAUREEN?

One evening as I walked the beach
'cause I just couldn't sleep,
I saw her sitting on a rock —
a sight my mind still keeps.

She held a sea shell to her ear
and waited for a sound,
I tossed a lily at her feet —
She slowly turned around.

I put my arms around her waist
and gently pulled her near.
She smiled when I held her tight
and whispered in her ear.

A strong wind came; the clouds grew dark
and lightning split the sky.
The thunder roared — it shook the earth,
and formed for her a pyre.

Now, as I walk along the shores,
I ask the good Lord, ''Why?''
With tear-filled eyes I'll mourn for her
until the day I die.

Michael D. McCracken

THE LAST TRAIL

As your sun slowly sets
One last, lonesome trail awaits —
Ride on, cowboy.
Ride on.

With saddlebags full of memories
And love bright shining
As the stars
It's time to say ''adios.''

Ride on, cowboy —
Beyond the sunset.
Ride on.

B. Jean Newton

ON THE DEATH OF BABY, AMY

for Darlene Harney, the mother

My baby, my baby, when you are so small,
Oh, why did you leave us, you'll never grow tall
I cannot believe it, understand it at all
God called you, you left us, but you had no choice
I still hear your footsteps, I still hear your voice

Oh, you are so young, just learning to talk
And play with your brother, and recently walk
I turn to the Bible to get some release
From the pain in my heart to offer me peace

No more can I hug you, I just want to die
My heart is so heavy, no more can I cry!
No more can I hold you, and rock you to sleep
'Til your eyelids get heavy and you fall fast asleep
So snug on my shoulder, where I held you so tight
Then I tucked you in bed, and kissed you goodnight.

I know we'll be with you, in heaven again
Where there is no sickness, no sorrow or pain
God picks the best jewels to be with the King
In heaven you'll blossom where angels do sing.

Agnes M. Westmoreland

TRUE LIBRA

At the start of each day, my mind seems to go
    every which way.
Sometimes so very slow, or to a creative flow.
Should I wash my hair for work, or to go out somewhere?
Do I really care which dress I wear?
Goodness me, I just don't know.

To answer the door or the phone?
Or pretend no one is home.
Have company or set quietly alone?
I wish someone could decide for me.
Not even sure then I would agree.

Will I ever see eye to eye with me?
I hope you're not mixed up this way.
My life is seldom dull is all I can say.
Just making up my mind keeps me busy all day.

Sherry Bischoff

HOMESICK

I'm homesick tonight for the state where I was born;
    for the rollings hills of Iowa and the green of the corn.
The old hometown with its Main Street wide:
    I want to visit again with friends by my side.
Just to visit awhile with old friends I've missed,
    to say hello, and shake hands, and even be kissed.
My mother is there on a farm north of town;
    my room, too, is ready, with the bed all turned down.
A huge family dinner would soon celebrate,
    the return of a wanderer to the old home state.
Oh yes, I'm homesick tonight, for the state where I was born,
    for the rolling hills of Iowa, and the green of the corn.

Earlus "Kay" Gannon

REMEMBERING

Dedicated to those of you who . . .

Remember the smells in your grandma's kitchen
Where bread cakes and "goodies" were prepared
Where there was a warm cozy feeling
An invitation to "set a spell and share"

Where those who came to our mountain home
"Come in," we'd say, "set a spell"
Most never got past the kitchen
Where they would relax and tell

Of other warm intimate kitchens
In their almost forgotten past
But which they still remembered
For those are the memories that last

Of Grandma's famous "goodies"
Which their mothers made and then
Either forgot or were too busy
To ever make them again

Ella Young Wood

ON THE RIVER OF LIFE

Lady of Love with the Child in your arms
hope, tenderness, mercy, faith in my youth,
I bring you my tears, the blood of my heart
dew on red rose to pin on your robe.
From it take the thorns that are piercing my soul.

To you come a mother, O Mother of God
in anguish and pain to plead for one loved.
Blue manthel Maria, Maria full of grace
to your sweet protection I commend my son.

Touch him that he'll know what's right and what's wrong;
preserve his intellect, his spirit free, his body strong . . .

On the River of Life:

Keep him sturdily swimming against the currents
of hate, crime, violence and drugs.
On fair weather, placid waters, hard working, in tune with learning,
at times playfully skipping from pebbles to logs
inspiringly writing his whimsical songs . . .

But more important than all of the above,
light his heart. In darkness remained after LSD,
and loving, my son, could not longer be.

Gloria Stella Avril

HUES OF LIVES

Winter gifts a cool blessing
    always preserving a hidden best
Spring softens life's sleeping assets
    renewing strength from our deepest chest:
Summer warms a provisional test
    resisting wrongs and showing kindness to guests
Fall is that beauty time of year full of color
    combining every hue with wisdom's zest!

Douglas Kendel

MY VISION

For I see a glow of gold,
Sinking in the breezy blue cold.
Oh, what a sight.
A sight to see.
A sunset gold.
Warm and glistening.
Feel the air,
Feel it touch you.
How it seems to hug you.
Touch my soul, touch it deep.
Breathless gasps,
My smile peeks.
Endless vision,
To wonder I see.
This day a glory.
No other will have this, this is my own.
Others share this sight,
They're all different from one another.
Description! Description!
For they come from the heart.

Christine Villanueva

GRIEF

Grief grips me like a choking cough,
And holds on tight — too tight.
Grief makes me question many things,
Was I wrong or was I right?
My body aches from head to toe,
My heart will surely break.
I know that grief must run its course,
But how long will it take?
A month, a year, perhaps two,
A lifetime, maybe so.
Someday I shall have peace again,
If grief will just let go.

Helena B. Schildknecht

I HELD YOUR HAND

I held your hand when first we met
And came to know your touch,
I held your hand, and as time passed
I loved you oh so much.

I held your hand when we were wed
To place a golden band,
And when you bore me children
Again, I held your hand.

I held your hand all through the years,
I know I always will,
Now that you're gone, in memories
I'm holding your hand still.

Gloria Yousha

MOTHER

I wish we had a few more years
When the memories of your love brings tears
As your spirit flies to the heavens above
You gave the world your boundless love

Our God has found a home for mother
A place where everyone loves their brother
Your gift was creating your beautiful Art
Colorful images live in your children's heart

Miles of hard roads along the way
Your smile and humor enhanced our day
You went to church to sing and pray
Your faith was strong and did not sway

I wish you had some more time here
When the time came you had no fear
Old age and suffering proclaim you a Saint
Now the clouds and sky are yours to paint

Wayne J. Klinge

WAYNE JOSEPH KLINGE. Born: Trenton, New Jersey, 1-30-45; Married: Patricia Louise Rieder Klinge, 4-25-83; Education: University of Wisconsin, 1974-75, Acting, Art; Academy of Health Sciences; U.S. Army, Fort Sam Houston, Texas, Diploma Medical Specialist course, 1981; U.S. Army Training Center, Fort Jackson, South Carolina, Diploma Unit Supply Specialist course, 1987; Occupations: Soldier, Actor, Artist, Medical specialist, Supply Sergeant; Awards: Golden Poet Awards, 1984-86, for 'The Rose,' 'Family Tree,' 'Actor'; Poetry: 'The Poet,' 1982; 'The Rose,' 'Family Tree,' 1984; 'Actor,' 1987; 'Deep Within,' *American Poetry Anthology,* 1984; Comments: *I write poetry in order to be in tune with my innermost feelings. I believe poetry has a way of uplifting our spirits when we are down. The poems I write give the reader a message of hope. They show expressions of love, keep the past alive and my imagination awake for future experiences. In my poetry I am able to see my destiny unfold through my words and deeds. Also in my poems I use rhyme and meter as a communicating tool for lovers of poetry.*

PAINTED AUTUMNS

Seasons rise like daily dawns
to lose and gain their splendor,
Friendships bloom and die as springs,
though lovers shall remember,
I secretly admire fall,
once all the year has passed,
A time of painted ecstasy,
that never seems to last,
A season filled by memories,
fall sleeping to the ground,
Where beauty mellows everything,
each time it comes around,
So quietly the calm sets in,
assuring love survived,
What all the year has done to me,
and strengthened me inside,
To those I knew and loved last spring,
who gave so much to me,
Remains the portraits of all we were,
in painted memories.

Corinne L. Smith

WILD WIND OF CAMERON

Wild wind doth blow at Cameron
Wreaking vengeance there
It howls along the canyons
And hillsides have blown bare.

In jail at old Fort Cameron
Our father realized
He had been forsaken
He would give his life.

Blow free, wild wind of Cameron
His doom was plain to see
His friends had all turned from him
They sealed the fate of John D. Lee.

Ye restless wind of Cameron
His diaries hold the proof
A century now is over
Time is on the side of truth.

Wild wind that blows at Cameron
Your howlings now may cease
Tender aching hearts of loved ones
Long last will rest in peace.

Wanda Lee Burrell

I see the wind before me
I hear its precious call
The fine traumatic splendor
Has echoed every hall

And yet I stay here waiting
For silence to succeed
To encompass every feeling
Of my extraordinary need.

Marianne Bartsch

HOPE: THE POETRY OF LIFE

Present:

Hope my Christian parents felt my gratitude for their training!
Hope my family's grateful for a Christian upbringing!
Hope my heirs continue with Christ for future living!
Hope for continued peace!

Future:

Hope temptations do not engulf our leaders!
Hope peaceful treaties are written with all neighbors!
Hope my country continues under God for daily living!
Hope for continued peace!

Immortality:

Hope; Nothing separated me from the love of God!
Hope; Jesus gave His life for my required ransom!
Hope; Faith in Jesus has brought me home to Heaven!
Hope; For continual peace!

Wilma Noe Payne

FAMILY: THE POETRY OF LIFE

Oh how I wish I would have suggested Mother's Day first!
What satisfaction it must have been when Father's Day officially began!
If we had a Children's Day would the parents hearts' influenced be
To have and hold their offspring in devout responsibility?

A Son's Day or a Daughter's Day could never be sufficient
For partiality should never ever be present!
Parents should show their Creator gratitude and love!
For all children are blessings only from above!

Wilma Noe Payne

UNWRITTEN BOOK

Once upon a time.
Fiction or non, a thin line with
you, us.
As the story goes on there is much color and depth.
Building our characters to what will happen next.
I can't decide now, I haven't written our ending yet.
Imagination brings
you, us
through many volumes.
Reality brings a bit of uncertainty.
Let me create and dream.

Cathy L. Daniels

THINKING OF YOU

I just wanted you to know how my thoughts lean toward you,
If once, a thousand times.
A certain place,
Although it's not really the place,
It's the way I felt when I was in this certain place,
With you.
I think of what it would mean to me if you were gone,
It would mean pain.

Cathy L. Daniels

MY SECRET FEELINGS OF DELIGHT AND DESPAIR!

Growing up is often a frightening time in life.
At this time, years ago, questions were not answered
As today — often the private, precious feelings are too open now.
Secret inner feelings of delight get turned to despair!

Being an only child, and leading a very sheltered life —
Loving books, music and drawing pictures at an early age,
I had many dreams of being a great singer in New York
Or becoming a very famous artist — especially of mountain scenes!

When I was ten years old I began to study music,
    later sang in an oratorio group,
Also became a church organist — and was painting
    many pictures of mountains.
I seemed to be living in a fantasy world of my own —
    loving and being loved.
Blessed with the true love of a wonderful, compatible man,
    my dreams coming true!

With marriage plans being made — friends and my mother
    to share this joy!
The loved one unexpectedly becoming very ill, and died very suddenly
One month before the Nuptial Day! The secret feelings of delight
Turned to despair — leaving only his true love
    locked in my sad heart!

Mildred A. Martin

THE JOY OF AN EVERLASTING FRIENDSHIP

While staying at my favorite hotel in Colorado
Having lunch with a very exciting man at Trader Vic's,
A fascinating lady wearing a Chanda hat
Was facing me, and smiled each time I glanced that way.

I was describing my stay and the overwhelming mountains,
As I had rented a car, taking a few friends on a mountain trip.
I had the courage to drive up to and along the Continental Divide
In the breath-taking mountains — then the descent from that height!

The very lovely lady stopped at our table as she was leaving.
She had heard my account of the thrill I felt
    during that mountain trip!
Handing me her card, she asked me to call her as soon as possible.
When I called she invited me to stop
    at their mountain home — Ernaloa!

Such a beautiful spot, where they lived, high in the mountains.
Several days later she came to take me, in a pink Cadillac,
    to their home.
We went to the Opera in Central City,
    to the Broadmoor in Colorado Springs,
Our friendship was growing by leaps and bounds
    as we enjoyed these things.

Such outgoing people, she and her husband — happy to share with me
The Park of the Red Rocks, The Denver Symphony
    performing that night!
A very deep and lasting relationship — friendship, love
    and understanding.
Both are gone now, but I will always feel
    their undying presence forever!

Mildred A. Martin

Shoestrings neat and fancy fair
Remind me then so unaware
When breathing fresh was in the air
My hair was soft and fancy fair

A babe is born and he is sworn
The water falls and you belong

A rapid rush of mixed emotion
Scourging scores of endless notion

Crushing rocks exerting force
Wasteless pits of foul remorse . . .

What is it then we may forget
Our shoestrings tied, a little wet,
But yet, so fancy fair within the air
My hair was soft, I didn't care.

Marianne Bartsch

MUTABILITY

The flower that smiles today
    Tomorrow dies;
All that we wish to stay,
    Tempts and then flies.
What is this world's delight?
Lightning that mocks the night,
  Brief even as bright.

Virtue, how frail it is!
    Friendship how rare!
Love, how it sells poor bliss
    For proud despair!
But we, though soon they fall,
Survive their joy and all
  Which ours we call.

Whilst skies are blue and bright,
    Whilst flowers are gay,
Whilst eyes that change ere night
    Make glad the day,
Whilst yet the calm hours creep,
Dream thou — and from thy sleep
  Then wake to weep.

Percy Bysshe Shelley

SONS BY A STEP

They're only 12 and 9
but they're always mine,
and they can be bad
and it's just a matter of time
before they want
no more nursery rhymes.
But in my eyes
they can do no wrong,
because they are loving stepsons.
Whether angels or not,
they're where my heart must belong . . .

Michael D. Emsley

THE LONELY SOUNDS

I have come to brush
the autumn leaves away
The grass has a soft touch to remind me
you lie in peace . . .

I hope it's beautiful where you are.

Our pet . . . *King* — listens attentively
to gentle winds caressing the grass
protecting me
while I arrange the roses I brought

Like the ones you used to send
to grace my world
they glisten with life
Love seems to be everywhere!

The wind sings
in deep restful prayer
Above the hills
the clouds weep . . . silently.

Victoria C. Ridgeway

FASCINATION IN SHADOW

Oftentimes . . . when it rains
I turn down the lights of evening
I recline . . . in silence
as if in a dream

I hear the faint murmur of voices
the echo of laughter
There is music that touches my senses.
Secret sounds . . . among the visions
of early times . . . when . . .
I was the one . . . you loved the best.
Ah yes!

Now that it's late . . . I can see . . .
the trees bent with the weight of rain
They seem to whisper
maybe . . . somewhere . . .

In another life . . . again.

Victoria C. Ridgeway

CONTENTMENT

Offered often, recognized seldom,
It comes to you and me —
A gift from the Holy Trinity.

Sense —
An inner calm, an absence of reason.

Taste —
The happiness it brings.

See —
The rewards of life.

Enjoy —
Contentment.

B. Jean Newton

GABRIEL'S ROSE

A tribute to Grandma

With respect for laws
Laid down by seasons
The rose withers
Without reason
Petals falling
Gently
From their glory
Taking with them
Life
Itself
Her majestic birth
A single seed
Sown underground
Beneath the earth
A spring day
With love
Had brought her
Now the winter
Sends her home

Jennifer Huerta

A THING OUT OF SEASON

The bitterness, the cold
  What has brought you
Only yesterday, bright warm hopes
  Surrounded us
Seems you've come as
  A thing out of season
A blizzard and it's
  Breathtaking purity
How can anything so cold
  Appear so peaceful
Icicles hang from
  Everything in sight
I, lost in a lonely blizzard
  Await the thaw
Puddles of misery,
  The only sign of a change
Only after the eternal wait
  Comes the budding hope
It too may have come as
  A thing out of season

Jennifer Huerta

WHEN DEPRESSION REIGNS

The misty clouds of darkness
shadow passages from pain
whispering your weakness
through the feeling of the rain.

A sad and lonely dancer
'tis the heart with broken vein,
ever searching for an answer
and the will to remain.

When depression reigns.

Brian Floyd Newton

GRANDPA, HERE COMES CHRISTY

'Mid the hush and the stillness of her hospital room,
  Their hearts with grief near bursting,
Her parents stand by her wee bedside;
  They've just said good-bye to Christy.

In a heavenly meadow eternally green,
  Beneath a shade-tree resting,
An old man sits near a happy brood
  Waiting for news of Christy.

On her knees by her bed in her far-away home,
  Another whose heart Heaven's touching
Whispers the message he's waiting to hear,
  ''Grandpa, here comes Christy!''

On a pure white blanket as soft as a cloud
  Five little cherubs are playing;
They pause in their tumbling and rolling about
  As Jesus appears leading Christy.

The old man stirs as the two draw near,
  And his eyes with joy grow misty;
He holds out his arms and she snuggles inside;
  ''Grandpa, here comes Christy!''

  Anona Canright Birtch

DAD'S FRONT YARD

Sometimes memory takes me back,
To Dad's front yard, full of lilac;

There too, grew the trees, the pineys, and the asparagus,
And there on warm summer days we played on a green carpet of grass;

It was there I learned to catch a ball, play crouquet,
and throw a horse shoe,
My, what fun in Dad's front yard, for every day, there were
exciting things to do;

We didn't need to run about, have fights, and scream and shout, nor
look for some strange sign;

For in Dad's front yard you could always find,
Something exciting, something funny, and something kind;

Oh, I'm grown up and older now,
Often life's road seems long and hard;

But if in my memory I can somehow,
Walk once more in Dad's front yard,

And in the shade of the trees' stand,
I'll find the peace I knew as a lad.

  Joe Martin

THE SIGN

Footprints in the saturated ground,
The rain is over and the sun is bound.
Giggling voices travel through the misty air,
As little splashing feet run like a hare.
Expressions of excitement while they run to the door,
The sign says *open* on the candy store.

  Steed Edwards

DRINKS ON ME

The other night I saw my favorite band play.
They were so good and they made me smile —
Lost in their creativity I became creative and thought . . .
What if there was no audience, but the chairs jumped around —
and started to cheer? What would the band say?

On the way home I kept singing their songs.
The songs are so good they made me smile —
Lost in the cheerful tunes I became silly and thought . . .
What if nobody had hair and the *in* thing of the summer was —
to get a suntan on your bald head? Ouch!

But then I listened to their songs.
They had meaning and rhythm and lots of purpose —
I became full of spirit and felt so good and thought . . .
Why can't everyone smile and find ways to help one another —
rather than hurt? *He* would be happy!

I think I'll go to Soul City with my electric honey.
G. P. and Chris Partland, the drinks are on me.
Thank God for guys like you.

  Jim Harris

HOW DO I LOVE YOU?

How do I love you?
Let me tell you how I love you.
I love you deeply in my very soul
and with my whole heart;
to the profoundest depth of my self
and with my entire being.
I love you as everyday's
most intense work under
the sun's light or the moon's rays.
I love you willingly, as humans fight for freedom;
I love you truly, as they search for truth.
I love you with the same intensity I needed
for my today's forgotten sadness, or my childhood's hopes.
I love you with a love I thought I had lost
with my gone desires — I love you with
the passion I have given to each one of my days,
and, if it is possible
I shall but love you always, just as I do today.

  Helen Williams

TIME ALONE

From moment to moment.
  Second to second.
    Minute to minute.
      Hour to hour.
As time passes along, it flows to another eternal existence.
  For man must accept all that is given.
    Or should he be that accepting?

Our acceptance of good becomes non-cerebral and natural.
  Only as the tide turns to the disfavor of man — does he then
    Become introspective.

Perhaps he will then receive a second breath.

  Bernard L. Ginsberg

CAPTURED WONDERS

Oh if time could stand still,
  And if so,
    For a moment,
      On the weathered
        Face of time.
How lonely
  The prisoned thoughts
    Of what wasn't,
      If only,
        And whys.
Silent yearnings
  Wearing cloaks of sadness,
    Echoing whispers
      On the breath
        Of mankind.
Fleeing hopes are soon captured
  By dreams,
    Wearing chains.
In the mind
  Hides the truth,
    Holding keys,
      Dangling freedom,
        In the face
          Of what is.

Jennifer Huerta

GRANDPA

It's cancer, they tell me —
It's eating him away.
They don't know how long it'll be
Before he goes God's way.

It scares me so much
To know I'm losing someone I love;
But his suffering will be gone
And he'll go above.

I love my grandpa dearly,
I hope he realizes this —
And before he goes to eternal sleep
I'll give him one more kiss . . .

Carol Vidrine

CHRISTMASTIME

The sun shines bright
Above the snow-capped mountains
Frost is everywhere
You can see the cold crispness in the air
Sleighbells ringing, all around the valley
Children singing merry Christmas carols

It's Christmastime once more
Time for Santa, Rudolf, and more
Laughter, gaiety, hearts filled with joy
Happiness all around the world

I love this merry season
If only this feeling of warmth
Could continue all year long.

June Drao

AND I WAS ONLY ME

As we went our separate ways tonight,
I noticed more than ever in my life . . .
As we hugged and said goodnight,
All of you were we —
And I was only me.

Grace Ramelle Dwoskin

HOLD MY HEART

I cannot hold my heart
Amid the clouds;
So I must live with
All that is today.

It is — well, strange I'd say
That when I'm here today,
I somehow find myself
— among the clouds.

Grace Ramelle Dwoskin

VACANCY

The wrenching continues inside my gut
  thunder pounds, my eyes
  cannot focus on life around me.

Bones disappear from fingers

hang loose
like slender pieces of silk
that fall from your braids.

Knees weaken, I fall
the weight of my body
creates a hollow

  where warm clay forms
  where the earth opens to me.

I am forced to smell
the sweetness of paths

  we once walked.

Sun's warmth blankets
my cold body.

Safe, I rest my eyes

  and leave a space behind.

Linda Born-Gibbs

THIS IS MINE

Miracles are without and still you have got
Miracle is how could it be
Miracle is I have no diploma or degree
Miracle is writing much
With nothing to write about
Miracle I don't know how to rhyme
I hear the sound and write it down
Miracles are not impossible with God
I said this from my heart
1974 I heard and I still hear
I'll write as long as he gives me
a sound or give me a song
Miracle I didn't finish high school
I didn't go to college
I didn't have no background
All that stuff is tuff
A Miracle in me I find
this is some of mine
In a vase of flowers love wraps in many colors
read the poems and figure me out

Rosa Lee King

GONE AWAY

So near yet so far,
  so close and yet,
    I cannot touch.
So happy yet so sad,
  so glad and yet,
    there are tears.
I felt your tender kiss,
  whisper-soft and warm.
I saw your sunny smile,
looked into your fiery eyes,
  and then it was gone —
Your eyes, and smile,
  your gentle kiss,
— gone . . .

Donna Wise

ONE IN A MILLION

Like a needle in a haystack,
  so did I find you.
Full of hidden desire,
  searching for an unknown.

One in a million,
  a lucky find
If once lost I'll never find another.

For it is said that there is
  but one true love —
And I have found
  the one true love that is
meant for me
  and mine to love.

Donna Wise

INNER VISIONS

In growing, we must not place ourselves in judgment of others, and those
we love, by dwelling only on the shortcomings each of us may have;
because things aren't accomplished our way.

Search deep, very deep, and find the good that is there. Touch it,
and remember, then store it with love, for you need it to live.

Do you live for power, or for life?
Do we strive to control, or to unite?
Are our goals to dominate, or to create?

So many are misled, because they want so much to believe in something
or someone.

Will not one submerge and withdraw, from the lack of being loved; Is it
reasonable to assume, that in order for motivation, there has to be a
need? Should we fantasize on what we might touch upon,
or treasure what we have?

Should we second-guess tomorrow, or give thanks and answer for today?
If life is an illusion of make-believe, then can there be any
one set pattern?

Don't we have to have hopes and dreams of our tomorrows, which
generate and carry us through our today? . . . *Huh?*

Wanda J. Pugh

WANDA JEAN PUGH. Born: Kansas City, Missouri, 12-24-35; Married:
Chester E. Pugh, 4-30-78; Education: Laney College, Chabot College; Oc-
cupation: Inventory Control Analyst; Awards: First Place, 1972, 1976, 1978;
Second Place, 1973; Poetry: 'My Mom,' 3-18-72; 'The Last Days,' 3-11-78;
'Each Other,' 1982; 'The Love Game,' 4-30-73; 'Inner Visions,' 7-30-76, all
American Poetry Anthology; Comments: *To love and honor God first, give
thanks and strive to develop this gift for writing. Give and share with others
along the way. To appreciate this precious life we've been given, and always
strive to do good from day to day.*

DON'T FORGET ME

Don't forget me when I'm dead and gone;
Make my memory linger on.

Remember all the good times we shared;
For you I really cared.

You said you would love me forever;
I hope we'll share our afterlife together.

Please remember something of me in everything you do;
I know if the situation were changed, I would of you.

Don't forget me when I'm dead and gone;
Make my memory linger on.

Kathleen Moore

WILL I EVER GET OVER YOU?

I finally got over you or so I thought.
Then memories of you came and teardrops they brought.
I was so happy, then all at once I was sad.
It made me upset and I felt really bad.
It all started because I thought you cared.
But the feelings *I* had, *we* never shared.
I tried to get over you, you have to believe me.
But the feelings I have can't be forgotten easily.
I know we made a deal and I'm really trying.
But sometimes those memories just leave me crying.
Will my feelings end? Will I ever get over you?
I'm not sure, but for our friendship's sake,
I sure hope I do.

Julie R. Hale

A DREAM FULFILLED

Oh, Martin, how we wept
How we longed to see your Dream fulfilled
But they took you away too soon.

And now, fifteen year later,
I sit, in awe, at your Resting Place
And looking at the Peaceful Island where you sleep,
I hear again the magnificent voice
Proclaiming that Dream.

And finally, I know that the Dream lives on
And finally, there is Peace in my Soul
And finally, I understand that you *gave us* the Dream
And we will keep it
Until it *is* fulfilled.

Again I weep, Martin
Tears of Joy this time because I share the Dream
And because you *were* here for awhile.

Katherine Scott Fitzgerald

CHANGES OF TIME

When I was a little girl,
I once said
''I can't wait till I'm eighteen
So I can dye my hair red
And wear some of those *long-heeled* shoes.''

When I was eighteen,
I didn't think I'd like myself
Too much with red hair,
And I could hardly walk in medium-heeled shoes!

And now that I'm older,
I thank Heaven I didn't dye my hair!
It has flecks of grey here and there,
But I rather like it.
And as for the shoes,
The heels on my daughters' shoes
Are *longer* than anything I will *ever* wear!

Isn't it funny how the greatest ideas
Can change with the passage of time.

Katherine Scott Fitzgerald

GHOSTS

When will the ghosts of the past
cease to haunt me?
Will they rise forever
filling me with the eeriness of doom?
Why must they continually feed
on my selflessness?
How do I stop their parasitic feast
with my insecurities as their prey?
How do I starve them
and put my guilt to rest?

Juanita E. Dorner

A MOTHER'S PRAYER

Blessed Lord, hear my prayer.
Be with my children
In all of their tomorrows,
The way you walked them
Through their yesteryears.

Their childhoods have slipped
Into mingled memories —
Sunshine, laughter, rain, and tears.
Into these memories
Daddy has slipped too.
Be with them Lord.

Let them know
Daddy won the race —
He vanquished suffering,
Gained eternal peace —
Heaven is his home.

B. Jean Newton

BELLA JEANNETTE (JEAN) NEWTON.
Born: Somerville, New Jersey; Married: Edward
L. Newton, 5-5-46; Widowed 5-4-72; Education:
Fayetteville Technical Institute, Fayetteville,
North Carolina, A.A.S, general education, 1978;
Sul Ross State University, Alpine, Texas, B.A.,
1980; Memberships: Council for Exceptional
Children; Association of Texas Professional
Educators; Awards: Golden Poet Award, 1987;
Silver Poet Award, for 'Silence,' 1986; Inclusion
in *Who's Who in American Education,* 1987-
1988; Poetry: 'Shades of Perplexity,' *American
Poetry Anthology,* 1986; 'Silence,' *Impressions,*
1986; 'Today,' 1986; 'Whispering Chimes,'
1977; Comments: *I am not really sure I have a
common theme in my poetry. I write when a feel-
ing or idea stirs within me. Most of my poetry
stems from happenings in my life that have led to
meditation, on my part, of both happy and sad
events.*

SELF-MYSTIQUE

Inside my heart is calmness
Great solitude that lures
My heart is of great fairness.

My spirit is glowing very strongly
That intactly compliment my heart
But my body is coping up wrongly.

I feel happy at inner side of me
Revealing it out seem deem
'cause my body is to act for me.

I keep fighting against the odd
Challenging the meanful temperament
Like being put in a pool of mud.

Sometimes I forget what is being human
As I strive hard against my destiny
Try to make myself a kind of human.

I wouldn't cope up being less of myself
Born to feel and think to make whole me
I have to make something out of myself.

Ferdson O. James

REBORN

The dawn
breaks the shadow of night.

The black sky
gives way to a beautiful orange haze
and is transformed to a deep, rich blue.

The birds
come alive with song.

The leaves
glisten with morning dew.

The fresh, crisp air
fills your lungs
as you remember yesterday
and silently pray for strength and humility.

As your senses reel
from this awesome beauty
something deep within seems to say,
''This is the beginning of forever.
Remember —
who you are.''

Charles E. Stickle

PASSION

Hot, like August sun —
Desire aching deep
With unleashed emotion,
Wanting to say
What's felt inside . . .
But, so afraid
That one-way signs —
Might be
At the next corner.

Linda Baron

A DEBT UNPAID

The pain seems unbearable.
The loss seems too great.
My fellowship with him has ended abruptly.

I sense the light rain
pelting the trees
are the tears of God
trickling
to the depths of my heart.

For He grieves with me
for this loss of a loved one,
bidding me to recall
a few words
of this kind and caring man.

I know he would sit eternally
at the right hand of God when he said,
''Please help me, Lord,
Don't let me think no evil thoughts.''

One day,
I pray,
I can thank him for sharing his wisdom.

Charles E. Stickle

A HAUNTING LOVE

Lines written from afar
Indicate the love is still lingering in my heart.
Following the paths you traveled,
Visions of pleasure unraveled.
Casting eyes upon the seas,
Reminds me of times you bend to please.

Simple expression of gratitude
Elicits watery sparks of affection too.
Big brown exciting eyes mirrored the happiness
Flooding deep inside.
From me, came a big contagious smile
Infested with pride.

Moments together cause time to sit in a void.
A haunting love is like an itch around the heart
That can't be reached or scratched.

Sam Brown

I NEED TO STUDY

I need to study 'cuz tests are near
My up-pop toaster body dear
Won't stay put
To read each page
My mind, it wants to disengage.
I know a magnet's
In my tum
It pulls me to the fridge, yum, yum.
And I just have to brush my hair
And hem up my new underwear.
My toenails look a bit too long,
I have to hear just one more song.
Oops, how could it now be so late?
I'll study on another date

    And then,

        I'll not procrastinate!

Linda Baron

THE STORM

Winging through the mists of time
Lighting the Earth with its magic power
Thundering its way into the heart & mind
The Storm — slashing rain upon parched land
Elements of fiery fury and fear that sear
The forest and scatter wild creatures
Suddenly, nature links our present, past, future
Reminds us of the cold, dark caves
Where our ancestors once huddled
In terror and awe
And momentarily, civilization forgotten,
Wet, chilled, and forlorn, we share
Thoughts they have known.
During the enlightening,
Frightening experience
Of the storm

Jessie Faulkner Cuedek

THE SONG OF THE WIND

As the wind moves along
Whistling its song
Hear it rustling in the shrubbery and the trees
Disturbing the leaves
With its deft motile touch
Providing incentive to the squirrels, the birds and bees
It rushes over the rooftops and down the chimney
With a grim muffled roar
And whisks into the house to greet us
As we open up the door
The wind sports around the hills and mountainside
Through the dense forest and open meadow
And drifts merrily over the lane
Or through the wide and scenic farmlands
Turning the blades of the windmill and the weather vane
O! The wind, the vital wind that blows
Passing through one's hair, ruffling their clothes
Touching one's hand and face
Imparting a soothing feeling of vigor
And of dignity and grace.

Harold E. J. Friedrichs

ELECTRIC EYE

They see us as sentries that ride the wire,
  using electric eyes that never tire.
I shoulder my rifle and lock the gate, avoiding the stares
  of unrest and hate.

In here I'm like no other, the protesters outside wouldn't
  call me *brother*.
The girl with the baby threw the first stone, I watched with
  wonder and felt chill to the bone.

In confusion I wait for them to move on.
I ride the wire and I'm alone, an ocean away from home.
I find no answers but more questions yet.

Their faces say, "Let us live and we'll move on."

I ride the wire with electric eyes, wondering, wondering
  if I'll die.
The bombing, the burnings, the voices outside the gate,
  fuel the fire of unrest and hate.
Will I die, will I die, I hear the voices telling me to go
  home, I stand the watch, I'm all alone.

Still I wait riding the wire and guarding the gate.

Michael Georgia

HOBO'S HEAVEN

If there is a place up in heaven
for the weary hobo, will the hobo
have to sleep out at night upon the ground
out in the rain and cold.

Will there be soup lines up in heaven
missions with hand-me-down clothes
will they let the hobo stay for more than one day
kick the hobo back out in the rain and cold.

Will there be empty boxcars up in heaven
where the hobo won't have to hide
or get kicked off the freight trains
in the snow and rain and left all alone
on the cold ground to die.

Will all my buddies that are hobos
be in heaven when I get there
I want to go to heaven's freight yards
and be with my buddies who are hobos
when I get to heaven so fair.

Jay Donald Foote

A TRILOGY

Where Are My Children?

Where have my children gone?
Much too busy with their own concerns to
  bother with an outgrown parent
They don't need a mother anymore;

I gave them life —
And what they do with it is none of my business —
But I'm still interested —
Where are they?

Happy Solo

Aloneness isn't that bad;
People assume it's sad,
It's not — it's restful
People can be tiresome
Silence is a lovely sound!

Status Quo

Our romance is as exciting
  as watching paint dry —
Nor will I cry!
Or is this romance?
I have more fun with a gaggle of
  giggley girls!

Jean Hillman-Foote

TO THE LADY

You stand there facing many people,
People from far and near.
Coming to see you,
Coming to pay homage to you.

We are proud of you.
We admire your strength and duration.
Lasting throughout the years,
Standing proud to welcome strangers.

You have faced many hardships,
Weathered many a storm.
Yet there you stand:
Tall, strong, solid, and firm.

To you we pay tribute!
To you we say Thank you!
Thank you for welcoming us here,
Thank you for being our model!

A model of truth, justice,
A model of liberty.
To you we show honor forever.
Thank you Ms. Liberty.

Edward H. Kwantes

DO YOU SEE THE PICTURE?

There was a dead man from Hoboken,
Who had died from all of his smokin,
    Leaving a wife in tears,
    And a widow for years,
Recalling his coffin and chokin.

Harry A. Fry

IT WON'T HAPPEN TO ME

Many are the examples
From which we all may learn;
Yet there are some people
The truth will surely spurn.

Constant use of alcohol
Those with cigarette breath;
Most any of the drugs
Can lead to early death.

Rogers and Len Bias
Athletes of some fame;
Somehow caught up in drugs
Death prematurely came.

The foolish have an answer
It sounds ever so sweet;
"Drugs won't bother me
I'm not an athlete."

If we play with fire
Our bodies we just may burn;
Death has no favorites
When will we ever learn?

Harry A. Fry

THE RUEFUL FIRE IN AN OLD STONE FIREPLACE

In thy glorious eyes it appears
to everlasting memories,
The burning of the maple tree wood
in an old stone fireplace
Seeing the flames red hot, still burning
as an obstacle on one's face
Just release me with fear and
without a natural trace
feeling the sensitivity of war and hunger
burst through thy veins
Keep me wondering will it defeat mine sane
In hoping the old stone wall fireplace
would come to cribbles and fall
So that of a new it would
    come to call.

Brenda Anthony

THE STRANGER AND I

I looked through
the misty morning fog
and saw an image of a face
I thought I knew,
then the sun rose
upon the land and dispersed
the haze to unveil
a stranger out of the blue.

Now in the aftermath
of what has passed
it's a matter of what
is to be said and heard,
the choice has been made
for the stranger and I,
that's why between each other
we say or hear not a word.

Jeffrey Adam Sager

PERSIAN WITCH

Persian Witch
like the coal her hair
its dust
her eyes
her heart
its hardness bare,
and burning fire
of hate and sin
within a soul of bleak despair
of hell's games and fantasies.
One must resist her kiss
to stay alive
because the lust for pain
is her only desire.

Gajef McNeil

TRAVELLERS

When the breezes say I'm going somewhere,
I prepare myself for a journey there.
Wondering where destiny will guide me,
the unknown incites curiosity.
I just got to move on to a new frontier,
the future at my front, the past at my rear.
A new way of life brings a new form of death
but in spite of it all I must do my best.
From the singers, I shall borrow a song
from the travellers a route to move along.

Gajef McNeil

GAJEF McNEIL. Born: Red Springs, North Carolina, 7-10-51; Education: Southern Illinois University, M.S., 1981; Ripon College, Ripon, Wisconsin, B.A., 1973; Occupations: Youth director, Attucks Youth and Community Services, Carbondale, Illinois; Memberships: Midwest Black Belt Federation, United States Aikido Federation; Poetry: 'A Love Poem,' 'Pearls of Life,' *Hearts on Fire,* 1987; Comments: *Through poetry I attempt to reveal the sweet simplicities and to sharpen the natural inclinations we all share towards the sensitivities of life be they the pains or the pleasures.*

AWARENESS

Spring promises,
breathes a winsome sigh;
contends expectantly.
Adept of time,
she admonishes gently
of the passing season;
she greets of new,
soft,
e'er of time approach.
Patient of her coming,
she knows of heart
along the journey,
success
is yet a bit of waiting;
'tis only then,
the tempo
as well assigned,
becomes the essence
of the newness,
rejoicing forth.
She arrives,
becomes,
is.

Marjorie Shirley Carder

THE WAR

The war was lost by the Pentagon; but *we* went *into the field.*
They played God almighty, with the politicians:
And left the troops in the worst indefensible positions
in world history!
The Pentagon ''waste basket'' *still* pumps ''paper''
currency to ''fire'' the furnaces of a ''hell of their *own* making''!
The ''bias'' is theirs, but, the crime is ''aided, *and* abetted,'' by
''local yokels,'' who keep *their* kids — ''navy goat'' —
at home, and working, safe and sound.
It has been the same in every war since it was
made ''legally'' feasible, and ''proper'' to ''buy'' your
way out of the ''legal''(?) draft! In the ''We hold
these *truths(?)* to be *self evident.*'' ''We are met
on a Great Battlefield?'' (Child's Play!) —
War, which, according to the 1976 World Almanac,
was the war with the ''highest number of deserters'' in
American history. The ''total terror'' wreaked upon
all returning veterans in continental U.S. *is* the
''worst.''

Richard C. Miller

HOMESICK SEASON

Fall's ambush left a haunting scent
   a subtle understatement of the magic waiting
     brought a treasured image
of the big, cream-coloured house
     brought a paradise illusion
         of irresistable Palominos
and the sapphire pond still holds my reflection
    summer shade leaves the senses in a copper gleam
      the rich array of fall softly intoxicates
        and a gentle mysterious allure penetrates
          there comes night-blooming jasmine
         with an overpowering luscious fragrance
the same as cut glass bottles of bubble bath crystals
       the breeze becomes less delicate
      while past fall images become more provocative
         feeling the silky temperature changes
taking invigorating walks under mauve skies
        colorless trees become cinnamon and gold.

Amy Julianne Smith

LET MY PEOPLE GO

Totally bewildered at the many things
That are going on in
America and South Africa, I say,
Let my people go!

The high and the mighty with their covetousness
And self-aggrandizement are liken unto an incurable wound
In the bowels of God's people.
Their corrupting influences oppress.
I say, *Let my people go!*

Social injustice and moral corruption
Are on every hand.
The rich have amassed great fortunes
By grinding the faces of the poor.
There is nothing but denunciations of justice
And dire threats and wrath.

I cry out for mercy:
Lord, let my people go!
Free them from these giants of selfishness and greed!

Ann Dubose Little

ROCK 'N' ROLL HALL OF FAME

Dedicated to Elvis, Jerry and Sam

Music! Is the name of the game.
Honor! Is the Hall of Fame.

Rock 'n' Roll is the type of music honored here.
The first 10 to receive this were this year
January 23, 1986, was the month, day and year.
Waldolf Astoria, New York, was the chosen site —
  What a beautiful place —
  What a beautiful night —
The music called Rock 'n' Roll has been around for a while.
They have never topped it for a better style.

Rock 'n' Roll takes its place in history,
Yea, that makes us smile.
Because Rock n' Roll has been around a while.

  Elvis Presley,
  Jerry Lee Lewis,
  Sam Phillips, too,
Were there in the beginning — when it was brand new.

They have rocked & rolled all the way to the Hall of Fame
Because they *love music* and
Music brought them fame.

Betty Brooks

BETTY JEAN BROOKS. Born: Memphis, Tennessee, 3-22-32; Education: High school, Olive Branch, Mississippi, 1950; Miller Hawkins College of Business, IBM Keypunch, 1969; Occupations: Sales, Cashier, Market Basket, Inc., Blair, Inc.; Memberships: Sponsor of G.O.P. Victory Fund and Ronald Reagan Presidential Foundation; Awards: 1987 Presidential Achievement Award for 'The American Bald Eagle,' 1987, dedicated to President Reagan; Golden Poet Award, 1987; Four Award of Merit Certificates; Poetry: 'The American Bald Eagle,' 'The Lady with a Lamp, 100th Anniversary,' 1987; 'Life's Journey,' 1987; 'Good Intentions,' 1962; 'Bundle of Love,' 1986; Comments: *The 'alpha and omega' of Elvis Presley's life: I am still his friend and follower after all these years. I have been asked many times to join one of his fan clubs, but I have chosen to stay an independent fan and friend.*

IMAGES

However we may try to live or die,
Life will never be complete without a song or cry.
The notes will follow the silver tears that fall,
And now we'll understand that we should walk — not crawl.

Life will always be green to the valleys of the scene;
And images will always be blue to the waters of the true.
Unless the sun will overlook them, they will remain the same;
And it will no longer be to them — as to us — a game.

Laura Geft

GOD'S BEAUTY

As I wake up to the morning light
And all the beauty that I see,
God, you are what makes life worth living to me.

The beauty of the autumn, the bright
colors of the trees, the melody and
buzz of the little birds and bees,
God, you are what makes life worth living to me!

And man, though we keep failing
And failing thee, yet you forgive
Through time, until eternity. God,
You are what makes life worth living to me.

Seeing the sunset in the west
And knowing, I am at peace with thee,
God, you are what makes life worthing living to me!

Peggy Duncan

PASSAGES

Knowing the first patches of frost in nature's quilt
Covers the sensuous growth of summer
Stand in the country road
And listen to the season's clock . . .
The harvest flies swarming
To a chilling climax
Run down to a hiss and a dull drone.
With eyes closed, breathe in and let
The spiced fragrance of old-fashioned pinks
Remind you of the seasoning in summer . . .
In Mother's garden, nectar from honeysuckle
Where shadows play, the taste of mint.
Walk in the open fields and let the heat
Of the day settle on you
Before the anaesthesia of autumn
Numbs the chain of life.
In the midst of a firefly galaxy
Linger as the first stars appear
After the soft flight of the gray moths
Hover in the dusk.

Lee Meyer Devine

LEE MEYER DEVINE. Born: Los Angeles, California, 1938; Education: B.A., Education, Elementary credential; Occupations: Artist, Poet; Former teacher, Children's librarian; Memberships: Charter member, National Museum of Women's Art, Washington, D.C.; Lahaina Arts Society, Maui, Hawaii; Group art shows, Rose Court, San Francisco, University of Pacific; Awards: Golden Poet Award, 1985-87; Grant Award, *Best New Poets of 1986,* American Poetry Association; Nine Honorable mention awards, 1985-87; Poetry: 'A Rose,' *America Sings,* 1950; Inclusion in 7 anthologies; Comments: *I am both an artist and a poet. I wrote and painted as a young person and have recently resumed my career at a rapid rate after raising four delightful children. I choose words that paint a poem with images. A fresh paper in the typewriter is the canvas awaiting creation.*

NOW THAT MY SEPARATION IS ENDING

Now that my separation is ending
Must I suddenly stop depending
On friends who may be tired of lending
Advice and efforts to console
Emotions occasionally beyond self-control

Now that my separation is ending
Must I attempt to convince others
Including my own sister and brothers
That decisions such as who should get the dryer
Just made tempers flare that much higher

Now that my separation is ending
Must I soon begin tending
To therapeutic methods of mending
Feelings of bitterness and pain
That simply cannot be allowed to remain.

Darlene Dixon

JOHN JENNON

John Lennon was more than a rock singer to me.
I'm glad that I was born in his time.
How happy am I that he touched my life and soul.
John's music, his words of peace and love, made me
The person I am today. I saw through his eyes truth and the beauty
of youth. To me he seemed like a father, I grew to love and
respect him for what and who he was . . . himself.
In his footsteps I walk today. John shall always feel like my
friend. I felt I could turn to him for whenever I was sad or
lonely and needed a special friend to talk to, I always
knew John would listen, I would write him, and soon as
the letter was in the box I could feel a glow come over me.
Somehow I knew John would read my letter.
Through John's music I learned about the beauty, the art, the music
and creativity. After he had gone I wept night and day.
My pillow was wet with tears. My face was full of fear,
suddenly I felt alone. To me the world no longer turned,
the sun no longer shined. The birds no longer sang.
If it was all there I wasn't aware of its presence.
The vigil was sad, but the saddest thing was losing you.

Jean Roberts

DISSOLUTION

Three women pale to alabaster
Jangled my bells and banged my doors
Uprooted from love
Slimmer than beeches in winter
They trembled and bowed
And spread their sorrow like ashes in Lent
Once told they told their stories twice
And told and told again
Of men who'd been their life
And were no longer theirs
Of having once been wives
They were like naiads melting through their eyes
They were like wraiths dissolving in the sun
They jangled my bells and banged my doors
Paled and melted and faded and thinned
Till I heard from them no more

Myrna Treston

WHAT WAS I BEFORE

Years ago, in another life
Did I dance and sing, was I happy and bright?
Was I heaped with problems and strife
Or did I travel and sail, do what was right?

Butcher, baker, smithy or trader
Did I ride a horse, did I walk the decks?
Was I a traveler, a salesman or raider?
Blaze new trails, have a dog named Rex?

Black or white, yellow or red?
Free as the sir or just a poor slave?
Did the ground or feathers make up my bed?
Was I afraid or gallant and brave?

Did I fight for my country or hide in disgrace?
Was I famous and rich or saddened and poor?
Did I have people whom I could embrace?
Was I alone and did I want more?

The answer I may never never know
I wonder and think, I hope and I pray
That I wasn't bad and evil and low
And hope that I am much better today.

Charles Rockyvich, Jr.

LOVE IN VAIN

I sit and dream of you each day
The sky is blue and bright
You're there in all my thoughts
Oh! You are quite a sight

Your lovely hair and pretty face
Haunt me day and night
To hold and have you for myself
I wish with all my might

If I just had the courage to say
The things I think and feel
Like the eagle soaring up on high
I'd fly the clouds, my heart would heal

What hope is in your heart
When the candles are burning low?
What song would stir your senses
When soft winds begin to blow?

My love for you is great
But silently I go
And watch you from afar
Because you have another beau

Charles Rockyvich, Jr.

TREASURES

Treasures of life if you want it.
Treasures of love if you wish it.
Treasures of youth if you desire to keep it.
Treasures of happiness if you feel it.
Treasures of beauty if you see it.
No gold, silver nor precious jewels can buy.
The only key is within your soul.
These are your treasures.

Curtis E. Blake

TO BE A KID AGAIN

To be a kid again
And roam the woods and tramp the hills
To lie and watch the clouds rolling by
Making up forms and shapes and things

To sit by the brook without a care
And watch the tadpoles swimming about
And look!
Is that a spider building a web?

There on a fence, a bird so small
It's red and brown and oh so free
A nest in the bushes, let's take a peek
See, four little eggs are nestled in there

Cows in the pasture with heads to the ground
Munching on grass without a sound
Down by the barn, the chickens are busy
Pecking and scratching and talking aloud

Under the oak tree we sit and rest
Then up again to run up the hill
What mysteries we see, what wonders there are
Being a kid is the wonder of all

Charles Rockyvich, Jr.

BEGINNINGS

Hopeful anticipation for fulfillment
of whimsical dreams;
Blissful joy which surrounds the
flirtations of a new start
And a fresh yearning to
conquer past defeats.
Fertile seeds of sprouting
accomplishments;
Tantilizing enlightenment
enveloping new strategies
And the gathering of stock
for the "better" tomorrow.

New Perspectives
New Plans
New Plateaus
A cycle that procreates existence.

Patricia Robinson Williams

MY GODCHILD

When I look at your picture
I start to tear.
Wishing so much that
You were here.
You're always such a good boy
When you're with me.
I may spoil you a bit,
But no one has to worry.
My Punky, my godchild,
My lovable boy.
You bring me so much cheer
And so much joy.
I can take you with me
Wherever I go.
You always have such a good time
And you let me know.
Punky, Faustine, my number one.
You don't mind when I call you son.

Kathy Bonito

LORD OF LOVE

Lord of Love, Lord of light
Look upon thy child tonight,
Ease the fret and daily care
That would each day my life ensnare.

Lord of mercy, Lord of grace
Show to me thy smiling face,
Banish all the doubt and fear
Ease the heartache, dry the tear.

Lord of joy, Lord of peace
Bring thy calmness, bring release,
Let me feel thy presence nigh,
Hear each plea, hear each sigh.

Lord of calm, Lord of rest
Help me bear each strain and test,
For I know thou will abide
Every moment by my side.

Cecile M. Greenland

WALKING WITH MY FRIEND

Walking with Jesus side by side,
He's my friend, counselor and guide,
He'll be with me whate'er betide;
Glory, Glory, Hallelujah!

So together along we go,
He loves me and I love Him so,
I never knew such love before;
Glory, Glory, Hallelujah!

Oh, how sweet to commune with Him,
On mountaintop or valley dim,
He forgives and keeps me free from sin;
Glory, Glory, Hallelujah!

Love divine,
Joy sublime,
Peace within,
What a friend;
Glory, Glory, Hallelujah!

Cecile M. Greenland

ON THE THRESHOLD

A little girl's questions

"Does God *really* hear me when I pray?"
Rebecca asked Grandpa one day;
"He's way up there in His beautiful Heaven,
and He *knows* that I am only seven!"

"He hears your prayers loud and clear,
it matters not the time of year;
Night and day, in winter or spring,
rich blessings will your prayers bring."

"But Grandpa, Heaven is *so* far away,
do you think that I'll go there someday?"
"It isn't all that far, my dear,
Take God's hand, He'll hold you near."

"But how far away *is* Heaven?
Oh Grandpa, tell me *please!*"
"Dear child, you're on the threshold,
when you're praying on your knees!"

Ralph Dietterick

SOMETIMES

Sometimes I'm not as caring
when I come home from work
it's just I'm tired, and had a long day
so if you feel it's you that has done something wrong,
don't feel that it's you in the way,
it's only selfish me.
Please understand me, and be patient
and soon you will see
I just need time for my tiredness
but I will come around
to hold you forever
and be as caring as I should
but most of all,
I'll be as understanding with love
just as you thought I would

Michelle Moreira

THE FERRIS WHEEL

Life may be described as a continuous motion of a Ferris wheel.
For when the wheel rotates and attains its zenith point, it
  becomes cerebrally pleasurable to man.

During the period of descent, whereupon, it reaches the lowest
  level, it becomes a test of cerebral endurance.

As the Ferris wheel continues in this manner, it becomes
  most important that an acceptance and sharing of these
  moments.

Only at times when the wheel reaches its lowest level will
  a reflection of true and genuine friendship be known.

Bernard L. Ginsberg

MEMORIAL

Endless monuments row after row.
How they get there one may not know.
Year after year new ones are added.
Others become crumpled and faded.

One lone tree sits off in the distance.
Can it be a symbol of some long resistance?
No, it is in memory of one that lies there.
And others will join him to lay down their care.

People walk by here stunned by the silence.
They remark on this and then return to the violence.
Countless flags flutter in the breeze.
Those that lay there were caught in a siege.

From an old war long since forgotten
Just so a new one can be begotten.
The names on the monuments pass in review.
Remembered now by only a few.
And the stillness is broken only by the hum
Of a boy and his mower working to overcome
  the grass that grows there.

John R. Clough

MY OTHER FLOWER GARDEN

I thought of the flower garden I wanted to grow,
There just wasn't time to plant and make row upon row.
Then I thought of the other garden I was growing,
With all the young lives that were defiantly showing.

The many seeds that had been sown down through the years,
Reaped, and garnered abundantly, with joy and with tears.
The effort was worth all that I had made,
The flowers had been grown without using a spade.

I looked at the flower garden I had helped grow.
I saw each one standing row upon row.
There were Johnny-Jump-Ups, with energy to spare,
There were some named Rose, with beauty so fair.

Jack-in-The-Pulpits, yes, several are preachers.
Touch-Me-Nots, who were touched, are now schoolteachers.
Even Mistress Mary, who was quite contrary,
Grew her own garden, and is now a missionary.

Flowers are beautiful and lovely to see.
Helping young lives is more beautiful to me.
Perhaps there will be flowers in Heaven, fair,
And upon entering, I can pick my share.

Mildred Quine Dennis

SUNSHINE ON A CLOUDY DAY

I'd think of you when you're far away,
You brought me the sun on a cloudy day.
I listened to you; the things I learned
Gave new meaning in a time when leaves turned.
Then came winter, the bitter cold,
And with it reality — there's nothing to hold.

But frigid memories in a warm heart
Soon would melt and spring would start.
The world revolves and life goes on,
As time passes the hurt is gone.
I have all the summers of my life left ahead
As I walk down the path that you once led.
I think of you, though you're far away,
You bring me the sun on a cloudy day.

Karin Greenwood

A TRIBUTE TO DAD AND GRANDPA

*Written in loving memory for my father,
Roy C. Dilka, who passed from this life
into the next on May 29th, 1987.*

Through the years we traveled on the road of life.
You had started the journey before us.
You struggled while we came to be.
Helping to mold our lives into the people we've chosen to be.
You always spoke your mind.
Speaking out for what you believed to be.
Like all parents;
Sometimes you became upset with things we do.
But no matter what the outcome.
You were still proud of us and your love never faded once.
You've gone ahead once more.
To start paving another path for us.
We shall cry, because we miss you.
We shall smile and remember you always.
A part of you will always live in each of us.
We love you, Dad, Grandpa.

Lois L. Selby

. . . AND THEY BUILT BRIDGES

The child cried out in fear;
the mother heard and comforted;
and they built bridges
to conquer the fear.

The husband and wife were silent;
they had argued and disagreed;
and they built bridges
to listen and understand.

The patient moaned in agony;
the doctor consoled and diagnosed;
and they built bridges
to overcome the pain.

Whenever someone cried
for help,
someone who could lend a hand
and a heart
heard;
and they built bridges
to reach each other.

Kelly Sharon

SILENT COMMUNICATION

Your silence hovers over me
like some threatening mystery,
its darkness embraces
all the missing traces
of our communication.

It says nothing
but lets me know everything,
what you show
will let me know
because this is our communication.

It is a darkness
that screams of hollowness,
but it is filled
with our unspoken, strong-willed
communication.

Kelly Sharon

HAPPINESS IS!

to gaze fondly on a loved face
to hold a precious body close
to stroke cherished flesh
to behold a beauteous form
to listen to gentle laughter
to share a tender moment
to give a gift of love
to receive a silent kiss
to help in time of need
to have it all
    summed up in you,
    Happiness is!

David Briggs

NIGHTFALL

Sun droops,
Darkness gathers,
Neon lights burst forth

Spinsters dream
Old men remember
Children cry
and night marches on

Listen!
Laughter, sadness,
tossing

Feel!
Sultry, stifling,
sweaty

and night wraps
itself
in black-face
grim and sightless.

Nightfall!

David Briggs

DEPARTURE FROM INIQUITY

Like a mighty weight upon your back,
Is not your burden too much to bear,
Look to wisdom for what you lack,
Let her exult you ever fair.

And will you fail to see this light,
That hope and wonder fired for thee,
Not for me you fight this fight,
Or give the sparrow to the tree.

If this then be your simple game,
The game that made for you this life,
Know you this, I played the same,
Now I look to end your strife.

And when at last yourself you see,
In all your glory and bright hope,
Know you then, that you are free.
No more to stumble, fall and grope.

I see a light far off, ahead,
A ship has sailed this tranquil sea,
No more turbulent days to dread,
At last, this raging storm you flee.

P. J. Parker

EVENING STAR

A
Star —
Pulsing
Silver
Against
 a
Black sky.
Shining,
Solitary,
Happy.

Christine Tatem

RAINDROPS GENTLY FALLING

Raindrops gently falling,
  Against the *window* pane;
Softly, yes so softly,
  They'd *trickle* down again.

Thunder in the distance,
  It rumbled through the *earth;*
Lightning all around the *sky,*
  Wind blowing for all it's worth.

I sat there *reminiscing,*
  Of the ''*storms*'' in my own life;
And I thought about the *man* I loved,
  Who didn't want his *wife.*

My *ears* could hear the *laughter,*
  My *heart* could feel the *love;*
My *eyes* could see the *family,*
  God had given *us* from *above.*

So many *happy* memories,
  I went through them *one by one;*
And as rain's *teardrops* stopped outside,
  Mine had just *begun!*

Elaine Charles

UPON THE NEXT HORIZON

Upon the *next horizon,*
  The sun above is *bright;*
And as the *colors* change their hue,
  And *gently* falls the night,

I watch the color's *splendor,*
  Purple's yellow mist;
And see the *sunset* God has made,
  With *radiant love* He kissed.

And over in the western *sky,*
  I see the *sun* descend;
And in *awe* I watch the patterns,
  As the day *begins* to end.

The day that *long-awaited,*
  Was *once* so far away;
Has now become an *afterthought,*
  Of *just* another day.

Looking in the distance,
  A *new horizon* will I see;
And *somewhere* down the road in time,
  Will be a *memory.*

Elaine Charles

WAITING

Lord, You have been here so very long
  and I have come so late.
You had watched, waited
  in love, as the father of that son.
You've drawn me safely, surely
  to the true Cup of life
To drink — and thirst no more!

Helen M. Williams

I've searched high;
I've searched low.
Listen for wisdom while the winds blow.
Asked the wise old owl.
   "Will he love me?
   Love me the way I love him?
   Or will I lose him?"
The wise old owl only scowls;
   "No one woman knows what beats in his heart and soul.
   He'll search all his life to find that happiness
   is in his heart.
   So place no chains on his feet.
   Let him be free and he will never flee thee."
I nodded and walked away.
I understood his words of wisdom.
For it took time for me to stop searching and see what was
   inside of me.
All the love, happiness and peace was resting in my soul.

Lois L. Selby

ILLUSIONS

Last Friday night, as the moon shined bright,
I saw reflections of you in the silvery light.

A vision of a lady, standing up high in the air,
Dressed in a white gown of satin, soft as her silky hair.

I paused and I pondered; I asked, "How can this be?"
"Is this an illusion, or is this reality?"

I stood and I stared, then I dropped on one knee;
The next thing I knew, I was with her on her balcony.

I said, "This is so real," as the image was now clear;
We talked so softly, for only each other to hear.

Then I touched and nibbled her ear, as she smiled with delight;
This was truly a real lady, in the silvery night.

We turned to each other and ever so gently, we kissed;
Locked in each other's arms, the rest of the night we missed.

And, when I awakened, I found myself home in my bed;
The lady in the night? had been just a "dream" in my head.

The reflection now faded, a sadness now grew;
A feeling of loneliness, for one so blue.

As for the likeness of the lady, whom I "thought," I once knew,
Will remain as a . . . memory, for only one, not two.

Richard D. Sempek

J is for Jesus Christ
E is for Everyone, He loves all of us
S is for Save, He will save you
U is for Understanding, that He is
S is for Salvation, He will give you

C is for Church, where we learn about Him
H is for Holy, that He is
R is for Ready, He's ready to help you
I is for Incredible, the things He can do
S is for Stars, He flung in the sky.
T is for Tomb, by the grave where He laid.

Celious Davis

BROTHER

Brother,
Go where your heart is and where the winds take you;
  it is there where you'll find your solitude.
Brave the rough seas and stormy winds,
  and stand firm against the rocky mountains and shores.
You will find there waiting at the end of every storm
  a ray of sunshine for every piece of hope.
And at the end of every storm find the satisfaction
  of being the victor, that you have triumphed
  in the face of all odds.
You have weathered every challenge hurled,
  and find the glory of having met your purpose
  with a humble heart and mind.
Be joyful, brother, and may you find your solitude.
Be strong in the face of all odds.

Erwin G. de la Paz

FOR BALANCHINE

Energy ticked you current, like no clock Fabergé crafted.
Essential! Elemental! Self-wound hands few could know.
Minus jewels but radiant! Wound to risky madness.

Heir to a revolution where some transcended mortality
through tidy steps you align, Museum dust coats no fevered phrase
nor can we dumbly stand in passive reverence.

Your springs were wound too tight. No midwife slapped those feet
to draw your cry, nor was it a mother's hand that paced
rushed rhythm to those dreams that scented God and wrote in light.

Your vision stretched us. What had been slipped dusty and was bound.
Your strength of tick retarded evanescence and left so hushed regard
for workings clear profound. The frailty ballet knew was gone.

Bounding, resounding theme echoes by fragment the malady's sustained.
Music is seen! Flat notes moved by compelling vitality reflect
a face of no limited digits, ticking a skewed circumference

by which the metered movement measures some result.
Not mortal, mechanized, nor God, you wound yourself
so easily we thought you set apart — immune.

Elizabeth Williams

BLUEBIRDS OF SUNSHINE

Two lovely bluebirds grace my neighbor's yard today.
They said 9 morning, sir" and chased my blues away.
Lori, a stately lass of 15 years and Lisa, but 13,
With sunny smiles the world endears.
Enraptured seemed they with the sunlit sky
As lovely natures to the world unfurled.
These fair maidens glistened in their warmth
And made my day a brighter ray of hope.
Ah, youth, where flows the hope, the joyous
Wonder, the inspiration for tomorrow.
Blessed are the young.

David James Platt

ONE COLD WINTER'S NIGHT

One cold and lonely winter's night,
  As I lay sleeping in my bed;
Something had awakened me,
  With *words* inside my head.

At first I tried to just ignore,
  All the *words* that came;
But I could not get back to sleep,
  On my dreaming I put the blame.

And then those *words* just wouldn't stop,
  And so on paper took;
The *message* that was coming fast,
  All in *poetry*, my hand just shook!

The ''first'' one I put in a real safe place,
  And didn't tell a soul;
It was a *blessing* from my *Lord*,
  And *His words*, they made me whole!

I treasured it and took it out,
  Time and time again;
And I thanked *Him* for the *words He gave*,
  In the *poetry* He did send!

Elaine Charles

THE LAWN KEEPER

He was only a boy,
An entrepreneur;
With big dreams, a heart,
And a tiny lawnmower.
I believe he was eight,
A thin scrap of a lad.
He'd only his mother,
And a mem'ry of dad.
But hustle he would,
Though little in size;
He made a mock of most boys,
More than twice his own size.
He worked hard for me,
And I paid him well;
What he did with the money,
He never did tell.
But he taught me a lesson,
I'll not soon forget;
He was more of a man,
Than some men I've met.

J. R. Moses

THE WINTER OF MY LIFE

It was a glorious springtime,
and the summer that followed was fair;
autumn was filled with ecstatic days —
I'm glad that I was there.

But winter is now upon me,
and I haven't the least regret;
I've always been blessed with happiness —
it's a thing that follows me yet.

Ralph Dietterick

MOMENTS

If moments of pleasure
Could be frozen in time
To be enjoyed again,
More than just in the mind;
What freezers we'd need!
To keep our memories safe,
So we could relive them,
Any time, any place.
Photographs help,
But they're lifeless things,
Without audio effects
To bring them some zing.
Movies are nice,
But some things are missed;
So only parts are seen,
Of moments of bliss.
But to freeze them in time,
Take out; view at will,
Then refreeze for safekeeping,
Would be a marvelous thrill.

J. R. Moses

LABOR OF LOVE

I sat on the ancient remnants
Of someone's labor of love.
'Twas once a home's foundation,
Now crumbled nearly to dust.

Rough stones once sealed together,
With water, sand, and clay,
Laid carefully to weather
The storms of yesterday.

I could see the vaguest outlines, there,
Of the rooms that made this home,
And imagined doors and windows
As though it were my own.

And near the crumbling, ancient stones
Of this home of yesterday,
Stood a gnarled and twisted, ageless tree
Where children used to play.

It's sad to see these crumbling ruins,
Soon to be no more than dust;
And not know at all the people
Who created this labor of love.

J. R. Moses

RAIN AND ARCTIC

Rain
 softly
  melting
   snow.
Quietly descending.
 Turning
   a
  poor
   sheepdog
    into
     a
   drowned
    rat.

Christine Tatem

FOR JERRY LEE MOORE

I'm not looking for forever
I know forever is just
Tomorrow for us.

I only want to know that you care
That's all I need
As long as you're here.

And to tell you what's on my mind
You know that no one else
Can listen as kind.

You seem to know me so well
But there are some feelings
I never can tell.

I'm not asking for all of your heart
Just a small piece
To hold in the dark.

I guess all of this is just to say
That I don't want to be someone
Who'll stand in your way.

I only want to become a part
Tucked deep away
Inside of your heart.

Lori Ann Burton

I CRY INSIDE

In a world where roles
  are all reversed
and everyone
  is so rehearsed
when wrong is right
  and right is wrong
and everyone
  just goes along
for the crazy ride
  they can't decide
which way to go
  It hurts me so
I cry inside
  . . . every time
the truth's denied
  but tears don't show
they just don't know
  the way I feel
the love that's real
  and not a fantasy.

J'Marie Floe

TRUE FRIEND

All through life 'til the very end,
The most wondrous things is a True Friend —
To share your troubles — laughter — tears —
Help you through sickness — all your fears —
Share your thoughts throughout the years.

Your friends may be many,
Or they may be few;
However, one *true friend* will do.

(This one's for you).

Elaine Meli

FROM THE WINDOW

After you left the house,
wearing pink bureau-lipstick and perfume dashes
I watched you grow small, below on the island path
in your old, flowered Mommy blouse
walking slowly, disappearing and reappearing among tall pine trees
and around the bends.

In the bright summer daylight my feet felt shy
and my knees got numb for you — I knew you had
loosened, stray hairs traveling along on your shoulders —
hairs that just keep falling.

Despite this, you kept on going — to be a part of the
summer crowd to make the scene at the library opening.

I didn't know where else I'd ever understood myself so well,
to the degree that I learned not to touch the stove top
back in early split-level childhood.

Seeing you walking alone, containing your pains
I felt proud of you, your thick, silver-white hair glistening,
the sunglasses protecting your recuperating eyes.

I recognized, once again, with familiar clarity
still, tears choked my sight,
that I loved you as only a mother can love her small child
or an aging daughter loves her aging mother.

Virginia Irwin

THE FAMILY

As one grows older in our society,
We recognize the importance of one's family.
A group characterized by cohesiveness,
Which withstands vicissitudes and stress.

Family members contribute love and care,
To promote the individual's health, welfare.
This special feeling of family togetherness,
Is the basis for security and happiness.

The family offers help and counseling,
With acceptance of our faults, failings.
We realize as we contemplate, analyze,
Collective family teamwork is best and wise.

As trials and tribulations arise,
They sometimes are blessings in disguise.
For the family furnishes strength, comfort in adversity,
Which enables the individual to find his own identity.

Families surmount problems with a winning combination;
Faith, trust, sympathy and cooperation.
Thus the individual gains confidence, self-esteem,
Whereby he may fulfill his destiny and dreams.

Phyllis Hefty

ABSOLUTION

How undefiled and perfect are we
Who look upon the glut and mental depravity
Of the human race with scorn. And judge them such.

Nor could I be found wanting. My thoughts are pure as lilies,
Vile curses never pass my lips; from my innermost being, never envy.
All *that* is beneath me, and shan't engulf my kind.
I sit in judgment against others in my mind.

Honest toil and labor use up my body strengths,
And toward my children, I have noble reflection.
Wild seeds along the way I've never sown,
Nor wretched left behind to pay the price of my transgression.
No one judges me.

Touch me not with vile disease, perfidious, false-hearted brother,
No shame is mine. Only cogency, goodness, and eternal virtues
Exude from my being. I am free from guilt or blame.
Faultless is my name. Absolution.

Carolyn Wolfe

IF FREEDOM'S STOLE

Buried deep in the soul of man is the longing to be free,
     An envy of the lark that sings,
     Of elk and deer, of honeybee,
     Of pheasant flocks and squirrels' play,
     Of rabbits o'er the glen;
He cannot see but this should be the life and likes of men.

Through balance of nature, undisturbed, each wildlife has its prey,
     And hides its young, and runs for holes,
     Escaping dangers of the day,
     And lives each hour to pass the night
     In crouched and fearful lair;
Lest it should be the victim of a hound, a fox, or bear.

Intellect of the human mind should warn man of his plight,
     For freedom's such a fleeting thing,
     Intangible, and blind to sight,
     One cannot grasp it in one's hand
     Or hide it in some vault;
Yet, he should know if freedom's stole, it surely is his fault.

Carolyn Wolfe

I DREAM OF A LOVE

I dream of a love
 as the days go gently by,
A love that shines as bright as the stars above,
 and for this love — I sometimes sit and cry.

I dream of a love
 that will mend my sad heart, when it is broken,
A love that's loving and peaceful as a dove,
 one that I can always keep as a token.

I dream of a love
 that will last through the years,
A love that will stay with me and never rove,
 a love that will be with me, whether in smiles or tears.

Celious Davis

MUSICAL LEAVES

If the world
shall not fear
such a faith
that is imminent

If the world
were as brilliant
as
the autumn leaves
femininely
falling,
with colors of spiritual shades
combined together

Then a lost mind,
or
a lost life
shall become the mystery
in a god's love

Garrison Leroy Moreland

FREEZING TIME

If I could freeze time,
I'd freeze every moment spent with you.
The good times and the bad,
For I've learned from both.

In a fragile icicle,
You'd find the first time we made love.
In the crystal flakes of frost —
I'd store the laughs we shared together
Then gently glaze them one or twice
With the tears that came along.

If I could freeze time,
The time would be with you.
There we'd be — the two of us . . .

Oh, but fantasy becomes reality.
There is no freezing time.
Our paths were meant to cross,
But not to merge.
How sad,
As I stand in this puddle of melted ice.

Linda Ann Gron

LIFE'S ROAD

At the end of our road
of life
When we meet Jesus face to
face
All things along the road of strife
Fade into oblivion within
the human race

The power Divine is for all time
as we travel this road of strife
His love is there to always
care
And offers eternal life.

Clara Fetterolf

MY LOVE

When I was young, I loved you as much as I
love you now, my Love.

With all the others that I knew, I loved you
more as now, my Love.

As we have grown older, and age has begun its
toll on us, the love that I have for you has
become stronger, my Love.

We still have each other, thru all the sickness,
happiness and unhappiness, poverty and
the wealth that we have shared, my Love.

As the props from our bodies pile high on the
dresser as we prepare to retire, you are as
beautiful as the first time that I saw you,
my Love.

You are my Love.

Curtis E. Blake

SMILE

Look around and see all the beauty
the world has to give,
lift your eyes and dry your tears
and cast your vision upon the earth.

The grass grows tall and green
with accents of wild flowers,
the sun shines bright and colors
the leaves high in the trees.

The rivers run deep and clear where
the little animals play their games,
while the birds serenade us with
tender songs of love.

Although it all dies in time
the memories live on forever,
so put aside your sorrow and
life your eyes with mine.

Take my hand and let me
lead you through this wonderland,
relax and smile for me.

Christopher A. Morris

blue corn tortillas

my eyes recall kachinas
my taste of blue corn
my talent for the hunt

my energy from mother earth
every day at dawn I dance
in my Indian dream

the green piñon tree branch
I carry my kiva root
to speak with the Great Spirit

and from my mother earth
I am energized each day
for I am Alberto, Indian blood.

Albert M. Gallegos

OLD LACE

I feel a warm glow . . .
And happiness abounds;
Feelings I have come to know
Because love is all around.

When I am with you
The love I feel is ecstatic;
Old emotions tried and true,
Like the day in the attic.

Our love was so new,
We discovered more each day;
In the midst of an old trunk and shoes,
You found lace to frame my face.

A wedding gown we found,
From another wedding true;
Lace, pearls, and love were bound,
In my mother's trunk given to me and you.

Joan Hughes Black

GRACE

My fondest memories
Begin with you near.
Your laughter and smile
Filled me with cheer.

You belonged to me
Because you were always there;
I tried not to see . . .
With others I had to share.

You are so smart!
You have your Ph.D. too!
But your gentle, compassionate heart
Has always remained true.

The love our mother had
Is continued in you.
I am happy and glad
To know perfect love and truth.

Diamonds, rubies, and pearls
Would not interest you;
But intelligent boys and girls
Make teaching your dream come true.

We were truly blessed!
With a universal bond,
Of love, faith and happiness,
Through family, God, and Jesus, His son.

Joan Hughes Black

THE BOTTOMLESS PIT

Out of the dregs and depths of despair
    Out of the bottomless pit
Wanders a man who had sunken there
    Still wearing the chains of it.

Where does he burrow — this vile objection
    Where does he lay down his head?
Why struggles this soul from hell's protection
    To face those he's injured instead?

Sufficient to him is his verdict to live out
    This punishment inflicted of many.
Contrary, ye ought rather to forgive
    And comfort him above any.

Lest through oppression, his grief is too great
    That he's smothered with over-much sorrow,
And wrapped in the chains of his mortal defeat
    To the bottomless pit he'll burrow.

Into the dregs and depths of despair
    Back to the bottomless pit
Wanders the soul who had climbed from there
    Dragged back by the chains of it.

Carolyn Wolfe

KATHRYN LUCILLE JACKSON. Pen Name: Carolyn Wolfe; Born: Ionia, Michigan, 10-2-14; Married: Dr. Gordon L. Birnie, D.D.S., (retired); Education: University of Michigan, B.A.; University of Michigan Graduate School, Horace Rackham, M.A., 1964 and 1965, after completing Music Education and raising two boys; Occupations: Retired music instructor, Journalism, English Literature, Creative Drama; Memberships: National Association of Professional Educators; International Lioness Club, Flint; Past choir director; First violin in Flint Symphony; Award: 'The Confounders'; Poetry: 'My Kids,' humorous poem, *American Poetry Anthology,* 1986; 'The Confounders,' 'The Silent House,' *In Quiet Places,* 1986; 'Lord, Take Me,' religious plea, *Words of Praise,* 1986; 'God's Orbit,'on infinity, *Today's Greatest Poems,* 1983; Other Writings: *Billy and the Boys,* children's book, fiction based on fact, 1969; Comments: *I am basically a religious person, and like to write themes that bring out integrity, honesty, love, deep emotional feelings, and beauty. Most of my poems are too long to fit into the mold required by poetry editors. I shortened 'The Creation of a Tree' to get it published, but some of my "story" poems are too long and each line too concise to comply.*

FALL

Changing colors like our lives
Turn season of compassion.
Fall slowly like Grand Central Station's movement
One track laid at a time.
Board the train slowly, people.
Remember there are four seasons.
Leaves, yes, leaves swept
over this painting of ground
long before your name was
known.

Zane Bond

JUDY

The strange part is that nothing would have happened,
    Had I had the luck, in this life, to meet you.
So many miles from Philly to Houston, and walls of religion, too.
All that we had in common, at least, the way that it seemed,
Was one certain hope for mankind, and for America, one special dream.
Those are what you died for, and as I read, it began coming through,
All the details of the life you led, I fell in love with my
    image of you.
So fascinating a background, of someone special and dear,
It would have been too right to be real, if we'd found
    each other here.
Now you know what I only hope for, about the future of our human race,
Perhaps we'll share what this world couldn't give us,
    When we meet in some place . . . not a place.

Guillaume-Georges Crepeau

PEOPLE IN THE WORLD TODAY

People are quick to slay rather than give their
fellow man a helping hand.

People are quick to kill rather than help someone to live.

People love to talk on the telephone gossiping and telling lies.

Instead of saying something kind about a person, people
rather kill a person's pride.

People are too busy worrying about what another has done
and who is running around with whose son.

People are so full of hate, they rather tell others
where they can go, rather than say hello.

People in the world today have forgotten God above.

People rather give in to Satan and show no love.

People should remember there is a cross to bear and most of all,

God has our record and is watching from above.

Joyce Hines

FLAMING SHADOWS

In the darkness
    a match is lit.

        A spark of light
                burns only for a moment,

        Then fades away
            in the night.

        It returns by striking again
           the hapless box from
                which it came.

When the heat disappears
    and the fire is gone,

        Another is there to
           take its place;

        Until its belly finally is empty
           and flaming shadows
             can no longer

        be cast.

Elizabeth Berlie

ANDY

Tears were streaming
Down my brother's face;
I did not know . . .
Whom to embrace.

I looked at you, my sister,
So stricken and pale . . .
You could not cry . . .
Would you ever get well?

Losing a child
Is more than one can bear;
Life had just begun
For Andy, one so good and fair!

He was warm and real,
Golden hair and eyes of blue;
We were given a taste
Of all that is good and true.

The pain as I write this
Is still so sharp and sad;
Andy, we still miss you,
Our precious, darling lad.

Joan Hughes Black

JOAN HUGHES BLACK. Born: Sylacauga, Alabama, 6-1-41; Married: Bobby Gene Black, 6-14-63; Education: B. B. Comer Memorial High School, Jacksonville State University, Auburn University at Montgomery; Occupation: American Sterilizer Company; Memberships: National Writers Club, Dalraida Baptist Church; Poetry: 'Father,' 1978; 'Mother,' 'The Fight for Lost Dreams,' 'Paradise,' 'To My Children'; all *American Poetry Anthology;* Themes: *The common themes in my poetry are family, home, nature, and love. The solitude and beauty of my father's and mother's home are something I yearn for an write about — with the wind blowing through the tall pines and the hushed, quiet splendor all around. My poetry is also inspired by a warm and loving family.*

THOUGHTS

I close my eyes and you are there,
The very first thought I have each day;
From sunup, to sundown
I see your smile, hear your laugh.

No matter where I am, what I am doing,
My thoughts turn to you,
Wondering if you need me as I need you,
Loving you more every minute, every hour.

The wish I make each day and night
Is that we may share our love,
Every minute, every hour, our whole life long,
Caring and sharing, giving and taking,
Always loving.

Angie Ferraro

THOUGHTS OF YOU

Thoughts of you
    Are crystal clear
They're all I think
    And all I fear

As friends and lovers
    Do we dare
To show each other
    That we care

Pain left us cautious
    Hesitant to call
We're both so afraid
    A heart will fall

Together we can find
    The courage to try
Holding each other
    Never needing to cry

Jayne Brock

STOPPING BY LIGHT

In the street
Up ahead, something
Reflects the sun.

The body before the mind
Drifts to the glittering light.

I am drawn to it
Like insects drawn to light
Out of darkness

Or like men I suppose
Drawn to wealth, who love
Both light and the cover of darkness.

When I get there I wonder
If it's money or something of value

But when I get there
It is merely broken glass instead,
Nothing more, scattering the sun.

A word is still attached
To a fragment of the broken wine bottle.
I wonder who has gone to pieces.

George D. Scott

You
were taken
so far
and so fast
and too soon I knew you —
all of the sudden
you were my past.
Words and plans
can ruin
a good love affair.
Sometime I think
I dreamed you up —
you were
never
really
there.

Korene Cleo Sizemore

WHAT MY FATHER SAID TO ME BEFORE HE DIED

When I am gone release me
Let me go. You must not tie
Yourself to me with tears. Be
Happy we had these many years.

I gave you my love, you can only
Imagine how much you gave to me in
Happiness. I thank you for the
Love you each have given me, but
Now, it's time I traveled on alone.
So bless also all the memories
Within your heart.

I won't be far away, for life always
Goes on. If you need me, just call.
And even though you can't see me or
Touch me, I'll be near. And if you
Listen with your heart, you will hear
My love around you soft and clear.

And then, when you must come this
Way, *alone,* I'll greet you with a
Smile and say, *welcome home.*

Albert M. Gallegos

IN A GARDEN

From the swirl of the world
Where no one is rude
You find sweet solitude
In a garden.

You are at ease
And you can appease
Yourself.
Kind flowers in bright dress
Caress your thoughts,
These products of the sod
Bring you closer to your God
In a garden.

Alice Compo

WISHFUL OF

I'm seven years old,
I sit out back on top of the
Wooden sawhorse and face a tree with
Broomstick in hand.

Only I'm not just seven, I'm a
Shining knight in armor.
I'm sitting on a white stallion
With my lance under arm and
I'm fighting off the evil dragon,
Rescuing the fair maiden.

Whack, smack, thump, I hit the dragon's bark.

My lance breaks, but that's okay — it's only
A broomstick and a stupid old tree.

And I'm really not seven but instead seventeen,
And even though I wish for,
There's really not, a fair maiden.

James C. L. Crabtree

OUR WORLD

A world of crime — who's the blame?
Are our children condemned to a world of flame?
Children taking what is not theirs,
   a society which is loosing its wares.
Death — by bullet, bomb, and disease,
   the world can no longer afford to appease!
Trash in the streets, the high seas, and numerous landfills,
   waterways, airways, polluted by our industrial mills!
Man against nature, nature against man,
   man against man!
Who will win?
Who will lose?

Glen R. Anderson

TO LINDA

First Love

Memories of you linger, Linda — within my mind,
Forever etched: like the Mona Lisa — beautiful, young,
Yet refined. Your girlish features: joyful and trusting —
   Giving and receiving our young love.
My sweet country girl, where have you gone?
Are you still there — on your father's farm? In
The old house with shutters of green, with:
   Creaking porch and tire swing.
Time flew by us as we ran through fields and trees,
Hand in hand through maple and pine — young sweet love:
Life's natural wine. Hayrides on cool October nights,
Holding each other close under gentle starlight.
Laughing and singing to old Mrs. Stone's: for hot chocolate,
And fresh cookies — still warm from the oven.
She brightened our spirits with story and song:
   Till it was time to go home.

I remember you, Linda: golden hair and eyes shining like
Blue fire. Thirty years we've been apart, Linda:
Someday I'll come back — joy of my heart.
                                         Love, Bruce

Bruce R. Humphreys

WHITNEY ROAD

Fields: patchwork quilts of green and gold,
White porches and blue shutters:
On large, friendly looking houses.
Ancient oak trees with tire swings
Hold children who laugh and sing.
Wheat and corn wave to say *good day;*
Wagons piled with sweet smelling hay, passing
Country folks who smile and call *hello,*
Tall maple trees dripping drops of delight,
Soon to be syrup on flapjacks light.

Whitney Road,
Memories still linger with childhood dreams:

Replaced by traffic and city scenes.
Concrete and steel no longer will do,
It's time to come back —
To Montville — Whitney Road,
And:
You.

Bruce R. Humphreys

CURTAIN CALL

My message to you is of *Love* — pure, unblemished
Pouring forth, unceasingly,
as a gentle brook caressing its bed of sand and stones —
and as the infinite particles of sand await the brook's
tender caresses,

I await your readiness for me!

Through eyes of interest and oftentimes in awe,
I watch you act, as the curtain draws open,
revealing the stage crowded with *players*

Through teasing eyes, you tantalize!
My desire heightens — taking on the strength of a magnet,
drawing, until I capture you!

We return to the blissful presence
The presence we knew when we first were . . .
. . . but, eventually, you succumb to the *players* —

Once more you create and act out illusion's roles!

C. Lewis Holland

PRESAGE

I heard a sadness upon the wind
and in the air between its breaths.
Such a moaning whisper that the trees trembled
each leaf shivering, sharing,
in harmony with that loneliness . . .
But so softly, ever so softly
their sound beneath that keening —
Until with a sigh they bowed
and thunder marched across the sky,
heaven releasing her tears,
and I bowed my head
and died.

Eyvonn Alberts

My Golden Corn Grows
By The Mesquite Bush
And When I Paint The Sky
My Pinto Waiting By The Mesa High
I Bring The Blue Into My Turquoise
Brush To Insure The Spirit
Of The Ancestors Waiting At My Side.

We Listen For The Coyote Howling
At Our Moon, Trying To Misuse Its Power
To Disperse And Ruin Our Flock
But All In The Great Spirit's Use Of
Time And Space. I Kneel To Pray
Atop my Taos Dwelling House.

Albert M. Gallegos

ALBERT M. GALLEGOS. Pen Name: Tobias Jarbos; Born: Belen, New Mexico, 7-11-36; Education: Loyola University, Chicago, M.A., Spanish literature, 1964; Governors State University, Park Forest, Illinois, M.A., Sociology, 1966; Occupations: Priest, University professor, Journalist — Communications; Memberships: Spanish-Portuguese Teachers' Association, P.A.D.R.E.S. NC News, S.T.L. Society; Writings: *Wise Owl of the Ballet (El Buhito Sabio del Ballet),* bilingual children's book, Aurora Press, Nashville, Tennessee; *A Christmas Story, An Easter Story,* bilingual children's books; Comments: *Poetry has a spiritual afterlife (another life) theme. Bilingual books and poetry appeal to the human insights into life with one another on this earth.*

REUNION

Although I haven't been in touch . . .
I want you still to know how much
I loved your son and hold him dear
Within my heart; he's gone yet near.

I've shared your thoughts, and thru the years
I've felt our loss and known your tears.
Whatever life yet holds in store
For me, I'll only miss him more.

With thanks to God for times we shared . . .
With thanks for knowledge that he cared,
I treasure memories of past
And know some things forever last!

Jeanine M. Droen

THOSE WERE THE DAYS!

Ah! To be just five!
Innocent, eyes wide!
Curiosities
Still determining
Days' activities.

Ah! To be just five!
None from me can hide!
Not butterflies . . . nor
Mother robin's nest
Nor gopher's front door.

Ah! To be just five!
Pleasures undenied!
Slides and swings, balloons
With happy faces
And Disney cartoons.

Why can't we stay five?
Simple, uncontrived?
With hidden treasure
Of four-leaf clovers;
Time without measure.

Jeanine M. Droen

EMPTINESS

I find an emptiness
Surrounding me
Engulfing me
Within its loneliness.

I call out in silence
But no one hears my plea.
Must I float in despair alone?
Help me!

Come forth with the force possessed
And spread it around.
Fulfill the emptiness and loneliness
That hath been found.

Fear arises when silence
Pushes itself from within.
No, it can't
Sink me deeper and deeper — in.

Where is the strength
Claimed to possess?
Hidden as my emptiness, and yet
Never longing to rest.

Dell Guerra

For Randall Ty

wild oats burnt i
smell them like new
bread i touch dried
husks sun-warmed i
crumble garlic crispy
sharp-scented cloves lush
blackberry vicious briars my
skin burns bleeds my
soul aches for the touch
you

Charlie Washburn

Miss the little girl
Whose picture hangs on the wall,
Whose memories still bring widening eyes,
And hard-to-hold tears.

Now the tears fall,
The memories rush out,
I miss the little girl
Whose memories are fixed in my heart,
Whose life made me laugh and cry.
I miss the little girl
Whose picture hangs on the wall
And echoes through my heart.

Have struggled, given in, faded away,
Tried to pretend it didn't exist.
Refused to accept she was gone.
I miss the little girl
Whose image is a picture,
Whose soul is deep within me.
I miss the little girl
Who called me Daddy.

Pat Willis

TO MY VALENTINE

Butterflies are special,
Their kiss as soft as dew.
I was blessed by three of those.
Now, can you guess who?

My silver eagles, now turned gold,
Like the skin of Zanny Lee,
All bring memories of life,
The day I was set free.

This Valentine I hope you'll like
And treasure in your heart,
Not unlike a year ago,
The light still glowing bright.

Though it blinded not my love for you,
Nor covered all your faults,
I'd love you anyway, my dear,
That love will never halt.

Farewell to old and torturous ways,
Farewell to sorrow and pain,
When my butterfly, turned eagle,
Comes to light again.

Jonnine Long

photo-tones

watching for you
mind glinting off
obsidian wet asphalt
bounces refracted
explodes
i see gray
in black and white
you see only
half-tones
i love hand tints.

Charlie Washburn

LOVE'S LESSONS

Ne'er love too deeply or like petals of a flow'r
Your heart will be crushed in twain
And having loved so deeply your tortured soul
Will ne'er love again

Ne'er love too wildly or like raging fires
Through bewitching while unchecked they burn
All beauty by untameness born
Once quenched will ne'er return

Ne'er love too freely nor too long
Or like dawn's rising sun
Few hours of beauty 'til turn of eve
Love's fleeting day is done

Love with only half yourself
With only half your heart
And when that half is torn in twain
Then love with the other part

Edelin C. Fields

EDELIN COLEMAN FIELDS. *A native Washingtonian, she attended Howard University and the University of the District of Columbia in working on her degree in Business Education. She served in administrative and managerial positions for a number of years in the Federal Government from which she is now retired. At present, she serves as Secretary to the Chairman of the Politics Department at the Catholic University of America. Her interests include poetry and church music. She has been published in a number of periodicals. Presently she plans to write several books and has already published two,* Taking Refuge Behind a Smile, *and* What's At the End of the Rainbow? *She is married to Freddie Fields and the mother of one son, Greig Coleman Fields.*

LIFE

She stood before me —
   so dainty,
   so pretty,
   dressed in her finest spring colors.
A sweet fragrance scented the air.
A bumblebee hovered overhead.
Not a word was said.
The wind gently blew.
The sun's rays filtered down between the thick white clouds.
High above a rocky precipice an eagle soared.
Down on a meadow a fawn suckled its mother.
Curiously watching nearby from the safety of its pond swam an otter.
Small robins chirped among the treetops.
I took this in from a distance.
All that I saw was good.
I wanted to see as much as I could.
It lingers on in my mind.
It was a very precious find.

Glen R. Anderson

THE INNOCENCE OF TRUST

We can always reach back only to remember,
the emotions that still glow like an ember.
Spellbound by time's essence in this potion,
I watched with rapture the unveiling emotion.

My heart beckons to feel, my eyes to behold,
the magic only your gentle touch could unfold.
My lips long to caress your tender face,
sheer anticipation makes my heart race.

I see the innocence of trust in your eyes,
and feel its growing depth in your sighs.
My emotions surface to meet your supple lips,
and your body surrenders to my fingertips.

More than just images that have found a way,
to become memories that cannot be taken away.
Your voice caresses this emotion that I'm feeling,
and I give in to your spell that sends me reeling.

Holding you in my arms I look into your eyes,
and I'm sailing across the endless blue skies.
Drawn by the magic of what tomorrow might hold,
and the dawning of emotions that might unfold.

Albert Duran

OLD AGE SHOWS NO MERCY

Oh bless these precious moments of childhood life. Cherish the youth you hold for old age shows no mercy.

Seek out the child that hides within your heart and never let it die.

Set it free from time to time and look through the eyes of a child. For old age shows no mercy.

Oh cherish the moments when life has blessed youth upon you. For if you don't the years will pass and rid the child's laughter from your heart.

Remember the memories of your youth to understand the children of today.

Laugh like a child and never really grow up for old age shows no mercy.

Alicha Martinez

KNOWLEDGE

Knowledge is like a fountain
   Wafting its freshness
Of sparkles like crystals,
   A feeling of ardent hope
With sequence of actions
   In a world of diverged fancy.

Knowledge shows patience
   In the discovery of light
Under rugged hills and hard rocks
   Where every creature dwells unharmed
With unlimited gifts of life,
   To stand strong and free
With lovers of original beauty.

Knowledge is prudence
   With the will to obey and serve
Able to learn and willing to share.
   Today and tomorrow will increase one moment
Of joy for the pursuit of unknown truth
   And knowledge like the cherry plant
Will flourish to reform the course of human needs.

Josephine I. Njoku

BEYOND THE HORIZON

Beyond the horizon
Beyond the ocean blue
Lie some different lands
Of different people
The same as me and you.

Though these distant lands be
Wilderness, desert sands
Or cultivated lands
Different race and creed
To all, life makes demands.

Yet we scheme and we dream
As we look far away
Of fortune and of fame
And bliss and happiness
Which might beyond us lay.

While hope springs eternal
Within our beating hearts
We are our dreams and our
Desires from day to day
Till life from us departs.

Elspeth Crebassa

ELSPETH CREBASSA. Born: Los Angeles, California; Married: Fred Langham, 12-29-29 (now divorced); Occupations: Steno-typist clerk, now on Social Security; Memberships: National Geographic Society, Audubon Society, The Planetary Society; Awards: Merit Awards, Golden Poet Awards, 1985-87; Poetry: 'Seasonal Changes,' *Our World's Best Loved Poems*, 5-84; 'Infinity,' *The Art of Poetry*, 8-2-85; 'Contrast,' *American Poetry Anthology, Vol VI*, 10-84; 'A Fall Walk,' *Best New Poets of 1986*, 'Tempestuous Love,' *Hearts on Fire, Vol. III*, 1986; Comments: *I like to make up poetry about the earth and its many interesting metamorphoses and I'm very happy that my poetry is liked.*

A TUNNEL TRIP

Let's take a trip through a tunnel!
The darkness seems so intense.
We grope for something to sustain,
To improve our steps, which delay to maintain.

We're on guard for a coming train
Speeding so fast, with so much noise,
Which compares to our daily living routines
With a busy life, many forms and scenes.

However, as we reach the far end
A round frame depicts such delight,
The beautiful world framed by heaven's blue
A delightful sight, as Christ lights, so true.

Beatrice Nelson

RUTHIE, CHUCK & DEAN

Bumbles in the Rhodies
A robin on the wing
The tulips and the peonies
Are all such special things.
Sleepy weepy willows
Whisper in the wind.
Springtime blossoms everywhere
As life about begins.
Springtime is a happy time
The time I spend with you
The thoughts of sunny daffodils
All kissed in morning dew
The scent of lilac everywhere
The robin on his wing
The love we share in Pittsburgh
Is such a special thing.

William D. Leavitt

PUZZLES

Why don't you love me
Why don't you care
When I reach out to you
Why aren't you there
It's hard to make rhyme
Or reason of this
No arms to hold me
No lips to kiss.

Where did I fail you
Where was I wrong
Whom was I kidding
As it took so long
For nothing to happen
Nothing for me
As I kept on looking
For the way it should be.

Life is a puzzle
With pieces that fit
And those that fit also
If you fiddle a bit,

Maybe . . .

William D. Leavitt

EVERLASTING LOVE

Each day we gaze into the sky
On bended knee we always try
We ask the Lord our day to bless
We praise Him for His glorious way
He watches o'er us night and day
God's gift to us is all around
The rolling hills with trees abound
Our meadows filled with streams and flowers
Happy are we in this world of ours
From lakes and mountains water flows
It feeds the valleys far below
Desert flowers in color array
God does it all in every way
We give Him our heart, unending trust
Ask and receive, the Lord is just
How can we thank Him, great as He is
Our love, our praises all are His.

Alvera L. Gartmann

YOU

You are magic
You're the sparkling ray of light
That moonbeams dance on
Making all so right.

You are a moment
Of ecstasy's sweet bliss
You are the morning
As she leaves her dewy kiss.

Because you're special
So easily we share
Life's happy moments
In love beyond compare.

And if the day should come
When you are gone from me
Each second will become
Almost eternity.

A tear of sorrow falls
In search of what's to be
I pray to God above
You will return to me.

William D. Leavitt

DEAR LORD

Written for the cardinals during the papal visit.

A tree began to grow
Great knowledge made it be.
I heard the bluebird sing
About life joyously.
A ray of hope we find
Radiates sweet charity.
And then the written word
Of God's reality.
I saw the dove of peace
Fly high into the air.
I heard a red rose speak
Of love beyond compare.
I lift my heart with love
And adoration too
For all the special gifts
God's love has given you.

And all mankind.

William D. Leavitt

I'LL BE ALL RIGHT

In the darkness of the night,
   As I read of Jesus' might,
The Holy Spirit brings the light,
   Fills my mind and makes it bright,
Raises it to a new height,
   Gives me more of an insight,
Shows me how and when to fight,
   Satan with his evil plight,
Insures me that — God is right,
   — Rescues me from sin's death bite,
Then lets me know — I'll be all right.

Jean P. Derby

DICENTRA.

RAIN CLOUDS

Clouds come
misty thunder
on the breath
of wind

Fish cry
rainbow bubbles
in the ocean
of tears

Showers sing
perfumed notes
it's the symphony
of joy

Swirling compassion
breaks the
silence of
the luminous eye

In the eye
of the universe
eternal peace
sighs in silence

Ted R. Holoway

I LOVE YOU, DAD

Many fathers can't be found
Of those that have gone away
But you have that extra-special something
And I'm glad you decided to stay.

There may be times you wonder
But don't ever feel defeated
Of the every bit of love you give
Every bit is needed.

And if there are times
That you ever feel rejected
Then let yourself be heard
For it must be corrected.

Because you're as special
As you make me feel
And the love is from the heart
No doubt it is real.

Many times may be good
But some times may be bad
But all through these times
I never stopped loving you, Dad.

Kimberly Thomas

JESSEE

He breathed —
Carved cells were now polished skin,
Wrapped in maternal blood.

He was both brother and son.
Father's eyes wrapped him
With paternal love.

I breathed —
And sensed the loss
Inside of one.

Patricia M. Stephens

MY GRANDMOTHER

She lay there in misery
Waiting for her call
And then it came
The day she left us all.

We knew that would happen
But like always, not when
She held out as best she could
She stayed strong until the end.

She looked away into the heavens
To a better awaiting home
Where all her burdens would be lifted
And all her pain would be gone.

It was a long lonely journey
For anyone to have to face
And if it had been God's will
I would have gladly taken her place.

And does that make me a fool?
It only begins to tell how much I loved her
And why so much?
She was my grandmother.

Kimberly Thomas

SURE AND STEADY

Sure and steady
Sets the pace
Sure and steady
Wins the race
Sure and steady
Overcomes haste
E-LIM-I-NA-TING
Needless waste.

Amyvonne Grogan

THE "WHY" OF CHRISTMAS

Some people don't believe
That Christmas can retrieve
All the memories of Love
All the blessings from above.

Why, just think! God sent His Son
To come down and dwell among
Poor folks of every race
Now, that's what I call Grace.

The miracles he performed
Thank God that He was born
I wish everyone knew "Why"
He came to Earth to live . . . and die!

In this commercializing world
The pace can leave you in a swirl
We spend one day with family and friends
Then, tomorrow, the Spirit ends.

But if we could just believe
That blessings of Love can be retrieved
By those to whom we would be true
Giving Peace and Joy the whole year through.

Desiré P. Grogan

METEMPSYCHOSIS

My eyesight is not as it should be
and my pulse is now quite faint.
I have trouble walking up the stairs
and my hands tremble when I paint.

My son-in-law called me this morning
and, oh, how I wish I was there.
A beautiful little baby was born
I wish we had that moment to share.

I told him to call if he wanted
and write whenever he could.
I felt guilty knowing I did not always
write when really I knew that I should.

Soon after my daughter went home
she had taken the time to write —
I read her words over and over and kept
her words under my pillow that night.

"His eyes are starting to focus, Dad,"
and she continued to say —
"His heartbeat gets stronger and stronger
with the passing of each day.

"One of my friends made the statement
that he looks a lot like you.
If only you could see him Dad
you would know that this is quite true."

I decided to write her a letter,
My letter began, "Dear Gwen,"
I wiped the tear that was on my face
and wrote, "Life is beginning again."

Patricia M. Stephens

THE SUBWAY

A million faces
Staring at me
Life is only
A maze, a sea

Try to make
This day of toil
Rushing, reeling
Through this world

Sifting and sorting
Trying for size
Did I do right
Was that wise

People are people
Wherever you go
The same old thing
No feeling, no show

I should speak out
Oh no! be calm
They really don't mean
To cause alarm

A sea of faces
Happy or sad
Life is not really
All that bad

Arise and go
Up from the ground
You are safe
No worry, a crown

Margaret J. Patterson

TAKE ME BACK

Take me back when days were young. A child's laughter in the sun.
Down a dusty road in the olden days, golden moments I can't forget.
Days of love but never tears. Drifting backwards through the years.
While a child dreams of his future, an old man dreams of his past.
Take me back to the good old days in the peaceful past,
Don't let me die in the frantic future.
So, take me back.

Alicha Martinez

ALICHA MARIE MARTINEZ. Born: Santa Ana, California, 2-6-71; Single; Education: Sophomore student; Poetry: 'America,' *American Poetry Anthology,* 1987; 'Old Age Shows No Mercy,' 'Take Me Back,' *Poetry of Life,* 1988; Comments: *When I write poetry I tend to write about life, of how I see it through the eyes of youth. I like to write seriously and express my feelings towards life. I hope my readers actually feel my poetry.*

NATURE'S MIRACLE

Whatever you wish to sing or say,
Perform it under a golden ray.
For you memories will last forever on,
And your jealousies will now be surprisingly gone.

Laura Geft

MY BUDDY IN POLICEMEN'S BLUE

Standing alone, something inside says, I'm scared . . .
When it hurts deep within, I begin to cry real tears . . .
I cared for my working buddy, dressed in his Policemen's Blue,
  shining brass buttons and how he wore his hat so well.
I cry when I think of those night shift stories he could tell.

Days, nights, he would walk proudly, as his duty, to the car in
  front . . . without fear . . .
My Buddy never thought of the danger so near.
I would tell him, "Be careful, be alert!"
Laughing, he would say, "Don't worry. I won't be hurt."
He never thought he walked with danger, in his Policemen's Blue . . .
Policeman badge shining as new, he believed everyone to be honest
  and true.

But, it didn't work that way, one fateful day . . .
Up there . . . I know he smiles at the ones he left behind . . .
Knowing my Buddy, he would say, "I reached the end of my lifeline."
I cared for my Buddy . . . dressed in his Policemen's Blue . . .
We always worked together . . . the whole shift through . . .
I begin to cry real tears . . . because I cared . . .

Marguerite G. Jones

IN THE MOONLIGHT WITH THE STARS PLAYING

The sun rays of light soon go dim and the evening
starts its slow and chilling course.
You and I alone in separate bedrooms, separate
places wishing, wishing one of us was there together.
Looking out my window, the light from the streetlamp
leaves shadows eerie and ironic, only invisible eyes
can detect movement in the shadows.
She is standing in her doorway, the moonlight outlining
her features, feasting gently over her body,
stimulating her to the quietness and the longingness
in her eyes.
Her eyes, my God! Her eyes light upon my person alone
and only alone, in private together in life alone to
ourselves in the moonlight with the stars playing.

Laura Gajdosik

UNEASE

How dare you be coy, when every fiber of my being screams
And yet your ploy would be accepted, could it be.
Alone I stood in fright and you enjoyed solace,
While you shared my plight with others and not me.
Yes there was suspicion but I could not prove a thing.
Unease without remission, followed me.
You ask, "What could I say?" And you will rationalize,
There is no other way that you could see.
And did I note contempt, as I reluctantly accepted,
Your half-amused attempt to baffle me.
To you its just a game and the total of my worth
Is diminished, in the name of shielding me.
For I cannot believe, in love without compassion
Nor mind and soul conceive all this for me.
You see I understand, and your motives are too clear.
I stepped too long to your command and now I see.

Theresa Strangi Mitchell

MY FRIEND

Today I learned of your Death my Friend
My tears did freely flow
To hear of it in such a way
dealt me a severe blow

You were so kind in life my Friend
to all who crossed your path
I know for sure, that God welcomed you with
arms that opened wide

No more you dream by the fires' hearth
No more you walk the beach
No more the toil of workaday life
Your goal you now have reached

Now, the grief and pain I feel
will take its time before I heal
from the loss of you my friend
My friend from the beginning and to the end

This life of yours is gone my Friend
It was not lived in vain
The happiness you gave to others
while on this earthly plane, will always be remembered
until we meet again.

Maureen B. Fuller

DADDY'S LITTLE GIRLS

Jessica & Alissa

I can't believe God gave you both to me.
I've loved you more than you've ever known.
You've made me proud as a Father could be,
I'll keep on lovin' you, even after you've grown.

I always dreamed of a family someday,
Not ever knowing you'd both come my way.
You've made my life worth living twice,
Having two little girls, sure is *nice*.

I used to sit and rock you to sleep,
Sing you songs, and a kiss on the cheek.
We'd dance to music, and play all day,
I love you both, what more can I say.

Even when, you both are grown,
I'll still be wishing you were home.
You're the best in this whole world,
And you'll always be, Daddy's little girls.

Jack Smith

MEMOIR

Oh! Comrades
  We're freedom doers
I look around
  Our world is full of miseries
My heart trembles
  Tears fill my eyes
Comrades are dying
  The wicked are rejoicing
They shall never relax —
Until we regain our right to sleep
  Comrades! We shall be free.

Omololu Sheriff Oketokun

GODCHILD

Her head feels light
And she cannot
keep from smiling
Her body feels
beautiful
He looks at her
with such love in his eyes
She cries
With love they created
a child
Visions and dreams
of their family
Does he want a son
Does she want a daughter
She could never choose
As she lies down
he kisses her
and gently places his hand
on their unborn blessing
She sleeps

Dianna Michelle

DESCRIPTION

Description!
What is a description?
But
I couldn't explain
the reason why
I tried to write
a photograph
but
I couldn't explain
the reason why
I tried
to write
a telegram
I cannot
write
a description
I cannot
tell
a lie

Mrs. Herbert Reeder

SOULS

Held by a cord
  just like a balloon
  our souls fly freely.
Our bodies
  their anchors
  provide the only shelter they need.
Above the rest of the world
  the soul sees through eyes of wisdom
  on a chain of thought leading to our bodies.
Of its many lives in the past
And of many to come in the future
We are to fly freely
  just like a balloon
  on our cord that leads us to Truth.

Angela M. Scattarelli

RAPE

I could not believe how you were nourished
  By sinister thoughts; I knew not
Your manhood grew and flourished.
  My heart burst with grief.
You were unsubdued and I was caught.
  I realize anger is but madness brief.

You shook my life from its stride
  And make me keep the golden rule;
  By giving in to flesh, you fool,
You took away my dignity, my pride
In myself, and started an endless tide
  Of guilt in me and hate for you.
  I think of my friend, your wife. How cruel!
How unfair for my soul to have died.

Dawn Kelly

ONLY YOU . . .

At the ailing of Grandmom Benko

Only you, Lord
Realize life's sorrows and grief
Move men's souls toward inner peace
Soothe one's mind with great release

Only you, Lord
Know what hearts have desired
Buttress your sheep when they grow tired
Instill a strength to be admired.

Only you, Lord
Should pass through two lovers' embrace
Guide our lives towards truth and grace
At a dateless time to behold! Your face.

Only you, Lord
Could design this master plan
Cast shadows over illusions of man
Frail shadows of paradise
Where time began . . .

Dr. Pamela Hall

WHAT ELSE BUT . . . SUNRISE

View from NJ/NY Conrail Line

Sitting at a train window
Before the break of dawn
Studying my own reflection in the glass
As the Ironhorse rambles on

Behind me, inside the train
Is light, and life, and warmth
Outside in the bleakest shadows
The day is not yet born

As moments evaporate
Into vapors of the past
The sun brings blue to a formless sky
And outlines of factories, black
Contrast

The daybreak, now, in splendor, Glory!
A brisk Fall day is made
As the images of life inside the train
And my own reflection fades.

Dr. Pamela Hall

THE ATTIC

I rush upstairs to the attic
Priceless treasures stored about.
In the trunk of my attic
Very fondly I caress,
The beautiful hat my mother wore
And hold it to my breast.
Old silver and china like gems I have stored,
Heirlooms all over the attic floor.
Quiet time to be alone
Reminiscing in the attic of my home.

Joy M. Parker

HOW MUCH DO THEY CARE?

Sitting on her steps at the close of day,
She carefully watched her children at play.
Pondering on things both here and there,
She wondered, ''How much do they care?''
Will they come home when they go away?
Will they write to me from day to day?
Do they know how they're wrapped up in my heart?
What hurt I will have when we're torn apart?
No, they can't know that 'til a farther day,
When their own dear children are going away.
Then God give them strength to let them go,
To make their own home filled with warmth and glow.

Myrtle Mitchell

LITTLE SISTER

My dear little sister, you're sixty today.
Let's go back through the years, if we may.
You were so tiny with eyes so blue,
We all fell in love right away with you.

You were coddled and petted by sisters three,
And loved by a brother to a high degree.
And Mother thought that none could compare
To her wee little girl with soft blonde hair.

Weighing twenty-five pounds at the age of five
We thought you the cutest girl alive.
Wearing a dress from a scrap of blue,
You looked like heaven with the sun shining through.

Your growing-up years were happy and gay,
To everyone you had kind things to say.
You had the honest square look of your dad
From the day you were just a wee little tad.

As life became more complex day by day
Your faith became deeper along the way;
You've been able to exemplify love and trust,
And making service for others a must.

So you've come to your last long years of rest,
Knowing you've always done your best.
By your children you'll be loved and caressed,
And by all others you'll forever be blessed.

Myrtle Mitchell

MYRTLE PRINCE MITCHELL. Born: Valley Mills, Texas, 12-29-1896; Died: 10-11-81; Education: Baylor University, Waco, Texas, B.A., 1941; Occupation: Public school teacher; Poetry: *Forget-Me-Nots of Love,* a collection of poems, 1978.

GOD, MY DIVINE HELPER ALWAYS

Behold, God is mine Helper (Psalms 54:4)

How it thrills my searching heart,
To find Thee here with me,
And to hear Thee say,
That Thou wilt be my Divine Helper Always.

God, as you know, I need Thy Help each day of my life,
I need Thy Help in all things great and small,
And, with Thee as my Divine Helper,
I know,
There will never be a river too deep for me to cross!
There will never be a mountain too high for me to climb!

Thy strength will help me to overcome any obstacle,
Thine Eyes will help me to see beyond the darkness
of despair and worry,
Thine Arms will help me,
Yes, Lord, all along the rough paths of confusion,
Yes, Thy Voice will help me,
With words of Comfort and Wisdom and Love.

O Lord,
How glorious to have Thee as my Divine Helper,
Always!

Janice Brown

YOU ARE THE REALITY OF MY DREAMS

If ever could be a time untouched by life itself;
It was that moment I realized with you how I felt.

You stepped into my life in the Autumn of my years;
Waltzing in like Spring, blooming with everything to share.

You brought with your confidence a new identity for me;
One, that at times, I do not feel deserving to be.

You are all the things I had dreamt of but never experienced myself;
And quite certain I would live to regret for never having felt;

I thought I was all there was to be;
Until you triggered a shadow from deep inside of me.

You are the entity of a dream, people dare to believe can be real;
Stepping forth out of the corners of my mind, allowing me to feel.

I am all the years that life has given to me;
Playing the parts as required by others to see.

With you there is no part for me;
For with you there is only me to be.

I need not portray a character you need to see;
For what I am and who you see is all I have to be.

For once in my life there is no chance I am taking;
For every moment spent with you I have lived my dreams in the awaking!

Bonnie Provenzano Antignani

WINDOWS IN OUR WORLD

A city window
Musty and gray
Each one representing
A slice of life
Unique unto itself
The windows are
Monstrously huge
And transparent
The life is veiled by
Microblinds
Which project a uniform façade
Try as you will
To peer through the glass
Yet the lifestyles inside
Remain dubiously masked

The City has so many windows

Dr. Pamela Hall

PAMELA ELIZABETH HALL. Born: Jacksonville, Florida, 9-10-57; Single; Education: Rutgers University, Rutgers College, B.A.; Pace University, New York City, M.A., Ph.D., Psychology; Occupation: Licensed psychologist, (NY/NJ); Memberships: American Psychological Association, New York Academy of Sciences; New York and New Jersey State Psychological Associations; Awards: Published in *Journal of Animal Learning and Behavior;* Poetry: 'A Woman in a Man's World,' 1985; 'Long Distance Loving,' 1982; 'Stability,' 1986; 'Wedding Day Jitters,' 1987; Other Writings: *The Psychological Effects of Divorce,* book, 1984, unpublished (currently being submitted for review); Themes: *Inner reflections on personal growth; self-development; interpersonal experiences and relationships; spiritual/inspirational; existential.*

MY LIFE HAS BEEN POETRY

With exemplary parents truly dear,
 A beautiful and loving beloved wife,
Four happy children, none without a peer,
 Living has been poetry all my life.
Parents, wife, and children more than Frank,
 An ordinary person, could expect,
Have made my life true poetry in rank
 Above my worth but which I must respect.

Dr. Frank E. Greene

SPACE — FRIENDS OR FOES?

They're out there, man, I'm sure they are.
But at this time they seem so far,
Yet if we knew the facts today
Maybe they're just a thought away.

These aliens could be friends or foes.
We cannot assume, as no one knows.
What will we do when the meeting comes
Open our hearts or fire guns?

Let's stop and think most carefully,
They could be just like you and me,
Which means they love and shed their tears
And live in hope, but have their fears.

That we, the aliens to them
Could be the cause of their mayhem.
Perhaps they'll come to us and teach
The things that now seem out of reach.

Just simple ways of living life,
Without the stress of wars and strife.
If that were so, the world could say
Thank God, at last we've found the way!

Mary Sheppard

TIME

Time, matter, space,
Relative to each other.
Yet each has its place
In this limitless space.
For time is ever — endless.

From time of birth to time spent on earth,
To some an eternity, to others a short span.
Time here is reckoned
To a split second.
For time is ever — endless.

The flowers, the trees,
Bloom and flourish.
The birds, the bees,
Live and nourish,
Only to die in time.
For time is ever — endless.

The clocks tick the minutes away,
Hour after hour,
Day by day on time.
For time is ever — endless.

Our earth, the planets, the sun,
Someday will be gone in time.
For time is ever — endless.

Ben Rubin

NIGHT WATCH

Suddenly awake was I . . .
A train, a cycle, or a cry?
So alert, I wondered why?

The rain had ceased.
All seemed at peace.
But slowly did my fear increase.

I raised my window open wide,
And breathed the fragrance from outside.

The full moon soft and silvery shone,
While spooky shadows crossed the lawn.

I saw the North Star's twinkling eye,
And saw the Big Bear standing by.

A sudden whistling loud and shrill!
I knelt so quiet, frozen still.

Then moving, but against my will,
I pushed the screen beyond the sill.

Below a dark form moved about.
So late, who would be walking out?

I watched his figure disappear
Across the lawn. Why did I fear?

But stealthily I moved . . . so still,
And pulled the window to the sill.

Then sliding quietly to bed,
I prayed, and soon the night was sped.

Winifred Murray

TOGETHER

Traveling down the hallways of life,
Go many a husband and his wife.

Some make detours along the way,
As from their mate they're wont to stray.

And some go on all through the years,
Sharing laughter, and yes, some tears.

Down the byways of life together they go,
Reaching and stretching they continue to grow.

Some have a family, and some perhaps none,
Together they play and make of work fun.

Making a home of a mansion, or hut,
Some have no pets, and some have a mutt.

Facing the storms of weather and strife,
Together they've gotten the best out of life.

Elizabeth Borselli

PARTING GRATITUDE

To Dr. "H"

My thought is this, as we disband:

If I could somehow make you understand
What your class-hour meant to me,
If I could write a Song of Gratitude
For viewpoints new I chanced to see, —

If you had known I felt unworthy
My unmade contributions seemed so meager,
If you had known my tongue, though mute,
Enslaved a spirit eager, —

If you could grasp my pathway glows
With the flame of keen determination,
My new-found torch, — "Creative Youth"
My source of inspiration, —

If you could come some autumn morn
To my studio room not far away,
My "vision" new you then might see, —
Perhaps you do, — I cannot say.

My thought amiss, please understand.

Edith Johnson

JOSEPH

In memory of Joseph Bernard, 1985-87

I was so shocked when I first saw you lying in your crib.
Even pictures of other children did not prepare me for you —
Those pictures had been of older children — not a baby.

I touched your hand and your small fingers gripped mine.
My heart opened and I loved you as I do other babies.
You laid your head on my shoulder, gripped my thumb and relaxed.
Your swollen eyes gazed into mine.

You were too weak and had been too sick during your short life so
You could not move like most eight-month-olds
But you turned from side to side and your bright eyes
   did not miss a thing.
You grasped your rattles and shook them.
You reached for the mobile above your bed.
You pushed my hands away when I suctioned your tracheostomy
And cried in silent frustration when I completed the task.

When your mother came home you smiled in your odd way and wiggled
And reached your hands to her.

No longer did I see your handicaps. To me you were a loving baby.

Diann Foster

COME AND SOAR

Could you see the beauty of a clear, blue sky,
if you never had to go through a storm?
If you never had to spend a night out in the cold,
how could you then appreciate the warm?
Would a rose ever seem so delicate and sweet,
if it weren't for the harshness of a thorn?
When you're feeling all alone in the cold, dark night,
don't you anticipate the bright, new morn?
So, then it is in life from time to time, My child,
sometimes it's hard for you to just believe.
But, didn't I tell you that I was by your side,
and don't you know that I would never leave?
Above the darkest storm, the sun still shines crystal clear;
the darkest hour is just before the dawn.
Come and soar with Me, above the clouds,
and I will hold you near,
take My hand, and you'll never be alone.

Wanda Drew

I WILL TRUST IN THEE

What time I am afraid, I will trust in Thee.
I praise Your word,
I will not fear,
what flesh can do to me.

As long as I have Jesus, I am never alone.
I call His name,
He comes to me,
and all my fears are gone.

He's given me a promise, one that I have proved.
He is my Rock,
my Salvation,
I shall not be moved.

Though trials come along my path, they won't conquer me.
I lift my hands,
and then I sing,
my song of victory.

What time I am afraid, I will trust in Thee.
I praise Your word,
I will not fear,
what flesh can do to me.

Wanda Drew

IF I COULD SEE

If I could see you, through the eyes of God,
I wouldn't see your face.
I would see the center of your heart,
the secret, hidden place.
Would I see an alter, to praise your Lord,
compassion for your brother,
would I see tears shed for the widow,
a helping hand to another?
Would I see your footsteps, straight and strong,
along the path you trod?
Would you be ashamed, if I could see,
You, through the eyes of God?

Wanda Drew

A PARENT

I am a Parent, and because so many people keep asking us
''Ungrateful Parents'' what we need,
I finally found an answer that I believe says everything.
I am a parent and this is what I need,
I need time to be alone . . . alone with my thoughts,
I need to be accepted for who I am,
I need to be loved by those who share my life with me,
I need a home that is rich in Love, Sharing and Caring.
I need to be heard sometimes . . . I just might have something
   to say that you need to hear,
I need to know more about myself . . . my feelings . . .
   my desires . . . my goals,
I need to know communication . . . so that the problems I have to
   face can be worked out.
I need to live my life one day at a time;
For only then will us ''Ungrateful Parents'' know
   that it is being fulfilled.
And, as I would live my life for you, so would I ask you to
   live your life for me.

Wanda L. Bell

MY BURNING TEARS

When I saw you yesterday I shed some burning tears
I remembered how it was, back, not so many years.
We had vowed to each other our deep, undying love.
I'd have given you anything, like the moon and stars above.
But you dreamed your dreams too fast and set your hopes too high.
And when you said ''We are through,'' I thought I'd surely die.
You said you had found another. He'd give you everything.
All I had to offer was just what life would bring.
But we cannot dwell upon the past when it's over and it's done.
We can only cherish the moments of happiness and fun.
You've gone your way and I've gone mine, never again to meet.
Except, perhaps, occasionally along life's busy street.
I wish nothing but the best for you in your remaining years.
And I'll walk alone in sorrow, and shed my burning tears.

Kenneth G. Rose

MOMENTS

The beauty of life is to seek by its living.
Our cares, fears, worries, disappointments,
And all the joys.
Yet we seek for even more.
We learn to face reality;
Trying to make this life a better place to be.
We search beyond reality —
Reasoning.
Asking always the question as to why;
Do we have the right?
For if we knew all the answers,
What knowledge could we seek of ourselves.
A heart full of memories;
Some to recapture, others only traces.
A pattern only once —
Each an original, authentic, unique.
Love that faded with the coming of its season;
Leaving only remembrance and wisdom of its passing.
Molded before the beginning;
To reshape after the past.

Ruby Pauline Cherry

MY PRAYER

At Thy feet, O Gentle Master, let me rest my wearisome load.
By Thy side, O Heavenly Father, let me tread that long, long road.
In Thy hands, for Thy forgiveness let me place my sin-filled life.
In Thy arms that Thou might keep me always safe from harm and strife.

Watch o'er me lest I wander in my own willful way.
Watch o'er me, Heavenly Father, keep me from sin's dread sway.
Let me dwell with Thee Forever.
Let me walk in Thy bright light.
Let me fear not Hell's damnation
Or fear not the black of night.

Thy rod and staff, they comfort me.
My cup You have runneth o'er.
Let me dwell with You forever,
Lord, keep me safe forevermore.

I pray I may be worthy to kneel there at Thy feet
To be with You forever when my life on earth is complete.

Dolores M. Mann

BELOVED

As the rose must die to bloom anew, also then must he.
Eyes closed in death, to open again a brighter world to see.
Life's heavy burden cast aside, his steps become much lighter.
The furrowed brows of stress are gone,
   his pathway appears much brighter.

The Heavenly Host is there on high and bids him come inside,
To a more spacious home than he's ever known;
   Heaven's gates are opened wide.
He has gone ahead to prepare a place where again we all may meet,
Where we will laugh, sing, and dance with joy;
   and worship at God's great feet.

He asks that we not cry for him and bids us feel no sadness,
He's playing there in Heaven's band those songs of joy and gladness.
So mourn no more for that dear one; of our eternal love, he knows.
Have faith, give thanks, be happy now,
   for he blooms there like that rose.

Dolores M. Mann

OUR 60TH ANNIVERSARY

My dear, some sixty years have passed
Where did they go so fast?
Seems only yesterday when of your love I asked.
You gave me all,
Summer, spring and fall.
You gave me all.
Four children blessed our lives
And made us love the more,
And made our lives forevermore.
A bond united us as one.
Summer, spring and fall,
You gave me all.
You gave me all.
My dear, I brush away a tear
Not of sadness, but of joy supreme.
The years complete and full.
Summer, spring, and fall,
You gave me all.
You gave me all.

David James Platt

A PART OF ME

Dedicated to my sister,
Carol Beebe Strite

My sister is a part of me,
Of that I'm not mistaken.
She gave me a new kidney
When both of mine were taken.
I didn't ask — she was there to offer,
It wasn't a question of now or later.
She gave the best she had to give;
She gave me a new life to live.
Now my sister is a part of me,
And, with much love, she will always be!

Delva L. Wolfe

CHILDISH BEHAVIOR

Roughly Bonnie yanked this tiny flower
   root and all
      from reddish-brown clay
then hastily pressed
   its golden head
      against her youthful cheek
before abruptly thrusting it aside
   and so it lay
      the stem broken
limp upon the newly mown grass
   before she ran into the house
      to fetch her favorite doll

Ridgely Lytle

FOOTPRINTS OF TIME

As I walked the beach one beautiful night
Listening to the sound of the waves
   Washing ashore
I wish with my life I had done so
   Much more
The happiness I so enjoyed — the sadness
   I so prolonged
I wasted too much time thinking of
   The things I didn't have
Instead of the things I had —
   For which I should have been glad
I look up at the stars — seeing
   Beauty in that darkness
And again listening to the waves
   Washing upon the shore
Knowing my footprints will soon be
   Washed away
Once again I know I should have taken
   Each day — day by day

Peggy Coburn Mathison

THAT AWFUL NOTE
IN FIRST GRADE

My teacher called me to her.
She'd found my awful note.
Reluctantly responding,
I thought on what I'd wrote.
Then how she brought my grandeur down
as I approached her desk.
She held the note before me
I cried and clutched my gown.
She put her arm around me
Forgave without a frown.

Ruth E. Beckwith

THE WORLD HAS
SET YOU FREE

To my beloved Frank

Two lives came to an end, my dear,
   The day you peacefully died;
You on your bed of linen white,
   I standing by your side.

You closed your eyes and saw naught here,
   Life's journey at an end;
Your gaze fixed on Eternity;
   What visions at the bend!

Your Maker welcomed you with joy;
   Though I saw none of this,
I saw the glow etched on your face;
   A rising surge of bliss!

Though all of me has gone with you,
   Selfish I must not be;
Your joys are now eternal joys;
   The world has set you free!

Louise Pannullo-Parnofiello

WHEN THE CLEAR CAN
BE SEEN FOREVER

Happy New Year
My dear friend
Please stay, don't go
Please go, don't stay

You tempt me with your love
All reasons being wrong
I am not your only lover
There are far too many others

All sense of logic leaves me
While in your ever presence
Hazy memories — fading to black
Remain after you have gone

You are a seducer and a temptor
You wreak havoc in my life
But somehow make it bearable
Until the next time

Be gone, Bitter Spirit!
Forget you ever knew me
Our party is over
And it is now time to leave

Joanne Erickson

HEADLINES

Necrophobia taps my shoulder.
tap after tap after tap after tap
Must keep myself distracted,
busily . . . I avoid disorder.

Still —

"Headlines" "Headlines"
Slap my brain onto frequent waves . . .
Zap my eyes into newsstand craze:

   ANDY WARHOL DEAD
   HOSPITAL TO BLAME?

"Headlines"
Sad mortality claims
immortal personage.
Something's wrong when righteous dies —
pages upon page upon GERALDINE PAGE

"Headlines" "Headlines"
So much we have to do . . .
"Deadlines" "Deadlines"
Tomorrow's show is through.

   the pulse of . . .
   Ian Russell Ayers

IAN RUSSELL AYRES. *"Shot by Roy Schatt. New York City. October 31, 1986. A photic shadow session."*

THE THREAD

To Elizabeth Browning, Keats,
Shakespeare, and the masters.

  See how it spans, the golden thread,
span in the annals of history
spotless like snow. Here the birds thread
lightly when they fly from place
to place, and carry with them
memories of sweet aroma.
The roots of the thread can be traced
to the rubber trees. How then
was this golden thread weaved?
The weaver was careful weaving it
until it reached its artistic perfection
and he occasionally stole glances
which amused the stars of the sky.
  It is this golden thread that binds
and inspires us to weave and produce
some of the finest artistic and lovely
expressions of our day.

Apostle J. P. K. Appiah, Jr.

ODE ON SOLITUDE

Happy the man whose wish and care
  A few paternal acres bound,
Content to breathe his native air,
          In his own ground.

Whose herds with milk, whose fields with bread,
  Whose flocks supply him with attire,
Whose trees in summer yield him shade,
          In winter fire.

Blest, who can unconcernedly find
  Hours, days, and years slide soft away,
In health of body, peace of mind,
          Quiet by day,

Sound sleep by night; study and ease,
  Together mixed; sweet recreation;
And innocence, which most does please
          With meditation.

Thus let me live, unseen, unknown;
  Thus unlamented let me die;
Steal from the world, and not a stone
          Tell where I lie.

Alexander Pope

IN REMEMBRANCE OF A TOUGH GUY

A tough guy doesn't care about anything, it seems.
He lives his own way, he creates his own dreams.
He doesn't reach out, he doesn't care.
When you're near him, you'd better beware.

He just shoves and pushes,
He doesn't hear you, he does what he wishes.
He must have it his way, for there's no other.
No one gets in his way, not even a brother.

A tough guy, does that describe him?
Or does he hide behind that steel armor, he calls skin.
Afraid that someone might see,
That inside he's just like you and me.

He can be hurt much more than most.
He can be touched by a small tiny tear,
And he'll hesitate when he comes up against fear.
Silently he knows God's there above,
And he'll fall apart when he's faced with true love.

He still roams today, that forgotten man from the fifties.
Still demanding his way, his mind full of memories
As he walks tall, alone through the eighties.

Izella Jean Morlan

ALONE

As I mourn on this barren island
A mystic fog, heavy and damp rolls in along the skyland
Frightened and restless I keep alert as to what evolves around me
The crying sea gulls, the foreboding sounds, and the whitecaps
  on the sea
Minute by minute the day enhances forth
Steadily the darkness thickens when I hear a disturbance far
  out from the north
Lonely and hopeless I pray only of home
But as I face this incident that has occurred I realize now
  and forever I shall remain Alone

Bethann Covone

BEST FRIENDS ALWAYS

Dedicated to my best friend, Gerald Duval

With hatred being the trend,
It's hard to find a good friend.
But I knew we'd be best friends always.

People think that it's incredible
That we're so inseparable.
They say we'll be best friends always.

Helping each other follow our dreams,
We have become the two-man team.
Together we're best friends always.

We have created a special bond.
You're someone I can really count on.
Through time we're best friends always.

Our friendship has remained strong
During all the adventures we've been through.
Our friendship means a lot to me
And I know it means a lot to you.

If we part from the fate of time,
You will always be kept in my mind.
Remember us forever as best friends always.

Shawn Killackey

SHAWN PATRICK KILLACKEY. Born: Pittsfield, Massachusetts, 8-11-65; Education: Berkshire Community College, Westfield State College, A.A., B.A. degrees in Fine Arts; Occupation: Commercial artist; Poetry: 'This Quest,' *American Poetry Anthology,* 1987; Comments: *In my poetry, I like to write about the events that are going on in my life; romance, friendships, or the different feelings that are stirring around inside of me.*

DESPERATE HEART

Lonely tears fall, but that's all right.
I can cry another night.
It doesn't matter who's been right or wrong.
I was the weak one, you were the strong.
You played on my emotions, and built me up for love.
And made me really believe your love was from above.
Now, I'm just a lonely desperate heart, you see.
Crying out for you, to please come back to me.
I need your love so desperately, I don't know what to do.
I hope and pray someday that you will love me too.
But desperation shows no pity.
I'm just a desperate heart in this big city.

Barbara Wirkowski

TRANSCENDING SEPARATENESS

Among us are those who have
   crystallized joy
As well as those with feelings
   vitalized by spirit
Keepers of the mind send out
   the cool breezes of intellect's
   discrimination
And our dwellings are watched over
   by workers mighty or humble
Those who by love overtake
   truth within
Bind us all together, transcending
   separateness,
By capturing truth beyond.

Wilson Reid Ogg

WILSON REID OGG. Born: Alhambra, California, 2-26-28; Single; Education: University of California, Berkeley, B.A., 1949; LL.B., J.D., 1952; Honorary Cultural Doctorate in the Philosophy of Law, World University, Roundtable, 1984; Occupations: Poet, Curator, Retired lawyer, Educator, Real estate executive; Memberships: World Literary Academy; Deputy Governor, ABIRA; Deputy Directory General, International Biographical Centre; Life Patron, BC; World Future Society, The Ina Coolbreth Circle; World Academy of Arts and Culture, Inc.; Awards: Second Prize Winner, 12-85, Literary Competition, World Institute of Achievement, for the poem 'My Escaping Self'; Second Prize Winner, 1-87, Literary Competition, World Institute of Achievement, for the poem 'The Summer Solstice'; Poetry: 'Interlude,' 'To Touch With Love,' *IBC Magazine,* Winter 1985; 'The Canopy of Love,' *The Ecphorizer,* 12-85; 'The Mystery of Love,' *The Ecphorizer,* 1-86; 'Tending to My Garden,' 'Our Shared Love,' newsletters, World Institute of Achievement, 6-86; 'Springtide,' 'Bitter Harvest,' 'Lost Innocence,' newletters, World Institute of Achievement, 11-85; 'Plunder Unearned,' 'Beauty,' 'Our Love Refreshed,' *VIDUA,* 9-86; 'When We Are One,' 'Our Love is One with Us,' *IBC Magazine,* Summer, 1986; 'Your Integrity Is One,' *American Poetry Anthology, Vol. VI, No. 5,* 1986; Comments: *My poetry combines analytical, romantic, and mysterious aspects of myself and nature. I find that only in poetry am I enabled to express meaningfully these contrasting aspects.*

FALLING STAR

*Dedicated to the memory of
Donald Joseph Ribeiro,
8-1-49—11-26-81,
A truly good man!*

I stare up into the ebony nothingness
on a cool autumn evening.
In the east, I see one small star.
Its light was so strong, it lit up
the night for miles.
In the west, I see a small dimly-lit star.
It approaches at a fast rate of speed
and a drunken manner.
I stare in horror
as the two stars collide.
The dim one staggers and fades.
The bright one falls to the earth.

Tears stream down many cheeks.
The world has lost a good man.

Lewis Fram

WHO CAN MATCH YOUR LOVE?

*Dedicated to: God
(Father, Son, Holy Spirit).*

I look out the windows of
my mind, and see visions
of your presence in all
I see.

Birds that fly so free,
Stars that shine so bright,
A seed that bursts into a tree,
A universe that knows no height.

Oh glorious Lord above,
So gracious like a dove.
Oh my glorious God above,
Who can match your gracious Love?

Giving life to all, spring,
Summer, winter, fall. And
like each passing season,
You even gave man a reason.

Taking him from being a sinner,
And making him a righteous winner.
Tell me, Who can match this love
from our glorious God above?

Michael A. Porter

LAVISHED

Each day I am becoming more aware
   of His Presence,
   and I am knowing
   that He is inside me,
   and not just way up there above.

Like candle wax — warm and mellow —
   and almost to the point of flowing,
   I am enveloped,
   as He lavishes me with love.

Julia Jones

FRIENDS ARE FOREVER

*Dedicated to: God,
friendship & my friends*

A friend will always care,
a friend will always share.
So remember, this friend
will always be there.

In a time of joy, in a
time of pain. Through
thick and thin, through
snow and rain.

Friends are forever, in
good and bad weather.
Friends always care, even
when the other isn't there.

A true friend will stand
by you, even when you've
done them wrong, that's
what makes this love strong.

So when you make a friend,
stand by them till the end.
Give them the gift of love,
something special from God above . . .

Michael A. Porter

DIMINISH ME

*News Item: Population Clock
in Smithsonian passes five
billion mark.*

   Diminish me
By some man's death? Hardly, but they
   Diminish me
By birth. Vast crowds will finish me
Those many islands made of clay
That clog the human sea each day
   Diminish me.

Joseph E. Barrett

EMPTY HOUSE

Empty house, and I know the reason why,
   you're not here to say hello or goodbye.
So many things to do,
   how can I think of anything else,
   seems I'm always thinking of you.
I try to be true, can't you see,
   pretty women make a fool out of me.
I want you back again,
   you will be my only lover
   and not just a friend.
I don't want an empty house,
   say you'll forgive a fool
   that has broken every rule.

Robert L. Willyard

EIGHTY FOUR SEASONS OF LOVE

As sure as the bright colored leaves
appear in the Fall.
As sure as God's earth shimmers in white each Winter,
turns to silky green each Spring.

As sure as the sun and rain
flow down from the sky.
Giving birth in living color,
as Spring changes over to Summer.

As sure as the seasons of time have come and gone,
the memory of our first kiss lingers on.
Twenty-one years have come and passed,
telling us our love will last.

Eighty-four good reasons,
tells my heart.
To love you, for another,
Eighty-four Seasons.

Izella Jean Morlan

COUNT YOUR BLESSINGS

We go through life each day
Never expecting tragedy to strike.
But there's no way of knowing
Just what our destinations are.
Through sheer experience we learn
To appreciate a duo combination
That we have available to us.
We have our wonderful God,
Who works true miracles in our lives,
Guiding us each day.
And we should never forget our admirable medical profession;
That is capable of its own wonders.
Facing real possibilities of losing someone dear
Makes us think.
Finally realizing just how much
We have to be thankful for,
Each and every day,
And whom we have to thank for it all.

Judy Johnson

WE ARE ALL SAILORS

During life we sail the coastline of this earth's reality,
the three-dimensional, concrete, touchable world.
We use its presence as a guide to navigate by,
and even take refuge in its harbors from the storms
which occur at sea.
But eventually we lose this coastline, and must
learn to navigate by the stars.
Perhaps we'd do well to note the correlation between
the two *now*, before the chance is gone, and
we must journey on the open sea,
alone.

David Emrich

SONG OF LOVE

You are aware, listen and hear.
That you are special! Near and dear.
To beloved is beautiful adorned in this
world to come.
Calmly I once searched for you in places to and from.
Casting my eyes down to abandon lust.
Our love based on trust, no one else only us.
Many come even their chief.
During darkness just like a thief.
Trying to destroy us with deceit.
Offering nothing declaring us grief.
Two hearts are we our belief.
Holding tightly cuddling like doves.
Having each other a blessing of love.

Judith St. Vic

A GIFT OF LOVE

One day, despite the snow and drift, I sought for you
a Christmas gift,
To somehow tell you just how true is my eternal love for you.

I hurried through the downtown Mall. The gifts were all
too large, too small.
I stumbled in and out the stores until the merchants
closed their doors.

I shuffled up and down the street, a hostage to my blistered feet.
My thoughts from here to there would shift, still searching for
the perfect gift.

For days I searched the village through, so wild to prove
my love for you.
Asleep, awake, I sought in vain, a gift that would
my love proclaim.

Then one day, quickly I perceived, my love, conveyed and so received,
Alone, unaided, knowing how, had surely found you long ere now.

My love, sustained and set apart, is locked forever in your heart.

Eugene Poulter

OH LET ME SPEAK

Sweet Muse, unloose the bands that bind my inarticulate tongue.
Oh let the restless rivers of my angry passions run.
Don't let the dead past pall the poet in this triumphant hour;
Nor parch the hand now pregnant with premeditated power.
Oh hush no more the rising tide of sound that strides the shore;
Nor quench the flame that lights the way where darkness
reigned before.
Let not the pen betray the penman's unprolific past,
But sound the trumpet, trumpeter, thine hour is come at last.
Now tune thine ear to those sweet lyrics he created best;
No more suppress the rising pulse that trembles in his breast.
See how the conquering hero comes with banners all unfurled.
Oh let his cry of victory be heard around the world!
For me no deathless grave, no farewell ballads left unsung.
Oh hear sweet Muse and heed the cry of my importunate tongue.

Eugene Poulter

TO BELIEVE

To become is to

believe.

To believe is to

achieve.

The things we find

most difficult to do,

Are found only in the mind.

For all it takes

is

you!

Rita M. Sutherby

I SEE THE RAINBOW,
YOU SEE THE GOLD

You and I have different lives
We have different things we despise
I look at the stars in the skies
You and I have different lives

I see the rainbow, you see the gold
I rebel, you do what you're told
You live your dreams, mine I still hold
I see the rainbow, you see the gold

You walk on the ground, I float in the air
You are concerned, I don't care
I've been selfish, while you share
You walk on the ground, I float in the air

I'm not you and you're not me
We both have different things we see
But Tracy, my sister, sweet and lovely
Don't ever forget that I love thee

Jessica Ann Hammer

THANK GOD FOR YOUR
BLESSINGS

Take a special day
to thank the Lord,
Your God, for all
the things He has given us.
With all the help
God has given us.
Where we may understand
the way we should
love and help out fellowmen
to understand the love
of Jesus Christ, who came to
this earth that we would be
saved from our sins.
God so loved us all that
He gave His only son
that we would be saved
from our sins.
Delight thyself
with the love
of God!

Zora B. Fetner

AUTUMN PEACE

All around me,
autumn maples.
All around me,
peace.

In the distance,
''Jesus Loves Me,''
and His love
is pealed.

All around me,
mighty oak trees.
All around me,
peace.

In the distance,
''Jesus Loves Me.''
In my heart,
I kneel.

Anne L. Emory

TEARDROPS ON
THE WINDSHIELD

There were teardrops on my windshield
as I drove home that night.
That lonely night,
my first night alone.
Without my husband,
who's never coming home.
They buried him today,
late this afternoon.
I've been there with him,
since late this afternoon.
But I'm going home now,
and I cannot cry.
Yet this night brought the rain,
so my windshield could cry —
Instead of I.

Mariah Lace

FOREVER

Loneliness comes
when you lose a friend
or a lover
Who helped you through your bad —
and sometimes good
times.

Why do we feel these things
as they happen —
but say nothing —

until they're gone . . .

forever?

Mary Prinzo

BORN OF GOD

The color of love is many,
six to be exact;
Violet, indigo, blue, yellow, orange, and red,
each with its own impact.

Violet, indigo, and blue are related,
belong to the royal class;
Each with a spiritual feeling,
that which is found in the Mass.

Yellow, orange, and red relate to sunshine,
the rising and setting of the sun,
Days that begin and end with promise,
a pledge to everyone.

Love is a beautiful rainbow,
a veritable divining-rod,
For we find at rainbow's end,
a true love born of God.

Luke N. Baxter

LUKE NATHANIEL BAXTER. Born: Van Buren, Arkansas, 9-12-15; Education: High school, 1933; Occupations: Poet, Painter, retired; Awards: Golden Poet Awards, 1985, 1986, 1987; Poetry: 'Best,' *American Poetry Anthology,* 1984; 'Education,' *The Art of Poetry,* 1985; 'First Love,' *Hearts on Fire, Vol. II,* 1985; 'Two Sides,' *Best New Poets of 1986;* 'A Time For Celebration,' *Words of Praise, Vol. III,* 1987; Themes: *Life! Its tragedy, triumph, ecstasy, sorrow.*

INNER VOICE

Whispers are heard with a
soft, gentle sound;
while shouts — or screams — are heard
blaring, screeching
into all ears.
Therefore, the inner voice — a voice heard
by *all* —
—*not by blaring,*
not by whispering,

but by
the expressions
we make
unintentionally.

Mary Prinzo

TO A WILD ROSE

I saw a wild, wayward rose in nature's verdant, emerald hair;
  A lovely form in pensive pose, presiding in that garden fair.
Perfection from the hand of God, a Venus blooming in the sod.
  So like a lovely, regal queen, clothed in her robes of velvet red.
I saw her there as in a dream, her perfume floating to my head.
  Her beauty flashed upon my sight like moonlight
  in the dark of night.
If I was drunk I could not tell. She scattered my defenses.
  Day after day she cast her spell upon my failing senses.
Her grace and beauty I could not deny. I was enslaved; I knew not why.
  I plucked her for my own to keep, forgetting that her life was cheap
Without so much as light or air, the essence of a life so fair.
  And so the flower pined for sun, her petals fading one by one;
Until at last she drooped and died and left protesting thorns
within my side;
  Her final, fainting breath a plea to once more rest upon
  her native lee.
    I saw a wild rose in nature's care.
      Ah, would that I had left her blooming there.

Eugene Poulter

I WALK ALONE

We began the journey down the long narrow road together.
To find happiness was our destiny.
I a few feet in front him never looking back, for I knew
that our love was so strong, that he would always be there.
As we walked and walked, I suddenly felt a cold breeze upon my back,
as though I was alone and without shelter.
I continued to walk trying to dismiss this annoying feeling,
yet the more I walked the more I felt the breeze.
I stopped, thinking to myself that it was silly to suspect
that if I turned around he would not be there,
yet as I turned I found that it was not silly at all,
for he had turned off somewhere along the way without signaling,
and all that was there,
was the long empty narrow road we had traveled together.
As I stood in the middle of the road,
I was faced with the decision of which path to follow.
To the right was the path for which we began,
and whose destiny I knew.
To the left was the path of unknown destiny.
I turned and continued down the unknown path in search of happiness,
never again looking back.

Andrea Landrum

IN THIS TIME OF SORROW

In this time of sorrow, the tunnel always seems the darkest.
You must put faith in the Heavenly Father as He has put faith in you
And only then will a ray of light come shining through.

Think not of it as the end of a life,
But the rebirth, a new beginning.

You must go forth in life,
For life is too short to stay where you are.

Grieve if you must, but don't grieve long,
For it has been placed in God's trust.

He has served His purpose on earth and has gone to serve
even a greater purpose,
Thy Father who art in heaven.

If there is love for Him in your heart,
Then of your life He shall always be a part.

Andrea Landrum

THE WINDS OF SUMMER

What do the winds of summer tell?
Happiness to my soul contemplating Beauty,
In a moment of life at summer night,
After the heat of day dissipates itself,
The cool air murmers to swaying leaves of trees.

A moment of meditation spells Eternity,
When my soul attains togetherness with Nature's Beauty,
The winds of summer night coincide,
With the harmonious air free of strife,
Then thoughts of peace and love prevail.

Meditation for peace brings happiness to my soul,
Happiness springs from the heart,
One truth the mind can safely tell,
Like a brother to the heart at peace:
''There is harmony in a breezy summer night.''

The loveliness of life returns on a summer night,
With the leaves of trees swaying gently to the wind,
The heart and mind attune themselves like twins,
To the harmony of Nature's whispering wind,
Then my soul is happy forever.

Rolando L. Boquecosa

A DELICATE BALANCE

Happiness returns to my mind and soul,
By remembering collegiate days and subjects.

My Bachelor of Arts degree is valuable,
Encompassing disparate subjects under the sun.

There is harmony of mind and heart,
A delicate balance achieved by Intellect.

My mind expands, my heart blossoms,
For things visible and invisible.

My heart beats for the glory of the flowers,
The swift flight of fireflies and butterflies.

My eyes had been the sparkle of a diamond,
In brilliant and changing colors reflecting sunlight.

My mind goes back to God who made the earth,
From where the diamond was completed to perfection.

My eyes had seen invisible specimen under a microscope,
A different world God has also made.

All Beauty God has made for men to study,
A delicate balance for mind and heart.

My soul appreciates the visible and intangible,
A harmony of Beauty only God can make.

Rolando L. Boquecosa

SUMMER AND FALL OF '82

Summer and Fall of '82
There wasn't much I didn't do.
He took me out partying to all kinds of places.
He even took me to drag races.
We went for walks in all kinds of weather.
We had nice talks, when we were alone together.
We're not with each other at this time.
But he'll always be in my heart and on my mind.

Kathy Bonito

40 AND PREGNANT

As the ball turned slowly blue
I could only sit and stare
A tear crept slowly down my cheek,
Somehow it wasn't fair.

I thought for a while about the future
As I said good-bye to a plan
But then my mind began to picture
A son who grows to be a man.

The joy slowly began to grow
As I thought of family, friends and fun
I could see the looks of their faces
When I finally had a son.

And now as the day grows close
And I wonder if I'm right
A son would be a grand thing
But a girl would be all right.

As I picture a day without babes
Or a smile for me he'd grant
With joy I soon begin to see
I'd rather be 40 and pregnant.

Sandra S. Oidtman

DO YOU BELIEVE
IN SANTA CLAUS?

Do you believe in miracles
Or are you just a hopeless cause
Have you ever seen the Land of Oz
Do you believe in Santa Claus

Do you believe in fairy tales
In your heart the magic dwells
Have you ever heard the Christmas bells
Or tossed pennies into wishing wells

Do you believe in fantasies
The wonderment within ourselves
Do you believe in little elves
Who live in forests by themselves

Do you believe in magic things
Like riding carpets through the sky
Do you believe that reindeer fly
Or must you know the how and why

Do you believe in Santa Claus
Without a reason just because

Robert James, Jr.

Across my aching soul
You've lain yourself
As a salve.

Opening my mind's eye
Awakened to the brilliance
The flowing beauty
Within us.

Gina Cestaro

GAUGIN, MATISSE,
CÉZANNE, MONET

On my canvas I create a world
Which I control and not it me.
A safe harbor, a quiet pasture,
A floral fantasy.
My pencil doesn't me betray.
Mistakes conveniently melt away.
If life could only be this way
Artists we all would be.

It doesn't hurt to run away.
Gaugin, Matisse, Cézanne, Monet
They all did it.
With their hands they found the way
To substitute for pain some play
And somehow in the doing they
Enriched our world beyond compare
By putting paint to canvas.

Ess Jay Nolan

PARIS LOVE

*Dedicated to my love
in the black coat
at the souvenir shop
along the Seine . . .
Pierre mon amour*

Where forth go you?
To be near my love
Across the ocean to the Seine
For there, I know my love waits
Silently and gently
Manly and distinct
Full of opulence and wit
Joy to my unknown eyes
Destiny awaits me
Smiles for my life with you
Finally caught in a web of glory
And ecstasy
I pray that your love
For me will always last
To where forth go I?
To the Seine and Paris
*Bonjour, c'est amour
Mon cherie, mon amour*

B. Devi

GOD'S GIFT

Ten tiny fingers
And ten tiny toes,
A little round face
And a cute little nose;
They belong to a babe,
Six pounds-three and one half
Named Steven Charles
Who made his debut
On June fifteenth,
The year eighty-seven,
At nineteen inches
He's not very tall,
But this little babe
Will be loved by all.
God Bless Him.

Lillian DeKeno

THE DIVORCE

The sands of time crumble away
beneath your feet.
You watch its setting suns
and rising moons meet.
Together in eternity they exist
one for each other,
Yet you feel their loneliness
for never touching one another.
They pass each other, revolving away
to the darkness again.
You reach to give them comfort,
but jerk away when you feel their pain.
You say you're sorry and a tear
of guilt fills your eye
As you walk away, knowing
that on you they can't rely.

Susan Anna Zell

BEAUTY IN THE EYE
OF THE BEHOLDER

Can you tell me where it's written,
Tell me where the rules must be,
To behold those things of beauty,
One must have eyes to see?

My fingers touch the velvety rose
And smell its fragrance rare.
I walk beneath the blossoming trees
While bird songs fill the air.

I sit beside the rippling brook,
Willows nodding in the breeze.
I taste the brackish, salty spray
Windswept from across the seas.

I hear the happy children play.
I hear the choir sing.
I hear the first drops of rain
Singing nature's hymn to Spring.

I thank you God, that I may have
These beauties to enjoy.
You've given me so very much,
With other senses to employ.

Dolores M. Mann

HEAR THE CRY
FROM DEEP WITHIN

My eyes are blind and it's
hard for me to find, when you're too kind

My ears are deaf, and my
heart was taken by theft

My mind is clear, but for
me to hear the cries of my
stronger inner emotions are fears

My arms, extended, cry out
in search of an
embracing acknowledgment
of my cry for *freedom!*

Melissa Belanger

A VAN DYCK pinx.   W. FRENCH sc.

INDIANA SUMMER
(On the Banks
of the Brandywine)

Dedicated to: J.W. White,
J.W. Whyte, Sr., J.W. Whyte, Jr.,
J. 'Dick' White, and
M.E. Starkweather

Hopscotch
  Along the rocks
Skimming at higher
  Velocities

We have come here to
  Create
Our own Summer Thing
  Zeroing in on

Yesterday's Visions
  Holding on &
Then letting go
  As we glide

With easiness
  into a free . . .
    ¡fall!

Earl M. (Suleiman) White

REASON

The fundamental cause of reason,
  Is man's rational nature.
    As he tries to unravel the problems,
He becomes articulate and sensory.

His sensory perceptions give him
  Ideas which become knowledge,
    All experience is based on senses,
Ideology is a form of sense perception.

I cannot form ideas before reason,
  Only rational truth is binding.
    All reason is a result of thought,
Understanding of man is intellectual.

His ideas are based on facts,
  Then he uses reason.
    The fatalist depends on chance,
Therefore, he is the opposite of reason.

The creditability of an object,
  Is to test its usefulness.
    Objects exist in space and time,
Because they are rational.

Honesty and integrity are signs
  Of good taste and morality,
    The likes and dislikes
Are part of a morbid personality.

Elizabeth Saltz

TO MY SON

You are almost whole again
  first off dope
    then married and children
      now off drinking and smoking.

My beautiful son
  almost a failure in life . . .

I am so proud of you
  of your stubbornness
    of your struggles . . .

You have achieved
  beyond the reality of a few years ago

You are the most beautiful
  son a woman can have.

Shirley Erbacher

ALWAYS CARING

The ocean is bright and
sand is soft and silky white.
Waves gently caressing, calming
fears and always caring.

They live together in total
harmony, one taking the other
giving, never hurting only
pleasing, always caring.

The evening has come
all others are gone and now
is our time to learn, from sand and
sea, to love but be always caring.

John J. McDonnell

JOHN JOSEPH McDONNELL. Born: Brooklyn, New York; Single; Education: Brookdale Community College, A.A. in Broadcasting; Kean College, B.A. in English; Occupation: Asst. grocery manager, Foodtown Supermarkets; Memberships: Kean College Alumni Association; Cousteau Society; Poetry: 'Warm Winter Afternoon,' *The Art of Poetry*, 6-85; 'To The Good Life,' *American Poetry Anthology*, 10-84; 'Writing on the Wall,' *Words of Praise, Vol. II*, 4-86; 'Cicada Song,' *Best New Poets of 1986*, 1-87; Comments: *I live near the shore and most of my work is a reflection of that. I try to use words to help me paint pictures with my poetry; the paper is my canvas, the pen, my brush and words are my paint. The poem is my final masterpiece.*

UNTITLED

Oh if Thy lips weren't for words
    But for kissing
I would kiss all,
The sky,
    The moon,
        The trees,
But mostly, Thy holiest of feet.

My Lord,
Lord of my soul,
I would betray You not with words
But with the meager way in which
My soul attempts to repay You
With my humblest of loves.

I give You all in which
You gave first.
I give You all of me.
My love,
    My soul,
        My gratitude,
And every ounce of glee.

Shani

A KIND OF COURAGE

Pretty Pat, whose chuckles
Drown out life's sour notes,
  Turns lemon gifts to lemonade
Or ice cream lemon floats.

  An orchard of lemon trees
Has dumped on Pretty Pat.
  She's ducked and squeezed and stirred,
And will laugh at even that.

  Now all you skeptic cynics
Just answer this charade:
  "Who's that darling dreamboat drifting
On a sea of lemonade?"

  Her laughter creates gales
To blow the boat ashore,
  Where, if she finds more lemons,
She'll just laugh some more.

  "What makes our Pat so giddy?"
The uninformed may ask,
  Well, rolling with the punches
Becomes a dizzy task.

Virginia F. Brown

PSYCHENTROPIC
METAMORPHOSIS

a butterfly
    flutters by
on tremulous ephemeral wings . . .
falters,
falling to my feet . . .
. . . and i blinked as i looked . . .
it had only been a leaf.

but in that split instant,
it had been
    a butterfly.

Brian Bywater

THE GOLDEN FOREST

There it lies in the midst of the sun-stricken hills
The finely contrasted flowers make a picturesque scene with
  their lacy petals and frills
The moss-covered ground remains layered with green
While the monstrous trees abounding the land add to the beauty
  with an overwhelming sheen
When the warmth of the sweet fragrant air is sent forth
The leaves begin to sway with a fluttery movement much like
  a moth
And the pond nearby with its glimmering shimmer follows with
  a tune as great as a chorus
For it plays of the magic of the Golden Forest

Bethann Covone

JESUS WITH LOVE, HAS COUNTED ME IN

Christians follow Jesus in this world
He delivers so freely our sorrows and sin
Surrender banners from hearts will unfurl
Jesus with love, has counted me in.

Christians love Jesus with peace serene
Burdens lifted, sweet comfort descends
He is our Redeemer, He is Supreme!
Jesus with love, has counted me in.

Christians pray to Jesus night and day
Blessings overflowing, He humbly sends
There is grace and forgiveness along the way
Jesus with love, has counted me in.

Every soul on earth longs for His way
A blessed release from burdens and sin
I have prepared for Homecoming Day
Jesus with love, has counted me in.

He knocked at my door, He is my friend
He won my heart, He counted me in.
Knocking, knocking again and again
I am at peace, He counted me in.

Margaret Kerr

DEAR JOHN

A Tribute To John Lennon

   This is just a line or so, to say how much we care.
The music that you've given us was all so much and
rare. This is just another line, to tell appreciation
of your musicianship, and the love and peace you shared.

   We loved you then, we love you now, God knows we
always will. We miss the most the love you gave,
and the soul that poured out from your pen.

   We never had the chance to see you, your death
came all too quick. It brought the tears we see
through now, we know your music will never quit. I
only hope that in my end, I'll get that chance to see
you, but until I do I'll wait my turn, my words not
finished yet.

   You were the best, and your greatness of soul
must have assured your place in Heaven, how untimely
it was and sad to say, John Lennon had to die that day.
It's in our hearts we know you're at peace, and your
music lives on and on.

Thomas W. Gales III

IN THE HANDS OF TIME

   Deep in the hands of time there are memories
beautiful and rich, of these we are weavers of
nine, as are the bad that we try to forget, and
as time heals all we shall weave in more good, as
in our Love we know we cannot neglect, and maybe
goals are just wishes, but we will keep on weaving
much like our Love we simply have to protect.

   So as time goes by and we put the bad behind,
the good will still remain and we'll share in each
other's mind. If all memories were meant to be just
a passing thing, my heart could never be the open
book it appears to be, the bad might remain then my
tears would flood like rain, so as time goes by we
know it's true that within our Love all the good memories
we share will help to ease our pain.

   As time goes by we'll play their little mind
games knowing full well we'll do it just to see,
if it can help then what the heck, let's do it once
again. As times goes by we may even see they're right
and remain in Love until the bitter end.

Thomas W. Gales III

OUT OF THE BLUE

   As I wade deeply in the sadness of my gloom,
I see open curtain sunlight shine through, as dust
gathers quickly upon the bronze box, with a body so
still awaiting earth to swallow it to its tomb.

   Trembling sadness no help within this room,
once more no sunlight, just grey clouds of doom,
I'm far away too blue. His time went on so swiftly,
no cards did he play to lose, time just stops the
joker's wild, then onwards and upwards into the
great sky blue.

   When our time comes, God springs up so suddenly
as if that's all there is to do, what about us the living,
won't You come help us from out of the blue?
With all the problems on earth, He cannot debate that
there's just too much killing, wars, injustice and hate,
we could use of His help to bring out more faith
for when it's our turn to go too, but even if He can't
He knows we'll always look up to His Holiness there
in His great yard blue.

Thomas W. Gales III

PENDULUM

We huddle at midpoint in search of objective
We spiral through space, yet through time march straight on
But where lies the truth in a clash of perspective
Is the treasure half-gathered, or is it half-gone

Now the motion is present, the forces eternal
We are all of a process, in progress somehow
Do the flames bless with warmth, or the fires wax infernal
Is the Golden Hour soon, or was it long before now

Of the past we're all purblind in the meanings we give
Of the future, all helpless to create or forget
Of the present, it is only by moments we live
And tomorrow's mock value lies in not being here yet

Martin Mitchell

TIME WARP

Suddenly the cars had crashed,
She sailed through glass so fast her
    Head and arms and ribs were smashed —
Yet she survived disaster.

    She struggled up through stitches
And splintered broken wrist,
    To speak in alien tongue, which is
The German railway list.

    ''Her mind is gone,'' the nurses said,
Knowing not of Jackie's trip.
    With German robbers in her head,
Jackie clutched her purse and grip.

    Three days she closely hovered
Deep in German castles where,
    Her heart's desire discovered,
She longed to stay right there.

    Lucky Jackie's past her pain,
Her scars are shrinking fast.
    Let's celebrate! She's home again
In the here and now at last!

Virginia F. Brown

PREFERENCE

After watching
  Three hours of
    Drama and mystery
      As recorded by
        The television eye.

I turned away
  Walked to the front porch,
    To watch the stars,
      The cheshire moon,
        The night birds floating by,
          My cat chasing imaginary
            Shadow moths.

I discovered
  That night
    I preferred
      Reality
        To fantasy.

Doris M. Compton

WHEN THE MOON
HANGS LOW IN THE SKY

When the moon hangs low in the sky
I can see you dancing there
From point to point
Easily sliding through the darkness
Occasionally swinging from a star.
I watch from where I rest
Within this tree.
I spread my limbs in anticipation
Of your inevitable fall to freedom

The sun now rises melting away the night
And I can hear your cries building
As you gracefully slip down
Through the blue
Into my loving.

Gina Cestaro

LONELY BEING

The cascade fills the emptiness,
Dew on the brow —
Refreshing the heat within the soul.

Flight of forgiveness,
Despair crashing inward
Episodic in nature,

Thrashing among the buds,
Bringing imbalances
To the roots.

The bond broken,
Empathy the halt
Rivulet evaporating.

Stress shooting asunder,
Atrophy destroying
The harmonious being.

Heartfelt,
    Sadness,
        Darkness.

Christopher Smith

CHRISTOPHER C. (CHARLES) SMITH. Born: Coatesville, Pennsylvania, 7-2-60; Education: Elizabethtown College, Elizabethtown, Pennsylvania, B.S., 12-83; Occupations: Teaching assistant, Department of Chemistry, Villanova University; Memberships: The Zoological Society of Philadelphia, The Wilderness Society, National Geographic Society, National Arbor Day Foundation, National Wildlife Federation; Poetry: 'Snowflake,' *American Poetry Anthology,* Spring 1987; *The Vanishing Child,* collection; Comments: *The poems are the result of inspirational energies flowing through my inner domain during professional experience in the mental health field: retarded clientele, and adjudicated juveniles. The message underlies the poems: a beautiful experience may result when working with the special public.*

I WAS BORN UNDER A
LUCKY STAR

I was born under a lucky star
Or I'd never have lived to find you
You'll always know, dear, wherever you are
My lucky heart will be true

I'd like to find it, wherever it shines
Only to thank it for making you mine

Guard now, my love, oh my lucky star
Until all my dreams have come true.

Katherine E. Cartwright

OH! THE SUNRISE
BATHED IN SPLENDOR

As I looked out through my window
The golden sun was rising clear
Up it came so bright! In splendor!
I could sense that God was near!

In a blaze of light and glory
Mirrored on the waters deep
Surrounded by the marshlands only
Caused my lonely heart to leap!

Oh! The thrill of glorious sunrise!
Oh! The blesséd hope it brings!
Each new day brings peace and pardon!
Causes hearts to laugh and sing!

''Oh! The sunrise bathed in splendor!''
Oh! The prize that we can claim!
Oh! The peace that dwells within us!
When we pray in ''Jesus' name!''

Mrs. La Forrest Lucas

DUSK

The colors we saw were incredible
Reds,
  Yellows,
    Oranges,
      Purples,
        Pinks,
          Blues,
All swirling together
  Rolling around with the clouds
It bursts the sky with brilliance
  It dazzles the eye.

There is nothing so beautiful.

A deer stands feeding in the grass;
    It sees us,
      But does not run.
      The awe of what it sees becomes the
center of its attention.

The world stands still to gaze.

And God shines through
    in His glory.

William R. Guerra

I have traveled a long road
The path through many sunrises
Now an ancient me
Seeks joy — not pride.
I laugh at those who have
        an answer.
For every day dawns still new
We carry with us past memories
That help the future to renew.

My feet upon the black soft earth
The smell of rotting seeds
Saved by the wind that flows
And time together.

Evelyn Miqdadi

I ROVE NEW YORK

Great towers reaching for the sky,
  Oh! How can they build so high?
Huge edifice in your glass shroud,
  Are you reaching for a cloud?
In a long canyon that stands fallow,
  I encounter some with a face sallow.
A group passes by, their faces dark.
  To the west, along some murky street,
  one hears the sound of a tropic beat.
Among the cars, the fumes from the gas,
  Someone shouts in a manner crass.
There, inside those low hovels,
  The inhabitants seem to be from the earth's bowels.
One must head away from there,
  Surely we deserve better fare.
The roar comes from a machine —
  Up goes another beam!
Now it's time to sit and dream.

Jim Henry

DENNIS AND THE DRAGONS

When Dennis comes to our house after school,
The Elves and Dwarves and Dragons tag along.
For Dennis thinks that fantasy is ''cool''
And who am I to tell him that he's wrong?

Bright swords and dashing figures join the throng
That sits upon our floor and speaks of doom
Which may befall the weakest or the strong
Enclosing them forever in the gloom
Of fallen heroes. Headed for the tomb
Untimely, sorcery and Wizards pass
While adolescent chatter fills the room
Till Dennis has to leave again. Alas,
I often wish the Elves and Dwarves could stay
While Dennis and the Dragons go away.

William V. Robertson

CIRCUMSTANCES ALTER CASES

November winds blows around you for the last time,
And now, unable to keep yourself together,
You lean against the wall, no longer able to stand
Upright . . . Broken . . . Unhinged . . . and I remember when
You were not so.
Many years have we been together, many miles have
We travelled, many things have we seen.
Long, the hours that I have held you and carried
You. Creeping November has come into your life,
Your blackness, still stark against November's grey,
The parting will be hard.
Still, I must go on while you cannot. Another, soon,
Must take your place, and we must part with care and
Memory, but twenty years is a long time for
An attaché case, and I will not grieve.

William V. Robertson

SONNET FOR A MISSPENT HOUR

We, in that hour we salvaged for our own,
Renounced the touch for which our bodies yearned,
As if by stern denial could be earned,
A recompense for things we left undone.

Yet underneath that coolly decorous tone,
A leaping, crackling flame of wanting burned,
And spoke to us, you said, of youth returned.
Our triumph of forbearance was hard won.

How staid my mind that once was bold and free,
That for convention proudly showed disdain,
And walked encircled in its own propriety!
Should I now seek that posture to regain,
And cast away the husk of undue piety,
Which made that stolen hour such exquisite pain?

Phyllis Brown

RETURN

A door was opened, our eyes met,
our smiles burst 'round us in a warm, gold shower
Of déjà vu.
We were not strangers.

A door was opened, a veil rent,
An aura whirled around us as an ancient power
Of love spilled through,
With present dangers.

The karmic thrust that moved us
Through our vortex of desire,
Has portents of recurrent fire,
With inference beyond our present scope.
And knowing of our phoenix course
Has charged my flagging field-force,
And filled my days with cosmic hope.

Phyllis Brown

A ROMANCE

My love, you are to me like a rainbow
In the sky so blue
Ever so constant and true
But elusive, that's you
Who am I? To sigh like the rain
On a wind-blotched landscape
And to try to escape the foreboding
Weather with a cape of leather.
But for you coming along to drive away
The threat in the weather
Whenever I come nether to whisper in your ear
Any sunshine behind my dark clouds
Would never reappear
And I would be a goner, that's for sure.
A catastrophe in the corner of our atmosphere.
Forgive me, sir, but
I must turn around and
Shed a tear, and
Thank the Lord Jehovah (with a wish and a hope)
That you are ever so near.

Caroline A. Connelly-Moore

MY BELOVED

*Written on the 1st
anniversary of his death*

Where are you, my beloved
Where did you go?
Where are you, my beloved
I miss you so

Where are you, my beloved
Where have you gone?
Where are you, my beloved
You left me so alone

Where are you, my beloved
Why were you taken?
Where are you, my beloved
You left me so forsaken

Come back to me, my beloved
When I called you came to me
And told me you'd love me
through all Eternity

Ella Young Wood

MY GEMS

For my children

I have no sparkling diamonds
No cultured pearls to show
For jewels and other trinkets
Are not my way, you know.

My diamond is my husband
A true and perfect one
My rubies are my two precious sons
My highly polished pearls
Are three lovely daughters
God has lent to me.

My gems have all been polished
Through years of rearing them
I know they will always sparkle
Until we meet again.

Vi Schoenbaum

SUNRISE

*This was written for my sister
who nags me to get up and watch
sunrises with her.*

I love to greet the new day
    with a sunrise fantastic and bright.
It is a daily promise from God
    that He will always bring the light.

If my day starts with a heartache,
    a sunrise can set it right;
It renews my faith in God's word
    as I view the beautiful sight.

But sunrises come so early —
    and I'm such a sleepyhead,
It is easier to wait for the end of the day,
    and watch His sunset signature instead.

Earlus ''Kay'' Gannon

IF ONLY I COULD
CRY ENOUGH TEARS

If only I could cry enough tears
To make you change your mind,
And think once more before you choose
To leave it all behind.

If only I could cry enough tears
To wash away the pain,
And make you think it's worth a chance
To try just once again.

It hurts so much to realize
Things aren't the way I planned,
If only I could cry enough tears
To make you understand.

I've tried to think just what went wrong,
But the answer I can't see.
If only I could cry enough tears
To bring you back to me.

If only I could cry enough tears
I'd write a brand new set of years.
I'd make a way through all your fears
If only I could cry enough tears.

David W. Edwards

DAVID WAYNE EDWARDS. Born: West Point, New York, 10-25-50; Education: Riverside City College, 1980-82; Education: Riverside City College, 1980-82; Occupation: Heavy equipment operator, rock plant; Memberships: Script coordinator for Christian theatre group, Corona, California; Poetry: 'When Love Became Real,' 'Davy,' 'If Time Ran Away,' *Hearts On Fire, A Treasury of Poems on Love, Vol IV,* 11-87; Comments: *Life can deal some hard blows, and no one is immune to them. I hope my poetry can help others see their pain in a new perspective so that they can come through each trial better than they did before.*

PARABOLA

The returning tribune
    with stolen horse
    let it drink;
    then yanked its head
    in new direction:
a swarm
    of bees
        had been disturbed
    and chased them
        for awhile.

The honest footman
    soaked his ''dogs,''
    took a bath,
    then searched for logs.
    He built a fire —
    cooked his meal —
    that's when
        the bees
        came
            back.

P. B. Quinn

SILHOUETTES OF LOVE

Scenes of lilacs bloom for us,
Overcoming in purple clouds
    all that we cherish.
Can we know love thus?

A winged instinct replies,
Holding desire from our longing:
    from moments and days
We touch with our eyes.

More fragrant in intrusion,
Your scent in tangled hair wears:
    yet my vision draws
Back from attraction.

In a stormy eloquence
Filled with beauty and brooding,
    our todays walk out
With our acceptance.

Worship in our tomorrow,
Finds us a place where lilacs bloom:
    and a shining ring
Welcomes our love, glow.

God, rights our name, and we bloom
In His impassioned beauty:
    a concept of love
Earthy dusts intomb.

Audrie M. Fiskaali

PRECIOUS MOMENTS

Don't waste a precious moment
    as you watch your grandchild grow.
For life goes by much too quickly,
    and they'll be grown before you know.

Take the time to read them stories,
    as you tuck them into bed.
Be part of their make-believe world,
    and the magical dreams that revolve in their head.

The most beautiful words in the world
    are when they say, *Grandma, I love you,*
For children speak straight from their heart,
    and the heart-spoken words are true.

Ann Lo Cascio

WHY?

Why do people I love have to drink?
There are so many other ways to solve problems.
Don't they love me anymore?
Life can't be that bad.
Don't they love themselves anymore?
You have to love yourself before you can love others.
Do they find solace in their alcohol?
If so, they are lying to themselves.
What are they looking for?
Life can be so confusing sometimes.
Will I end up like them someday?
The thought sends chills down my spine.
Does everybody solve their problems this way?
Drinking can't be the absolute answer for everybody.
Why do they drink at all?
They say alcohol is bad for your system.
Why does anybody do what they do?
We all do things that others think are crazy.
Can't we work things out together?
People have been known to work things out by talking.
  Haven't they?

Stacey "Tina Marie" Dorchester

I CAN GO WHERE NO ONE ELSE CAN

Today is certainly a day to dream.
The rain falls from the sky,
And it does not look like it will stop.
If this keeps up all day
I think I will scream.
It is best to remain calm, so I will,
And I will go where no one else can.
I will go to a grassy knoll
And ride upon a sunbeam.
When I reach the end
It won't be raining anymore.
I will run and play with the fairy folk
And we will be very happy.
The birds will sing and the flowers will grow,
Because this is my dream.
Then when it is over I will go home,
And maybe the rain will stop.
If it hasn't I will go back to my dream.

Stacey "Tina Marie" Dorchester

LOOKING AT YOU

I saw the pain within your heart,
And your need for a new start.

For life has somehow gotten old,
True happiness is only for the bold.

I want to lift you up and show you a better day,
So you will know that sadness isn't there to stay.

Life is learning and growing,
And through experience comes the knowing.

Fill your heart with love and light,
And listen to your soul, it's right.

Don't drown yourself in misery,
Release yourself and you'll be free.

You are only responsible to yourself,
It is your poverty or your wealth.

It is your choice to be happy or sad,
To ride calm seas or to be mad.

Your destiny is yours alone,
It matters not what others condone.

You have all the answers within yourself,
They're yours to see, or put on a shelf.

Take hold and you will see,
How you've been your own worst enemy.

Find the goodness in your heart and let it fill the air,
For you're a wonderful person with so much to share.

Koleen Gilstad

PATTY AND PAUL

*A true romance of a modern Chinese
poet and his second wife.*

Life with army officer Libby was a misery.
To others, with great admiration,
A happy couple in a wealthy society.
To Patty, the tough and rough husband
Had everything, but her heart.
Daytime she put on smiles with tears.
At night she sobbed on pillows with pains.

One day, the sun shone on her
When she met Poet Paul.
Their eyes met, so were their hearts,
The flames of love burning within them.
Like her, he was married by arrangement.
For love, freedom and beauty,
Undaunted, they got married.

After the storm, the rainbow was shortlived.
From all sides, they felt the pressures.
Fearlessly they fought on and on.
Before leaving by air, Paul assured Patty his love.
But, fate played the game,
As Paul vanished in the flame.

Christina Ching Tsao

MOMENTS

Dedicated to Brian Evans Baldwin, whose friendship shall always be treasured.

you entered the confusion of my life
knowing not what was dwelling there.
you stayed and searched, seeking not
the imperfections of my humanness,
but rather exposing qualities
that lie sleeping among insecurities.
you guided me through the darkness
stopping to light candles of trust
and friendship.
my trembling self was held and hugged
after tales of woe from wrong roads taken.
you helped me to laugh and grow.
taught me how to pronounce Van Gogh,
and count my hair (all of them!).
and though our paths have parted
your enduring friendship has
gifted me with memories to warm
my heart for a lifetime.

Juanita E. Dorner

QUALITIES

A measure of *kindness* and a
    share of human *compassion*
A meter of *unselfishness*
    and a liter of
        sensitivity —

Some creative vision and a glimmer
    of *hope*
Deep abiding *faith* and a capacity
    to *love*

            Stable routes
                to
            happiness
                and
            success!

Patricia Robinson Williams

ENLIGHTENMENT: THE OBITUARY

I thought I knew him well,
Until I read his obituary.
A quiet elderly gentleman
Who always greeted me at church.
I knew he came from the city
To retire in our little town.

But now I saw him as he was:
A hero; received the Medal of Honor.
A diplomat; served in foreign lands.
A linguist; fluent in seven tongues.

If only I had known!
Yet I had missed it all,
Until I read his obituary.

Virginia E. Cruikshank

BE STILL AND KNOW THAT I AM GOD

It is now nineteen years ago
when my beloved husband
left for the Heavenly
Home to rest. Since then,
I have missed him every day
and every hour.
But through God's help,
and mercy, I am happy that my
Heavenly Father has
always been my refuge and my deliverer.
With the help of my children, I am
well taken care of.
And by keeping myself busy, in
my church and temple work,
I am happy to serve God with
love and prayer. The Lord is
my light and my salvation, of whom
shall I fear? The Lord is the
strength of my life, of whom
shall I be afraid?

Sister Gay G. Cabotaje

GAY GABBUAT CABOTAJE. Pen Name: Sister Gay G. Cabotaje; Born: Solano, Nueva Vizcaya, Philippines, 10-8-08; Married: Dr. Pablo V. Cabotaje, 3-13-39 (deceased); Education: University of the Philippines, B.A., Philosophy, 1937; Philippine Christian University, B.S., Education, 1960; Occupations: High school english teacher, retired; Poetry: 'To My Beloved Mother,' 1-8-85; 'Praises Be Unto God On High,' *Words of Praise*, 7-10-86; 'Take Everything To God In Prayer,' *Best New Poets of 1986*, 11-30-86; 'Be Still and Know That I Am God,' *The Poetry of Life, Vol. I*, 9-28-87; Comments: *I want to share my love for God with others. I want to give thanks to my Heavenly Father for the millions of blessings that He give to me and my children and grandchildren every day and every hour. My poetry conveys my complete faith and trust in God who loves me and who careth for me. I am a special child of God, my eternal father. God is my refuge and He is my deliverer. And He's my strength from day to day. And I know that if I will always try to do His will and try to serve Him with love and joy in my heart, He will always take care of me; hence the verse, ''Be still and know that I am God,'' is really His word of truth.*

FOR GAY

Tell me why, oh God!
. . . A beautiful creature,
a child, has to die?
And does my life have to go on?
. . . this emptiness inside,
the endless, muffled cry
of agony and despair . . .
the futility of it all!
Why, oh why? God!
. . . a child?

Does not the flower also die?
The wind in the trees
            after the storm!
The last echoes of a prayer . . .
like the melody, the refrain
            when a song is no more!

G. Maria de Archangelis

THE PROFILE OF A DEMOCRATIC WOMAN

The Democratic Woman
in days of yore
was determined to prove
that she could endure.

She trailed the man
and the political crew
as she learned to unify
the old and the new.

The Democratic Woman
stands *tall and bold*.
She dares to attain
her political *goal*.

The Democratic Woman
is Loyal and Great
as she serves her party,
her country, and her state.

Margaret J. Patterson

POETRY CREATED

Sleight of hand
    wielding its sword
        destroys to create;

Perfect white mottles
    to accommodate
        verse . . .

    Wisdom
        coyly phrased

    Relaying a message
        to generations . . .

    Answering mysteries
        and creating more to be pondered.

A poet propines in solitude —
    Annotator of mankind.

Barbara Siegfried

THE LORD CALLED

Moments before Momma passed away
These are the words that I heard her say,
''The Lord entered in, He just came through the door.''
When Momma was gone the rest of the family went to
    the hospital's lower floor.
But I stayed behind sitting in the hall right outside her door.
I couldn't leave her, I just couldn't let go.
Then I heard a voice call me by name.
It was so real, I heard it so plain.
I looked around quickly to see who had called ''Marge.''
There was no one in sight
I saw no one with me in the hallway that night.

Marjorie Rinkel Graumenz

MARJORIE RINKEL GRAUMENZ. Born: Farina, Fayette County, Il-
linois, 3-18-27; Married: Elroy Graumenz, 8-18-46; Education: 8th grade;
GED, 1980; Occupations: Housewife, Grandmother of 24 grandchildren;
Award: Demo record, 'Unique Love'; Poetry: 'My Fountain Pen,' *Gove
News,* 1939; 'Life on Mars,' *Our Twentieth Century's Greatest Poems,* 1982;
'Loving Father,' *Our Western World's Greatest Poems,* 1983; 'Joshua,'
American Poetry Anthology, Vol. VI, No. 3, 1986; 'Family Tree, Part 2,' *Best
New Poets of 1986,* American Poetry Association, 1986; Comments: *The
poem, 'The Lord Called,' is a true happening; the photo is a picture of my
mother at the age of 16 (Jane Elizabeth Dixon Rinkel).*

A GLORIOUS NEWNESS

Sometimes I get a sadness,
Sometimes I experience suffocation;
But today I watched a world outside myself.
Sunrise, sunset and, in between,
A shower enhancing the greenery of spring.

I gave a sigh at the sudden sight
Of a red-breasted bird so joyous in flight.
I marveled at the quietness of squirrels
As they frolicked about, in the trees and out.

I came upon happily chattering girls
Playing jacks, hopscotch and jump-the-rope
On sidewalks now warmed by a bright sun.

I broke into a smile
As bicyclists pedaled gracefully by,
Around boys noisily gathered in the street
Playing their wonderful games of fun.

Gazing up soon afterward,
I felt overwhelmed at the beauty of the sky.
I gave thanks in my heart;
And, yes, Lord, I knew why.

Lester E. Garrett

REDEMPTION

Heavenly angels & cherubim white dressed before
    the altar of God.
Tabernacle of Gold shedding the lust of centuries.
White wings of providential peace, alternating
    the adoration of eternity.
Flowers sending messages of immortality, cospersed
Roses & beautiful carnations emanating the fragrance
Of hopeful days ahead. Expecting the promised ark
Of cherubim & seraphim from ur' world range,
Tredding by destiny, roaring to earth from
Distant Uranus where myriads of nuclei-star are
Silvery dusting the panorama of earthly things decay.
Illustrating the universe through theories, while
The crisp, perennial turn-wheel of Uranus sends
Tulips, magnolias and white-snow roses, like the
Hope-light in Emmaus when the saviour appeared
Between two beloved disciples transtuling the
''Hickarae'' sacred host: Jesus broke it and
Consumating with those who loved Him, disappeared
        in impassible redemption!
    Mysterium Urani Aeterni!
    Mysterium Amoris et Fidei.

Allan De Fiori

I HEAR YOUR ANGER FROM WITHIN

Sip some wine maybe you'll feel fine
Drink some beer let's hear a cheer
Are you hooked did your mind shake
Did your feelings break when you found love was late
Was it something that you ate that makes your thoughts want sin
Are these your real feelings coming from within

I hear your anger from within
Do you still feel the thrill that makes life seem very nice
Testing emotions that feed your thoughts
Are you alive filling your ego with desperation
Did your personality get caught in a mirror of illusions
Have you found a way in and out of yesterday's and today's confusion

Maybe you should not drink while your mind thinks
Let's cheer if you make it through another year
I have felt your pain do not be ashamed
Sometimes you lose that what you try and gain
Let go of what is not then begin
I hear your anger from within

Melvin Sykes

GIVE LIFE AN EGO

Do you have a map that shows you where life is really at
Looking for love somewhere within the treasures of remembrance
We should not forget the roads we struggle making up some shade
before tomorrow fades

Trash and waste that gives our bitter minds such a bad taste
There's a sun that we still get inner pleasures from
It gives life in return sometimes revealing what we learn
Turn me on turn me off
Is it because of my gas an electric bill

Know map whatever happens where's my graduation cap that's supposed
to be on my head that keeps my thoughts from being misled

Without the joy life brings we become like children playing
Without love that we all need we find life not so good
With inner faith we keep on going time becomes not such a waste

Melvin Sykes

A time for all seasons
  a blending of reasons
So meets the snow and the fire,
  bringing rain in our lives.

People darkening,
  and lightning (side by side)
So meets the snow and the fire,
  bringing the rain into our lives.

A time for all seasons
  a blending of reasons,
As a stream flows,
  from a mountain's many lives.

As a stream flows,
  from a mountain's many lives,
So formed an earthbound fire,
  from the skies.

People darkening,
  and lightning,
Born of a mountain's moving,
  from a fire inside.

As a stream flows,
  from a mountain's many lives,
People darkening,
  and lightning side by side
                side by side.

Cathleen Chesrow

CATHLEEN GWEN CHESROW. Born: Chicago, Illinois, 1-16-47; Divorced, 1979; Education: Art Institute of Chicago, BFA; Monte Foreman Photo Research, Inc.; Horsemanship certification; Occupations: Writer, Artist, Photographer, Videographer, Horsewoman; Memberships: LaPorte County, Indiana Sheriff's Association; The Smithsonian Associates; The Chicago Council on Foreign Relations; American Museum of Natural History; Poetry: 'Songwriter,' *In The Area,* newspaper, 9-23-85; 'Single Parent Family,' *American Poetry Anthology,* 1983; 'Lightning,' 1986; Comments: *I write for that unspoken word, that glance, that touch; the depth of feelings and understanding still to be discovered and named. Being held in writing, these frontiers of human experience and expression are thereby held in trust for future generations.*

You are the endless beauty
of the rolling waves
at night;
the new moon charting a
pathway across the water
to our feet.

You are the priceless wonder
of a single rose
a gift,
given with love to mark
our anniversary of
one week.

You are the aching, sobbing sadness
of your music
that echoed
all my tears that fell for all
my losses which now seem
just rehearsals

        for the loss
        of you . . .

Jean E. Judy

TO THE HEARTBREAK OF ALZHEIMER'S

Let me be your memory
For I remember you when . . .
We'd build a barn and
Set a fence to keep the cattle in.

We'll laugh at the ways of others
We'll cry when a loved one goes
We'll till the fields and make them grow
Then we'll go where nobody knows.

Let me be your eyes
For I can show you the lights . . .
We'd look at the sky and
Wonder at the stars at night.

We'll see little children running
Away from a bull so fierce
We'll watch the darkness swallow us up
And together we'll shed our tears.

Let me be your will
For I can give you strength . . .
Just like you gave it to me
Endless, tireless, never-ending strength.

We'll span the miles you've traveled before
We'll find a new meaning in every new day
We'll know and believe that heaven is ours
We'll feel fulfilled and here we'll stay.

I will be you and you can be me
So you will feel the love we share
Just please remember me . . .
Because when you need me
I promise — I will be there.

Claire Vallot Peyton

THE THOUGHTS AND IMAGINATIONS OF THEIR HEARTS WERE ONLY EVIL CONTINUALLY

The thoughts and imaginations of his
heart were only evil continually.
He will die without making amends.

The thoughts and imaginations of his
heart were only evil continually.
He is to be cut off.

The thoughts and imaginations of his
heart were only evil continually.
The fierceness and wrath of
Almighty God rests upon him until
he repents.

Conclusion:

All are brought to disrepute.
All are overcome.

She who hath not an husband has many
more children, than she that hath
an husband.

Estella M. McGhee-Siehoff

WEAR NO SHAME OUT OF AFRICA

From when time was young, siege
Has been laid to every culture
On earth; an unbroken circle.

Wear no shame out of Africa:

She gave birth to yesterday;
So the scholars say.

Through her strife of desolation
And separation, many a kingdom
Rose and fell; from altered rules:

Yet . . . she still stands, after losing
Millions to the struggles against
The odds; she has played the game
Well.

Wear no shame out of Africa:

She gave birth to yesterday;
So the scholars say.

Doris Reynolds

MEDITATING

This morning came the early dawn — It was so
lively, brisk and clear — I took an early
morning walk — Some thoughts I needed to steer
— I talked with the wind — And the many little
birds — They listened very carefully — And
seemed to understand each word — They sensed
I was walking — And thinking all alone — I had
so much to think about — Just thinking on my own
— So many things I must do — So many letters
to write and say — So many things to make —
Before the holidays — But first I needed to see
— God's world afresh — anew — To see the sparkling
diamonds — While wet with frost and dew —
My Dear, I wish that you — Could have been there
with me — And saw the world wake up — In such
blissful ecstasy — Someday soon again My Darlin'
— We will walk and talk together — Oh yes, we
will enjoy our days — No difference what the
weather — Mornings are so beautiful — When all
the world is bright — You see the Master Painter
— Blends his color scenes just right!

Ruth F. Teeters

FIELDS OF HOME

The many things that worried me — Departed
from me yesterday — Among the fields —
Where as a youth — I did work and play —
Among the budding trees — And in the babbling
streams — Among the sweet singing birds —
And in the flowers of Spring — The fears and
tears — Of the long ago past — I threw them
all away — I became as a little child — I
could laugh - could run - and play — Among the
sunny fields — Of green green grass —
Recalling the sweet aroma — Of new-mown hay —
Among the paths of yesterday — Now overgrown
with mossy-sod — I left all my worries — All
ill thoughts — Out in the fields with God —

Ruth F. Teeters

MORNING IS SO SPECIAL

Morning is like a brand new garment — So fresh
— So unused — So unspoiled — You want to wear
it — To try it on — Before it becomes —
Wrinkled or soiled — No matter what the color
— If it be sunny or gray — You want to
wear it — Don it quickly — Before it slips
away — Garbed in fresh morning — What could
ever go wrong — Morning is so sunny — So peaceful
— Life is so entirely new — Filled
with hopeful expectations — Of what lies ahead
for you — Morning promises fulfillment —
Of exciting satisfying pleasures — Filled with
thrilling mysteries — Of exciting satisfying
pleasures — Filled with thrilling mysteries
— Of unexpected treasures — Morning is so
special — Bubbling with exciting plans —
So don this special time — And wear it while
you can —

Ruth F. Teeters

THE PAINS OF THE FAITHFUL ONE

I loved him from the depth of my being
My world became his world to rule as king
 I would have given him my last heartbeat
His cut was sudden and everlasting.

Reflecting on a life I chose to take
Was like a sleep I tried lax to awake
 Only after the heartache took a seat
The faithful one saw her painful mistake.

I now exist only on memories
When you have loved — had loved someone truly
 Accept forgiveness is a fool's defeat
If he returned, what once was could not be.

Darlene Pitts

VOYAGE HOME

He slept with a wish in the bowel of his ship
That was to change his destiny

He was proud to serve in his Navy Corps
With pride and dignity

He chores while on board — with faith in his Lord
He completed faithfully

He felt no fear and was so unaware
Sailing the Gulf in tranquility

The Persian Gulf cradled his ship and rocked him to sleep
Unaware of his shattered liberty

The Iraqi war plane fired — two missiles in the side
Of his ship of serenity

With no evasive action — the USS Stark stood at attention
Engulfed in a horror of reality

In the burning sound as the destruction bound
He was lifted in His simplicity

Cradled in His arms he surrendered all his harms
He went Home for all eternity

Valentina M. Panzone

VALENTINA M. PANZONE. Born: Canonsburg, Pennsylvania, 2-14-22;
Married: James V. Panzone, 1940; Education: South Macomb Community
College, Warren, Michigan, A.A., 1962; Wayne University, Detroit,
Michigan, B.A., 1964; Eastern Michigan University, M.A., 1966, Ed.S.,
1968; Occupations: Retired Special Education Teacher, Counselor,
Psychologist; Membership: American Poetry Association; Awards: Golden
Poet Awards, 1985-87; Poetry: 'The Convalescent Home Guest,' *American
Poetry Anthology,* 1985; 'My Stranger,' *Our World's Most Cherished Poems,*
1985; 'Approaching The Statue, 1919,' *Best New Poets of 1986;* 'The Part-
ing,' 1986; 'Cycle of Love,' *Hearts on Fire, Vol. IV,* 1987.

THANKFULLY YOURS SWEET WILLIAM

I'm thankful for the little things
You very often do.
I'm thankful for your gentle voice
And each tender ''I love you.''
I'm thankful for your knowing glance
And that twinkle in your eye.
I'm thankful for your loving arms
That hold me when I cry.
I'm thankful for your strength and love
And for your faithful heart.
I'm thankful you keep me with you
Even when we are apart.
I'm thankful that I've found a man
As good and kind as you.
I'm thankful for each chance to say
''My Angel, I love you!''
You'll always be my shining knight,
My champion, my love.
Yes, I'm thankful for you, My Sweet,
So very thankful for your love.

Donna J. Nixon

MY PROUD VETERAN

*Recently in our home town,
the AR Viet Nam vets were honored with
a memorial and dedication. This
poem was inspired as I stood beside.*

Mere words cannot convey
how proudly I stood with you,
my veteran.

My proud veteran with
the silent tears streaming
from your eyes.

Your tears were for
the many, many men who could not stand
where we stood today.

Your tears were for the wives,
or mothers, or fathers
who stood alone today.

I cry with you, my proud veteran,
for I am a part of you
and wish to share your pain.

So stand tall
My Proud Veteran,
for I am proud of you.

Dena Luttrell

THE FALLING DREAM

*To my parents, Joy and Simon
Wexler with love and gratitude*

Late night hours of impromptu introspection
floating
in ponds of coffee tasting of cold sweat
the falling dream
Jolted awake clutching at blankets
gasping short mouthfuls of fear-weighted air
the falling dream
suddenly
nothing exists beneath my feet
the world dissolves
        and I fall forever
            (dream time)
Then one night,
frightened beyond caring,
I simply allowed the fall to continue
and found myself
free to fly.

Marci W. Maitland

PRETTY FLOWERS

I see you pretty flowers
As you run and you play;
I see you pretty flowers,
As you steal my heart away.

I see you pretty flowers,
As you spread your joy abound;
I see you pretty flowers,
As you sleep so peaceful and sound.

The love I have for you pretty flowers,
Is more than you'll ever know;
And I see you pretty flowers,
As each passing year you grow.

It won't be long pretty flowers,
Until you'll be all grown;
I'll miss your sweet fragrance,
When you're out and gone.

You remind me pretty flowers,
Of some of the things I did;
And I'll always love you pretty flowers,
For you'll always be my kids.

Fletcher J. Eller

OH LORD, OPEN OUR EYES

Oh Lord, open our eyes
    To the truth that is in you
        Only you

We cannot see, for we are blind
    Though we search night and day
We need your guiding hand
    And your light to show the way

Lead us to your living water
    Guard us with every step we take
Help us to see your love eternal
    And teach us with each choice we make

Vivian L. Hayward

FREE THIS LONELINESS WITHIN

Must I endure these endless days?
Your love remains, remains always,
The memories, all, will live again.
Oh free this loneliness within.

It seems you're ever near to me.
In dreams of loveliness I see.
As the endless day now begins,
Release this loneliness within.

Will memories haunt me all my days?
Will dreams return of you always?
The pain, I thought, someday will end
To free the loneliness within.

Will lonely days return anew?
Or must I forget a life with you?
A troubled heart yearns deep within,
Someday, someday will live again.

Please free this loneliness, I see,
As all the dreams return to me.
A weary heart will not be vain,
From loneliness be free again.

Albert S. Owens

IN GOD'S TIME

*Written for the parents of and
dedicated to my niece, Katherine
Raelynn Pomroy, who by faith was
born fulfilling God's promise
to answered prayers.*

1987, the 28th of May
    Was born to us a girl.
Wrapped in *answered prayers*
    And more precious than the world!

She's been a long time coming
    We've waited so many years.
Not ever grasping parenthood
    Was just one of our numerous fears.

Katelyn is our dream come true
    After twelve long years of trying.
With the birth of this little babe
    End so much agony and crying.

Praying with such empty arms
    Has taken patience and grace.
But in the end — all's come to pass
    As we see her face to face.

As new parents we're found to be
    We shall try to do our best.

We know that God in all His *mercy*
    Will keep our family blest.

Kathy Bess Thibodaux

YOU CAN'T KEEP MY HEART

I remember so well the day that I met you.
It was then that I knew I would never forget you.
It was on that sweet day you took something of mine.
I wanted you to have it, but now it is time.
I know that everything is all over now.
It happened so fast. I don't even know how.
But since you are leaving, you must give it back.
There are too many things that my life seems to lack.
It wasn't my love that for you was so deep.
Nor was it my pride. At least that I will keep.
It wasn't my tears. No, those I can hide.
Nor was it my memories. I kept those inside.
At the time that I met you, I was falling apart.
So you entered my life, but you kept my heart.
You can take back your dreams that were so much like mine.
You can take back your laugh that was so like a chime.
You can take back your love. I know it was true.
You can take with you my words, ''I love you, too.''
You can walk out of my world and into your land,
But you can't walk away with my heart in your hand.

Lori Simonton

SOUTHERN LADY — YANKEE SNOW

How does a lady maintain dignity and charm
When each day fresh white mounds appear?
Another snow storm!

Try as I may, I lose all grace
As I step outside on this lovely ice,
  and invariably, land on my face!

Others have no problem remaining upright.
An enjoyable sport awaited by most.
But me? I slip and slide as on a
  roller-coaster in flight.

Gliding across the sparkling white snow,
Broken bones and bruises are of no concern,
  Only whose eyes have seen and who might know!

Must *I* be the star of this seasonal production,
As the female clown of comedy favorites?
I desire only poise, and less bumpy introductions!

Melba J. Hrncir

MEMORIES OF YOU

As we set here, gazing into the sea, I think of you
As time goes by you see I'm watching.

As the tides comes in they huff and puff, they are short and tall
They achieve so much and so precious here to me
My memories are passes fresh and sweet
Today is almost gone, so let's take it.
I will never pass this way again
But to me you are always here with me, you see.
When I gaze at the sea you will always be the one I
  feel is so close to me.
Only God knows how close I feel your precious love and
  tender memories
That we shared together
When we were here together and you are here with me.

Rea Wallace

BLOOD TIES

The ties of blood are tugging at my heart today.
I want to feel my mother's nearness, hug her tight to me,
Tell her I love her and always will.
But she is in one state and I am in another.
And telephoning is not enough.
I leaf through my photo albums, poring over her laughing eyes,
Her workworn hands, her face so full of living.
I think of the years we shared,
Of the long journey I have taken from her belly to my womanhood.
Of the birth we struggled through together,
Our closeness in my infancy, our survival of my adolescence.
I worry that she will die too soon
And leave me wracked with guilt that I spent so little time with her.
I fear that she will die too late, and suffer before her passing.
If only I were God, and could ensure her a happy life
  and a painless death!
I must learn to release my mother
Let her go her way without my wishes and regrets,
As she has done with me.
But meanwhile my soul cries out for her presence.
And if that is childish, then I shall be a child all my life.

Binkie Johnson

MEMORIES OF PEANUT

A funny-looking little dog, you walked into our yard
(I didn't think that losing you was going to be so hard).
A nervous little pup you were with very little hair,
But you were cute in spite of it and I soon came to care.
The time was spring of '73 when I first saw your face,
I tried to find your family (they didn't leave a trace).
Up and down the road we went, I held you in my arms,
Street by street, but no one knew. To keep you? I had qualms.
But you were sweet and funny, yes funny, I repeat,
And oh, so small, so after all, how much food could you eat?
Oh Peanut, I will miss you, I love you and, you see,
What makes it even harder still . . . I know how you loved me.

Gloria Yousha

WHY DO I LOVE HER?

Someone asked me today, ''Why do you love her so?''
For the first time I thought, and wondered at the *why*.
Why do I stop breathing, whenever I see her go?
And when my breath returns, why comes it as a sigh?

I love the rhythm of her body as she walks,
The poise with which she meets whatever comes her way,
The music of her voice, whenever I hear her talk,
The honesty of purpose, she shows every day.

Ah yes, I love her laugh, it comes first to her eyes,
I love her gentleness, her love of flowers and life,
And her laughter, teases me, haunts me and taunts me,
I love her understanding nature, that soothes my strife.

Like a benediction, this thought I clearly see,
I love her, yes, I love her, for she first loved me!

Joseph H. Avellone

"VIETNAM" — SOMEONE ELSE'S WAR

They were drafted into a war,
Made to fit into a plan,
To fight for someone else's land.

They were young and unprepared,
Gripped by fear,
With no time to care.

They learned to hear through silence,
Death was always near.

They are back now in what they called the
World, still trying to understand
the injustice of it all.

Beryl Ellison

ON THE PAIN OF THE HUMAN CONDITION . . .

On the pain of the human condition . . .
An anguish that words fail to soothe
How sketchy our feelings
When expressed to others
Though their condition may be
not far removed.

Why does language fall short
of human experience?
When to describe it
We patented this tool
We formed it, we shaped it
We made up some rules
Then to ensure its immortality
We taught it in school

We project it, respect it
And continually progress
But we still have emotions
That cannot be expressed!

Dr. Pamela Hall

HOW DID YOU GROW TO BE SO WISE?

How did you grow to be so wise?
Always you have seemed to be
Content and free.
How did you grow to be so sage?
For one of such a tender age.

Always you have seemed to know
Whatever was right to do;
Whatever was best.
Yet, you have always seemed to live
In harmony with joy . . . with zest!

There never seems to be
The worry, fret or fuss
That always plagued the rest of us.
What is the secret you possess?
What is your power? Come . . . Confess!

For one of such a tender age,
How did you grow to be so sage?

Mertie Elizabeth Boucher

LONELY ARTS

Alone
is Not lonely;
procreative
is Not creative —
witness Hitler.

by Myself,
I write of Others.
childless, I create
people on paper.

why shun solitude?
praise multitude?
few Cannot procreate.
Few ever seek
Oneness with Oneself.

Those who Create
Isolate; Learn
of themSelves
to teach Others.

Joan M. Schumack

JOAN MARIA SCHUMACK. Born: Methoni, Greece, 11-4-53; Education: Marquette University, B.A., Journalism, 1976; graduate work in journalism, Marquette University; Occupations: Freelance Journalist; Editor, Publisher, & Founder of *Ethnos,* an ethnic publication for the Greek Community in Wisconsin; Memberships: Society of Professional Journalists, Women in Communication, Philhellenic Greek Professional Society; Awards: National Council of Teachers of English Award, 1972; Society of Professional Journalists, Mark of Excellence Award, 1975; Comments: *Poetry has served as my wellspring of creativity. I wrote extensive poetry as a youngster, then abandoned it in favor of articles and essays. As an adult, I have come full circle. Poetry once again provides the soil from which my other writing grows.*

TWILIGHT IMAGE

The western sky now gold in color
Spectacular sunset unlike no other
A lonely cowboy heading home
Through bramble, brush and thorn.

The evening air perfumed with sage
As he rode across the range
With thought of home and who waits there
An ageless love of one yet fair.

His voice in song slowly drifts
In the saddle his body shifts
Hanging high the evening star
The mellow sound from his guitar.

In the distance cattle lowing
Beneath the moon coyote howling
Sweet scent of lilac in the breeze
Humble abode 'neath cottonwood trees.

Body frayed but filled with peace
Trusting fully, never to cease
A gentle touch for his faithful mare
The cowboy . . . lowered his head in prayer.

Jeannie Davis Weaver

JEANNIE DAVIS WEAVER. Born: Waynesville, North Carolina, 3-17-38; resides in southeastern Idaho; Married: Kenneth Weaver, M.D.; Physician, Researcher, Writer; Education: Arkansas School of Arts, Haywood Technical College, Greenville School Interior Design, T.V. News Photography; Occupations: Private Investigator (17 years); Entertainer (professional); Songwriter, Writer, Artist, former Model; Membership: Tennessee Frontiersmen, an historic muzzle-loading group dedicated to reviving the past in drama, exhibition and film, chartered by State of Tennessee (only female member); Awards: 1986, 1989 poetry contest, Laureate Press; Poetry: 'Country Heaven,' 'Greener Pastures,' 'Just a Dream,' 'Attic Treasures,' 'Lord, I Forgot to Pray,' 'It's Been So Long Ago,' all songs; Poetry published in: *American Poetry Anthology, Volume VI; Ideals* magazine; *Diversion* Magazine; *Homecoming News; Impressions; Relics and Treasures of Yesteryear,* self-published; Comments: *Nostalgic expression through poetry and song allows rebirth of an era bygone. Today is the past of each tomorrow from yesterday. This day, our memories borrow reviving characters, sights and scents; reliving pleasant past events. In each memory, a treasure . . . packed away, lying dormant, somewhere, along our way.*

A TRAGEDY THAT BROUGHT
US TO OUR KNEES

My mother was a mother of twelve, she taught us how
to live and to stay out of hell. She would cook the meals
and clean the house, and then she would rid the house from
all the mouse. She loved to work day by day, until one day
I heard her say, "There is a pain in my side, how can I bear
it, seems I am always in despair."

Then one day I heard her pray, "Lord forgive me for my
wrongness each day."

Then tragedy swept across my home, leaving me without
a place to belong. It took my mother and father
too, now I don't know what I must do. My mother lies so
stiff and cold, she didn't have a chance to grow old.
She struggled for life night and day until God came and
took her away.

Father, he tried to hold on, until he realized that
he was all alone. He gave up the ghost and said once
more, "I'll meet her there on the other shore."

Bertha M. Zackery

FRIENDSHIP

When the two men met for the first time
They did not think much about the meeting.
But time would draw the two back together,
Time and time again. Then they would talk
With each other on the telephone a lot. They
Got to be very friendly with each other and
Would help each other out administratively
Wise. Included in this help, they would send
Each other circulars and other pamphlets
That each other would be interested in. Since
Both were due to retire sometime soon,
They were naturally glad to hear each
Other's voice and see each other when they could.
After they retired; they just kept up their
Friendship and became very close friends.

Michael Swartwood

A DIRTY OLD MAN

Don't care if'n I don't go nowhar,
    I'd have to wash and comb my hair.
Shoes untied, got a crick in my back,
    Cain't bend over for to tie up the slack.
Cain't turn around, got a hole in my breeches,
    No eyes back thar to see to sew on any stitches.
Sittin' around all day, sweat a-runnin' off my chin,
    Open up the door and the flies swarm in.
Old gray mare chawin' on the cellar door,
    Looked out the winder and she chawed some more.
Planted some poppin' corn up the hill a pace,
    It got so bloomin' hot it popped all over the place.
Turned in the chickens fer to eat up the corn,
    They thought it was snow and was all froze the next morn.
Thar hain't no school in our home town,
    The woodpeckers et the school house down.
Hain't had a bath fer the last month or so,
    The water dried up down at the ol' fishin' hole.
Don't care if'n I don't go nowhar,
    I'd have to wash and comb my hair.

Wanda Lee Burrell

THE MELTING POT

Little brown boy, what is your fate?
Born in a nation of racial hate.

Little red boy, you don't understand
The conflict and contention throughout the land.

Little yellow boy, skipping to school
Do you know the meaning of the golden rule?

Little black boy, so carefree and gay,
What are your dreams for a later day?

I see you standing in front of the crowd
Your head held high, you've a right to be proud

Encore after encore comes from the throng —
As you lift your baton to the strains of the song.

The scene is changing, you're dressed in white,
I see quick movement under bright light

The scalpel moves swiftly under your hand
Your service is sought throughout the land.

Black, white, yellow, brown or red,
Genius holds no preference to race, 'tis said.

I challenge the nation, who dares lift a hand?
The future depends on the youth of this land.

Wanda Lee Burrell

GONE AWAY

One day, when you have gone away,
I'll know where to find you, along the Piscataway —
canoeing its intricate streams and main.
Perhaps singing under a protected canopy of leaves
or listening to whippoorwills through the trees.
Your shimmering glory at sunset
reflects shadows of sea gulls,
wingspread and spirits soaring
through passionate evening into morning.

One day, when I have gone away,
among fields of daffodils I'll stay —
dancing in a yellow skirt, reciting sonnets
about the blooming spring and resignation of autumn.
My fragrant company abounds in narrow groves
of dogwood and trumpet creepers, until
a June breeze sweeps me to shallow bay.
A beautiful memory
drifting down the Piscataway.

Lynn Ware

UNENDING MEMORIES

I will always love you,
these deep feelings are engraved in my heart,
just to see you, be with you and talk to you
fills me with happiness and warmth,
until I have to part,
then the memories leave your smile in my heart,
yeah,
the memories leave your sweet smile in my heart.

Brian Floyd Newton

THE EYES OF LOVE

Childhood eyes are renewed again, and the eyes
of passion have now brightened within. I've been
waiting for you, waiting for you, in my dreams.

Eyes of Love, recaptured again, and the lust
for life, rekindled within. At last you've
come to me, come to me, you're here with me.

Life is good for us willing to dream, and the
love you bring is endless it seems. We can
have it all, have it all, if we please.

Childhood eyes are renewed again, and the
eyes of love are recaptured within. It's a
beautiful world, beautiful world, for those
who dream.

Childhood eyes renewed again.

Eyes of Love recaptured within.

It's a beautiful world, beautiful world, for those
who dream.

Celeste Noel Perkins

FROST PATTERN

The frost pattern on the window, resembles your
face. I guess it could be my tears distorting
my outlook, distorting my outlook. I remember
that you said hold on, hold on to what we've got,
but it's been three days and two days seemed like
forever.

I understand that you had to leave. New Mexico or
something, but that's not a consolation for holding
you, for holding you. Well, you said that you'd be
back, oh how I want to believe that, but it's been
three days and now you're two thousand miles away.

Could it possibly be time to start over? I've
already packed, I packed up my things. To the
town or the city? To the town or the city? It's
been three days, but the frost pattern just won't
melt away. The frost pattern stays and it stays.

Celeste Noel Perkins

GOLD ON THE MOUNTAIN

Like the gold rush to the mountains, it could be our only
chance. Oh, to fulfill the dreams we harbor, if we will only
take the chance.

On our journey to the mountain, it will take all that we have.
Does gold really line the mountain, will we have it in our hand?

While excitement fills our wonder, defeat is ready at our heels.
All the glory of the mountain, I have to see it to know it's real.

I see the gold rushing from the mountain, in all its beauty I
can't describe. Take your chance and go to the mountain, it has
been waiting for you and I. There's gold, gold, gold on the
mountain.

Celeste Noel Perkins

Though the winds may blow in every direction
why do I earnestly await a sign of perfection to a misty day?
Return to me I say, a cosmetic tranquility of new hopes and
dreams, an abundant array, lathered, and aside from all schemes
of an ogre not yet fortunate to be redeemed as a servant dwelling
on a simple homesite as fresh and as wide as the ocean
casts waves, the tide reaches its high. So then do I.

Now grateful for my place in the sun and
fortunate to know of its mist
yet reluctant to search furthermore in time
I cast my light finally realizing my crime.

Marianne Bartsch

EXCUSE ME

Excuse me, are you — are you
who I think you are

You've changed a trifle bit

Excuse me, are you — are you
My love from years ago
The one who promised, to never let me go

Your hair's a little different

Excuse me, are you — are you
One who has traveled from afar
The one I used to adore

You look a little taller

Excuse me, are you — are you
My long lost love
Tell me you traveled the world, to find me once more

Your face has changed a bit

Excuse me, sir, I must really know
Oh I beg your pardon, sir,
I thought you were my love from years ago.

June Drao

IF ONLY

I walk along the quiet shores, thinking only
if you were with me once more
If just one more time, you could be by my side
your arms around me, holding me so tight
If only we could laugh, like we used to do
make jokes at the bad times, look forward to the new
If only I could feel your warm tender kiss
just one more time
and know that you'll be forever mine
If only I could hold you and tell you I love you
If only — if only — if only
I can only repeat
as I continue to walk quietly along the beach

June Drao

BONNIE A COUNTRY SCHOOLMARM

There is not enough darkness
   in all the world
To put out the light of one
   small candle.
      An old Chinese proverb

With her one small candle
She touched the wicks of others
And lighted country roads
Of dirt, crushed stone and gravel
And helped them to become
Illuminated thoroughfares and
Impressive boulevards where
More enlightened people
Live, visit and travel.

Her candlelight reflections
Will glow on and on and on
Until every human thirsting
Brain and cell are gone.

Dorothy Moore

THE PLAYFUL BREEZE

Today an impish little breeze
   Went dancing down the hill
      Twirling the sweet wild roses
         Partners in his quadrille
         Whistling through swaying grass
      The freshest songs he knew
   Tickling the tiny toes
Of spiders wet with dew.

His game of hide-and-seek
   Was really lots of fun
      Until the scarecrow's silly wink
         Motioned which way he'd gone.
         He shook the half-locked door
      Of milkweed's silken store
   And chuckled as he puffed
To launch airships galore.

But rainclouds spoiled his fun
   And sent him home to stay:
      "Someday I'll grow so very big
         I'll blow those clouds away!"

Vera Shaw

WHY, WHY, WHY

As a parent how did I fail?
   What in the living hell did I do?
What did I do to deserve your hate?
   Other than keep you out of jail
Think always first of you
   Help keep your affairs straight
Be there when you needed me
   Defend you to others
All of this falls on barren ground
   As you are no longer around
You've hied off to some strange place
   Where strangers now share your grace
Your invalid mother sits and cries
   I wipe the tears from her eyes
Should I now take all the blame
   Because you now hate your given name?

Wesley M. Alden

OUR SONNY

*Our thirty-six year old son was
killed in a helicopter crash*

He was our first born
A beautiful baby on a beautiful morn.
He was a precious child, so smart
And so dear to my heart.
He was a special love
sent from Heaven above.
He grew in body and mind,
he taught us all to be kind
to all God's creatures, great and small
(even snakes, for goodness' sakes)
His unique talent was helpful to all.
He was a remarkable young man
who from adversity never ran.
He was brave, strong and true
His favorite color was blue
He was his own man!
He was a gentle man!
He was a gentleman!

Hesse G. Byrd

MY NEW LIFE AS GRANDMA OF JESSICA FRANCES

My life began many a year ago —
But now I know
What life means,
For I am grandma of Jessica
Frances,
A darling "blue-eyed blonde,"
One of whom I'm more than fond,
Sure she cries but what
Baby doesn't?
She wouldn't be a baby if she wasn't
(Crying that is).
Then she babbles, coos and smiles,
Catching my heart with lovestrings,
She'll hold me forever,
And I'll never
Let her go.
For I know I'm grandma of
Jessica Francis,
And that is the poetry
Of *my* life!

Jacqueline Adam

THE ROAD TO PEACE

Whispered words of silence,
   So gently shines the moon.
A guiding light,
   Showing me the road to peace.

Singing sweetly of life,
   Caressing his Mother Earth.
Soothing her wounds,
   Lighting the road to peace.

Let us follow the path,
   Let no one stray.
For within the light, the answer,
   The road to peace.

Cheryl Paris

THE PANGS OF PAIN AND PASSION

I know I had so many pains
   The day when he left me
When he gave me pangs of pain
   And the passion I could see

He always meant so much to me
   He never let me down.
Because he meant so much to me
   He will always wear a crown.

We had so many different pains
   And many different times
When different things were found
   We even heard church chimes.

We try and think of different things
   And always try to be
The ones we always think we are
   And he meant so much to me.

Nancy Quinn

PHILOSOPHY . . . THE QUESTIONS OF LIFE

*To my devoted parents, who have
influenced my questions of life*

Here I stand
All alone between myself
And the world
Wondering what my purpose of life is
And if I should do that or this
   Should I think only of logic
   Separating my life's magic?
   Or will I trust only my emotions
   In every situation?
   Or would I fill my head and heart
   With beliefs till I depart?
   Or should I admire my values
   While I ignore my failures?
This is philosophy
   Thoughts
      Feelings
         Beliefs
            Values
The questions of life!

Junghee Kim

WHAT A FEELING

I am holding to my dignity no matter what it costs
if I abandoned love and joy
Roses and delicious fruit
for a lion or a tiger
With an orchard plenty roaring
Lord — let not this secret feeling
Be for a thirsty beast
through whirlwind disasters and disappointments
I am not the best not trying to be the worst
equally I'll be fair I'll put joy into the air
I'll nurture it with love I do care
if I am not good for you — you won't let me be
are you a gloomy forest of thorns
exposed to fury elements
are you hungry and thirsty
Just to torture me
My guard too far to protect me I am very weak
You are too near you won't forget to reach
a secret feeling overpowering me
My body is larger than the feeling but my feeling squeezes me.

Rosa Lee King

NOW I HAVE HOPE

I felt pain I have hurt a loved one gone
life brought gain life brought loss
you and I will wait as this was meant to be
experiences and time change things around
I have lost a part of me
Now I have hope
it was a life for me
Not to hold and not for me to keep
Not to tuck away in a safe place
or in a draw benease
friend whatever the kind mother father
sister brother husband wife children
you only have memories of love and of years
Can you do what's been done days past and gone
I thought all love was gone time passes years on
I thought again the greatest love man knows
Will give peace of mind to all mankind
the Jesus that in each of you will give joy instead
and pull you out of the cloud and take me out the rain
and let sunshine out again

Rosa Lee King

THREE WISHES

If I were given three wishes today,
I'd wish not for money, riches, or popularity:
    but for something I could have forever!
My first wish would be for a true friendship with those whom
    I am the closest:
    having neverending happiness —
    we would never part ways or lose touch again.
My second wish would be for your love:
    a love I've wanted since we first met, but have been too
    shy to ask —
    a love that would last until the end of time.
My third wish would be to never lose sight of my hopes and
    dreams:
    in case you feel I am not the one to receive your love,
    I need dreams to keep from falling apart —
    and a hope that our friendship would not be lost
    over a misled love.

Tracy Barankiewicz

LIFE IS

Life is a challenge, full of ups and downs,
Life is joy, flowing all around,
Life is each day, with each step that comes our way,
Life is right now, when you're alive —
Life is a dream, always wanting to come true,
Life is the future, wondering what it holds for you,
Life is a shadow, following you everywhere you go,
Life is today, and not tomorrow —
Life is a hope, that keeps coming your way,
Life is a mystery, always wondering why it came,
Life is a gift, given to you and me,
Life is for free, each day we can breathe —
Life is a moment, each one coming your way,
Life is your mind and the direction you will take,
Life is from your heart, with you all the time,
Life is what you are, going through changing times —
Life is a play, each person going their way,
Life is a script, written out each day,
Life is God, and the love He gave,
Life is Jesus, the love God made —

Benjamin E. Thompkins, Jr.

THAT BURNING FLAME

My love for you is a burning flame,
And in my heart has played a game.
It's the winner of, of the champion of my life
It gives me power every hour.
It keeps me strong I am not alone.
I say these things because they are true,
That burning flame that's in my heart is you.

For your love has ignited a flame in my heart,
That will melt us together and nothing can take us apart.
In my life it's a gleaming light
That lights my world and makes it bright.
It broadens my path from day to day,
My love for you can never stray.
Your recipe of burning love has made a
Steaming brew,
That burning flame that's in my heart is you.

Without you my world would turn to a volcano,
It would erupt and explode.
Then all our love would turn to ash,
With its lava spilled and my heart unfilled.
Please tell me what would I do,
That burning flame that lights my world,
Is the love I have within my heart for you.

Josephine Dicks

FORGIVE ME

*Dedicated to my mom with a big
thanks for seeing me through this*

Forgive me is all of you that I must ask —
To live any longer would be a difficult task —

I have gone through so much sorrow and so much pain —
I feel like I have all to lose and nothing to gain —

Forgive me because I chose to part —
And remember that I truly love you with all my heart . . .

Ruthie Mac

IN THE DARKNESS OF YOUR MIND

In the darkness
    of your mind . . .

There's a Helter Skelter View
Micro-dots and Visions
That can make you come unglued.

Everything happens
    so quickly
One cannot stop
Winding down
    takes forever

To the shadows
    of your mind

They keep saying
    These things take time.

So you work back
    toward reality

From the darkness
    of your mind.

Sharon Derrico

WARNING: TO ALL THE BIRDS THAT EVER THOUGHT TO FLY

If you don't have a love nest
 to call your very own

Your companion will be loneliness
 your heart won't have a home

The minutes will be hours
 turned into years

The sea will be an ocean
 from the droplets of your tears

If you give up that love nest
 to take wing
  to fly

You'll only bat your wings at air
 and never touch the sky

So build your little love nest
 where birds in love fly

Furnish it with kindness
 and a thoughtfulness of mind

Be ever oh so patient
 be her valentine

Keep your little love nest
 for your very own

Hold her ever gently
 and never
  ever roam.

Betty Jame

ON VIEWING A STATUE OF GEORGE WASHINGTON

Is this the hand that raised the sword
That set our country free?
Is this the man that signed the scroll
That gave us liberty?

Is this the commander who led his troops
Through battles far and wide?
Is this the patriot who suffered so
When his comrades bled and died?

Is this the statesman who led our nation
Towards our chosen destiny?
Is this the president who governed
With such integrity?

Is this the American who did
What no other man has done?
Yes, this is the father of our country.
This is George Washington!

H. G. Brady

FISHING

(When I did)

long hot cozy afternoons
sweating beads of love
of interest

talking about the moment
                    no more
Dad and myself
almost duplicates of each other
drifting peacefully upon the gentle
rippled water

my turn to row

he's ready

"even strokes" Dad speaks
he is so right

diamond-like sparkles
when the excitement has been reeled in

scales upon the bottom of the boat

Dad always caught the biggest fish
but there were times when I did

William Capozzi

HE DRANK MY BROTHER TO DEATH

Thanks to a man who didn't think
    and filled himself
        with plenty of "drinks"
Got in a van —
    hit a man —
    "left him for dead,"
That's what he said.

Our parents lost a son.
I had three brothers,
Now I'm less one.

He was a father —
    daughters, three.
Their daddy's gone —
The (man?) drinks "free."

A young woman —
    her husband lost
The (man?) still drinks "free."
Hop's life paid the cost!

Nic

POEMS FOR THE NEW GENERATION

BETTER RUN

Happen to meet a violent man
Be among those who also ran
Take no chance get away fast
To stick around may be your last
For a violent man has no control
Fool around with him may never grow old

BAD NIGHT

In early morning the rooster crows
To let you know of last night's woes

EXIT PLEASE

Where's the head and not the tail
Yelled old Jonah inside the whale

THE OLD WEST

This man of the West always carried a gun
Face to face in a fight he always won
So good with a gun called him a sinner
In every challenge he was a winner
Shot him in the back cowardly thing to do
This fast gun sure was through

R. W. Champion

YOU'RE SO SPECIAL

You're so very special to me,
You opened my eyes and you made me see.
Where there was sadness you gave me joy,
And to me you're like a baby's toy.
You're so special, so very special to me.
And I love you, love you, love you, love you,
Yes I do.

Where I was low you lifted me higher,
Where I was so cold you gave me fire.
Now my warm love for you,
Goes deeper than the ocean,
And higher than the sky so blue.
You're so special, so very special to me.
And I love you, love you, love you, love you,
Yes I do.

You're my sweet buzzing honeybee with your honey,
Melting all in my ecstasy.
When I look in your eyes, I feel your power,
And I know I need you every hour.
You're so special, so very special to me.
And I love you, love you, love you, love you,
Yes I do.

Josephine Dicks

IN MY LIFE THERE WILL ALWAYS BE YOU

I can't go anywhere except you are there.
We are oneness in love because we cared.
You are that special someone in my life.
Through sickness and in health,
Through all troubles and strife.
Your tenderness has put me through.
And in my life there will always be you.

You are the one that God has created for me,
To have and to hold until eternity.
This relationship of ours,
Has such strong and lasting power.
The closeness of our togetherness
Is the essence of it all.
I'll always love you no matter what befalls.
I'll find a clue.
For in my life there will always be you.

Our love is strong, our love is tough,
And it's everlasting for the two of us.
I've accepted the intimacy that God has provided to be.
Now I've made a commitment to you, can't you see.
Sharing and caring in everything we do,
For in my life there will alway be you.

Josephine Dicks

THE NIGHT LIVES

Today is now lost in the past. All the colors of day,
yellow, red, and blue have merged into one black mask.
Only the two extreme colors are left.
The darkness of black and the light from the stars.
The absence of color.
The wind is still. The ocean is flat and motionless,
the sea gulls and ducks at rest.

In the distance a very dull misty glow begins to appear.
There is something lurking in the blackness of night.
The night is waking up, coming to life. Now,
a warm creamy gold glow is rising out there.
It seems to be suspended in blackness.
The shape is round and cheesy-looking with a mock smile.

Lazy thin clouds pass gently across its face.
The flow is getting less yellow, or more white.

A full moon! The night lives. The night lives.

Sam Brown

IN THE GARDEN MY DEAR

Come into the garden,
where man and woman have an array
of beautiful colors to choose from.

You're looking at an artist palette.
Beginning with white, black, yellow, orange, red,
tan and hundreds or more shades of brown.

In the Garden My Dear

Give you a high yellow, fellow?
How about a red hot one over there?
Don't frown. I'll get you the pretty brown.

In the garden, we are the true melting pot.

Come to our garden for a natural tan, one
that will never change, peel, flake or disappear.
Do you hear?

In the Garden My Dear.

Sam Brown

SECRET LETTERS

I've kept the cards and letters
Through the years you've sent to me,
They're in a secret hiding place
For no one else to see.

They're carefully tied with a ribbon
That once was bright and blue,
The color now has faded
But the message still is new.

Sometimes when I'm lonely
The letters beckon me,
To come again to the hiding place
No one knows but me.

I carefully open each envelope
Every word read again with my heart,
And live for a while in hours once yours and mine
Before time broke our worlds apart.

Mildred M. Byrd

GOOD-BYE TO A FRIEND

A friend of mine left me today,
We were friends for a brief while.
Our paths crossed but only once in a long period of time,
But when we met it was a special day.

He was at the end of a long journey,
And mine had just begun.
He was aged, his travels many.
I was young, with desire to travel many a journey.

My friend died today.
A part of me died with him,
But a part of him will be with me all the way.

Our parting was special,
He held my hand and I held his.
He turned to me with feeble eyes
And told me to "Reach for the skies!"

A friend of mine left today.
We were friends for a brief while.
But our friendship will last always!

Edward H. Kwantes

SAY HELLO AND SAY GOOD-BYE

Say Hello and say Good-bye,
Hello to someone who has grown,
Grown to be a confident and strong person,
Good-bye to the person you always thought I was.

Struggling through time
I slowly have had a change of mind.
By becoming this person
Have left you behind.

You have always thought yourself as:
Superior, intelligent, charming, and above all others.
Making everyone around you
Feel worthless and non-existent.

I am now a better person,
One of worth and one who can understand others.
I am sorry you are left behind,
But I must go onward and forward.

Say Hello and say Good-bye.
Good-bye to the person who used to love you,
Hello to the person who loves himself once again.

Edward H. Kwantes

MY LOVE

I can say that you, my love, are truly my best friend —
Your loving support is something of which I can always depend.

You have been my listening ear and the shoulder I could lean on —
And you, my love, are always there for me to depend upon.

You have shared my good times with me
  and helped me through the bad —
Whenever I was unhappy, it also made you sad.

Whatever seems to happen, you are there and quick to defend —
I know that you will be with me, my love, until the bitter end . . .

Ruthie Mac

TOO LATE

"It's too late," you whispered.
Three dreaded words; ones I didn't want to hear,
  but needed to, so I asked, and you answered.
"I'll always love you," I thought,
  fighting back a flood of tears that threatened to flow,
  but I couldn't let them, not now; not till later.
It seems that time and circumstances worked against us,
  coming between us; tearing us apart;
  and putting far too much distance between us —
  physically and emotionally.
I just hope that someday
  we can bridge that gap
  and be friends again.
And I promise when that times comes,
if you won't whisper,
I won't cry.

Carolynn Jerome

THE BABY COLT ON THE PRAIRIE

Yesterday I stumbled across a beautiful scene
It was so much creativity in his first try,
That its yearning to go forward made me cry
He was so very brave but small
And yet wanting to kick and fly
Falling and falling, he never for a moment
Gave up hope, I left him that way
And the very next day feeling so excited
About the young colt, I skipped, and I
Rolled down the hillside, through the
Flowers and brush to see him again
And to my surprise! The struggling colt
On the prairie had disappeared, and above
The soft blue sky, I saw him fly, passing me by.
Thence wondering was it a trick of the eye
Or was he something I'd adore to experience
Come true and never die.

Brenda Anthony

BRENDA LEE ANTHONY. Pen Name: Queen Bee; Born: Scotland Neck, North Carolina; Single; Education: Attending school at N.A. Institute for Writers; Occupation: Salesperson; Memberships: Songwriter's Club of America; Poetry: 'African Drums,' 'The Cry of Hunger,' 'Resume to Jesus'; Other Writings: "The Darkness in the House with the Rising Sun," short story; Themes: *The fulfilling caresses of life itself, the dream and hope that every man carries hidden deep within his soul, adventure and suspense, the heights and depths of experiencing joy and pain.*

COUNTRY MUSIC IN HEAVEN

Dedicated to the late
Rosamond Baker, my mother.

You gave me life and love, and taught me all you knew
and I guess that's what mothers are for;
When the angels came and you had to leave . . . its true
and every day I miss you more and more;

I hope there's roses and flying swings
and rainbow-colored leaves that fall;
Little kids and sparkling things
Crystal birds . . . and most of all
I pray there's . . . country music in Heaven;

It always took so little to make you smile
your zest for life should be an inspiration;
You proved each and every day, in your own style
that mothers are the good Lord's best creation;

I hope there's kittens and football games
and puppy dogs to fetch a ball;
Memories . . . and stars of fame
Fireworks . . . and that's not all
I pray there's . . . country music in Heaven.

Marlene Kasprzak

BEAUTY IN THE BLACKBIRD

I discovered the essence of beauty in a pretty blackbird.
We caught each other's attention because we stared each
other dead in the eye. There seemed to be a mutually warm
sensation. Blackbird, teach me to fly.

Staring through a bush while the sun catoptrically provided
the right shade of light, it was then that I knew what art
was all about. Art is a spirit. It makes so many marvelous
things like the bird and the flower. It adds to the fact
that the bird's color was a velvet black robe with shades of
purple and blue as its feathers fold. Majestic is not even
the word. Majestic in form is the pretty Blackbird.

Right on for the Artist for His art is appealing. Beauty is
a feeling because of art. Quite a calm picture perfect.
So, the message of art was transmitted to me via the bird.
Art is supreme, it is in all things. I was so much into this
rapture that something became a part of me. It seemed as
though I heard Blackbird speak these words, ''I will teach
you how to soar like an eagle, how to ride the winds over
wide terrain, how to touch the significance of art in wisdom,
because Blackbird is my name.''

Gajef McNeil

THE COLOSSAL MISS LIBERTY

She towers as ''The New Colossus'' on Liberty Island —
The majestic symbol of freedom to all around the world.
She stands supremely alone with her torch held high in hand;
Yet she stands not alone, for in spirit we beside her stand;
In spirit, we are with her and are part of her and she of us;
In spirit, we are all of us and forever with her bound thus.
Still, this towering and stately lady holds up for us more
   than the lamp:
She holds up that right to be free, which is the very soul
   of freedom's stamp!

Joseph Bonsignore

A HUMAN TRAGEDY

No one knows the pain and suffering
that befall me,
when the ketchup runs out.
My hot dog stands alone before me,
estranged,
naked on its bun,
crying out for union with its favorite fruit.
I grab the tall, sleek bottle I purchased
for a dollar, thirty nine,
and tap, tap, tap
gently at first . . .
then with increasing vigor,
begging,
pleading for the thick, rich, tomatoey substance
to flow forth in all its fullness.
But my anticipation is alas answered
with emptiness.
And grudgingly,
I realize my life is empty, too,
until my next trip to Safeway.

James Cappel

ONE LOOK FROM AN ETERNAL LOVER'S EYES

An eternal lover's look has mystifying eloquence sublime,
A look of divinity such as no other eyes can mime;
The epitome of romantic lovers' feeling
Is this supreme expression all revealing.

As Gibran effuses, ''Love is the poet's elation,''
For poets revel in lovers' adulation.
Yet, no instinctive word of poets electrifies
Compared to an intuitive look from a lover's eyes.

The look of love is a subtle nuance and shading,
Growing and blossoming with sharing depths pervading.
The countenance of angels which radiates and multiplies
Is reminiscent of those inspiring looks from a lover's eyes.

There is no sensation like loving ecstatically,
Intimate gazes shared between lovers dramatically;
The hearing of exquisitely unspoken words entrances
As in enraptured silence soulmates exchange glances.

All the love rhymes of poets cannot fully express,
For they seem to grow pale . . . and, even . . . colorless;
Albeit, no matter how eloquent,no word sanctifies
Compared to one sacred look from an eternal lover's eyes!

EveLyn Russell

SCHOOL LIFE

When I was younger in my high school days,
I had lots of enemies and lots of pain.
I went to school day after day saying
I'll get through this in my own special way.
I come home crying and ashamed of being laughed at
and called names.
The friends I had said not to worry or be sad.
The friends I had were special and dear.
They were with me through laughter and tears.
When my senior year came I was feeling different
and was no longer ashamed. I was looking toward the
future as the year was coming to the end, of leaving
my childhood and my adulthood was near.

Julie Farris

GUIDING STAR

Smile as beautiful as the rainbow free.
Yesterday a star, today a guiding light,
Leading America through the night.
A gem in my heart carrying him into eternity.
People see he went far.
Autograph from a movie star, Reagan became our president,
A special gift that God sent.
Without neglect, to open a gate,
To help end all world-wide hate.
In the 1950s he gave gentle concern for this little girl.
Ronald visited our theatre so small,
With a question so tall, "What can I do for you?"
I handed him my little autograph book,
Fascinated by his glamorous made-up look.
I learned about movies, kings and queens,
In what seemed to be my home, a world within me.
Mr. Reagan gave a swirl and now the cares
This fine president shares
With America the great!

Bonnie Simmons Peter

BONNIE HELEN SIMMONS PETER. Born: Pontiac, Michigan; Occupations: Songwriter, Author, Poet; Memberships: National Association of Players, Top Records Songwriters Association, Songwriters Club of America; Awards: Golden Poet Awards, 1985-87; 12 Awards of Merit; Winner of round No.1 of the Great American Screen Test; Poetry: 'Peace to Mother Earth,' 1987; 'Silver Lake Within My Soul,' poem and song, *Country Creations,* Nashville, 1987; Other Writings: 'Put a Smile Upon Your Make-up,' song and video, Magic Key Productions, 1987; "Polished Walls of Memory," potential Top 20 hit songs, *Songs of Love, Songs of Life,* record album, 1987; *Blue Scarlet,* non-fiction book, 1986; "Magnificent Trifle," short story; Numerous unpublished songs and poems; Manuscript for 'Black & White Lily'; Themes: *Living, love.* Comments: *I have great dreams and expectations. My ambition is to publish a series of children's books, and a book helpful to health and diet. I hope to produce a doll named Blue Scarlet.*

ANGELISA

Was there ever one more fair, more beautiful than her?
She, Angelisa, is the one to whom I refer.
Above all beauties, she is the one that I prefer —
Of that, I am sure; of such beauty I do not err.

Were there ever eyes more blue, so blue, and hair so fair?
No — Angelisa's eyes and hair are beyond compare —
This, believe me, to the whole wide world I would declare —
Such eyes, so blue; such hair, so fair — a sight oh so rare!

Was there ever such a form more deserving of fame?
No — Angelisa's form puts all others to swift shame!
Of that form, of her flawless face, in love I became —
This I say again and again still in full declaim!
And if ever the world sees her, me they would not blame —
Ever Angelisa — she stands alone as her name!

Joseph Bonsignore

PUNCTUATION

A stranger semantic duo
has not existed
than that
implied
in a coupling
of erraticism
with
otherworldly patience.

A more peculiar lexical analysis
has not been pursued
than that
required
to reconcile
rebellion
with
spiritual hope.

Such contradictory lexical semantics
abides —
in the most miraculous human feeling of *all:*
Unconditional *love.*

Patricia Robinson Williams

NO WORDS

Now I write this just for you;
these mere words will have to do.
For no measure can express
how He fills our emptiness,
Or how He always holds us in His loving hand;
His love so gentle, like that of a lamb.
I thank Him for the gifts He longs to give;
like that of a friend, that makes it easier to live.
I have no words that I can give to you;
only a picture of a rose, as it opens to morning dew.
You're as precious as a petal, so gentle and soft;
for it's people like you, that send my heart aloft.
Someday our Lord will reveal to you
the feelings I have, as no words could ever do.

Bryan Humphrey

FANTASIES

Sitting here in the darkness
All alone.
My thoughts and dreams
Are all my own.
Things are really mixed up
In my mind.
Someday I hope my dreams
I can find.
I have this Fantasy.
Will it ever become a Reality?
I think about it a lot.
I fantasize about it too.
Getting things started — well, in that department
I don't know what to do.
Someday, perhaps, one of my dreams
Will come true.
If I really try hard enough,
Maybe even two.

Kathy Bonito

OUR GIFT

I thank the Lord for granting me,
The chance of meeting you.
And pray that He will continue to see,
How rare we'd be, we two.

It seems that hurt and heartaches,
Have been the course we've both been through.
But now He's given us the chance,
To never again feel blue.

For you have gone and brought to me,
The one and only thing,
That I have found I've needed so,
Yet no one else could bring.

The sincerity from in your eyes,
And the warmth in your gentle touch,
Have made me realize the joys in life,
I missed so very much.

The strength and the desire, to be an active part again,
Of life and nature's beauty, as I felt it was back then,
Were all but drained, before I knew you, from deep within my soul,
'Til the softness of your face, your kiss, made me again feel whole.

Dawne Lepore

EXPERIENCE

Veinte-cinco y medio

I had experienced all those years;
All those lonely years that have gone by
I had known that all my fears would never die
I was hoping that someday, somehow, sometime, and someway,
All my fears would fade away
All those lonely years that have gone by will end up as one more tear

I'm in reality now;
I could never tell how I'm going to be
If only you were here with me now;
I know that we will always be as one for eternity, for immortality,
 'til the end of time totally . . .
. . . all so sweet, Becky.

Ernie H-Donez

ERNIE H-DONEZ. Pen Name: E. H-D; Born: Harlingen, Texas, 3-11-58; Single; Education: Tulelake High School, 1978; College of the Desert, 1983; Disabled; Awards: Excellence in Creative Writing, Annual Rotary Awards, 4-28-86; Writings: 'A Clown,' poem, song, 11-16-81; 'Much More Than Before,' poem, song, short story, 1-4-83; 'A Summer In Tule,' poem, song, 1-16-78; 'I'll Get By On My Own,' poem, song, short story, 12-31-84; 'Bare,' poem, song, 3-9-82; Comments: *I want to tell the whole wide world how they made me feel.*

CAMARADERIE

I want to help you smile again;
Not ridicule your pain — your sorrow.
I want to lift you up
So that you won't only see the dinginess of the ground,
But also the glory of the sun
That shines upon you.
I want to teach you the levity of laughter:
So that you may learn
To lighten your burden with mirth;
Learning the folly and splendor
It is to be human.
I want to pull you close,
And let you rest upon me,
So that you may gather strength anew.
I want . . . to be . . . your friend.

John Wills

FREE SOUL

Viewed on the coast the wondering savage stand,
Uncouth, and fresh from her Creator's hand;
While woods and fangling brakes, where wild she ran,
Bore a rough semblance of primeval woman . . .
A form like this, illustrious souls, of yore,
Your own Marinite's sea-girt land wore . . .
Rude as the wilds around her sylvan home,
In freedom's grandeur see the love child roam;
Bare were her limbs, and strong with toil and cold,
By untamed nature cast in giant mould.
In the depth of Tamalpais groves,
She dwells with does that gain unenvied loves:
Or joins in social isles the mirthful band,
Or leads the dance on Native's strand.
There sits the Power, from busier scenes convey'd,
There walks with Nature over the unbounded shade;
There soothed to rest, and pleased with artless strains,
Restores a golden age on Marin's meadowed plains.

Mark Richards

THE LITTLE ONES KNOW

Never were you as you appeared.
While you had other men's respect
At home you were feared.
Neighbors and friends saw you as honest and just
But the little ones knew you were not one to trust.
Their minds have been tainted
Their dreams darkly painted.
Hearts become as rust
From loneliness, shame, and mistrust.
Remember the game — remember it well
Secret! Secret! Never to tell.
Yet feverishly they search to find a way
To free themselves from yesterday.
Tomorrow's freedom — will it ever be?
You're the one who holds the key
Or is it held by the little ones . . . we.

Dolores Marie Torres

CREATION

I stand amongst the tall and stately giants,
Which begin in the earth and reach for the sky,
Truly the bridge between heaven and earth,
So much more than I.

Within mother earth they begin as seed,
Drawing water and food,
They sprout to receive —
The open air and sunlight.

The day, the night, the dawn and twilight,
The turning of every season —
Nurtures their growth,
'Til they have far surpassed man,
Touching the very sky above!
Even then their root remains, growing stronger.

What creature, what object attends such growth?
What captivates and enchants,
Drawing a feeling of envy and admiration?
Something as simple as a tree!

Harriet R. Measures

A MOMENT

A moment is but a fleeting memory
Of a special time shared together.

It may be a smile . . . it may be a look,
A funny conversation . . . a new and wonderful discovery,
A sentimental day spent together.

A moment is but a fleeting memory
To be relived over and over again.
Nothing can compare with a moment
Because it is so perfect, quaint, and special.

A walk in the rain . . . A bright sunny day,
Your eyes meet his . . . Lips touch in a kiss.
I love you is unspoken, yet written in the eyes
Of adoration.

A moment of tenderness . . .
Moments bittersweet . . .
Moments of fond remembrance.

A moment is but a fleeting memory . . .
Given, shared, and treasured through time.

Angela S. Wright

OH, GIVE ME A PIECE . . .

Oh, give me a piece of that far-off land,
And I would be happy to shake your hand.
Just a piece of that land is all I need;
Give me no more than that to plant my seed.

These few seeds of mine need just such a place,
For in a near land these seeds would not sprout,
Let alone grow in too near and large space:
Such are these rare seeds, of that have no doubt.

So, give me a piece of that far, far plot:
To sprout and to grow these seeds need that spot,
As such men as I need some special ground
On which to grow and live and not be bound —
Unlike most others who easily are —
Some men, I and my seeds need to live far.

Joseph Bonsignore

FRIENDSHIP

My friend is so sweet and dear.
I care for him deeply even when he's not near.
He cares for me, though I know how much he cares
scares me so.
I don't want to hurt him or lead him on.
I just want us to stay friends forevermore.
We're so good together and have lots of fun,
we act as if we're the only ones beneath the sun.
He's the only one I can talk to when I'm feeling blue,
and after we talk I feel good as new. He understands me
and the things I do, even when I'm in the wrong he's
there for me too.
Now here's a good friend and that's all he is,
so how do I tell him what he doesn't want to hear?

Julie Farris

JULIE ANN FARRIS. Born: Xenia, Ohio, 7-3-65; Education: Wright State University; Occupation: Store clerk; Awards: Literary magazine in high school; Poetry: 'Birds,' American Poetry Association.

BESIDE MY MARY

Her smile carried laughter and memories of spring
Her caresses were as soft as a meadowlark's wing.
Perfumed like honey made by the bees
And a voice as soft as the wind in the trees.
Footsteps so light as she danced around
It always surprised me when they made a sound.
Hands that were tender and loving to touch
They brought me moments that I miss so much.
She carried gently the keys to my heart
Life was so lonely when we were apart.
She caused the moments that gave life its worth.
But fate wasn't kind, she's asleep in the earth.
Lonely I wander. Each night I roam.
Waiting for God to call me back home.
I fill up my nights and all of my days
Waiting to be where my sweet Mary lays.

So when I die, just take me please
To where I always long to be
And there in peaceful silence,
Lay me beside my Mary.

Norris D. Hertzog

STANZAS

When A Man Hath No Freedom To fight For At Home

When a man hath no freedom to fight for at home,
  Let him combat for that of his neighbors;
Let him think of the glories of Greece and of Rome,
  And get knocked on his head for his labors.

To do good to mankind is the chivalrous plan,
  And is always as nobly requited;
Then battle for freedom wherever you can,
  And, if not shot or hanged, you'll get knighted.

George Gordon, Lord Byron

THE DREAMER

Rain patters by the window
Where I read by light,
Sluicing all through my soul.
Torn between love of knowledge
And love for her, I turn
A page. Seeing nothing fixed or solid,
And how roots are ripped from soil
As the tree fallen in the night
To remind one of another day's toil,
I smell the damp dusty earth
Of human strife, where men burn,
And think, Is death better than birth?

But the dream comes and goes;
Memory slogs in a muddy wake
At daybreak. When the mind bows
In weariness like a man bent
As time wears his back,
Shall I go in the way he went?
Night leaves my soggy books on the sill,
Dawn greets me with whiskey shakes and a wavering will.

George D. Scott

BOUNTY BEAUX

He doesn't ask for very much,
just a kindly word and a gentle touch;
A bit of food and a good warm bed,
usually up close beside my head.

Now I'm not rich but he don't care,
what I have, with him I'll share;
His soft brown eyes communicate,
his wishes to me, inviolate.

For this he wags his friendly tail —
a walk along a forest trail;
He never gives me any sass,
as he sniffs at every tree we pass.

His wagging tail — it never quits,
it lifts me when I'm in the pits;
From him I get this rich reward —
days in which I'm never bored.

You can have your gems and precious gold,
but on Bounty Beaux I'm really sold;
He sticks to me like Elmer's Glue,
a loving friend that's tried and true — my buddy.

Ralph Dietterick

TWO KNOCKS

He left for the war the night we were wed.
Nine months later his son I bore.
A knock at the door —
The message read, "We regret to inform you . . ."
Our generation thought we saw
The war that would end all war.

Our son grew into a fine young man.
The call went out — war anew.
Our boy was one of the chosen few.
A knock at the door —
The message read, "We regret to inform you . . ."
Like father — like son.

Elaine Meli

BANFF SUNSET

The setting sun with burning beams
crowns old Mount Rundle's head,
mirrored in Vermillion's dreams,
the dancer and the lake are wed.

She dips her toes, the ripples crease
atop the head sunk in the glade,
watches the ripples ring reprise,
sees the stairway to heaven displayed,
makes the majestic mountain rise,
and praise her music to the skies.

The last of sun's life-giving rays,
the warm kiss on snow in crag's crevasse
feeds clear water to the rippling lake;
leaving us mortals marvelling en masse
that nature bears these for our sake
of the glorious sight to partake.

After this unparalleled array
the night gives promise of more glorious day:
the sun arising with burning beams
bouncing off the mountain golden streams.

Voinoff Voyo Miljevich

VOIN VOINOFF MILJEVICH. Pen Name: Vojo Voinoff; Born: Montenegro, Yugoslavia; Married: July, 1950; Now divorced from Janice (music teacher and composer); Education: Grade 12 in Montenegro and Macedonia; University of Calgary, Alberta, accounting and commercial law, 1963-65; Occupations: Freelance interpreter/translator, Photographer, Writer; Memberships: Writers Guild of Alberta, Past president of Canadian Authors Association, Calgary branch, presently Okanagan branch, CAA; Awards: Creative writing scholarships, 1964, 1966, from Canadian Womens Press Club and C.F.C. Radio and T.V., Calgary and Edmonton, Alberta; Poetry: 'Inch By Inch Rip-Off,' 9-83; 'Dogged By Paparazzi,' 9-84; Other Writings: *Broken Lullabies,* play, 1-66; "Plain English," essay, 11-80; "New Year Happiness is Within Us," article, 1-87; Themes: *Eternal optimism, humorous side of life, and love of the land.*

THE FEEDER

In the morning many different
types of birds come to eat
at the feeder. Soon the time
comes to build nests and mate.

We smile to see the little ones
stretching their necks out and
crying for food. The parents
feed them and soon the nestlings
try their wings. We watch as
they learn to fly to the feeder.

One day a zone-tailed hawk flies
to a branch and quietly sits in
the tree. Then with a swoop he
catches a thrush. In an explosion
of feathers he is off somewhere to
eat what he has caught.

We sit first in amazement, then in
anger. But it passes as we realize
that the birds we feed are not ours
and that Nature's way is cruel.

Semino

LIGHT-TRAILING SHADOW

First the wick in the glass Shivah-lamp
doubled over once when ignited
burning like two separate flames
but did join together after awhile
leaving a normal burning flame
with a fleeting shadow of itself
inside its glass-perimeter curve.

Observing the impossible
the wonder of the doubling wick
the shadow of the dancing flame
reflex of consuming pain within me
to the memory of my recent mate
a feeling I had buried twice
my first loss all over again . . .

Howard Deutsch

WHOSE JOY IS THIS

Whose joy is this, can you safely tell?
No one else matters half so much —
They cannot see us walking hereby
Among the flowers we love to smell.

Our friends will think us queer
When we laugh at wit not seen —
Or when we dance to music,
The poetry they cannot hear.

My dear lady, will you think of me
When proud April's trim turns winter white
And rose petals long crushed, are bottled
And tossed in the lake tide to the sea?

But we must continue our walk,
For the morning sun has risen
Upon the garden path of roses
And there are many flowers to see
There are so many flowers to see.

James Symmons

IMCOMPLETE

If I could go to the blue hills
Whose cloaks are flung against the sky
I would be no closer to you, for if I did
Other horizons I would find,
Skyline upon skyline stretching
To the uttermost range
Of hills that meet the eye.

The sea, the restless reaching tide
Comes and goes in its appointed way,
And leaves no message,
No syllable, no sigh,

To let me know that where you are
There's something that is incomplete
And will not be made whole
Until I am with you.

Genieva B. Pawling

GENIEVA BOUTON PAWLING. Born:
Troupsburg, 3-21-98; Married: Kenneth Rawling
(deceased); Education: High school; Occupations:
Schoolteacher in rural schools; Memberships: National Writers' Club; Awards: 5th Prize in Clover
Contest for 'Dona Belle,' Honorable Mention,
1977; Poetry: 'Aunt Sofrony's Cellar'; 'Sackcloth,' *Jean's Journal;* 'Etiquette,' *Wall Street
Journal;* Other Writings: *Over My Shoulder,* historical book; *Echoes of Woodhull,* historical
book.

AFTER ALL

I very often sit and meditate
After death comes, what then will be my fate?
On which planet will I indeed reside
Or will I be a comet? Who will decide?
Perhaps I'll be a star shining brightly
Looking down on a troubled world nightly.
Think I'd like to be a fleecy, white cloud
Drifting along changing shapes, feeling proud.
If by chance I should be any of these
Will I travel to wherever I please?
Maybe I will be sent to some strange land
I'll be alone and I won't understand.
Would be nice to twinkle and drift near home
So those I left behind won't be alone.
From a white to a black cloud I may change
I will hear them say, "She is in a rage!"
And so, God, please, do listen to my plea
Far up in the sky I would like to be.
And where I do orbit on you depends
I'd like to be near to watch over my friends.

June Alexander

TOWARDS A GOAL

What makes a person what he is
With one a dud and one a whiz
I can not find the reason why
One person does not even try
While others driven on by fate
Come charging from the starting gate
I've watch'd these scenes throughout the years
Where one gets boos, another cheers
I have not found what makes this tick
X Factor seems to be the trick
The force that drives you to a goal
May be imbedded in your soul.

Sol Finkelman

SOLITAIRE

Tonight, I'm playing "Solitaire"
Wondering whether it's my fate
To be lucky in cards, or love?
Am I the Queen of Hearts
And will I find my King
Or just a Jack of Diamonds?
These cold, cruel, cardboard characters
Filled with strange symbols
What do they know of love?
All the plays are numbered
There's no chance for romance.
Perhaps, it's like love's passion, a delusion?

Oh, at last, I've won!
But what have I done?
This lonely night has ended
Is there another, not yet begun?

Jessie Faulkner Cuedek

ANGEL OF THE LIGHT

Oh, holy angel of my delight,
Stand by me in every fright,
To soothe the pangs
That he inflicts with fangs.

Satan prowls in many a man;
Disguised in her as a fan.
To weight the mind and then snare,
Entangling it from your sweet care.

If each could just know,
How strong you are against the foe.
To beckon His grace-filled light
That channels all His might.

Oh, guardian angel, I love you so;
And, even with out my asking, you go
By my side, leading toward heaven's way,
To guide, with His light, each and every day.

Carla Ann Bouska Lee

FARAWAY FRIENDS

So far away the miles between us,
Yet our friendship has never faded.
Often my thoughts have turned to you,
Wishing the miles were never there,
Wanting to hear the sound of your voices,
Needing your friendship to keep it together,
Knowing you would always be there,
If I were to call or drop a line.
So many things have changed our lives,
The things we do each passing day,
Routines that once were standard
Now are forgotten with new innovations;
Though all these things have come about
Still there is one thing never forgotten —
That is our friendship so long a companion;
No amount of time, nor distance in miles,
Can remove from my heart the love for my friends,
Never forgotten.

Angie Ferraro

NO ONE THERE

I need someone to hold me, to tell me that they care,
Someone who wraps themselves around me,
Then tells me I am safe from the world out there;
The hours seem long and endless
As the night spreads its darkness,
No one is there to console me,
No one to say they care,
No one there to wrap around me;
As the day has lost its glare,
As night comes to all the world,
No one is there, no one is there.

Angie Ferraro

OLD ORCHARD BEACH

I heard the bells of old St. Margaret's ring
I smelled the ocean's spray and then remembering
When I was just a child, no more than eight or nine
This very special place, this very special time.

French fries from yesterday and the sandy boardwalk too
As ghosts began to play a magic game for you.
I introduced you to my early days gone by.
We shared this happy place, just you and I.

We found a special world complete with lilac.
Cherry blossoms pink and iris bloomed for you
To make this special time of sweet reunions new,
A very special time for me to share with you.

In just the past two years we've kindled loves anew.
We found the Pittsburgh joys
And Maine came shining through.
A time when old friendships became all bright and new
And I began to love again with you.

If I were asked to share life's greatest moment through,
I'd live that day again in Maine with you.

William D. Leavitt

MOTHER

I walked down to the sea today.
My toes touched the golden shore.
I remembered years past in the summertime
and my thoughts went evermore.
To Mother sweet in the golden sun, kissed by the rolling sea.
How much love I had for her and the love she gave to me.
In the summertime on the golden shore
Kissed by the shimmering sea.
I think about my mother's smile so special then to me.
I think about her loving touch, my hand, my heart, my mind.
My mother, me, and the rolling sea in our special place and time.
No matter if the winter's cold has touched the wind to chill
As the snow drifts deep and icicles, I have my memories still
Of Momma sweet on the golden shore kissed by the shimmering sea.
And she will live on forevermore within my memories.

William D. Leavitt

SUMMER REUNION

I went home to the state of Maine to see my family
To see if the echoes in my mind had some reality.

Buildings I remember — faces from the past
Although it seems so different now as thirty years elapsed.

Searching for your loved ones, finding them, such joy.
Remembering all the happy times this meeting we employ
To talk about the yesterdays and on to days to come.
We laugh about the days gone by anticipating fun.

Joanne is a pussycat, her humor warm and dry.
Jeannie such a pretty thing, but her story makes you cry.

Harold and Ellen and Stella and Aunt and Old Orchard by the sea.
Steven, Chip and Janny, too, how much they mean to me.

I traced a footprint in the sand in Old Orchard by the sea
And shared a week of yesterdays with those so close to me.

Ruth and Chuck and Mark and I walked on the sandy shore
Lobsters and clams and French fries too, and lilac evermore.

William D. Leavitt

TO JANEY WITH LOVE

When I see the birds so sweetly grace the sky
When I hear the children's laughter or their cry
When I reflect the magic that is me
I praise the Lord who brought this all to be.

He is the Lord
The father of life's radiant energy.
He is the Lord
Creator of this life for you and me
And when I see
His presence through the sunny rays so bright
On the other side of darkness there is light.

And when the end is here as life must go its way
The spirit now returns upon the words we pray
To bring it safely back through life's sweet mystery
To live a thousand times in God's sweet energy.

He is the Lord
He'll take us through the sunny rays of bright
He is the Lord
The other side of darkness, He is the light
He is the Lord.

William D. Leavitt

THE SOURCE OF KNOWLEDGE

The force of nature reigns supreme
The force of mankind but a dream
We march and strut in grand parades
But these are merely grand charades
Each time we think we know much more
We find we have not reach'd the core
There are some things beyond our ken
That were not meant for mortal men
But bit by bit all in due course
We're getting closer to the Source
Our scientists will soon unfold
A plan they think as good as gold
And while it will seem good to man
We still must wait for Heaven's plan.

Sol Finkelman

SOL FINKELMAN. Born: Warsaw, Poland, 1918; Married: Gay Newnam Propp; Education: Baruch School of Business, B.B.A.; City College of New York; Occupation: CPA; Memberships: American Institute of L.P.A.A., California and New York Societies of C.P.A.s, International Platform Association, Commonwealth Club, Public library board member; Writings: Numerous articles published in jewelry and furniture trade magazines; Comments: *My poems express my thoughts on the meaning of life and love in terms all can understand. They also contain my views on contemporary political characters and activities.*

THE FALLEN SNOW

The snow had fallen softly
Through the long cold winter night.
Everything was covered now
In a blanket soft and white.

The snow piles deeply by the fence
And up against the house.
And out across the smooth white top
Were tracks of a little mouse.

You could almost feel the silence.
Just the slightest sound of wind
As it whispered through the branches
Of the trees around the bend.

Lorraine Chappell

THE INNER VOICE

I have an Inner Voice
That cries out to be heard;
It struggles with my consciousness,
Eludes each spoken word.
It lives within my being
And snuggles there inside
And when I call, in search of it,
It runs away to hide.
I face the outside world, it seems
With armor free to spare
But every overt gesture made
Belies what lies in there.
And so — though not what I might show
The outer world by choice,
There is a part that stays apart:
It is the Inner Voice.

P. K. Newman

P. K. NEWMAN. Born: Indianapolis, Indiana, 11-5-54; Education: Michigan State University, B.A., Psychology, 1976; also have some post-graduate education in advertising/marketing; Occupation: Free-lance Designer; Publications/Awards, 1971-72; National Poetry Press; American Poetry Press; Massport Authority Essay Award; Massachusetts Commission on Employment of the Handicapped, Government Essay/Research Award; Poetry: 'The Well,' 'Loving,' 'The Dream,' *American Poetry Anthology*, 1987.

LONGINGS

I dream of a day,
    Without envy and hate.

Long for a week, free
    Of a Boss who berates,

Desire a month of Liberation
    From Women who dissipate.

As for those spoilers of the Moment,
    A Year would be great.

Margaret T. McGarry

IN MY DREAMS

I walk in a shaded woodland.
I sit by a quiet stream.
I see the beautiful wild flowers.
But only in my dreams.

I see the snowflakes falling.
I see the trees so green.
I hear the wild birds calling.
But only in my dreams.

I see the mountains rise above me.
I see the moon as it palely gleams.
I see my sweetheart waiting for me.
But only in my dreams.

I strum my guitar softly
And listen as the music seems
To waft its way to heaven
But only in my dreams.

I've gone away and left my
Woodlands, fields and streams
But always I'll return
But only in my dreams.

Lorraine Chappell

NEEDLESS LONELINESS

Who can be lonely alone
with or without a telephone?
Since God is everywhere,
There's no need for despair!
Only this fact can end
a lonely soul's sadness
and change its life
into one of gladness!
What we long for is
God inside ourselves!
We need never be lonely
for we are never alone!
God's reflection is
in every form.
This beauty and love
make us feel warm.
So try to see it
wherever you may roam.
Then you will find
you are never alone!

Clodah G. Summer

WHEN LITTLE THINGS HAPPEN

We outgrow the little things
that seem big when they happen,
but are really small if we recall
how young and unaware we were then.
When little things happen
in our childhood days,
we cry out in protest
or gulp down our tears
to hide our deep hurts for years!
Then comes the time we see
things more important
that cancel out our hurts of the past.
Scares though they may be
on our personality,
we grow in depth and compassion
for others who need a friend
when little things seem like big things
to the young soul, evolving by
living, learning and loving
in spite of hurts and disappointments!

Clodah G. Summer

PROMISED FREEDOM

Most learned and yet most unordered,
We're ball-and-chained to contradictions,
Wherein flesh remains legal guardian,
Binding us with earthly restrictions.

Discontent with our destiny, we attempt
Endless maneuvers to obtain the key.
All prove futile 'til the day of reckoning,
For only Christ has the power to free.

Sheila Wells Hughes

SHEILA WELLS HUGHES. Born: Mt. Sterling, Kentucky, 3-3-49; Married: Frank M. Hughes; Education: George Rogers Clark High School, Winchester, Kentucky; Occupations: Housewife and mother of two sons, Kevin and Michael; Former secretary at Lexington Blue Grass Army Depot; Poetry: 'Slumbering People,' 1986; 'Don't Be Foolish,' 'God's Homework,' 'Deception — A Cancerous Sore,' 1987; Comments: *It's so gratifying when we can unleash the depths of our soul to others so that they might share in our wondrous experiences of life. This is what I attempt to do when I write poetry.*

MISSING YOU

Droplets of water tumble . . . roll
As raindrops splash on moss-covered rocks

Leaves and twigs bob and swirl
Wandering from bank to bank
Carried along by the brook's current

Overhead, branches of trees
That line the water's edge
Bend and sway . . . rustle
From the stormy breeze

Leaves drift by
In their erratic . . . fluttering journey
Searching for a resting place
On the fern-strewn forest floor

Like the objects of this rainy, grey
Fall-colored day
My thoughts wander, float and drift

And I am here in the rain
Myself . . . alone . . . *Missing you*

William K. Brobst

RECESS

In the school yards gazing —
At children playing —
Swings are swaying —
Skies are now changing —
Talking to my friends —
Enjoying the trends —
Hoping these good times would never end.
Met a girl who I adored —
Fantastic looks that couldn't be ignored —
Hoping a relationship might be in store —
All the moments that were once here —
Were so happy and free of fear —
Merely a story I wished to share.

Joseph R. Carchia

JOSEPH RAYMOND CARCHIA. Pen Names: Rocky, Rocco; Born: Providence, Rhode Island, 11-27-60; Education: High school; Occupations: Currently in medical field; Poetry: 'Lost in Love,' *Hearts on Fire*, 11-86; 'Grasping for Love,' *Best New Poets*, 3-87; 'Only My Tears,' *Words of Praise*, 7-87; Comments: *Ever since I was a child, I dreamed of seeing my name in a book. (As for my work, in due time it will become better). I thank God I have been accepted.*

LITTLE PEOPLE

Hello there, little man (lady),
They say you're just a child,
And that you're into everything,
And about to drive them wild.

Well, you can't tell them yet,
But in a year or two,
You can explain to them,
You're learning by all you do.

And when you grow up,
And reach for a book,
You won't knock over things,
For them to get so shook.

And you wonder how they can be so young,
And still be so wise,
And yet can't remember how it was,
When they were just your size.

As a matter of fact,
You could show them all
Things they daily miss
Now that they are tall.

I guess they can't remember
How it was to see things so near the floor,
Like — their knees, chair seats and table legs
Until picked up so they could see more.

And maybe they don't remember
How it was to get new teeth,
The kind that grow in,
Not fitted by someone in a white sheath.

Of course you can't tell them
That not all of your days are bright,
You'd think they didn't know
How it is to not feel just right.

And if you could talk
You wouldn't need to whine so much
For you could tell them you hurt somewhere
And not try to show them by where you clutch.

You see them look and touch
When they carry you in a store,
But when you reach to examine something,
They slap and say, "No more!"

Yes little man (lady), they call you
A child, a kid, or a brat,
But they should remember
When *they* were where you're at.

Right now you're little people
But one day you too will be big and tall,
So remember to have patience,
With parents, and all.

Elizabeth Borselli

OUR DAY IN THE CHICKEN HOUSE

Chickens, chickens, how they lay
Eggs, eggs, in the nest to gather each day,
Up early to feed them, the day to start
Feeding, picking up eggs, and carrying out dead ones till dark.

People who never worked in a place like this
Can figure that the job they have is ''mere bliss,''
Dust, nest to fill once a week, is work for pay
You put all you got into it, but work hard all day.

Some work very hard, as each day we see the sun
Morning, noon, and night after many hours their work is done,
Chickens, roosters, eggs, are grown, for our need
People who make this possible, do all a good ''deed.''

Baskets by the dozens, with eggs, all sizes, piled up high
These are gathered each day, and these dozens nearly reach the sky,
See your neighbor, who gathers eggs, in house numbered ''three''
Day of rest from seeing eggs, and hens, is ''day off'' you feel free.

We worked for people so nice, too much ''dust'' couldn't take it
Then we talked and told them we couldn't go on and we'd have to quit,
Good place, nice people, all the eggs we needed, also had good pay
It was long, hard work to do, we hated to leave them and go away.

Gloria Barber

SCARED

  I'm scared
 Not hiding in a corner scared
Not being beaten up by the class bully scared,
  But scared
 Scared of losing what means everything to me
 Scared of my family leaving because I'm not free
Not scared like a child being spanked by his parents
  But trembling all over scared
  Scared of what's in store for me
 Scared of what might happen to my family
   Scared!
 Scared of what being locked up could do to my life
  Scared of having to face my angry wife
  Just scared!
Scared of not being accepted as the person I really am
  Yes, I'm scared
 Scared not of dying, but staying alive
Scared not of losing, but participating in life
  Scared!

Marc Dudley

JOURNEY

Time with you is infinite. In love, with no beginning,
no end. Just as we are, they way we've always been.
Passions, long smouldering, burst into flame, blazing
with ecstasy inside me.
In the stillness, your heart beats with mine. Tenderly
together, we share the silence. We need no words.
We speak of love through our eyes, by our touch.
Through the ages, united by emotion, ours is
everlasting.

Korena Gilham

A WOMAN'S DREAM

Here I sleep at night, dreaming,
I reach over to love you and to touch you.
I awake to find that it is only a dream.

I begin to dream once more
Of a wonderland with beautiful sights
For us to see, but I awake.
I am surprised that again it is only a fantasy.

Wonderland is a place for fantasy,
For finding thoughts and exploring minds.
In my wild dream, my beautiful dream,
We start to notice each other,
And begin a lovemaking relationship.
We wander to a deserted island.
There is nothing around us for miles.

We start to put our arms around each other
In the cool air by the sea.
It gets dark, the stars come out,
And you build a fire to keep us warm.

We walk along the seashore,
You smile and hold me close,
Whispering love poems from deep within your soul.
We sleep together as husband and wife.

Here I sleep at night, loving you,
Then I awake to realize it is only a dream.

Ginger Chapman

UNSPOKEN LOVE

When you were an infant, I carried you down the path of life;
Then, so sure of your protection, so sure that I was right.

And when you took your first steps, I walked behind you down the path;
To catch you when you fell when you moved too fast.

When you learned to walk, we walked hand and hand;
Always right beside me you would always stand.

And then the time came you needed to walk alone;
I watched in the distance to make certain you found your way home.

When you became independent and had the thirst to change direction;
A few steps I was behind shadowed by your reflection.

And when you fell and experienced the pain;
My heart was right behind you calling your name.

When you ran fast ahead just to challenge me;
I knew side by side we would always be.

I wanted to race ahead of you to pave each path smooth;
But that would have only robbed you of the ability to choose.

And when you chose paths that I could not agree;
Somehow, someway, I knew they would always lead back to me.

Remember, always move ahead never looking back with regrets;
Because each time you move, your life is being molded by your steps.

And no matter what the roads may bring or where they may lead;
On the path in your heart I will always be.

When the time comes that my road must end;
You must walk for both of us until for your heart I shall send!

Bonnie Provenzano Antignani

HOLD THE THOUGHT

When times are tough
And tempers get rough —
Be still and remember . . .
God cares!

When lonely and blue
With no one to turn to —
Look up and tell yourself . . .
God cares!

When laughs aren't shared
Nor feelings ever spared —
With courage repeat again . . .
God cares!

When loved ones die
And you wonder why —
The answer never changes . . .
God cares!

Sheila Wells Hughes

FAMILY

There's beauty in the land we live
That calls from everywhere
But beauty in your family
Is to know that you care
When sometime travels far and wide
To find a life anew
We find a life of loneliness
That brings us back to you
You can't imagine how you're missed
Or how you're needed too
No matter how independent
We still depend on you
It is because we need your love
Your arms to hold us tight
To let us know when things get tough
They're soon to be all right
Or just to let us know you're there
And we can come to you
To find the comfort that you give
And give some comfort too

Joyce Banks Piggue

THE FREEDOM OF
TREES IN WINTER

Like the trees
for some time
bearing colors
first green
then orange
and now brown
I, too
am slowly
pushing free
free from the burden
of bloom
and foliage
and fertility
like the trees
unimpeded now
I learn to grow
invisibly
into the winter
of my life

Maria Maxfield

I REMEMBER . . .

I remember, I remember,
In the hot September days
Of my childhood, precious childhood,
In the fading summer haze.

Spending visits, final visits,
Sleeping in my cousin's bed,
Before the school bell's dinging, ringing,
Called me back to books unread.

Country town, buildings brown
And cream and white, 'neath shimmering sky,
Spent time playing, always saying,
"It won't be long till we say good-bye."

Until the winter, cold, cold winter
Comes the next long holiday.
Time forgets, I'm old and yet
It seems as though were yesterday.

Joyce Wallace

THE CORE AND THE SHELL

All of mine
who are gone
reside in crevices
where memories abide
come back to me
as they were
in life
and like those
whom they have known
in their own time
since man
acquired conscience
beholden of decrees
to be and leave
traces of his presence
for us to find
the sweetness
in the core
or the shell
a perpetual void
may hold . . .

Howard Deutsch

THAT SOLID BOND

It began in the year of '86,
She and I close friends became,
As if we two were meant to meet,
For neither had one to call his own,
And somehow knew that this was it.
Each day that passed, our time consumed
In joyous revelations felt,
Did bring us closer, tick by tick,
Until our path's design was clear.
And on that day that we were wed,
The flowers filled the air with sweet,
And birds sang clearly their songs of love
For this, the bond, we two did seal.
Ah, precious love we did ignite —
May you burn forevermore,
And as these days pass into years,
Give strength to keep these bonds in place.

Les Race

THE SEARCH

Mirrors on a placid sea,
thoughts, reflecting all the past;
solitude, the cure for me,
freedom soul, free at last.

Reasons now, becoming clear,
among the misty web-spun mind;
friends and lovers, held so dear,
friends, not lovers, so hard to find.

So many people among the friends,
sharing much, but none so real;
so many beginnings, so many ends,
to share so much, but never feel.

Looking for love, prepared to hail,
the faulty promises of wedding chimes;
the dismal ache, of search and fail,
the lonely reality, of endless times.

Searching and searching, fore and hind,
longing for love, among the Blue;
endless searches, never to find,
never to found . . . 'til there was You.

Glenn T. Fugitt

YOU ARE

Soft Rose-like dawning of the morn
  Now lends its glow to me,
With inspiration daily born
  Whispering that you'll ever be.
And, *you are* here.

Ah, warm the Winter Sun at noon
  Dispelling chill of night,
A promise that now, sure and soon,
  Your dear love will bring me light.
For, *you are* dear.

Oh, mellow lamp at evening's shade
  So gently marks the way,
With strength that keeps me unafraid
  You blessing every closing day.
'Cause, *you are* near.

I would the firelight yet gleam
  Now in your loving eyes,
Sweet treasures of the past can seem
  Lost in a dim paradise.
Still, *you are* here.

Alfred W. Hicks

A DAD WHO KNOWS WHERE HE'S GOING

For my dad on Father's Day, June 21, 1987

It's not every family who can honestly say
  They're content when enduring rough going
But happy are we that we can withstand
  With a Dad who knows where he's going.

This world is full of pitfalls it's true
  And the evils and snares are frustrating
As duties abound and success is found
  With a Dad who knows where he's going.

When God made the world, He made good men
  And women who share in the choosing
And to women who doubt, and who feel left out
  Be wise, never fear that you're losing.

A woman can dream and hope and trust
  That she'll have a family worth loving
With a contender for right, who walks in the Light
  A Dad Who Knows Where He's Going!

   Amyvonne Grogan

AMYVONNE GROGAN. Born: Washington, D.C., 6-20-53; Education: Boston University, B.A., Music Education and Therapy, 1975; Bowie State College, M.A., Special Education, 1976; Trinity College, Washington, D.C., Post-Graduate studies; recipient of Advanced Professional Certificate; Occupation: Special Education Instructor, 10 years, Prince George's County School System of Maryland; Memberships: Prince George's County Educator's Association; Boston University Alumni Association; Comments: *My inspiration for writing poetry originated in my family: my mother, Earlean S. Grogan, and my sister, Desiré. Also, the unique individuals with whom I have worked through the years provide many themes that I should like to integrate with stylistic topography and illustrations in my own book.*

FIRST WALK ALONE

Mommy told me that I may
Walk alone to school today.
She told me not to stop and play,
Because I must be on time.
Look both ways when you cross the streets.
Don't talk to strangers that you meet,
Or anyone offering you candy to eat.

I walked up the block (there were many more).
I turned to wave to Mommy standing at the door.
She looked strange,
Like when she is going to cry.
So was I.
I called back, "Mommy, don't you worry, I will hurry —
You see, I'm all grown up today!"

I *ran!*

   Elaine Meli

CHRISTMAS JOY

Though the world seems dark and gray today
There was a bright yellow star that spread its rays
A long time ago in a town forlorn
To announce that a King had just been born.

The shepherds and kings came from far and near
Even wise men came with gifts so rare
And though people came with all kinds of things
Somehow they knew He was King of Kings.

Some didn't understand the purpose of His coming
The world from its sins He came for redeeming
And though He was born of a lowly estate
They knew He was Lord! He was King! He was Great!

We mark our calendars, the 25th of December
In the hope that we, too, might try to remember
The Peace, Love, and Joy that filled every man's heart
In this world where we live. We must do our part.

To let the meaning of Christmas within us abide.
The warm glow of brotherhood must be felt deep inside.
So, Merry Christmas, Glad Tidings, Best Wishes, Good Cheer!
And may you be blest in this coming New Year.

   Desiré P. Grogan

A LITTLE PEACE OF HEAVEN

Dedicated, with love, to my sister Susie

Born on January Twenty-one,
It was a girl, he wanted a son.
They named her Anastasia Esin
A radiant beauty, without and within.
Youthful and untouched by sin.

A smiling child, a laughing heart —
Her life and learning just beginning to start.
Loved by many in so short a time
But God said unto her "Bring your soul to mine."
She departed to Him in 1981, the day, March 9.

No words can express the sorrow, the pain,
Shared by her Mom and Dad, shared one and the same.
Her Mom carried her there beneath her heart
And shared a love of which no one else could take part.

We are separated now only by God's will —
Pray for us Anastasia, for we need help still.
Pray until God's face we see
And we find our littlest angel of our family tree.

   Patricia M. Stephens

SOFIA

That ecstatic charge that permeates the air
Tells me without a glance she must be there,
And though my head is bent with toil of the morn,
At that magic moment I am completely reborn
From the dismal reality to the enchanted sublime.
Until her arrival, the fates mark time.
Then, a spiritual uplift, an urge to sigh
As the statuesque Sofia passes me by:
A picture of poise, of warmth, of grace,
Of symmetrical perfection from toe to face;
And, though this ardor she may ne'er return,
'Tis my plight to hope, to wait, to yearn.

   Lawrence Di Lorenzo

THE REAL WORLD

You feel weak, you're all alone
Curled up in the corner, in the lonely zone
By the thick walls that block
You think there's no way through
But there is one way out, and it's up to you.

You think to yourself, *I feel like I'll fade.*
So you still continue to fight the truth
Which is really that you're afraid
Afraid of facing the real world
Afraid of accepting your problems at hand
And trying to do things from where you stand.

Finally you figure out the maze
That has put you through a lot of craze
You know now you have to be strong,
And you've learned that it took long
To know that people love you.

Now you're strong and feel free
But in order to keep the feeling
You must keep the key
The key that will open the door to *The Real World!*

Keri Weintraub

MY FRIEND

I felt lost in a soul-enveloping blackness.
And you said:
    ''It's only dark where you are, now.''

I felt like I wanted to curl up in a cocoon,
To stagnate, where I did not have to move.
And you said:
    ''You only want to return to the womb
    where it's warm and secure.''

I said I could only crawl.
And you said:
    ''Crawling is demeaning;
    you can stand upright, with your shoulders back
    and your head held high.''

I could not share this devastating, pain-filled,
Soul-searching experience with you, but you attempted to understand.
And you said:
    ''I know where you are, I don't know why you are there;
    but, I am here for you . . . to continue being
    your friend.''

Marcia Eckel Robinson

A NEW DAY

The yesterdays of life are over and a new day has begun.
Yesterdays were the failures and defeats and victories of life's road.
A new day to begin over, a day to relive life to its fullest.
A new day to battle and climb the mountains and valleys on life's road.
The new day of God is for His people to continue their travels for life.
A new day to battle, a new day to claim the victories of life.
The new day of life, to learn of God and to be taught of God.
The day day is of God, rejoice in that day that God has given us.
For God wishes His people to continue on the road of life.
Continue until another day of life.

David A. Sigler

THE MIRACLE OF THY PEACE

Oh Father, Creator of my spirit,
Thank Thee for Thy healing, gentle waves of peace . . .
Which bathed and becalmed my anguished, ravaged soul.

None but Thee, indwelling me,
Could have wrought so great a Miracle as this —
When I was lost and drowning in such dark, tidal waves of despair,
Smashing and crashing down upon the mind and heart and soul of me —

Then to be spiritually lifted,
Above this scene of rampant, dreadful destruction,
To a far clime, which somehow began to live, within my mind;

Then its comforting, strengthening Reality,
Began to trickle down into the sacred regions
Of my heart, of my soul.

And the power-filled assurance came from Thee,
That despite this seeming tragedy . . .
All would be well, All would be for the good and necessary learning
Of these two loved ones, so near and dear to me.

And with this new knowledge,
Possessed within my mind, my heart, my soul,
I began to sing!

Marcia Eckel Robinson

REQUEST

Remember . . .
        My dear child,
        That which you have learned
        Of value to your soul,

        As you have traveled through
        Life's many teaching schools
        Of myriad expressions and of
        Myriad experiences;

You have the
        Responsibility . . .
        Opportunity . . . and the
        Privilege . . .

Of teaching
And sharing
        With your fellow brothers and sisters;
        As you meet them along
        The winding paths of eternal life,
        That lead ever upward.

Marcia Eckel Robinson

DADDY'S GIRLS WEEP

For Daddy's girls, death is hard to take;
It's just another cruel quirk of fate.

A special bond between fates exists here;
Love without ownership, enfringements or fear.

A daddy's love for his daughter is of the purest find
Repaid in multiple degrees by daughters who love in kind.

When daughters weep at dad's eternal sleep,
At least they know their greatest fear cannot repeat.

Sont

UNFILLED LOVE

Have I not given to thee, my love, the full contents of my soul?
And yet you rebuke me.
Have I not given to thee, the sweet fragrances of the earth,
That were prepared by the Gods?
And still my love, you rebuke me.
Have I not given to thee, my love,
A rainbow of flowers that danced in the green meadows,
And the Gods sprinkled them with fresh morning dew?
And behold, my love again rebukes me.
Cannot my love feel the compassion that flows through my veins?
Nor hear the cries of the Gods as the gifts they prepared?
If my love is left unfilled, then to whom am I to?
If I am to no one, then am I not a beginning without an end,
And an end without beginning?
So then my love, as my soul flies into the hand of death,
For whom will the mourners toll?

Edward W. Green

DEAR DADDY . . .

In loving memory of my dad

Dear Daddy . . . I miss you. I still love you so.
It's hard for me to understand why you had to go.
Since you've been away, I feel so alone.
It's so different now, no place is home.
Sometimes I pretend to show and spread cheer,
When all I remember is when you were here.
I'm writing this letter so that I may learn.
For surely I know . . . you will not return.
So I must ask you now, ''Do you remember?
All the things that we shared before that September?''
Because I want you to know just who I am.
The things I can't do. The things that I can.
I always try to make *you* proud of *me*.
But I can't help but wonder — do you even see?
Because if I thought for a minute that you didn't know,
Then I would realize that there's no place to go.
So Daddy, remember . . . I'll love you forever.
And I know that one day we will all be together.
I know you loved me, and you know I love you.
So Dad, please don't worry . . . because God loves us, too.

Lori Simonton

GONE

Grief is a sort of . . . semi-private affair,
Where agonies pour out in voice and prayer,

But after the floods, and the cries, and the wails,
Some tranquility and peace finally prevails

For life keeps flowing on, in its tireless stream —
Placid, then rippling over rocks to make frothy cream.

It reaches the ocean and pushes ripples in its wake,
Home at last, as it merges from river or lake.

The waves roll upward and onward to shore
While clouds form a cover, and rain comes once more,

Bringing new life to follow the old,
It's the way God designed it to unfold.

Elizabeth Borselli

MY TEACHER AND MY GUIDE

To Miss Terrey: my friend at R.M.V.T.S.

When someone teaches you a valuable lesson,
how can you just say, ''Thank you''?
When they share with you experience,
how do you show your appreciation?
Learning is a process that involves time.
You never stop learning till the day you die.
No matter how much you try to avoid it,
knowledge just soaks right in.
At times, you may try to reject it,
but it can't be forgotten.

It takes such a giving person
to share that kind of knowledge.
To give what they first learned,
and teach what is so hard;
to pass a gift of unmeasured price,
that increases in value as it is shared;
the giver gives with love
even when the receiver denies.
How can you show appreciation
when you receive a gift worth life itself?

Loni E. Krick

DEATH CAN BE POETIC

While poetry exudes with life and gleam
    And seems untouched by ''passing away,''
Death opens a door which makes most of us beam
    At eternal joy for which at death we pray.
My brother, sister, and my mother too,
    Have passed into eternal peace and rest
Through Death's door long before their times were due,
    They learned that poetry ''of life'' was jest.

Dr. Frank E. Greene

SOUL SEARCHING

There comes an hour of soul searching,
  An hour one could regret;
An hour of reminiscing
  The things we should forget;

Of happy days, yet fraught with pain,
  Of planning days, yet all in vain;
Of heart-break days so filled with tears,
  Because of many unproved fears.

Commitments made must still be kept.
  Though thoughts of dear ones intercept.
To face the Lord one day we must,
  And He will bless us in our trust.

Oh do confess the Lord will bless whoever serves Him well,
And recognize there is no prize in serving Him in hell.

So when the ailing, aching feet no longer want to trod,
May those who love and truly serve return once more to God.

And there for sure our hearts are pure,
  Our days no longer sad;
And entering in devoid of sin,
  Our loved ones will be glad.

Bertha Larsen

THE JOY OF JESUS

Sometimes we tend to go our own way
but if we stay right with Jesus, He'll mend our day.
The Joy of Jesus is like no other ever known
it's a blessed reminder, we just can't do it on our own.
It's good to know that we can call on each other
when we need a big sister or a brother.
If you don't know the Joy of Jesus, just call on me
and He will teach us, as one with Thee
How to reach out and touch someone's heart
and with the Joy of Jesus, we can give others a new start.
The Joy of Jesus can turn a heart of stone
into something precious, and a joy to call our own.
I will forever seek the thing that from Satan frees us
and I will forever thank Thee, for the Joy of Jesus.

Bryan Humphrey

MY LOVING LOVABLE WIFE — ELLA

Without the comfort of my loving wife,
  Whose companion I have been for sixty years,
For me there's no poetry of life,
  The smiles of joy would be transformed to tears.
Immeasurably beloved by my devoted mind
  For more than a common lifetime way;
No word of my devotion can I find
  Ineffable like *poems* must it stay.
"Complete" is just a hint of what I feel.
  It falls far short of my consuming love
Which raised my life to heights beyond the real
  And leaves me staring up for what's above
With Ella's love and my devotion true,
  "Complete" is just a word, not something new.

Dr. Frank E. Greene

LIFE

Life is like a staircase, as ever upward it goes,
And step by step we follow, as we learn and grow.

Step one we are born in a strange new place,
Where gradually we learn we're of the human race.

From toddler to child, each a step of its own,
We become teenagers and think the child we've outgrown.

With Mom and Dad by our side
We somehow through those years slide.

And can hardly wait as adulthood we feel beckoning,
Little knowing the responsibilities it holds for our reckoning.

Still the stairs keep going up
With trials and troubles mixed with happiness to sup.

Some slip and stumble
And trudge on with a grumble.

Some live each day the best they can,
And give with a smile and helping hand.

Some learn early, moderation in all,
And get strength from God whenever they call.

Elizabeth Borselli

THE PERFECT POEM

Dedicated to
Ted & Marge Schlobohm

If, as they say, our favorite dreams can oftentimes come true,
I hope the one I dream each night's the one they've reference to,
The one in which my *three*-score years are suddenly but *one*,
And all my aches and pains have vanished — along with the sun!

I see, in dreams, my happy days, so many years ago,
When, as a youth, inspired by love, emotions I would show,
And ev'ry poem that I wrote would emphasize a theme —
A budding poet I would be — yes, that was quite a scheme!

But that was many years ago, and while my poems do rhyme,
I'm driven by this dream — each night — to write a poem sublime,
A poem just so perfect that it catches every eye,
And as the moving words are read, produce a tear or sigh!

A poem so sweet that every child can use it as a guide,
So strong that ev'ry mother's son is touched, deep down inside,
And even those with troubled hearts can find an inner peace
By reading those few gentle words — may wonders never cease!

For through this poem, which, in my dreams, I write the perfect way,
Each one of us can touch the stars, inspired every day
We read the words, which stir our hearts, thus lend a helping hand
As, awkwardly, we make our way to our own "Promised Land"!

Lee M. Schlobohm

TO A SON'S WEDDING

Dedicated to Steven Schlobohm

They say that love's a two-way street, and I believe it's true,
For if you live the "Golden Rule," you'll find love comes to you!
For what you give is what you get, in every little way,
I wish the best for you, my son, on this — your wedding day!

A father's wish is for his son to have a happy life,
To have his own career, and home, and find a loving wife!
My fervent wish for you, of course, is that my wish comes true,
And that this bride you've asked to wed will bring true love to you!

So let the wedding march begin, with music loud and strong,
And let the preacher say the words, let someone sing a song!
And when you trade those golden rings, and promise to be true,
It indicates you'll give your love — so it comes back to you!

One ring would bring you joy and love, throughout your married life,
The two rings that you give today will make you "Man and Wife"!
And as you wend your way through Life, if clouds obscure the sun,
Remember, there's no darkness if you're with your "Special One"!

Lee M. Schlobohm

A HUMAN BEING IS SUCH
A REMARKABLE THING!

An assortment of things assembled is ''Man,''
A head, two feet and also two hands,
The hands to work, the head to think,
The feet to take you to get a drink!

And then, don't forget, there's a heart that beats
Endlessly on — and on — and on —
Though just taken for granted, it still repeats
Its lifegiving thrust through night and morn —

What a remarkable thing we are!
We have thoughts. They lead us to make or mar.
We have feelings as all of our parts express
Strength and good things, or a life that's a mess!

Each little part needs to maintain perfection
So the majestic whole can maintain direction
To complete the plans each one may conceive
To bring them great joy — or cause them to grieve!

There are no words to fully contain
A proper description of
God's Perfect Man!

Cee Cee

TOYS

I still remember when I was a little boy
How I loved to play with all my fav'rite toys.
I remember my sleek, golden race car,
And the styrofoam plane that always flew far.
I remember a yellow bear named Winnie-the-Pooh
Who through thick and thin would be there to talk to.
And I knew a space man from the planet Kaldoze
Who defended from evil a palace of Legos.

But now that I'm older — older and wiser.
Through years of schooling you've taught me to be
A quick cold concise fast fact analyzer.
But where'd you put my toys? Where can they be?
What happened to my orange crate scooter?
What happened to my brave Pooper Trooper?

I know some are lost and some hid away,
(In fact, I found my old sled yesterday!)
But I see all the kids, and all that they do,
And hate how you'll take their toys away too.
I look at those kids — those girls and those boys,
And wonder what happened to all of my toys.

Paul Gregory

RAIN

What a glorious feeling —
        Mother Earth is happy again.
No longer must she roll
        In clouds of dust —
No longer must her children
        Die of thirst.
All the busy streams —
        The brooks — are being fed —
Sweet fragrant flowers,
        Are lifting their heads.
God's blessed sun will
        Soon shine again —
But, until then — thank You, Father
        For the sweet, refreshing rain!

Joy S. Pearce

TO KRP

In all your grace you came to me today,
Your gentle beauty shining true and bright;
And, therein lost, no words I found could say
How blest I was to bathe within your light.

Your ey shining true and bright;
And, therein lost, no words I found could say
How blest I was to bathe within your light.

Your eyes shone like the greenest, fertile mead
Beneath your sunlit locks of golden hair.
While watching you I felt my spirit freed;
So blest was I to be transported there.
I marvelled in the meadows of your eyes,
And as the loving grasses stroked my heart
I raised my eyes, beheld the golden sky,
And wondered if I did deserve such art.

Then, as your spirit drifted 'cross those pastures,
And as you held me in your gracious rapture,
I thought: perhaps deserve it all I did,
Perhaps, in part, it's shaped by love I give.

Paul Gregory

A TIME TO TURN

No ordinary day has crossed my way;
The hand of destiny has touched me.
I, who have lived for myself now see,
That blessed glimpse of necessity.
It may have been her smile that changed a hardened heart,
Or maybe it was a faith undying that shone so bright.
Whatever cause did have its say,
The result is compassion fulfilled —
A miracle for which the multitudes pray.
My soul has turned — it is no longer tinged with gray.
The angels which have taken my hand
Have kept me from going astray.
If my spirit should pass into eternity's clay
Before the end of this wondrous day,
Then let all creation feel free to say,
A lonely child has come home to stay.

Ronald Russell Enders

YOUR ROCKING CHAIR

The other day I fixed your rocking chair.
I remember seeing it sitting there
With every arm and backbar loose,
I'd often thought, oh, what's the use,
Why bother — let it lie.

Then one day it seemed the time
To put that chair back on the line.
So I took my hammer and my glue;
With each repair I thought of you,
And I found that I began to cry.

I cried for all those happy days
When our baby rocked and laughed and played.
I cried for the mistakes I'd made.
I cried because I wished you'd stayed.

When my crying and repairs were through,
I rocked in your chair like I used to do.
Seems funny, but no matter what we've been through,
I find that I still care for you.

David W. Edwards

TWO NEW LIVES

Is there really any way that we can travel through the past
To start anew to build on dreams we once hoped were going to last?
Will all the years that have come and gone as we each went our own ways
Be a wall that feelings hide behind, or a door to brighter days?

　　Can it be that though we were apart
　　Hard lessons we each took to heart
　　Have prepared us for a brand new start?
　　Two new lives lived as one?

　　Can we see within each other's eyes
　　A way our hearts can harmonize?
　　Can there a new light now arise
　　As with the morning sun?

Is there really any way that we can travel on through time
To picture what may lie ahead for your life and for mine?
So many years still yet to come! When all is said and done,
Can we build a dream upon the promise of two new lives lived as one?

David W. Edwards

A WALL OF WIND

In front of my eyes on the neighbor's wall,
Yonder, yes, there, there,
Where the figures of hay in mud
Are glowing as talismen of time.

Once through a window in this wall,
A magus gave me a sad mysterious smile.
I saw it through a frame of milky fog;
Then the window closed.

The wall scans me, this everybody's neighbor's wall,
And drains me of my eyes' colors.
I say we all fall as well as the wall's figures,
And our fall is without dimension.

You say you are a hard believer:
With your fall the world falls.
But I remember the magus,
The closing of the window.

But Ali, Mawlana, Omar and Attar say:
You are a little figure in this wall,
With hay color and a little muddy shadow,
The wind is the brick and mud of the wall.

Hassan Kaseem

REDBIRDS IN THE PEPPER BUSH

The redbirds come to feel the cool of the well's water.
They light in the tall, green pepper bush,
And rest awhile for the next turn
Of heaven's rainbow, as it arcs its push
From north to south and cools the earth,
From which the seeds, of many types,
Have pushed through the earth their girth,
And nestled down, in drops so cool, hypos
Themselves for a long night's rest;
And, then, awake with morning's sun,
They stretch their arms, their leaves, their life
Through all the day, 'til sun is done;
Transformed, filling basket of farmer's wife,
So all may eat, and love, and live
In this great place we are given
With God's grace, to make our living.

Jenny Gale

A BUNDLE OF LOVE

　　Little Alex, so full of charm.
　　Running around, or on my arm.
　　Playing games like hide and seek,
　　She always makes my heart go weak.

　　A curious little bundle of fun,
　　It wasn't long 'til she had me won.
　　With rarely a tear in her pretty blue eyes,
　　This little child, a miracle in disguise.

　　She's always so happy, morning to night,
　　Exploring her world with eyes so bright.
　　We take for granted 'til she shows us anew
　　That everything is fresh as the morning dew.

　　She won my heart the very first day.
　　What she gives to me I can never repay.
　　As you grow, may you always find
　　Only the good, the sweet and kind.

　　Little Alex, with a spirit so high,
　　She could reach above and touch the sky.
　　Little Alex, with a heart so pure,
　　The love you inspire will ever endure.

Carol M. Marfuta

YVONNE

A friend's introduction to her, girl of black and blue
the revealing conversation, insured remembering too
An occurring impression of the her that should have been
angered at the destruction of a mother's obsession.

Yvonne, underdog to silence
blond casualty of violence
Yvonne is gentle inspiration
a bond for loyal dedication

Glimpsing past her shell, a soul of innocence
knew skeletons of hell and lacked all confidence
Couldn't tell if she was perceiving or even if she was receiving
gazing in her eyes another look, she wasn't so mysterious.

The children of anguish, afflicted by adult kin
like Yvonne, please relinquish with a heart over brim
Origin is of no concern, they've omitted life's limb
share the gift to learn you see, they're undiminished within.

Yvonne, underdog to silence
blond casualty of violence
Yvonne is gentle inspiration
a bond for this loyal dedication.

K. R. Ollis

WHEN THE REAL DOCTOR CALLS

''He don't need 'no' doctor anymore'':
He's had them by the score.
Everything they did to him made him sore,
Left him each time worse than before.
No, he doesn't need doctors anymore.

Then he was blessed by a house call.
A different doctor quietly came into his room,
Sat down and gently held his hand;
Bent low, and whispered ''My boy,
'Tis time for you to come home.''
The youth would rather have stayed,
Even though here his doctors had betrayed,
'Til life had become a medical jail.

His pained eyes looked far away from there,
Into blazing rays shining into eternity,
The real doctor who had come to call, spoke,
''Your place now is beyond that lighted wall.''
The son of man smiled at those bright lights,
Fading into the loving arms of God,
The real Father/Doctor of us all.

V. S. Lewis

SCARLETT O'HARA
THE ONE THE ONLY

Scarlett and her ''Rhett'': everyone knows of their rosy love story.
It's one-of-a-kind to end all great loves, with the usual worry.
Now, there is a group that wants to re-create and carry it along.
Would a ''concocted'' script for a brand new picture show be
    right or wrong?
Scarlett and Rhett are no more — shouldn't be seen on
    any type screen.
Their curtain came down, as well it should, for they both
    pulled its rope.

When love leaves from one or both that's it: It's over —
    there's no hope.
They can't resurrect these two out of the rubble the North
    left behind.
So, let their affair end on the last page of a great book,
    and be kind.
Its memories are sweet; though full of defeat, in spite of the
    rebel yell.
They lost each other; as the South lost its cause:
    what's more to tell?
Besides, what fun it is to make up endings that turn out just swell.

Please let the beauty and glory of their love last in memory,
Like those ''blue and gray'' soldiers who rest in the cold,
    old ground.
For fighting to save ''then,'' for us ''now,'' everybody's
    ''Old Glory.''
So, right hand to your head to salute our flag —
    the cause of the story.
There is only one Scarlett: therefore, only one Rhett Butler.
They both went away, back then, to where the wind blows-s-s.

Leave their names, please, with those of the others,
    in perpetual repose.
                For the wind now blows in peace.

V. S. Lewis

LOSS OF A LOVED ONE

The greatest sorrow that anyone is ever asked to bear
Is the knowledge that a loved one will no longer be there.
When you lost your loved one your sorrow ran deep
And you thought that probably forever you'd weep.
But on a restless night to follow, when hardly you slept
You finally understood, even though gone,
    in your heart they could always be kept
So your life goes on, even though theirs has now ended.
Before long you'll find that your heart, has just about mended.
After all, it's not as though we'll never see them again
Be someday in the future, God will reunite us with them.

Patty Maben

LIVELY SPIRIT

Remove the earth, so I can see his face again.
I would not mind seeing his fine, lean, young face then!
Twenty years have passed since rifles wailed,
And as many seas of life have since been sailed.
In my dream, I see only the lively spirit;
Tall marine, laggard? No! He would not bear it!
I know I would see, without earth, alone,
The impatient, happy smile of strong face bone.
As he asked, I helped him from the casket grey;
He said he was in a hurry, on his way.
''Let's go to Gran'ma's; she wants to bake a cake
For you,'' he said. ''Tell her, a small one to make.
I'm in a hurry, and I want you to know,
I have a very important place to go!''
While deep in my mind, two faces I see —
In my heart, always, only one will be.
His lively spirit, strong face bone, and bright eyes
I will always love, though his tender body dies.

Jenny Gale

LOOKING BACK

At age sixteen I look ahead and plan and dream and silently
wonder what lies ahead. Proms, weddings, baby buntings

At age twenty-two I look ahead and plan and dream and silently
wonder what lies ahead
At twenty-three I look back and ponder

At thirty-two I look back and wonder and ponder
Bicycle rides, kites in the sky, soccer, baseball, gymnastics
and birthday parties
At thirty-two I silently ponder

At forty-two and not yet gray I do not look back and wonder why
Why did he take them away
I look back and ponder

Linda S. Fulton

ANTONIO

In the emergency room cubicle
Antonio lies on a stretcher,
blood-stained, wrinkled sheet beneath him,
tubes invade his body.

He groans, ''Nurse, nurse.''
I, a volunteer,
go to him.
He asks to have his head raised,
a cold drink of water.
I put a wet piece of gauze to his dry, cracked lips,
a wet towel on his hot forehead.

Jean Willard

A VISIT FROM MY GRAND-DAUGHTER

Dedicated to
All My Grand-daughters

I saw a pretty girl today, a-wandering through my house,
Although, at first, she was as quiet as the proverbial mouse!
But when she started mixing dough, and doughnuts did appear,
I realized just who it was — 'twas my grand-daughter dear!
She came to spend a day or two — we had some jolly times —
Like renting ''fins'' and ''beachballs,'' and saying silly rhymes!
And, later on, we took a rest, and walked upon the sand —
I sure enjoyed that little walk, as we went hand-in-hand!
We also took a ride to town, to shop for things to eat,
Then stopped in at the ''movie-house'' —
        watched from a front-row seat!
I even sacrificed my nap, so we would have the time
To wander through the shady park — it didn't cost a dime!
We even took some roses red to ''Great Grandmother S.,''
Who thanked my ''girly'' with a kiss, and a sincere ''God-bless!''
We then left town, and started home, so that the dark we'd beat,
We got home just in time for buns — and hot dogs —
        what a treat!
Then, when the daylight turned to dark,
        we watched ''Pink Panther Man,''
I really had a super time — I hope she'll come again!

Lee M. Schlobohm

LEE MERLE SCHLOBOHM. Born: Hobart, Indiana; Married: Lucille Anne Stevens, 4-19-42; Education: Portage High School, Crisman, Indiana, 5-20-40; Occupations: U.S. Air Force Captain, Celestial & Radar Navigator, Bombardier, B-29 bomber, 1940-46; City Fire Chief, San Luis Obispo, California, 1957-77, retired; Memberships: International Association of Fire Chiefs, California Fire Chiefs' Association, Tri-counties Fire Chiefs' Association, California State Firemen's Association; Poetry: 'Lo, The Mighty Hunter,' 1948, *Santa Clara County Firemen's Association Newsletter; The Schlobohm Collection,* 60 original poems, 1987 (to be published); Other Writings: ''The Red Scourge,'' science-fiction story, 1948, *Family Newsletter;* ''A Second Chance,'' short story, 1970, *Family Newsletter;* Comments: *Themes for the majority of my poems include personal thoughts for special occasions, importance of family love, and putting into words the private feelings relating to family members and close personal friends.*

REMEMBERING

The blue sky stretches forth to touch the bands
Which hold the dome of heaven. On her breast
The grey lake snuggles peacefully at rest
While lazy winds play hopscotch on the sands,
And dusk creeps silently into the day,
Spreading its mystery. The evening star,
Like a flirting maiden, is near, then far,
Fleetingly evasive, then back to stay.

Lighting with blood-red hue this great expanse,
The full moon blushes with womanly grace
And gives to the universe one embrace,
Then goes her way without a backward glance.

There, silently, until the dawn returns
Our newborn love, in cool enchantment, burns.

Colleen Barton

DAMN IT, LOVE ME!

If you must walk away
Please walk away slowly,
Listen to your heart
And promise me this only:

If you must close the door between us,
Promise you'll keep the key.
And as distance grows between us,
Promise you'll think of me.

If you can love me, then damn it, love me!
Let's share dreams and fears and hearts and tears and laughter.
If you don't love me, then don't love me.
Be honest with yourself first, and with me after.

But if you walk away
Please walk away slowly,
Listen to your heart
And think of me.

Kendell W. Spencer

GRANDPA'S GIRL

My grandfather was always there when I was a child.
I was his favorite: grandpa's little girl.
I was special in his eyes, a gift from heaven,
the joy of his life: a golden-haired doll to love.

The old man died and was buried on a hill.
His memories ever in my heart, I still talked to him.
Years later, I had a child, a tiny baby,
fragile fighter, doomed to die: a golden-haired baby.

Such love, such agony when her clear blue eyes closed.
I placed her into a small pink-velvet coffin
while grief tore at my soul
the baby of my dreams was gone, forever on the hill

I left her on the hill next to my grandpa's grave
a new tiny child to be loved by the old man;
a little girl who lived only two days
now dead forever, beyond heaven

I sent her to be my grandpa's little girl

Nancy Hoekstra

CONTEST WINNERS

FIRST PRIZE
ADRIAN

The brown, watery spine of the city slithers to the sea.
The Jewish Cemetery: your body in a plain pine box hovers
over the earth's abyss.

A strange, cold April afternoon — the buildings downtown look
gray and somber. Rain clouds fill the sky.

No trees or flowers here: only gray-white stones and earth.
Your friends huddle together — they still feel the cold.
They look like black sparrows or a Henry Moore sculpture
— a family of adults.

The ground feels hard and old today — only I can see — the earth
spins around the sun, the moon in tow. The Rabbi speaks
about your life, your friendships.

Back in our cars, the car doors slam, the mourners leave:
back to their lives, the Sunday dinner, the New York
Times.

As we slip into our warm beds tonight, you are underground.
I danced in your arms there. We were best man and woman of
honor at our friends' wedding. I turn to kiss my love.

Charlotte Tapley

SECOND PRIZE
UNTITLED

looking back
    the end of our path —
mother waving

Charles B. Rodning

THIRD PRIZE
AN ENGLISH LESSON

I stand before the row of students
who expect me to be very brilliant,
and I do not feel like being brilliant at all.

They are so young, so eager to learn,
and I have a splitting headache,
tortured by remorse, self-pity, guilt.

Today I teach them English tenses,
English grammar soothes me, being so lucid.
Perhaps I am not a failure, after all.

I wind my alarm clock every day,
and am seldom late for my classes.

The students trust me though I seldom smile.
Sometimes it seems to me
that I am more feared than respected.

When I stand alone before the blackboard
with a piece of chalk in my hand,
I regain confidence and am young again,
no longer embittered or vulnerable.

Tadeusz Rybowski

FOURTH PRIZE
I WILL WAKE UP SLOWLY THIS MORNING

I will wake up slowly this morning.
I will let sleep peel from me
a little at a time.

My mouth's still tasting
the words I know I've spoken
during the night —
loose beads now.
It must have been an ample dream.

And the laughter, the strange sound
that came out of me in the dark,
still seems to fill my mouth.
It was ilke the laughter of a girl
being paid a compliment.

I wonder what passed through me
that I should laugh in my sleep.
I wonder what happiness it is
that I keep so well hidden.

I will wake up slowly this morning.
That sound
must last me for a long time.

Flavia Prishtina

FIFTH PRIZE
FOR BERNHARD GOETZ

Frightened, I look into the great matters
Of my insignificant life. Hear quiet rustles
Breaking out from the crevices of walls
And from the ceiling and I don't know
What to fear and where to hide.

I watch how the mad dogs devour
The intestines of this city, how they jump
For the throat of the defenseless and the child
Within me dies and I change into a rat.

In the desert of my bad times
My eyes swell bloodshot.
You say: "Stop complaining, you have
To learn from the caveman how to fight
And stir up fire from nothing.

White brothers, black brothers
Black brothers, white brothers
There is no freedom in this America
Freedom is the absence of fear."

Adam Szyper

THE LAST TEST AND PROOF

How soon others grow tired of their own stimulus,
break apart, move through a room of solitude,
open a door, begin again.
Each of us have made this attempt,
forgetting the one lying next to you
must also work hard to forget,
even during a good night's sleep.

Together, we are awake beating our wings.
We've awakened new worlds of light,
returning the darkness
to its own natural place.
We tell ourselves the normal problems
will not touch us
with so much belief.

And as we believe we outline the growth
of this last test that proves
there is an eternal expansion of time
between the ripening of the fruit
and the moment it falls from the tree.

William Dwyer

SPANS

Near Jeffersonville, near Kennedy Bridge,
which sways when fog straddles the Ohio River,
Second Street Bridge hangs midstream, pilings
untethered by midmorning haze. When I was
seven, my family drove across
to Louisville in my grandfather's Ford,
which smelled of Ben-Gay, while rain gusted
under the running boards. I scrunched down
the front seat, complained I could not see
over the dash. Saturdays my father would
plunk out Fats Waller songs on the upright
piano and tell stories of the Flood, which
drowned the town courthouse, swept away his
birth certificate. When, as usual, my mother
said he could not prove he lived, he'd look
into the darkened mirror of my face and find
his full lips, his gap-toothed grin. Now
when I ask what happened in the Flood, she
always says: ''the flood of '32? or '35?
What flood, child?''

Martha M. Vertreace

DREAM

You left roses on my doorstep — red, white and yellow,
buds, fluffy open ones, delicate pinks.

You were in my garden last night. You could have been
anybody — it was dark, no moon or stars to light your way.
I know your walk, your essence — I hid in the oak tree.

The night air sweet with honeysuckle, I saw a moment of
you in a flash of a headlight. My eyes long for your
shadow, your fire.

I lie down in my soft bed. My life curls around me
like smoke from a pipe. I sink down in my pillows
and dream — I am swimming in a cool pool — going farther
away from you. I see my life extending out in its
usual measured pattern — a bath of reality.

My lips, my hands, my breasts burn for you — the places you
have touched me. I walk down the thin aisle of a country
church in a white lace dress, white Gardenias pinned
in my hair. Do you wait for me?

Charlotte Tapley

THE HARROWING

Coming late in April, home,
I found the field
Between the house and cemetery
Turned for harrowing —
Your illness coming
As the seed went in —
A gauzy droning
Past the curtained room.

The earth, regardless,
Churned itself to corn,
The tasseling coming on
As you went down.

By harvest
You were gone,

Today the field waves parchment
In the wind
And stubble glints
Like nails
In the late sun.

Jean Holmes Wilson

TENTH PRIZE
BIRDS

Black crows sit on the tree
behind the window;
it is winter, and the snow is thick.

Immobile and monumental, they grow out
of the trunk, wingless.

I sit in the heated room, typing a poem,
and I do not feel sorry for them;
after all, they are just birds.

Midnight is nearing, time is running out;
I quickly finish typing my page,
and fold it gently in two.

A part of my heart is gone;
I feel exhausted
and void.

Black crows sit outside on the tree:
patient, solemn, immobile.

Tadeusz Rybowski

ELEVENTH PRIZE
MARBLES FROM A JAR

I pushed,
pulled,
and grunted.
Work seemed all consuming.
My body in a rubber band
almost ready to snap.
I sit in front of the T.V.
watching people change the
world, as a slow sad song
plays on the stereo,
and my life becomes a blur.
A blur that is gone, before it's
in my grasp.
And the years are marbles
falling from a jar.
They can't be stopped,
no one's ever
quick enough.

John White

TWELFTH PRIZE
LOST SUMMER

I wake alone and reach for the familiar presence.
But she fell on the tennis court
    and wears a cast all the way up her arm
    and sleeps by herself.

The dream is very real . . .
I am at a writer's conference.
A visiting poet, tall, dark-haired, dark-eyed
stands in the center of an admiring group.
I maneuver my way to face her.
Blurt out my admiration for her work.
The lovely eyes briefly meet mine, move beyond.
I withdraw.

Down the street someone whistles to a dog.
The dream recedes to join the doomed summer,
trips deferred, tomato plants slowed by the cold,
attacked by snails and worms,
flat tires, broken fan belts, radiators boiling over.

My companion cries softly in the cool night.
Her arm itches, and she can't scratch
    under the heavy cast.

Robert M. Tarleton

HONORABLE MENTIONS
in alphabetical order

HONORABLE MENTION
TO LOU

I remember that window's blistered paint
from the heat of all those summers.
It had rust stains from the six-penny nails that
were stuck out part way.
And the faded curtain lace browned
by winter's ice inside was still plainly beautiful
as it hung — ancient.

We had lain beneath the window pane,
heard patters of fall rain following the tempo
of crackling fire.
It was good on those dark nights,
with you and your Italian dinners.
It was good to come to see you, knowing
a touch would be there.
But, it would be hard from outside that window,
when you looked to me on splashing wet sidewalks,
my back moving up towards the District lights.

Richard Armstrong

PRIDE

Wrong?

Who me?
I couldn't be!

Well, maybe —
Possibly —
Just this once . . .

Mrs. David L. Baird

DR. ROSENQUIST'S OFFICE

Of course, he offers me the green chair by the window.
I can see three flights down through the rain-stained glass.
On my left, his smugly crowded bookshelves
Watch me scornfully.

He lights my Camel cigarette and asks how I am feeling.
I play with my ashes in his heavy, pink marble ashtray.
And I tell him again about the dream, the rough hands at my throat.
He listens without blinking.

And I talk about my veins; they are strangling me,
I can hardly breathe.
He waves his sanity over my head, like a gaudy ostrich plume fan.
I mash my cigarette into his ashtray,
Pretending not to notice him staring at my breasts.

He knows I love him, the bastard.
I tell him how much his cactus annoys me.
Staring hard at the small birds trapped in the twining
Ivy patterning his carpet,
I twirl a strand of hair around my finger.

He smiles at me,
''Would you like another cigarette?''

Rosemary L. Bauman

IMPROVISATION

Children play games in which
Characters are rotated, roles
Are reversed. An Asian boy
Once taught me a game where
Boys line up behind each other,
Three or four with hands touching
The one in front, forming a ''dragon.''
A single boy is left out, and he
Tries to catch the dragon's tail
While the dragon's head in turn
Pursues him. Then they all change
Places; each one in his turn
Is the dragon's pursuer.
Such improvisations of the spirit
Are difficult for grown men,
Who tend to see themselves
Only as pursued or pursuer
At any given time, and lack
The pliability of children, the agility
To somersault from one position to another.

George N. Braman

WALK

It is the beginning again, but this
time it is new. My boy is going away
to school. He wants to go alone, insists

that every kid walks it alone this way.
''But oh,'' I feel like crying, ''You are mine.
Mine for God's sake. Please.'' But I don't. I say,

''Please watch for bikes.'' He looks at me, eyes
slightly startled by the sudden release.
I tap his perfect nose; he blinks and says

Thanks. As he leaves I feel my fear increase
at the sight of that small, windbreakered back.
Those perfect bones, that lovely chest. My keys

are in my left-hand pocket. The one mac
I can find in the closet is one of
his mother's: navy-blue, with ducks. The back

of it stretches over my shoulders. Love,
I think, has made me crazy. I pause in
the rain, watching his tiny body move.

Jessica Burstein

PLAIN

I'm only 9,
I'm plain old fine.
My face is plain,
I'm not so vain.
I'm not to like,
I'm not to hate.
That's because
I'm not so great.
I have a plain old cat,
a plain old dog,
a plain old mouse,
a plain old frog.
My life has always
been like this,
I never will be full of bliss!

Sean Carney

A TRUE STORY

Bought a yogurt for $.75 from the vending machine
For Sunday morning breakfast.
It was Cherry yogurt, the only flavor in the machine,
And the taste I desire least.
Oh well, better than a donut or cake or
The other hi-calorie junk they stock.
    I select a plastic spoon,
    Depart the satellite and
    Meander back to the crib
    To slowly enjoy my feast.

In our wooden oasis I lift the lid and prepare to dine.

    What's this!

    It's all watery!

    Could it be old?

    I check the date on the lid —

''Best Eaten Before January Fourth''

Today is January Sixth.

    I eat it anyway.
    And hope for the best.

        Leon E. Chamberlain

THE EXIT PLEASE

Where's the head
And not the tail
Yelled old Jonah
Inside the whale

        R. W. Champion

UNTITLED

My imagination:
it works two ways,
for the good of it
and for the bad of it.

        Sydney M. Conover

HONDA

Roaring down the twisting highway
In my little imported deathtrap
Advertising my realization,
That life has no purpose
My existence is meaningless

Suddenly around a curve
The pale immortal moon
Flashes between two mountains
Just briefly enough to remind me
Not to take myself so seriously

        Melinda Correll

HAIKU

raindrop etchings
on its floury surface
dirt road
and Kansas summer

        L. K. Cox

THE NAKED MAN CRIES

Where do I put sleep?
I have no hidden pockets
In which to keep dreams

        James Dierken

MAKING LOVE

Making love
is like
a house
with the front door open
welcoming you
into the warmth
and the mysterious comfort
of each
and every room.

        Deirdre Duffy

A BRIDGE AND A GOING UNDER

In memory of Peter Deland

''What is great in man is that he is a bridge
and not an end: what can be loved in man is
that he is an *overture* and a *going under*.''
        — Nietzsche

Others knew you better, intimate fathoms:
the prisoner-of-war nightmares translated
into speech: puns, gibes, *ripostes*
were an extended family, a place to be
safe. And speech was your pleasure:
temporary refuge! quips, malaprops, *bons
mots,* the more outlandish the better.
The slow rhetorical blade of langpleasure:
temporary refuge! quips, malaprops, bons
mots, the more outlandish the better.
The slow rhetorical blade of language
was too dull for your wit, self-sharpening.
In your grip, our numb thoughts quickened:
you helped us to own that swift shattering
of the known you lived with. *What is truth?*
Emotional shrapnel. And we listened: you
were a bridge, Peter, and a going under,
faith that survived its wounding . . .
runs of glancing words.

        Charles Fishman

SHADOWS OF MOTHERHOOD

Shadows, like oversized giants,
   lean against pale yellow walls
      then fall on a tiny white elephant
        in an unoccupied cradle.
Eerie patches of geometrical designs
   fill the night hours with puzzles,
      as sleepless eyes revolve around
        the merry-go-round room.
Questions fill the yellow spaces between right-angled darkness.

Tricia Ann Fordham

TRYST

Come, my latter-day Lindbergh
Fly with me over the north Atlantic to Norway.
Share a mystic cruise in slate green fjords
We'll wrap ourselves in furs and gaze at the clear
          midnight sky
Laugh at sailors speaking Norwegian who sound like
      they have marbles in their mouths.
If you ignore my plumpness
I'll ignore your hairpiece.
Gawky teenage sweethearts, remember us —
Arms linked to keep warm. Crunching, stamping
our feet in the snow.
Snowflakes circling.
Window shopping at the festive windows on the Plaza.
Spanish arabesque buildings outlined in thousands
of colored lights.
A magic romantic evening which never happened.
But could have
Should have.

Gerry Frerichs

AN OFFICE AT CLOSING

Good-byes are said, and the light goes out,
   almost as though it knew its cue.
Just then the door slams shut, locked, secure.
The walls begin to settle, and crack.
Are there really noises if no one hears?

Papers are piled high on the desks
   waiting to be filed or discarded in the morning.
In a dormant state they will sit, until someone wants to work.
The coffee pot no longer perks, and the typewriters are also silent,
Perhaps they are sleeping.
The trash cans are empty, a pleasant sight, yet somehow sad too.
There is no one around to use them.
Ashtrays with the leftover butts of those last-minute cigarettes,
Seem to be saying, ''Use me, for I am lonely.''

The mice scurry about, as they know at this time they are safe, free.
Occasionally a security guard will rattle the door from the outside.
He is thinking to himself, ''No more business today.''
The empty chairs, and desks make up a vacant room.
It's calm and peaceful there.
If only, just for one night, I could sit in a corner there,
Just to clear my head, and think.

Cynthia L. Gardner

NINE PLANETS IN SEVEN DAYS

Shopping in Saturn on Saturday night.
Off to Pluto on a three-minute flight.
Solar cafés on Vulcan and Mars,
Lunar aesthetics in asteroid bars.
Androids in Celluloid; celestial chic,
Lingerie in laser; the century slick.
Mutant maquillage in pomegranate and puce,
Venusian veils, Uranian looks.
Dinner in Jupiter, Neptune Hotel.
Mercury's posh, but the airport was hell!
What a vacation!
I should've had ten . . .
Nine planets in seven days!
Never again!

Khimm Graham

REMEMBERING THE BARN

I remember so clearly that familiar brown barn
glued against a taupe horizon
melancholy memories of childhood passing through
I can still see bursts of sunlight
thrusting their way through the broken-down doors
dancing fairies upon the dried out hay
Just like they used to do
I turn my head to catch a glimpse of a spider scurry
across the dirt floor
Years ago, I would have had nightmares about
it
But now — the sight of that insect seems almost consoling
the sweet smell of fresh cut grass
fills the barn
I cross my feet and use one hand
to lean on a rafter
only to get a hand full of
splinters
It seems as though they were waiting all these years for me
Nothing has changed

Margaret Hall

FRIENDLY DIVORCE

Outside of me, I see
the toes of moddish boots, a patch of plaid wool skirt,
black stockinged knees,
the placid patina of the auto's hood.
The manicured, beringed fingers on the wheel are mine;
and mine the spotless lace at either wrist.
I view it all from a protected place,
behind Italian lenses.

Inside of me, I hear
a grieving peasant woman cry aloud.
She sinks to her knees, pounding the earth,
as I turn the key.
Dirt and tears streak her face,
as the engine starts.
Her frantic fingers tear at my eyes,
as I pull away.

Ann Hill-Beuf

PERCEPTION

You keep on,
touching me
with your fantasy.

Anne Animus

DRESDEN

Our fears touched their fears in Dresden
one bright blue day while the Elbe blinked
in dazzling sunshine as we faltered
and nervously moved across East Germany,
the Deutsche Demokratische Republik,
and saw the cathedrals in ruined chinks.

In the bright light we heard that Americans
perpetrated this destruction and began the war
while even today like a vulture our president
wants to bomb the innocent, such lore
we could not refute as we were visitors
with our own fears of police and more.

Yet, with a smile from our child to theirs,
touched fingers and friendly advice
we recognized their individual sacrifice
and will entice all to put aside the hatred
caused by people using bloody devices
where old men can say twice perhaps, not thrice!

Nancy Hoekstra

DRIVING FOR LOSS

Long night
so long
night as grey
as your hand
on the wheel
driving on

empty through a town
edged up to a dream
of dust and storefronts.
A man walks slowly
to a corner of traffic

lights marking hours
between cars, your
car that won't stop
even in that noiseless
place. His face, dark

stubble, heavy lids
lined with night
travels along with
you like a mirror.

Marcia L. Hurlow

TWO SHOWS FOR THE PRICE OF ONE

the girl handing out tickets makes our decision for us
sleigh-ride together jingles from the screen
people laugh popcorn crunches
do you love me more than anyone more than anything
more than food clothing shelter
i ask my mate
would you run gleefully through life naked for me
no she replies
we hang out in the back seat of the last row
huddled in quiet anticipation
waiting for the first customers to enter for the next show
a kid shows up and walks into his friend's coca cola
we laugh and wish we could sip a coke ourselves
but we're afraid we'll get busted.

mikel k

THE SHOPPING STREET

The shopping street runs along a hillside, which may be
why it still has stores and has not been made into a mall.
It's located on both sides of a major east-west avenue.

The intersecting streets allow many customers from apartment
buildings to walk to the stores, seven bus lines bring people.

Sixty years ago it was trolleys and suburbanites as well as
local people. Before the street roadway was repaved sections
of the old trolley tracks poked through the paving.

On one of our corners there was a children's garment shop,
featuring pretty party dresses for little girls. It was
superseded for awhile by a popular discount drug store.

Many of the stores used to be swankier — a dignified grand
piano salesroom became a popular electronics showcase. The
confectionery store's successors are fast food places.

There is still a mixture of appearances of people and languages —
different languages than sixty years ago.

Wooden strollers and wicker carriages have changed to folding
plastic strollers, but the mothers and grandmothers seem to fuss
over and care about the youngsters as much as they did sixty years ago.
Again there is a children's garment shop with pretty party dresses.

Florence K. McCarthy

AFTER MY MOTHER'S FUNERAL

The house lies deep inside the womb
of darkness.
These are no small hours.
These hours are huge.

How much we need to fall asleep —
the curtains drawn, warm blankets
this winter night,
all the doors closed.

She instead
can sleep anywhere now.
Even inside that box
we left under the rain
for the gravediggers.

Flavia Prishtina

SOLITAIRE

You sit there playing solitaire
While I knit and purl.
The radio declares
The futility of hope for peace;
The dog lies sleeping on the couch,
And all within the room is quiet, restful —
All except my fragmented thought
That jumps and hops and torments my breast.
I busy myself with the knit and purl of life,
Find tasks to do and errands to run,
And across from me sits you.

Sometimes I venture to put forth my hand
Tentatively, toying with the hope you might respond,
But you look at me as though to say,
''What's got in to you?''
I look at other men sometimes
And wonder how their hands would feel
In caresses only you should give
And lonely, turn to knit and purl again
A winter occupation for a droughty spring.

Lewetta Russell

SUFFERING

It is supposed to do you good
I never had a piece
Of it offered to me in my life
I'd as life not had

Today in mistake
I spread sour pit cherry jam
All on my toast myself

I didn't want that either

But that I had
     had have have

Richard Russell

SUPPLICANT

Jesse James visited
My great-grandfather's place outside
Sikeston Mo my father told us

Said Jesse thanked Grandma
For the coffee he had the kindest
Eyes Grandma said
Grandpa for the four horses

Grandpa said he wouldn't have dreamed
Of not helping Jesse and not just because
Grandma was kin to Jesse somewhere
Down the line

Grandpa said it was in his eyes
When Jess said horses

Why Grandpa said anybody
Would have helped Jesse

Richard Russell

A SLIM MODERN GIRL GOES ANTIQUING IN CONNECTICUT

Tall mirrors dim in darkened frames turn lithe young
women into ladies with hourglass figures, and a slim
modern girl hastens to escape their lying reflections.
Oak-framed paintings hold high-collared men with calm
eyes that acknowledge high masculine worth, and pale
stolid women in full dark dresses validate male claims . . .
All are securely in possession of a world they think
shall never change, but is due to soon pass into history's
merciless book, to be known forever as: ''The Victorians.''

Elegant oval mirrors send slender images back from gold
glittery frames and flatteringly enchant the eyes of all
who pass. The slim modern girl stops and smiles. Finely
wrought frames hug canvasses of slick men and sleek women
with short shiny hair, dressed in blazing colors, and they
hold glinting cigarette holders in smiling quirky mouths . . .
All are securely in possession of a world they think
shall never change, but is due to soon pass into history's
merciless book, to be forever known as: ''Art Deco.''

The slim modern girl learns a lesson.

Vee Shanahan

LOVE LOST

Fall is long in coming
quick in going
yet hardly perceptible
the very instant when the last leaf
finally falls
disconnects, separates
loses itself.
Like a long love newly lost
it is hard to recall
exactly when it goes
uproots,
splinters off
scatters debris —
hard to remember
when the memory of it
no longer lingers
in the residue of discarded
dreams —
decomposes like dry
fallen leaves.

M. Norris Stanton

OFTEN TIRED OF WHAT I DO

Often tired of what I do
I come to a tropical rain forest
To a Caribbean coastal floodplain
In Costa Rica.

Rain cascades down, wind moves swiftly
As I watch red frogs, violet butterflies
And yellow flowers under the huge canopy
Of a ceiba tree.

From dense shade I enter
The scattered light gaps of the forest
Where I drink the sun mixed with drops of water
Till somebody starts blowing the horn.

Often on the way to the office
I cross the street on a red light.
Among angry glances I know what they think
But I just smile and keep walking.

Adam Szyper

REASSURED

You know that pillow I hug
every night when I go to sleep,
well,
I don't need it anymore —

Pamela Y. Tagami

UNTITLED

The difference between
now and then,
is me. . . .

Pamela Y. Tagami

THE HEALING

We drive through the blue fields of grass
dotted with white lilies-of-the-valley
and hold our breath.
We forget the cement flower pots
on our windowsill
the tulips crushed together
in caked soil.
We forget the books collecting dust
on our shelves
warped leather bindings
yellowed paper.
We forget the delicate thread
which binds us
the tangles our words form.
The air is still between us.
The orange sky yawns on the horizon,
blackbirds slice through clouds,
droning cicadas follow us past watermelon orchards
past miles of cornfields
and deep into the hush of the countryside.

Katherine Tassi

VINCENT IN FLAMES

Snow fell the afternoon that Vincent came to Arles,
Two Place Lamartine. False teeth clacked behind

his unkempt beard which grew between leather wrinkles
in his cheeks. Village children stoned him, believed

his carmine hair, turquoise eyes, proof of fever since he
lived on cafe-au-lait with dark rye bread. Japanese prints

of peonies and half-mad sunflowers papered his walls after
another argument: Gauguin threw away some twisted oil tubes.

Their Yellow House melted like fresh butter into pale citron.

''Life is after all enchanting,'' he wrote Theo from his Poet's Garden
where Petrarch and Dante sang to him alone of lovers found and lost

in the mistral; where cypresses shot like flames into the stars
through his eyelashes; on his canvases, haggard scratchings.

He heard the rasp of crows who claimed the wheatfield's gold;
their great black wings skimmed grain like a reaper's scythe.

Gauguin could only see the razor glint in Van Gogh's eyes;
their silence, cobalt blue; their rage, vermilion.

Martha M. Vertreace

LETTERS I NEVER WROTE

I want you to read the words in my mind,
the ones that I meant but never sent.

The ones you were waiting to hear
when all you got in the mail
were coupons for laundry detergent
and mailgrams announcing the
Random House Sweepstakes.

The ones that would explain
why I left without leaving
the keys to the front door,
a forwarding address.

Tamara R. Wells

PLAY DOH: or,
YOU CAN WRITE
A POEM ON ANYTHING

Expectant pressure
on the plastic pump
and pasta-for-two
(Cheerful Tearful and
Baby Wetums
have ladies' appetites)
curls out in
perfect tubes.
Soup noodles ooze
in arcs of
to-be-dissected
s*t*a*r*s*
and petits fours of pieces
are served up
on lids of
Mason jars.

Jean Holmes Wilson

SHADOWED.

INDEX